THE EDUCATED READER

THE EDUCATED READER

GERALD LEVIN

Professor Emeritus of English
University of Akron

Harcourt Brace Jovanovich, Publishers

San Diego   New York   Chicago   Austin   Washington, D.C.
London   Sydney   Tokyo   Toronto

Cover: "Santa Fe in Winter" by Carol Mothner, 1985–86. Photo courtesy of the Gerald Peters Gallery, Santa Fe, New Mexico, and Dallas, Texas.

The painting "La chute d'Icare" ("The Death of Icarus") by Pieter Bruegel the Elder is reprinted on page 177 by permission of the Musées Royaux des Beaux-Arts de Belgique, Brussels.

ISBN: 0-15-520717-2
Library of Congress Catalog Card Number: 87-81889
Printed in the United States of America

Preface

The Educated Reader is a collection of essays, fiction, poetry, and a play directed to students at all levels. The book is designed for courses concerned with critical reading and writing or those that make the discussion of ideas an integral part of composition. The chief purpose of this book is to introduce ideas and issues and some approaches to them that a well-educated person should possess.

The reading selections present important ideas and experiences from various intellectual and artistic perspectives. By *perspective* I mean the particular way a philosopher, an imaginative writer, a social scientist, a psychologist, a biologist, or a medical doctor would interpret an experience or idea. Thus Stanley Milgram writes as a social psychologist on why people obey and disobey authority; Hannah Arendt writes as a political scientist in attempting to explain the authoritarian character of Adolf Eichmann. A philosopher of law, Sissela Bok, seeks to define the responsibilities of doctors to their patients; in his short story, William Carlos Williams writes from his own experience as a medical doctor on how particular doctors perform their jobs and define their responsibilities. The issues, perspectives, and opinions represented in each section are not the only ones that exist; they are intended to be representative.

The book presents not only various perspectives, but also important genres. These include autobiography and memoir, the philosophical dialogue and essay, the critical and the argumentative essay, satire, the formal address, the research report, poetry, drama, the short story, and the novella. The introduction to each section gives an overview of the topic and essential background and facts. It also describes the content of the section's readings and identifies the perspectives they represent. The introduction to each selection suggests ways to read the selection; several of them discuss the characteristics of the particular genre. The questions and suggested writing assignments give students opportunities to discuss the ideas contained in the selections and how the ideas are expressed or represented. Suggestions for additional reading are provided for each writer. The Instructor's Manual contains additional background and definitions, as well as suggestions for using the selections. Excisions have not been made from the selections; each is a complete poem, story, play, or section or chapter of a book. Exceptions are the self-contained excerpts from Rousseau's *Emile* and Machiavelli's *Art of War*. The notes throughout the book are the editor's unless otherwise stated.

In selecting the materials for this book, I have drawn on my experience with numerous students who, in composition courses, have read with me and written about some of the writers presented in this book. I also have learned much from my students in courses in medical humanities and the literature of medicine, at the University of Akron and Northeastern Ohio Universities College of Medicine, with whom I have discussed several of the selections on medicine and biomedical issues contained in this book.

I thank the following reviewers, who made valuable suggestions on the organization of the book and the reading selections: Angela Williams (The Citadel), Dale Silviria (University of California at Los Angeles), and Joanne Muratori (New York University). To my acquisitions editor at Harcourt Brace Jovanovich, Marlane Agriesti Miriello, a person of exceptional judgment and good sense, I am indebted for suggesting this reader and for her invaluable advice at all stages of work on the manuscript. To Carole Hallenbeck, who edited the manuscript with so much care, I am indebted for improving many sentences and clarifying many ideas. I wish to express thanks also to Kim Svetich, the production editor, and to Cathy Reynolds, the designer, for their fine work on the book. As always, I have had the steady encouragement and help of my wife, Lillian Levin.

Gerald Levin

Contents

Preface   V

General Introduction   1

PART ONE

GENERAL PERSPECTIVES   5

YOUTH AND EXPERIENCE   7

Michel de Montaigne, *Of the Inconsistency of Our Actions*   8
       Translated by E. J. Trechmann
The sixteenth-century French essayist considers the relationship between our character and our actions.

Albert Schweitzer, *I Resolve to Become a Jungle Doctor*   16
       Translated by C. T. Campion
The twentieth-century French theologian and musician explains why he decided as a young man to become a doctor and go to French Equatorial Africa.

Frederick Douglass, *A Change Came o'er the Spirit of My Dream*   24
A former slave who devoted his life to liberating and improving the lives of black people describes how, as a young man, he discovered the reason for slavery and oppression.

Maya Angelou, *Graduation*   32
At their graduation in a segregated Southern town, black boys and girls reject the idea that they are fated to be "maids and farmers, handymen and washerwomen" and find a way to express pride in their race.

Nathaniel Hawthorne, *My Kinsman, Major Molineaux*   42
Arriving in a New England colonial town, a young man has trouble finding his wealthy kinsman, who will help him make his fortune.

Dylan Thomas, *Poem in October, Fern Hill, Poem on His Birthday*   56
The Welsh poet celebrates the joys of growing up and the pride of youth.

EDUCATION   65

    Jean-Jacques Rousseau, *Emile*, from Book 2   67
           Translated by Barbara Foxley
"Nature provides for the child's growth in her own fashion, and this should never be thwarted," writes the eighteenth-century French social philosopher.

    John Stuart Mill, *Childhood and Early Education*   87
A nineteenth-century English philosopher describes his unusual education, which began with the study of Greek at the age of three.

    Margaret Mead, *The Child's World*   102
Describing the Manus children of New Guinea, an American anthropologist asks whether a price is paid when children grow up isolated from the responsibilities and tensions of the adult world.

    Susan Allen Toth, *Preparation for Life*   111
A teacher and writer describes how various jobs in an Iowa town in the 1950s prepared her for womanhood.

    Lincoln Steffens, *I Become a Student*   129
It is possible to get an education, a twentieth-century journalist suggests, if the student knows "how to circumvent the faculty, the other students, and the whole college system of mind-fixing."

    William Wordsworth, *Resolution and Independence*   134
An encounter with an old leech-gatherer teaches a young man what to value in life.

ART AND LIFE   141

    Plato, *The Republic*, Part 5   142
           Translated by F. M. Cornford
A Greek philosopher considers the role of literature in the education of young people in an ideal society.

    Sigmund Freud, *Creative Writers and Day-Dreaming*   155
           Translated by I. F. Grant Duff
The Viennese psychologist and founder of psychoanalysis compares the creative writer to a child at play and considers the nature of art.

    Alexander Solzhenitsyn, *Nobel Lecture*   163
           Translated by F. D. Reeve
The contemporary Russian novelist argues that a nation that loses its literature loses its memory and its spirit.

    W. H. Auden, *Musée des Beaux Arts*   177
The paintings of a sixteenth-century Flemish artist show that artists can teach us much about human suffering.

AIMS OF LIVING   181

Ralph Waldo Emerson, *Self-Reliance*   182
"Nothing can bring you peace but yourself. Nothing can bring you peace but the triumph of principles."

Albert Schweitzer, *Essays: Riddles of Existence, The Will to Live*   201
        Translated by C.T. Campion
The French doctor and missionary describes how he discovered a "reverence for life" and lived by it.

E. M. Forster, *What I Believe*   207
Personal relationships are "something comparatively solid in a world full of violence and cruelty."

Paul Tillich, *The Lost Dimension of Religion*   215
"Being religious means asking passionately the question of the meaning of our existence and being willing to receive answers, even if the answers hurt."

Will Herberg, *The Religion of Americans and American Religion*   223
Catholics, Protestants, and Jews in America share attitudes and values that form an "American religion."

Graham Greene, *The Last Pope*   241
An English novelist asks whether an age of war, injustice, and cruelty can be called "Christian" and "civilized"?

Albert Camus, *The Guest*   249
        Translated by Justin O'Brien
A schoolmaster in Algeria, ordered by a police official to take an accused killer to prison, must decide whether to act against his conscience.

Leo Tolstoy, *The Death of Ivan Ilych*   259
        Translated by Louise and Aylmer Maude
A magistrate dying of a mysterious illness begins to question how he has lived his life.

PEOPLE AND STEREOTYPES   299

Mary Wollstonecraft, *A Vindication of the Rights of Woman*, Chapter 3   300
The eighteenth-century English feminist considers the effects of inadequate education and other deprivations on the lives of women.

Stephen Jay Gould, *Human Equality Is a Contingent Fact of History*   312
"My visceral perception of brotherhood harmonizes with our best biological knowledge."

Robert Coles, *Those Proud and Set Faces*   321
A social worker tries to understand Southern white people trying to survive in a large Northern city.

Martin Luther King, Jr., *Letter from Birmingham Jail*   329
The civil rights leader explains to clergymen in Birmingham, Alabama, why blacks must resort to nonviolent direct action to secure social equality and justice.

Eudora Welty, *Where Is the Voice Coming From?*   343
A Southern white man describes how he stalked a black civil rights leader and shot him to death.

Wright Morris, *A Fight between a White Boy and a Black Boy in the Dusk of a Fall Afternoon in Omaha, Nebraska*   348
Returning in later years to the scene of a fight between a white boy and a black boy, a man wonders why the episode stays in his memory.

PEOPLE AND SOCIETY   353

Henry David Thoreau, *Resistance to Civil Government*   354
"Can there not be a government in which majorities do not virtually decide right and wrong, but conscience?"

George Orwell, *Reflections on Gandhi*   370
Orwell asks whether Gandhi's pacifism and philosophy of nonviolent direct action were antihuman and out of touch with political realities in the twentieth century.

Hannah Arendt, *Duties of a Law-Abiding Citizen*   378
A political scientist examines the mentality of Adolf Eichmann and other Nazis who slaughtered millions of Jews.

Stanley Milgram, *Obedience and Disobedience to Authority*   390
A social psychologist conducts an experiment to discover why people perform acts that violate their moral inclinations and conscience.

Nadine Gordimer, *The Smell of Death and Flowers*   411
A young South African woman volunteers to join a protest against apartheid and wonders why she has.

Irving Feldman, *The Pripet Marshes*   427
A poet mentally transports Jewish friends and relatives to a Russian village and then tries to imagine what happens to them when a German death squad arrives.

PART TWO

PERSPECTIVES ON CONTEMPORARY ISSUES   431

RESPONSIBILITIES OF THE SCIENTIST   433

T. H. Murray, *Ethical Issues in Genetic Engineering*   433
Experiments with recombinant DNA raise various ethical issues.

Jeremy Rifkin, *Creating the Efficient Gene*   446
The experiments proposed by genetic engineers present a danger different from those of other scientific experiments.

Elliot S. Gershon, *Should Science Be Stopped? The Case of Recombinant DNA Research*   453
Banning experiments with recombinant DNA is unjustified and will be devastating to scientific research.

Lewis Thomas, *The Hazards of Science*   464
"*Is there a limit to scientific inquiry not set by what is knowable but by what we ought to be knowing?*"

RESPONSIBILITIES OF THE DOCTOR   471

Mack Lipkin, *On Lying to Patients*   471
A medical doctor argues that it is sometimes impossible to tell a patient the whole truth about an illness.

Sissela Bok, *Lies to the Sick and Dying*   475
A legal philosopher asks whether it is ever right to deny patients the facts about their illness.

William Carlos Williams, *Jean Beicke*   489
A doctor treating a sick child wonders why doctors and nurses work to save patients they consider hopeless or destined to live painful lives.

James F. Childress, *Who Shall Live when Not All Can Live?*   497
When medical resources such as dialysis machines are scarce, how should they be allocated?

Jules Romains, *Knock*   509
        Translated by James Gidney
An enterprising doctor uses interesting methods to turn a poor medical practice into a lucrative one.

POPULATION AND HUMAN LIFE   545

René Dubos, *Population Density and Human Life*   546
The question raised by population growth is not how many people can be fed or how many the earth can hold, but "what can be done to maintain the qualities that give to human life its peculiar characteristics."

Richard Selzer, *Abortion*   552
A medical doctor describes his feelings and thoughts about an abortion he witnesses.

Jonathan Swift, *A Modest Proposal*   558
A witness to the suffering of poor people in eighteenth-century Ireland proposes a remedy that he believes many Irish and their English landlords and governors will find practical.

Garrett Hardin, *Triage*   566
Society must develop a policy for the allocation of food and other scarce natural resources.

Arthur Hugh Clough, *The Latest Decalogue*   579
A nineteenth-century English poet suggests how people of his time modernized the Ten Commandments.

WAR   581

Nigel Calder, *Looking for the Exit*   582
Calder considers the possibilities for nuclear disarmament in the 1980s.

Niccolo Machiavelli, *The Art of War*, from Book 1   590
        Translated by Allan H. Gilbert
"A well-ordered city will then decree that this practice of warfare shall be used in times of peace for exercise and in times of war for necessity and for glory, and will allow the public alone to practice it as a profession, as did Rome."

William James, *The Moral Equivalent of War*   601
The twentieth-century American philosopher considers ways to limit and possibly eradicate war.

Lewis Mumford, *The Origins of War*   611
Mumford asks whether war originates in a human disposition to violence or in particular needs of a society or culture.

Pope John XXIII, *Pacem in Terris*, Parts III and IV   621
"There can be . . . no doubt that relations between states, as between individuals, should be regulated not by the force of arms but by the light of reason, by the rule, that is, of truth, of justice, and of active and sincere cooperation."

Herbert Read, *The Execution of Cornelius Vane*   633
A young soldier about to be executed for desertion during World War One questions the justice of his sentence.

Author Index   641

THE
EDUCATED
READER

GENERAL INTRODUCTION

The Aim of This Book

The essays, dialogues, stories, poems, and the play in this book deal with related experiences and ideas from different perspectives or outlooks. The word *perspective* refers generally to the special viewpoint of a writer, to habitual ways of interpreting or understanding experience. The writer's past experiences gradually form this outlook; new experiences and perceptions continually modify it. The word *perspective* also refers to the particular assumptions and methodology of a discipline or science. We thus refer to the perspectives of the humanities or the sciences. Part One of this book presents various viewpoints and outlooks toward a wide range of experiences and ideas; Part Two does the same, but also shows how writers in various disciplines discuss important contemporary issues.

Although a person's experiences of growing up, getting an education, and becoming acquainted with various kinds of people are similar to other people's experiences, they are never the same. Our upbringing and our culture affect us more than we realize. The South African young woman described by Nadine Gordimer in her short story faces decisions, and so did the young Frederick Douglass in the slave-owning South and the young Maya Angelou in twentieth-century Arkansas. The very different values and attitudes of their worlds shaped these young people's decisions in ways they could not fully understand or control. Writers like Jean-Jacques Rousseau and Margaret Mead, living in different centuries and in very different societies, also wrote from different assumptions shaped by their culture and philosophy.

Each section of this book draws on different kinds of writing—autobiography, fiction, poetry, philosophical, expository, and argumentative essays. Does it matter that one writer explores experiences and ideas fictionally and another writer explores them philosophically or technically—perhaps through the assumptions and methods of a particular social science or school of philosophy? Certainly the aims of a story and a technical essay seem at first markedly different, particularly if we regard fiction as a form of entertainment. Even Sir Philip Sidney's classic statement that the aim of imaginative literature is "to teach and delight" would seem to separate the stories in this book from that writing whose purpose is mainly to instruct and persuade. Yet readers of Nadine Gordimer, Eudora Welty, Leo Tolstoy, and Albert Camus would find it difficult to apply Sidney's definition to those writers' stories. To "teach" indeed suggests that the writer has a single aim or a clear message in mind in the course of writing. Yet, as numerous writers have testified, the act of writing is often an act of discovery of meanings that never become fixed. The decision to write is often the decision to explore experiences that evade definition or exact interpretation.

"No man draws a definite outline of his life, and we only think it out in details," the French essayist Michel de Montaigne writes in the essay that opens this book. The philosopher and the social scientist deal with human life and experience abstractly; therefore, they are able to discover patterns and thus give life a single fixed order. But this reduction of experience to fixed laws and categories is deceptive. The nicely defined "problem" that the social scientist examines leads most often to tentative conclusions and not to "solutions"—to new problems that may require a different kind of investigation. The investigation itself is often a matter of dispute among the scientists themselves. And the intuition and imagination that artists and writers depend upon are no less important to the philosopher and the social scientist. In the fieldwork she did in New Guinea, Margaret Mead depended upon the same powers of imagination and observation.

So in referring to *perspectives* we are not referring to independent acts performed by individuals different in mental capacity, experience, or training. At various times each of us may function as a reporter, an artist, a philosopher, or a researcher. This book illustrates the various modes of observation, reporting, and imagining that writers employ. It does not seek to do what only the systematic study of literature, philosophy, art, and the sciences can do for us, but it shows that these studies are really more similar and interdependent than day-to-day classroom experience suggests.

How to Read This Book

We do not read or view an essay, a story, a poem, a film, and a play in exactly the same way. How we approach any one of these depends on what we seek from it. Sometimes we read to be entertained; turning the pages of a magazine, we glance at stories and photographs, pausing at times when one captures our attention. Other times we read because we seek to converse silently with the writer we have chosen to make our companion, and other times we read to learn something. Perhaps a deeper motive exists for other reading we do. We noted that writers seek in the act of writing to discover what it is they have experienced and thought. Readers do the same. We read because we wish to know ourselves.

The advice to read with an open mind is a cliché, but one worth repeating. An open mind means more than an openness to new experiences and ideas. A mind that is open is skeptical; it gives an idea a fair hearing, at the same time looking for evidence and watching how the writer puts that evidence to use. A skeptical attitude is particularly necessary because the printed page seems to give authority to the words and we perhaps want them to contain the "answer" to the question or issue of the essay. Each writer, as we said at the beginning, looks at experiences and ideas from a particular perspective; each narrative, description, explanation, and argument has been shaped by a way of seeing—from the way the writer sees the world, based on the way the culture has taught the writer to do so. As we read we need to be aware of these perspectives—the connections, similarities, differences, interdependencies. In writing, too, we must keep in mind that no single perspective or point of view gives the whole truth about human experience or the world.

Each way of seeing gives us a rich and significant view of the world that is nevertheless limited. But this limitation proves unexpectedly a source of further insight both into ourselves and into the world. In learning to read better, the reader is like an instrument that probes the visible world to its limits and then seeks to probe the world from a new physical vantage point or perspective. The same is true of our writing, whether it is inspired by our observations of life or by the reading we do. Reading and writing, together, develop a particular kind of intellect that one writer has defined as humanistic:

> The intellect is common to us all. The use of intellect for the discovery of what we may become is the work of humanistic study. For what humanists study is what some have been and done which is worthy of attention and even emulation. When we use our minds to explore the potentialities of imagination, we come to history, philosophy, and literature. For these disciplines explore the great works of imagination and passion (not alone of intellect) and allow us to experience, in the deeds and vision of other men and women, those hitherto unimagined thoughts, unseen visions, unheard sounds, and unplumbed depths of mature emotion, by which we may measure and shape our own capacity and so transcend our small and limited selves.—Jacob Neusner, "To Weep with Achilles," *The Chronicle of Higher Education,* January 29, 1979

PART ONE

GENERAL PERSPECTIVES

YOUTH AND EXPERIENCE

*T*he story, essays, and poems in this section on youth and experience reveal very different people as well as backgrounds. The sixteenth-century France that shaped the life and influenced the writings of Michel de Montaigne was a far different world from the Arkansas town that Maya Angelou describes or the Wales that influenced Dylan Thomas as a writer. Family, society, religion, the prevailing culture—all are decisive influences in everyone's life, and they can tell us much about choices and goals. Yet the sum of these influences, if a writer could identify all of them, cannot tell us the truly important things we want to know. The English novelist Virginia Woolf expresses this fact in a discussion of what biographers miss in the lives of the people they write about:

> Yet it is by such invisible presences that the "subject of this memoir" is tugged this way or that every day of his life; it is they that keep him in position. Consider what immense forces society brings to play upon each of us, how that society changes from decade to decade; and also from class to class; well, if we cannot analyze these invisible presences, we know very little of the subject of the memoir; and again how futile life-writing becomes. I see myself as a fish in a stream; deflected; held in place; but cannot describe the stream.
> —*Moments of Being*

Often the choices and goals that guide the writer, indeed the whole of the past, are as mysterious as "invisible presences" that are unanalyzable:

> Looking back, then, at Kensington Gardens, though I can recover incidents, many more than I have patience to describe, I cannot recover, save by fits and starts, the focus, the proportions of the external world. It seems to me that a child must have a curious focus; it sees an air-ball or a shell with extreme distinctness; I still see the air-balls, blue and purple, and the ribs on the shells; but these points are enclosed in vast empty spaces. —*Moments of Being*

For Virginia Woolf the act of writing was an effort to recover the past, but that past cannot be wholly recovered. As we read essays, stories, and poems about youthful experiences, we need to keep in mind that facts are what recollection and imagination conceive them to be.

How imaginative a work is depends on its type or form. The choice of a particular genre—whether the work is to be an essay, a story, or a poem—is the choice of a way of seeing. Here is Virginia Woolf struggling with her way of seeing in her diary entry on the characters of a novel she was writing:

> I am not trying to tell a story. Yet perhaps it might be done in that way. A mind thinking. They might be islands of light—islands in the stream that I am trying to convey; life itself going on. The current of the moths flying strongly this way. A lamp and a flower pot in the center. The flower can always be changing. But there must be more unity between each scene than I can find at present. Autobiography is might be called. —*A Writer's Diary*, May 28, 1929

The decision to write a story, a novel, a poem, or an essay might seem to depend on the writer's aptitude or preference. Virginia Woolf was so much dependent on her words to understand herself and her world that she probably would not have chosen to paint a picture instead of writing a novel. Yet the writing of the novel, the diary entry suggests, was for her much like the act of painting. The primary need of the artist is to express one's personal life or sense of the world. That need is an ongoing one; the world is never fully expressed, nor is the understanding of one's own life or other people's lives. Certainly the materials of expression must be at hand for the writer or the artist.

Each develops a craft by learning the fundamentals and practicing them. Often mastery of the craft comes through the act of expression. But the act of imagination and understanding is an achievement that comes for every writer and artist through successive attempts and failures. The writer seeks to discover the world through a perspective offered by the genre. The essays, stories, and poems in this section show each writer seeking not only a perspective but also a genre or form through which to express a truth about the self or the world.

*On the Inconsistency of Our Actions**

Michel de Montaigne

> *It is usual to describe the late-sixteenth-century French writer Michel de Montaigne (1533–1592) as representative of the French Renaissance—like the earlier Italian Renaissance, a period in which individualism and self-expression were important values. This commonplace is not so much untrue as a half-truth, for individual art and thought had existed in the Middle Ages. Yet strong personalities*

---

*Translated by E. J. Trechmann.

like Dante three centuries earlier, at the beginning of the fourteenth century, and the later Montaigne made literature much more a vehicle for personal expression than did medieval writers; Dante used poetry and Montaigne the essay to define their own natures.

Montaigne was born in the southwestern seaport city of Bordeaux, into a family that made its fortune selling wine and fish. Montaigne's father, a Catholic and a soldier in the army of Francis I, was twice mayor of the city; his Spanish-Jewish mother was Protestant. Michel was raised a Catholic; two of the other eight children in the family were Calvinist. This diversity suggests that Michel grew up in a family of independent minds. No member was more independent than his father, who gave his infant son a tutor that spoke to the boy only in Latin.

Montaigne was thoroughly educated in classical literature, which he quoted frequently in his essays, and in later years he studied law. During his career of public service as a legal counselor and member of the Bordeaux parliament, he made the friendship of a young nobleman three years his senior, the author of an unpublished republican tract. The influence of this friend deepened the more when he died of the plague in 1563. One writer suggests that the essays that Montaigne began writing, after retiring about 1571 to his family estate, were a continuation of an ongoing dialogue with his deceased friend. But Montaigne was by no means a recluse: he had married in 1565, and he fathered six daughters—only one of whom lived beyond childhood. Between 1581 and 1585 he was, like his father, mayor of Bordeaux. He was occasionally active in court politics and was the friend of both the Catholic king Henry III and the Protestant Henry of Navarre, who, after turning Catholic, was crowned Henry IV of France in 1589.

Que sais-je?—"What do I know?" This question was one of several mottos on the ceiling of his library. Another was the statement "The for and against are both possible." In essays written over a period of twenty years, Montaigne examined the world from the perspective of his own life. Formal essays had been written in classical times and were written by his own contemporaries; Montaigne created the personal essay, which, unlike the formal essay, would range from subject to subject, guided by his intellect and curiosity. He writes in his essay "Of Vanity": "For my part, the very fact of being tied to what I have to say is enough to put me off it." And in another:

For many years now my thoughts have had no other aim but myself, I have studied and examined myself only, and if I study any other things, it is to apply them immediately to, or rather, within, myself. And I do not think I go wrong if, as is done in other incomparably less profitable sciences, I communicate what I have learned in this one, although I am not very well satisfied with the progress I have made therein. There is no description equal in difficulty to a description of oneself, and certainly none in profitableness. —*Essays*, Book 2, "Of Preparation"

The three volumes of essays (published in various editions beginning in 1581) are an autobiography of Montaigne's mind. For Montaigne the essay is what the word itself suggests—an essay or trial, an attempt rather than a completed effort. The essays reveal a man in wonder at his own thoughts. Each thought has value and therefore need not be refined or qualified; feelings and experiences are various and unending; truth is to be discovered through reflection. No single essay can contain the whole truth about either Montaigne himself or people in general. The reader must therefore be prepared for the unusual and the expected. Transitions can be abrupt. Montaigne seldom builds an argument; one reflection follows another, often without concern for consistency:

> Reader, permit this test-piece also to pass muster, and this third addition to the other parts of my portrait. I add, but I do not correct. Firstly, because it appears reasonable that one who has handed his work over to the world has no further claim on it. Let him state his views better elsewhere, if he can, and not adulterate the work he has sold. —*Essays*, Book 3, "Of Vanity"

The essays of Montaigne need not be read consecutively. The reader will gain considerable pleasure in looking over the collected essays and reading at will. The range of topics is wide. The essay on cannibals is of unusual interest, for Montaigne had seen Indians from the New World at the court in Rouen. Montaigne's long apology for the theologian Raimond Sebond, perhaps his most famous work, reminds many readers of Shakespeare's Hamlet— a play that may allude to Montaigne's searching examination of the perennial question, What is man? His essay on the inconsistency of our actions is not so profound an essay and yet asks important questions about human nature.

They who make a practice of comparing human actions are never so perplexed 1
as when they try to piece them together and place them in the same light, for they commonly contradict one another so strangely that it seems impossible they should have come out of the same shop. Marius the younger is now a son of Mars, now a son of Venus.[1] Some one said that Pope Boniface the Eighth entered upon his charge like a fox, behaved therein like a lion, and died like a dog.[2] And who could believe that it was Nero, the very image of cruelty, who, when the sentence of a condemned criminal was brought to him to be signed in the usual way, exclaimed, "Would to God that I had never learned to write!" So grieved was he in his heart to doom a man to death!

The world is full of such examples, nay, any man may provide such an abun- 2
dance of them out of his own experience, that I sometimes wonder to see intelligent

[1]Marius the Younger (109–82? B.C.), the Roman official who unsuccessfully opposed the dictator Sulla, was the adopted son of the great Roman general and politician Gaius Marius. The historian Plutarch wrote of the younger Marius: "His martial intrepidity and ferocious behavior at first procured him the title of the son of Mars, but his conduct afterwards denominated him the son of Venus."
[2]The medieval pope Boniface VIII (1235?–1303) asserted the temporal supremacy of the papacy. He died during his imprisonment by his enemy, Philip IV of France.

men at pains to sort the pieces, seeing that irresolution is, in my view, the most common and conspicuous defect of our nature: witness that famous line of Publilius the writer of low comedies,

> Poor is the plan that never can be changed. (PUBLILIUS SYRUS.)

It seems reasonable to judge a man by the most ordinary acts of his life, but in 3 view of the natural instability of our habits and opinions, I have often thought that even good authors are wrong in obstinately attributing to us a steadfast and consistent character. They hit upon a general feature in a man and arrange and interpret all his actions in accordance with this fanciful conception; and if they are unable to twist them sufficiently, set them down to dissimulation. Augustus has escaped them, for we see in this man, throughout the course of his life, so manifest, abrupt, and continual a variety of actions, that he has slipped through the fingers of even the most daring critics, and been left undecided. I find nothing more difficult to believe than man's consistency, and nothing more easy than his inconsistency. If we examine him in detail and judge of his actions separately, bit by bit, we shall most often find this true.

Throughout ancient history it would be difficult to choose a dozen men who 4 have steered their lives in one certain and constant course, which is the principal aim of wisdom. For, to comprise it all in one word, as an ancient writer says,[3] and to embrace all the rules of life in one, is "to wish and not to wish always the same thing. I will not vouchsafe to add, he says, provided the wish be right; for if it be not right, it is impossible it should be always the same". I once learned indeed that vice is no more than want of rule and moderation, and that it is consequently impossible to associate it with consistency. It is a saying attributed to Demosthenes, "that the beginning of all virtue is consultation and deliberation; and the end and perfection, constancy". If reason directed our course we should choose the fairest; but no one has thought of that:

> He scorns that which he sought, seeks what he scorned of late;
> He flows and ebbs, his whole life contradiction. (HORACE.)

Our ordinary practice is to follow the inclinations of our appetite, to right, to 5 left, up hill, down dale, as we are borne along by the wind of opportunity. We do not consider what we wish except at the moment of wishing it, and we change like that animal which takes its colour from what it is laid upon. What we have but now determined we presently alter, and soon again we retrace our steps: it is nothing but wavering and uncertainty;

> We are led as a puppet is moved by the strings. (HORACE.)

We do not go, we are carried along, like things floating, now smoothly, now perturbedly, according as the water is angry or calm;

> We see them, knowing not
> What 'tis they want, and seeking ever and ever
> A change of place, as if to drop the burden. (LUCRETIUS.)

---

[3]The Roman philosopher Seneca (4 B.C.–A.D. 65) committed suicide on the order of the emperor Nero.

Every day a new fancy; and our humours move with the changes of weather:

> So change the minds of men, like days
> That Father Jove sends down to earth,
> To alternate 'twixt wet and fine. (HOMER.)

We waver between different minds; we wish nothing freely, nothing absolutely,   6
nothing constantly. Should any man prescribe and establish definite laws and a definite
policy in his own head, he would present throughout his life a shining example of even
habits, an order and an unfailing relation of one action to another.

(Empedocles remarked in the inhabitants of Agrigentum this discrepancy, that   7
they abandoned themselves to their pleasures as if they were to die on the morrow, and
that they built as if they were never to die.)[4]

The reason will be easily found, as we see in the case of the younger Cato; he   8
who touches one note of the keyboard touches all: there is a harmony of sounds, all in
perfect tune with each other, which is not to be mistaken. With us, on the other hand,
the rule is: so many actions, so many particular judgements to be passed. The surest,
in my opinion, would be to refer them to the nearest circumstances, without seeking
any farther, and without drawing from them any other inferences.

It was told me, during the tumultuous times our poor State had to go through,   9
that a young woman who lived quite near to where I then was, had thrown herself from
a high window to avoid the forcible caresses of a poor knave of a soldier who was quar-
tered in her house; the fall did not kill her, and, repeating the attempt on her life, she
would have cut her throat with a knife, but was prevented; not however without inflict-
ing a serious wound. She herself then confessed that the soldier had done no more than
importune her with gifts, entreaties, and solicitations, but that she feared he would in
the end proceed to violence. And all this, her words, her mien, and the blood which testified to her virtue, in the true manner of a second Lucretia!

Now I have heard, as a fact, that, both before and after, she was a wench not 10
very difficult to come by. As the tale has it, "Be as handsome and as fine a gentleman
as you will, when you have failed in your pursuit, do not immediately conclude an inviolable chastity in your mistress; it does not follow that the muleteer will not find his opportunity."

Antigonus, having taken a liking to one of his soldiers, on account of his virtue 11
and valour, ordered his physicians to attend him for a persistent internal malady which
had long tormented him, and perceiving that after his cure he went much more coldly
to work than before, asked him what it was that had so altered and cowed him. "You
yourself, Sire, he replied, by delivering me from the ill which made me indifferent to
life."[5] A soldier of Lucullus, having been plundered by enemies, devised a bold stroke for
his revenge; when he had retrieved his loss with interest, Lucullus, whose good opinion

---

[4]According to legend, the fifth-century Greek philosopher Empedocles jumped into the Mount Etna volcano,
perhaps to create the belief that he was a god who had vanished suddenly. Cato the Younger (95–46 B.C.), the
Roman Stoic philosopher, also committed suicide on hearing of a military victory by his political enemy Julius Caesar.

[5]Antigonus was the Macedonian general of Alexander the Great. Lucullus was a Roman general, famous for
his lavish feasts and patronage of the arts.

he had gained, tried to induce him, with the best persuasions he could think of, to undertake some risky business;

> With words that might have stirred a coward's heart. (HORACE.)

Employ, he replied, some wretched soldier who has been plundered;   12

> Though but a rustic clown, "he'll go
> Who's lost his money-belt," he said; (HORACE.)

and resolutely refused to go.

When we read that Mahomet having furiously rated Chasan, chief of his Janis-13 saries, for allowing his line of troops to be broken by the Hungarians, and bearing himself like a coward in the battle; and that Chasan made no reply but, alone and just as he was with his weapon in his hand, rushed furiously into the first body of enemies that he met with, and was immediately overwhelmed; it was not so much a justification of his conduct as a change of mood, not so much natural prowess as a new spite.

Do not think it strange that the man who was so venturesome yesterday should 14 prove such a poltroon on the morrow; either anger, or necessity, or company, or wine, or the sound of the trumpet had put his heart into his belly; it was not a courage thus formed by reason, but a courage stiffened by those circumstances; it was no marvel if other contrary circumstances made a new man of him.

These so supple changes and contradictions which we manifest have made 15 some to imagine that we have two souls, others, that we have two powers which, each in its own way, accompany and stir us, the one to good, the other to evil, since so abrupt a diversity is not to be reconciled with a single subject.

Not only does the wind of accidents stir me according to its blowing, but I am 16 also stirred and troubled by the instability of my attitude; and he who examines himself closely will seldom find himself twice in the same state. I give to my soul now one face, now another, according to the side to which I turn it. If I speak differently of myself, it is because I regard myself differently. All the contradictions are to be found in me, according as the wind turns and changes. Bashful, insolent; chaste, lascivious; talkative, taciturn; clumsy, gentle; witty, dull; peevish, sweet-tempered; mendacious, truthful; knowing, ignorant; and liberal and avaricious and prodigal: all this I see in myself in some degree, according as I veer about; and whoever will study himself very attentively will find in himself, yea, in his judgement, this discordance and unsteadiness. I can say nothing of myself absolutely, simply, and steadily, without confusion and mixture, nor in one word. *Distinguo* is the most universal member of my logic.

Though I am ever inclined to speak well of what is good, and rather to interpret 17 favourably the things that are capable of such interpretation, yet such is the strangeness of our nature that we are often driven to do good, even by vice; if it were not that well-doing is judged by the intention alone.

Therefore a courageous deed ought not to imply a valiant man: the man who 18 is really brave will be always so, and on all occasions. If valour were a habit, and not a sudden eruption, it would make a man equally resolute for all emergencies, the same alone as in company, the same in single combat as in a battle; for let them say what they will, there is not one valour for the pavement and another for the field. As bravely would he bear sickness in his bed as a wound in camp, nor would he fear death in his own home any more than in an assault. We should not see the same man charge with brave assurance into the breach, and afterwards worrying, like a woman, over the loss of a lawsuit or a son. When, though afraid of infamy, he bears up against poverty; when, though wincing at a surgeon's lancet, he stiffly faces the enemy's sword, the action is praiseworthy, but not the man.

Many Greeks, says Cicero,[6] cannot look upon an enemy, and are brave in sick- 19 ness. The Cimbrians and Celtiberians, quite the contrary: *For nothing can be consistent that has not reason for its foundation* (Cicero).

No valour could be more extreme in its kind than Alexander's; but it is of one 20 kind only, and is not complete enough, nor universal on all occasions. Incomparable though it be, it has its blemishes. So it is that we see him so desperately disturbed by the slightest suspicions that his subjects may be plotting against his life, and carried away in his investigations to such violent and indiscriminate acts of injustice, and haunted by a fear that upsets his natural good sense. The superstition too with which he was so strongly tainted bears some likeness to pusillanimity. And the excess of his penitence for the murder of Clytus is also evidence of uneven temper.

Our actions are but a patchwork (*they despise pleasure, but are cowardly in* 21 *pain; they are indifferent to fame, but infamy breaks their spirit),* and we try to gain honour by false pretences. Virtue will not be wooed but for her own sake, and if we sometimes borrow her mask for some other purpose, she will very soon snatch it from our face. When the soul is once steeped in it, the dye is strong and vivid, and will not go without taking the skin with it. Wherefore, to judge a man, we must long and carefully follow his traces. If constancy does not stand firm and wholly on its own foundation, *if the path of life has not been well considered and preconcerted* (Cicero); if changing circumstances make him alter his pace (I should say his route, for the pace may be accelerated or retarded by them), let him go: that man will go *A vau le vent* (down the wind), as the motto of our Talebot has it.[7]

It is no wonder, says an ancient writer,[8] that chance has so great a hold over 22 us, since we live by chance. Unless a man has directed his life as a whole to a certain fixed goal, he cannot possibly dispose his particular actions. Unless he have an image of the whole in his mind, he cannot possibly arrange the pieces. How can a painter lay in a stock of colours, if he knows not what he is going to paint? No man draws a definite outline of his life, and we only think it out in details. The archer must first know at what he is aiming, and then accommodate his hand, his bow, the string, the arrow, and his movements, accordingly. Our plans go wrong because they have neither aim nor direction. No wind serves the ship that has no port of destination.

I cannot agree with those judges who, on the strength of seeing one of his trag- 23 edies, declared in favour of Sophocles, when accused by his son of being incapable of managing his domestic affairs. Nor do I hold with the conclusions arrived at by the Pari-

---

[6]Cicero (106–43 B.C.), the great Roman orator and philosopher, influenced writers and speakers of the sixteenth century both as a thinker and Latin stylist. His orations have remained models of organization and argument up to our time.

[7]Probably the English Earl of Shaftesbury, who died near Montaigne's estate in 1453, during the long war between England and France.

[8]The philosopher Seneca.

ans who were sent to reform the Milesians. Visiting the island, they remarked the best-cultivated lands and the best-kept country-houses, and made a note of their owners; and then, having called an assembly of the citizens in the town, they appointed these owners the new governors and magistrates, concluding that, being careful of their private affairs, they would be equally careful of those of the public.

We are all made up of bits, and so shapelessly and diversely put together, that 24 every piece, at every moment, plays its own game. And there is as much difference between us and ourselves, as between us and others. *Be sure that it is very difficult to be always the same man* (Seneca). Since ambition can teach a man valour, temperance, and liberality, yea and justice too; since greed can implant in the heart of a shop-apprentice, bred up in obscurity and neglect, the confidence to entrust himself, so far from the domestic hearth, to the mercy of the waves and angry Neptune in a frail bark; since it teaches also discretion and prudence; and since Venus herself can put resolution and temerity into the boy who is still under the discipline of the rod, and embolden the heart of the tender virgin in her mother's arms,

> With Love for guide,
> Alone the maid steps o'er her prostrate guards,
> And steals by night into the young man's arms; (TIBULLUS.)

it is not enough for a sober understanding to judge us simply by our external actions: we must sound the innermost recesses, and observe the springs which give the swing. But since it is a high and hazardous undertaking, I would rather that fewer people meddled with it.

Questions

1. Does Montaigne merely note or call attention to irresolution as "the most common and conspicuous defect of our nature" (paragraph 2) and also to "the natural instability of our habits and opinions" (paragraph 3)? Or does he give an explanation for these qualities?
2. Does his self-portrait in paragraphs 16–17 provide an explanation or increase your understanding of his view of human nature?
3. What is Montaigne trying to show through the young woman described in paragraphs 9–10 and through Antigonus, the soldier of Lucullus, and Chasan in paragraphs 11–13?
4. How does Montaigne define vice in paragraph 4? By implication, then, what is virtue? Is he suggesting that the rational man who consults and deliberates is always a virtuous man? Is the harmonious person described in paragraph 8?
5. What is the purpose of the discussion of valor and cowardice in paragraphs 18–22?
6. Why does Montaigne turn to the role of chance in human life in paragraph 22 and to Sophocles, the Greek dramatist, in paragraph 23? How are these topics related to the rest of the essay?
7. How are the ideas of paragraph 24 related to the rest of the essay?
8. Does the essay contain a central idea or thesis that organizes the many ideas and illustrations? Or is the essay a loosely organized series of reflections on human actions and human nature?

Suggestions for Writing

1. Discuss the qualities you share with Montaigne and those that are different. Present these in an essay as informal and free-ranging as you wish.
2. Explain in your own words the idea of virtue implied in Montaigne's essay and illustrate it. Then discuss the extent to which Montaigne's idea of virtue is your own.
3. Compare the development of ideas in "On the Inconsistency of Our Actions" with those of another essay by Montaigne or an essay by Samuel Johnson, Charles Lamb, William Hazlitt, Robert Louis Stevenson, or another essayist who writes about human actions or human nature.

Additional Reading

Auerbach, Erich. *Mimesis: The Representation of Reality in Western Literature.* Chapter 12. Princeton: Princeton University Press, 1953.

Frame, Donald M. *Montaigne: A Biography.* New York: Harcourt Brace Jovanovich, 1965.

———. *Montaigne's Discovery of Man: The Humanization of a Humanist.* New York: Columbia University Press, 1955.

———. *Montaigne's Essays: A Study.* Englewood Cliffs: Prentice-Hall, 1969.

Montaigne, Michel de. *The Essays.* Trans. E. J. Trechmann. London: Oxford University Press, 1935.

———. *Complete Works: Essays, Travel Journal, Letters.* Newly trans. by Donald M. Frame. Stanford: Stanford University Press, 1957.

Tilley, Arthur A. *Studies in the French Renaissance.* Cambridge, England: Cambridge University Press, 1922.

I Resolve to Become a Jungle Doctor

Albert Schweitzer

Few men or women of the twentieth century better exemplify the ideal of the whole person than does Albert Schweitzer, the German theologian, philosopher, musician, and doctor. In his autobiography Out of My Life and Thought, *Schweitzer tells us of his childhood in Upper Alsace, where his father was a Lutheran minister and his paternal grandfather had been a schoolteacher and organist; his mother was the daughter of a Protestant clergyman. At the age of five, Schweitzer began receiving piano lessons from his father; he soon was taking lessons at the organ and at nine began performing in public. In 1893, he entered Strassburg University to study philosophy and theology—and during an interruption of his studies for military serv-*

ice, he pursued an inquiry into the life of Jesus. Passing his theological examination in 1898, he studied philosophy and theology in Paris and Berlin, completed a doctoral degree in theology at Strassburg, and wrote books on religious subjects and on the composer Johann Sebastian Bach. He later collaborated on an edition of Bach's organ works. In 1905, he made a resolution to become a medical doctor and work in Africa.

Schweitzer received his medical degree in 1911 and in 1912 married Hélène Bresslau, a young woman he had met in Strassburg ten years earlier—a person of independent mind who worked with sick children in a state orphanage and with unmarried mothers. In 1913 Schweitzer founded a hospital at Lambaréné in French Equatorial Africa, where he practiced medicine the rest of his life. A trained nurse, his wife worked with Schweitzer at his hospital until her death in 1957. Though she and Schweitzer made occasional visits to Europe and the United States, they lived most of their life at Lambaréné and Dr. Schweitzer continued writing on religion and philosophy and playing the organ. In 1952 he received the Nobel Peace Prize. Schweitzer died in 1965.

His essays in the Aims of Living section of this book represent the philosophical thought of his later years. The excerpt from a chapter in his autobiography reprinted here describes Schweitzer's decision to become a medical doctor. Schweitzer writes in a later passage:

> I wanted to be a doctor that I might be able to work without having to talk. For years I had been giving myself out in words and it was with joy that I had followed the calling of theological teacher and of preacher. But this new form of activity I could not represent to myself as being talking about the religion of love, but only as an actual putting it into practice. Medical knowledge made it possible for me to carry out my intention in the best and most complete way, wherever the path of service might lead me. In view of the plan for Equatorial Africa, the acquisition of such knowledge was especially indicated because in the district to which I thought of going a doctor was, according to the missionaries' reports, the most needed of all needed things. They were always complaining in their magazine that the natives who visited them in physical suffering could not be given the help they desired. To become one day the doctor whom these poor creatures needed, it was worthwhile, so I judged, to become a medical student.

On October 13th, 1905, a Friday, I dropped into a letter box in the Avenue de la Grande Armée in Paris, letters to my parents and to some of my most intimate acquaintances, telling them that at the beginning of the winter term I should enter myself as a medical student, in order to go later on to Equatorial Africa as a doctor. In one of them I sent in the resignation of my post as principal of the Theological College of St.

Thomas because of the claim on my time that my intended course of study would make.

The plan which I meant now to put into execution had been in my mind for a   2
long time, having been conceived so long ago as my student days. It struck me as incomprehensible that I should be allowed to lead such a happy life, while I saw so many people around me wrestling with care and suffering. Even at school I had felt stirred whenever I got a glimpse of the miserable home surroundings of some of my schoolfellows and compared them with the absolutely ideal conditions in which we children of the parsonage at Günsbach lived. While at the university and enjoying the happiness of being able to study and even to produce some results in science and art, I could not help thinking continually of others who were denied that happiness by their material circumstances or their health. Then one brilliant summer morning at Günsbach, during the Whitsuntide holidays—it was in 1896—there came to me, as I awoke, the thought that I must not accept this happiness as a matter of course, but must give something in return for it. Proceeding to think the matter out at once with calm deliberation, while the birds were singing outside, I settled with myself before I got up, that I would consider myself justified in living till I was thirty for science and art, in order to devote myself from that time forward to the direct service of humanity. Many a time already had I tried to settle what meaning lay hidden for me in the saying of Jesus! "Whosoever would save his life shall lose it, and whosoever shall lose his life for My sake and the Gospels shall save it." Now the answer was found. In addition to the outward, I now had inward happiness.

What would be the character of the activities thus planned for the future was   3
not yet clear to me. I left it to circumstances to guide me. One thing only was certain, that it must be directly human service, however inconspicuous the sphere of it.

I naturally thought first of some activity in Europe. I formed a plan for taking   4
charge of abandoned or neglected children and educating them, then making them pledge themselves to help later on in the same way children in similar positions. When in 1903, as warden of the theological hostel, I moved into my roomy and sunny official quarters on the second floor of the College of St. Thomas, I was in a position to begin the experiment. I offered my help now here, now there, but always unsuccessfully. The constitutions of the organizations which looked after destitute and abandoned children made no provision for the acceptance of such voluntary co-operation. For example, when the Strasbourg orphanage was burnt down, I offered to take in a few boys, for the time being, but the superintendent did not even allow me to finish what I had to say. Similar attempts which I made elsewhere were also failures.

For a time I thought I would some day devote myself to tramps and discharged   5
prisoners. In some measure as a preparation for this I joined the Rev. Augustus Ernst at St. Thomas' in an undertaking which he had begun. He was at home from one to two P.M. and ready to speak to anyone who came to him asking for help or for a night's lodging. He did not, however, give the applicant a trifle in money, or let him wait till he could get information about his circumstances. He would offer to look him up in his lodging house that very afternoon and test the statements he had volunteered about his condition. Then, and then only, would he give him help, but as much , and for as long

a time, as was necessary. What a number of bicycle rides we made with this object in the town and the suburbs, and very often with the result that the applicant was not known at the address he had given. In a great many cases, however, it provided an opportunity for giving, with knowledge of the circumstances, very seasonable help. I had some friends, too, who kindly placed a portion of their wealth at my disposal.

Already, as a student, I had been active in social service as a member of the student association known as the Diaconate of St. Thomas, which held its meetings in St. Thomas' College. Each of us had a certain number of poor families assigned to him, which he was to visit every week, taking to them the help allotted to them and making a report on their condition. The money we thus distributed we collected from members of the old Strasbourg families who supported this undertaking, begun by former generations and now carried on by us. Twice a year, if I remember right, each of us had to make his definite number of such begging appeals. To me, being shy and rather awkward in society, these visits were a torture. I believe that in these preparatory studies for the begging I have had to do in later years I sometimes showed myself extremely unskillful. However, I learned through them that begging with tact and restraint is better appreciated than any sort of stand-and-deliver approach, and also that the correct method of begging includes the good tempered acceptance of a refusal. 6

In our youthful inexperience we no doubt often failed, in spite of the best intentions, to use all the money entrusted to us in the wisest way, but the intentions of the givers were nevertheless fully carried out in that it pledged young men to take an interest in the poor. For that reason I think with deep gratitude of those who met with so much understanding and liberality our efforts to be wisely helpful, and hope that many students may have the privilege of working, commissioned in this way by the charitable, as recruits in the struggle against poverty. 7

While I was concerned with tramps and discharged prisoners it had become clear to me that they could only be effectively helped by a number of individuals who would devote themselves to them. At the same time, however, I had realized that in many cases these could only accomplish their best work in collaboration with organizations. But what I wanted was an absolutely personal and independent activity. Although I was resolved to put my services at the disposal of some organization, if it should be really necessary, I nevertheless never gave up the hope of finding a sphere of activity to which I could devote myself as an individual and as wholly free. That this longing of mine found fulfillment I have always regarded as a signal instance of the mercy which has again and again been vouchsafed to me. 8

One morning in the autumn of 1904 I found on my writing table in the college one of the green-covered magazines in which the Paris Missionary Society reported every month on its activities. A certain Miss Scherdlin used to put them there knowing that I was specially interested in this society on account of the impression made on me by the letters of one of its earliest missionaries, Casalis by name, when my father read them aloud at his missionary services during my childhood. That evening, in the very act of putting it aside that I might go on with my work, I mechanically opened this magazine, which had been laid on my table during my absence. As I did so, my eye caught the title of an article: *Les besoins de la Mission du Congo* ("The needs of the Congo Mission"). 9

It was by Alfred Boegner, the president of the Paris Missionary Society, an Alsa- 10
tian, and contained a complaint that the mission had not enough workers to carry on
its work in the Gaboon, the northern province of the Congo Colony. The writer expressed his hope that his appeal would bring some of those "on whom the Master's eyes
already rested" to a decision to offer themselves for this urgent work. The conclusion
ran: "Men and women who can reply simply to the Master's call, 'Lord, I am coming,'
those are the people whom the Church needs." Having finished the article, I quietly
began my work. My search was over.

My thirtieth birthday a few months later I spent like the man in the parable 11
who "desiring to build a tower, first counts the cost whether he have wherewith to complete it." The result was that I resolved to realize my plan of direct human service in
Equatorial Africa.

With the exception of one trustworthy friend no one knew of my intention. 12
When it became known through the letters I had sent from Paris, I had hard battles to
fight with my relations and friends. Almost more than with my contemplated new start
itself they reproached me with not having shown them so much confidence as to discuss
it with them first. With this side issue they tormented me beyond measure during those
difficult weeks. That theological friends should outdo the others in their protests struck
me as all the more preposterous, because they had, no doubt, all preached a fine
sermon—perhaps a very fine one—showing how St. Paul, as he has recorded in his letter to the Galatians, "conferred not with flesh and blood" beforehand about what he
meant to do for Jesus.

My relatives and my friends all joined in expostulating with me on the folly of 13
my enterprise. I was a man, they said, who was burying the talent entrusted to him and
wanted to trade with false currency. Work among savages I ought to leave to those who
would not thereby be compelled to leave gifts and acquirements in science and art unused. Widor, who loved me as if I were his son, scolded me as being like a general who
wanted to go into the firing line—there was no talk about trenches at the time—with
a rifle. A lady who was filled with the modern spirit proved to me that I could do much
more by lecturing on behalf of medical help for natives than I could by the action I contemplated. That saying from Goethe's *Faust* ("In the beginning was the Deed"), was now
out of date, she said. Today propaganda was the mother of happenings.

In the many verbal duels which I had to fight, as a weary opponent, with people 14
who passed for Christians, it moved me strangely to see them so far from perceiving that
the effort to serve the love preached by Jesus may sweep a man into a new course of life,
although they read in the New Testament that it can do so, and found it there quite in
order. I had assumed as a matter of course that familiarity with the sayings of Jesus
would produce a much better appreciation of what to popular logic is nonrational, than
my own case allowed me to assert. Several times, indeed, it was my experience that my
appeal to the act of obedience which Jesus' command of love may under special circumstances call for, brought upon me an accusation of conceit, although I had, in fact, been
obliged to do violence to my feelings to employ this argument at all. In general, how
much I suffered through so many people assuming a right to tear open all the doors and
shutters of my inner self!

As a rule, too, it was of no use allowing them, in spite of my repugnance, to 15 have a glimpse of the thoughts which had given birth to my resolution. They thought there must be something behind it all, and guessed at disappointment at the slow growth of my reputation. For this there was no ground at all, seeing that I had received, even as a young man, such recognition as others usually get only after a whole life of toil and struggle. Unfortunate love experiences were also alleged as the reason for my decision.

I felt as a real kindness the action of persons who made no attempt to dig their 16 fists into my heart, but regarded me as a precocious young man, not quite right in his head, and treated me correspondingly with affectionate mockery.

I felt it to be, in itself, quite natural that relations and friends should put before 17 me anything that told against the reasonableness of my plan. As one who demands that idealists shall be sober in their views, I was conscious that every start upon an untrodden path is a venture which only in unusual circumstances looks sensible and likely to be successful. In my own case I held the venture to be justified, because I had considered it for a long time and from every point of view, and credited myself with the possession of health, sound nerves, energy, practical common sense, toughness, prudence, very few wants, and everything else that might be found necessary by anyone wandering along the path of the idea. I believed myself, further, to wear the protective armor of a temperament quite capable of enduring an eventual failure of my plan.

As a man of individual action, I have since that time been approached for my 18 opinion and advice by many people who wanted to make a similar venture, but only in comparatively few cases have I taken on me the responsibility of giving them immediate encouragement. I often had to recognize that the need "to do something special" was born of a restless spirit. Such persons wanted to dedicate themselves to larger tasks because those that lay nearest did not satisfy them. Often, too, it was evident that they had been brought to their decisions by quite secondary considerations. Only a person who can find a value in every sort of activity and devote himself to each one with full consciousness of duty, has the inward right to take as his object some extraordinary activity instead of that which falls naturally to his lot. Only a person who feels his preference to be a matter of course, not something out of the ordinary, and who has no thought of heroism, but just recognizes a duty undertaken with sober enthusiasm, is capable of becoming a spiritual adventurer such as the world needs. There are no heroes of action: only heroes of renunciation and suffering. Of such there are plenty. But few of them are known, and even these not to the crowd, but to the few.

Carlyle's *Heroes and Hero Worship* is not a profound book.*   19

Of those who feel any sort of impulse, and would prove actually fitted, to devote 20 their lives to independent personal activity, the majority are compelled by circumstances to renounce such a course. As a rule this is because they have to provide for one or more dependents, or because they have to stick to their calling in order to earn their own living. Only one who thanks to his own ability or the devotion of friends is in

---

*In *On Heroes, Hero Worship, and the Heroic in History* (1841) the Scottish writer Thomas Carlyle distinguishes various heroes, including kings and others who, like Oliver Cromwell and Napoleon Bonaparte, act on their visions of what life should be.

worldly matters a free man, can venture nowadays to take the path of independent activity. This was not so much the case in earlier times because anyone who gave up remunerative work could still hope to get through life somehow or other, while anyone who thought of doing the same in the difficult economic conditions of today would run the risk of coming to grief not only materially but spiritually as well.

I am compelled, therefore, not only by what I have observed, but by experience 21 also, to admit that worthy and capable persons have had to renounce a course of independent action which would have been of great value to the world, because circumstances rendered such a course impossible.

Those who are so favored as to be able to embark on a course of free personal 22 activity must accept this good fortune in a spirit of humility. They must often think of those who, though willing and capable, were never in a position to do the same. And as a rule they must temper their own strong determination with humility. They are almost always destined to have to seek and wait till they find a road open for the activity they long for. Happy are those to whom the years of work are allotted in richer measure than those of seeking and waiting! Happy those who in the end are able to give themselves really and completely!

These favored persons must also be modest so as not to fly into a passion at the 23 opposition they encounter; they have to meet it in the temper which says: "Ah, well, it had to be!" Anyone who proposes to do good must not expect people to roll stones out of his way, but must accept his lot calmly if they even roll a few more upon it. A strength which becomes clearer and stronger through its experience of such obstacles is the only strength that can conquer them. Resistance is only a waste of strength.

Of all the will for the ideal which exists in mankind only a small part can be 24 manifested in action. All the rest is destined to realize itself in unseen effects, which represent, however, a value exceeding a thousandfold and more that of the activity which attracts the notice of the world. Its relation to the latter is like that of the deep sea to the waves which stir its surface. The hidden forces of goodness are embodied in those persons who carry on as a secondary pursuit the immediate personal service which they cannot make their life work. The lot of the many is to have as a profession, for the earning of their living and the satisfaction of society's claim on them, a more or less soulless labor in which they can give out little or nothing of their human qualities, because in that labor they have to be little better than human machines. Yet no one finds himself in the position of having no possible opportunity of giving himself to others as a human being. The problem produced by the fact of labor being today so thoroughly organized, specialized, and mechanized depends only in part for its solution on society's not merely removing the conditions thus produced, but doing its very best to guard the rights of human personality. What is even more important is that sufferers shall not simply bow to their fate, but shall try with all their energy to assert their human personality amid their unfavorable conditions by spiritual activity. Anyone can rescue his human life, in spite of his professional life, who seizes every opportunity of being a man by means of personal action, however unpretending, for the good of fellow men who need the help of a fellow man. Such a man enlists in the service of the spiritual and good. No fate can prevent a man from giving to others this direct human service side by side with his life work. If so much of such service remains unrealized, it is because the opportunities are missed.

That everyone shall exert himself in that state of life in which he is placed, to 25 practice true humanity toward his fellow men, on that depends the future of mankind. Enormous values come to nothing every moment through the missing of opportunities, but the values which do get turned into will and deed mean wealth which must not be undervalued. Our humanity is by no means so materialistic as foolish talk is continually asserting it to be. Judging by what I have learned about men and women, I am convinced that there is far more in them of idealist will power than ever comes to the surface of the world. Just as the water of the streams we see is small in amount compared to that which flows underground, so the idealism which becomes visible is small in amount compared with what men and women bear locked in their hearts, unreleased or scarcely released. To unbind what is bound, to bring the underground waters to the surface: mankind is waiting and longing for such as can do that.

Questions

1. What thought or realization made Schweitzer resolve to become a medical doctor? Does he say or imply that his decision was entirely rational—made consciously and without reservation?
2. What does Schweitzer suggest are the right and wrong reasons or motives for making such a decision? Under what circumstances would he have discouraged someone from making a similar decision?
3. What service can those dissuaded from this course perform in the world? Is this service always one of direct action?
4. What image of the ideal human being emerges in the discussion of those who sought to dissuade Schweitzer and his opposition to them? Does Schweitzer state this ideal directly?
5. Is this autobiographical essay informative or persuasive, or possibly both? Is Schweitzer perhaps writing a sermon?

Suggestions for Writing

1. Schweitzer says this of people who seek a field of action: "Such persons wanted to dedicate themselves to larger tasks because those that lay nearest did not satisfy them" (paragraph 18). He is alluding here to Carlyle's statement in his semiautobiography *Sartor Resartus* that in a world that seems godless and without purpose the human being can show the universe to be purposeful by doing work at hand and in this way acting as a purposeful being:

> I too could now say to myself: Be no longer a Chaos, but a World, or even Worldkin. Produce! Produce! Were it but the pitifullest infinitesimal fraction of a Product, produce it, in God's name! 'Tis the utmost thou hast in thee: out with it, then. Up, up! Whatsoever thy hand findest to do, do it with thy whole might. Work while it is called Today; for the Night cometh, wherein no man can work.—"The Everlasting Yea"

Discuss the extent to which Schweitzer would agree or disagree with this statement. Cite statements in his autobiographical essay to support your answer.

2. Discuss the extent to which a similar decision of your own was guided by ideals or principles rather than practical considerations.
3. Compare Schweitzer's account of his resolution with that of one of the following people who made similar decisions to devote their lives to the service of others. Use your comparison to reach a relative estimate of character or the nature of the resolution or decision:
   a. St. Augustine, *Confessions*, Book 6
   b. Helen Keller, *The Story of My Life*
   c. Mohandas Gandhi, *The Story of My Experiences with Truth*
   d. Bertrand Russell, *Autobiography*
   e. Leo Tolstoy, *Confession*

Additional Reading

Brabazon, James. *Albert Schweitzer: A Biography.* New York: Putnam's, 1975.

Cousins, Norman. *Dr. Schweitzer of Lambaréné.* New York: Harper and Row, 1960.

Marshall, George, and David Poling. *Schweitzer: A Biography.* New York: Doubleday, 1971.

Schweitzer, Albert. *African Notebook: Reminiscences including Hospital Life and Scenes.* Trans. Mrs. C. E. B. Russell. Bloomington: Indiana University Press, 1958.

————. *Memoirs of Childhood and Youth.* Trans. C. T. Campion. New York: Macmillan, 1949.

————. *On the Edge of the Primeval Forest: Experiences and Observations of a Doctor in Equatorial Africa.* Trans. C. T. Campion. New York: Macmillan, 1948.

————. *Out of My Life and Thought: An Autobiography.* Trans. C. T. Campion. New York: Holt, 1933.

————. *The Philosophy of Civilization.* Trans. C. T. Campion. New York: Macmillan, 1953.

————. *Reverence for Life.* Trans. Reginald H. Fuller. New York: Harper and Row, 1969.

"A Change Came o'er the Spirit of My Dream"

Frederick Douglass

As a free man living in the pre–Civil War North, Frederick Augustus Washington Bailey adopted the name by which he is known today. The chapter reprinted here from My Bondage and My Freedom, *published in 1855—one of several versions of his autobiography— describes his experiences as a black slave in the 1820s. Douglass was born in 1818 on the Maryland farm of a slaveowner, Aaron Anthony.*

Descended from West Indies blacks brought to Maryland, his mother, Harriet Bailey, was a slave in the household. Douglass later suspected that Anthony was his father: "He was admitted to be such by all I ever heard speak of my parentage," Douglass wrote in 1845. "The opinion was also whispered that my master was my father; but of the correctness of this opinion, I know nothing; the means of knowing was withheld from me." The autobiographies reveal changes in Douglass's perception of Anthony and indeed of his life from early manhood to his late years. In the 1855 autobiography, Douglass states that his father was "nearly white" and gives a graphic description of the man: "Most of his leisure was spent in walking, cursing and gesticulating, like one possessed by a demon. Most evidently, he was a wretched man, at war with his own soul, and with all the world around him." In his 1881 Life and Times of Frederick Douglass, *he writes, "Of my father I know nothing."*

 But the brutalities black people and Douglass himself suffered were not the result of sadism and warped minds alone. In his biography of Douglass, Dickson J. Preston quotes the statement of a Maryland act governing blacks—in force until 1809—that they "have no Sense of Shame, or Apprehensions of future Rewards or Punishments" and therefore could not be governed by English law alone. When Anthony died in 1826, Douglass was sent to the Baltimore house of Hugh Auld, the brother of his owner Thomas Auld. Hugh Auld's young wife Sophia started to teach him to read and write, but stopped when her husband objected. Contrary to what Hugh Auld told his wife, no Maryland law forbade doing so. Although most youths today take the opportunity to learn how to read and write for granted, Douglass could not, and after Auld's interference he proceeded to teach himself through books in the house.

 Douglass lived under other masters, including a "slave breaker" who beat him frequently and severely. One failed escape led to imprisonment, from which he was rescued by Thomas Auld, who then apprenticed him to a ship caulker. In 1838, he succeeded in escaping to New York City, where he married a free-born black woman to whom he had become engaged in Maryland. After moving to New Bedford, Massachusetts, he took the name Frederick Douglass. On hearing William Lloyd Garrison and other abolitionists, Douglass became active in the antislavery movement, traveling widely and publishing a leading abolitionist journal. In 1845 he traveled in England and Ireland; he returned in 1847, after buying his freedom with $710 raised by British friends. On his travels in the United States he was on occasion attacked by sympathizers of slave owners. Thought to have been an accomplice in John Brown's unsuccessful raid on Harper's Ferry, he fled to England in 1859—returning six months later on hearing that his daughter Annie had died.

 At the beginning of the Civil War, Douglass helped organize black regiments; he also pressed for the Emancipation Proclamation. Convinced that blacks would advance only through political action, he was active in the Republican Party—serving in a number of adminis-

trative and diplomatic posts under several presidents and working until his death in 1895 to improve the lives of American black people. "The real question," Douglass said toward the end of his life, "is whether American justice, American liberty, American civilization, American law, and American Christianity can be made to include and protect alike and forever all American citizens. . . ."

Douglass is an important figure in black American history for many reasons. Kenneth Rexroth suggests one of them:

> Although his adult life was spent almost entirely with white people, Frederick Douglass chose to think as a black man. This in itself was no small accomplishment. It is more difficult to avoid becoming an *assimilado* than, for Douglass at least, to escape from slavery. —"Frederick Douglass," *Classics Revisited*

I lived in the family of Master Hugh, at Baltimore, seven years, during which 1 time—as the almanac makers say of the weather—my condition was variable. The most interesting feature of my history here, was my learning to read and write, under somewhat marked disadvantages. In attaining this knowledge, I was compelled to resort to indirections by no means congenial to my nature, and which were really humiliating to me. My mistress—who, as the reader has already seen, had begun to teach me—was suddenly checked in her benevolent design, by the strong advice of her husband. In faithful compliance with this advice, the good lady had not only ceased to instruct me, herself, but had set her face as a flint against my learning to read by any means. It is due, however, to my mistress to say, that she did not adopt this course in all its stringency at the first. She either thought it unnecessary, or she lacked the depravity indispensable to shutting me up in mental darkness. It was, at least, necessary for her to have some training, and some hardening, in the exercise of the slaveholder's prerogative, to make her equal to forgetting my human nature and character, and to treating me as a thing destitute of a moral or an intellectual nature. Mrs. Auld—my mistress—was, as I have said, a most kind and tender-hearted woman; and, in the humanity of her heart, and the simplicity of her mind, she set out, when I first went to live with her, to treat me as she supposed one human being ought to treat another.

It is easy to see, that, in entering upon the duties of a slaveholder, some little 2 experience is needed. Nature has done almost nothing to prepare men and women to be either slaves or slaveholders. Nothing but rigid training, long persisted in, can perfect the character of the one or the other. One cannot easily forget to love freedom; and it is as hard to cease to respect that natural love in our fellow creatures. On entering upon the career of a slaveholding mistress, Mrs. Auld was singularly deficient; nature, which fits nobody for such an office, had done less for her than any lady I had known. It was no easy matter to induce her to think and to feel that the curly-headed boy, who stood by her side, and even leaned on her lap; who was loved by little Tommy, and who loved little Tommy in turn; sustained to her only the relation of a chattel. I was *more* than that, and she felt me to be more than that. I could talk and sing; I could laugh and weep; I could reason and remember; I could love and hate. I was human, and she, dear lady, knew and felt me to be so. How could she, then, treat me as a brute, without a mighty struggle with all the noble powers of her own soul. That struggle came, and the will and power of the husband was victorious. Her noble soul was overthrown; but, he that overthrew it did not, himself, escape the consequences. He, not less than the other parties, was injured in his domestic peace by the fall.

When I went into their family, it was the abode of happiness and contentment. 3 The mistress of the house was a model of affection and tenderness. Her fervent piety and watchful uprightness made it impossible to see her without thinking and feeling—*"that woman is a christian."* There was no sorrow nor suffering for which she had not a tear, and there was no innocent joy for which she had not a smile. She had bread for the hungry, clothes for the naked, and comfort for every mourner that came within her reach. Slavery soon proved its ability to divest her of these excellent qualities, and her home of its early happiness. Conscience cannot stand much violence. Once thoroughly broken down, *who* is he that can repair the damage? It may be broken toward the slave, on Sunday, and toward the master on Monday. It cannot endure such shocks. It must stand entire, or it does not stand at all. If my condition waxed bad, that of the family waxed not better. The first step, in the wrong direction, was the violence done to nature and to conscience, in arresting the benevolence that would have enlightened my young mind. In ceasing to instruct me, she must begin to justify herself *to* herself; and, once consenting to take sides in such a debate, she was riveted to her position. One needs very little knowledge of moral philosophy, to see *where* my mistress now landed. She finally became even more violent in her opposition to my learning to read, than was her husband himself. She was not satisfied with simply doing as *well* as her husband had commanded her, but seemed resolved to better his instruction. Nothing appeared to make my poor mistress—after her turning toward the downward path—more angry, than seeing me, seated in some nook or corner, quietly reading a book or a newspaper. I have had her rush at me, with the utmost fury, and snatch from my hand such newspaper or book, with something of the wrath and consternation which a traitor might be supposed to feel on being discovered in a plot by some dangerous spy.

Mrs. Auld was an apt woman, and the advice of her husband, and her own expe- 4 rience, soon demonstrated, to her entire satisfaction, that education and slavery are incompatible with each other. When this conviction was thoroughly established, I was most narrowly watched in all my movements. If I remained in a separate room from the family for any considerable length of time, I was sure to be suspected of having a book, and was at once called upon to give an account of myself. All this, however, was entirely *too late*. The first, and never to be retraced, step had been taken. In teaching me the alphabet, in the days of her simplicity and kindness, my mistress had given me the *"inch,"* and now, no ordinary precaution could prevent me from taking the *"ell."*

Seized with a determination to learn to read, at any cost, I hit upon many expe- 5 dients to accomplish the desired end. The plea which I mainly adopted, and the one by which I was most successful, was that of using my young white playmates, with whom I met in the street, as teachers. I used to carry, almost constantly, a copy of Webster's spelling book in my pocket; and, when sent of errands, or when play time was allowed me, I would step, with my young friends, aside, and take a lesson in spelling. I generally paid my *tuition fee* to the boys, with bread, which I also carried in my pocket. For a single biscuit, any of my hungry little comrades would give me a lesson more valuable to me than bread. Not every one, however, demanded this consideration, for there were those who took pleasure in teaching me, whenever I had a chance to be taught by them. I am strongly tempted to give the names of two or three of those little boys, as a slight testimonial of the gratitude and affection I bear them, but prudence forbids; not that it would injure me, but it might, possibly, embarrass them; for it is almost an unpardonable offense to do anything, directly or indirectly, to promote a slave's freedom, in a slave state. It is enough to say, of my warm-hearted little play fellows, that they lived on Philpot street, very near Durgin & Baily's shipyard.

Although slavery was a delicate subject, and very cautiously talked about 6 among grown up people in Maryland, I frequently talked about it—and that very freely—with the white boys. I would, sometimes, say to them, while seated on a curb stone or a cellar door, "I wish I could be free, as you will be when you get to be men." "You will be free, you know, as soon as you are twenty-one, and can go where you like, but I am a slave for life. Have I not as good a right to be free as you have?" Words like these, I observed, always troubled them; and I had no small satisfaction in wringing from the boys, occasionally, that fresh and bitter condemnation of slavery, that springs from nature, unseared and unperverted. Of all consciences, let me have those to deal with which have not been bewildered by the cares of life. I do not remember ever to have met with a *boy*, while I was in slavery, who defended the slave system; but I have often had boys to console me, with the hope that something would yet occur, by which I might be made free. Over and over again, they have told me, that "they believed *I* had as good a right to be free as *they* had;" and that "they did not believe God ever made any one to be a slave." The reader will easily see, that such little conversations with my play fellows, had no tendency to weaken my love of liberty, nor to render me contented with my condition as a slave.

When I was about thirteen years old, and had succeeded in learning to read, 7 every increase of knowledge, especially respecting the FREE STATES, added something to the almost intolerable burden of the thought—"I AM A SLAVE FOR LIFE." To my bondage I saw no end. It was a terrible reality, and I shall never be able to tell how sadly that thought chafed my young spirit. Fortunately, or unfortunately, about this time in my life, I had made enough money to buy what was then a very popular school book, viz: the "Columbian Orator." I bought this addition to my library, of Mr. Knight, on Thames street, Fell's Point, Baltimore, and paid him fifty cents for it. I was first led to buy this book, by hearing some little boys say that they were going to learn some little pieces out of it for the Exhibition. This volume was, indeed, a rich treasure, and every opportunity afforded me, for a time, was spent in diligently perusing it. Among much other interesting matter, that which I had perused and reperused with unflagging satisfaction, was a short dialogue between a master and his slave. The slave is represented as having been recaptured, in a second attempt to run away; and the master opens the dialogue with an upbraiding speech, charging the slave with ingratitude, and demanding to know what he has to say in his own defense. Thus upbraided, and thus called upon to reply, the slave rejoins, that he knows how little anything that he can say will avail, seeing that he is completely in the hands of his owner; and with noble resolution, calmly says, "I submit to my fate." Touched by the slave's answer, the master insists upon his further speaking, and recapitulates the many acts of kindness which he has performed toward the slave, and tells him he is permitted to speak for himself. Thus invited to the debate, the quondam slave made a spirited defense of himself, and thereafter the whole argument, for and against slavery, was brought out. The master was vanquished at every turn in the argument; and seeing himself to be thus vanquished, he generously and meekly emancipates the slave, with his best wishes for his prosperity. It is scarcely necessary to say, that a dialogue, with such an origin, and such an ending—read when the fact of my being a slave was a constant burden of grief—powerfully affected me; and I could not help feeling that the day might come, when the well-directed answers made by the slave to the master, in this instance, would find their counterpart in myself.

This, however, was not all the fanaticism which I found in this Columbian Orator. 8 I met there one of Sheridan's mighty speeches, on the subject of Catholic Emancipation, Lord Chatham's speech on the American war, and speeches by the great William Pitt and by Fox.* These were all choice documents to me, and I read them, over and over again, with an interest that was ever increasing, because it was ever gaining in intelligence; for the more I read them, the better I understood them. The reading of these speeches added much to my limited stock of language, and enabled me to give tongue to many interesting thoughts, which had frequently flashed through my soul, and died away for want of utterance. The mighty power and heart-searching directness of truth, penetrating even the heart of a slaveholder, compelling him to yield up his earthly interests to the claims of eternal justice, were finely illustrated in the dialogue, just referred to; and from the speeches of Sheridan, I got a bold and powerful denunciation of oppression, and a most brilliant vindication of the rights of man. Here was, indeed, a noble acquisition. If I ever wavered under the consideration, that the Almighty, in some way, ordained slavery, and willed my enslavement for his own glory, I wavered no longer. I had now penetrated the secret of all slavery and oppression, and had ascertained their true foundation to be in the pride, the power and the avarice of man. The dialogue and the speeches were all redolent of the principles of liberty, and poured floods of light on the nature and character of slavery. With a book of this kind in my hand, my own human nature, and the facts of my experience, to help me, I was equal to a contest with the religious advocates of slavery, whether among the whites or among the colored people, for blindness, in this matter, is not confined to the former. I have met many religious colored people, at the south, who are under the delusion that God requires them to submit to slavery, and to wear their chains with meekness and humility. I could entertain no such nonsense as this; and I almost lost my patience when I found any colored man weak enough to believe such stuff. Nevertheless, the increase of knowledge was attended with bitter, as well as sweet results. The more I read, the more I was led to abhor and detest slavery, and my enslavers. "Slaveholders," thought I, "are only a band of successful robbers, who left their homes and went into Africa for the purpose

---

*Douglass was reading the speeches of eighteenth-century members of parliament. Richard Brinsley Sheridan (1751–1816), the dramatist and statesman, defended the American cause in the Revolutionary War. The elder William Pitt (1708–1778), First Earl of Chatham, opposed taxation of the American colonists; his son, William Pitt (1759–1806), an English prime minister, favored abolition of slavery. So did the orator and statesman Charles James Fox (1749–1806).

of stealing and reducing my people to slavery." I loathed them as the meanest and the most wicked of men. As I read, behold! the very discontent so graphically predicted by Master Hugh, had already come upon me. I was no longer the light-hearted, gleesome boy, full of mirth and play, as when I landed first at Baltimore. Knowledge had come; light had penetrated the moral dungeon where I dwelt; and, behold! there lay the bloody whip, for my back, and here was the iron chain; and my good, *kind master,* he was the author of my situation. The revelation haunted me, stung me, and made me gloomy and miserable. As I writhed under the sting and torment of this knowledge, I almost envied my fellow slaves their stupid contentment. This knowledge opened my eyes to the horrible pit, and revealed the teeth of the frightful dragon that was ready to pounce upon me, but it opened no way for my escape. I have often wished myself a beast, or a bird—anything, rather than a slave. I was wretched and gloomy, beyond my ability to describe. I was too thoughtful to be happy. It was this everlasting thinking which distressed and tormented me; and yet there was no getting rid of the subject of my thoughts. All nature was redolent of it. Once awakened by the silver trump of knowledge, my spirit was roused to eternal wakefulness. Liberty! the inestimable birthright of every man, had, for me, converted every object into an asserter of this great right. It was heard in every sound, and beheld in every object. It was ever present, to torment me with a sense of my wretched condition. The more beautiful and charming were the smiles of nature, the more horrible and desolate was my condition. I saw nothing without seeing it, and I heard nothing without hearing it. I do not exaggerate, when I say, that it looked from every star, smiled in every calm, breathed in every wind, and moved in every storm.

I have no doubt that my state of mind had something to do with the change in 9 the treatment adopted, by my once kind mistress toward me. I can easily believe, that my leaden, downcast, and discontented look, was very offensive to her. Poor lady! She did not know my trouble, and I dared not tell her. Could I have freely made her acquainted with the real state of my mind, and given her the reasons therefor, it might have been well for both of us. Her abuse of me fell upon me like the blows of the false prophet upon his ass; she did not know that an *angel* stood in the way; and—such is the relation of master and slave—I could not tell her. Nature had made us *friends;* slavery made us *enemies.* My interests were in a direction opposite to hers, and we both had our private thoughts and plans. She aimed to keep me ignorant; and I resolved to know, although knowledge only increased my discontent. My feelings were not the result of any marked cruelty in the treatment I received; they sprung from the consideration of my being a slave at all. It was *slavery*—not its mere *incidents*—that I hated. I had been cheated. I saw through the attempt to keep me in ignorance; I saw that slaveholders would have gladly made me believe that they were merely acting under the authority of God, in making a slave of me, and in making slaves of others; and I treated them as robbers and deceivers. The feeding and clothing me well, could not atone for taking my liberty from me. The smiles of my mistress could not remove the deep sorrow that dwelt in my young bosom. Indeed, these, in time, came only to deepen my sorrow. She had changed; and the reader will see that I had changed, too. We were both victims to the same overshadowing evil—*she,* as mistress, *I,* as slave. I will not censure her harshly; she cannot censure me, for she knows I speak but the truth, and have acted in my opposition to slavery, just as she herself would have acted, in a reverse of circumstances.

Questions

1. Douglass grows into many kinds of knowledge as a result of Mrs. Auld's kindness to him and his first experience with reading. What set Mrs. Auld apart from other white people Douglass had known, and what knowledge does he gain of people in general through Mrs. Auld?
2. What insight does this knowledge of people give Douglass into slave owners?
3. What experiences lead Douglass to realize that slavery is neither God-ordained nor a necessary and inescapable condition?
4. What audience is Douglass addressing: a special audience familiar with the institutions of slavery and the lives of slaves, a general audience unfamiliar with them, or a general audience that varies in knowledge?
5. Does Douglass build from broad truths to particular perceptions and applications, or do broad truths emerge from particular experiences and perceptions? Does Douglass state the full meaning of his experiences for the reader?

Suggestions for Writing

1. Develop an idea presented in this essay from your own experience and point of view—for example, "Conscience cannot stand much violence" (paragraph 3). Qualify the statement if you disagree with it in part or as a whole. Be specific in your details of your experience.
2. Narrate an unusual experience that taught you a surprising truth about people. Give specific details about the experience and the persons involved.
3. Narrate your own first experience or a later experience with reading. Discuss the effects of this experience, and draw general conclusions as Douglass does.

Additional Reading

Bontemps, Arna. *Free at Last: The Life of Frederick Douglass.* New York: Dodd, Mead, 1971.

Douglass, Frederick. *The Frederick Douglass Papers, Series One: Speeches, Debates, and Interviews. Volume I: 1841–1846.* Ed. John W. Blassingame, et al. New Haven: Yale University Press, 1979.

Douglass, Frederick. *The Life and Writings of Frederick Douglass.* 5 vols. Ed. Philip S. Foner. New York: International Publishers, 1950–1975.

Foner, Philip S. *Frederick Douglass.* New York: Citadel, 1964.

Huggins, Nathan Irvin. *Slave and Citizen: The Life of Frederick Douglass.* Boston: Little, Brown, 1980.

Preston, Dickson J. *Young Frederick Douglass: The Maryland Years.* Baltimore: Johns Hopkins University Press, 1980.

Graduation

Maya Angelou

At the age of three, Marguerite Johnson (later Maya Angelou) traveled from Long Beach, California, with her brother Bailey to live with a grandmother and an uncle in Stamps, Arkansas. Her parents were on the verge of breaking up. "Years later," Angelou writes in the first of her autobiographies, "I discovered that the United States had been crossed thousands of times by frightened Black children traveling alone to their newly affluent parents in Northern cities, or back to grandmothers in Southern towns when the urban North reneged on its economic promises." In the early 1930s, her grandmother, whom she called "Momma," ran the only black general store in Stamps. Angelou says of her: "Knowing Momma, I knew that I never knew Momma. Her African-bush secretiveness and suspiciousness had been compounded by slavery and confirmed by centuries of promises made and promises broken. We have a saying among Black Americans which describes Momma's caution. 'If you ask a Negro where he's been, he'll tell you where he's going.'"

In her autobiography I Know Why the Caged Bird Sings, *Angelou gives a graphic account of black life in a segregated Southern town. She and her brother were later to live with their mother in San Francisco. A dancer and an actress as well as a journalist and poet, Angelou toured for the State Department in* Porgy and Bess, *acted in the television series* Roots, *wrote for newspapers in Egypt and Ghana, and worked as a coordinator for the Southern Christian Leadership Conference. Angelou describes these experiences in later volumes of her autobiography—*Gather Together in My Name, Singin' and Swingin' and Gettin' Merry like Christmas, and The Heart of a Woman. *These books and her several volumes of poetry, recently collected in* Maya Angelou: Poems, *tell us of the problems the black woman in America encounters in growing up and making a career. This chapter from* I Know Why the Caged Bird Sings *gives insight into feelings of black children on the threshold of entering a larger world.*

The children in Stamps trembled visibly with anticipation. Some adults were 1
excited too, but to be certain the whole young population had come down with graduation epidemic. Large classes were graduating from both the grammar school and the high school. Even those who were years removed from their own day of glorious release were anxious to help with preparations as a kind of dry run. The junior students who were moving into the vacating classes' chairs were tradition-bound to show their talents for leadership and management. They strutted through the school and around the campus exerting pressure on the lower grades. Their authority was so new that occasionally if they pressed a little too hard it had to be overlooked. After all, next term was coming, and it never hurt a sixth grader to have a play sister in the eighth grade, or a tenth-year student to be able to call a twelfth grader Bubba. So all was endured in a spirit of shared understanding. But the graduating classes themselves were the nobility. Like travelers with exotic destinations on their minds, the graduates were remarkably forgetful. They

came to school without their books, or tablets or even pencils. Volunteers fell over themselves to secure replacements for the missing equipment. When accepted, the willing workers might or might not be thanked, and it was of no importance to the pregraduation rites. Even teachers were respectful of the now quiet and aging seniors, and tended to speak to them, if not as equals, as beings only slightly lower than themselves. After tests were returned and grades given, the student body, which acted like an extended family, knew who did well, who excelled, and what piteous ones had failed.

Unlike the white high school, Lafayette County Training School distinguished 2 itself by having neither lawn, nor hedges, nor tennis court, nor climbing ivy. Its two buildings (main classrooms, the grade school and home economics) were set on a dirt hill with no fence to limit either its boundaries or those of bordering farms. There was a large expanse to the left of the school which was used alternately as a baseball diamond or a basketball court. Rusty hoops on the swaying poles represented the permanent recreational equipment, although bats and balls could be borrowed from the P. E. teacher if the borrower was qualified and if the diamond wasn't occupied.

Over this rocky area relieved by a few shady tall persimmon trees the graduat- 3 ing class walked. The girls often held hands and no longer bothered to speak to the lower students. There was a sadness about them, as if this old world was not their home and they were bound for higher ground. The boys, on the other hand, had become more friendly, more outgoing. A decided change from the closed attitude they projected while studying for finals. Now they seemed not ready to give up the old school, the familiar paths and classrooms. Only a small percentage would be continuing on to college—one of the South's A & M (agricultural and mechanical) schools, which trained Negro youths to be carpenters, farmers, handymen, masons, maids, cooks and baby nurses. Their future rode heavily on their shoulders, and blinded them to the collective joy that had pervaded the lives of the boys and girls in the grammar school graduating class.

Parents who could afford it had ordered new shoes and ready-made clothes for 4 themselves from Sears and Roebuck or Montgomery Ward. They also engaged the best seamstresses to make the floating graduating dresses and to cut down secondhand pants which would be pressed to a military slickness for the important event.

Oh, it was important, all right. Whitefolks would attend the ceremony, and two 5 or three would speak of God and home, and the Southern way of life, and Mrs. Parsons, the principal's wife, would play the graduation march while the lower-grade graduates paraded down the aisles and took their seats below the platform. The high school seniors would wait in empty classrooms to make their dramatic entrance.

In the Store I was the person of the moment. The birthday girl. The center. 6 Bailey had graduated the year before, although to do so he had had to forfeit all pleasures to make up for his time lost in Baton Rouge.

My class was wearing butter-yellow piqué dresses, and Momma launched out 7 on mine. She smocked the yoke into tiny crisscrossing puckers, then shirred the rest of the bodice. Her dark fingers ducked in and out of the lemony cloth as she embroidered raised daisies around the hem. Before she considered herself finished she had added a crocheted cuff on the puff sleeves, and a pointy crocheted collar.

I was going to be lovely. A walking model of all the various styles of fine hand 8 sewing and it didn't worry me that I was only twelve years old and merely graduating from the eighth grade. Besides, many teachers in Arkansas Negro schools had only that diploma and were licensed to impart wisdom.

The days had become longer and more noticeable. The faded beige of former 9 times had been replaced with strong and sure colors. I began to see my classmates' clothes, their skin tones, and the dust that waved off pussy willows. Clouds that lazed across the sky were objects of great concern to me. Their shiftier shapes might have held a message that in my new happiness and with a little bit of time I'd soon decipher. During that period I looked at the arch of heaven so religiously my neck kept a steady ache. I had taken to smiling more often, and my jaws hurt from the unaccustomed activity. Between the two physical sore spots, I suppose I could have been uncomfortable, but that was not the case. As a member of the winning team (the graduating class of 1940) I had outdistanced unpleasant sensations by miles. I was headed for the freedom of open fields.

Youth and social approval allied themselves with me and we trammeled memo- 10 ries of slights and insults. The wind of our swift passage remodeled my features. Lost tears were pounded to mud and then to dust. Years of withdrawal were brushed aside and left behind, as hanging ropes of parasitic moss.

My work alone had awarded me a top place and I was going to be one of the first 11 called in the graduating ceremonies. On the classroom blackboard, as well as on the bulletin board in the auditorium, there were blue stars and white stars and red stars. No absences, no tardinesses, and my academic work was among the best of the year. I could say the preamble to the Constitution even faster than Bailey. We timed ourselves often: "WethepeopleoftheUnitedStatesinordertoformamoreperfectunion . . ." I had memorized the Presidents of the United States from Washington to Roosevelt in chronological as well as alphabetical order.

My hair pleased me too. Gradually the black mass had lengthened and thick- 12 ened, so that it kept at last to its braided pattern, and I didn't have to yank my scalp off when I tried to comb it.

Louise and I had rehearsed the exercises until we tired out ourselves. Henry 13 Reed was class valedictorian. He was a small, very black boy with hooded eyes, a long, broad nose and an oddly shaped head. I had admired him for years because each term he and I vied for the best grades in our class. Most often he bested me, but instead of being disappointed I was pleased that we shared top places between us. Like many Southern Black children, he lived with his grandmother, who was as strict as Momma and as kind as she knew how to be. He was courteous, respectful and soft-spoken to elders, but on the playground he chose to play the roughest games. I admired him. Anyone, I reckoned, sufficiently afraid or sufficiently dull could be polite. But to be able to operate at a top level with both adults and children was admirable.

His valedictory speech was entitled "To Be or Not to Be." The rigid tenth-grade 14 teacher had helped him write it. He'd been working on the dramatic stresses for months.

The weeks until graduation were filled with heady activities. A group of small 15 children were to be presented in a play about buttercups and daisies and bunny rabbits. They could be heard throughout the building practicing their hops and their little songs that sounded like silver bells. The older girls (non-graduates, of course) were assigned to the task of making refreshments for the night's festivities. A tangy scent of ginger, cinnamon, nutmeg and chocolate wafted around the home economics building as the budding cooks made samples for themselves and their teachers.

In every corner of the workshop, axes and saws split fresh timber as the 16 woodshop boys made sets and stage scenery. Only the graduates were left out of the general bustle. We were free to sit in the library at the back of the building or look in quite detachedly, naturally, on the measures being taken for our event.

Even the minister preached on graduation the Sunday before. His subject was, 17 "Let your light so shine that men will see your good works and praise your Father, Who is in Heaven." Although the sermon was purported to be addressed to us, he used the occasion to speak to backsliders, gamblers and general ne'er-do-wells. But since he had called our names at the beginning of the service we were mollified.

Among Negroes the tradition was to give presents to children going only from 18 one grade to another. How much more important this was when the person was graduating at the top of the class. Uncle Willie and Momma had sent away for a Mickey Mouse watch like Bailey's. Louise gave me four embroidered handkerchiefs. (I gave her three crocheted doilies.) Mrs. Sneed, the minister's wife, made me an underskirt to wear for graduation, and nearly every customer gave me a nickel or maybe even a dime with the instruction "Keep on moving to higher ground," or some such encouragement.

Amazingly the great day finally dawned and I was out of bed before I knew it. 19 I threw open the back door to see it more clearly, but Momma said, "Sister, come away from that door and put your robe on."

I hoped the memory of that morning would never leave me. Sunlight was itself 20 still young, and the day had none of the insistence maturity would bring it in a few hours. In my robe and barefoot in the backyard, under cover of going to see about my new beans, I gave myself up to the gentle warmth and thanked God that no matter what evil I had done in my life He had allowed me to live to see this day. Somewhere in my fatalism I had expected to die, accidentally, and never have the chance to walk up the stairs in the auditorium and gracefully receive my hard-earned diploma. Out of God's merciful bosom I had won reprieve.

Bailey came out in his robe and gave me a box wrapped in Christmas paper. He 21 said he had saved his money for months to pay for it. It felt like a box of chocolates, but I knew Bailey wouldn't save money to buy candy when we had all we could want under our noses.

He was as proud of the gift as I. It was a soft-leather-bound copy of a collection 22 of poems by Edgar Allan Poe, or, as Bailey and I called him, "Eap." I turned to "Annabel Lee" and we walked up and down the garden rows, the cool dirt between our toes, reciting the beautifully sad lines.

Momma made a Sunday breakfast although it was only Friday. After we finished 23 the blessing, I opened my eyes to find the watch on my plate. It was a dream of a day. Everything went smoothly and to my credit. I didn't have to be reminded or scolded for anything. Near evening I was too jittery to attend to chores, so Bailey volunteered to do all before his bath.

Days before, we had made a sign for the Store, and as we turned out the lights 24 Momma hung the cardboard over the doorknob. It read clearly: CLOSED. GRADUATION.

My dress fitted perfectly and everyone said that I looked like a sunbeam in it. 25 On the hill, going toward the school, Bailey walked behind with Uncle Willie, who muttered, "Go on, Ju." He wanted him to walk ahead with us because it embarrassed him to have to walk so slowly. Bailey said he'd let the ladies walk together, and the men would bring up the rear. We all laughed, nicely.

Little children dashed by out of the dark like fireflies. Their crepe-paper dresses 26 and butterfly wings were not made for running and we heard more than one rip, dryly, and the regretful "uh uh" that followed.

The school blazed without gaiety. The windows seemed cold and unfriendly 27 from the lower hill. A sense of ill-fated timing crept over me, and if Momma hadn't reached for my hand I would have drifted back to Bailey and Uncle Willie, and possibly beyond. She made a few slow jokes about my feet getting cold, and tugged me along to the now-strange building.

Around the front steps, assurance came back. There were my fellow "greats," 28 the graduating class. Hair brushed back, legs oiled, new dresses and pressed pleats, fresh pocket handkerchiefs and little handbags, all homesewn. Oh, we were up to snuff, all right. I joined my comrades and didn't even see my family go in to find seats in the crowded auditorium.

The school band struck up a march and all classes filed in as had been re- 29 hearsed. We stood in front of our seats, as assigned, and on a signal from the choir director, we sat. No sooner had this been accomplished than the band started to play the national anthem. We rose again and sang the song, after which we recited the pledge of allegiance. We remained standing for a brief minute before the choir director and the principal signaled to us, rather desperately I thought, to take our seats. The command was so unusual that our carefully rehearsed and smooth-running machine was thrown off. For a full minute we fumbled for our chairs and bumped into each other awkwardly. Habits change or solidify under pressure, so in our state of nervous tension we had been ready to follow our usual assembly pattern: the American national anthem, then the pledge of allegiance, then the song every Black person I knew called the Negro National Anthem. All done in the same key, with the same passion and most often standing on the same foot.

Finding my seat at last, I was overcome with a presentiment of worse things to 30 come. Something unrehearsed, unplanned, was going to happen, and we were going to be made to look bad. I distinctly remember being explicit in the choice of pronoun. It was "we," the graduating class, the unit, that concerned me then.

The principal welcomed "parents and friends" and asked the Baptist minister 31 to lead us in prayer. His invocation was brief and punchy, and for a second I thought we were getting back on the high road to right action. When the principal came back to the dais, however, his voice had changed. Sounds always affected me profoundly and the principal's voice was one of my favorites. During assembly it melted and lowed weakly into the audience. It had not been in my plan to listen to him, but my curiosity was piqued and I straightened up to give him my attention.

He was talking about Booker T. Washington, our "late great leader," who said 32 we can be as close as the fingers on the hand, etc. . . . Then he said a few vague things about friendship and the friendship of kindly people to those less fortunate than themselves. With that his voice nearly faded, thin, away. Like a river diminishing to a stream and then to a trickle. But he cleared his throat and said, "Our speaker tonight, who is also our friend, came from Texarkana to deliver the commencement address, but due to the irregularity of the train schedule, he's going to, as they say, 'speak and run.' " He said that we understood and wanted the man to know that we were most grateful for the time he was able to give us and then something about how we were willing always to adjust to another's program, and without more ado—"I give you Mr. Edward Donleavy."

Not one but two white men came through the door offstage. The shorter one 33 walked to the speaker's platform, and the tall one moved over to the center seat and sat down. But that was our principal's seat, and already occupied. The dislodged gentleman bounced around for a long breath or two before the Baptist minister gave him his chair, then with more dignity than the situation deserved, the minister walked off the stage.

Donleavy looked at the audience once (on reflection, I'm sure that he wanted 34 only to reassure himself that we were really there), adjusted his glasses and began to read from a sheaf of papers.

He was glad "to be here and to see the work going on just as it was in the other 35 schools."

At the first "Amen" from the audience I willed the offender to immediate death 36 by choking on the word. But Amens and Yes, sir's began to fall around the room like rain through a ragged umbrella.

He told us of the wonderful changes we children in Stamps had in store. The 37 Central School (naturally, the white school was Central) had already been granted improvements that would be in use in the fall. A well-known artist was coming from Little Rock to teach art to them. They were going to have the newest microscopes and chemistry equipment for their laboratory. Mr. Donleavy didn't leave us long in the dark over who made these improvements available to Central High. Nor were we to be ignored in the general betterment scheme he had in mind.

He said that he had pointed out to people at a very high level that one of the 38 first-line football tacklers at Arkansas Agricultural and Mechanical College had graduated from good old Lafayette County Training School. Here fewer Amen's were heard. Those few that did break through lay dully in the air with the heaviness of habit.

He went on to praise us. He went on to say how he had bragged that "one of 39 the best basketball players at Fisk sank his first ball right here at Lafayette County Training School."

The white kids were going to have a chance to become Galileos and Madame 40 Curies and Edisons and Gauguins, and our boys (the girls weren't even in on it) would try to be Jesse Owenses and Joe Louises.

Owens and the Brown Bomber were great heroes in our world, but what school 41 official in the white-goddom of Little Rock had the right to decide that those two men must be our only heroes? Who decided that for Henry Reed to become a scientist he had to work like George Washington Carver, as a bootblack, to buy a lousy microscope? Bailey was obviously always going to be too small to be an athlete, so which concrete angel glued to what country seat had decided that if my brother wanted to become a lawyer he had to first pay penance for his skin by picking cotton and hoeing corn and studying correspondence books at night for twenty years?

The man's dead words fell like bricks around the auditorium and too many set- 42 tled in my belly. Constrained by hard-learned manners I couldn't look behind me, but to my left and right the proud graduating class of 1940 had dropped their heads. Every girl in my row had found something new to do with her handkerchief. Some folded the tiny squares into love knots, some into triangles, but most were wadding them, then pressing them flat on their yellow laps.

On the dais, the ancient tragedy was being replayed. Professor Parsons sat, a 43 sculptor's reject, rigid. His large, heavy body seemed devoid of will or willingness, and his eyes said he was no longer with us. The other teachers examined the flag (which was draped stage right) or their notes, or the windows which opened on our now-famous playing diamond.

Graduation, the hush-hush magic time of frills and gifts and congratulations 44 and diplomas, was finished for me before my name was called. The accomplishment was nothing. The meticulous maps, drawn in three colors of ink, learning and spelling deca-syllabic words, memorizing the whole of *The Rape of Lucrece*—it was for nothing. Donleavy had exposed us.

We were maids and farmers, handymen and washerwomen, and anything 45 higher that we aspired to was farcical and presumptuous.

Then I wished that Gabriel Prosser and Nat Turner had killed all whitefolks in 46 their beds and that Abraham Lincoln had been assassinated before the signing of the Emancipation Proclamation, and that Harriet Tubman had been killed by that blow on her head and Christopher Columbus had drowned in the *Santa Maria*.

It was awful to be Negro and have no control over my life. It was brutal to be 47 young and already trained to sit quietly and listen to charges brought against my color with no chance of defense. We should all be dead. I thought I should like to see us all dead, one on top of the other. A pyramid of flesh with the whitefolks on the bottom, as the broad base, then the Indians with their silly tomahawks and teepees and wigwams and treaties, the Negroes with their mops and recipes and cotton sacks and spirituals sticking out of their mouths. The Dutch children should all stumble in their wooden shoes and break their necks. The French should choke to death on the Louisiana Pur-chase (1803) while silkworms ate all the Chinese with their stupid pigtails. As a species, we were an abomination. All of us.

Donleavy was running for election, and assured our parents that if he won we 48 could count on having the only colored paved playing field in that part of Arkansas. Also—he never looked up to acknowledge the grunts of acceptance—also, we were bound to get some new equipment for the home economics building and the workshop.

He finished, and since there was no need to give any more than the most per- 49 functory thank-you's, he nodded to the men on the stage, and the tall white man who was never introduced joined him at the door. They left with the attitude that now they were off to something really important. (The graduation ceremonies at Lafayette County Training School had been a mere preliminary.)

The ugliness they left was palpable. An uninvited guest who wouldn't leave. The 50 choir was summoned and sang a modern arrangement of "Onward, Christian Soldiers," with new words pertaining to graduates seeking their place in the world. But it didn't work. Elouise, the daughter of the Baptist minister, recited "Invictus," and I could have cried at the impertinence of "I am the master of my fate, and I am the captain of my soul."

My name had lost its ring of familiarity and I had to be nudged to go and re- 51 ceive my diploma. All my preparations had fled. I neither marched up to the stage like a conquering Amazon, nor did I look in the audience for Bailey's nod of approval. Marguerite Johnson, I heard the name again, my honors were read, there were noises in the audience of appreciation, and I took my place on the stage as rehearsed.

I thought about colors I hated: ecru, puce, lavender, beige and black.   52

There was shuffling and rustling around me, then Henry Reed was giving his 53 valedictory address, "To Be or Not to Be." Hadn't he heard the whitefolks? We couldn't *be,* so the question was a waste of time. Henry's voice came out clear and strong. I feared to look at him. Hadn't he got the message? There was no "nobler in the mind" for Negroes because the world didn't think we had minds, and they let us know it. "Outrageous fortune"? Now, that was a joke. When the ceremony was over I had to tell Henry Reed some things. That is, if I still cared. Not "rub," Henry, "erase." "Ah, there's the erase." Us.

Henry had been a good student in elocution. His voice rose on tides of promise 54 and fell on waves of warnings. The English teacher had helped him to create a sermon winging through Hamlet's soliloquy. To be a man, a doer, a builder, a leader, or to be a tool, an unfunny joke, a crusher of funky toadstools. I marveled that Henry could go through with the speech as if we had a choice.

I had been listening and silently rebutting each sentence with my eyes closed; 55 then there was a hush, which in an audience warns that something unplanned is happening. I looked up and saw Henry Reed, the conservative, the proper, the A student, turn his back to the audience and turn to us (the proud graduating class of 1940) and sing, nearly speaking,

> "Lift ev'ry voice and sing
> Till earth and heaven ring
> Ring with the harmonies of Liberty . . ."

It was the poem written by James Weldon Johnson. It was the music composed by J. Rosamond Johnson. It was the Negro national anthem. Out of habit we were singing it.

Our mothers and fathers stood in the dark hall and joined the hymn of encour- 56 agement. A kindergarten teacher led the small children onto the stage and the buttercups and daisies and bunny rabbits marked time and tried to follow:

> "Stony the road we trod
> Bitter the chastening rod
> Felt in the days when hope, unborn, had died.
> Yet with a steady beat
> Have not our weary feet
> Come to the place for which our fathers sighed?"

Every child I knew had learned that song with his ABC's and along with "Jesus 57 Loves Me This I Know." But I personally had never heard it before. Never heard the words, despite the thousands of times I had sung them. Never thought they had anything to do with me.

On the other hand, the words of Patrick Henry had made such an impression 58 on me that I had been able to stretch myself tall and trembling and say, "I know not what course others may take, but as for me, give me liberty or give me death."

And now I heard, really for the first time: 59

> "We have come over a way that with tears
>   has been watered,
> We have come, treading our path through
>   the blood of the slaughtered."

While echoes of the song shivered in the air, Henry Reed bowed his head, said 60 "Thank you," and returned to his place in the line. The tears that slipped down many faces were not wiped away in shame.

We were on top again. As always, again. We survived. The depths had been icy 61 and dark, but now a bright sun spoke to our souls. I was no longer simply a member of the proud graduating class of 1940; I was a proud member of the wonderful, beautiful Negro race.

Oh, Black known and unknown poets, how often have your auctioned pains 62 sustained us? Who will compute the lonely nights made less lonely by your songs, or by the empty pots made less tragic by your tales?

If we were a people much given to revealing secrets, we might raise monu- 63 ments and sacrifice to the memories of our poets, but slavery cured us of that weakness. It may be enough, however, to have it said that we survive in exact relationship to the dedication of our poets (include preachers, musicians and blues singers).

Questions

1. In the opening paragraphs, is Angelou describing the grammar school and high school graduation of children who feel themselves to be Americans? Or do the children already have the sense, before Mr. Edward Donleavy speaks, that they are black Americans graduating from black schools?
2. How does Angelou make us experience what the children feel in listening to Mr. Donleavy? Are the other children as conscious as Angelou of the meaning of his words?
3. Does Henry Reed make the decision to sing the "Negro national anthem," or was the anthem scheduled as part of the graduation ceremony? Do Henry and the others present experience the same feelings that Angelou does in singing the anthem?
4. How does the anthem illustrate Angelou's statement, quoted earlier, "If you ask a Negro where he's been, he'll tell you where he's going"?
5. Does Angelou state a thesis, or does she instead allow the episode to make its own points?

6. What, in general, is Angelou saying through the episode about the origins of selfhatred and the ways to overcome it? Would Frederick Douglass agree?

Suggestions for Writing

1. Describe a ceremony or an episode that contained unexpected moments and led you to discoveries about yourself and your world. Let your reader experience what you did by giving details as vivid as Angelou's.
2. Develop the following statement from your own experience of music and literature:

> It may be enough, however, to have it said that we survive in exact relationship to the dedication of our poets (include preachers, musicians and blues singers).

3. Compare the attitude toward being black expressed by Frederick Douglass and Maya Angelou. Discuss how you discover this attitude in noting similarities and differences.
4. Compare Angelou's account of facing the world as a black person with the account of similar experiences in one of the following autobiographies. Use your comparison to develop a point or idea:
   a. *Autobiography of Malcolm X*
   b. Claude Brown, *Manchild in the Promised Land*
   c. Mary E. Mebane, *Mary: An autobiography* and *Mary, Wayfarer*
   d. Alex Haley, *Roots*
5. The autobiography has been used by other minority writers to characterize both their personal life and that of their families or their people. Among these are Maxine Hong Kingston's *The Woman Warrior,* M. Scott Momaday's *The Way to Rainy Mountain,* I. B. Singer's *In My Father's Court,* Edward Rivera's *Family Installments,* and Richard Rodriguez's *Hunger of Memory.* Autobiographies that focus on the experiences and trials of growing up include Mary McCarthy's *Memories of a Catholic Girlhood* and Susan Allen Toth's *Blooming: A Small-Town Girlhood* (a chapter from which appears later in this book) and *Ivy Days: Making My Way Out East.* Analyze a chapter in one of these books to characterize or comment on the author and the world described.

Additional Reading

Angelou, Maya. *All God's Children Need Traveling Shoes.* New York: Random House, 1986.
———. *Gather Together in My Name.* New York: Random House, 1974.
———. *The Heart of a Woman.* New York: Random House, 1981.
———. *I Know Why the Caged Bird Sings.* New York: Random House, 1970.
———. *Singin' and Swingin' and Gettin' Merry like Christmas.* New York: Random House, 1976.

My Kinsman, Major Molineux

Nathaniel Hawthorne

The American writer Nathaniel Hawthorne was born in Salem, Massachusetts, in 1804. His father, a sea captain, died in Dutch Guiana when Nathaniel was four. Raised by his reclusive mother, he immersed himself in books and the history of his family and town. (One of his ancestors was a judge at the witch trials in colonial Salem in the late seventeenth century.) Most of Hawthorne's fiction is set in Puritan New England. Hawthorne began his writing career shortly after graduating from Bowdoin College in 1825. His stories appeared in literary magazines of the day and were collected in Twice-Told Tales, published in two series in 1837 and 1842. In addition to writing fiction, Hawthorne worked at the Boston Custom House from 1839 to 1841. In 1842 he married Sophia Peabody following a long engagement and moved to nearby Concord. From 1846 to 1849 Hawthorne worked as a surveyor in Salem. A collection of his stories, Mosses from the Old Manse, *was published in 1849; the novels* The Scarlet Letter, The House of the Seven Gables, *and* The Blithedale Romance *appeared in 1850, 1851, and 1852, respectively; other collections of stories appeared in later years. Hawthorne also wrote a biography of President Franklin Pierce, a Bowdoin friend, served as American consul at Liverpool, England, and traveled in Italy. On his return to the United States, he lived in Concord until his death in 1864.*

Hawthorne wrote many historical and allegorical tales in which the characters are symbolic or representative of a historical attitude or type. Although the characters are richly drawn, readers sometimes disagree on how complex in motive and feeling some of the major ones are. The hero of "My Kinsman, Major Molineux" raises this question. Some readers find Robin a complex character; others find him simple—mysterious neither in his motive for seeking his kinsman, Major Molineux, nor in his feelings toward him. The story concerns youth and experience, but Hawthorne does not speak to the reader directly about the meaning of what happens to Robin or about the kind of story he has written. In deciding how to interpret the story, the reader must pay close attention to the setting and action of the story and the behavior of the characters.

After the kings of Great Britain had assumed the right of appointing the colonial governors, the measures of the latter seldom met with the ready and generous approbation which had been paid to those of their predecessors, under the original charters. The people looked with most jealous scrutiny to the exercise of power which did not emanate from themselves, and they usually rewarded their rulers with slender gratitude for the compliances by which, in softening their instructions from beyond the sea, they had incurred the reprehension of those who gave them. The annals of Massachusetts Bay will inform us, that of six governors in the space of about forty years from the surrender of the old charter, under James II, two imprisoned by a popular insurrection; a third, as Hutchinson inclines to believe, was driven from the province by the whizzing of a musket-ball; a fourth, in the opinion of the same historian, was hastened to his grave by continual bickerings with the House of Representatives; and the remaining two, as well as their successors, till the Revolution, were favored with few and brief intervals of peaceful sway. The inferior members of the court party, in times of high political excitement, led scarcely a more desirable life. These remarks may serve as a preface to the following adventures, which chanced upon a summer night, not far from a hundred years ago. The reader, in order to avoid a long and dry detail of colonial affairs, is requested to dispense with an account of the train of circumstances that had caused much temporary inflammation of the popular mind.

It was near nine o'clock of a moonlight evening, when a boat crossed the ferry with a single passenger, who had obtained his conveyance at that unusual hour by the promise of an extra fare. While he stood on the landing-place, searching in either pocket for the means of fulfilling his agreement, the ferryman lifted a lantern, by the aid of which, and the newly risen moon, he took a very accurate survey of the stranger's figure. He was a youth of barely eighteen years, evidently country-bred, and now, as it should seem, upon his first visit to town. He was clad in a coarse gray coat, well worn, but in excellent repair; his under garments were durably constructed of leather, and fitted tight to a pair of serviceable and well-shaped limbs; his stockings of blue yarn were the incontrovertible work of a mother or a sister; and on his head was a three-cornered hat, which in its better days had perhaps sheltered the graver brow of the lad's father. Under his left arm was a heavy cudgel formed of an oak sapling, and retaining a part of the hardened root; and his equipment was completed by a wallet, not so abundantly stocked as to incommode the vigorous shoulders on which it hung. Brown, curly hair, well-shaped features, and bright, cheerful eyes were nature's gifts, and worth all that art could have done for his adornment.

The youth, one of whose names was Robin, finally drew from his pocket the half of a little province bill of five shillings, which, in the depreciation in that sort of currency, did but satisfy the ferryman's demand, with the surplus of a sexangular piece of parchment, valued at three pence. He then walked forward into the town, with as light a step as if his day's journey had not already exceeded thirty miles, and with as eager an eye as if he were entering London city, instead of the little metropolis of a New England colony. Before Robin had proceeded far, however, it occurred to him that he knew not whither to direct his steps; so he paused, and looked up and down the narrow street, scrutinizing the small and mean wooden buildings that were scattered on either side.

"This low hovel cannot be my kinsman's dwelling," thought he, "nor yonder old house, where the moonlight enters at the broken casement; and truly I see none hereabouts that might be worthy of him. It would have been wise to inquire my way of the ferryman, and doubtless he would have gone with me, and earned a shilling from the Major for his pains. But the next man I meet will do as well."

He resumed his walk, and was glad to perceive that the street now became wider, and the houses more respectable in their appearance. He soon discerned a figure moving on moderately in advance, and hastened his steps to overtake it. As Robin drew nigh, he saw that the passenger was a man in years, with a full periwig of gray hair, a wide-skirted coat of dark cloth, and silk stockings rolled above his knees. He carried a long and polished cane, which he struck down perpendicularly before him at every step; and at regular intervals he uttered two successive hems, of a peculiarly solemn and sepulchral intonation. Having made these observations, Robin laid hold of the skirt of the old man's coat, just when the light from the open door and windows of a barber's shop fell upon both their figures.

"Good evening to you, honored sir," said he, making a low bow, and still retaining his hold of the skirt. "I pray you tell me whereabouts is the dwelling of my kinsman, Major Molineux."

The youth's question was uttered very loudly; and one of the barbers, whose razor was descending on a well-soaped chin, and another who was dressing a Ramillies wig, left their occupations, and came to the door. The citizen, in the mean time, turned a long-favored countenance upon Robin, and answered him in a tone of excessive anger and annoyance. His two sepulchral hems, however, broke into the very centre of his rebuke, with most singular effect, like a thought of the cold grave obtruding among wrathful passions.

"Let go my garment, fellow! I tell you, I know not the man you speak of. What! I have authority. I have—hem, hem—authority; and if this be the respect you show for your betters, your feet shall be brought acquainted with the stocks by daylight, tomorrow morning!"

Robin released the old man's skirt, and hastened away, pursued by an ill-mannered roar of laughter from the barber's shop. He was at first considerably surprised by the result of his question, but, being a shrewd youth, soon thought himself able to account for the mystery.

"This is some country representative," was his conclusion, "who has never seen the inside of my kinsman's door, and lacks the breeding to answer a stranger civilly. The man is old, or verily—I might be tempted to turn back and smite him on the nose. Ah, Robin, Robin! even the barber's boys laugh at you for choosing such a guide! You will be wiser in time, friend Robin."

He now became entangled in a succession of crooked and narrow streets, which crossed each other, and meandered at no great distance from the water-side. The smell of tar was obvious to his nostrils, the masts of vessels pierced the moonlight above the tops of the buildings, and the numerous signs, which Robin paused to read, informed him that he was near the centre of business. But the streets were empty, the shops were closed, and lights were visible only in the second stories of a few dwelling-houses. At length, on the corner of a narrow lane, through which he was passing, he beheld the broad countenance of a British hero swinging before the door of an inn, whence proceeded the voices of many guests. The casement of one of the lower windows was thrown back, and a very thin curtain permitted Robin to distinguish a party at supper, round a well-furnished table. The fragrance of the good cheer steamed forth into the outer air, and the youth could not fail to recollect that the last remnant of his travelling stock of provision had yielded to his morning appetite, and that noon had found and left him dinnerless.

"Oh, that a parchment three-penny might give me a right to sit down at yonder table!" said Robin, with a sigh. "But the Major will make me welcome to the best of his victuals; so I will even step boldly in, and inquire my way to his dwelling."

He entered the tavern, and was guided by the murmur of voices and the fumes of tobacco to the public-room. It was a long and low apartment, with oaken walls, grown dark in the continual smoke, and a floor which was thickly sanded, but of no immaculate purity. A number of persons—the larger part of whom appeared to be mariners, or in some way connected with the sea—occupied the wooden benches, or leather-bottomed chairs, conversing on various matters, and occasionally lending their attention to some topic of general interest. Three or four little groups were draining as many bowls of punch, which the West India trade had long since made a familiar drink in the colony. Others, who had the appearance of men who lived by regular and laborious handicraft, preferred the insulated bliss of an unshared potation, and became more taciturn under its influence. Nearly all, in short, evinced a predilection for the Good Creature in some of its various shapes, for this is a vice to which, as Fast Day sermons of a hundred years ago will testify, we have a long hereditary claim. The only guests to whom Robin's sympathies inclined him were two or three sheepish countrymen, who were using the inn somewhat after the fashion of a Turkish caravansary; they had gotten themselves into the darkest corner of the room, and heedless of the Nicotian atmosphere, were supping on the bread of their own ovens, and the bacon cured in their own chimney-smoke. But though Robin felt a sort of brotherhood with these strangers, his eyes were attracted from them to a person who stood near the door, holding whispered conversation with a group of ill-dressed associates. His features were separately striking almost to grotesqueness, and the whole face left a deep impression on the memory. The forehead bulged out into a double prominence, with a vale between; the nose came boldly forth in an irregular curve, and its bridge was of more than a finger's breadth; the eyebrows were deep and shaggy, and the eyes glowed beneath them like fire in a cave.

While Robin deliberated of whom to inquire respecting his kinsman's dwelling, he was accosted by the innkeeper, a little man in a stained white apron, who had come to pay his professional welcome to the stranger. Being in the second generation from a French Protestant, he seemed to have inherited the courtesy of his parent nation; but no variety of circumstances was ever known to change his voice from the one shrill note in which he now addressed Robin.

"From the country, I presume, sir?" said he, with a profound bow. "Beg leave to congratulate you on your arrival, and trust you intend a long stay with us. Fine town here, sir, beautiful buildings, and much that may interest a stranger. May I hope for the honor of your commands in respect to supper?"

"The man sees a family likeness! the rogue has guessed that I am related to the Major!" thought Robin, who had hitherto experienced little superfluous civility.

All eyes were now turned on the country lad, standing at the door, in his worn three-cornered hat, gray coat, leather breeches, and blue yarn stockings, leaning on an oaken cudgel, and bearing a wallet on his back.

Robin replied to the courteous innkeeper, with such an assumption of confidence as befitted the Major's relative. "My honest friend," he said, "I shall make it a point to patronize your house on some occasion, when"—here he could not help lowering his voice—"when I may have more than a parchment three-pence in my pocket. My present business," continued he, speaking with lofty confidence, "is merely to inquire my way to the dwelling of my kinsman, Major Molineux."

There was a sudden and general movement in the room, which Robin interpreted as expressing the eagerness of each individual to become his guide. But the innkeeper turned his eyes to a written paper on the wall, which he read, or seemed to read, with occasional recurrences to the young man's figure.

"What have we here?" said he, breaking his speech into little dry fragments. " 'Left the house of the subscriber, bounden servant, Hezekiah Mudge,—had on, when he went away, gray coat, leather breeches, master's third-best hat. One pound currency reward to whosoever shall lodge him in any jail of the province.' Better trudge, boy; better trudge!"

Robin had begun to draw his hand towards the lighter end of the oak cudgel, but a strange hostility in every countenance induced him to relinquish his purpose of breaking the courteous innkeeper's head. As he turned to leave the room, he encountered a sneering glance from the bold-featured personage whom he had before noticed; and no sooner was he beyond the door, than he heard a general laugh, in which the innkeeper's voice might be distinguished, like the dropping of small stones into a kettle.

"Now, is it not strange," thought Robin, with his usual shrewdness,—"is it not strange that the confession of an empty pocket should outweigh the name of my kinsman, Major Molineux? Oh, if I had one of those grinning rascals in the woods, where I and my oak sapling grew up together, I would teach him that my arm is heavy though my purse be light!"

On turning the corner of the narrow lane, Robin found himself in a spacious street, with an unbroken line of lofty houses in each side, and a steepled building at the upper end, whence the ringing of a bell announced the hour of nine. The light of the moon, and the lamps from the numerous shop-windows, discovered people promenading on the pavement, and amongst them Robin had hoped to recognize his hitherto inscrutable relative. The result of his former inquiries made him unwilling to hazard another, in a scene of such publicity, and he determined to walk slowly and silently up the street, thrusting his face close to that of every elderly gentleman, in search of the Major's lineaments. In his progress, Robin encountered many gay and gallant figures. Embroidered garments of showy colors, enormous periwigs, gold-laced hats, and silver-hilted swords glided past him and dazzled his optics. Travelled youths, imitators of the European fine gentlemen of the period, trod jauntily along, half dancing to the fashionable tunes which they hummed, and making poor Robin ashamed of his quiet and natural gait. At length, after many pauses to examine the gorgeous display of goods in the shop-windows, and after suffering some rebukes for the impertinence of his scrutiny into people's faces, the Major's kinsman found himself near the steepled building, still unsuccessful in his search. As yet, however, he had seen only one side of the thronged street; so Robin crossed, and continued the same sort of inquisition down the opposite pavement, with stronger hopes than the philosopher seeking an honest man, but with no better fortune. He had arrived about midway towards the lower end, from which his course began, when he overheard the approach of some one who struck down a cane on the flag-stones at every step, uttering at regular intervals, two sepulchral hems.

"Mercy on us!" quoth Robin, recognizing the sound.

Turning a corner, which chanced to be close at his right hand, he hastened to pursue his researches in some other part of the town. His patience now was wearing low, and he seemed to feel more fatigue from his rambles since he crossed the ferry, than from his journey of several days on the other side. Hunger also pleaded loudly within him, and Robin began to balance the propriety of demanding, violently, and with lifted cudgel, the necessary guidance from the first solitary passenger whom he should meet. While a resolution to this effect was gaining strength, he entered a street of mean appearance, on either side of which a row of ill-built houses was straggling towards the harbor. The moonlight fell upon no passenger along the whole extent, but in the third domicile which Robin passed there was a half-opened door, and his keen glance detected a woman's garment within.

"My luck may be better here," said he to himself.

Accordingly, he approached the door, and beheld it shut closer as he did so; yet an open space remained, sufficing for the fair occupant to observe the stranger, without a corresponding display on her part. All that Robin could discern was a strip of scarlet petticoat, and the occasional sparkle of an eye, as if the moonbeams were trembling on some bright thing.

"Pretty mistress," for I may call her so with a good conscience, thought the shrewd youth, since I know nothing to the contrary,—"my sweet pretty mistress, will you be kind enough to tell me whereabouts I must seek the dwelling of my kinsman, Major Molineux?"

Robin's voice was plaintive and winning, and the female, seeing nothing to be shunned in the handsome country youth, thrust open the door, and came forth into the moonlight. She was a dainty little figure, with a white neck, round arms, and a slender waist, at the extremity of which her scarlet petticoat jutted out over a hoop, as if she were standing in a balloon. Moreover, her face was oval and pretty, her hair dark beneath the little cap, and her bright eyes possessed a sly freedom, which triumphed over those of Robin.

"Major Molineux dwells here," said this fair woman.

Now, her voice was the sweetest Robin had heard that night, yet he could not help doubting whether that sweet voice spoke Gospel truth. He looked up and down the mean street, and then surveyed the house before which they stood. It was a small, dark edifice of two stories, the second of which projected over the lower floor, and the front apartment had the aspect of a shop for petty commodities.

"Now, truly, I am in luck," replied Robin, cunningly, "and so indeed is my kinsman, the Major, in having so pretty a housekeeper. But I prithee trouble him to step to the door; I will deliver him a message from his friends in the country, and then go back to my lodgings at the inn."

"Nay, the Major has been abed this hour or more," said the lady of the scarlet petticoat; "and it would be to little purpose to disturb him to-night, seeing his evening draught was of the strongest. But he is a kind-hearted man, and it would be as much as my life's worth to let a kinsman of his turn away from the door. You are the good old gentleman's very picture, and I could swear that was his rainy-weather hat. Also he has garments very much resembling those leather small-clothes. But come in, I pray, for I bid you hearty welcome in his name."

So saying, the fair and hospitable dame took our hero by the hand; and the touch was light, and the force was gentleness, and though Robin read in her eyes what he did not hear in her words, yet the slender-waisted woman in the scarlet petticoat proved stronger than the athletic country youth. She had drawn his half-willing footsteps nearly to the threshold, when the opening of a door in the neighborhood startled the Major's housekeeper, and, leaving the Major's kinsman, she vanished speedily into her own domicile. A heavy yawn preceded the appearance of a man, who, like the Moonshine of Pyramus and Thisbe, carried a lantern, needlessly aiding his sister luminary in the heavens. As he walked sleepily up the street, he turned his broad, dull face on Robin, and displayed a long staff, spiked at the end.

"Home, vagabond, home!" said the watchman, in accents that seemed to fall asleep as soon as they were uttered. "Home, or we'll set you in the stocks by peep of day!"

"This is the second hint of the kind," thought Robin. "I wish they would end my difficulties, by setting me there to-night."

Nevertheless, the youth felt an instinctive antipathy towards the guardian of midnight order, which at first prevented him from asking his usual question. But just when the man was about to vanish behind the corner, Robin resolved not to lose the opportunity, and shouted lustily after him,—

"I say, friend! will you guide me to the house of my kinsman, Major Molineux?"

The watchman made no reply, but turned the corner and was gone; yet Robin seemed to hear the sound of drowsy laughter stealing along the solitary street. At that moment, also, a pleasant titter saluted him from the open window above his head; he looked up, and caught the sparkle of a saucy eye; a round arm beckoned to him, and next he heard light footsteps descending the staircase within. But Robin, being of the household of a New England clergyman, was a good youth, as well as a shrewd one; so he resisted temptation, and fled away.

He now roamed desperately, and at random, through the town, almost ready to believe that a spell was on him, like that by which a wizard of his country had once kept three pursuers wandering, a whole winter night, within twenty paces of the cottage which they sought. The streets lay before him, strange and desolate, and the lights were extinguished in almost every house. Twice, however, little parties of men, among whom Robin distinguished individuals in outlandish attire, came hurrying along; but, though on both occasions, they paused to address him, such intercourse did not at all enlighten his perplexity. They did but utter a few words in some language of which Robin knew nothing, and perceiving his inability to answer, bestowed a curse upon him in plain English and hastened away. Finally, the lad determined to knock at the door of every mansion that might appear worthy to be occupied by his kinsman, trusting that perseverance would overcome the fatality that had hitherto thwarted him. Firm in this resolve, he was passing beneath the walls of a church, which formed the corner of two streets, when, as he turned into the shade of its steeple, he encountered a bulky stranger, muffled in a cloak. The man was proceeding with the speed of earnest business, but Robin planted himself full before him, holding the oak cudgel with both hands across his body as a bar to further passage.

"Halt, honest man, and answer me a question," said he, very resolutely. "Tell me, this instant, whereabouts is the dwelling of my kinsman, Major Molineux!"

"Keep your tongue between your teeth, fool, and let me pass!" said a deep, gruff voice, which Robin partly remembered. "Let me pass, or I'll strike you to the earth!"

"No, no, neighbor!" cried Robin, flourishing his cudgel, and then thrusting its larger end close to the man's muffled face. "No, no, I'm not the fool you take me for, nor do you pass till I have an answer to my question. Whereabouts is the dwelling of my kinsman, Major Molineux?"

The stranger, instead of attempting to force his passage, stepped back into the moonlight, unmuffled his face, and stared full into that of Robin.

"Watch here an hour, and Major Molineux will pass by," said he.

Robin gazed with dismay and astonishment on the unprecedented physiognomy of the speaker. The forehead with its double prominence, the broad hooked nose, the shaggy eye-brows, and fiery eyes were those which he had noticed at the inn, but the man's complexion had undergone a singular, or, more properly, a twofold change. One side of the face blazed an intense red, while the other was black as midnight, the division line being in the broad bridge of the nose; and a mouth which seemed to extend from ear to ear was black or red, in contrast to the color of the cheek. The effect was as if two individual devils, a fiend of fire and a fiend of darkness, had united themselves to form this infernal visage. The stranger grinned in Robin's face, muffled his party-colored features, and was out of sight in a moment.

"Strange things we travellers see!" ejaculated Robin.

He seated himself, however, upon the steps of the churchdoor, resolving to wait the appointed time for his kinsman. A few moments were consumed in philosophical speculations upon the species of man who had just left him; but having settled this point shrewdly, rationally, and satisfactorily, he was compelled to look elsewhere for his amusement. And first he threw his eyes along the street. It was of more respectable appearance than most of those into which he had wandered; and the moon, creating, like the imaginative power, a beautiful strangeness in familiar objects, gave something of romance to a scene that might not have possessed it in the light of day. The irregular and often quaint architecture of the houses, some of whose roofs were broken into numerous little peaks, while others ascended, steep and narrow, into a single point, and others again were square; the pure snow-white of some of their complexions, the aged darkness of others, and the thousand sparklings, reflected from bright substances in the walls of many; these matters engaged Robin's attention for a while, and then began to grow wearisome. Next he endeavored to define the forms of distant objects, starting away, with almost ghostly indistinctness, just as his eye appeared to grasp them; and finally he took a minute survey of an edifice which stood on the opposite side of the street, directly in front of the church door, where he was stationed. It was a large, square mansion, distinguished from its neighbors by a balcony, which rested on tall pillars, and by an elaborate Gothic window, communicating therewith.

"Perhaps this is the very house I have been seeking," thought Robin.

Then he strove to speed away the time, by listening to a murmur which swept continually along the street, yet was scarcely audible, except to an unaccustomed ear like his; it was a low, dull, dreamy sound, compounded of many noises, each of which was at too great a distance to be separately heard. Robin marvelled at this snore of a sleeping town, and marvelled more whenever its continuity was broken by now and then a distant shout, apparently loud where it originated. But altogether it was a sleep-inspiring sound, and, to shake off its drowsy influence, Robin arose, and climbed a window-frame, that he might view the interior of the church. There the moonbeams came trembling in, and fell down upon the deserted pews, and extended along the quiet aisles. A fainter yet more awful radiance was hovering around the pulpit, and one solitary ray had dared to rest upon the open page of the great Bible. Had nature, in that deep hour, become a worshipper in the house which man had builded? Or was that heavenly light the visible sanctity of the place,—visible because no earthly and impure feet were within the walls? The scene made Robin's heart shiver with a sensation of loneliness stronger than he had ever felt in the remotest depths of his native woods; so he turned away and sat down again before the door. There were graves around the church, and now an uneasy thought obtruded into Robin's breast. What if the object of his search, which had been so often and so strangely thwarted, were all the time mouldering in his shroud? What if his kinsman should glide through yonder gate, and nod and smile to him in dimly passing by?

"Oh that any breathing thing were here with me!" said Robin.

Recalling his thoughts from this uncomfortable track, he sent them over forest, hill, and stream, and attempted to imagine how that evening of ambiguity and weariness had been spent by his father's household. He pictured them assembled at the door, beneath the tree, the great old tree, which had been spared for its huge twisted trunk and venerable shade, when a thousand leafy brethren fell. There, at the going down of the summer sun, it was his father's custom to perform domestic worship, that the neighbors might come and join with him like brothers of the family, and that the wayfaring man might pause to drink at that fountain, and keep his heart pure by freshening the memory of home. Robin distinguished the seat of every individual of the little audience; he saw the good man in the midst, holding the Scriptures in the golden light that fell from the western clouds; he beheld him close the book and all rise up to pray. He heard the old thanksgivings for daily mercies, the old supplications for their continuance, to which he had so often listened in weariness, but which were now among his dear remembrances. He perceived the slight inequality of his father's voice when he came to speak of the absent one; he noted how his mother turned her face to the broad and knotted trunk; how his elder brother scorned, because the beard was rough upon his upper lip, to permit his features to be moved; how the younger sister drew down a low hanging branch before her eyes; and how the littlest one of all, whose sports had hitherto broken the decorum of the scene, understood the prayer for her playmate, and burst into clamorous grief. Then he saw them go in at the door; and when Robin would have entered also, the latch tinkled into its place, and he was excluded from his home.

"Am I here, or there?" cried Robin, starting; for all at once, when his thoughts had become visible and audible in a dream, the long, wide, solitary street shone out before him.

He aroused himself, and endeavored to fix his attention steadily upon the large edifice which he had surveyed before. But still his mind kept vibrating between fancy and reality; by turns, the pillars of the balcony lengthened into the tall, bare stems of pines, dwindled down to human figures, settled again into their true shape and size, and then commenced a new succession of changes. For a single moment, when he deemed himself awake, he could have sworn that a visage—one which he seemed to remember, yet could not absolutely name as his kinsman's—was looking towards him from the Gothic window. A deeper sleep wrestled with and nearly overcame him, but fled at the sound of footsteps along the opposite pavement. Robin rubbed his eyes, discerned a man passing at the foot of the balcony, and addressed him in a loud, peevish, and lamentable cry.

"Hallo, friend! must I wait here all night for my kinsman, Major Molineux?"

The sleeping echoes awoke, and answered the voice; and the passenger, barely able to discern a figure sitting in the oblique shade of the steeple, traversed the street to obtain a nearer view. He was himself a gentleman in his prime, of open, intelligent, cheerful, and altogether prepossessing countenance. Perceiving a country youth, apparently homeless and without friends, he accosted him in a tone of real kindness, which had become strange to Robin's ears.

"Well, my good lad, why are you sitting here?" inquired he. "Can I be of service to you in any way?"

"I am afraid not, sir," replied Robin, despondingly; "yet I shall take it kindly, if you'll answer me a single question. I've been searching, half the night, for one Major Molineux; now, sir, is there really such a person in these parts, or am I dreaming?"

"Major Molineux! The name is not altogether strange to me," said the gentleman, smiling. "Have you any objection to telling me the nature of your business with him?"

Then Robin briefly related that his father was a clergyman, settled on a small salary, at a long distance back in the country, and that he and Major Molineux were brothers' children. The Major, having inherited riches, and acquired civil and military rank, had visited his cousin, in great pomp, a year or two before; had manifested much interest in Robin and an elder brother, and, being childless himself, had thrown out hints respecting the future establishment of one of them in life. The elder brother was destined to succeed to the farm which his father cultivated in the interval of sacred duties; it was therefore determined that Robin should profit by his kinsman's generous intentions, especially as he seemed to be rather the favorite, and was thought to possess other necessary endowments.

"For I have the name of being a shrewd youth," observed Robin, in this part of his story.

"I doubt not you deserve it," replied his new friend, good-naturedly; "but pray proceed."

"Well, sir, being nearly eighteen years old, and well grown, as you see," continued Robin, drawing himself up to his full height, "I thought it high time to begin in the world. So my mother and sister put me in handsome trim, and my father gave me half the remnant of his last year's salary, and five days ago I started for this place, to pay the Major a visit. But, would you believe it, sir! I crossed the ferry a little after dark, and have yet found nobody that would show me the way to his dwelling; only, an hour or two since, I was told to wait here, and Major Molineux would pass by."

"Can you describe the man who told you this?" inquired the gentleman.

"Oh, he was a very ill-favored fellow, sir," replied Robin, "with two great bumps on his forehead, a hook nose, fiery eyes; and, what struck me as the strangest, his face was of two different colors. Do you happen to know such a man, sir?"

"Not intimately," answered the stranger, "but I chanced to meet him a little time previous to your stopping me. I believe you may trust his word, and that the Major will very shortly pass through this street. In the mean time, as I have a singular curiosity to witness your meeting, I will sit down here upon the steps and bear you company."

He seated himself accordingly, and soon engaged his companion in animated discourse. It was but of brief continuance, however, for a noise of shouting, which had long been remotely audible, drew so much nearer that Robin inquired its cause.

"What may be the meaning of this uproar?" asked he. "Truly, if your town be always as noisy, I shall find little sleep while I am an inhabitant."

"Why, indeed, friend Robin, there do appear to be three or four riotous fellows abroad to-night," replied the gentleman. "You must not expect all the stillness of your native woods here in our streets. But the watch will shortly be at the heels of these lads and"—

"Ay, and set them in the stocks by peep of day," interrupted Robin, recollecting his own encounter with the drowsy lantern-bearer. "But, dear sir, if I may trust my ears, an army of watchmen would never make head against such a multitude of rioters. There were at least a thousand voices went up to make that one shout."

"May not a man have several voices, Robin, as well as two complexions?" said his friend.

"Perhaps a man may; but Heaven forbid that a woman should!" responded the shrewd youth, thinking of the seductive tones of the Major's housekeeper.

The sounds of a trumpet in some neighboring street now became so evident and continual, that Robin's curiosity was strongly excited. In addition to the shouts, he heard frequent bursts from many instruments of discord, and a wild and confused laughter filled up the intervals. Robin rose from the steps, and looked wistfully towards a point whither people seemed to be hastening.

"Surely some prodigious merry-making is going on," exclaimed he. "I have laughed very little since I left home, sir, and should be sorry to lose an opportunity. Shall we step round the corner by that darkish house, and take our share of the fun?"

"Sit down again, sit down, good Robin," replied the gentleman, laying his hand on the skirt of the gray coat. "You forget that we must wait here for your kinsman; and there is reason to believe that he will pass by, in the course of a very few moments."

The near approach of the uproar had now disturbed the neighborhood; windows flew open on all sides; and many heads, in the attire of the pillow, and confused by sleep suddenly broken, were protruded to the gaze of whoever had leisure to observe them. Eager voices hailed each other from house to house, all demanding the explanation, which not a soul could give. Half-dressed men hurried towards the unknown commotion, stumbling as they went over the stone steps that thrust themselves into the narrow footwalk. The shouts, the laughter, and the tuneless bray, the antipodes of music, came onwards with increasing din, till scattered individuals, and then denser bodies, began to appear round a corner at the distance of a hundred yards.

"Will you recognize your kinsman, if he passes in this crowd?" inquired the gentleman.

"Indeed, I can't warrant it, sir; but I'll take my stand here, and keep a bright lookout," answered Robin, descending to the outer edge of the pavement.

A mighty stream of people now emptied into the street, and came rolling slowly towards the church. A single horseman wheeled the corner in the midst of them, and close behind him came a band of fearful wind-instruments, sending forth a fresher discord now that no intervening buildings kept it from the ear. Then a redder light disturbed the moonbeams, and a dense multitude of torches shone along the street, concealing, by their glare, whatever object they illuminated. The single horseman, clad in a military dress, and bearing a drawn sword, rode onward as the leader, and, by his fierce and variegated countenance, appeared like war personified; the red of one cheek was an emblem of fire and sword; the blackness of the other betokened the mourning that attends them. In his train were wild figures in the Indian dress, and many fantastic shapes without a model, giving the whole march a visionary air, as if a dream had broken forth from some feverish brain, and were sweeping visibly through the midnight streets. A mass of people, inactive, except as applauding spectators, hemmed the procession in; and several women ran along the sidewalk, piercing the confusion of heavier sounds with their shrill voices of mirth or terror.

"The double-faced fellow has his eye upon me," muttered Robin, with an indefinite but an uncomfortable idea that he was himself to bear a part in the pageantry.

The leader turned himself in the saddle, and fixed his glance full upon the country youth, as the steed went slowly by. When Robin had freed his eyes from those fiery ones, the musicians were passing before him, and the torches were close at hand; but the unsteady brightness of the latter formed a veil which he could not penetrate. The rattling of wheels over the stones sometimes found its way to his ear, and confused traces of a human form appeared at intervals, and then melted into the vivid light. A moment more, and the leader thundered a command to halt: the trumpets vomited a horrid breath, and then held their peace; the shouts and laughter of the people died away, and there remained only a universal hum, allied to silence. Right before Robin's eyes was an uncovered cart. There the torches blazed the brightest, there the moon shone out like day, and there, in tar-and-feathery dignity, sat his kinsman, Major Molineux!

He was an elderly man, of large and majestic person, and strong, square features, betokening a steady soul; but steady as it was, his enemies had found means to shake it. His face was pale as death, and far more ghastly; the broad forehead was contracted in his agony, so that his eyebrows formed one grizzled line; his eyes were red and wild, and the foam hung white upon his quivering lip. His whole frame was agitated by a quick and continual tremor, which his pride strove to quell even in those circumstances of overwhelming humiliation. But perhaps the bitterest pang of all was when his eyes met those of Robin; for he evidently knew him on the instant, as the youth stood witnessing the foul disgrace of a head grown gray in honor. They stared at each other in silence, and Robin's knees shook, and his hair bristled, with a mixture of pity and terror. Soon, however, a bewildering excitement began to seize upon his mind; the preceding adventures of the night, the unexpected appearance of the crowd, the torches, the confused din and the hush that followed, the spectre of his kinsman reviled by that great multitude,—all this, and, more than all, a perception of tremendous ridicule in the whole scene, affected him with a sort of mental inebriety. At that moment a voice of sluggish merriment saluted Robin's ears; he turned instinctively, and just behind the corner of the church stood the lantern-bearer, rubbing his eyes, and drowsily enjoying the lad's amazement. Then he heard a peal of laughter like the ringing of silvery bells; a woman twitched his arm, a saucy eye met his, and he saw the lady of the scarlet petticoat. A sharp, dry cachinnation appealed to his memory, and standing on tiptoe in the crowd, with his white apron over his head, he beheld the courteous little innkeeper. And lastly, there sailed over the heads of the multitude a great, broad laugh, broken in the midst by two sepulchral hems; thus, "Haw, haw, haw,—hem, hem,—haw, haw, haw, haw!"

The sound proceeded from the balcony of the opposite edifice, and thither Robin turned his eyes. In front of the Gothic window stood the old citizen, wrapped in a wide gown, his gray periwig exchanged for a nightcap, which was thrust back from his forehead, and his silk stockings hanging about his legs. He supported himself on his polished cane in a fit of convulsive merriment, which manifested itself on his solemn old features like a funny inscription on a tombstone. Then Robin seemed to hear the voices of the barbers, of the guests of the inn, and of all who had made sport of him that night. The contagion was spreading among the multitude, when all at once, it seized upon Robin, and he sent forth a shout of laughter that echoed through the street,—every man shook his sides, every man emptied his lungs, but Robin's shout was the loudest there. The cloud-spirits peeped from their silvery islands, as the congregated mirth went roaring up the sky! The Man in the Moon heard the far bellow. "Oho," quoth he, "the old earth is frolicsome to-night!"

When there was a momentary calm in that tempestuous sea of sound, the leader gave the sign, the procession resumed its march. On they went, like fiends that throng in mockery around some dead potentate, mighty no more, but majestic still in his agony. On they went, in counterfeited pomp, in senseless uproar, in frenzied merriment, trampling all on an old man's heart. On swept the tumult, and left a silent street behind.

"Well, Robin, are you dreaming?" inquired the gentleman, laying his hand on the youth's shoulder.

Robin started, and withdrew his arm from the stone post to which he had instinctively clung, as the living stream rolled by him. His cheek was somewhat pale, and his eye not quite as lively as in the earlier part of the evening.

"Will you be kind enough to show me the way to the ferry?" said he, after a moment's pause.

"You have, then, adopted a new subject of inquiry?" observed his companion, with a smile.

"Why, yes, sir," replied Robin, rather dryly. "Thanks to you, and to my other friends, I have at last met my kinsman, and he will scarce desire to see my face again. I begin to grow weary of a town life, sir. Will you show me the way to the ferry?"

"No, my good friend Robin,—not to-night, at least," said the gentleman. "Some few days hence, if you wish it, I will speed you on your journey. Or, if you prefer to remain with us, perhaps, as you are a shrewd youth, you may rise in the world without the help of your kinsman, Major Molineux."

Questions

1. How does the opening description of Robin's dress and appearance characterize him? What additional qualities emerge in his encounters with the old man on the street

and the people in the tavern? Does Robin seem to you a complex character at this point in the story?

2. Does the scene with the woman in the scarlet petticoat show other qualities? Is Hawthorne revealing Robin's character gradually, or does he establish Robin's character fully in the opening scenes and then show this character acting?

3. The writer of fiction, Hawthorne states in a preface, knows how to "manage his atmospherical medium as to bring out or mellow the lights and deepen and enrich the shadows of the picture." What shadows does Hawthorne create, and to what purpose does he put them? Would the effect be different if most of the events occurred during the day?

4. How does Hawthorne characterize Major Molineux in the account of his visit to his cousin's farm and in his brief appearance toward the end of the story? Do the opening details on colonial Massachusetts explain the treatment he receives, or is the answer to be found in the character of the man? Or are both of these important to understanding what happens?

5. How do you explain Robin's behavior when he finally sees Major Molineux? Do the events leading up to this encounter and Robin's views up to this point prepare you for what he does? Does Robin seem more complex than he did at the beginning, or is he essentially the same character?

6. What is the implication of the end of the story? Are we to find Robin admirable or contemptible, or are we to make no judgment about him?

7. Do you find a moral in this story? Is it a parable—a story that teaches a lesson? Or is it a mystery story, its characters finally not complex when the mystery is unraveled? Or is the story more realistic than either a parable or a mystery story—a revelation of complex character and motives?

Suggestions for Writing

1. Setting is often as important as character in the realistic story, for the realist shows people acting in a particular time and place. The setting may also provide part of the explanation for what characters think, feel, and do. Analyze a paragraph from "My Kinsman, Major Molineux" to show what the setting reveals about Robin. Use your analysis to define the kind of story Hawthorne has written.

2. Write an analysis of Robin's character, centering on the final scenes of the story. Use your analysis to decide whether Hawthorne has created a simple or a complex character.

3. Many of Hawthorne's stories—for example, "Young Goodman Brown," "The Birthmark," and "Rappaccini's Daughter"—raise interesting questions about motivation and setting. Compare the principal male character in one of the stories with Robin to determine who is the more complex and why.

Additional Reading

Bell, Millicent, ed. *Nathaniel Hawthorne. Vol. II: Novels.* Library of America. New York: Viking, 1983.

Crews, Frederick. *The Sins of the Father: Hawthorne's Psychological Themes.* New York: Oxford University Press, 1966.

Matthiessen, F. O. *American Renaissance: Art and Expression in the Age of Emerson and Whitman.* New York: Oxford University Press, 1941.

Pearce, Roy Harvey, ed. *Nathaniel Hawthorne. Vol. I: Tales and Sketches.* Library of America. New York: Viking, 1981.

Van Doren, Mark. *Nathaniel Hawthorne.* New York: Sloane, 1949.

Waggoner, Hyatt H. *Hawthorne: A Critical Study.* Rev. ed. Cambridge: Harvard University Press, 1963.

Poems

Dylan Thomas

Dylan Thomas lived a life as exuberant and complex as his poetry. Born in 1914 in Swansea, Wales, Thomas made the seaside town the subject of many sketches and stories. Though his father, a schoolmaster, wanted him to attend a university, he chose instead to begin a career as a writer. Thomas's first book of poems, published when he was twenty, received immediate recognition. During his short life, he wrote poems, stories, plays, and movie scripts; toward the end of his life, he traveled in the United States giving readings of his poetry. In her famous memoir, Leftover Life to Kill, *his Irish wife Caitlin describes their stormy marriage and the alcoholism that led to Thomas's tragic death in 1953 in New York City.*

His biographer Constantine Fitzgibbon tells us that Thomas saw in the Welsh town of his youth the meeting place of the Welsh and English languages and cultures, the idioms and rhythms of which he unites in his poetry, though he wrote in English. It was also the boundary between land and sea and ancient and modern Wales—the contrasting farming and mining villages. Thomas describes this world in his memoir A Child's Christmas in Wales *and his verse play* Under Milk Wood. *The experiences of his childhood and young manhood are the subject of many of his stories and poems, like the three reprinted here. His poetry explores contrasting moods and perceptions, which his often-complex metaphors seek to resolve. There were personal conflicts that Thomas needed to resolve as well. His letter to the novelist Pamela Hansford Johnson in 1933 reveals qualities not always apparent in his poetry:*

Automatic writing is worthless as literature, however interesting it may be to the psychologist and pathologist. So perhaps, after all I am nothing but a literary oddity, a little freak of nature whose madness runs into print rather than into ravings and illusions. It may be, too, an illusion that keeps me writing, the illusion of myself as some misunderstood poet of talent.

But Thomas also understood the nature of his achievement as a poet. He wrote the following to a young scholar:

I am a painstaking, conscientious, involved and devious craftsman in words, however unsuccessful the result so often appears, and to whatever wrong uses I may apply my technical paraphernalia. I use everything and anything to make my poems work and move in the directions I want them to: old tricks, new tricks, puns, portmanteau-words, paradox, allusion, paranomasia, paragram, catachresis, slang, assonantal rhymes, vowel rhymes, sprung rhythm. Every device there is in language is there to be used if you will. Poets have got to enjoy themselves sometimes, and the twistings and convolutions of words, the inventions and contrivances, are all part of the joy that is part of the painful, voluntary work.

Poem in October

It was my thirtieth year to heaven
Woke to my hearing from harbour and neighbour wood
And the mussel pooled and the heron
Priested shore
The morning beckon
With water praying and call of seagull and rook
And the knock of sailing boats on the net webbed wall
Myself to set foot
That second
In the still sleeping town and set forth.

My birthday began with the water-
Birds and the birds of the winged trees flying my name
Above the farms and the white horses
And I rose
In rainy autumn
And walked abroad in a shower of all my days.
High tide and the heron dived when I took the road
Over the border
And the gates
Of the town closed as the town awoke.

A springful of larks in a rolling
Cloud and the roadside bushes brimming with whistling
Blackbirds and the sun of October
Summery
On the hill's shoulder,
Here were fond climates and sweet singers suddenly
Come in the morning where I wandered and listened
To the rain wringing
Wind blow cold
In the wood faraway under me.

Pale rain over the dwindling harbour
And over the sea wet church the size of a snail
With its horns through mist and the castle
Brown as owls
But all the gardens
Of spring and summer were blooming in the tall tales
Beyond the border and under the lark full cloud.
There could I marvel
My birthday
Away but the weather turned around.

It turned away from the blithe country
And down the other air and the blue altered sky
Streamed again a wonder of summer
With apples
Pears and red currants
And I saw in the turning so clearly a child's
Forgotten mornings when he walked with his mother
Through the parables
Of sun light
And the legends of the green chapels

And the twice told fields of infancy
That his tears burned my cheeks and his heart moved in mine.
These were the woods the river and sea
Where a boy
In the listening
Summertime of the dead whispered the truth of his joy
To the trees and the stones and the fish in the tide.
And the mystery
Sang alive
Still in the water and singingbirds.

And there could I marvel my birthday
Away but the weather turned around. And the true

Joy of the long dead child sang burning
          In the sun.
        It was my thirtieth
Year to heaven stood there then in the summer noon
Though the town below lay leaved with October blood.
          O may my heart's truth
            Still be sung
        On this high hill in a year's turning.

Fern Hill

Now as I was young and easy under the apple boughs
About the lilting house and happy as the grass was green,
        The night above the dingle starry,
          Time let me hail and climb
        Golden in the heydays of his eyes,
And honoured among wagons I was prince of the apple towns
And once below a time I lordly had the trees and leaves
          Trail with daisies and barley
        Down the rivers of the windfall light.

And as I was green and carefree, famous among the barns
About the happy yard and singing as the farm was home,
        In the sun that is young once only,
          Time let me play and be
        Golden in the mercy of his means,
And green and golden I was huntsman and herdsman, the
                  calves
Sang to my horn, the foxes on the hills barked clear and cold,
          And the sabbath rang slowly
        In the pebbles of the holy streams.

All the sun long it was running, it was lovely, the hay
Fields high as the house, the tunes from the chimneys, it
                  was air
        And playing, lovely and watery
          And fire green as grass.
        And nightly under the simple stars
As I rode to sleep the owls were bearing the farm away,
All the moon long I heard, blessed among stables, the night-
                  jars
        Flying with the ricks, and the horses
          Flashing into the dark.

And then to awake, and the farm, like a wanderer white
With the dew, come back, the cock on his shoulder: it was all

Shining, it was Adam and maiden,
    The sky gathered again
    And the sun grew round that very day.
So it must have been after the birth of the simple light
In the first, spinning place, the spellbound horses walking
        warm
        Out of the whinnying green stable
        On to the fields of praise.

And honoured among foxes and pheasants by the gay house
Under the new made clouds and happy as the heart was long,
    In the sun born over and over,
        I ran my heedless ways,
        My wishes raced through the house high hay
And nothing I cared, at my sky blue trades, that time allows
In all his tuneful turning so few and such morning songs
        Before the children green and golden
        Follow him out of grace,

Nothing I cared, in the lamb white days, that time would
        take me
Up to the swallow thronged loft by the shadow of my hand,
    In the moon that is always rising,
        Nor that riding to sleep
        I should hear him fly with the high fields
And wake to the farm forever fled from the childless land.
Oh as I was young and easy in the mercy of his means,
        Time held me green and dying
        Though I sang in my chains like the sea.

Poem on His Birthday

    In the mustardseed sun,
    By full tilt river and switchback sea
        Where the cormorants scud,
    In his house on stilts high among beaks
        And palavers of birds
    This sandgrain day in the bent bay's grave
        He celebrates and spurns
    His driftwood thirty-fifth wind turned age;
        Herons spire and spear.

        Under and round him go
    Flounders, gulls, on their cold, dying trails,
        Doing what they are told,

Curlews aloud in the congered waves
   Work at their ways to death,
And the rhymer in the long tongued room,
   Who tolls his birthday bell,
Toils towards the ambush of his wounds;
   Herons, steeple stemmed, bless.

   In the thistledown fall,
He sings towards anguish; finches fly
   In the claw tracks of hawks
On a seizing sky; small fishes glide
   Through wynds and shells of drowned
Ship towns to pastures of otters. He
   In his slant, racking house
And the hewn coils of his trade perceives
   Herons walk in their shroud,

   The livelong river's robe
Of minnows wreathing around their prayer;
   And far at sea he knows,
Who slaves to his crouched, eternal end
   Under a serpent cloud,
Dolphins dive in their turnturtle dust,
   The rippled seals streak down
To kill and their own tide daubing blood
   Slides good in the sleek mouth.

   In a cavernous, swung
Wave's silence, wept white angelus knells.
   Thirty-five bells sing struck
On skull and scar where his loves lie wrecked,
   Steered by the falling stars.
And to-morrow weeps in a blind cage
   Terror will rage apart
Before chains break to a hammer flame
   And love unbolts the dark

   And freely he goes lost
In the unknown, famous light of great
   And fabulous, dear God.
Dark is a way and light is a place,
   Heaven that never was
Nor will be ever is always true,
   And, in that brambled void,
Plenty as blackberries in the woods
   The dead grow for His joy.

There he might wander bare
With the spirits of the horseshoe bay
   Or the stars' seashore dead,
Marrow of eagles, the roots of whales
   And wishbones of wild geese,
With blessed, unborn God and His Ghost,
   And every soul His priest,
Gulled and chanter in young Heaven's fold
   Be at cloud quaking peace,

   But dark is a long way.
He, on the earth of the night, alone
   With all the living, prays,
Who knows the rocketing wind will blow
   The bones out of the hills,
And the scythed boulders bleed, and the last
   Rage shattered waters kick
Masts and fishes to the still quick stars,
   Faithlessly unto Him

   Who is the light of old
And air shaped Heaven where souls grow wild
   As horses in the foam:
Oh, let me midlife mourn by the shrined
   And druid herons' vows
The voyage to ruin I must run,
   Dawn ships clouted aground,
Yet, though I cry with tumbledown tongue,
   Count my blessings aloud:

   Four elements and five
Senses, and man a spirit in love
   Tangling through this spun slime
To his nimbus bell cool kingdom come
   And the lost, moonshine domes,
And the sea that hides his secret selves
   Deep in its black, base bones,
Lulling of spheres in the seashell flesh,
   And this last blessing most,

   That the closer I move
To death, one man through his sundered hulks,
   The louder the sun blooms
And the tusked, ramshackling sea exults;
   And every wave of the way
And gale I tackle, the whole world then,

With more triumphant faith
Than ever was since the world was said,
Spins its morning of praise,

I hear the bouncing hills
Grow larked and greener at berry brown
Fall and the dew larks sing
Taller this thunderclap spring, and how
More spanned with angels ride
The mansouled fiery islands! Oh,
Holier then their eyes,
And my shining men no more alone
As I sail out to die.

Questions

1. What similarities and differences do you notice in the expression of emotions, perceptions, or ideas in "Poem in October" and "Fern Hill"? Do the poems express the same
   attitude toward young manhood?
2. What is Thomas saying about youth and time in "Fern Hill"? In what sense did time
   hold him "green and dying"? What are the "chains" referred to in the final line of the
   poem? Does Thomas seek to resolve the contrasting or paradoxical emotions, perceptions, and ideas he explores?
3. What is the general theme of "Poem on His Birthday," and how does Thomas develop
   it? Is Thomas exploring a single idea or attitude, or does the poem range from one
   idea or attitude to others? Do you find the structure of the poem—the buildup of
   emotion, image, and idea—different from that in "Poem in October" and "Fern
   Hill"? Does the poem develop similar attitudes or ideas?
4. Is there a dominant metaphor that organizes the many metaphors of "Poem on His
   Birthday"? Or does Thomas present a series of related metaphors that express an attitude or develop an idea?
5. What qualities do these poems share? Do they express a characteristic attitude toward
   youth or toward life generally?

Suggestions for Writing

1. Paraphrase the final stanza of one of the poems, explaining images, metaphors, and
   the like through earlier images, metaphors, and ideas in the poem. Then write one
   or two paragraphs discussing what the stanza loses in paraphrase.
2. Compare key lines in the three poems to define the qualities that distinguish Dylan
   Thomas as a poet. Single out a quality that most distinguishes Thomas from other
   poets you have read—possibly another poet who has written about the feelings or experiences of youth.
3. Characterize Dylan Thomas on the basis of these three poems. Then discuss the extent to which you find an expression of the same qualities in his other poems, stories,
   or letters.

Additional Reading

FitzGibbon, Constantine. *The Life of Dylan Thomas*. Boston: Little, Brown, 1965.

Holbrook, David. *Dylan Thomas: The Code of Night*. Tuscaloosa: University of Alabama Press, 1972.

Olson, Elder. *The Poetry of Dylan Thomas*. Chicago: University of Chicago Press, 1954.

Tindall, William York. *A Reader's Guide to Dylan Thomas*. New York: Farrar, Straus and Giroux, 1962.

Thomas, Dylan. *The Poems*. New York: New Directions, 1971.

———. *Collected Letters*. Ed. Paul Ferris. New York: Macmillan 1985.

———. *Collected Stories*. New York: New Directions, 1984.

———. *Quite Early One Morning*. New York: New Directions, 1954.

———. *A Portrait of the Artist as a Young Dog*. New York: New Directions, 1940.

EDUCATION

The essays in this section consider kinds of education from various perspectives or points of view. The section opens with the eighteenth-century philosopher Jean-Jacques Rousseau's often-quoted discussion of how to educate children. The essays by John Stuart Mill and Margaret Mead describe the education of one child in the early nineteenth century and that of children in a traditional society in New Guinea. Susan Allen Toth describes how a young woman in our own society "prepares for life," and Lincoln Steffens discusses how to survive a college education. Wordsworth's poem concerns truths learned from a strange encounter.

Some of the writers in this and later sections share a perspective that deserves comment, namely, that personal experience and observation are sources of important truths. This is an assumption that most of us take for granted, yet personal experience and observation have not always been so highly regarded. Rousseau's work illustrates the empirical study of people and society inaugurated in his century, which we refer to today as the "social sciences." You will recognize in Rousseau a familiar idea—that of the noble savage, the "natural" human being that is corrupted and made vicious by society and its institutions. How did Rousseau develop this idea? In his *Discourse on the Origin of Inequality* of 1754, Rousseau recognized the revolutionary nature of the method he was proposing for studying the human being—that is, the observation of people in a natural state in order to learn truths about society and government:

> The very study of the original man, of his real wants, and the fundamental principles of his duty, is besides the only proper method we can adopt to obviate all the difficulties which the origin of moral inequality presents, on the true foundations of the body politic, on the reciprocal rights of its members, and on many other similar topics equally important and obscure.

Familiar with modern statistical surveys of public opinion and behavior, the modern reader may not appreciate how much of a break with the past this statement represents. We know what traditional societies are like from studies Margaret Mead and other anthropologists have conducted "in the field." Jane Goodall, Farley Mowat, Barry

Lopez, and other observers of animal life tell us that we can best understand animals by studying them in their natural environments. Yet it was by no means obvious in Rousseau's time that people observed in a natural or urban setting could provide bases for generalizing about what humans are or can become. It was common for Rousseau's predecessors to reason about human nature, society, government, and ethics in a much different way—from truths derived from biblical and religious doctrine, "natural law," and other authoritative sources. Truths about people and their world were deduced directly from these "givens." Some earlier philosophers, for example, began with the "given" that humans are rational beings and asked what this truth entails.

In the new science of the seventeenth and eighteenth centuries, observations and measurements led to hypotheses, which were then tested by further observation and experiment. Thinkers and writers of that age were also influenced by the analytic method of the seventeenth-century French philosopher Descartes, who reduced things to their components and moved from simple truths about the self and the world to complex ones—as in the famous statement of Descartes, "I think, therefore I am." In that age of "enlightenment," many scientists and philosophers believed that reason is an independent source of truth or "enlightenment," as Plato had held in the ancient world (see p. 142). But others like Descartes recognized that many "first principles" remained beyond human inquiry. "Nothing seems to me more absurd," Descartes wrote in his *Rules for the Direction of the Understanding,* " . . . than to dispute boldly on the mysteries of nature, on the influence of the heavens on our earth, on the prediction of the future, and the like, as many do, and yet never to have inquired whether human reason is adequate for the discovery of these things."

Deductive reasoning still played an important role in mathematical physics. And deduction was for most experimental scientists the counterpart of inductive reasoning; the scientist then and now makes deductions in drawing conclusions from observations and experiments. The change in the attitude toward deduction is evident in the eighteenth-century French writer Voltaire, who satirizes the older deductive method of philosophizing—the process of broad inference from assumed truths, or first principles—in his novel *Candide* (1759). In the following passage, the comical philosopher Pangloss is explaining why he and the innocent hero of the novel are fortunate to be living in the best of all possible worlds:

> " 'Tis demonstrated," said he, "that things cannot be otherwise; for, since everything is made for an end, everything is necessarily for the best end. Observe that noses were made to wear spectacles; and so we have spectacles. Legs were visibly instituted to be breeched, and we have breeches. Stones were formed to be quarried and to build castles; and My Lord has a very noble castle; the greatest Baron in the province should have the best house; and as pigs were made to be eaten, we eat pork all the year round; consequently, those who have asserted that all is well talk nonsense; they ought to have said that all is for the best."

Voltaire concludes his novel with the advice that "we must cultivate our gardens"—that is, limit our speculations about life and perform the work we each do best. Not all essayists since the age of Rousseau and Voltaire have given the same advice; Emerson, Schweitzer, Thoreau, and other writers later in this book generalize broadly about people and life—outside the restrictions that modern essayists often set for themselves. But many of the essays in this section show this limitation and dependence on personal experience and observation.

Emile, from Book 2*

Jean-Jacques Rousseau

Jean-Jacques Rousseau was born in 1712, the son of a Geneva watchmaker. His mother having died shortly after his birth, Rousseau and his brother lived for a time with their father and then with an uncle. Apprenticed to an engraver who beat him, Rousseau fled to Savoy, now a part of southwestern France; later he lived with a second "mama," Mme. de Warens, one of many lovers he describes in his Confessions. *"I loved too sincerely, too completely, I venture to say, to be able to be happy easily," Rousseau wrote about himself during these years. "Never have passions been at once more lively and purer than mine; never has love been tenderer, truer, more disinterested."*

For many years Rousseau lived with Mme. de Warens, traveling frequently, working at various jobs, and slowly absorbing the literature and ideas of Newton, Leibniz, Voltaire, and other writers of the Enlightenment (see p. 66), a period in which established ideas in science, religion, and politics were being examined critically. After parting from Mme. de Warens, he went to Paris, and in 1846 began an eight-year relationship with Thérèse Levasseur. Rousseau placed each of their five children in an orphanage at birth—later pleading poverty and remorse, but nonetheless furious with Voltaire for revealing the fact. Receiving the first prize of the Dijon Academy in 1850 for a discourse, he began the series of books that eventually forced him to flee to England. His most famous political tract, The Social Contract, *was published in 1762—the same year as* Emile, *a treatise on education in the form of a novel. In 1767 Rousseau returned to France, where he lived until his death in 1778.*

The "original man," a major theme of Rousseau's many books, is the subject of Emile. *"God makes all things good," Rousseau begins the book; "man meddles with them and they become evil. He forces one soil to yield the products of another, one tree to bear another's fruit." A few pages later, he defines nature by contrasting it with the society and environment that warp the child:*

> We are born sensitive and from our birth onwards we are affected in various ways by our environment. As soon as we become conscious of our sensations we tend to seek or shun the things that cause them. . . . These ten-

---

*This excerpt consists of the first half of Book 2. The notes throughout are Rousseau's.

dencies gain strength and permanence with the growth of
reason, but hindered by our habits they are more or less
warped by our prejudices. Before this change they are
what I call Nature within us.

*Everything, says Rousseau, "should therefore be brought into har-
mony with these natural tendencies." The pages that follow describe
the education of the boy Emile according to nature. Rousseau introduces ideas promoted today by educational reformers who argue that
formal schooling stunts children by imposing artificial restraints
on them. Many of the issues debated today are discussed in
these pages, translated by Barbara Foxley.*

We have now reached the second phase of life; infancy, strictly so-called, is 1
over; for the words *infans* and *puer* are not synonymous. The latter includes the former,
which means literally "one who cannot speak"; thus Valerius speaks of *puerum
infantem.* But I shall continue to use the word child (French *enfant)* according to the
custom of our language till an age for which there is another term.

When children begin to talk they cry less. This progress is quite natural; one 2
language supplants another. As soon as they can say "It hurts me," why should they cry,
unless the pain is too sharp for words? If they still cry, those about them are to blame.
When once Emile has said, "It hurts me," it will take a very sharp pain to make him cry.

If the child is delicate and sensitive, if by nature he begins to cry for nothing, 3
I let him cry in vain and soon check his tears at their source. So long as he cries I will
not go near him; I come at once when he leaves off crying. He will soon be quiet when
he wants to call me, or rather he will utter a single cry. Children learn the meaning of
signs by their effects; they have no other meaning for them. However much a child
hurts himself when he is alone, he rarely cries, unless he expects to be heard.

Should he fall or bump his head, or make his nose bleed, or cut his fingers, I 4
shall show no alarm, nor shall I make any fuss over him; I shall take no notice, at any
rate at first. The harm is done; he must bear it; all my zeal could only frighten him more
and make him more nervous. Indeed it is not the blow but the fear of it which distresses
us when we are hurt. I shall spare him this suffering at least, for he will certainly regard
the injury as he sees me regard it; if he finds that I hasten anxiously to him, if I pity him
or comfort him, he will think he is badly hurt. If he finds I take no notice, he will soon
recover himself, and will think the wound is healed when it ceases to hurt. This is the
time for his first lesson in courage, and by bearing slight ills without fear we gradually
learn to bear greater.

I shall not take pains to prevent Emile hurting himself; far from it, I should be 5
vexed if he never hurt himself, if he grew up unacquainted with pain. To bear pain is his
first and most useful lesson. It seems as if children were small and weak on purpose to
teach them these valuable lessons without danger. The child has such a little way to fall
he will not break his leg; if he knocks himself with a stick he will not break his arm; if
he seizes a sharp knife he will not grasp it tight enough to make a deep wound. So far
as I know, no child, left to himself, has ever been known to kill or maim itself, or even
to do itself any serious harm, unless it has been foolishly left on a high place, or alone
near the fire, or within reach of dangerous weapons. What is there to be said for all the

paraphernalia with which the child is surrounded to shield him on every side so that he grows up at the mercy of pain, with neither courage nor experience, so that he thinks he is killed by a pin-prick and faints at the sight of blood?

With our foolish and pedantic methods we are always preventing children from learning what they could learn much better by themselves, while we neglect what we alone can teach them. Can anything be sillier than the pains taken to teach them to walk, as if there were any one who was unable to walk when he grows up through his nurse's neglect? How many we see walking badly all their life because they were ill taught? 6

Emile shall have no head-pads, no go-carts, no leading-strings; or at least as soon as he can put one foot before another he shall only be supported along pavements, and he shall be taken quickly across them.[1] Instead of keeping him mewed up in a stuffy room, take him out into a meadow every day; let him run about, let him struggle and fall again and again, the oftener the better; he will learn all the sooner to pick himself up. The delights of liberty will make up for many bruises. My pupil will hurt himself of-tener than yours, but he will always be merry; your pupils may receive fewer injuries, but they are always thwarted, constrained, and sad. I doubt whether they are any better off. 7

As their strength increases, children have also less need for tears. They can do more for themselves, they need the help of others less frequently. With strength comes the sense to use it. It is with this second phase that the real personal life has its begin-ning; it is then that the child becomes conscious of himself. During every moment of his life memory calls up the feeling of self; he becomes really one person, always the same, and therefore capable of joy or sorrow. Hence we must begin to consider him as a moral being. 8

Although we know approximately the limits of human life and our chances of attaining those limits, nothing is more uncertain than the length of the life of any one of us. Very few reach old age. The chief risks occur at the beginning of life; the shorter our past life, the less we must hope to live. Of all the children who are born scarcely one half reach adolescence, and it is very likely your pupil will not live to be a man. 9

What is to be thought, therefore, of that cruel education which sacrifices the present to an uncertain future, that burdens a child with all sorts of restrictions and be-gins by making him miserable, in order to prepare him for some far-off happiness which he may never enjoy? Even if I considered that education wise in its aims, how could I view without indignation those poor wretches subjected to an intolerable slavery and condemned like galley-slaves to endless toil, with no certainty that they will gain any-thing by it? The age of harmless mirth is spent in tears, punishments, threats, and slav-ery. You torment the poor thing for his good; you fail to see that you are calling Death to snatch him from these gloomy surroundings. Who can say how many children fall victims to the excessive care of their fathers and mothers? They are happy to escape from this cruelty; this is all that they gain from the ills they are forced to endure: they die without regretting, having known nothing of life but its sorrows. 10

---

[1]There is nothing so absurd and hesitating as the gait of those who have been kept too long in leading-strings when they were little. This is one of the observations which are considered trivial because they are true.

Men, be kind to your fellow-men; this is your first duty, kind to every age and 11 station, kind to all that is not foreign to humanity. What wisdom can you find that is greater than kindness? Love childhood, indulge its sports, its pleasures, its delightful instincts. Who has not sometimes regretted that age when laughter was ever on the lips, and when the heart was ever at peace? Why rob these innocents of the joys which pass so quickly, of that precious gift which they cannot abuse? Why fill with bitterness the fleeting days of early childhood, days which will no more return for them than for you? Fathers, can you tell when death will call your children to him? Do not lay up sorrow for yourselves by robbing them of the short span which nature has allotted to them. As soon as they are aware of the joy of life, let them rejoice in it, so that whenever God calls them they may not die without having tasted the joy of life.

How people will cry out against me! I hear from afar the shouts of that false 12 wisdom which is ever dragging us onwards, counting the present as nothing, and pursuing without a pause a future which flies as we pursue, that false wisdom which removes us from our place and never brings us to any other.

Now is the time, you say, to correct his evil tendencies; we must increase suf- 13 fering in childhood, when it is less keenly felt, to lessen it in manhood. But how do you know that you can carry out all these fine schemes; how do you know that all this fine teaching with which you overwhelm the feeble mind of the child will not do him more harm than good in the future? How do you know that you can spare him anything by the vexations you heap upon him now? Why inflict on him more ills than befit his present condition unless you are quite sure that these present ills will save him future ill? And what proof can you give me that those evil tendencies you profess to cure are not the result of your foolish precautions rather than of nature? What a poor sort of foresight, to make a child wretched in the present with the more or less doubtful hope of making him happy at some future day. If such blundering thinkers fail to distinguish between liberty and licence, between a merry child and a spoilt darling, let them learn to discriminate.

Let us not forget what befits our present state in the pursuit of vain fancies. 14 Mankind has its place in the sequence of things; childhood has its place in the sequence of human life; the man must be treated as a man and the child as a child. Give each his place, and keep him there. Control human passions according to man's nature; that is all we can do for his welfare. The rest depends on external forces, which are beyond our control.

Absolute good and evil are unknown to us. In this life they are blended to- 15 gether; we never enjoy any perfectly pure feeling, nor do we remain for more than a moment in the same state. The feelings of our minds, like the changes in our bodies, are in a continual flux. Good and ill are common to all, but in varying proportions. The happiest is he who suffers least; the most miserable is he who enjoys least. Ever more sorrow than joy—this is the lot of all of us. Man's happiness in this world is but a negative state; it must be reckoned by the fewness of his ills.

Every feeling of hardship is inseparable from the desire to escape from it; every 16 idea of pleasure from the desire to enjoy it. All desire implies a want, and all wants are painful; hence our wretchedness consists in the disproportion between our desires and our powers. A conscious being whose powers were equal to his desires would be perfectly happy.

What then is human wisdom? Where is the path of true happiness? The mere 17 limitation of our desires is not enough, for. if they were less than our powers, part of our faculties would be idle, and we should not enjoy our whole being; neither is the mere extension of our powers enough, for if our desires were also increased we should only be the more miserable. True happiness consists in decreasing the difference between our desires and our powers, in establishing a perfect equilibrium between the power and the will. Then only, when all its forces are employed, will the soul be at rest and man will find himself in his true position.

In this condition, nature, who does everything for the best, has placed him 18 from the first. To begin with, she gives him only such desires as are necessary for self-preservation and such powers as are sufficient for their satisfaction. All the rest she has stored in his mind as a sort of reserve, to be drawn upon at need. It is only in this primitive condition that we find the equilibrium between desire and power, and then alone man is not unhappy. As soon as his potential powers of mind begin to function, imagination, more powerful than all the rest, awakes, and precedes all the rest. It is imagination which enlarges the bounds of possibility for us, whether for good or ill, and therefore stimulates and feeds desires by the hope of satisfying them. But the object which seemed within our grasp flies quicker than we can follow; when we think we have grasped it, it transforms itself and is again far ahead of us. We no longer perceive the country we have traversed, and we think nothing of it; that which lies before us becomes vaster and stretches still before us. Thus we exhaust our strength, yet never reach our goal, and the nearer we are to pleasure, the further we are from happiness.

On the other hand, the more nearly a man's condition approximates to this 19 state of nature the less difference is there between his desires and his powers, and happiness is therefore less remote. Lacking everything, he is never less miserable; for misery consists, not in the lack of things, but in the needs which they inspire.

The world of reality has its bounds, the world of imagination is boundless; as 20 we cannot enlarge the one, let us restrict the other; for all the sufferings which really make us miserable arise from the difference between the real and the imaginary. Health, strength, and a good conscience excepted, all the good things of life are a matter of opinion; except bodily suffering and remorse, all our woes are imaginary. You will tell me this is a commonplace; I admit it, but its practical application is no commonplace, and it is with practice only that we are now concerned.

What do you mean when you say, "Man is weak"? The term weak implies a rela- 21 tion, a relation of the creature to whom it is applied. An insect or a worm whose strength exceeds its needs is strong; an elephant, a lion, a conqueror, a hero, a god himself, whose needs exceed his strength is weak. The rebellious angel who fought against his own nature was weaker than the happy mortal who is living at peace according to nature. When man is content to be himself he is strong indeed; when he strives to be more than man he is weak indeed. But do not imagine that you can increase your strength by increasing your powers. Not so; if your pride increases more rapidly your strength is diminished. Let us measure the extent of our sphere and remain in its centre like the spider in its web; we shall have strength sufficient for our needs, we shall have no cause to lament our weakness, for we shall never be aware of it.

The other animals possess only such powers as are required for self- 22 preservation; man alone has more. Is it not very strange that this superfluity should make him miserable? In every land a man's labour yields more than a bare living. If he were wise enough to disregard this surplus he would always have enough, for he would never have too much. "Great needs," said Favorin, "spring from great wealth; and often the best way of getting what we want is to get rid of what we have." By striving to increase our happiness we change it into wretchedness. If a man were content to live, he would live happy; and he would therefore be good, for what would he have to gain by vice?

If we were immortal we should all be miserable; no doubt it is hard to die, but 23 it is sweet to think that we shall not live for ever, and that a better life will put an end to the sorrows of this world. If we had the offer of immortality here below, who would accept the sorrowful gift?[2] What resources, what hopes, what consolation would be left against the cruelties of fate and man's injustice? The ignorant man never looks before; he knows little of the value of life and does not fear to lose it; the wise man sees things of greater worth and prefers them to it. Half knowledge and sham wisdom set us thinking about death and what lies beyond it; and they thus create the worst of our ills. The wise man bears life's ills all the better because he knows he must die. Life would be too dearly bought did we not know that sooner or later death will end it.

Our moral ills are the result of prejudice, crime alone excepted, and that de- 24 pends on ourselves; our bodily ills either put an end to themselves or to us. Time or death will cure them, but the less we know how to bear it, the greater is our pain, and we suffer more in our efforts to cure our diseases than if we endured them. Live according to nature; be patient, get rid of the doctors; you will not escape death, but you will only die once, while the doctors make you die daily through your diseased imagination; their lying art, instead of prolonging your days, robs you of all delight in them. I am always asking what real good this art has done to mankind. True, the doctors cure some who would have died, but they kill millions who would have lived. If you are wise you will decline to take part in this lottery when the odds are so great against you. Suffer, die, or get better; but whatever you do, live while you are alive.

Human institutions are one mass of folly and contradiction. As our life loses its 25 value we set a higher price upon it. The old regret life more than the young; they do not want to lose all they have spent in preparing for its enjoyment. At sixty it is cruel to die when one has not begun to live. Man is credited with a strong desire for self-preservation, and this desire exists; but we fail to perceive that this desire, as felt by us, is largely the work of man. In a natural state man is only eager to preserve his life while he has the means for its preservation; when self-preservation is no longer possible, he resigns himself to his fate and dies without vain torments. Nature teaches us the first law of resignation. Savages, like wild beasts, make very little struggle against death, and meet it almost without a murmur. When this natural law is overthrown reason establishes another, but few discern it, and man's resignation is never so complete as nature's.

Prudence! Prudence which is ever bidding us look forward into the future, a fu- 26 ture which in many cases we shall never reach; here is the real source of all our troubles! How mad it is for so short-lived a creature as man to look forward into a future to which he rarely attains, while he neglects the present which is his? This madness is all

---

[2]You understand I am speaking of those who think, and not of the crowd.

the more fatal since it increases with years, and the old, always timid, prudent, and mi-
serly, prefer to do without necessaries to-day that they may have luxuries at a hundred.
Thus we grasp everything, we cling to everything; we are anxious about time, place,
people, things, all that is and will be; we ourselves are but the least part of ourselves.
We spread ourselves, so to speak, over the whole world, and all this vast expanse becomes sensitive. No wonder our woes increase when we may be wounded on every side.
How many princes make themselves miserable for the loss of lands they never saw, and
how many merchants lament in Paris over some misfortune in the Indies!

Is it nature that carries men so far from their real selves? Is it her will that each 27
should learn his fate from others and even be the last to learn it; so that a man dies
happy or miserable before he knows what he is about. There is a healthy, cheerful,
strong, and vigorous man; it does me good to see him; his eyes tell of content and well-
being; he is the picture of happiness. A letter comes by post; the happy man glances at
it, it is addressed to him, he opens it and reads it. In a moment he is changed, he turns
pale and falls into a swoon. When he comes to himself he weeps, laments, and groans,
he tears his hair, and his shrieks re-echo through the air. You would say he was in con-
vulsions. Fool, what harm has this bit of paper done you? What limb has it torn away?
What crime has it made you commit? What change has it wrought in you to reduce you
to this state of misery?

Had the letter miscarried, had some kindly hand thrown it into the fire, it 28
strikes me that the fate of this mortal, at once happy and unhappy, would have offered
us a strange problem. His misfortunes, you say, were real enough. Granted; but he did
not feel them. What of that? His happiness was imaginary. I admit it; health, wealth, a
contented spirit, are mere dreams. We no longer live in our own place, we live outside
it. What does it profit us to live in such fear of death, when all that makes life worth living is our own?

Oh, man! live your own life and you will no longer be wretched. Keep to your 29
appointed place in the order of nature and nothing can tear you from it. Do not kick
against the stern law of necessity, nor waste in vain resistance the strength bestowed on
you by heaven, not to prolong or extend your existence, but to preserve it so far and so
long as heaven pleases. Your freedom and your power extend as far and no further than
your natural strength; anything more is but slavery, deceit, and trickery. Power itself is
servile when it depends upon public opinion; for you are dependent on the prejudices
of others when you rule them by means of those prejudices. To lead them as you will,
they must be led as they will. They have only to change their way of thinking and you
are forced to change your course of action. Those who approach you need only contrive
to sway the opinions of those you rule, or of the favourite by whom you are ruled, or
those of your own family or theirs. Had you the genius of Themistocles,[3] viziers, courti-
ers, priests, soldiers, servants, babblers, the very children themselves, would lead you
like a child in the midst of your legions. Whatever you do, your actual authority can
never extend beyond your own powers. As soon as you are obliged to see with another's

[3]"You see that little boy," said Themistocles to his friends, "the fate of Greece is in his hands, for he rules his
mother and his mother rules me, I rule the Athenians and the Athenians rule the Greeks." What petty creatures we should often find controlling great empires if we traced the course of power from the prince to those
who secretly put that power in motion.

eyes you must will what he wills. You say with pride, "My people are my subjects." Granted, but what are you? The subject of your ministers. And your ministers, what are they? The subjects of their clerks, their mistresses, the servants of their servants. Grasp all, usurp all, and then pour out your silver with both hands; set up your batteries, raise the gallows and the wheel; make laws, issue proclamations, multiply your spies, your soldiers, your hangmen, your prisons, and your chains. Poor little men, what good does it do you? You will be no better served, you will be none the less robbed and deceived, you will be no nearer absolute power. You will say continually, "It is our will," and you will continually do the will of others.

There is only one man who gets his own way—he who can get it single-handed; 30 therefore freedom, not power, is the greatest good. That man is truly free who desires what he is able to perform, and does what he desires. This is my fundamental maxim. Apply it to childhood, and all the rules of education spring from it.

Society has enfeebled man, not merely by robbing him of the right to his own 31 strength, but still more by making his strength insufficient for his needs. This is why his desires increase in proportion to his weakness; and this is why the child is weaker than the man. If a man is strong and a child is weak it is not because the strength of the one is absolutely greater than the strength of the other, but because the one can naturally provide for himself and the other cannot. Thus the man will have more desires and the child more caprices, a word which means, I take it, desires which are not true needs, desires which can only be satisfied with the help of others.

I have already given the reason for this state of weakness. Parental affection is 32 nature's provision against it; but parental affection may be carried to excess, it may be wanting, or it may be ill applied. Parents who live under our ordinary social conditions bring their child into these conditions too soon. By increasing his needs they do not relieve his weakness; they rather increase it. They further increase it by demanding of him what nature does not demand, by subjecting to their will what little strength he has to further his own wishes, by making slaves of themselves or of him instead of recognising that mutual dependence which should result from his weakness or their affection.

The wise man can keep his own place; but the child who does not know what 33 his place is, is unable to keep it. There are a thousand ways out of it, and it is the business of those who have charge of the child to keep him in his place, and this is no easy task. He should be neither beast nor man, but a child. He must feel his weakness, but not suffer through it; he must be dependent, but he must not obey; he must ask, not command. He is only subject to others because of his needs, and because they see better than he what he really needs, what may help or hinder his existence. No one, not even his father, has the right to bid the child do what is of no use to him.

When our natural tendencies have not been interfered with by human preju- 34 dice and human institutions, the happiness alike of children and of men consists in the enjoyment of their liberty. But the child's liberty is restricted by his lack of strength. He who does as he likes is happy provided he is self-sufficing; it is so with the man who is living in a state of nature. He who does what he likes is not happy if his desires exceed his strength; it is so with a child in like conditions. Even in a state of nature children only enjoy an imperfect liberty, like that enjoyed by men in social life. Each of us, unable to dispense with the help of others, becomes so far weak and wretched. We were meant to be men, laws and customs thrust us back into infancy. The rich and great, the very kings themselves are but children; they see that we are ready to relieve their misery; this makes them childishly vain, and they are quite proud of the care bestowed on them, a care which they would never get if they were grown men.

These are weighty considerations, and they provide a solution for all the con- 35 flicting problems of our social system. There are two kinds of dependence: dependence on things, which is the work of nature; and dependence on men, which is the work of society. Dependence on things, being non-moral, does no injury to liberty and begets no vices; dependence on men, being out of order,[4] gives rise to every kind of vice, and through this master and slave become mutually depraved. If there is any cure for this social evil, it is to be found in the substitution of law for the individual; in arming the general will with a real strength beyond the power of any individual will. If the laws of nations, like the laws of nature, could never be broken by any human power, dependence on men would become dependence on things; all the advantages of a state of nature would be combined with all the advantages of social life in the commonwealth. The liberty which preserves a man from vice would be united with the morality which raises him to virtue.

Keep the child dependent on things only. By this course of education you will 36 have followed the order of nature. Let his unreasonable wishes meet with physical obstacles only, or the punishment which results from his own actions, lessons which will be recalled when the same circumstances occur again. It is enough to prevent him from wrong doing without forbidding him to do wrong. Experience or lack of power should take the place of law. Give him, not what he wants, but what he needs. Let there be no question of obedience for him or tyranny for you. Supply the strength he lacks just so far as is required for freedom, not for power, so that he may receive your services with a sort of shame, and look forward to the time when he may dispense with them and may achieve the honor of self-help.

Nature provides for the child's growth in her own fashion, and this should 37 never be thwarted. Do not make him sit still when he wants to run about, nor run when he wants to be quiet. If we did not spoil our children's wills by our blunders their desires would be free from caprice. Let them run, jump, and shout to their heart's content. All their own activities are instincts of the body for its growth in strength; but you should regard with suspicion those which others must carry out for them. Then you must distinguish carefully between natural and artificial needs, between the needs of budding caprice and the needs which spring from the overflowing life just described.

I have already told you what you ought to do when a child cries for this thing 38 or that. I will only add that as soon as he has words to ask for what he wants and accompanies his demands with tears, either to get his own way quicker or to over-ride a refusal, he should never have his way. If his words were prompted by a real need you should recognise it and satisfy it at once; but to yield to his tears is to encourage him to cry, to teach him to doubt your kindness, and to think that you are influenced more by his importunity than your own good-will. If he does not think you kind he will soon think you unkind; if he thinks you weak he will soon become obstinate; what you mean to give must be given at once. Be chary of refusing, but, having refused, do not change your mind.

---

[4]In my *Principles of Political Law* it is proved that no private will can be ordered in the social system.

Above all, beware of teaching the child empty phrases of politeness, which 39 serve as spells to subdue those around him to his will, and to get him what he wants at once. The artificial education of the rich never fails to make them politely imperious, by teaching them the words to use so that no one will dare to resist them. Their children have neither the tone nor the manner of suppliants; they are as haughty or even more haughty in their entreaties than in their commands, as though they were more certain to be obeyed. You see at once that "If you please" means "It pleases me," and "I beg" means "I command." What a fine sort of politeness which only succeeds in changing the meaning of words so that every word is a command! For my own part, I would rather Emile were rude than haughty, that he should say "Do this" as a request, rather than "Please" as a command. What concerns me is his meaning, not his words.

There is such a thing as excessive severity as well as excessive indulgence, and 40 both alike should be avoided. If you let children suffer you risk their health and life; you make them miserable now; if you take too much pains to spare them every kind of un-easiness you are laying up much misery for them in the future; you are making them delicate and over-sensitive; you are taking them out of their place among men, a place to which they must sooner or later return, in spite of all your pains. You will say I am falling into the same mistake as those bad fathers whom I blamed for sacrificing the present happiness of their children to a future which may never be theirs.

Not so; for the liberty I give my pupil makes up for the slight hardships to 41 which he is exposed. I see little fellows playing in the snow, stiff and blue with cold, scarcely able to stir a finger. They could go and warm themselves if they chose, but they do not choose; if you forced them to come in they would feel the harshness of constraint a hundredfold more than the sharpness of the cold. Then what becomes of your griev-ance? Shall I make your child miserable by exposing him to hardships which he is per-fectly ready to endure? I secure his present good by leaving him his freedom, and his fu-ture good by arming him against the evils he will have to bear. If he had his choice, would he hesitate for a moment between you and me?

Do you think any man can find true happiness elsewhere than in his natural 42 state; and when you try to spare him all suffering, are you not taking him out of his nat-ural state? Indeed I maintain that to enjoy great happiness he must experience slight ills; such is his nature. Too much bodily prosperity corrupts the morals. A man who knew nothing of suffering would be incapable of tenderness towards his fellow-creatures and ignorant of the joys of pity; he would be hard-hearted, unsocial, a very monster among men.

Do you know the surest way to make your child miserable? Let him have every- 43 thing he wants; for as his wants increase in proportion to the ease with which they are satisfied, you will be compelled, sooner or later, to refuse his demands, and this unlooked-for refusal will hurt him more than the lack of what he wants. He will want your stick first, then your watch, the bird that flies, or the star that shines above him. He will want all he sets eyes on, and unless you were God himself, how could you satisfy him?

Man naturally considers all that he can get as his own. In this sense Hobbes' 44 theory is true to a certain extent: Multiply both our wishes and the means of satisfying them, and each will be master of all. Thus the child, who has only to ask and have, thinks himself the master of the universe; he considers all men as his slaves; and when you are at last compelled to refuse, he takes your refusal as an act of rebellion, for he thinks he has only to command. All the reasons you give him, while he is still too young to reason, are so many pretences in his eyes; they seem to him only unkindness; the sense of injustice embitters his disposition; he hates everyone. Though he has never felt grateful for kindness, he resents all opposition.

How should I suppose that such a child can ever be happy? He is the slave of 45 anger, a prey to the fiercest passions. Happy! He is a tyrant, at once the basest of slaves and the most wretched of creatures. I have known children brought up like this who expected you to knock the house down, to give them the weather-cock on the steeple, to stop a regiment on the march so that they might listen to the band; when they could not get their way they screamed and cried and would pay no attention to any one. In vain everybody strove to please them; as their desires were stimulated by the ease with which they got their own way, they set their hearts on impossibilities, and found themselves face to face with opposition and difficulty, pain and grief. Scolding, sulking, or in a rage, they wept and cried all day. Were they really so greatly favoured? Weakness, combined with love of power, produces nothing but folly and suffering. One spoilt child beats the table; another whips the sea. They may beat and whip long enough before they find contentment.

If their childhood is made wretched by these notions of power and tyranny, 46 what of their manhood, when their relations with their fellow-men begin to grow and multiply? They are used to find everything give way to them; what a painful surprise to enter society and meet with opposition on every side, to be crushed beneath the weight of a universe which they expected to move at will. Their insolent manners, their childish vanity, only draw down upon them mortification, scorn, and mockery; they swallow insults like water; sharp experience soon teaches them that they have realised neither their position nor their strength. As they cannot do everything, they think they can do nothing. They are daunted by unexpected obstacles, degraded by the scorn of men; they become base, cowardly, and deceitful, and fall as far below their true level as they formerly soared above it.

Let us come back to the primitive law. Nature has made children helpless and 47 in need of affection; did she make them to be obeyed and feared? Has she given them an imposing manner, a stern eye, a loud and threatening voice with which to make themselves feared? I understand how the roaring of the lion strikes terror into the other beasts, so that they tremble when they behold his terrible mane, but of all unseemly, hateful, and ridiculous sights, was there ever anything like a body of statesmen in their robes of office with their chief at their head bowing down before a swaddled babe, addressing him in pompous phrases, while he cries and slavers in reply?

If we consider childhood itself, is there anything so weak and wretched as a 48 child, anything so utterly at the mercy of those about it, so dependent on their pity, their care, and their affection? Does it not seem as if his gentle face and touching appearance were intended to interest every one on behalf of his weakness and to make them eager to help him? And what is there more offensive, more unsuitable, than the sight of a sulky or imperious child, who commands those about him, and impudently assumes the tones of a master towards those without whom he would perish?

On the other hand, do you not see how children are fettered by the weakness 49 of infancy? Do you not see how cruel it is to increase this servitude by obedience to our caprices, by depriving them of such liberty as they have? a liberty which they can scarcely abuse, a liberty the loss of which will do so little good to them or us. If there is nothing more ridiculous than a haughty child, there is nothing that claims our pity like a timid child. With the age of reason the child becomes the slave of the community; then why forestall this by slavery in the home? Let this brief hour of life be free from a yoke which nature has not laid upon it; leave the child the use of his natural liberty, which, for a time at least, secures him from the vices of the slave. Bring me those harsh masters, and those fathers who are the slaves of their children, bring them both with their frivolous objections, and before they boast of their own methods let them for once learn the method of nature.

I return to practical matters. I have already said your child must not get what [50] he asks, but what he needs;[5] he must never act from obedience, but from necessity.

The very words *obey* and *command* will be excluded from his vocabulary, still [51] more those of *duty* and *obligation;* but the words strength, necessity, weakness, and constraint must have a large place in it. Before the age of reason it is impossible to form any idea of moral beings or social relations; so avoid, as far as may be, the use of words which express these ideas, lest the child at an early age should attach wrong ideas to them, ideas which you cannot or will not destroy when he is older. The first mistaken idea he gets into his head is the germ of error and vice; it is the first step that needs watching. Act in such a way that while he only notices external objects his ideas are confined to sensations; let him only see the physical world around him. If not, you may be sure that either he will pay no heed to you at all, or he will form fantastic ideas of the moral world of which you prate, ideas which you will never efface as long as he lives.

"Reason with children" was Locke's chief maxim; it is in the height of fashion [52] at present, and I hardly think it is justified by its results; those children who have been constantly reasoned with strike me as exceedingly silly. Of all man's faculties, reason, which is, so to speak, compounded of all the rest, is the last and choicest growth, and it is this you would use for the child's early training. To make a man reasonable is the coping stone of a good education, and yet you profess to train a child through his reason! You begin at the wrong end, you make the end the means. If children understood reason they would not need education, but by talking to them from their earliest age in a language they do not understand you accustom them to be satisfied with words, to question all that is said to them, to think themselves as wise as their teachers; you train them to be argumentative and rebellious; and whatever you think you gain from motives of reason, you really gain from greediness, fear, or vanity with which you are obliged to reinforce your reasoning.

Most of the moral lessons which are and can be given to children may be re- [53] duced to this formula:

> *MASTER.* You must not do that.
> *CHILD.* Why not?

---

[5]We must recognise that pain is often necessary, pleasure is sometimes needed. So there is only one of the child's desires which should never be complied with, the desire for power. Hence, whenever they ask for anything we must pay special attention to their motive in asking. As far as possible give them everything they ask for, provided it can really give them pleasure; refuse everything they demand from mere caprice or love of power.

MASTER. Because it is wrong.
CHILD. Wrong! What is wrong?
MASTER. What is forbidden you.
CHILD. Why is it wrong to do what is forbidden?
MASTER. You will be punished for disobedience.
CHILD. I will do it when no one is looking.
MASTER. We shall watch you.
CHILD. I will hide.
MASTER. We shall ask you what you were doing.
CHILD. I shall tell a lie.
MASTER. You must not tell lies.
CHILD. Why must not I tell lies?
MASTER. Because it is wrong, etc.

That is the inevitable circle. Go beyond it, and the child will not understand 54 you. What sort of use is there in such teaching? I should greatly like to know what you would substitute for this dialogue. It would have puzzled Locke himself. It is no part of a child's business to know right and wrong, to perceive the reason for a man's duties.

Nature would have them children before they are men. If we try to invert this 55 order we shall produce a forced fruit immature and flavourless, fruit which will be rotten before it is ripe; we shall have young doctors and old children. Childhood has its own ways of seeing, thinking, and feeling; nothing is more foolish than to try and substitute our ways; and I should no more expect judgment in a ten-year-old child than I should expect him to be five feet high. Indeed, what use would reason be to him at that age? It is the curb of strength, and the child does not need the curb.

When you try to persuade your scholars of the duty of obedience, you add to 56 this so-called persuasion compulsion and threats, or still worse, flattery and bribes. Attracted by selfishness or constrained by force, they pretend to be convinced by reason. They see as soon as you do that obedience is to their advantage and disobedience to their disadvantage. But as you only demand disagreeable things of them, and as it is always disagreeable to do another's will, they hide themselves so that they may do as they please, persuaded that they are doing no wrong so long as they are not found out, but ready, if found out, to own themselves in the wrong for fear of worse evils. The reason for duty is beyond their age, and there is not a man in the world who could make them really aware of it; but the fear of punishment, the hope of forgiveness, importunity, the difficulty of answering, wrings from them as many confessions as you want; and you think you have convinced them when you have only wearied or frightened them.

What does it all come to? In the first place, by imposing on them a duty which 57 they fail to recognise, you make them disinclined to submit to your tyranny, and you turn away their love; you teach them deceit, falsehood, and lying as a way to gain rewards or escape punishment; then by accustoming them to conceal a secret motive under the cloak of an apparent one, you yourself put into their hands the means of deceiving you, of depriving you of a knowledge of their real character, of answering you and others with empty words whenever they have the chance. Laws, you say, though binding on conscience, exercise the same constraint over grown-up men. That is so, but what are these men but children spoilt by education? This is just what you should avoid.

Use force with children and reasoning with men; this is the natural order; the wise man needs no laws.

Treat your scholar according to his age. Put him in his place from the first, and 58 keep him in it, so that he no longer tries to leave it. Then before he knows what goodness is, he will be practising its chief lesson. Give him no orders at all, absolutely none. Do not even let him think that you claim any authority over him. Let him only know that he is weak and you are strong, that his condition and yours puts him at your mercy; let this be perceived, learned, and felt. Let him early find upon his proud neck, the heavy yoke which nature has imposed upon us, the heavy yoke of necessity, under which every finite being must bow. Let him find this necessity in things, not in the caprices[6] of man; let the curb be force, not authority. If there is something he should not do, do not forbid him, but prevent him without explanation or reasoning; what you give him, give it at his first word without prayers or entreaties, above all without conditions. Give willingly, refuse unwillingly, but let your refusal be irrevocable; let no entreaties move you; let your "No," once uttered, be a wall of brass, against which the child may exhaust his strength some five or six times, but in the end he will try no more to overthrow it.

Thus you will make him patient, equable, calm, and resigned, even when he 59 does not get all he wants; for it is in man's nature to bear patiently with the nature of things, but not with the ill-will of another. A child never rebels against, "There is none left," unless he thinks the reply is false. Moreover, there is no middle course; you must either make no demands on him at all, or else you must fashion him to perfect obedience. The worst education of all is to leave him hesitating between his own will and yours, constantly disputing whether you or he is master; I would rather a hundred times that he were master.

It is very strange that ever since people began to think about education they 60 should have hit upon no other way of guiding children than emulation, jealousy, envy, vanity, greediness, base cowardice, all the most dangerous passions, passions ever ready to ferment, ever prepared to corrupt the soul even before the body is full-grown. With every piece of precocious instruction which you try to force into their minds you plant a vice in the depths of their hearts; foolish teachers think they are doing wonders when they are making their scholars wicked in order to teach them what goodness is, and then they tell us seriously, "Such is man." Yes, such is man, as you have made him. Every means has been tried except one, the very one which might succeed—well-regulated liberty. Do not undertake to bring up a child if you cannot guide him merely by the laws of what can or cannot be. The limits of the possible and the impossible are alike unknown to him, so they can be extended or contracted around him at your will. Without a murmur he is restrained, urged on, held back, by the hands of necessity alone; he is made adaptable and teachable by the mere force of things, without any chance for vice to spring up in him; for passions do not arise so long as they have accomplished nothing.

Give your scholar no verbal lessons; he should be taught by experience alone; 61 never punish him, for he does not know what it is to do wrong; never make him say,

---

[6]You may be sure the child will regard as caprice any will which opposes his own or any will which he does not understand. Now the child does not understand anything which interferes with his own fancies.

"Forgive me," for he does not know how to do you wrong. Wholly unmoral in his actions, he can do nothing morally wrong, and he deserves neither punishment nor reproof.

Already I see the frightened reader comparing this child with those of our time; 62 he is mistaken. The perpetual restraint imposed upon your scholars stimulates their activity; the more subdued they are in your presence, the more boisterous they are as soon as they are out of your sight. They must make amends to themselves in some way or other for the harsh constraint to which you subject them. Two schoolboys from the town will do more damage in the country than all the children of the village. Shut up a young gentleman and a young peasant in a room; the former will have upset and smashed everything before the latter has stirred from his place. Why is that, unless that the one hastens to misuse a moment's licence, while the other, always sure of freedom, does not use it rashly. And yet the village children, often flattered or constrained, are still very far from the state in which I would have them kept.

Let us lay it down as an incontrovertible rule that the first impulses of nature 63 are always right; there is no original sin in the human heart, the how and why of the entrance of every vice can be traced. The only natural passion is self-love or selfishness taken in a wider sense. This selfishness is good in itself and in relation to ourselves; and as the child has no necessary relations to other people he is naturally indifferent to them; his self-love only becomes good or bad by the use made of it and the relations established by its means. Until the time is ripe for the appearance of reason, that guide of selfishness, the main thing is that the child shall do nothing because you are watching him or listening to him; in a word, nothing because of other people, but only what nature asks of him; then he will never do wrong.

I do not mean to say that he will never do any mischief, never hurt himself, 64 never break a costly ornament if you leave it within his reach. He might do much damage without doing wrong, since wrong-doing depends on the harmful intention which will never be his. If once he meant to do harm, his whole education would be ruined; he would be almost hopelessly bad.

Greed considers some things wrong which are not wrong in the eyes of reason. 65 When you leave free scope to a child's heedlessness, you must put anything he could spoil out of his way, and leave nothing fragile or costly within his reach. Let the room be furnished with plain and solid furniture; no mirrors, china, or useless ornaments. My pupil Emile, who is brought up in the country, shall have a room just like a peasant's. Why take such pains to adorn it when he will be so little in it? I am mistaken, however; he will ornament it for himself, and we shall soon see how.

But if, in spite of your precautions, the child contrives to do some damage, if 66 he breaks some useful article, do not punish him for your carelessness, do not even scold him; let him hear no word of reproval, do not even let him see that he has vexed you; behave just as if the thing had come to pieces of itself; you may consider you have done great things if you have managed to hold your tongue.

May I venture at this point to state the greatest, the most important, the most 67 useful rule of education? It is: Do not save time, but lose it. I hope that every-day readers will excuse my paradoxes; you cannot avoid paradox if you think for yourself, and whatever you may say I would rather fall into paradox than into prejudice. The most dangerous period in human life lies between birth and the age of twelve. It is the time when errors and vices spring up, while as yet there is no means to destroy them; when the means of destruction are ready, the roots have gone too deep to be pulled up. If the infant sprang at one bound from its mother's breast to the age of reason, the present type of education would be quite suitable, but its natural growth calls for quite a different training. The mind should be left undisturbed till its faculties have developed; for while it is blind it cannot see the torch you offer it, nor can it follow through the vast expanse of ideas a path so faintly traced by reason that the best eyes can scarcely follow it.

Therefore the education of the earliest years should be merely negative. It con- 68 sists, not in teaching virtue or truth, but in preserving the heart from vice and from the spirit of error. If only you could let well enough alone, and get others to follow your example; if you could bring your scholar to the age of twelve strong and healthy, but unable to tell his right hand from his left, the eyes of his understanding would be open to reason as soon as you began to teach him. Free from prejudices and free from habits, there would be nothing in him to counteract the effects of your labours. In your hands he would soon become the wisest of men; by doing nothing to begin with, you would end with a prodigy of education.

Reverse the usual practice and you will almost always do right. Fathers and 69 teachers who want to make the child, not a child but a man of learning, think it never too soon to scold, correct, reprove, threaten, bribe, teach, and reason. Do better than they; be reasonable, and do not reason with your pupil, more especially do not try to make him approve what he dislikes; for if reason is always connected with disagreeable matters, you make it distasteful to him, you discredit it at an early age in a mind not yet ready to understand it. Exercise his body, his limbs, his senses, his strength, but keep his mind idle as long as you can. Distrust all opinions which appear before the judgment to discriminate between them. Restrain and ward off strange impressions; and to prevent the birth of evil do not hasten to do well, for goodness is only possible when enlightened by reason. Regard all delays as so much time gained; you have achieved much, you approach the boundary without loss. Leave childhood to ripen in your children. In a word, beware of giving anything they need to-day if it can be deferred without danger to to-morrow.

There is another point to be considered which confirms the suitability of this 70 method: it is the child's individual bent, which must be thoroughly known before we can choose the fittest moral training. Every mind has its own form, in accordance with which it must be controlled; and the success of the pains taken depends largely on the fact that he is controlled in this way and no other. Oh, wise man, take time to observe nature; watch your scholar well before you say a word to him; first leave the germ of his character free to show itself, do not constrain him in anything, the better to see him as he really is. Do you think this time of liberty is wasted? On the contrary, your scholar will be the better employed, for this is the way you yourself will learn not to lose a single moment when time is of more value. If, however, you begin to act before you know what to do, you act at random; you may make mistakes, and must retrace your steps; your haste to reach your goal will only take you further from it. Do not imitate the miser who loses much lest he should lose a little. Sacrifice a little time in early childhood, and it will be repaid you with usury when your scholar is older. The wise physician does not hastily give prescriptions at first sight, but he studies the constitution of the sick man before he prescribes anything; the treatment is begun later, but the patient is cured, while the hasty doctor kills him.

But where shall we find a place for our child so as to bring him up as a senseless 71 being, an automaton? Shall we keep him in the moon, or on a desert island? Shall we remove him from human society? Will he not always have around him the sight and the pattern of the passions of other people? Will he never see children of his own age? Will he not see his parents, his neighbors, his nurse, his governess, his man-servant, his tutor himself, who after all will not be an angel? Here we have a real and serious objection. But did I tell you that an education according to nature would be an easy task? Oh, men! is it my fault that you have made all good things difficult? I admit that I am aware of these difficulties; perhaps they are insuperable; but nevertheless it is certain that we do to some extent avoid them by trying to do so. I am showing what we should try to attain, I do not say we can attain it, but I do say that whoever comes nearest to it is nearest to success.

Remember you must be a man yourself before you try to train a man; you your- 72 self must set the pattern he shall copy. While the child is still unconscious there is time to prepare his surroundings, so that nothing shall strike his eye but what is fit for his sight. Gain the respect of every one, begin to win their hearts, so that they may try to please you. You will not be master of the child if you cannot control every one about him; and this authority will never suffice unless it rests upon respect for your goodness. There is no question of squandering one's means and giving money right and left; I never knew money win love. You must neither be harsh nor niggardly, nor must you merely pity misery when you can relieve it; but in vain will you open your purse if you do not open your heart along with it, the hearts of others will always be closed to you. You must give your own time, attention, affection, your very self; for whatever you do, people always perceive that your money is not you. There are proofs of kindly interest which produce more results and are really more useful than any gift; how many of the sick and wretched have more need of comfort than of charity; how many of the oppressed need protection rather than money? Reconcile those who are at strife, prevent lawsuits; incline children to duty, fathers to kindness; promote happy marriages; prevent annoyances; freely use the credit of your pupil's parents on behalf of the weak who cannot obtain justice, the weak who are oppressed by the strong. Be just, human, kindly. Do not give alms alone, give charity; works of mercy do more than money for the relief of suffering; love others and they will love you; serve them and they will serve you; be their brother and they will be your children.

This is one reason why I want to bring up Emile in the country, far from those 73 miserable lacqueys, the most degraded of men except their masters; far from the vile morals of the town, whose gilded surface makes them seductive and contagious to children; while the vices of peasants, unadorned and in their naked grossness, are more fitted to repel than to seduce, when there is no motive for imitating them.

In the village a tutor will have much more control over the things he wishes 74 to show the child; his reputation, his words, his example, will have a weight they would never have in the town; he is of use to every one, so every one is eager to oblige him, to win his esteem, to appear before the disciple what the master would have him be; if vice is not corrected, public scandal is at least avoided, which is all that our present purpose requires.

Cease to blame others for your own faults; children are corrupted less by what 75 they see than by your own teaching. With your endless preaching, moralising, and pedantry, for one idea you give your scholars, believing it to be good, you give them twenty more which are good for nothing; you are full of what is going on in your own minds, and you fail to see the effect you produce on theirs. In the continual flow of words with which you overwhelm them, do you think there is none which they get hold of in a wrong sense? Do you suppose they do not make their own comments on your long-winded explanations, that they do not find material for the construction of a system they can understand—one which they will use against you when they get the chance?

Listen to a little fellow who has just been under instruction; let him chatter 76 freely, ask questions, and talk at his ease, and you will be surprised to find the strange forms your arguments have assumed in his mind; he confuses everything, and turns everything topsy-turvy; you are vexed and grieved by his unforeseen objections; he reduces you to be silent yourself or to silence him: and what can he think of silence in one who is so fond of talking? If ever he gains this advantage and is aware of it, farewell education; from that moment all is lost; he is no longer trying to learn, he is trying to refute you.

Zealous teachers, be simple, sensible, and reticent; be in no hurry to act unless 77 to prevent the actions of others. Again and again I say, reject, if it may be, a good lesson for fear of giving a bad one. Beware of playing the tempter in this world, which nature intended as an earthly paradise for men, and do not attempt to give the innocent child the knowledge of good and evil; since you cannot prevent the child learning by what he sees outside himself, restrict your own efforts to impressing those examples on his mind in the form best suited for him.

The explosive passions produce a great effect upon the child when he sees 78 them; their outward expression is very marked; he is struck by this and his attention is arrested. Anger especially is so noisy in its rage that it is impossible not to perceive it if you are within reach. You need not ask yourself whether this is an opportunity for a pedagogue to frame a fine disquisition. What! no fine disquisition, nothing, not a word! Let the child come to you; impressed by what he has seen, he will not fail to ask you questions. The answer is easy; it is drawn from the very things which have appealed to his senses. He sees a flushed face, flashing eyes, a threatening gesture, he hears cries; everything shows that the body is ill at ease. Tell him plainly, without affectation or mystery, "This poor man is ill, he is in a fever." You may take the opportunity of giving him in a few words some idea of disease and its effects; for that too belongs to nature, and is one of the bonds of necessity which he must recognise. By means of this idea, which is not false in itself, may he not early acquire a certain aversion to giving way to excessive passions, which he regards as diseases; and do you not think that such a notion, given at the right moment, will produce a more wholesome effect than the most tedious sermon? But consider the after effects of this idea; you have authority, if ever you find it necessary, to treat the rebellious child as a sick child; to keep him in his room, in bed if need be, to diet him, to make him afraid of his growing vices, to make him hate and dread them without ever regarding as a punishment the strict measures you will perhaps have to use for his recovery. If it happens that you yourself in a moment's heat depart from the calm and self-control which you should aim at, do not try to conceal your fault, but tell him frankly, with a gentle reproach, "My dear, you have hurt me."

Moreover, it is a matter of great importance that no notice should be taken in 79 his presence of the quaint sayings which result from the simplicity of the ideas in which he is brought up, nor should they be quoted in a way he can understand. A foolish laugh may destroy six months' work and do irreparable damage for life. I cannot repeat too often that to control the child one must often control oneself.

I picture my little Emile at the height of a dispute between two neighbors going 80 up to the fiercest of them and saying in a tone of pity, "You are ill, I am very sorry for you." This speech will no doubt have its effect on the spectators and perhaps on the disputants. Without laughter, scolding, or praise I should take him away, willing or no, before he could see this result, or at least before he could think about it; and I should make haste to turn his thoughts to other things, so that he would soon forget all about it.

I do not propose to enter into every detail, but only to explain general rules and 81 to give illustrations in cases of difficulty. I think it is impossible to train a child up to the age of twelve in the midst of society, without giving him some idea of the relations between one man and another, and of the morality of human actions. It is enough to delay the development of these ideas as long as possible, and when they can no longer be avoided to limit them to present needs, so that he may neither think himself master of everything nor do harm to others without knowing or caring. There are calm and gentle characters which can be led a long way in their first innocence without any danger; but there are also stormy dispositions whose passions develop early; you must hasten to make men of them lest you should have to keep them in chains.

Our first duties are to ourselves; our first feelings are centered on self; all our 82 instincts are at first directed to our own preservation and our own welfare. Thus the first notion of justice springs not from what we owe to others, but from what is due to us. Here is another error in popular methods of education. If you talk to children of their duties, and not of their rights, you are beginning at the wrong end, and telling them what they cannot understand, what cannot be of any interest to them.

Questions

1. How does Rousseau arrive at the definition of human happiness stated in paragraph 17?
2. Rousseau states in paragraph 18 that nature "does everything for the best." How has he illustrated this premise in earlier paragraphs?
3. What does Rousseau mean by *imagination* in paragraphs 18 and 20? If imagination is "boundless" and therefore a source of human discontent, how can nature do "everything for the best"?
4. What laws does Rousseau seem to have in mind in arguing that law provides a cure for the social evil discussed in paragraph 35? How does that paragraph help to explain what Rousseau means by the *general will?*
5. In what sense should the child be "dependent on things only" (paragraph 36)? Is Rousseau saying that only material things are real and sources of pleasure? Or does he mean something else?
6. What does Rousseau mean by *power* in paragraphs 18, 30, and 36? Is he referring to physical strength, dominance over others, or material wealth? Why is power not a source of happiness?

7. According to paragraph 37, how can the parent or teacher distinguish between a false need and a real need? Why does Rousseau stress this difference?
8. Those who recommend force in dealing with children probably will agree that "if children understood reason they would not need education" (paragraph 52). Would Rousseau ever strike a child? Is Rousseau contradicting himself in stating, "Use force with children and reasoning with men," (paragraph 57) and, "Let him only know that he is weak and you are strong" (paragraph 58)?
9. According to paragraph 63, in what sense is selfishness both good and bad? What is the measure or definition of good and bad for Rousseau?
10. In paragraph 67 Rousseau asks the reader to excuse his paradoxes. To what paradoxes is he referring?

Suggestions for Writing

1. Rousseau states in paragraph 55: "Nature would have them children before they are men. . . . Childhood has its own ways of seeing, thinking, and feeling." Discuss how he explains and illustrates this in the whole essay.
2. Discuss your agreement or disagreement with one of Rousseau's ideas. Explain the basis of your agreement or disagreement—perhaps beliefs you hold about children and people in general, or personal experience and observation, or the teachings of your parents or church.
3. Discuss how different a school you attended would have been if Rousseau had been in charge. Give particular examples from your personal experience and observation.

Additional Reading

Blanchard, William. *Rousseau and the Spirit of Revolt.* Ann Arbor: University of Michigan Press, 1967.
Chapman, John William. *Rousseau—Totalitarian or Liberal?* New York: Columbia University Press, 1956.
Crocker, Lester G. *Jean-Jacques Rousseau. Volume 1: The Great Quest, 1712–1758. Volume 2: The Prophetic Voice, 1758–1778.* New York: Macmillan, 1968–1973.
Guehenno, Jean. *Jean-Jacques Rousseau* (2 vols.). Trans. John and Doreen Weightmann. New York: Columbia University Press, 1966.
Perkins, Merle L. *Jean-Jacques Rousseau on the Individual and Society.* Lexington: University of Kentucky Press, 1973.
Rousseau, Jean-Jacques. *Confessions.* Trans. J. M. Cohen. Baltimore: Penguin, 1953.
———. *Émile.* Trans. Barbara Foxley. Everyman's Library. London: Dent, 1911.
———. *Minor Educational Writings.* Trans. William H. Boyd. New York: Columbia Teachers College, 1962.
———. *The Social Contract.* Rev. ed. Trans. G. D. H. Cole. Everyman's Library. London: Dent, 1973.
Temmer, Mark J. *The Art and Influence of J.-J. Rousseau.* Chapel Hill: University of North Carolina Press, 1973.

Childhood and Early Education

John Stuart Mill

John Stuart Mill (1806–1873) was the son of Harriet and James Mill—a follower of Jeremy Bentham, the founder of Utilitarianism, an early-nineteenth-century philosophical movement. The remarkable education that Mill describes in the opening chapter of his autobiography, reprinted here, was conducted by his father. Whatever the benefits and deficiencies of his education may have been, it prepared Mill to undertake a career as a man of letters. Before he was twenty years old, he helped found the Utilitarian Society and the influential Westminster Review—the political journal of the Utilitarians—which he later edited. In 1823 he began his long career in the East India Company, where his father also was employed.

What he describes in his autobiography as a "crisis in my mental history" occurred in 1826 when he discovered that his feelings had for some reason deadened. Mill blamed the emphasis on intellectual analysis in his education:

> For I now saw, or thought I saw, what I had always before received with incredulity—that the habit of analysis has a tendency to wear away the feelings: as indeed it has, when no other mental habit is cultivated, and the analyzing spirit remains without its natural complements and corrections.

Those "complements" were the feelings or "passive susceptibilities" that his education had failed to develop:

> The maintenance of a due balance among the faculties now seemed to me of primary importance. The cultivation of the feelings became one of the cardinal points in my ethical and philosophical creed.

Through the poetry of Wordsworth, Mill slowly developed powers of imagination and emotion, which promoted his recovery.

Bentham's well-known definition of goodness and happiness was quantitative: "The greatest happiness of the greatest number is the foundation of morals and legislation." Mill's experiences led him to rethink this and other tenets of Utilitarianism. Bentham was thinking of the needs of society and not of the qualitative experience of the individual, and Mill challenged this emphasis. In his essay on Bentham, Mill (1838) says the following: "Man is never recognized by him as being capable of pursuing spiritual perfection as an end; of desiring, for its own sake, the conformity of his own character to his standard of excellence, without hope of good or fear of evil from other source than his own inward consciousness." Nor did Bentham recognize "the love of loving, the need of a sympathizing support, or of objects of admiration and reverence."

Among the qualitative experiences that Mill was to explore in major essays were the nature of literature in The Thoughts of Poetry and Its Varieties *(1883), the development of the individual in his great essay* On Liberty *(1859), and the education of women in* The Subjection of Women *(1869). He was strongly influenced in the writing of this last book by Harriet Taylor, a woman of considerable intellect that Mill met in 1831 and married in 1851, two years after the death of her husband. In his autobiography, published in 1873, Mill raised important questions about the abilities of children. "What I could do, could assuredly be done by any boy or girl of average capacity and healthy physical constitution," Mill says late in the chapter of that autobiography that follows.*

It seems proper that I should prefix to the following biographical sketch, some 1
mention of the reasons which have made me think it desirable that I should leave behind me such a memorial of so uneventful a life as mine. I do not for a moment imagine that any part of what I have to relate, can be interesting to the public as a narrative, or as being connected with myself. But I have thought that in an age in which education, and its improvement, are the subject of more, if not of profounder study than at any former period of English history, it may be useful that there should be some record of an education which was unusual and remarkable, and which, whatever else it may have done, has proved how much more than is commonly supposed may be taught, and well taught, in those early years which, in the common modes of what is called instruction, are little better than wasted. It has also seemed to me that in an age of transition in opinions, there may be somewhat both of interest and of benefit in noting the successive phases of any mind which was always pressing forward, equally ready to learn and to unlearn either from its own thoughts or from those of others. But a motive which weighs more with me than either of these, is a desire to make acknowledgment of the debts which my intellectual and moral development owes to other persons; some of them of recognized eminence, others less known than they deserve to be, and the one to whom most of all is due,[1] one whom the world had no opportunity of knowing. The reader whom these things do not interest, has only himself to blame if he reads farther, and I do not desire any other indulgence from him than that of bearing in mind, that for him these pages were not written.

I was born in London, on the 20th of May 1806, and was the eldest son of James 2
Mill, the author of the History of British India. My father, the son of a petty tradesman and (I believe) small farmer, at Northwater Bridge, in the county of Angus, was, when a boy, recommended by his abilities to the notice of Sir John Stuart, of Fettercairn, one of the Barons of the Exchequer in Scotland, and was, in consequence, sent to the University of Edinburgh at the expense of a fund established by Lady Jane Stuart (the wife of Sir John Stuart) and some other ladies for educating young men for the Scottish Church. He there went through the usual course of study, and was licensed as a Preacher, but never followed the profession; having satisfied himself that he could not believe the doctrines of that or any other Church. For a few years he was a private tutor in various families in Scotland, among others that of the Marquis of Tweeddale; but

----

[1]Mill's wife.

ended by taking up his residence in London, and devoting himself to authorship. Nor had he any other means of support until 1819, when he obtained an appointment in the India House.

In this period of my father's life there are two things which it is impossible not 3 to be struck with: one of them unfortunately a very common circumstance, the other a most uncommon one. The first is, that in his position, with no resource but the precarious one of writing in periodicals, he married and had a large family; conduct than which nothing could be more opposed, both as a matter of good sense and of duty, to the opinions which, at least at a later period of life, he strenuously upheld. The other circumstance, is the extraordinary energy which was required to lead the life he led, with the disadvantages under which he laboured from the first, and with those which he brought upon himself by his marriage. It would have been no small thing, had he done no more than to support himself and his family during so many years by writing, without ever being in debt, or in any pecuniary difficulty; holding, as he did, opinions, both in politics and in religion, which were more odious to all persons of influence, and to the common run of prosperous Englishmen, in that generation than either before or since; and being not only a man whom nothing would have induced to write against his convictions, but one who invariably threw into everything he wrote, as much of his convictions as he thought the circumstances would in any way permit: being, it must also be said, one who never did anything negligently; never undertook any task, literary or other, on which he did not conscientiously bestow all the labour necessary for performing it adequately. But he, with these burthens on him, planned, commenced, and completed, the History of India; and this in the course of about ten years, a shorter time than has been occupied (even by writers who had no other employment) in the production of almost any other historical work of equal bulk, and of anything approaching to the same amount of reading and research. And to this is to be added, that during the whole period, a considerable part of almost every day was employed in the instruction of his children: in the case of one of whom, myself, he exerted an amount of labour, care, and perseverance rarely, if ever, employed for a similar purpose, in endeavouring to give, according to his own conception, the highest order of intellectual education.

A man who, in his own practice, so vigorously acted up to the principle of los- 4 ing no time, was likely to adhere to the same rule in the instruction of his pupil. I have no remembrance of the time when I began to learn Greek. I have been told that it was when I was three years old. My earliest recollection on the subject, is that of committing to memory what my father termed Vocables, being lists of common Greek words, with their signification in English, which he wrote out for me on cards. Of grammar, until some years later, I learnt no more than the inflexions of the nouns and verbs, but, after a course of vocables, proceeded at once to translation; and I faintly remember going through Æsop's Fables, the first Greek book which I read. The Anabasis,[2] which I remember better, was the second. I learnt no Latin until my eighth year. At that time I had read, under my father's tuition, a number of Greek prose authors, among whom I remember the whole of Herodotus, and of Xenophon's Cyropædia and Memorials of Socrates; some of the lives of the philosophers by Diogenes Laertius; part of Lucian, and

---

[2]Of Xenophon, the Greek historian and student of Socrates; the *Anabasis* is an account of a Greek expedition against the Persians in 401 B.C.

Isocrates ad Demonicum and ad Nicoclem. I also read, in 1813, the first six dialogues (in the common arrangement) of Plato, from the Euthyphron to the Theætetus inclusive: which last dialogue, I venture to think, would have been better omitted, as it was totally impossible I should understand it. But my father, in all his teaching, demanded of me not only the utmost that I could do, but much that I could by no possibility have done. What he was himself willing to undergo for the sake of my instruction, may be judged from the fact, that I went through the whole process of preparing my Greek lessons in the same room and at the same table at which he was writing: and as in those days Greek and English Lexicons were not, and I could make no more use of a Greek and Latin Lexicon than could be made without having yet begun to learn Latin, I was forced to have recourse to him for the meaning of every word which I did not know. This incessant interruption he, one of the most impatient of men, submitted to, and wrote under that interruption several volumes of his History and all else that he had to write during those years.

      The only thing besides Greek, that I learnt as a lesson in this part of my child-   5
hood, was arithmetic: this also my father taught me: it was the task of the evenings, and I well remember its disagreeableness. But the lessons were only a part of the daily instruction I received. Much of it consisted in the books I read by myself, and my father's discourses to me, chiefly during our walks. From 1810 to the end of 1813 we were living in Newington Green, then an almost rustic neighbourhood. My father's health required considerable and constant exercise, and he walked habitually before breakfast, generally in the green lanes towards Hornsey. In these walks I always accompanied him, and with my earliest recollections of green fields and wild flowers, is mingled that of the account I gave him daily of what I had read the day before. To the best of my remembrance, this was a voluntary rather than a prescribed exercise. I made notes on slips of paper while reading, and from these, in the morning walks, I told the story to him; for the books were chiefly histories, of which I read in this manner a great number: Robertson's histories, Hume, Gibbon; but my greatest delight, then and for long afterwards, was Watson's Philip the Second and Third. The heroic defence of the Knights of Malta against the Turks, and of the revolted provinces of the Netherlands against Spain, excited in me an intense and lasting interest. Next to Watson, my favorite historical reading was Hooke's History of Rome. Of Greece I had seen at that time no regular history, except school abridgments and the last two or three volumes of a translation of Rollin's Ancient History, beginning with Philip of Macedon. But I read with great delight Langhorne's translation of Plutarch. In English history, beyond the time at which Hume leaves off, I remember reading Burnet's History of his Own Time, though I cared little for anything in it except the wars and battles; and the historical part of the Annual Register, from the beginning to about 1788, where the volumes my father borrowed for me from Mr. Bentham left off. I felt a lively interest in Frederic of Prussia during his difficulties, and in Paoli, the Corsican patriot; but when I came to the American War, I took my part, like a child as I was (until set right by my father) on the wrong side, because it was called the English side. In these frequent talks about the books I read, he used, as opportunity offered, to give me explanations and ideas respecting civilization, government, morality, mental cultivation, which he required me afterwards to restate to him in my own words. He also made me read, and give him a verbal account of, many books which would not have interested me sufficiently to induce me to read them of myself: among

others, Millar's Historical View of the English Government, a book of great merit for its time, and which he highly valued; Mosheim's Ecclesiastical History, McCrie's Life of John Knox, and even Sewell's and Rutty's Histories of the Quakers. He was fond of putting into my hands books which exhibited men of energy and resource in unusual circumstances, struggling against difficulties and overcoming them: of such works I remember Beaver's African Memoranda, and Collins's account of the first settlement of New South Wales. Two books which I never wearied of reading were Anson's Voyage, so delightful to most young persons, and a Collection (Hawkesworth's, I believe) of Voyages round the World, in four volumes, beginning with Drake and ending with Cook and Bougainville. Of children's books, any more than of playthings, I had scarcely any, except an occasional gift from a relation or acquaintance; among those I had, Robinson Crusoe was preeminent, and continued to delight me through all my boyhood. It was no part however of my father's system to exclude books of amusement, though he allowed them very sparingly. Of such books he possessed at that time next to none, but he borrowed several for me; those which I remember are, the Arabian Nights, Cazotte's Arabian Tales, Don Quixote, Miss Edgeworth's "Popular Tales," and a book of some reputation in its day, Brooke's Fool of Quality.

In my eighth year I commenced learning Latin, in conjunction with a younger 6 sister, to whom I taught it as I went on, and who afterwards repeated the lessons to my father: and from this time, other sisters and brothers being successively added as pupils, a considerable part of my day's work consisted of this preparatory teaching. It was a part which I greatly disliked; the more so, as I was held responsible for the lessons of my pupils, in almost as full a sense as for my own: I however derived from this discipline the great advantage, of learning more thoroughly and retaining more lastingly the things which I was set to teach: perhaps, too, the practice it afforded in explaining difficulties to others, may even at that age have been useful. In other respects, the experience of my boyhood is not favorable to the plan of teaching children by means of one another. The teaching, I am sure, is very inefficient as teaching, and I well know that the relation between teacher and taught is not a good moral discipline to either. I went in this manner through the Latin grammar, and a considerable part of Cornelius Nepos and Cæsar's Commentaries, but afterwards added to the superintendance of these lessons, much longer ones of my own.

In the same year in which I began Latin, I made my first commencement in the 7 Greek poets with the Iliad. After I had made some progress in this, my father put Pope's translation into my hands. It was the first English verse I had cared to read, and it became one of the books in which for many years I most delighted: I think I must have read it from twenty to thirty times through. I should not have thought it worth while to mention a taste apparently so natural to boyhood, if I had not, as I think, observed that the keen enjoyment of this brilliant specimen of narrative and versification is not so universal with boys, as I should have expected both a *priori*[3] and from my individual experience. Soon after this time I commenced Euclid, and somewhat later, algebra, still under my father's tuition.

From my eighth to my twelfth year the Latin books which I remember reading 8 were, the Bucolics of Virgil, and the first six books of the Æneid; all Horace except the

---

[3]Prior to experience.

Epodes; the fables of Phædrus; the first five books of Livy (to which from my love of the subject I voluntarily added, in my hours of leisure, the remainder of the first decad); all Sallust; a considerable part of Ovid's Metamorphoses; some plays of Terence; two or three books of Lucretius; several of the Orations of Cicero, and of his writings on oratory; also his letters to Atticus, my father taking the trouble to translate to me from the French the historical explanations of Mongault's notes.[4] In Greek I read the Iliad and Odyssey through; one or two plays of Sophocles, Euripides, and Aristophanes, though by these I profited little; all Thucydides; the Hellenics of Xenophon; a great part of Demosthenes, Æschines, and Lysias; Theocritus; Anacreon; part of the Anthology; a little of Dionysius; several books of Polybius; and lastly, Aristotle's Rhetoric, which, as the first expressly scientific treatise on any moral or psychological subject which I had read, and containing many of the best observations of the ancients on human nature and life, my father made me study with peculiar care, and throw the matter of it into synoptic tables.[5] During the same years I learnt elementary geometry and algebra thoroughly, the differential calculus and other portions of the higher mathematics far from thoroughly: for my father, not having kept up this part of his early acquired knowledge, could not spare time to qualify himself for removing my difficulties, and left me to deal with them, with little other aid than that of books: while I was continually incurring his displeasure by my inability to solve difficult problems for which he did not see that I had not the necessary previous knowledge.

As to my private reading, I can only speak of what I remember. History continued to be my strongest predilection, and most of all ancient history. Mitford's Greece I read continually. My father had put me on my guard against the Tory prejudices of this writer, and his perversions of facts for the whitewashing of despots, and blackening of popular institutions. These points he discoursed on, exemplifying them from the Greek orators and historians, with such effect that in reading Mitford, my sympathies were always on the contrary side to those of the author, and I could, to some extent, have argued the point against him: yet this did not diminish the ever new pleasure with which I read the book. Roman history, both in my old favorite, Hooke, and in Ferguson, continued to delight me. A book which, in spite of what is called the dryness of its stile, I took great pleasure in, was the Ancient Universal History: through the incessant reading of which, I had my head full of historical details concerning the obscurest ancient people, while about modern history, except detached passages such as the Dutch war of independence, I knew and cared comparatively little. A voluntary exercise to which throughout my boyhood I was much addicted, was what I called writing histories. I successively composed a Roman history, picked out of Hooke; an abridgment of the Ancient Universal History; a History of Holland, from my favorite Watson and from an anonymous compilation; and in my eleventh and twelfth year I occupied myself with writing what I flattered myself was something serious. This was no less than a history of the Roman Government, compiled (with the assistance of Hooke) from Livy and Dionysius: of which I wrote as much as would have made an octavo volume, extending to the epoch of the Licinian Laws. It was, in fact, an account of the struggles between the patricians

9

---

[4]Mill lists various Roman poets, dramatists, and philosophers.
[5]Mill lists various Greek poets, rhetoricians, and dramatists. The *Anthology* is a collection of about 6,000 elegiac poems by about 300 Greeks writers.

and plebeians, which now engrossed all the interest in my mind which I had previously felt in the mere wars and conquests of the Romans. I discussed all the constitutional points as they arose: though quite ignorant of Niebuhr's researches, I, by such lights as my father had given me, vindicated the Agrarian Laws on the evidence of Livy, and upheld to the best of my ability the Roman democratic party. A few years later, in my contempt of my childish efforts, I destroyed all these papers, not then anticipating that I could ever feel any curiosity about my first attempts at writing and reasoning. My father encouraged me in this useful amusement, though, as I think judiciously, he never asked to see what I wrote; so that I did not feel that in writing it I was accountable to any one, nor had the chilling sensation of being under a critical eye.

But though these exercises in history were never a compulsory lesson, there 10 was another kind of composition which was so, namely writing verses, and it was one of the most disagreeable of my tasks. Greek or Latin verses I did not write, nor learnt the prosody of those languages. My father, thinking this not worth the time it required, contented himself with making me read aloud to him, and correcting false quantities. I never composed at all in Greek, even in prose, and but little in Latin: not that my father could be indifferent to the value of this practice, in giving a thorough knowledge of those languages, but because there really was not time for it. The verses I was required to write were English. When I first read Pope's Homer, I ambitiously attempted to compose something of the same kind, and achieved as much as one book of a continuation of the Iliad. There, probably, the spontaneous promptings of my poetical ambition would have stopped; but the exercise, begun from choice, was continued by command. Conformably to my father's usual practice of explaining to me, as far as possible, the reasons for what he required me to do, he gave me, for this, as I well remember, two reasons highly characteristic of him. One was, that some things could be expressed better and more forcibly in verse than in prose: this, he said, was a real advantage. The other was, that people in general attached more value to verse than it deserved, and the power of writing it was, on this account, worth acquiring. He generally left me to choose my own subjects, which, as far as I remember, were mostly addresses to some mythological personage or allegorical abstraction; but he made me translate into English verse many of Horace's shorter poems: I also remember his giving me Thomson's "Winter" to read, and afterwards making me attempt (without book) to write something myself on the same subject. The verses I wrote were of course the merest rubbish, nor did I ever attain any facility of versification, but the practice may have been useful in making it easier for me, at a later period, to acquire readiness of expression.[6] I had read, up to this time, very little English poetry. Shakespeare my father had put into my hands, chiefly for the sake of the historical plays, from which however I went on to the others. My father never was a great admirer of Shakespeare, the English idolatry of whom he used to attack with some severity. He cared little for any English poetry except Milton (for whom he had the highest admiration), Goldsmith, Burns, and Gray's Bard, which he preferred to his Elegy: perhaps I may add Cowper and Beattie. He

---

[6]In a subsequent stage of boyhood, when these exercises had ceased to be compulsory, like most youthful writers I wrote tragedies; under the inspiration not so much of Shakespeare as of Joanna Baillie, whose "Constantine Paleologus" in particular appeared to me one of the most glorious of human compositions. I still think it one of the best dramas of the last two centuries. [Mill]

had some value for Spenser, and I remember his reading to me (unlike his usual practice of making me read to him) the first book of the Fairie Queene; but I took little pleasure in it. The poetry of the present century he saw scarcely any merit in, and I hardly became acquainted with any of it till I was grown up to manhood, except the metrical romances of Walter Scott, which I read at his recommendation and was intensely delighted with; as I always was with animated narrative. Dryden's Poems were among my father's books, and many of these he made me read, but I never cared for any of them except Alexander's Feast, which, as well as many of the songs in Walter Scott, I used to sing internally, to a music of my own: to some of the latter indeed I went so far as to compose airs, which I still remember. Cowper's short poems I read with some pleasure, but never got far into the longer ones; and nothing in the two volumes interested me like the prose account of his three hares. In my thirteenth year I met with Campbell's Poems, among which Lochiel, Hohenlinden, the Exile of Erin, and some others, gave me sensations I had never before experienced from poetry. Here, too, I made nothing of the longer poems, except the striking opening of Gertrude of Wyoming, which long kept its place in my feelings as the perfection of pathos.

During this part of my childhood, one of my greatest amusements was experi- 11 mental science; in the theoretical, however, not the practical sense of the word; not trying experiments, a kind of discipline which I have often regretted not having had—nor even seeing, but merely reading about them. I never remember being so wrapt up in any book, as I was in Joyce's Scientific Dialogues; and I was rather recalcitrant to my father's criticisms of the bad reasoning respecting the first principles of physics which abounds in the early part of that work. I devoured treatises on Chemistry, especially that of my father's early friend and schoolfellow Dr. Thomson, for years before I attended a lecture or saw an experiment.

From about the age of twelve, I entered into another and more advanced stage 12 in my course of instruction; in which the main object was no longer the aids and appliances of thought, but the thoughts themselves. This commenced with Logic, in which I began at once with the Organon, and read it to the Analytics inclusive, but profited little by the Posterior Analytics,[7] which belong to a branch of speculation I was not yet ripe for. Contemporaneously with the Organon, my father made me read the whole or parts of several of the Latin treatises on the scholastic logic; giving each day to him, in our walks, a minute account of what I had read, and answering his numerous and searching questions. After this, I went, in a similar manner, through the "Computatio sive Logica" of Hobbes, a work of a much higher order of thought than the books of the school logicians, and which he estimated very highly; in my own opinion beyond its merits, great as these are. It was his invariable practice, whatever studies he exacted from me, to make me as far as possible understand and feel the utility of them: and this he deemed peculiarly fitting in the case of the syllogistic logic, the usefulness of which had been impugned by so many writers of authority. I well remember how, and in what particular walk, in the neighbourhood of Bagshot Heath (where we were on a visit to his old friend Mr. Wallace, then one of the Mathematical Professors at Sandhurst) he first attempted by questions to make me think on the subject, and frame some conception of what constituted the utility of the syllogistic logic, and when I had failed in this, to make me understand it by explanations. The explanations did not make the matter at all clear to me

---

[7]The *Organon* of Aristotle, which includes the "Prior Analytics" and the "Posterior Analytics."

at the time; but they were not therefore useless; they remained as a nucleus for my observations and reflections to crystallize upon; the import of his general remarks being interpreted to me, by the particular instances which came under my notice afterwards. My own consciousness and experience ultimately led me to appreciate quite as highly as he did, the value of an early practical familiarity with the school logic. I know of nothing, in my education, to which I think myself more indebted for whatever capacity of thinking I have attained. The first intellectual operation in which I arrived at any proficiency, was dissecting a bad argument, and finding in what part the fallacy lay: and though whatever capacity of this sort I attained, was due to the fact that it was an intellectual exercise in which I was most perseveringly drilled by my father, yet it is also true that the school logic, and the mental habits acquired in studying it, were among the principal instruments of this drilling. I am persuaded that nothing, in modern education, tends so much, when properly used, to form exact thinkers, who attach a precise meaning to words and propositions, and are not imposed on by vague, loose, or ambiguous terms. The boasted influence of mathematical studies is nothing to it; for in mathematical processes, none of the real difficulties of correct ratiocination occur. It is also a study peculiarly adapted to an early stage in the education of philosophical students, since it does not presuppose the slow process of acquiring, by experience and reflection, valuable thoughts of their own. They may become capable of disentangling the intricacies of confused and self-contradictory thought, before their own thinking faculties are much advanced; a power which, for want of some such discipline, many otherwise able men altogether lack; and when they have to answer opponents, only endeavour, by such arguments as they can command, to support the opposite conclusion, scarcely even attempting to confute the reasonings of their antagonists; and therefore, at the utmost, leaving the question, as far as it depends on argument, a balanced one.

During this time, the Latin and Greek books which I continued to read with my [13] father were chiefly such as were worth studying not for the language merely, but also for the thoughts. This included much of the orators, and especially Demosthenes, some of whose principal orations I read several times over, and wrote out, by way of exercise, a full analysis of them. My father's comments on these orations when I read them to him were very instructive to me. He not only drew my attention to the insight they afforded into Athenian institutions, and the principles of legislation and government which they often illustrated, but pointed out the skill and art of the orator—how everything important to his purpose was said at the exact moment when he had brought the minds of his audience into the state most fitted to receive it; how he made steal into their minds, gradually and by insinuation, thoughts which if expressed in a more direct manner would have roused their opposition. Most of these reflections were beyond my capacity of full comprehension at the time; but they left seed behind, which germinated in due season. At this time I also read the whole of Tacitus, Juvenal, and Quintilian. The latter, owing to his obscure stile and to the scholastic details of which many parts of his treatise are made up, is little read and seldom sufficiently appreciated. His book is a kind of encyclopædia of the thoughts of the ancients on the whole field of education and culture; and I have retained through life many valuable ideas which I can distinctly trace to my reading of him, even at that early age. It was at this period that I read, for the first time, some of the most important dialogues of Plato, in particular the Gorgias, the Protagoras, and the Republic. There is no author to whom my father thought himself more indebted for his own mental culture, than Plato, or whom he more frequently recommended to young students. I can bear similar testimony in regard to myself. The Socratic method, of which the Platonic dialogues are the chief example, is unsurpassed as a discipline for correcting the errors, and clearing up the confusions incident to the *intellectus sibi permissus*,[8] the understanding which has made up all its bundles of associations under the guidance of popular phraseology. The close, searching *elenchus* by which the man of vague generalities is constrained either to express his meaning to himself in definite terms, or to confess that he does not know what he is talking about; the perpetual testing of all general statements by particular instances; the siege in form which is laid to the meaning of large abstract terms, by fixing upon some still larger class-name which includes that and more, and dividing down to the thing sought— marking out its limits and definition by a series of accurately drawn distinctions between it and each of the cognate objects which are successively parted off from it—all this, as an education for precise thinking, is inestimable, and all this, even at that age, took such hold of me that it became part of my own mind. I have felt ever since that the title of Platonist belongs by far better right to those who have been nourished in, and have endeavoured to practise Plato's mode of investigation, than to those who are distinguished only by the adoption of certain dogmatical conclusions, drawn mostly from the least intelligible of his works, and which the character of his mind and writings makes it uncertain whether he himself regarded as anything more than poetic fancies, or philosophic conjectures.

In going through Plato and Demosthenes, since I could now read these au- 14 thors, as far as the language was concerned, with perfect ease, I was not required to construe them sentence by sentence, but to read them aloud to my father, answering questions when asked: but the particular attention which he paid to elocution (in which his own excellence was remarkable) made this reading aloud to him a most painful task. Of all things which he required me to do, there was none which I did so constantly ill, or in which he so perpetually lost his temper with me. He had thought much on the principles of the art of reading, especially the most neglected part of it, the inflexions of the voice, or *modulation* as writers on elocution call it (in contrast with *articulation* on the one side, and *expression* on the other), and had reduced it to rules, grounded on the logical analysis of a sentence. These rules he strongly impressed upon me, and took me severely to task for every violation of them: but I even then remarked (though I did not venture to make the remark to him) that though he reproached me when I read a sentence ill, and *told* me how I ought to have read it, he never, by reading it himself, *shewed* me how it ought to be read. A defect running through his otherwise admirable modes of instruction, as it did through all his modes of thought, was that of trusting too much to the intelligibleness of the abstract, when not embodied in the concrete. It was at a much later period of my youth, when practising elocution by myself, or with companions of my own age, that I for the first time understood the object of his rules, and saw the psychological grounds of them. At that time I and others followed out the subject into its ramifications, and could have composed a very useful treatise, grounded on my father's principles. He himself left those principles and rules unwritten. I regret that when my mind was full of the subject, from systematic practice, I did not put them, and our improvements of them, into a formal shape.

---

[8]The mind left without guidance (a phrase of Sir Frances Bacon in *Novum Organum*).

A book which contributed largely to my education, in the best sense of the 15 term, was my father's History of India. It was published in the beginning of 1818. During the year previous, while it was passing through the press, I used to read the proofsheets to him; or rather, I read the manuscript to him while he corrected the proofs. The number of new ideas which I received from this remarkable book, and the impulse and stimulus as well as guidance given to my thoughts by its criticisms and disquisitions on society and civilization in the Hindoo part, on institutions and the acts of governments in the English part, made my early familiarity with it eminently useful to my subsequent progress. And though I can perceive deficiencies in it now as compared with a perfect standard, I still think it, if not the most, one of the most instructive histories ever written, and one of the books from which most benefit may be derived by a mind in the course of making up its opinions.

The Preface, among the most characteristic of my father's writings, as well as 16 the richest in materials of thought, gives a picture which may be entirely depended on, of the sentiments and expectations with which he wrote the History. Saturated as the book is with the opinions and modes of judgment of a democratic radicalism then regarded as extreme; and treating with a severity at that time most unusual the English Constitution, the English law, and all parties and classes who possessed any considerable influence in the country; he may have expected reputation, but certainly not advancement in life, from its publication; nor could he have supposed that it would raise up anything but enemies for him in powerful quarters: least of all could he have expected favour from the East India Company, to whose commercial privileges he was unqualifiedly hostile, and on the acts of whose government he had made so many severe comments: though, in various parts of his book, he bore a testimony in their favour, which he felt to be their just due, namely, that no government had on the whole given so much proof, to the extent of its lights, of good intention towards its subjects; and that if the acts of any other government had the light of publicity as completely let in upon them, they would, in all probability, still less bear scrutiny.

On learning, however, in the spring of 1819, about a year after the publication 17 of the History, that the East India Directors desired to strengthen the part of their home establishment which was employed in carrying on the correspondence with India, my father declared himself a candidate for that employment, and, to the credit of the Directors, successfully. He was appointed one of the Assistants of the Examiner of India Correspondence; officers whose duty it was to prepare drafts of despatches to India, for consideration by the Directors, in the principal departments of administration. In this office, and in that of Examiner, which he subsequently attained, the influence which his talents, his reputation, and his decision of character gave him, with superiors who really desired the good government of India, enabled him to a great extent to throw into his drafts of despatches, and to carry through the ordeal of the Court of Directors and Board of Control, without having their force much weakened, his real opinions on Indian subjects. In his History he had set forth, for the first time, many of the true principles of Indian administration: and his despatches, following his History, did more than had ever been done before to promote the improvement of India, and teach Indian officials to understand their business. If a selection of them were published, they would, I am convinced, place his character as a practical statesman fully on a level with his eminence as a speculative writer.

This new employment of his time caused no relaxation in his attention to my 18 education. It was in this same year, 1819, that he took me through a complete course of political economy. His loved and intimate friend, Ricardo, had shortly before published the book which formed so great an epoch in political economy;[9] a book which never would have been published or written, but for the entreaty and strong encouragement of my father; for Ricardo, the most modest of men, though firmly convinced of the truth of his doctrines, deemed himself so little capable of doing them justice in exposition and expression, that he shrank from the idea of publicity. The same friendly encouragement induced Ricardo, a year or two later, to become a member of the House of Commons; where during the few remaining years of his life, unhappily cut short in the full vigour of his intellect, he rendered so much service to his and my father's opinions both in political economy and on other subjects.

Though Ricardo's great work was already in print, no didactic treatise embody- 19 ing its doctrines, in a manner fit for learners, had yet appeared. My father, therefore, commenced instructing me in the science by a sort of lectures, which he delivered to me in our walks. He expounded each day a portion of the subject, and I gave him next day a written account of it, which he made me rewrite over and over again until it was clear, precise, and tolerably complete. In this manner I went through the whole extent of the science; and the written outline of it which resulted from my daily *compte rendu*,[10] served him afterwards as notes from which to write his Elements of Political Economy. After this I read Ricardo, giving an account daily of what I read, and discussing, in the best manner I could, the collateral points which offered themselves in our progress. On Money, as the most intricate part of the subject, he made me read in the same manner Ricardo's admirable pamphlets, written during what was called the Bullion controversy. To these succeeded Adam Smith; and in this reading it was one of my father's main objects to make me apply to Smith's more superficial view of political economy, the superior lights of Ricardo, and detect what was fallacious in Smith's arguments, or erroneous in any of his conclusions. Such a mode of instruction was excellently calculated to form a thinker; but it required to be worked by a thinker, as close and vigorous as my father. The path was a thorny one even to him, and I am sure it was so to me, notwithstanding the strong interest I took in the subject. He was often, and much beyond reason, provoked by my failures in cases where success could not have been expected; but in the main his method was right, and it succeeded. I do not believe that any scientific teaching ever was more thorough, or better fitted for training the faculties, than the mode in which logic and political economy were taught to me by my father. Striving, even in an exaggerated degree, to call forth the activity of my faculties, by making me find out everything for myself, he gave his explanations not before, but after, I had felt the full force of the difficulties; and not only gave me an accurate knowledge of these two great subjects, as far as they were then understood, but made me a thinker on both. I thought for myself almost from the first, and occasionally thought differently from him, though for a long time only on minor points, and making his opinion the ultimate standard. At a later period I even occasionally convinced him, and altered his opinion on some points of detail: which I state to his honour, not my own. It at once exemplifies his perfect candour, and the real worth of his method of teaching.

---

[9]The economist David Ricardo (1772-1823) published *Principles of Political Economy and Taxation* in 1817.
[10]Account.

At this point concluded what can properly be called my lessons. When I was 20 about fourteen I left England for more than a year; and after my return, though my studies went on under my father's general direction, he was no longer my schoolmaster. I shall therefore pause here, and turn back to matters of a more general nature connected with the part of my life and education included in the preceding reminiscences.

In the course of instruction which I have partially retraced, the point most su- 21 perficially apparent is the great effort to give, during the years of childhood, an amount of knowledge in what are considered the higher branches of education, which is seldom acquired (if acquired at all) until the age of manhood. The result of the experiment shews the ease with which this may be done, and places in a strong light the wretched waste of so many precious years as are spent in acquiring the modicum of Latin and Greek commonly taught to schoolboys; a waste, which has led so many educational reformers to entertain the ill-judged proposal of discarding these languages altogether from general education. If I had been by nature extremely quick of apprehension, or had possessed a very accurate and retentive memory, or were of a remarkably active and energetic character, the trial would not be conclusive; but in all these natural gifts I am rather below than above par. What I could do, could assuredly be done by any boy or girl of average capacity and healthy physical constitution: and if I have accomplished anything, I owe it, among other fortunate circumstances, to the fact that through the early training bestowed on me by my father, I started, I may fairly say, with an advantage of a quarter of a century over my contemporaries.

There was one cardinal point in this training, of which I have already given 22 some indication, and which, more than anything else, was the cause of whatever good it effected. Most boys or youths who have had much knowledge drilled into them, have their mental capacities not strengthened, but overlaid by it. They are crammed with mere facts, and with the opinions or phrases of other people, and these are accepted as a substitute for the power to form opinions of their own. And thus, the sons of eminent fathers, who have spared no pains in their education, so often grow up mere parroters of what they have learnt, incapable of using their minds except in the furrows traced for them. Mine, however, was not an education of cram. My father never permitted anything which I learnt, to degenerate into a mere exercise of memory. He strove to make the understanding not only go along with every step of the teaching, but if possible, precede it. Anything which could be found out by thinking, I never was told, until I had exhausted my efforts to find it out for myself. As far as I can trust my remembrance, I acquitted myself very lamely in this department; my recollection of such matters is almost wholly of failures, hardly ever of success. It is true, the failures were often in things in which success in so early a stage of my progress, was almost impossible. I remember at some time in my thirteenth year, on my happening to use the word idea, he asked me what an idea was; and expressed some displeasure at my ineffectual efforts to define the word: I recollect also his indignation at my using the common expression that something was true in theory but required correction in practice; and how, after making me vainly strive to define the word theory, he explained its meaning, and shewed the fallacy of the vulgar form of speech which I had used; leaving me fully persuaded that in being unable to give a correct definition of Theory, and in speaking of it as something which might be at variance with practice, I had shewn unparalleled ignorance. In this he seems, and perhaps was, very unreasonable; but I think, only in being angry at my failure. A pupil from whom nothing is ever demanded which he cannot do, never does all he can.

One of the evils most liable to attend on any sort of early proficiency, and which 23 often fatally blights its promise, my father most anxiously guarded against. This was self conceit. He kept me, with extreme vigilance, out of the way of hearing myself praised, or of being led to make self-flattering comparisons between myself and others. From his own intercourse with me I could derive none but a very humble opinion of myself; and the standard of comparison he always held up to me, was not what other people did, but what a man could and ought to do. He completely succeeded in preserving me from the sort of influences he so much dreaded. I was not at all aware that my attainments were anything unusual at my age. If I accidentally had my attention drawn to the fact that some other boy knew less than myself—which happened less often than might be imagined—I concluded, not that I knew much, but that he, for some reason or other, knew little, or that his knowledge was of a different kind from mine. My state of mind was not humility, but neither was it arrogance. I never thought of saying to myself, I am, or I can do, so and so. I neither estimated myself highly nor lowly: I did not estimate myself at all. If I thought anything about myself, it was that I was rather backward in my studies, since I always found myself so, in comparison with what my father expected from me. I assert this with confidence, though it was not the impression of various persons who saw me in my childhood. They, as I have since found, thought me greatly and disagreeably self-conceited; probably because I was disputatious, and did not scruple to give direct contradictions to things which I heard said. I suppose I acquired this bad habit from having been encouraged in an unusual degree to talk on matters beyond my age, and with grown persons, while I never had inculcated on me the usual respect for them. My father did not correct this ill breeding and impertinence, probably from not being aware of it, for I was always too much in awe of him to be otherwise than extremely subdued and quiet in his presence. Yet with all this I had no notion of any superiority in myself; and well was it for me that I had not. I remember the very place in Hyde Park where, in my fourteenth year, on the eve of leaving my father's house for a long absence, he told me that I should find, as I got acquainted with new people, that I had been taught many things which youths of my age did not commonly know; and that many persons would be disposed to talk to me of this, and to compliment me upon it. What other things he said on this topic I remember very imperfectly; but he wound up by saying, that whatever I knew more than others, could not be ascribed to any merit in me, but to the very unusual advantage which had fallen to my lot, of having a father who was able to teach me, and willing to give the necessary trouble and time; that it was no matter of praise to me, if I knew more than those who had not had a similar advantage, but the deepest disgrace to me if I did not. I have a distinct remembrance, that the suggestion thus for the first time made to me, that I knew more than other youths who were considered well educated, was to me a piece of information, to which, as to all other things which my father told me, I gave implicit credence, but which did not at all impress me as a personal matter. I felt no disposition to glorify myself upon the circumstance that there were other persons who did not know what I knew; nor had I ever flattered myself that my acquirements, whatever they might be, were any merit of mine: but, now when my attention was called to the subject, I felt that what my father had said respecting my peculiar advantages was exactly the truth and common sense of the matter, and it fixed my opinion and feeling from that time forward.

It is evident that this, among many other of the purposes of my father's scheme 24
of education, could not have been accomplished if he had not carefully kept me from
having any great amount of intercourse with other boys. He was earnestly bent upon my
escaping not only the ordinary corrupting influence which boys exercise over boys, but
the contagion of vulgar modes of thought and feeling; and for this he was willing that
I should pay the price of inferiority in the accomplishments which schoolboys in all
countries chiefly cultivate. The deficiencies in my education were principally in the
things which boys learn from being turned out to shift for themselves, and from being
brought together in large numbers. From temperance and much walking, I grew up
healthy and hardy, though not muscular; but I could do no feats of skill or physical
strength, and knew none of the ordinary bodily exercises. It was not that play, or time
for it, was refused me. Though no holidays were allowed, lest the habit of work should
be broken, and a taste for idleness acquired, I had ample leisure in every day to amuse
myself; but as I had no boy companions, and the animal need of physical activity was
satisfied by walking, my amusements, which were mostly solitary, were in general of a
quiet, if not a bookish turn, and gave little stimulus to any other kind even of mental
activity than that which was already called forth by my studies. I consequently remained
long, and in a less degree have always remained, inexpert in anything requiring manual
dexterity; my mind, as well as my hands, did its work very lamely when it was applied,
or ought to have been applied, to the practical details which, as they are the chief interest of life to the majority of men, are also the things in which whatever mental capacity
they have, chiefly shews itself. I was constantly meriting reproof by inattention, inobser-
vance, and general slackness of mind in matters of daily life. My father was the extreme
opposite in these particulars: his senses and mental faculties were always on the alert;
he carried decision and energy of character in his whole manner, and into every action
of life: and this, as much as his talents, contributed to the strong impression which he
always made upon those with whom he came into personal contact. But the children of
energetic parents, frequently grow up unenergetic, because they lean on their parents,
and the parents are energetic for them. The education which my father gave me, was in
itself much more fitted for training me to *know* than to *do*. Not that he was unaware
of my deficiencies; both as a boy and as a youth I was incessantly smarting under his severe admonitions on the subject. There was anything but insensibility or tolerance on
his part towards such shortcomings: but, while he saved me from the demoralizing effects of school life, he made no effort to provide me with any sufficient substitute for its
practicalizing influences. Whatever qualities he himself, probably, had acquired without
difficulty or special training, he seems to have supposed that I ought to acquire as easily.
He had not, I think, bestowed the same amount of thought and attention on this, as on
most other branches of education; and here, as well as in some other points of my tuition, he seems to have expected effects without causes.

Questions

1. What features of his early education does Mill stress in his account of his regimen of
   reading? Would Rousseau have approved of this regimen?
2. What is the tone of Mill's account? Is it matter of fact, self-satisfied, astonished,
   angry, or openly critical? Or is the tone ironic—implying an attitude that Mill prefers
   not to state?

3. Does Mill approve of his father's prohibition against his playing with other boys? Would he have been happier, healthier, or manually dextrous if he had played with them?
4. What is Mill's attitude toward his father? Does he state this attitude directly, or must you infer it from his account of his education?
5. What is Mill's purpose in writing, and how do you know?

Suggestions for Writing

1. Compare the influence of Mill's father on his early education with the influence of your parents on yours. Use your comparison to arrive at a relative estimate or judgment of both and to develop a thesis.
2. Do you agree with Mill's view of his education discussed in the introduction to the reading selection? What merits and deficiencies would you emphasize? Do you agree with Mill that "any boy or girl of average capacity and healthy physical constitution" could do the same as he?
3. Discuss what Rousseau probably would have said about Mill's early education and upbringing. Support your discussion with references to both Rousseau and Mill.

Additional Reading

Anschutz, Richard Paul. *The Philosophy of J. S. Mill.* Oxford: Clarendon Press, 1953.

Mazlish, Bruce. *James and John Stuart Mill: Father and Son in the Nineteenth Century.* New York: Basic Books, 1975.

Mill, John Stuart. *Autobiography.* Ed. Jack Stillinger. Boston: Houghton Mifflin, 1969.

Packe, Michael St. John. *The Life of John Stuart Mill.* London: Secker and Warburg, 1954.

Robson, John M. *The Improvement of Mankind.* Toronto: University of Toronto Press, 1968.

The Child's World

Margaret Mead

Margaret Mead (1901–1979) received her M.A. in psychology in 1924 and her Ph.D. in anthropology in 1929 from Columbia University. Her fieldwork in the Samoan Islands in 1925 and 1926 provided the material for her book Coming of Age in Samoa *(1928). Mead based* Growing Up in New Guinea *(1930) on field studies with the Manus of New Guinea in 1928. In* New Lives for Old *(1956), Mead describes her second visit to the Manus in 1953. In 1928 she had assumed Manus children and adults were little aware of one another; in 1953 she re-*

alized that this assumption was false. Children had been choosing not to participate in adult life, sharing their parents' view that life is burdensome.

In her introduction to Letters from the Field *Mead describes fieldwork as "the unique, but also cumulative, experience of immersing oneself in the ongoing life of another people, suspending for the time both one's beliefs and disbeliefs, and of simultaneously attempting to understand mentally and physically this other version of reality." Following her studies of adolescence in Samoa, she decided to study preadolescents and how they thought. She wished to discover whether Freud and other psychologists were right in claiming that "primitive people, civilized children, and neurotics are alike in their patterns of thought." The following chapter from* Growing Up in New Guinea *discusses another aspect of the life of the children of Manus, the largest of the Admiralty Islands northwest of New Guinea. To Rousseau, these would have been children in an original state of nature; Mead's account suggests that Rousseau may have found life in New Guinea surprising and complex.*

THE major issues of the adult world are thus ignored by Manus children. They 1 are given no property and they acquire none. There are none of those collections of shells, odd shaped stones, fish spines, seeds, etc., which clutter the secret caches of American children and have led to the construction of theories of a "collecting stage" in childhood. No child under thirteen or fourteen had any possessions except his canoe or bow and arrow, furnished him by adults. Spinning tops of seeds are made with some labour, only to be discarded after an hour's play. The short sticks used as punts, the mock spears, the dart, serve a few hours' use and are thrown away. The beaded anklets and armbands are made by the parents, placed on the children and taken off again at the parents' whim. The child does not complain. Even the new and strange objects which we brought to the village were not hoarded. The children scrambled eagerly for bits of coloured ribbon or tinsel, the tin wrappings of films or rolls of exposed and used film, but they never kept them. After I threw away about one hundred wooden film spools, an accidental discard left one camera without a spare spool. I asked the children to bring back one of the dozens they had picked up in the preceding weeks. After an hour, a fourteen-year-old boy finally found one which had been put away in his mother's work box; all the others had disappeared.

But this dissipation of property, so eagerly clutched and so swiftly relinquished, 2 was not due to destructiveness. Objects were lost far oftener than broken. Indeed, the children showed a touching care of a toy while they were still interested in it; a respect for property far exceeding our children's. I shall never forget the picture of eight-year-old Nauna mending a broken penny balloon which I had given him. He would gather the edges of the hole into a little bunch and painstakingly, laboriously, wind it about with raffia-like grass. The hole made temporarily fast, he would inflate the balloon, which a moment later would collapse and have to be mended again. He spent three hours at this labour of love, never losing his temper, soberly tying up the rotten flimsy material with his sturdy grass string. This was typical of their care of material things, an attitude instilled into them as children. But their elders had been at no pains to give them any pattern of collecting things for themselves or hoarding their small possessions.

Similarly in social organisation, the children found no interesting adult pat-   3
tern upon which they could draw. The kinship system with its complex functions and
obligations of relatives was not taught them, it was too complicated for them to grasp
readily themselves. Their habitual contempt for grown-up life kept them from drawing
on it for play purposes. Occasionally, about once a month, a group would make slight
mimetic play with it—stage a payment for a marriage, or pretend that one of their number was dead and that tobacco must be given away for his death feast. Just once I saw
the small girls pretending to keep house. Twice the fourteen-year-old boys dressed up
as girls, donned grass skirts and calico cloaks and dashed about in gay imitation of
betrothed maidens avoiding tabu relatives. Four times the six-year-olds built imitation
houses of tiny sticks. When one stops to compare this lack of imaginative play with a
large, free play group among our own children—with its young pirates, Indians, smug-
glers, "sides," its clubs, secret societies, pass words, codes, insignia, initiations, the difference is striking.

Here in Manus are a group of children, some forty in all, with nothing to do but   4
have a good time all day long. The physical surroundings are ideal, a safe shallow la-
goon, its monotony broken by the change of tide, by driving rains and occasional frightening whirlwinds. They are free to play in every house in the village, indeed the reception section of the house is often hung with children's swings. They have plenty of
materials ready to hand, palm leaves, raffia, rattan, bark, seeds (which the adults make
into tiny charm cases), red hibiscus flowers, coconut shells, pandanus leaves, aromatic
herbs, pliant reeds and rushes. They have materials in plenty with which they could imitate any province of adult life—playing at trade or exchange, or the white man's trade
store which a few of them have seen, of which all of them have heard. They have canoes
of their own, small ones, entirely their own, the larger ones of their parents in which
they are always free to play. But do they ever organise a boat's crew, choose captain and
pilot, engineer and helmsman, reproduce the crew of the white man's schooner of
which they have heard so many tales from returned work boys? Never once in the six
months I spent in close contact with them did I see this happen. Or did they pluck large
shrubs, fashion spears, whiten their bodies with lime, advance in a war fleet formation
upon the village as their elders did at great ceremonies? Did they build themselves small
dancing pole platforms in imitation of their elders? Did they catch small turtles and beat
miniature drums in triumph over their catch? They never did any of these things. They
put on seeds instead of shells and practiced with the little blunt spears their elders had
taught them to make. They beat toy drums when the young men drummed for a dance,
but they held no dances of their own.

They had no sort of formal organisation, no clubs, no parties, no codes, no se-   5
cret societies. If races were held, the older boys simply divided the children up into fairly
equal teams, or selected pairs who were matched physically. But there was nothing permanent about these teams, no continuous rivalry between the children. Leadership
there was, but only the spontaneous, free sort due to intelligence and initiative. Very
loose age groups, never exclusive, never permanent, tended to form about special activities, as a fishing trip a little afield of the village for part of an afternoon; stepping-stone
groups also formed for a few minutes' play—of one adolescent, a twelve-year-old, a
seven-year-old, and possibly a baby brother. These serial groupings were partly dependent upon neighbourhood or relationship, but even these were fluid—the smaller children retained no permanent allegiances to older ones.

Their play was the most matter of fact, rough and tumble, non-imaginative ac- 6
tivity imaginable; football, wrestlings of war, a few round games, races, boat races, making figures in the water, distorting their shadows in the moonlight while the person
who was "it" had to guess their identity. When they were tired they gathered in groups
and sang long monotonous songs over and over:

> I am a man.
> I have no wife.
> I am a man. I have no wife
> I will get a wife in Bunei.
> From my father's cross cousins,
> From my father's cross cousins.
> I am a man,
> I am a man, I have no wife—

Or they made string figures, or burnt decorative scars on each other's arms 7
with red hot twigs.

Conversation turned on who was oldest, who tallest, who had the most burned 8
beauty spots, whether Nane caught a turtle yesterday or to-day, when the canoe would
be back from Mok, what a big fight Sanau and Kemai had over that pig, how frightening
a time Pomasa had on the shipwrecked canoe. When they do discuss events of adult life
it is in very practical terms. So Kawa, aged four, remarked, "Kilipak, give me some
paper." "What do you want it for?" "To make cigarettes." "But where's the tobacco coming from?" "Oh, the death feast." "Whose?" "Alupu's." "But she's not dead yet." "No,
but she soon will be."

Argumentative conversations sometimes ending in fisticuffs were very com- 9
mon. They had an enormous passion for accuracy, a passion in which they imitated
their elders, who would keep the village awake all night over an argument as to whether
a child, dead ten years, had been younger or older than some person still living. In arguments over size or number attempts at verification were made, and I saw one case of attempted experiment. In the midst of several exciting days, during a death in the village,
I had less time than usual for meals, and a can of fruit, of a size usually consumed at
one meal, did for two. Pomat, the little table boy, commented on it, but Kilipak, the
fourteen-year-old cook, contradicted him. I had never divided a can of peaches between
two meals. All the other boys, the children who haunted the house, the married couple
who were temporarily resident, my two adolescent girls, were drawn into the argument,
which lasted for forty-five minutes. Finally Kilipak declared in triumph, "Well, we'll try
it out; we'll give her another can of the same kind tomorrow. If she eats them all, I'm
right; if she doesn't, you are."

This interest in the truth is shown in adult life in various ways. Pokenau once 10
dropped a fish's jawbone out of his betel bag. Upon being questioned, he said he was
keeping it to show to a man in Bunei who had declared that this particular fish had no
teeth. Another man returned from working for a scientific-minded German master to
announce to his astonished companions that his master said New Guinea was once
joined to Australia. The village took sides on the question and two young men fought
each other over the truth of the statement. This restless interest in the truth takes its
most extreme form when men try out the supernatural world; disbelieving the results
of a séance, they will do something which, if the séance were true, would endanger their
lives.

So the form of children's conversation is very like their elders'—from them 11 they take the delight in teaching and repetitious games, the tendency to boasting and recrimination, and the violent argument over facts. But whereas the adults' conversation turns about feasts and finances, spirits, magic, sin, and confession, the children's, ignoring these subjects, is bare and dull, preserving the form only, without any interesting content.

The Manus have also a pattern of desultory, formal conversation, comparable 12 to our talk about the weather. They have no careful etiquette, no series of formal pleasantries with which to bridge over awkward situations; instead meaningless, effortful chatter, is used. I participated in such a conversation in the house of Tchanan, where the runaway wife of Mutchin had taken refuge. Mutchin had broken his wife's arm, and she had left him and fled to her aunts. Twice he had sent women of his household to fetch her and twice she had refused to return to him. On this occasion I accompanied her sister-in-law. The members of her aunt's family received us; the runaway remained in the back of the house, cooking over a fire. For an hour they sat and talked, about conditions at the land market, fishing, when certain feasts were to be held, when some relatives were coming from Mok. Not once was the purpose of the visit mentioned. Finally a young man adroitly introduced the question of physical strength. Some one added how much stronger men were than women; from this the conversation shifted to men's bones and women's bones, how easily broken the latter were, how an unintentional blow from a well-meaning man might shatter a woman's frail bone. Then the sister-in-law rose. The wife spoke no word, but after we had climbed down into the canoe, she came slowly down the ladder and sat in the stern. This oblique conversational style is followed by some children when talking with adults. They make prim little statements which apply to any topic under discussion. So Masa, when her mother mentions a pregnant woman in Patusi remarks, "The pregnant woman who was at our house has gone home." She is then silent again until some other topic gives her a chance to make a brisk comment.

The adults give the children no story-telling pattern, no guessing games, rid- 13 dles, puzzles. The idea that children would like to hear legends seems quite fantastic to a Manus adult. "Oh, no—legends are for old people. Children don't know legends. Children don't listen to legends. Children dislike legends!" And the plastic children accept this theory which contradicts one of our firmest convictions, the appeal of stories to children.

The simple narration of something seen or experienced does occur, but flights 14 of fancy are strictly discouraged by children themselves. "And then there was a big wind came up and the canoe almost upset." "Did it upset?" "Well, it was a big wind." "But you didn't go into the water, did you?" "No-oo." The insistence on fact, on circumstantial accounts, on accuracy in small points, all serve as checks upon the imagination.

So the story-telling habit, the delight in story, is entirely absent. Imaginative 15 speculation about what is happening on the other side of the hill, or what the fish are saying, is all completely lacking. And the "why?" element in children's conversation with adults is superseded by the "what?" and "where?" questions.

Yet this does not mean a lack of intelligence on the children's part. Pictures, 16 advertisements in magazines, illustrations of stories, they greeted with interest and delight. They pored for hours over an old copy of *Natural History,* explaining, wondering, admiring. Every explanatory comment of mine was eagerly remembered and woven into new interpretations. Their alert minds had been neither dulled nor inhibited. They took to any new game, new pictures, new occupations, with far greater eagerness than did the little Samoans, smothered and absorbed in their own culture. Drawing became an absorbing passion with them. Tirelessly they covered sheet after sheet of paper with men and women, crocodiles and canoes. But unused to stories, unpractised in rearing imaginary edifices, the content of the realistic drawings was very simple: two boys fighting, two boys kicking a ball, a man and his wife, a crew spearing a turtle, a schooner with a pilot. They drew nothing with plot. Similarly, when I showed them ink blots and asked for interpretations, I got only straight statement, "It's a cloud," "It's a bird." Only from one or two of the adolescent boys whose thinking was being stimulated by the thought of the other lands they would see as work boys, gave such interpretations as "a cassowary" (which he had never seen), a motor car, or a telephone. But the ability of children in this society of developing whole plots from the stimulus of an ambiguous ink blot was lacking.

Their memories were excellent. Trained to small points and fine discrimina- 17 tions they learned to distinguish between beer bottles of medicines in terms of slight differences in size of label or number of words on the label. They could recognize each other's drawings of four months before.

In other words they were in no sense stupid children. They were alert, intelli- 18 gent, inquisitive, with excellent memories and receptive minds. Their dull unimaginative play life is no comment upon their minds, but rather a comment upon the way in which they were brought up. Cut off from the stimulation of adult life, they were never asked to participate in it. They took no part at feasts or ceremonies. The grown ups did not give them patterns of clan loyalty or chieftainship which they could use in their organisation of their children's group. The intricate interrelations of the grown-up world, the relationships between cross cousins with its jesting, cursing, blessing; the ceremonial of war, the mechanics of séances, any one of these would have given the children amusing material for imitation if only the adults had given them a few hints, had aroused their interest or enlisted their enthusiasms.

The Plains Indian life with its buffalo hunt, its pitching and breaking up of 19 camp, its war conventions, does not provide any more vivid material for its children than does the Manus life. But the Cheyenne mother makes her child a little tipi in which to play house. The Cheyenne household greets the diminutive hunter's slain bird as a great addition to the family cook pot. In consequence the children's camp of the Plains, which reproduces in mimetic play the whole cycle of adult activities, forms the centre of Cheyenne children's play interest.

If on the other hand, the Manus had willfully, aggressively excluded the chil- 20 dren, shut doors against them, consistently shooed them off the ceremonial scene, the children might have rallied to positive defensive measures. This has happened with Kaffir children in South Africa where the world of grown ups treat children as little nuisances, lie to them, pack them off to watch the grain fields, forbid them even to eat the small birds of their own catch. This play group of children, put on its mettle by adult measures, organises into a children's republic with spies and guards, a secret language, outlaw conventions of its own, which reminds one of city boys' gangs to-day. Either active enlistment of the children as on the Plains, or active suppression, as among the

Kaffirs, seems to produce a more varied, richer child life. Even in Samoa, which does neither but gives every child tasks graded to its skill, the children's life is given content and importance because of the responsibilities placed upon them, because they are part of a whole dignified plan of life.

But the Manus do none of these things. The children are perfectly trained to 21 take care of themselves; any sense of physical insufficiency is guarded against. They are given their own canoes, paddles, swings, bows and arrows. They are regimented into no age groups, made to submit to no categories of appropriate age or sex behaviour. No house is denied to them. They frolic about under foot, in the midst of the most important ceremonies. And they are treated as lords of the universe; their parents appear to them as willing, patient slaves. And no lord has ever taken a great interest in the tiresome occupations of slaves.

As in the social organisation, so with the religious life. There is a ready-made 22 adult content in which the children are given no part. Their invisible playmates are given them, pedigree complete, making no appeal to the imagination and no plea for its exercise.

In the less formal thought and play of children, which seems more spontane- 23 ous than their attitudes towards the finished system of religion which they have to learn by rote, a contrast with our own children is also seen. The habits of personalising inanimate things, of kicking the door, blaming the knife, apostrophising the chair, accusing the moon of eavesdropping, etc., are lacking in Manus. Where we fill our children's minds with a rich folklore, songs which personalise the sun, the moon, and the stars, riddles and fairy tales and myths, the Manus do nothing of the sort. The Manus child never hears of "the man in the moon," or a rhyme like Jean Ingelow's:

> "Oh, moon, have you done something wrong in Heaven,
> That God has hidden your face?
> I hope if you have, you will soon be forgiven,
> And shine again in your place."

nor hears his older sister dance to:

> "Turn off your light, Mr. Moon Man,
> Go and hide your face behind the clouds.
> Can't you see the couples all spooning?
> Two's a company and three's a crowd.
> When a little lad and lady
> Find a spot all nice and shady,
> It's time to say good-night.
> When you want to spoon,
> Say, 'Please, Mr. Moon,
> Be a good sport and turn off your light.' "

His parents and grandparents have given him no rich background upon which to embroider ideas about the moon, and he thinks of the moon as a light in the sky which is there and not there, periodically. He does not think the moon is a person. He believes it cannot see because "it has no eyes." His view of the moon is a matter-of-fact, naturalistic view, uncorrected by science, of course, for, like his untutored father, he believes that sun and moon alike proceed across the sky. His folklore gives him no help and the

Manus language is cool and bare, without figures of speech or rich allusiveness. It is a language which neither stimulates the imagination of children nor provides material for adult poetry. It is a rigorously matter-of-fact language where ours is filled with imagery and metaphor.

So where we give the moon sex and speak of her as "she," the Manus language, 24 which makes no distinction between he, she, and it, all of which are "third person singular," gives no personalising suggestion. Nor are verbs which apply to persons applied to the moon. The moon "shines," but it never smiles, hides, marches, flirts, peeps, approves; it never "looks down sadly," or "turns away its face." All the impetus to personalisation which our rich allusive language suggests to a child are absent.

I couldn't even persuade children to cast the blame upon inanimate objects. To 25 my remarks, "It's a bad canoe to float away," the other children would reply, "—but Popoli forgot to tie it up" or "Bopau didn't tie it fast enough." This suggests that this "natural" tendency in our children is really taught them by their parents.

Their attitude towards any sort of pretense or make believe is symbolised by the 26 reply of a small girl when I questioned the only group of children which I ever saw playing house. They were pretending to grate coconuts and the little girl said *"grease e joja,"* "this is our lie." The word *grease* is pidgin English for flattery or deceit. It has found its way into the native tongue as a deceit or lie. The little girl's answer contained a condemnation of their make believe play.

From this material it is possible to conclude that personalising the universe is 27 not inherent in child thought, but is a tendency bequeathed to him by his society. The young baby's inability to differentiate or at least to respond differentially to persons and things, is not in itself a creative tendency which makes an older child think of the moon, the sun, boats, etc., as possessed of will and emotion. These more elaborate tendencies are not spontaneous but are assisted by the language, the folk lore, the songs, the adult attitude towards children. And these were the work of poetic adult minds, not the faulty thinking of young children.

Whether or not an adult philosophical system of religion or science will appeal 28 to the child is not a function of the child mind but of the way the child is brought up. If the parents use matter of fact methods of suppression and invoke the child's size, age, physical incapacity, the child may respond with seven league boots and attendant genii, ideas drawn not out of its head, but from the folk lore which it has been taught. But if an unscientific point of view is used as a disciplinary method, as when the child tears a book and the adult says, "Don't pull the cover off that book. Poor book! How would you like to have your skin pulled off like that?" the same aged child can reply in the most superior tone, "Pooh, don't you know that books can't feel? Why, you could tear and tear and tear and it would never feel it. It's like my back when it's numb." The naturalistic approach is no less congenial to the child than the supernatural; his acceptance of one rather than of the other will depend on the way they are presented to him and the opportunities which arise for their use.

Children are not naturally religious, given over to charms, fetishes, spells, and 29 ritual. They are not natural story tellers, nor do they naturally build up imaginative edifices. They do not naturally consider the sun as a person nor draw him with a face.*

---

*In thirty thousand drawings, not one case of personalising natural phenomena or inanimate objects occurred. [Mead's note]

Their mental development in these respects is determined not by some internal necessity, but by the form of the culture in which they are brought up.

    The Manus play life gives children freedom, wonderful exercise for their bodies, 30
teaches them alertness, physical resourcefulness, physical initiative. But it gives them
no material for thought, no admired adult pattern to imitate, no hated adult pattern to
aggressively scorn, no language rich in figures of speech, no wealth of legend and folk
tale, no poetry. And the children, left to themselves, wrestle and roll—and even these
games are stimulated by passing adult interest—tumble and tussle, evolving nothing of
interest except general good spirits and quick wits. Without food for thought, or isolation, or physical inferiority to compensate for, they simply expend their boundless physical energy, and make string figures in the shade in complete boredom when they are
weary.

Questions

1. How are Manus children different from Plains Indian and Samoan children in their
   play? How does Mead explain these differences?
2. What kind of evidence does Mead present for her conclusions in paragraphs 28–31?
   Does she theorize at any point in the essay about the nature of children generally?
3. What does she mean by the word *religious* in paragraph 22 and later paragraphs?
   Does a religious attitude constitute belief in a supernatural being for Mead?
4. Is Mead critical of the upbringing of Manus children, or is she merely comparing
   their upbringing with that of other children? Does she state or imply what physical
   and mental powers are needed to make a person happy, and what kind of society she
   most and least approves? Can you tell what she values in life, or are these things impossible to determine from this chapter alone?
5. To what extent do the Manus parents follow Rousseau's precepts in *Emile?* Would
   Rousseau approve of treating children as "lords of the universe" (paragraph 21)?

Suggestions for Writing

1. Discuss the extent to which Rousseau and Mead agree on the nature of imagination
   and the role it plays in the life of children. Discuss also whether they reach similar
   or different conclusions about this role.
2. Compare an aspect of your own upbringing with that of the Manus children. Use your
   own experience to confirm, qualify, or reject an idea Mead reaches on this matter.

Additional Reading

Howard, Jane. *Margaret Mead: A Life.* New York: Simon and Schuster, 1954.
Mead, Margaret. *And Keep Your Powder Dry: An Anthropologist Looks at America.* New
    York: Morrow, 1971.
———. *Blackberry Winter: A Memoir.* New York: Morrow, 1972.
———. *Coming of Age in Samoa.* New York: Morrow, 1971.

———. *Culture and Commitment.* New York: Doubleday, 1970.
———. *Growing Up in New Guinea.* New York: Morrow, 1962.
———. *Letters from the Field: 1925–1975.* New York: Harper and Row, 1978.
———. *New Lives for Old.* New York: Morrow, 1956.
Mead, Margaret, and Rhoda Metraux. *Aspects of the Present.* New York: Morrow, 1981.
———. *A Way of Seeing.* New York: McCall, 1970.

Preparation for Life

Susan Allen Toth

Susan Allen Toth grew up in Ames, Iowa, which she describes in the first of her autobiographies, Blooming. *Her second,* Ivy Days, *describes her life at Smith College. Later Toth attended the University of California at Berkeley and the University of Minnesota, and she now teaches English at Macalester College in St. Paul, Minnesota.*

In the opening essay of Blooming, *Toth suggests how difficult it is to recall details of people, rooms, smells, things, episodes as they actually existed, and how people thought and felt. It is particularly difficult to describe the changes that have occurred in the lives of women:*

I have some of the same difficulty trying to explain to friends who did not grow up in a small Midwestern college town in the 1950s what life was like then. Those "old days" have disappeared into an irretrievable past that seems only faintly credible to those who did not live it. Does any girl today have the chance to grow up as gradually and as quietly as we did? In our particular crucible we were not seared by fierce poverty, racial tensions, drug abuse, street crime; we were cosseted, gently warmed, transmuted by slow degrees. Nonetheless we were being changed, girls into women. The kind of woman we thought we would become was what Ames, Iowa, saw as the American ideal. She shimmered in our minds, familiar but removed as the glossy cover of the Sears, Roebuck catalogue. There she rolled snowballs with two smiling red-cheeked children, or unpacked a picnic lunch on emerald grass as an Irish setter lounged nearby, or led a cherubic toddler into blue water. Her tall, handsome husband hovered close, perhaps with his hand protectively on her shoulder. Pretty and well dressed, she laughed happily into the KodaColor sunshine that flooded her future.

Toth adds that few women today "would fit into such a simple picture": "Many of us have gone through painful reassessments that have made us question the kinds of assumptions upon which we so confidently based our lives. We look to the past to discover how we got here from there." In the following later essay from Blooming, *Toth describes the jobs that prepared the adolescent girl of the 1950s for womanhood and marriage.*

"No allowance this week, Jennie, twice you didn't get your bed made," I say 1
regretfully but firmly, in my best parental voice of authority and responsibility. "I know," she answers cheerfully. "That's okay. I don't really need the money anyway." She is probably right, I think gloomily as I chalk up one more defeat for the Protestant work ethic. With two grandmothers, a weekend present-giving father, and an indulgent mother, why should she feel the need to earn money? What, besides a dog, does she want that she hasn't got? My attempts at starting Jennifer on an allowance have been a failure. Current child-care experts offered me two opinions: give money but don't require chores, because children should simply expect to help around the house anyway; give money and require chores, because children need to learn the connection between work and money. Anyone who grew up in Ames when I did would have unhesitatingly chosen the second approach. But I have become out-of-date.

In Ames everyone worked. Fathers had jobs and mothers were homemakers, 2
a word religiously observed in a town whose college was famed for its Division of Home Economics. Some mothers had outside jobs, not for pleasure but because they needed the money. Everyone knew that Mrs. McCallum clerked at the Hy Valu because her husband drank, Mrs. Olson managed the Dairy Dreme because her husband had deserted their family, my mother taught because she was a widow and had to support two daughters. A few other women, mainly faculty wives, worked even though they were securely married; but they were idiosyncratic individuals who somehow made their own rules and were not judged by ours.

As soon as I can remember, my friends and I wanted to get jobs. We looked for- 3
ward to being sixteen, the magic age when most employers would be able to put us legally on their payrolls. Until then, we had to scrabble furiously for what summer and after-school jobs we could dig up in a small town whose work force did not usually expand at the times we were available. All girls babysat. Boys mowed lawns, raked leaves, shoveled walks and delivered papers. In junior high school, we all detasseled corn in the summer. But by high school, we began to look more seriously for jobs that might "lead to something," jobs that seemed more important, jobs that offered what our high-school vocational counselor portentously called "preparation for life." As a sixteen-year-old reporter on the Ames Daily Tribune, I did a photo feature on teenagers' summer jobs, ostentatiously lugging my large black box camera around town to interview my friends. Kristy ran the elevator between the basement, first, and second floors of Younkers; Jack washed dishes at the Iowa State Union cafeteria; Emily was a carhop at the A&W Root Beer Stand; Patsy clerked at her aunt's fabric store; Charlie was cutting and hauling sod on an outlying farm. Kristy told me, confidentially, that her job was numbingly dull; Jack was planning to quit in a few weeks, when he'd saved enough for golf clubs; Emily hated the rude jibes she had to endure with her tips; Patsy didn't get along with her old-maid aunt; and Charlie said his job was about as much fun as football practice, and a lot dirtier. But we were all proud of ourselves, and the Ames

Daily Tribune *was proud too: my pictures ran on the front page, a visible testament to the way the younger generation was absorbing the values of its elders.*

    Besides the prestige that went with holding a job, a public acknowledgment 4 *that we were almost ready to enter the grown-up world, we of course wanted the money. All of us had small allowances, and we sighed together with agonized desire when we window-shopped on Saturday afternoons. Most of us schemed and planned from junior high on how to stretch our baby-sitting money, detasseling pay, and allowances into an annual first-day-of-school outfit and a formal for the Christmas Dance. In August I both sewed and plotted about how to spend my summer's accumulated earnings. At first my atlas and guide was the August issue of* Seventeen, *then, by the end of high school, the college issue of* Mademoiselle. *Thick as catalogues, bulging with advertisements, they offered page after page of tempting photographs, models I knew I'd never really resemble but whose clothes might just make me passable at a distance. Ames had never seen such exotic outfits: Bermuda shorts with raccoon jackets flung over them, blazers, Chanel suits. Eagerly I read the copy, absorbing the ease, the self-confidence the models exuded. "Jenny Blair, a senior at Southwest High, will enter Penn in the fall. Here she dashes to a tennis date in a crisp skirted outfit in white pique. Note the casual fling of her silk jacquard scarf." I didn't know anyone who had a tennis outfit. Since I didn't play tennis myself, I was able to pass over Jenny Blair without too much envy. But the next page! "Scotty Wales will party tonight in this red striped jersey two-piece pull-on outfit. Later she can wear the top with her gray flannel slacks." Scotty, who was sixteen, according to the text, looked more like twenty: smooth, sleek, gleaming red lipstick. I noted the price of the red striped wool jersey: $35. Almost half my budget of $77.40, counting the bonus I'd get from having stuck the whole detasseling season. Over many long hot afternoons, I made notes, added figures, shuffled priorities, folded back pages until my fingers were black with newsprint. Occasionally I asked my mother's advice. "That seems awfully like the striped dress you have, dear," she'd say discouragingly. Or, "That is nice, but my, it's expensive. I wouldn't spend all that money if I were you." Finally, "Maybe you'll have time to make a new dress."*

    Money, money, money. How I wanted it then, as I tried to reduce my shopping 5 *list to the size of my budget. In the end I never bought anything from the magazines anyway. Their world was too remote from mine, and I settled for what I could find on sale downtown in Ames. Years later, when I was married, I suddenly had access to a joint income that was more than enough to permit an occasional extravagance. I soon opened a charge account at Peck & Peck, where I'd vainly dreamed hours away on college afternoons. Browsing there one day, I saw a handsome plaid wool suit that cost more than I had ever paid before, and bought it. I never wore it much. It didn't matter to me like the orange print cotton dress with a tucked midriff I'd bought one fall at Younkers for $14.98. I'd tried on a whole rack that day, consulted my friends, thought my purchase over for two days; when I decided to take the orange dress home, I carefully paid out money from my small horde saved from clearing dishes at the Memorial Union, baby-sitting, and assisting at playground dramatics. I didn't have to ask my mother's permission to charge it. I wore that dress till deodorant rotted its armpits. It was a tangible proof of my earning power and my growing independence.*

Aside from basic money management, what did I actually learn from all my   6
summer and after-school jobs? Each one may have given me some small skills, but the
cumulative effect was to deepen my belief that work was the essential aspect of grown-
up life. Even now, I am sometimes filled with anxieties at the prospect of stretches of
free time. When I do not immediately rush to fill that time with work, I have to fight
off guilt, struggling mentally against a picture of a Real Grown-up shaking a finger at
me, someone with the droning voice of our high-school career counselor, but with firm
overtones of former employers, teachers, even my mother. "This," the voice beats re-
lentlessly into my ear, "is your preparation for life."

I wanted a paper route, but I baby-sat instead. Perhaps that disappointment was itself   7
a preparation for life. All during grade school I longed to deliver the afternoon Ames
Daily Tribune, but since our neighborhood had plenty of boys to do it, my applications
were always turned down. No girls were allowed to carry the more prestigious morning
Des Moines *Register*. But the undernourished *Tribune*, desperate for carriers, sometimes had to let a girl or two onto its list. My friend Shirley Conover was one of them.
Although I didn't share Shirley's passions for softball, climbing trees, and dogs, she let
me wistfully tag along many afternoons on her paper route. Making sure a *Tribune*,
neatly rolled and rubber-banded, was carefully slipped inside every front door for blocks
seemed the height of responsibility and importance. Sometimes, after careful instructions, Shirley let me take a whole block by myself. Shirley's route even carried us out
of her neighborhood, on the edge of Campustown, into strange apartment buildings,
where we crept down dark carpeted halls, and along streets where I didn't know anyone,
up long sidewalks guarded by dogs, onto screened porches where the sound of an opening door made me jump. I felt as though we were being given privileged glimpses into
unknown lives. The money, Shirley told me proudly, wasn't as much as her brother
made from the *Register*, but it was lots more than she got baby-sitting. And it sure was
lots more fun.

All girls in Ames, even Shirley, baby-sat. When we were eleven or twelve, old   8
enough for our mothers to approve our staying out late at night, we were expected to
accept baby-sitting jobs eagerly. Although I had no younger brothers or sisters, and
knew nothing about infants or even toddlers, grown-ups evidently assumed that the
mere fact of my sex qualified me to care for their children. They also assumed I wanted
to. I had, in truth, no particular love for babies or young children, a passion I only later
acquired, and then selectively, when I had my own child. Despite my popularity as a sitter, which was probably based mostly on my proximity, I suspect I had no particular talent either. Even today, I cannot quiet crying babies, and small children do not rush to
sit in my lap. But since baby-sitting was often the only available money-making opportunity for me, I naturally seized it. Between my sister and me, the Allen girls had a
monopoly for years on Oakland Street and Franklin Avenue.

Perhaps I felt inadequate as a baby-sitter because I was haunted by the memory   9
of Marcia Fitzpatrick. When I was very young, she had been my favorite sitter, one I
loved so much I used to beg my mother, "Can't you go out tonight, Mommy? Couldn't
you get Marcia Fitzpatrick to come?" My mother tells me I even offered to take money
from my piggy bank to pay for Marcia's visits. Although I barely remember how she
looked, other than a kind and friendly face, what really enthralled me about Marcia was

her storytelling. She had a genius for making up stories about a character called Snoopy Mouse, who was often threatened by a clever but villainous Reddy Fox, and her "Snoopy stories," as we called them, were long, inventive, and exciting. My mother used to urge Marcia to write them down, but, shy and self-effacing, she always blushed and shook her head. When I was ten or eleven, old enough myself to baby-sit, I tried to recreate her marvelous stories, vaguely recalling stray incidents, shamelessly plagiarizing what I could, haphazardly adding from my own small store of imaginative power. I felt I was trying to carry on Marcia's tradition, but with woeful inadequacy. "Give us another Snoopy story!" My little charges would ask, and my heart would sink. Even my own attention would wander from my threadbare plottings, and I would find myself repeating, adding another chase or explosion, abruptly ending when I was too weary to carry on.

When I finally realized that I was apt to be a sitter for at least several years, I 10 decided that I should approach the job in a more organized fashion. If all my resources were my small cache of patched-up Snoopy stories, I would run out quickly. So, adapting an idea from some project in my Camp Fire book, I made a baby-sitting box. With a small capital from my proceeds, I invested in several dime-store toys, tiny cars, inch-long dolls, rubber ball, new crayons, colored paper, blunt scissors, paste, a few cheap Golden Books. As part of my organization, I painstakingly lettered a series of information blanks, asking my employer-parents to list their telephone number, name of family doctor, and so on. Armed with this box, I marched off to my assignments feeling somehow that I was prepared, not, perhaps, a Marcia Fitzpatrick, but at least a girl who looked as though she knew what she were doing. The mere appearance of professionalism, I learned early in my work experience, was sometimes good enough.

Even with my baby-sitting box, however, I had my problems. Having been 11 gently raised by my mother, but having fought hand-to-hand battles with my older sister, I was never quite sure how to discipline small children. Should I coax or spank? I myself had almost never been spanked, and it seemed sadistic. Scolding, yelling, screaming didn't work. Other than threatening early bedtime, which was useless in the middle of the afternoon, I had to resort to pleading and bribes. This damaged my self-respect and also led me into playing many unwanted games of tag, hopscotch, or ring-around-the-rosy, most of which seemed both boring and beneath my dignity, and all of which I had to be careful to let my charges win.

I both feared and longed for the time when the children would go to bed. When 12 the house was quiet at last, I would get to explore, wandering among rooms furnished differently from ours at home, admiring velvet sofas or shell collections or silver tea services. Though I seldom touched anything I shouldn't, I felt a little like a thief. Even a promised snack in the refrigerator tasted like forbidden fruit. Mostly, though, I delved into libraries. At the Kendalls' I could always count on a collection of *Reader's Digests* and condensed *Reader's Digest* books, neither of which my mother ever bought. After avidly devouring all the true adventures, jokes, and poignant spiritual confessions in the *Digest*, I palpitated through the condensations of *Mrs. Mike, Anna and the King of Siam*, and dozens of other popular novels that Mrs. Erhard at the Ames Public Library would not yet let me check out. A night at the Smiths' was always a feast of romance too, with heaps of old *Ladies Home Journals, Woman's Home Companions, Coronets, McCall's*, stashed in a basement corner where I soon discovered them. I was fascinated by the marriage-counseling articles, never really believing that this marriage could be saved until the absolute last minute, and I thrived on the fiction. While movies formed many of my images of love and marriage, the stories in *McCall's* and the *Journal* confirmed them. Would a small-town girl (like me) be happy in a big city (no) until she met a lonely, sandy-haired, cheerful young man who turned out to be from a town near hers? (Well . . .) Would they fall in love? (Yes.) Would they return to Rock's Corners? (Yes, yes.) Would he be the town's new pharmacist, and would she love raising a houseful of children? (Yes, yes, yes.) At the end of such stories I tried not to compare the heroines' obvious virtues, their sweetness, good temper, and love of children, with my own irritation as I had finally salted away a runny-nosed little Smith in his rather smelly crib. One night, just after I had closed a *Journal* with a sigh of satisfaction, still blissfully seeing myself in the arms of my childhood sweetheart, who had forgiven me and taken me back after I had gone to the country-club dance with a black-haired, flirtatious, and dangerous young man who kept a pocket flask in his glove compartment, I heard little Tommy Smith cry. Dashed back to earth, I plodded dutifully up the stairs to his room. There he sat in his crib, wide awake, silent now, looking rather proudly at the corner of his crib. There, compact and irrefutable, was a large brown glob. It was several moments before I realized, with horrified amazement, that it was . . . "B.M.," said Tommy proudly. I ran for the bathroom and a piece of toilet paper, gingerly wrapping the glob for deposit and then with a fresh piece scrubbing away at the brown smear on the sheet. I felt shaken. Somehow I could not find a bridge between the world I had just left between those glossy magazine covers and the world of Tommy's poop.

My fear at the children's bedtime was simply that of being in a strange house 13 after dark. Closely nurtured, sheltered by my mother in the safest of homes, I was ill prepared for lurking dangers beyond it. Since Ames had a minuscule record of murders and molestations, I do not know what I was afraid of, though I could probably guess. All I knew was that I was scared of noises and of uncurtained windows, black glass that reflected back my own image but did not permit me to see what was outdoors. I wondered who might be hiding in the backyard, looking in. As I lay curled on the sofa, every gurgle of a water heater or click of a refrigerator made me jump. In one new house, heated by a fancy arrangement of hot-water pipes running along the walls, I was driven into near-terror by the constantly changing liquid murmurs. At most houses, though, I eventually drifted into a groggy somnolence, ready to leap up when I heard the front door open. Though parents assured me I should go to sleep when they stayed out late, I never felt quite right about leaving my job unattended. Baby-sitting was an uneasy business.

Besides baby-sitting, young girls in Ames could sometimes get part-time jobs 14 housecleaning, another skill most grown-ups assumed came with gender. Most grownups, not all. My first house-cleaning job was with an exception, old Mrs. Werdle, a crotchety widow who lived next door to one of Mother's friends. This friend, a kindly neighbor, knew Mrs. Werdle, crippled from arthritis and rheumatism, badly needed help. She called my mother, who asked me, and next Saturday, cheerful and willing, I arrived at the Werdle house. My cheerfulness soon waned. Old Mrs. Werdle, it seemed, did not trust me. She didn't think I knew how to vacuum or dust properly, and she wanted to be sure I didn't cheat her out of her twenty-five cents an hour. Much of that unpleasant morning has disappeared, but I still can see myself, crouched on hands and knees, washing the floor, while Mrs. Werdle sat a few inches behind me, doubled over on a small stool, peering over my shoulder to make sure I scrubbed all the way into the corners. I don't think I minded the hard work, the dark and musty house, or even Mrs. Werdle's snappish tongue, as much as I was wounded by her assumption that I didn't know how to work. "A good hard worker" was a phrase of highest approbation in Ames, and I knew I was one. I was so angry with Mrs. Werdle that I refused to return to her house. Even baby-sitting held less indignity.

Some time after the Werdle incident, my mother asked me if I would consider 15 one more cleaning job. A colleague of hers, a bachelor who sometimes took Mother to an occasional party, needed a replacement for his cleaning lady for a few weeks. He would pay fifty cents an hour. And, my mother added, he would be at work himself while I cleaned; I'd have the apartment to myself. I multiplied fifty cents quickly several times and accepted. Work conditions seemed ideal, and in fact they were: privacy, a chance to work at my own pace, good pay. The only problem with cleaning for Mr. Sanders was that I couldn't find anything to clean. A meticulous man, he kept his apartment so tidy, dusted, and swept that I felt real frustration when I vacuumed. I couldn't tell afterward what I had done except by watching the fine marks the vacuum wheels left on the carpet. If I managed to find a stray crumb under a sofa pillow, I was delighted. In the bathroom Mr. Sanders had showed me how to use Jonny Mops, a refinement we didn't have at home. But while I dutifully scrubbed around the toilet bowl, I never found a ring to erase or a spot to remove. Though Mr. Sanders seemed pleased with my work, I was relieved when his cleaning lady returned from vacation. I was tired of creeping carefully backward out his door so I wouldn't disturb the telltale vacuum wheel marks on the floor. They were, I felt, the only sign I had been there at all.

At about twelve or thirteen, I was old enough for a uniform. That was one of 16 the few rewards of clearing dishes from the Grill at the Iowa State Memorial Union. In summer not many college students used this large dining room that sprawled like an underground auditorium in a windowless basement. Jammed full of people during the school year, the heavy dark oak tables and chairs were mostly empty now, a sea of shiny surfaces stretching across the floor. Often I was the only clearing girl on duty in the deserted room, watching from a distance until two or three girls scraped their chairs back, strolled out the door, and left their coffee cups and pie saucers waiting for me. I was supposed to carry the dishes to the kitchen and wipe off the tables with a greasy rag, whose mildewy, sour smell can still waft acridly under my nose if I close my eyes and pretend I'm wearing my yellow cotton uniform and dirty white apron. The Union allowed only one apron a day.

Working at the Union made me realize how lonely you feel when you are invisi- 17 ble on the job. Sometimes older high-school kids I recognized wandered into the Grill for a Coke or a hamburger, but I couldn't go over and talk to them. Once in a while someone would nod at me and wave, and from my corner by the dishtrays I nodded and waved back. The supervisor was very firm about clearing girls mixing with the customers. I was often bored, too, waiting idly for some table to empty. Late in the afternoon, when I often worked, I would sometimes sneak a quarter into the jukebox so I could listen to music, trying to stay near the machine till my three records had ended, hoping the supervisor wouldn't suddenly march through the Grill and notice an uncleared table at the other end. Slowly wiping down the dark varnished surfaces, watching my rag make greasy circles, I swayed a little in time to the music. I always played mildly sad love songs, Sinatra, Perry Como, the Four Aces, so I could pretend the echoing Grill was just a garden in the rain, a dance floor where someone was playing the Beguine, a mountain top where love was a many-splendored thing. Anonymous in my uniform, moving around the quiet room, I felt as though I were an unseen ghost in an echoing empty space. I was living in the midst of the world of college, but the world had vanished. Leaving this cave, with its heavy oak furniture and gleaming dark surfaces, and emerging into the late-afternoon sunlight, I always experienced a kind of time warp. I was suddenly free and thirteen again, stretching cramped muscles, racing home happily on my bicycle to dinner and a movie with my girlfriends.

My only excitement at the Grill came from foreign students. By the 1950s, 18 many young men from developing or war-torn countries were drawn to Iowa State to study agriculture, industrial arts, or engineering. Lonely and at loose ends in the summer, they would often congregate in the Grill for card games and company. Unlike the regular Iowa State men, who ignored me, the Indians or Germans or Filipinos tried to flirt with me in their broken English, rapidly commenting in their own language, poking each other if they thought someone had gotten a response. My mother had taught me never to strike up conversations with strange men, and I usually confined myself to polite smiles and shakes of the head. Eventually they would give up and go back to cards, only glancing occasionally in my direction. After they had left, I would sometimes find a few nickels and dimes scattered for me under their plates. Those were the only tips I ever got.

One summer clearing tables at the Grill was enough to convince me that I 19 needed another job. Stacking dishes, I knew, wasn't going to lead to anything; I should be exercising my talents, such as they were. So I was delighted to be asked to serve as assistant to the Ames Playground Drama Director, who happened to be a neighbor, friend and faculty colleague of my mother's. A vivacious, assertive woman who frightened me a little by her sheer energy and organization, Dorothy Mae Frankel would certainly teach me something.

What I learned that summer may have been, in retrospect, preparation for cer- 20 tain aspects of college teaching: the ability to perform under unfavorable conditions, the instant tailoring of material to fit the audience, the necessity to keep going no matter what. Every weekday noon, just as the sun shone hottest, Mrs. Frankel honked her car outside my door. Sleepy from the heat, thinking longingly of our cool dark basement with its old rocking chair and a pile of books, I hurried out, slid gingerly across the hot plastic seat, and squinted my eyes as we barreled toward the concrete and brown grass of the city playgrounds. Mrs. Frankel crisply outlined our schedule for the afternoon: Whittier, Welch, a longer stop at Roosevelt.

When we arrived at the first playground, its harried director, relieved to see us, 21 blew long blasts on her whistle to assemble the children in whatever shade we could find. Hurrying behind Mrs. Frankel, I lugged with me a bulging laundry basket filled with old costumes and a few props, a fancier version of a "dress-up box" intended to keep some of the smaller children amused. Older children could be given scripts, dittoed poems, or short stories to act out. But first they all needed to be warmed up, and I was the crowd-pleaser. After everyone had more or less quieted down, settling haphazardly into the dirt or forming into rows under the nudging of the playground director, I stepped determinedly forward. Mrs. Frankel had taught me a simple narrative, "Bear

Hunt," with sounds and gestures, about an Indian, a journey, his fright and his sudden retreat. It must be an old camp favorite, and any summer now I expect Jennifer to come home with her version of it. The trick was to get the crowd of restless children to copy my actions, join in, and then, reversing the narrative, speed up as fast as possible for the Indian's return trip. This led to a wonderful hullabaloo of sounds, hands drumming on knees, growls, screams, general shouting and hallooing, ending in a hysterical collapse of giggles, shoving, and war whoops. If I had done well, hurrying fast enough to get everyone thoroughly excited, Mrs. Frankel waited a few moments and then told me to do it once more, "now that everyone's got it." If the group was quick and lively, I improvised and added a little new material, evoking squeals of glee. By this time our audience was hooked. Hoarse but game, I began beating on my knees once more. After three playgrounds, and eight or nine Bear Hunts, I was exhausted. Bear Hunts rang in my head at night. But I had done them well, Mrs. Frankel assured me, and I could do them again tomorrow at a new set of playgrounds.

Following the Bear Hunt, Mrs. Frankel divided the children into groups for in- 22 stantaneous versions of "Hansel and Gretel," "Rumpelstiltskin," or improvised plays based on the costume basket. If too many children had drifted away, we would combine into one group, and I took some of the parts myself. Then Mrs. Frankel directed me too, which, I felt, threatened my shaky position of authority, but I knew we had to keep the show going. So I only grumbled inwardly, wrapped an old velvet skirt over my head, and cackled, as directed, like a witch or a wicked stepmother. It might be humiliating, but it would pass the time: half an hour more, and we could all go home.

Promoting Bear Hunts to hot, restless children was only one of the ways I 23 learned about salesmanship, which I grew up intuitively recognizing as the backbone of the Ames work ethic. Selling a product and selling yourself were inextricable. My earliest lesson in this axiom was during the annual drive to sell Camp Fire candy. Even as a young Bluebird, I was eligible to peddle my boxes of candy at fifty cents a box, and I responded eagerly to the challenge. Whoever sold the most boxes would be awarded a free week at Camp Hantesa, a resident camp on the Des Moines River, with real cabins, tents, and teepees. I was beside myself with anxiety and ambition. Most of my friends were Camp Fire Girls too, and they had first dibs on their own neighborhoods. That didn't leave much free territory, though I was out knocking on doors the very afternoon the sales sheets were distributed. After covering a mile around our house, and often discovering a particular block had been picked clean by some nearby Camp Fire Girl, I had a brilliant idea. I shared it with no one but my mother, who could be trusted to keep it safe from my rivals. I would peddle my candy in Pammel Court.

Pammel Court, which still stands amazingly more or less intact, was a cluster 24 of prefabricated metal buildings hastily thrown up at the edge of the Iowa State campus after World War II to house the flood of returning veterans and their families. "Married student housing" is a dingy-sounding phrase, but it was almost too glamorous a description for Pammel Court. The rows of silver barracks looked like a prison camp, only it lacked barbed wire and guards. In summer, the corrugated roofs baked their inhabitants like ovens; in winter, wind blew through the uninsulated walls lined with cardboard. Tiny squares of worn grass were sometimes cultivated into foot-long gardens, but mainly children played in the Pammel streets, which were dirt tracks running between the barracks, or in a small playground somewhere in the middle of the complex. Years later, when I was older, I was told that Pammel residents had a wonderful community spirit, but when I was only ten, all I could see were battered screens, running noses, tiny rooms, and tired-looking women at the door.

Pammel Court, however, had two distinct advantages for the candy-seller: a 25 compact population and plenty of mothers. I knew that I could cover many more families in an afternoon at Pammel than I could by trudging up long sidewalks or crossing endless lawns. The women who opened their plastic storm doors to me in Pammel were young enough to remember their own Camp Fire days, sympathetic to a friendly child, ready with a smile if not always with money. So I filled my old red wagon with boxes of candy, asked my mother to drive me to the entrance, and began a long tour of Pammel Court, dragging the wagon behind me. My only difficulty was in remembering which rows I'd already traveled, since they all looked alike. The candy sold quickly. When my wagon was empty, I took future orders, noting names and addresses on my sales sheet. Though it seems to me I spent weeks and weeks in Pammel, feeling the hot sun beat down on my unshaded back, hearing babies crying from inside the dark little rooms, kicking the early-autumn dust with my sneakers, it was probably only several afternoons after school. When I had filled several sheets with orders, I was exhausted, both from my long tramps around Pammel and from the energy my salesmanship required, the cheerful smile, polite inquiry, eagerness. My list was impressive, though, and I dreamed of walking up to the podium at the annual Camp Fire Fair, where awards would be announced.

But I didn't win a prize. Worn out from my exertions, perhaps susceptible to 26 the first flu bugs of the oncoming winter, I got sick. I had to stay in bed for days, and even when I got up again, Mother wouldn't let me out of the house for long. Home from school, I collapsed in a tired little heap on my bed; outside the weather had changed, the wind howled, rain poured. No trips to Pammel Court. When the last call went out to our Camp Fire troop for ordering boxes from the supplier, I wasn't there to hear it. After I was well again, a girlfriend and I practiced bedrolls so we could do a team demonstration at the Camp Fire Fair. Mother said she thought she could afford to send me to Camp Hantesa for a week anyway. The next year I didn't try to sell much candy, and I never went back to Pammel Court. I was afraid some of the women whose orders had never arrived might remember me and ask what had happened.

I didn't give up the idea of selling, however, since I could tell I had a certain 27 persuasive skill. Perhaps what I needed was a more secure home base, I thought, none of this door-to-door stuff. Somehow I learned that the supermarket across from Welch Junior High needed an after-school salesgirl in its bakery department, and I applied. Tying on a white apron, cleaner than the one I'd worn at the Union Grill, I presided over a small corner of the store, tucked behind the checkout stands, just inside the large plate-glass window that faced Welch School. There I could sit on the window ledge, looking onto the sidewalk and playgrounds, or I could burrow back against the wall to read or do homework on a small stool. It was like having a window on the world, which passed me by a few inches away. My friends hammered on the double-paned glass, made funny faces, tried to shout through; but, afraid to break the silence of the store, I only gestured back. I had withdrawn into a kind of cocoon, sweet and sticky, with only the buzz of shoppers and the rattle of shopping carts for company. For two hours all I said, like a recording, was "May I help you?" "Here you are." "Thank you."

Few customers drifted to my corner of the Hy-Valu, since the bakery depart- 28 ment was small, its goods delivered twice a week and often stale. Sometimes the same decorated cake would wait in the case from one Monday to the next. After four or five days, I was allowed to label items "day old" and sell them at half price. Uneasy at this shady practice, I often whispered advice across the counter: "I'd skip the bismarcks today," or "I think those cookies have been around a while." I alerted the pleasant-looking customers, and let unpleasant ones take their chances. Mostly I sat, read, ate glazed doughnuts and tried to stay awake. At least when I was bored at the Union Grill, I could move around, wiping tables or adjusting salt shakers. Here I had no space, just a window ledge, a stool, and hot afternoon sun warming my back through the window. When I had cleaned empty trays, stacked rows of cookies more artistically, shooed stray flies out of the case, and dusted the countertop, I had nothing else to do. Eventually the boredom, sleepiness, and general heaviness of the job weighed me down so much I quit. I had gained five pounds.

If drowsing my way through a dull afternoon was not my idea of a good job, 29 neither was hard physical labor. For two summers, at thirteen and fourteen, when I was too young to do anything else, I detasseled corn, a job that lasted only three or four weeks, but one so strenuous and numbingly exhausting that it later seemed to have stretched over the whole summer.

During that brief time, hordes of teen-agers were hauled into the local seed 30 farms, where half- or quarter-mile rows of corn alternated, one male row to four female rows. In order for the plants to crossbreed correctly, the tassels had to be removed from the female cornstalks. A swift tug at the tall silky stem, a toss to the ground, another tug at the next tassel. Repetitive, numbing work, but it was good money. White's Hybrid Seed Farms, the biggest employer, offered a bonus: fifty cents an hour if you quit, but sixty-five if you stuck the whole season. Both summers I worked to what I thought was the limit of my endurance to earn that fifteen-cent-an-hour bonus.

Signing up for a detasseling crew didn't take much: a phone call, then a written 31 statement of age, address, and height. A few very tall girls were put into special foot crews, but most of us were automatically assigned to machines. No boys worked on machines; we understood that it was tougher to do the work on foot. A day detasseling began at six A.M., when my alarm went off, so I could be dressed and waiting at the corner gas station by seven for a pickup truck. The driver didn't wait; he had to gather teen-age girls all over Ames. We all wore varieties of the same uniform: swimming suits, over which we pulled jeans or shorts, shirts, and large floppy hats. Early mornings in the field were cool and dewy, and we'd shiver a little as the wet stalks brushed our thighs. But by midday we'd be so hot and sweaty that we'd gratefully peel down as far as possible, hosing each other off in the farmyard where we took our lunch break. Now we huddled in the truck, keeping out of the cold breeze that whipped our faces if we stood up too far. I loved the ride into the country, jouncing in the box, watching the morning brighten on the fields around us. I wished we could just keep driving.

Once the truck dropped us in the White Farms parking lot, we waited for other 32 trucks or cars, bringing girls from outlying farms or from small towns farther away. On the first day we were quickly divided into crews and assigned to machines. We would keep the same driver, always a man, for the whole season. He was our field boss, who reported if we slacked off or caused trouble, who could queer our bonus, who reigned an absolute dictator from his metal seat high above us. One lucky crew drew Ben Bowie, a handsome older Ames High boy. At lunchtime one of my friends on Ben's machine would always tell me whom he'd flirted with that day. My crew, however, got Pancho, so christened on our first day by someone who was struck by his fat red face under an enormous Mexican sombrero. He was much older, perhaps in his twenties, crude and ignorant, as well as paunchy. We had to humor him constantly, laughing at his dirty stories, many of which I didn't understand, answering his questions, smiling pleasantly. Fortunately we couldn't hear him often over the roar of the machine. If only, I thought, I could have gotten Ben Bowie.

Describing a detasseling machine to a college roommate was once so difficult 33 I was finally reduced to drawing a picture of a sort of mechanical spider. I think of that picture now, seeing Pancho as the two beady eyes at the spider's head. From a tractorlike seat, Pancho drove a machine that consisted of an engine, with two platforms on each side of it, and four branching metal arms that were suspended from the center at distances adjusted to the corn rows, each with its own platform. We girls stood on the platforms, leaning over metal encircling rods that prevented us from falling, and pulled the tassels from the cornstalks as the machine huffed along. Pancho was supposed to cover a certain amount of territory each day, and he set the speed we had to follow. Relentlessly, inexorably, the machine moved down the rows, while we plucked, yanked, pulled. If Pancho speeded up too much, we started to miss stalks, and then he swore loudly, stopped the machine, and waited for us to dismount, hurry back on foot, and get the missed tassels. He slowed then for a while, but before long he speeded up again. Of course he couldn't always see every tassel, or watch all of us at once, and sometimes we let a tassel slip by unnoticed. I was too squeamish to grasp the stalks that were covered with insects, or the ones distorted by smut, a fungus that makes the stalk swell and rot. If Pancho caught me shirking a bloated stalk, he shouted, stopped the machine, and I angrily stomped down the row, grabbed the stalk by its roots, and just pulled the whole plant out. As long as the tassel wasn't going to pollinate, Pancho didn't care. Otherwise the machine didn't stop until we'd reached the end of a half-mile row. Then we dismounted, drank from the lukewarm cooler of water strapped to the machine, stretched our cramped muscles, applied more suntan lotion, and climbed wearily back on board for another row.

Row breaks and lunchtime were our only real chances for conversation, though 34 you could sometimes shout to the girl standing on the platform next to you. At lunchtime we had chatted briefly while eating our gooey peanut-butter or soggy creamcheese sandwiches, splashing in the hose, or stretching prone on the green mown grass of the Whites' front yard. I remember broken bits of talk with other girls on my machine as part of my education. Usually three or four were girls I didn't know, from farms or small towns I never visited, girls who seemed older, with bigger busts, redder lipstick, real swearwords. They often understood Pancho's dirty jokes and could top them. One girl even told me she thought Pancho was "kind of cute." These girls talked of dances, beer, cruising, necking. They were tough, unafraid of smut, mildew, or insects; grasping an infected stalk firmly, they'd simply wipe their slimy hands on their shorts. "For God's sake," one called after me as I ran back to bend over a mildewed stalk, "what the hell are you scared of? Them things won't bite you." Pancho grinned in approval. "You know," he said several times a day, usually when we were slowly rolling back and forth to different fields, "you Ames kids are sure picky. Real snotty. Hey, Sue! Emily! Whaddya think? Are all Ames girls snotty?" My friend Emily and I looked at each other, reddened, and were silent. The other girls laughed. One, older at fifteen than I'd be at twenty, was engaged, she said, to a man who was taking over his father's farm soon. Then they'd get married. She didn't own a swimsuit, so when the sun glared directly overhead, she stripped off her shirt to a dingy gray cotton bra, sagging from the weight of her heavy breasts. It was so thick and laced with elastic that it hid her body better than a swimsuit might. Even Pancho, after a few wolf whistles and lewd remarks, which she ignored, didn't seem to find the sight very exciting and soon turned his attention to someone else. I was embarrassed for her, and glad that she pulled her shirt on again when the machine turned onto the road to head back to the farm at the end of the day.

Piling into our pickup truck, carrying our wadded clothes and lunchpails, we 35 lay back for the hot, dusty trip home. After being dropped off, I dragged myself the few blocks to my house, and a long tepid bath. Dirt caked the sides of the tub. After dinner I was too tired to go out, even to a movie. Falling into bed like a stone, my reddened back stinging, my face flushed from too much sun, I tried to think of the wonderful tan I'd have, the money I'd make if I stuck the whole season. I was asleep even before it got dark outside.

After two seasons of detasseling, I was through. I had earned my bonus and a 36 sense of survival with it. Now finally old enough for real summer jobs, I wanted glamour. Aided by persistence, luck, and perhaps a mention of my father, whom he said he'd known, I persuaded the general manager of the college radio and television station to hire me at fifteen as a courier and part-time receptionist. As courier, I'd carry mail back and forth from the television station to the third story of the nearby communications building. As receptionist, I'd answer the phone and type simple letters for secretaries who were taking vacations. I was thrilled. To work inside WOI-TV! Mingle with celebrities! Watch live shows! Every day I dressed carefully, my prettiest circle skirts, fresh ribbons around my ponytail. Every day something magical might happen, though I wasn't certain exactly what. Being so close to the entertainment industry, who could tell?

What I mainly saw, however, were closed doors. No one was allowed into a stu- 37 dio when a show was on. What I heard were tired, irritable voices, hassling over timing, guests, and the deadline of another show tomorrow. I particularly admired a young director from Chicago, Len Finkelstein, who came to WOI-TV that summer and left the next year; black-haired, sharp-nosed, and wiry, he snapped out commands to everyone around him, including the old-timers who had been with the station since television came to Ames. They didn't much like his arrogance, I could see, but he had a convincing big-city air about him: "We did it that way in Chicago," he'd say, or "Ed Murrow once told me, confidentially, of course . . ." Sometimes he wandered into the cubicle where pretty Liz Woods perched, when she wasn't planning her morning women's show. "Liz," he crooned, "geez, I miss that city so much. How do you all *stand* it here? I mean, year after year?" She laughed and their voices sank to a low murmur I couldn't hear.

Beauty, polish, and self-confidence floated around Liz like an expensive per- 38 fume. All the men in the station scrambled after her, finding excuses to sit on her desk, ask her if she wanted coffee, offer to run her home. She was careless of them; of her desk, piled high with mail and packages; of her expensive wardrobe, which even I could tell hadn't been bought in Ames. Once in the women's room, where Liz changed clothes, leaving some on hangers, others strewn on the floor, I saw in a corner a bundle that looked familiar. I unrolled it. It was a matching cashmere skirt-and-sweater set, in a lovely powder blue, which I'd admired the previous week as Liz had sailed around the offices, her hand patting her slim hips. I had never owned a cashmere sweater. This one had a smear of makeup on it now, as did the soiled skirt. They lay in the corner, waiting for someone, not Liz, to take them to the cleaners or perhaps even give them up for good. I carefully smoothed and folded them and put them back in the corner. When I quit my job a month later, they were still there. As I think now of my brief introduction to the mystique of television, my first image is a dirty, crumpled cashmere sweater.

I didn't quit WOI because I didn't like my job, but because I got one better. For 39 several years, probably since I was ten or eleven, I had timidly knocked on the glass door of the Ames *Daily Tribune*'s publisher, an old man with a sharp wit, good business sense, and a fondness for enterprise in young people. He laughed at first when I explained I wanted to work on the newspaper, I was going to be a reporter someday, I could write well already, I was editing the junior-high paper. But he treated me seriously too, listened to my whole application, then patted me on the shoulder as he dismissed me. "Come back in a year or two," he said, "and we'll see." I kept coming back, he was encouraging but noncommittal, until that summer I was fifteen. Then suddenly the society editor got sick and needed an operation. Mr. Skaggs called my mother. Would I like to come to work as soon as possible, just until the society editor got back? She was sure I would, I had a talk with the station manager next day, and I left for the *Tribune* offices the following morning.

From that summer on, all the way through college, I spent my summers filling 40 vacation spots and doing odd jobs at the *Tribune*. My first editor, Clarence, a gentle, quiet man, spoiled me; pleased at what he kindly said was my quickness and rapid progress, he taught me a few basics about type, headlines, and layout and then left me to do what I wanted. As long as I clocked forty hours a week, I could go out evenings on a feature assignment, come in late next morning, leave early in the afternoon. He encouraged and praised me. The second editor, Rob, who arrived my second year, was a much younger and tenser man, who thought I had become an office pet; he wanted me to go back and start from the ground up. I learned from both of them, though not always what they thought they were teaching me. Of course I acquired some basic journalistic skills, memorizing the right questions, compiling data, editing and proofing, juggling headlines. I also began to understand for the first time how one could be passionately committed to a job well done. Most of the day our small newsroom was in chaos, five of us elbow-to-elbow, phones ringing, old typewriters clacking, doors constantly swinging open to the business office on one side, the back room and presses on the other. But when the first paper rolled off the presses, and our editor carried in five copies and flung them down on the one big desk we all shared, suddenly the room was silent. Except for the flap of turning pages, small grunts of approval and whispers of dismay, we were all studying our work, adjusting our expectations to results, quietly noting what we might do differently next time. I always felt a certain amazement at seeing a whole paper, neat and finished, emerge from our slapdash, frantic efforts of the hours before. There it was until tomorrow.

Although moving relentlessly down a row of corn on a detasseling machine 41 held its own tension, until my summers on the *Tribune* I never really understood what working under pressure meant. Despite my love for the work, that pressure may be the main reason I eventually decided newspaper life wasn't for me. At first I mostly worried about typing. Just before I came to the *Tribune,* I bought a typing book and managed to learn the keyboard. But faced with a crotchety, oversized machine, and a story to be retyped within an hour, I quickly had to get a steady rhythm, and get it fast. As work piled up on my share of the desk, I was constantly aware of the huge clock on the wall above us, its minute hand sweeping by. If I looked too long at it, it mesmerized me, until someone else at the desk poked me. Then I'd snap back to attention, and bury myself in my rewrites again. I had always been a perfectionist in my writing, toying with my English essays, adding flourishes to my poems, rewriting and finally printing them all carefully by hand. Now I had to pick words quickly, not always wait for the right ones to appear, ignore unanswered questions if I couldn't find solutions right away, read quickly and make as few corrections as possible. When my galleys came back from the shop, I could sometimes sweet-talk Harley, the gray-haired, grandfatherly typesetter who liked me, into making a few cosmetic changes, but if Rob, the editor, caught me, he was furious. "Harley's got other things to do than pretty up your prose," he'd say. "Get your picture caption on my desk right now and let that story go." When I left the office in the afternoon, I was exhausted, my stomach in knots, my shoulders tight from having hunched over my typewriter.

Much of the fun of my job, aside from the daily delirious pleasure of seeing my 42 writing, and sometimes my by-line, in print, came from faking a certain professionalism. From my first summer, when I filled the women's page with recipes (when I didn't cook), articles on child care (when I didn't have a child), fashion (when I read only *Seventeen*), and marriage (what I knew least of all), I took great glee in posing as a grownup who was an expert in all these matters. Scissoring out syndicated columns, clipping from the wire service, and even fabricating some stories myself, I applied what I thought was my own superior intelligence and common sense. One of my mother's friends, upon hearing of my new job, laughed and said to me, "Oh, don't worry, Susan, you'll do fine. Nobody reads the women's page anyway." I was a little hurt, but I knew she wasn't entirely right. Once in a while a reader would call in to complain that I'd missed a typesetting error, slipping two cups of salt into a recipe instead of two tablespoons. And all the women in outlying small towns read their local "correspondence columns," filled with items about baby showers, bridge clubs, out-of-town visitors, and birthdays.

Families, down to the last cousin, always read the detailed wedding stories it 43 was then the *Tribune*'s principle to print in full: I had to ascertain whether the soloist sang "I Love You Truly" or "The Voice That Breath'd o'er Eden," if the bride wore pearls that were a gift of the groom, whether she carried a bouquet of stephanotis or white roses, the length of her veil and the style of her bridesmaids' gowns, who cut the cake, what the bride wore as a going-away outfit. Most of these details I merely copied from the *Tribune*'s standard wedding form, but sometimes deciphering handwriting or unscrambling description led me into omissions or vague generalities: "The bride, in a white scoop-necked gown, wore pearls." Then I might have to confront a critical mother, who had driven all the way from a little town an hour away, storming into the newsroom, demanding to see the Society Editor, and blinking, open-mouthed, at a fifteen-year-old with intense self-possession that I fought hard to keep from slipping. I wore heavy earrings in those days to balance the flippancy of my ponytail. With my swishing crinolines and round-collared blouses, and a furious blush when I was upset, I must have been a strange sight in that clacking, ringing, little newsroom. If I couldn't soothe my angry critic, Rob usually stepped in; I was always surprised at the iron quality he could suddenly assume. After the mother had left, he would turn to me, the iron only slightly softened, and snap, "Next time, Allen, get it right." Years later, when I was married in Ames, I made sure the organist played Handel, the wedding cake was chocolate, and nobody gave me pearls.

So I knew I had an audience, even if it wasn't my mother's friends. Most of 44 them depended for news on the Des Moines paper and claimed they only read the *Trib* for grocery ads. "Too big to line your drawers and too small to wrap the garbage in," wisecracked our neighbor Mr. Ball. I had the freedom to make mistakes without fearing that I would damage either my or the *Tribune*'s reputation forever.

Since I was so young, the other reporters and even the subjects I was some- 45 times sent to interview took an amused interest in me and offered me all the help I wanted. When my job eventually involved filling any gap or need in the editorial department, I found myself by turns society editor, religion editor, farm editor, and general reporter. The only department no one trusted me with, quite rightly, was sports. As farm editor for three weeks the summer I was sixteen, I only had to copy-edit news releases and prepare the layout of the weekly farm page, which my editor supervised closely. But I did have to make several trips into the country, nervously driving the *Tribune* staff car, which, since I barely knew how to shift, I usually kept in first or second gear. My most important job was to interview the Mystery Farm of the Week. An aerial photographer was hired to zoom over surrounding farms and snap pictures, one of which appeared on Monday, with a Mystery Caption. Readers were invited to send in their guesses about whose farm it was. On Friday, farm-page day, the *Tribune* ran a long feature, with lots of pictures, about the family who lived there. It was my job to do the feature.

On my first visit to a Mystery Farm, I tried to do it alone. Now sixteen, I wanted 46 to carry off my job like a pro. Since I constantly ground the old Plymouth's gears and killed its engine at every stop sign, I was already shaken by the time I crawled up the long dirt drive to the Janacek farm. Once safely inside the Janaceks' kitchen, I felt more at home; Mrs. Janacek, kindly and talkative, chatted easily with me about her life. I was able to understand something about her routine and ask fairly intelligent questions about her baking, sewing, church circle, and prize-winning honey. But when Mr. Janacek stamped in from the barn, his heavy boots and overalls thick with mud, I was daunted. Pleased with the idea of a newspaper story, he was eager to help too. But I didn't know what to ask him. "How are the crops?" I ventured weakly. He answered, and I took copious notes, but he might as well have been speaking in Greek. He took me around the farm, where I snapped dozens of pictures with my heavy box camera, having no idea what I was photographing or why. "What kind of pigs are those?" I occasionally managed, or "Isn't the corn unusually high for this time of year?" Mr. Janacek either assumed I knew more than I let on or pretended not to notice.

When I had returned to the office, and my developed photographs lay scattered 47 around my desk, I felt utterly defeated. I had no idea what to write under any of them. Then, like a deus ex machina, John Crawford, the county agent, appeared in the newsroom door. Soon I was to learn how important and respected a man he was in the countryside around Ames; now I was merely grateful that someone with answers could help me with my story. He was easy to ask, a friendly, open man, with sandy hair, a sun-burned face, and ready jokes. My editor always took time for a cup of coffee when John stopped by the newsroom. John took a quick look at my rough copy and began to laugh, checking himself only when he saw my wounded face. "Next week, Susan, why don't you let me come along with you?" he asked gently, sliding into an empty chair and grabbing a pencil. I could see him choking down laughter as he made notes on my copy.

I must have learned something about farm life from those weeks as farm editor, 48 including two afternoon trips tagging behind John Crawford. I even have a graying snapshot John took of me standing in a cornfield; I am wearing huge organdy earrings shaped like butterflies, a full-skirted summer dress, and high heels. I look hot, plump, and out of place. My editor stuck this snapshot on our bulletin board with the label, "Our farm editor: Iowa raises corn and pork," and I immediately went on a diet. Yet only last year, when a friend who had given up teaching Latin for farming began talking about his heifers, I let slip that I didn't know cows had to give birth in order to give milk. For almost four decades, I had assumed that when female calves grew up, they simply became cows and began to give milk nonstop. My own breast-feeding experience had never suggested to me anything about other animals. John Crawford would have been amused.

When we were short on local news, the editor often suggested topics to me for 49 long pictorial features, usually about Ames residents with unusual hobbies or exotic travel experiences. One day he assigned me to interview Willie Tallman about the pipe organ he was building in his basement. For three years I'd taken organ lessons myself, and I was confident I could do an informed piece. I talked to Willie at his real-estate office one afternoon and then spent a long evening in his basement, taking pictures and scribbling notes. Though the story wasn't as promising as I'd hoped, I turned in several pages of typescript to my editor next afternoon with the feeling of a job well done. After spending a half-hour in the back room checking on my pictures and captions, I returned to the newsroom to find my managing editor, the women's editor, the sportswriter and the general reporter all convulsed in laughter. "What's so funny?" I asked innocently. "Nothing, nothing," breathed the sports editor, trying to suppress his snorts. Even Rob had a grin on his face when he said, "Here's your copy, Susan. I've made a few changes. Run it back to Harley now."

Changes? In *my* copy? I snatched the manuscript and glanced over it. Every- 50 where I'd written the word *organ,* he had inserted the prefix "pipe." I couldn't under-stand why. "Hey, Rob," I said complainingly, "this sounds funny. How come you want me to repeat 'pipe' all the time?" The sportswriter began to snort again. Mary Ann, the women's editor, beckoned to me. "Come on, kid, let's go to the ladies' room," she said firmly. I followed, still puzzled and irritated by the laughter behind me. Once we were squeezed into the tiny dark room, she said, "Susan. Listen. You just can't print the sen-tence, 'Most nights Willie plays around with his organ.'" "Why not?" I asked belligerently. She paused, herself evidently puzzled about what to say next: "You know what organ means, don't you?" she finally asked. "Of course," I said, getting even an-grier. "Does it mean anything besides pipe organ?" "It's his thing," she said, looking embarrassed. She gestured vaguely toward her crotch. "Didn't you know?"

I was struck silent. That had never occurred to me. How stupid, I thought. 51 Grown-ups have such dirty minds. None of my friends would laugh at something like that. But I blushed anyway at my innocence. Mary Ann thoughtfully left me alone in the ladies' room, and I stayed there for some time, splashing my cheeks with cool water. When I walked back into the newsroom, everyone was bent assiduously over his work. I snatched the revised copy and carried it out to the typesetter. But for weeks afterward, the sportswriter would ask me if I was going out that night and if my date was planning to play a little on his organ.

From gearshifts and pork production statistics to double-entendres, my sum- 52 mers on the *Tribune* were educational. But probably the *Tribune*'s most important contribution was to show me day after day how wildly various life was. Poring over a wire story about famine in India, or correcting a local correspondent's excesses about a golden wedding in Zearing, I was exposed to overwhelming trivia inflated to importance and overwhelming importance reduced to trivia. I began to acquire a fledgling ironic sense, a perspective that permanently altered the way I looked at things. So much was funny, even absurd, and I had to pretend it wasn't; or it wasn't funny at all, but I had to refuse to take it too seriously. One long hot summer, the last I worked on the *Tribune,* a really big story broke in Ames. In one of the steaming tin bungalows of Pammel Court, a young husband had gone berserk and killed his three small children. His wife had escaped. Writers and photographers alit from Des Moines, our editor himself went out to the college to handle the story, and I was the only one left in the newsroom when Rob returned, sober-faced, late in the day. "Okay," he said shortly, "there's only one thing I want you to do before you go. Call Mrs. Johnson and talk to her." "You mean his *wife?*" I asked incredulously. "That's right," he said, and banged the door into the back room. I sat numbly and stared at my telephone. What in the world would I say? Would I ask her if he was crazy? Had he always been crazy? How did she feel about it? My stomach began to sicken. Twenty minutes later Rob walked in. "Well?" he asked. "Is the story ready?" "I can't do it, Rob," I said. Tears trembled in my eyes. "I just can't do it." He looked at me. I looked at him. Then he sighed. "No, of course you can't," he said. "I can't do it either. Forget it." He took the typescript from the desk and disappeared.

That's the way I like to think it happened. Remembering that hot afternoon, 53 my shock at the murder, the shiver with which I drove by Pammel Court on my way home that night, I feel the incident strongly but am uncertain of its details. Although I can recall many of the minutiae of my childhood, I have had to invent the dialogue between Rob and me. Somehow I've drawn a curtain over that afternoon. Eager as I was to prove myself a real reporter, curious, shut out from the scene of the crime, it might well have been I who suggested to Rob that I call the wife, not the other way around. He may have rejected *my* request. Since I like to remember myself as sensitive and tenderhearted, I may have constructed this dialogue in self-defense. All I am sure of is that the idea of calling the wife came up and that it was rejected.

But if my last vivid memory of working at the *Tribune* is shrouded in moral 54 confusion, that in itself has a truth of its own. All the lessons I learned in my jobs as I was growing up in Ames now seem to me ambiguous. I wonder about the hypocrisy with which I approached baby-sitting, the intensity with which I hustled Camp Fire candy, my brooding melancholy as a Union Grill waitress. Only my summers in the cornfields have a kind of awful simplicity. When I left Ames, I took with me an underlying sense of a work ethic that highlighted dedication but left much else in shadow. Perhaps that inconclusiveness was a most important preparation for life.

Questions

1. What differences between present and past does Toth explore in the opening pages? Does she refer to or hint at these differences in the pages that follow? What is the implication of the title?
2. What sense of "shadow" or "inconclusiveness"—referred to in the concluding paragraph—does Toth convey in narrating some of her experiences?
3. How would you characterize the tone of the narrative? Is it humorous, nostalgic, ironic, or neutral throughout, or does another word better describe the tone? Does the tone change from paragraph to paragraph or episode to episode?
4. Is Toth commenting on experiences of both male and female adolescence, or is she concerned with female adolescence only? Does she suggest that the work experiences of boys were substantially different from those of girls?
5. In what ways does Toth make the reader aware of changes in how she thinks and feels about life in the 1980s.

Suggestions for Writing

1. Discuss a few key differences between the lives of the Manus children described by Margaret Mead and the children that Toth describes. Draw a conclusion from this comparison—a judgment, perhaps on the gains and losses in the lives of both.
2. Discuss the differences between your own work experiences as an adolescent and those Toth describes. Draw a conclusion of your own from this comparison.

Additional Reading

Toth, Susan Allen. *Blooming: A Small-Town Girlhood*. Boston: Little, Brown, 1982.
———. *Ivy Days: Making My Way Out East*. Boston: Little, Brown, 1984.

I Become a Student

Lincoln Steffens

Though Lincoln Steffens is best known today for his famous autobiography, he was known in his own day as one of America's great investigative or "muckraking" reporters. Steffens was born in San Francisco in 1866. After graduating from the University of California at Berkeley in 1889, he studied for several years in Germany and France. He began his career as a journalist in 1892 as a reporter for the New York Evening Post; *he was later managing editor and staff writer for* McClure's *and wrote for and edited other periodicals. Steffens used his columns to expose social and political corruption and inspired other journalists to write similar exposes. Upton Sinclair's journalistic novel* The Jungle *(1906), which describes the horrendous Chicago stockyards, and Ida Tarbell's* The History of the Standard Oil Company *(1904) encouraged reforms in industry and business. Steffens collected his own writings in* The Shame of the Cities *(1904) and later books. He died in 1936.*

Published in 1931, The Autobiography of Lincoln Steffens *is both a personal account of Steffens' career as a journalist and a social and political history of his time. In the chapter reprinted here, Steffens describes his dissatisfaction with the Berkeley of his day. Earlier in the book, Steffens describes the university system of the 1880s:*

> There were no moot questions in Berkeley. There was work to do, knowledge and training to get, but not to answer questions. I found myself engaged, as my classmates were, in choosing courses. The choice was limited and, within the limits, had to be determined by the degree we were candidates for. My questions were philosophical, but I could not take philosophy, which fascinated me, till I had gone through a lot of higher mathematics which did not interest me at all. If I had been allowed to take philosophy, and so discovered the need and the relation of mathematics, I would have got the philosophy and I might have got the mathematics which I miss now more than I do the Hegelian metaphysics taught at Berkeley. Or, if the professor who put me off had taken the pains to show me the bearing of mathematical thought on theoretical logic, I would have undertaken the preparation intelligently. But no one ever developed for me the relation of any of my required subjects to those that attracted me; no one brought out for me the relation of anything I was studying to anything else, except, of course, to that wretched degree. Knowledge was absolute, not relative, and it was stored in compartments, categorical and independent. The relation of knowledge to life, even to student life, was ignored, and as for questions, the professors asked them, not the students; and the students, not the teachers, answered them—in examinations.

It is possible to get an education at a university. It has been done; not often, ₁ but the fact that a proportion, however small, of college students do get a start in interested, methodical study, proves my thesis, and the two personal experiences I have to offer illustrate it and show how to circumvent the faculty, the other students, and the whole college system of mind-fixing. My method might lose a boy his degree, but a degree is not worth so much as the capacity and the drive to learn, and the undergraduate desire for an empty baccalaureate is one of the holds the educational system has on students. Wise students some day will refuse to take degrees, as the best men (in England, for instance) give, but do not themselves accept, titles.

My method was hit on by accident and some instinct. I specialized. With several ₂ courses prescribed, I concentrated on the one or two that interested me most, and let-

ting the others go, I worked intensively on my favorites. In my first two years, for example, I worked at English and political economy and read philosophy. At the beginning
of my junior year I had several cinches in history. Now I liked history; I had neglected
it partly because I rebelled at the way it was taught, as positive knowledge unrelated to
politics, art, life, or anything else. The professors gave us chapters out of a few books
to read, con, and be quizzed on. Blessed as I was with a "bad memory," I could not commit to it anything that I did not understand and intellectually need. The bare record of
the story of man, with names, dates, and irrelative events, bored me. But I had
discovered in my readings of literature, philosophy, and political economy that history
had light to throw upon unhistorical questions. So I proposed in my junior and senior
years to specialize in history, taking all the courses required and those also that I had
flunked in. With this in mind I listened attentively to the first introductory talk of Professor William Cary Jones on American constitutional history. He was a dull lecturer,
but I noticed that, after telling us what pages of what books we must be prepared in, he
mumbled off some other references "for those that may care to dig deeper."

When the rest of the class rushed out into the sunshine, I went up to the pro- 3
fessor and, to his surprise, asked for this memorandum. He gave it to me. Up in the library I ran through the required chapters in the two different books, and they differed
on several points. Turning to the other authorities, I saw that they disagreed on the
same facts and also on others. The librarian, appealed to, helped me search the book-
shelves till the library closed, and then I called on Professor Jones for more references.
He was astonished, invited me in, and began to approve my industry, which astonished
me. I was not trying to be a good boy; I was better than that: I was a curious boy. He
lent me a couple of his books, and I went off to my club to read them. They only deepened the mystery, clearing up the historical question, but leaving the answer to be dug
for and written.

The historians did not know! History was not a science, but a field for research, 4
a field for me, for any young man, to explore, to make discoveries in and write a scientific report about. I was fascinated. As I went on from chapter to chapter, day after day,
finding frequently essential differences of opinion and of fact, I saw more and more work
to do. In this course, American constitutional history, I hunted far enough to suspect
that the Fathers of the Republic who wrote our sacred Constitution of the United States
not only did not, but did not want to, establish a democratic government, and I dreamed
for a while—as I used as a child to play I was Napoleon or a trapper—I promised myself
to write a true history of the making of the American Constitution. I did not do it; that
chapter has been done or well begun since by two men: Smith of the University of Washington and Beard[1] (then) of Columbia (afterward forced out, perhaps for this very
work). I found other events, men, and epochs waiting for students. In all my other
courses, in ancient, in European, and in modern history, the disagreeing authorities
carried me back to the need of a fresh search for (or of) the original documents or other

---

[1] James Allen Smith (1860–1924) was professor of political science at the University of Washington from 1897
to his death; he is the author of the influential *The Spirit of American Government* (1907). Charles Austin
Beard (1874–1948), Professor of Politics at Columbia University, resigned in 1917 in protest over the firing
of faculty who objected to U.S. involvement in World War One; he is the author of *An Economic Interpretation of the Constitution of the United States* (1913).

clinching testimony. Of course I did well in my classes. The history professors soon knew me as a student and seldom put a question to me except when the class had flunked it. Then Professor Jones would say, "Well, Steffens, tell them about it."

Fine. But vanity wasn't my ruling passion then. What I had was a quickening 5 sense that I was learning a method of studying history and that every chapter of it, from the beginning of the world to the end, is crying out to be rewritten. There was something for Youth to do; these superior old men had not done anything, finally.

Years afterward I came out of the graft prosecution office in San Francisco with 6 Rudolph Spreckels, the banker and backer of the investigation. We were to go somewhere, quick, in his car, and we couldn't. The chauffeur was trying to repair something wrong. Mr. Spreckels smiled; he looked closely at the defective part, and to my silent, wondering inquiry he answered: "Always, when I see something badly done or not done at all, I see an opportunity to make a fortune. I never kick at bad work by my class: there's lots of it and we suffer from it. But our failures and neglects are chances for the young fellows coming along and looking for work."

Nothing is done. Everything in the world remains to be done or done over. 7 "The greatest picture is not yet painted, the greatest play isn't written (not even by Shakespeare), the greatest poem is unsung. There isn't in all the world a perfect railroad, nor a good government, nor a sound law." Physics, mathematics, and especially the most advanced and exact of the sciences, are being fundamentally revised. Chemistry is just becoming a science; psychology, economics, and sociology are awaiting a Darwin, whose work in turn is awaiting an Einstein. If the rah-rah boys in our colleges could be told this, they might not all be such specialists in football, petting parties, and unearned degrees. They are not told it, however; they are told to learn what is known. This is nothing, philosophically speaking.

Somehow or other in my later years at Berkeley, two professors, Moses and 8 Howison, representing opposite schools of thought, got into a controversy, probably about their classes. They brought together in the house of one of them a few of their picked students, with the evident intention of letting us show in conversation how much or how little we had understood of their respective teachings. I don't remember just what the subject was that they threw into the ring, but we wrestled with it till the professors could stand it no longer. Then they broke in, and while we sat silent and highly entertained, they went at each other hard and fast and long. It was after midnight when, the debate over, we went home. I asked the other fellows what they had got out of it, and their answers showed that they had seen nothing but a fine, fair fight. When I laughed, they asked me what I, the D.S.,[2] had seen that was so much more profound.

I said that I had seen two highly-trained, well-educated Masters of Arts and 9 Doctors of Philosophy disagreeing upon every essential point of thought and knowledge. They had all there was of the sciences; and yet they could not find any knowledge upon which they could base an acceptable conclusion. They had no test of knowledge; they didn't know what is and what is not. And they have no test of right and wrong; they have no basis for even an ethics.

Well, and what of it? They asked me that, and that I did not answer. I was 10 stunned by the discovery that it was philosophically true, in a most literal sense, that

---

[2]Steffens's college nickname, "damn stinker."

nothing is known; that it is precisely the foundation that is lacking for science; that all we call knowledge rested upon assumptions which the scientists did not all accept; and that, likewise, there is no scientific reason for saying, for example, that stealing is wrong. In brief: there was no scientific basis for an ethics. No wonder men said one thing and did another; no wonder they could settle nothing either in life or in the academies.

I could hardly believe this. Maybe these professors, whom I greatly respected, 11 did not know it all. I read the books over again with a fresh eye, with a real interest, and I could see that, as in history, so in other branches of knowledge, everything was in the air. And I was glad of it. Rebel though I was, I had got the religion of scholarship and science; I was in awe of the authorities in the academic world. It was a release to feel my worship cool and pass. But I could not be sure. I must go elsewhere, see and hear other professors, men these California professors quoted and looked up to as their high priests. I decided to go as a student to Europe when I was through Berkeley, and I would start with the German universities.

My father listened to my plan, and he was disappointed. He had hoped I would 12 succeed him in his business; it was for that that he was staying in it. When I said that, whatever I might do, I would never go into business, he said, rather sadly, that he would sell out his interest and retire. And he did soon after our talk. But he wanted me to stay home and, to keep me, offered to buy an interest in a certain San Francisco daily paper. He had evidently had this in mind for some time. I had always done some writing, verse at the poetical age of puberty, then a novel which my mother alone treasured. Journalism was the business for a boy who liked to write, he thought, and he said I had often spoken of a newspaper as my ambition. No doubt I had in the intervals between my campaigns as Napoleon. But no more. I was now going to be a scientist, a philosopher. He sighed; he thought it over, and with the approval of my mother, who was for every sort of education, he gave his consent.

Questions

1. How does Steffens illustrate "the whole college system of mind-fixing"? Are the faculty chiefly to blame, or are they, too, victims of the system?
2. What system does Steffens recommend for "circumventing" the faculty, the other students, and the system?
3. Is Steffens saying that there are no answers to the large questions of life? Is the purpose of education to make one aware that there are no answers? Or is Steffens making a different point?
4. What aims of education would Steffens support in addition to those he states? What in the essay suggests these aims?
5. To what extent does Steffens reflect the assumptions of Rousseau on education?

Suggestions for Writing

1. Discuss the extent to which your own experience corresponds to the description of university courses in the introduction to the reading selection and in the excerpt. Note both similarities and differences and try to account for the differences.

2. Discuss the extent to which Steffens's characterization of university life in the introduction excerpt fits your own experience in high school or college. Try to account for the differences and draw a conclusion from your analysis.
3. Discuss what your goals in college are and how you developed them. Then discuss the obstacles you face now and expect to face in realizing these goals.

Additional Reading

Kaplan, Justin. *Lincoln Steffens.* New York: Simon and Schuster, 1974.
Steffens, Lincoln. *Autobiography.* 2 vols. New York: Harcourt Brace Jovanovich, 1968.
————. *The Shame of the Cities.* New York: Hill and Wang, 1957.
Weinberg, Arthur, and Lila Weinberg, eds. *The Muckrakers: The Era in Journalism that Moved America to Reform—The Most Significant Magazine Articles of 1902–1912.* New York: Simon and Schuster, 1961.

Resolution and Independence

William Wordsworth

The English poet William Wordsworth (1770–1850) was born in Cockermouth, in the mountainous northwest region of England known as the Lake District. As a young man he attended Cambridge University and afterwards he traveled in France, Switzerland, and Italy and lived for a year in revolutionary France before returning to England. Wordsworth had fallen in love with a Frenchwoman, Annette Vallon, but war between France and England prevented him from immediately returning to her and their daughter, and long separation seems to have discouraged later marriage. In 1793 he published poems describing his travels in the Alps. With his friend Samuel Taylor Coleridge, Wordsworth published Lyrical Ballads *in 1798. Following a stay in Germany with his sister, he returned with her to Grasmere, a village not far from his birthplace. In 1802 Wordsworth married Mary Hutchinson, and in 1813 he, his sister, and his wife and children moved a short distance to Rydal Mount, a large house close to the town of Ambleside. By this time Wordsworth had written his greatest poems.*

Much of Wordsworth's poetry describes his youthful experiences in the Cumbrian mountains and valleys of the Lake District. In his long autobiographical poem The Prelude, *begun in 1799 and finished in 1805, Wordsworth traces the growth of his imagination. Toward the beginning of the poem, Wordsworth states his central theme—how the world of nature generated in him the powers of feeling and sympathy:*

Ah, not in vain ye beings of the hills,
And ye that walk the woods and open heaths
By moon or starlight, thus, from my first dawn
Of childhood, did ye love to intertwine
The passions that build up our human soul
Not with the mean and vulgar works of man,
But with high objects, with eternal things,
With life and Nature, purifying thus
The elements of feeling and of thought,
And sanctifying by such discipline
Both pain and fear, until we recognize
A grandeur in the beatings of the heart.

*In a great poem, "Resolution and Independence," written in
1802, Wordsworth describes another experience that shaped his life—
his encounter with a leech gatherer, a person who collected leeches by
wading into still water and letting them gather on the body. Leeches
were used widely by physicians to draw blood from patients. In the
course of the poem, Wordsworth recalls other young poets whose lives
began in happiness—Thomas Chatterton who died by poison at the age
of seventeen and the Scottish poet Robert Burns, "who walked in glory
and in joy" behind his plough.*

1

There was a roaring in the wind all night;
The rain came heavily and fell in floods;
But now the sun is rising calm and bright;
The birds are singing in the distant woods;
Over his own sweet voice the stock dove broods;   5
The jay makes answer as the magpie chatters;
And all the air is filled with pleasant noise of waters.

2

All things that love the sun are out of doors;
The sky rejoices in the morning's birth;
The grass is bright with raindrops; on the moors   10
The hare is running races in her mirth;
And with her feet she from the plashy earth
Raises a mist; that, glittering in the sun,
Runs with her all the way, wherever she doth run.

3

I was a Traveler then upon the moor;   15
I saw the hare that raced about with joy;
I heard the woods and distant waters roar;

Or heard them not, as happy as a boy:
The pleasant season did my heart employ:
My old remembrances went from me wholly;   20
And all the ways of men, so vain and melancholy.

4

But, as it sometimes chanceth, from the might
Of joy in minds that can no further go,
As high as we have mounted in delight
In our dejection do we sink as low;   25
To me that morning did it happen so;
And fears and fancies thick upon me came;
Dim sadness—and blind thoughts, I knew not, nor could name.

5

I heard the skylark warbling in the sky;
And I bethought me of the playful hare: 30
Even such a happy Child of earth am I;
Even as these blissful creatures do I fare;
Far from the world I walk, and from all care;
But there may come another day to me—
Solitude, pain of heart, distress, and poverty.   35

6

My whole life I have lived in pleasant thought,
As if life's business were a summer mood;
As if all needful things would come unsought
To genial faith, still rich in genial good;
But how can he expect that others should   40
Build for him, sow for him, and at his call
Love him, who for himself will take no heed at all?

7

I thought of Chatterton,[1] the marvelous Boy,
The sleepless Soul that perished in his pride;
Of him who walked in glory and in joy   45
Following his plow, along the mountainside;[2]
By our own spirits are we deified:
We Poets in our youth begin in gladness,
But thereof come in the end despondency and madness.

---

[1] The English poet Thomas Chatterton (1752–1770), who died in the year of Wordsworth's birth.
[2] The Scottish poet Robert Burns (1759–1796), who also died a young man.

8

Now, whether it were by peculiar grace,   50
A leading from above, a something given,
Yet it befell that, in this lonely place,
When I with these untoward thoughts had striven,
Beside a pool bare to the eye of heaven
I saw a Man before me unawares: 55
The oldest man he seemed that ever wore gray hairs.

9

As a huge stone is sometimes seen to lie
Couched on the bald top of an eminence;
Wonder to all who do the same espy,
By what means it could thither come, and whence;   60
So that it seems a thing endued with sense:
Like a sea beast crawled forth, that on a shelf
Of rock or sand reposeth, there to sun itself;

10

Such seemed this Man, not all alive nor dead,
Nor all asleep—in his extreme old age;   65
His body was bent double, feet and head
Coming together in life's pilgrimage;
As if some dire constraint of pain, or rage
Of sickness felt by him in times long past,
A more than human weight upon his frame had cast.   70

11

Himself he propped, limbs, body, and pale face,
Upon a long gray staff of shaven wood;
And, still as I drew near with gentle pace,
Upon the margin of that moorish flood
Motionless as a cloud that old Man stood,   75
That heareth not the loud winds when they call,
And moveth all together, if it move at all.

12

At length, himself unsettling, he the pond
Stirred with his staff, and fixedly did look
Upon the muddy water, which he conned,   80
As if he had been reading in a book;
And now a stranger's privilege I took,
And, drawing to his side, to him did say,
"This morning gives us promise of a glorious day."

13

A gentle answer did the old Man make,   85
In courteous speech which forth he slowly drew;
And him with further words I thus bespake,
"What occupation do you there pursue?
This is a lonesome place for one like you."
Ere he replied, a flash of mild surprise   90
Broke from the sable orbs of his yet-vivid eyes.

14

His words came feebly, from a feeble chest,
But each in solemn order followed each,
With something of a lofty utterance dressed—
Choice word and measured phrase, above the reach   95
Of ordinary men; a stately speech;
Such as grave livers do in Scotland use,
Religious men, who give to God and man their dues.

15

He told, that to these waters he had come
To gather leeches, being old and poor: 100
Employment hazardous and wearisome!
And he had many hardships to endure:
From pond to pond he roamed, from moor to moor;
Housing, with God's good help, by choice or chance;
And in this way he gained an honest maintenance.   105

16

The old Man still stood talking by my side;
But now his voice to me was like a stream
Scarce heard; nor word from word could I divide;
And the whole body of the Man did seem
Like one whom I had met with in a dream;   110
Or like a man from some far region sent,
To give me human strength, by apt admonishment.

17

My former thoughts returned: the fear that kills;
And hope that is unwilling to be fed;   115
Cold, pain, and labor, and all fleshly ills;
And mighty Poets in their misery dead.
—Perplexed, and longing to be comforted,
My question eagerly did I renew,
"How is it that you live, and what is it you do?"

18

He with a smile did then his words repeat;   120
And said that, gathering leeches, far and wide
He traveled, stirring thus about his feet
The waters of the pools where they abide.
"Once I could meet with them on every side,
But they have dwindled long by slow decay;   125
Yet still I persevere, and find them where I may."

19

While he was talking thus, the lonely place,
The old Man's shape, and speech—all troubled me:
In my mind's eye I seemed to see him pace   130
About the weary moors continually,
Wandering about alone and silently.
While I these thoughts within myself pursued,
He, having made a pause, the same discourse renewed.

20

And soon with this he other matter blended,   135
Cheerfully uttered, with demeanor kind,
But stately in the main; and, when he ended,
I could have laughed myself to scorn to find
In that decrepit Man so firm a mind.
"God," said I, "be my help and stay secure;   140
I'll think of the Leech Gatherer on the lonely moor!"

Questions

1. Under what circumstances does the speaker encounter the leech gatherer? Why were these circumstances unusual?
2. What comparisons does the speaker use to describe the leech gatherer? How do these comparisons convey the qualities that impress the speaker as being unusual?
3. What does the speaker gain in conversing with the old man? Is it the man himself or his appearance or his words—or the sum of these—that produces the effect on the speaker?
4. Does the speaker state what he has gained—or does he let the reader make this discovery from the details of the encounter?

Suggestions for Writing

1. Explain how the title of Wordsworth's poem relates to the poem itself. Does Wordsworth refer directly to the qualities stated in the title?

2. Discuss the impression you get of William Wordsworth with the impression you get of Dylan Thomas in his poems. Use your comparison to pinpoint what seems to you the most striking similarity or difference. Analyze key lines in the poems of the two writers to explain your impression.
3. Compare the experience described in "Resolution and Independence" with the chance experience in one of the following poems. Use your comparison to develop an idea relating to the poets.
   a. Percy Bysshe Shelley, "Ode to the West Wind"
   b. John Keats, "Ode to a Nightingale"
   c. Thomas Hardy, "The Darkling Thrush"
   d. Robert Frost, "Two Tramps in Mud Time"

Additional Reading

Darbashire, Helen. *The Poet Wordsworth.* Oxford, England: Clarendon Press, 1950.

Ferry, David. *The Limits of Mortality: An Essay on Wordsworth's Major Poems.* Middletown, Conn.: Wesleyan University Press, 1959.

Gill, Stephen, and Frank Kermode, eds. *William Wordsworth.* Oxford Authors series. Oxford, England: Oxford University Press, 1984.

Hartman, Geoffrey H. *Wordsworth's Poetry: 1787–1814.* Rev. ed. New Haven: Yale University Press, 1972.

Moorman, Mary. *William Wordsworth: A Biography. Volume 1: The Early Years, 1770–1803. Volume 2: The Later Years, 1803–1850.* Oxford: Clarendon Press, 1957, 1963.

Perkins, David. *Wordsworth and the Poetry of Sincerity.* Cambridge, Mass.: Belknap-Harvard University Press, 1964.

Woodring, Carl. *Wordsworth.* Cambridge: Harvard University Press, 1968.

ART AND LIFE

*T*he nature of art and its role in our lives has been a concern of philosophers at least from the time of Plato in ancient Greece. Many people seem to think this topic is interesting only to those with the leisure to enjoy the arts, but a theory of art has important bearing for a society and a culture. Disinterest in the question of art is most common in cultures where a particular view of art has found wide acceptance and therefore is unquestioned. The situation is similar with the sciences.

The science historian Thomas S. Kuhn suggests that in times when standard ways of thinking are challenged and are in danger of becoming superseded, theorizing becomes important. Kuhn calls the interrelated body of assumptions and methods of inquiry that distinguish a particular view of the world a "paradigm." When an existing paradigm is not questioned, scientists take it for granted; they feel no need to defend its assumptions or their applications. However, when a paradigm comes under repeated challenge, scientists do reexamine and defend its assumptions or "first principles" and its applications. Physicists today take the atomic theory of matter for granted; they do not, like scientists in earlier times, have to defend the idea that solid bodies consist of tiny particles that are invisible to the naked eye. Nor do they need to defend their applications of the atomic theory in such fields as chemistry, microbiology, and physics. Biologists today face a different situation; though genetics is now an established science, evolutionists under attack from creationists defend their assumptions as Darwin did in the nineteenth century. The current debate between evolutionists and creationists is a debate on the prevailing paradigm of human development.

Less prominent but of no less importance is the disagreement in many parts of the world over the definition of art. In the United States and other countries the disagreement centers on definitions of obscenity and pornography. The issue is not merely what kinds of magazines and books should be on display in grocery stores or in libraries; much more is at stake—a whole body of assumptions, many of them unstated. For many people the banning of magazines and books (or the limiting of their audiences) is really a question of freedom of thought and action; for others, the question has bearing on the nature of art itself and what it contributes to a society and culture. In Chile, South Africa, and other countries, art is a vital means of personal expression and protest, as it is for blacks, women, and other minorities in the United States. In the Soviet Union art has long been a battleground; dissident writers and artists suffer imprisonment or the threat of imprisonment.

Though most writers, artists, and composers agree on the need for freedom, they are not united by common beliefs or goals; they take different stands on such issues as obscenity, pornography, and censorship. The English novelist Doris Lessing suggests that literature today reveals "a confusion of standards and the uncertainty of values." In the nineteenth century, she points out, writers had "neither religion nor politics nor aesthetic principles in common," nor do they have these in common today; but nineteenth-century writers did share certain values and "a climate of ethical judgment" that Lessing finds absent today. Lessing defines some of these values and what she believes the writer should be in our age in this passage:

> Once a writer has a feeling of responsibility, as a human being, for the other human beings he influences, it seems to me he must become a humanist, and must feel himself as an instrument of change for good or for bad. That image of the pretty singer in the ivory tower has always seemed to me a dishonest one. Logically he should be content to sing to his image in the mirror. The act of getting a story or a novel published is an act of communication, an attempt to impose one's personality and beliefs on other people.
> —"The Small Personal Voice"

Later in the same essay she states that:

> Artists are the traditional interpreters of dreams and nightmares, and this is no time to turn our backs on our chosen responsibilities, which is what we should be doing if we refused to share in the deep anxieties, terrors, and hopes of human beings everywhere.

Would all writers, musicians, and artists accept this definition of what they do? The writers reprinted here deal with this question in various ways, directly and indirectly. From the perspectives of philosophy, religious belief, depth psychology, and art itself, they ask what art is and what it can do.

The Republic, Part 5

Plato

The Greek philosopher Plato was born about 427 and died about 347 B.C., the son of a distinguished Athenian family. As a young man, he became a student of Socrates (469–399 B.C.), a sage who re-

putedly carved statues that stood near the Acropolis and who fought in the Peloponnesian War between Athens and Sparta—and who, according to legend, once saved his own life by glaring at the Spartans. An argumentative man, Socrates took delight in debating wise men and philosophers; eventually he gathered students into an informal school. Charged with impiety and corrupting Athenian youth, Socrates was put to death. Plato later founded his own school, the Academy. Both men and women attended; the related subjects mathematics and philosophy were the center of the curriculum—an inscription above the door warned "Let no one without geometry enter here." F. M. Cornford, the translator of the following pages from The Republic, *states that, influenced by the Peloponnesian War's effects and the memory of Socrates, Plato "from first to last, was chiefly bent on the question how society could be reshaped so that man might realize the best that is in him."*

Socrates is the central character in the dialogues that Plato wrote in his later years. These dialogues are not formal treatises or verbatim transcripts from memory; they are literary essays in which Plato dramatizes his old teacher and those with whom he conversed and debated. The dialogues are seldom, however, debates that reach a middle ground or compromise between diverse points of view and ideas. Rather, Socrates asks questions that elicit truths known to him but not immediately known to those with whom he converses. Bertrand Russell describes the method of inquiry:

> The matters that are suitable for treatment by the Socratic method are those as to which we have already enough knowledge to come to a right conclusion, but have failed, through confusion of thought or lack of analysis, to make the best logical use of what we know. A question such as "what is justice?" is eminently suited for discussion in a Platonic dialogue. We all freely use the words "just" and "unjust," and, by examining the ways in which we use them, we can arrive inductively at the definition that will best suit with usage. All that is needed is knowledge of how the words in question are used.—*A History of Western Philosophy*

In seeking answers, Socrates draws on prior knowledge of a special kind. Plato's "Doctrine of Ideas" explains what this knowledge is: it consists of Forms that we knew in a world of timeless Being before our birth. In the words of Cornford, "The Forms . . . are not laws of the sequence or coexistence of phenomena, but ideals, or patterns, which have a real existence independent of our minds, and of which the many individual things called by their names in the world of appearances are like images or reflections." In the trauma of birth, we forget these ideas or forms that, nonetheless, continue to exist in the mind. This is the central belief of Plato's rationalism: true knowledge (as distinguished from belief) is of Ideas, or Forms, of which things in the changing world—the world of Becoming—are copies.

In The Republic *Socrates begins his inquiry into the ideal state or society by seeking to clarify the meaning of the word* justice. *Then he describes at length a society that fits that definition. The section of* The Republic *reprinted here discusses the role of art in this society. The discussion develops an earlier one in which, having put restrictions on what schoolchildren may impersonate, Socrates proposes to put severe restrictions on poets and storytellers:*

> Suppose, then, that an individual clever enough to assume any character and give imitations of anything and everything should visit our country and offer to perform his compositions, we shall bow down before a being with such miraculous powers of giving pleasure; but we shall tell him that we are not allowed to have any such person in our commonwealth; we shall crown him with fillets of wool, anoint his head with myrrh, and conduct him to the borders of some other country. For our own benefit, we shall employ the poets and story-tellers of the more austere and less attractive type, who will reproduce only the manner of a person of high character and, in the substance of their discourse, conform to those rules we laid down when we began the education of our warriors.
> —*The Republic,* Chapter 9

Returning to this consideration, Socrates brings the young men with whom he has been conversing to the reasons for these rules.

Indeed, I continued, our commonwealth has many features which make me think it was based on very sound principles, especially our rule not on any account to admit the poetry of dramatic representation. Now that we have distinguished the several parts of the soul, it seems to me clearer than ever that such poetry must be firmly excluded.

What makes you say so?

Between ourselves—for you will not denounce me to the tragedians and the other dramatists—poetry of that sort seems to be injurious to minds which do not possess the antidote in a knowledge of its real nature.

What have you in mind?

I must speak out, in spite of a certain affection and reverence I have had from a child for Homer, who seems to have been the original master and guide of all this imposing company of tragic poets. However, no man must be honoured above the truth; so, as I say, I must speak my mind.

Do, by all means.

Listen then, or rather let me ask you a question. Can you tell me what is meant by representation in general? I have no very clear notion myself.

So you expect me to have one!

Why not? It is not always the keenest eye that is the first to see something.

True; but when you are there I should not be very desirous to tell what I saw, however plainly. You must use your own eyes.

Well then, shall we proceed as usual and begin by assuming the existence of a single essential nature or Form for every set of things which we call by the same name? Do you understand?

I do.

Then let us take any set of things you choose. For instance there are any number of beds or of tables, but only two Forms, one of Bed and one of Table.

Yes.

And we are in the habit of saying that the craftsman, when he makes the beds or tables we use or whatever it may be, has before his mind the Form of one or other of these pieces of furniture. The Form itself is, of course, not the work of any craftsman. How could it be?

It could not.

Now what name would you give to a craftsman who can produce all the things made by every sort of workman?

He would need to have very remarkable powers!

Wait a moment, and you will have even better reason to say so. For, besides producing any kind of artificial thing, this same craftsman can create all plants and animals, himself included, and earth and sky and gods and the heavenly bodies and all the things under the earth in Hades.

That sounds like a miraculous feat of virtuosity.

Are you incredulous? Tell me, do you think there could be no such craftsman at all, or that there might be someone who could create all these things in one sense, though not in another? Do you not see that you could do it yourself, in a way?

In what way, I should like to know.

There is no difficulty; in fact there are several ways in which the thing can be done quite quickly. The quickest perhaps would be to take a mirror and turn it round in all directions. In a very short time you could produce sun and stars and earth and yourself and all the other animals and plants and lifeless objects which we mentioned just now.

Yes, in appearance, but not the actual things.

Quite so; you are helping out my argument. My notion is that a painter is a craftsman of that kind. You may say that the things he produces are not real; but there is a sense in which he too does produce a bed.

Yes, the appearance of one.

And what of the carpenter? Were you not saying just now that he only makes a particular bed, not what we call the Form or essential nature of Bed?

Yes, I was.

If so, what he makes is not the reality, but only something that resembles it. It would not be right to call the work of a carpenter or of any other handicraftsman a perfectly real thing, would it?

Not in the view of people accustomed to thinking on these lines.

We must not be surprised, then, if even an actual bed is a somewhat shadowy thing as compared with reality.

True.

Now shall we make use of this example to throw light on our question as to the true nature of this artist who represents things? We have here three sorts of bed: one which exists in the nature of things and which, I imagine, we could only describe as a product of divine workmanship; another made by the carpenter; and a third by the painter. So the three kinds of bed belong respectively to the domains of these three: painter, carpenter, and god.

Yes.

Now the god made only one ideal or essential Bed, whether by choice or because he was under some necessity not to make more than one; at any rate two or more were not created, nor could they possibly come into being.

Why not?

Because, if he made even so many as two, then once more a single ideal Bed would make its appearance, whose character those two would share; and that one, not the two, would be the essential Bed. Knowing this, the god, wishing to be the real maker of a real Bed, not a particular manufacturer of one particular bed, created one which is essentially unique.

So it appears.

Shall we call him, then, the author of the true nature of Bed, or something of that sort?

Certainly he deserves the name, since all his works constitute the real nature of things.

And we may call the carpenter the manufacturer of a bed?

Yes.

Can we say the same of the painter?

Certainly not.

Then what is he, with reference to a bed?

I think it would be fairest to describe him as the artist who represents the things which the other two make.

Very well, said I; so the work of the artist is at the third remove from the essential nature of the thing?

Exactly.

The tragic poet, too, is an artist who represents things; so this will apply to him: he and all other artists are, as it were, third in succession from the throne of truth.

Just so.

We are in agreement, then, about the artist. But now tell me about our painter: which do you think he is trying to represent—the reality that exists in the nature of things, or the products of the craftsman?

The products of the craftsman.

As they are, or as they appear? You have still to draw that distinction.

How do you mean?

I mean: you may look at a bed or any other object from straight in front or slantwise or at any angle. Is there then any difference in the bed itself, or does it merely look different?

It only looks different.

Well, that is the point. Does painting aim at reproducing any actual object as it is, or the appearance of it as it looks? In other words, is it a representation of the truth or of a semblance?

Of a semblance.

The art of representation, then, is a long way from reality; and apparently the reason why there is nothing it cannot reproduce is that it grasps only a small part of any object, and that only an image. Your painter, for example, will paint us a shoemaker, a carpenter, or other workman, without understanding any one of their crafts; and yet, if he were a good painter, he might deceive a child or a simple-minded person into thinking his picture was a real carpenter, if he showed it them at some distance.

No doubt.

But I think there is one view we should take in all such cases. Whenever someone announces that he has met with a person who is master of every trade and knows more about every subject than any specialist, we should reply that he is a simple fellow who has apparently fallen in with some illusionist and been tricked into thinking him omniscient, because of his own inability to discriminate between knowledge and ignorance and the representation of appearances.

Quite true.

Then it is now time to consider the tragic poets and their master, Homer, because we are sometimes told that they understand not only all technical matters but also all about human conduct, good or bad, and about religion; for, to write well, a good poet, so they say, must know his subject; otherwise he could not write about it. We must ask whether these people have not been deluded by meeting with artists who can represent appearances, and in contemplating the poets' work have failed to see that it is at the third remove from reality, nothing more than semblances, easy to produce with no knowledge of the truth. Or is there something in what they say? Have the good poets a real mastery of the matters on which the public thinks they discourse so well?

It is a question we ought to look into.

Well then, if a man were able actually to do the things he represents as well as to produce images of them, do you believe he would seriously give himself up to making these images and take that as a completely satisfying object in life? I should imagine that, if he had a real understanding of the actions he represents, he would far sooner devote himself to performing them in fact. The memorials he would try to leave after him would be noble deeds, and he would be more eager to be the hero whose praises are sung than the poet who sings them.

Yes, I agree; he would do more good in that way and win a greater name.

Here is a question, then, that we may fairly put to Homer or to any other poet. We will leave out of account all mere matters of technical skill: we will not ask them to explain, for instance, why it is that, if they have a knowledge of medicine and not merely the art of reproducing the way physicians talk, there is no record of any poet, ancient or modern, curing patients and bequeathing his knowledge to a school of medicine, as Asclepius did. But when Homer undertakes to tell us about matters of the highest importance, such as the conduct of war, statesmanship, or education, we have a right to inquire into his competence. "Dear Homer," we shall say, "we have defined the artist as one who produces images at the third remove from reality. If your knowledge of all that concerns human excellence was really such as to raise you above him to the second rank, and you could tell what courses of conduct will make men better or worse as individuals or as citizens, can you name any country which was better governed thanks to your efforts? Many states, great and small, have owed much to a good lawgiver, such as Lycurgus at Sparta, Charondas in Italy and Sicily, and our own Solon. Can you tell us of any that acknowledges a like debt to you?"

I should say not, Glaucon replied. The most devout admirers of Homer make no such claim.

Well, do we hear of any war in Homer's day being won under his command or thanks to his advice?

No.

Or of a number of ingenious inventions and technical contrivances, which would show that he was a man of practical ability like Thales of Miletus or Anacharsis the Scythian?[1]

Nothing of the sort.

Well, if there is no mention of public services, do we hear of Homer in his own lifetime presiding, like Pythagoras, over a band of intimate disciples who loved him for the inspiration of his society and handed down a Homeric way of life, like the way of life which the Pythagoreans called after their founder and which to this day distinguishes them from the rest of the world?

No; on the contrary, Homer's friend with the absurd name, Creophylus,[2] would look even more absurd when considered as a product of the poet's training, if the story is true that he completely neglected Homer during his lifetime,

Yes, so they say. But what do you think, Glaucon? If Homer had really possessed the knowledge qualifying him to educate people and make them better men, instead of merely giving us a poetical representation of such matters, would he not have attracted a host of disciples to love and revere him? After all, any number of private teachers like Protagoras of Abdera and Prodicus of Ceos[3] have succeeded in convincing their contemporaries that they will never be fit to manage affairs of state or their own households unless these masters superintend their education; and for this wisdom they are so passionately admired that their pupils are all but ready to carry them about on their shoulders. Can we suppose that Homer's contemporaries, or Hesiod's, would have left them to wander about reciting their poems, if they had really been capable of helping their hearers to be better men? Surely they would sooner have parted with their money and tried to make the poets settle down at home; or failing that, they would have danced attendance on them wherever they went, until they had learnt from them all they could.

I believe you are quite right, Socrates.

We may conclude, then, that all poetry, from Homer onwards, consists in representing a semblance of its subject, whatever it may be, including any kind of human

---

[1]Thales (early sixth cent.) made a fortune out of a corner in oil-mills when his knowledge of the stars enabled him to predict a large olive harvest, thus proving that wise men could be rich if they chose (Aristotle, *Politics*, i. II). Anacharsis was said to have invented the anchor and the potter's wheel (Diog. Laert. i. 105). [The notes in this selection are those of the translator, F. M. Cornford.]

[2]Creophylus's name is supposed to be derived from two words meaning "flesh" and "tribe." He is said to have been an epic poet from Chios.

[3]Two of the most famous Sophists of the fifth century. Plato's *Protagoras* gives a vivid picture of them on a visit to a rich patron at Athens.

excellence, with no grasp of the reality. We were speaking just now of the painter who can produce what looks like a shoemaker to the spectator who, being as ignorant of shoemaking as he is himself, judges only by form and colour. In the same way the poet, knowing nothing more than how to represent appearances, can paint in words his picture of any craftsman so as to impress an audience which is equally ignorant and judges only by the form of expression; the inherent charm of metre, rhythm, and musical setting is enough to make them think he has discoursed admirably about generalship or shoemaking or any other technical subject. Strip what the poet has to say of its poetical colouring, and I think you must have seen what it comes to in plain prose. It is like a face which was never really handsome, when it has lost the fresh bloom of youth.

Quite so.

Here is a further point, then. The artist, we say, this maker of images, knows nothing of the reality, but only the appearance. But that is only half the story. An artist can paint a bit and bridle, while the smith and the leather-worker can make them. Does the painter understand the proper form which bit and bridle ought to have? Is it not rather true that not even the craftsmen who make them know that, but only the horseman who understands their use?

Quite true.

May we not say generally that there are three arts concerned with any object—the art of using it, the art of making it, and the art of representing it?

Yes.

And that the excellence or beauty or rightness of any implement or living creature or action has reference to the use for which it is made or designed by nature?

Yes.

It follows, then, that the user must know most about the performance of the thing he uses and must report on its good or bad points to the maker. The flute-player, for example, will tell the instrument-maker how well his flutes serve the player's purpose, and the other will submit to be instructed about how they should be made. So the man who uses any implement will speak of its merits and defects with knowledge, whereas the maker will take his word and possess no more than a correct belief, which he is obliged to obtain by listening to the man who knows.

Quite so.

But what of the artist? Has he either knowledge or correct belief? Does he know from direct experience of the subjects he portrays whether his representations are good and right or not? Has he even gained a correct belief by being obliged to listen to someone who does know and can tell him how they ought to be represented?

No, he has neither.

If the artist, then, has neither knowledge nor even a correct belief about the soundness of his work, what becomes of the poet's wisdom in respect of the subjects of his poetry?

It will not amount to much.

And yet he will go on with his work, without knowing in what way any of his representations is sound or unsound. He must, apparently, be reproducing only what pleases the taste or wins the approval of the ignorant multitude.

Yes, what else can he do?

We seem, then, so far to be pretty well agreed that the artist knows nothing worth mentioning about the subjects he represents, and that art is a form of play, not to be taken seriously. This description, moreover, applies above all to tragic poetry, whether in epic or dramatic form.

Exactly.

But now look here, said I; the content of this poetical representation is something at the third remove from reality, is it not?

Yes.

On what part of our human nature, then, does it produce its effect?

What sort of part do you mean?

Let me explain by an analogy. An object seen at a distance does not, of course, look the same size as when it is close at hand; a straight stick looks bent when part of it is under water; and the same thing appears concave or convex to an eye misled by colours. Every sort of confusion like these is to be found in our minds; and it is this weakness in our nature that is exploited, with a quite magical effect, by many tricks of illusion, like scene-painting and conjuring.

True.

But satisfactory means have been found for dispelling these illusions by measuring, counting, and weighing. We are no longer at the mercy of apparent differences of size and quantity and weight; the faculty which has done the counting and measuring or weighing takes control instead. And this can only be the work of the calculating or reasoning element in the soul.

True.

And when this faculty has done its measuring and announced that one quantity is greater than, or equal to, another, we often find that there is an appearance which contradicts it. Now, as we have said, it is impossible for the same part of the soul to hold two contradictory beliefs at the same time. Hence the part which agrees with the measurements must be a different part from the one which goes against them; and its confidence in measurement and calculation is a proof of its being the highest part; the other which contradicts it must be an inferior one.

It must.

This, then, was the conclusion I had in view when I said that paintings and works of art in general are far removed from reality, and that the element in our nature which is accessible to art and responds to its advances is equally far from wisdom. The offspring of a connexion thus formed on no true or sound basis must be as inferior as the parents. This will be true not only of visual art, but of art addressed to the ear, poetry as we call it.

Naturally.

Then, instead of trusting merely to the analogy from painting, let us directly consider that part of the mind to which the dramatic element in poetry appeals, and see how much claim it has to serious worth. We can put the question in this way. Drama, we say, represents the acts and fortunes of human beings. It is wholly concerned with what they do, voluntarily or against their will, and how they fare, with the consequences which they regard as happy or otherwise, and with their feelings of joy and sorrow in all these experiences. That is all, is it not?

Yes.

And in all these experiences has a man an undivided mind? Is there not an internal conflict which sets him at odds with himself in his conduct, much as we were saying that the conflict of visual impressions leads him to make contradictory judgements? However, I need not ask that question; for, now I come to think of it, we have already agreed that innumerable conflicts of this sort are constantly occurring in the mind. But there is a further point to be considered now. We have said that a man of high character will bear any stroke of fortune, such as the loss of a son or of anything else he holds dear, with more equanimity than most people. We may now ask: will he feel no pain, or is that impossible? Will he not rather observe due measure in his grief?

Yes, that is nearer the truth.

Now tell me: will he be more likely to struggle with his grief and resist it when he is under the eyes of his fellows or when he is alone?

He will be far more restrained in the presence of others.

Yes; when he is by himself he will not be ashamed to do and say much that he would not like anyone to see or hear.

Quite so.

What encourages him to resist his grief is the lawful authority of reason, while the impulse to give way comes from the feeling itself; and, as we said, the presence of contradictory impulses proves that two distinct elements in his nature must be involved. One of them is law-abiding, prepared to listen to the authority which declares that it is best to bear misfortune as quietly as possible without resentment, for several reasons: it is never certain that misfortune may not be a blessing; nothing is gained by chafing at it; nothing human is matter for great concern; and, finally, grief hinders us from calling in the help we most urgently need. By this I mean reflection on what has happened, letting reason decide on the best move in the game of life that the fall of the dice permits. Instead of behaving like a child who goes on shrieking after a fall and hugging the wounded part, we should accustom the mind to set itself at once to raise up the fallen and cure the hurt, banishing lamentation with a healing touch.

Certainly that is the right way to deal with misfortune.

And if, as we think, the part of us which is ready to act upon these reflections is the highest, that other part which impels us to dwell upon our sufferings and can never have enough of grieving over them is unreasonable, craven, and faint-hearted.

Yes.

Now this fretful temper gives scope for a great diversity of dramatic representation; whereas the calm and wise character in its unvarying constancy is not easy to represent, nor when represented is it readily understood, especially by a promiscuous gathering in a theatre, since it is foreign to their own habit of mind. Obviously, then, this steadfast disposition does not naturally attract the dramatic poet, and his skill is not designed to find favour with it. If he is to have a popular success, he must address himself to the fretful type with its rich variety of material for representation.

Obviously.

We have, then, a fair case against the poet and we may set him down as the counterpart of the painter, whom he resembles in two ways: his creations are poor things by the standard of truth and reality, and his appeal is not to the highest part of the soul, but to one which is equally inferior. So we shall be justified in not admitting him into a well-ordered commonwealth, because he stimulates and strengthens an element which threatens to undermine the reason. As a country may be given over into the power of its worst citizens while the better sort are ruined, so, we shall say, the dramatic poet sets up a vicious form of government in the individual soul: he gratifies that senseless part which cannot distinguish great and small, but regards the same things as now one, now the other; and he is an image-maker whose images are phantoms far removed from reality.

Quite true.

But, I continued, the heaviest count in our indictment is still to come. Dramatic poetry has a most formidable power of corrupting even men of high character, with a few exceptions.

Formidable indeed, if it can do that.

Let me put the case for you to judge. When we listen to some hero in Homer or on the tragic stage moaning over his sorrows in a long tirade, or to a chorus beating their breasts as they chant a lament, you know how the best of us enjoy giving ourselves up to follow the performance with eager sympathy. The more a poet can move our feelings in this way, the better we think him. And yet when the sorrow is our own, we pride ourselves on being able to bear it quietly like a man, condemning the behaviour we admired in the theatre as womanish. Can it be right that the spectacle of a man behaving as one would scorn and blush to behave oneself should be admired and enjoyed, instead of filling us with disgust?

No, it really does not seem reasonable.

It does not, if you reflect that the poet ministers to the satisfaction of that very part of our nature whose instinctive hunger to have its fill of tears and lamentations is forcibly restrained in the case of our own misfortunes. Meanwhile the noblest part of us, insufficiently schooled by reason or habit, has relaxed its watch over these querulous feelings, with the excuse that the sufferings we are contemplating are not our own and it is no shame to us to admire and pity a man with some pretensions to a noble character, though his grief may be excessive. The enjoyment itself seems a clear gain, which we cannot bring ourselves to forfeit by disdaining the whole poem. Few, I believe, are capable of reflecting that to enter into another's feelings must have an effect on our own: the emotions of pity our sympathy has strenghtened will not be easy to restrain when we are suffering ourselves.

That is very true.

Does not the same principle apply to humour as well as to pathos? You are doing the same thing if, in listening at a comic performance or in ordinary life to buffooneries which you would be ashamed to indulge in yourself, you thoroughly enjoy them instead of being disgusted with their ribaldry. There is in you an impulse to play the clown, which you have held in restraint from a reasonable fear of being set down as a buffoon; but now you have given it rein, and by encouraging its impudence at the theatre you may be unconsciously carried away into playing the comedian in your private life. Similar effects are produced by poetic representation of love and anger and all those desires and feelings of pleasure or pain which accompany our every action. It waters the growth of passions which should be allowed to wither away and sets them up in control, although the goodness and happiness of our lives depend on their being held in subjection.

I cannot but agree with you.

If so, Glaucon, when you meet with admirers of Homer who tell you that he has been the educator of Hellas and that on questions of human conduct and culture he deserves to be constantly studied as a guide by whom to regulate your whole life, it is well to give a friendly hearing to such people, as entirely well-meaning according to their lights, and you may acknowledge Homer to be the first and greatest of the tragic poets; but you must be quite sure that we can admit into our commonwealth only the poetry which celebrates the praises of the gods and of good men. If you go further and admit the honeyed muse in epic or in lyric verse, then pleasure and pain will usurp the sovereignty of law and of the principles always recognized by common consent as the best.

Quite true.

So now, since we have recurred to the subject of poetry, let this be our defence: it stands to reason that we could not but banish such an influence from our commonwealth. But, lest poetry should convict us of being harsh and unmannerly, let us tell her further that there is a long-standing quarrel between poetry and philosophy. There are countless tokens of this old antagonism, such as the lines which speak of "the cur which at his master yelps," or "one mighty in the vain talk of fools" or "the throng of all-too-sapient heads," or "subtle thinkers all in rags." None the less, be it declared that, if the dramatic poetry whose end is to give pleasure can show good reason why it should exist in a well-governed society, we for our part should welcome it back, being ourselves conscious of its charm; only it would be a sin to betray what we believe to be the truth. You too, my friend, must have felt this charm, above all when poetry speaks through Homer's lips.

I have indeed.

It is fair, then, that before returning from exile poetry should publish her defence in lyric verse or some other measure; and I suppose we should allow her champions who love poetry but are not poets to plead for her in prose, that she is no mere source of pleasure but a benefit to society and to human life. We shall listen favourably; for we shall clearly be the gainers, if that can be proved.

Undoubtedly.

But if it cannot, then we must take a lesson from the lover who renounces at any cost a passion which he finds is doing him no good. The love for poetry of this kind, bred in us by our own much admired institutions, will make us kindly disposed to believe in her genuine worth; but so long as she cannot make good her defence we shall, as we listen, rehearse to ourselves the reasons we have just given, as a counter-charm to save us from relapsing into a passion which most people have never outgrown. We shall reiterate that such poetry has no serious claim to be valued as an apprehension of truth. One who lends an ear to it should rather beware of endangering the order established in his soul, and would do well to accept the view of poetry which we have expressed.

I entirely agree.

Yes, Glaucon; for much is at stake, more than most people suppose: it is a choice between becoming a good man or a bad; and poetry, no more than wealth or power or honours, should tempt us to be careless of justice and virtue.

Your argument has convinced me, as I think it would anyone else.

Questions

1. Plato is an idealist in arguing that Forms or Ideas are the "perfectly real" things; the realist, by contrast, would argue that material objects (chairs and tables) are real and ideas only the abstractions we make of these. How does Socrates defend the idealist position through his discussion of the divine craftsman?
2. How does Socrates use this idealist argument to show that artists (and tragic poets like Homer) are inferior craftsman?
3. If they are inferior craftsmen, what must we no longer claim for artists and tragic poets?
4. What argument is Socrates developing about the bridle maker and the horseman and the instrument maker and the flute player? Is this argument essential to the case Socrates is making against the artist?
5. What other cases does Socrates make against the artist and poet? Given these arguments, why would he anoint the artist with myrrh and then lead him to the borders of the republic?
6. How does Socrates show at the end of this section that the issues of art and life are basic social questions?
7. Is Socrates saying that all art is inferior and destructive of character, or does he distinguish between good and bad art and condemn only bad art?
8. How persuasive do you find the arguments of the dialogue? Do you agree that art has the power to make people bad? Or should we look at art as a form of play that can relieve tension and strong emotion?

Suggestions for Writing

1. Argue whether controversial books like *Catcher in the Rye* should be kept off the shelves of school libraries because they are charged to contain bad language or characters that children should not emulate. Identify and answer arguments of those who hold views opposite to yours.
2. Argue whether pro football and hockey should be banned from television because they are violent sports and therefore may encourage violence. In the course of your argument, state what position Socrates would take on the issue, and defend or attack his position.

Additional Reading

Cornford, Francis M. *Before and After Socrates.* Cambridge, England: Cambridge University Press, 1932.

Hamilton, Edith, and Huntington Cairns, eds. *The Collected Dialogues of Plato.* Princeton: Princeton University Press, 1961.

Havelock, Eric A. *Preface to Plato.* Cambridge, Mass.: Belknap-Harvard University Press, 1963.

Shorey, Paul. *The Unity of Plato's Thought.* Chicago: University of Chicago Press, 1933.

Taylor, A. E. *The Mind of Plato.* Ann Arbor: University of Michigan Press, 1960.

Creative Writers and Day-Dreaming

Sigmund Freud

No theory of art and literature provides more of a contrast to the moral view of Plato than that of Sigmund Freud (1856–1939). The great Viennese psychologist and founder of psychoanalysis was well equipped to write about art. He had a wide knowledge of modern and classical literature, which he read in the original Greek and Latin. His native language was German, but he had learned Hebrew as a youth, and he was fluent in French, Spanish, Italian, and English (as a young man he had translated writings of John Stuart Mill into German). Freud was an unusually gifted science writer—able to present his ideas with considerable persuasiveness. His contribution to German literature received recognition in the award of the Goethe Prize in 1930.

For Freud art begins in the euphoric, conflict-free play of childhood—the pleasure the child derives from the free play of the faculties for their own sake, as in pleasure derived from the sound of nonsense words. Art, Freud suggests in Jokes and Their Relation to the Unconscious *(1905), engages us in euphoric play, as in innocent jokes that make us smile. As we grow up, however, the "pleasure-ego" of childhood changes under pressure from the world (and from within the child) into a "reality-ego." A new kind of play comes into being—one shaped by the reality-ego that helps us cope with the demands of the world. Emotions that we are forced in everyday living to suppress we can momentarily express in jokes that release tension by venting aggressive or forbidden feelings and thoughts. Art is still play, but it is play of a serious kind.*

Freud is referring to the two kinds of play—the euphoric and noneuphoric—in the opening paragraphs of "Creative Writers and Day-Dreaming." It is the second kind that he is referring to in the statement, "The opposite of play is not what is serious but what is real." The artist may be euphoric, as in music that we find exuberant and tension-free. But "reality"—the outer world—and the mature ego shun the impulses we expressed for a time in infancy. These impulses continue to exist, however, and can produce neurosis even though repressed. The artist, Freud suggests, is unusually gifted in sublimating or transforming these impulses into useful ones that can be put to the service of living. They are also put to use in allowing us to gain pleasure in watching a serious play like Hamlet. *We gain pleasure from the play of impulses or emotions—normally under repression—that are aroused and ultimately relieved when the tensions of the tragedy are resolved. The serious art of tragedy is pleasurable, then, in a special way and is no longer euphoric.*

Freud increasingly stressed and wrote about this second, noneuphoric art, which draws on unfulfilled tensions or longings of childhood—in the words of this essay, on phantasies that have become "over-luxuriant and over-powerful." When these phantasies are so

*powerful that they awaken repressed impulses and control adult be-
havior, the artist suffers neurosis. This is the meaning of Freud's statement that art can border on the psychopathic. Freud recognizes a euphoric art in this essay, but he also takes account of noneuphoric art.
It is his general view of the origin of art in play and phantasy that
deserves careful attention, because it raises the question whether art
truly has a therapeutic role to play—in addition to the entertainment
role most of us would agree art has. The bracketed notes are those of
Freud's editor, James Strachey. The translator is I. F. Grant Duff.*

We laymen have always been intensely curious to know—like the Cardinal who 1
put a similar question to Ariosto—from what sources that strange being, the creative
writer, draws his material, and how he manages to make such an impression on us with
it and to arouse in us emotions of which, perhaps, we had not even thought ourselves
capable. Our interest is only heightened the more by the fact that, if we ask him, the
writer himself gives us no explanation, or none that is satisfactory; and it is not at all
weakened by our knowledge that not even the clearest insight into the determinants of
his choice of material and into the nature of the art of creating imaginative form will
ever help to make creative writers of *us*.

If we could at least discover in ourselves or in people like ourselves an activity 2
which was in some way akin to creative writing! An examination of it would then give
us a hope of obtaining the beginnings of an explanation of the creative work of writers.
And, indeed, there is some prospect of this being possible. After all, creative writers
themselves like to lessen the distance between their kind and the common run of humanity; they so often assure us that every man is a poet at heart and that the last poet
will not perish till the last man does.

Should we not look for the first traces of imaginative activity as early as in 3
childhood? The child's best-loved and most intense occupation is with his play or
games. Might we not say that every child at play behaves like a creative writer, in that
he creates a world of his own, or, rather, re-arranges the things of his world in a new
way which pleases him? It would be wrong to think he does not take that world seriously; on the contrary, he takes his play very seriously and he expends large amounts
of emotion on it. The opposite of play is not what is serious but what is real. In spite of
all the emotion with which he cathects his world of play, the child distinguishes it quite
well from reality; and he likes to link his imagined objects and situations to the tangible
and visible things of the real world. This linking is all that differentiates the child's 'play'
from 'phantasying'.

The creative writer does the same as the child at play. He creates a world of 4
phantasy which he takes very seriously—that is, which he invests with large amounts
of emotion—while separating it sharply from reality. Language has preserved this relationship between children's play and poetic creation. It gives [in German] the name of
'*Spiel*' ['play'] to those forms of imaginative writing which require to be linked to tangible objects and which are capable of representation. It speaks of a '*Lustspiel*' or
'*Trauerspiel*' ['comedy' or 'tragedy': literally, 'pleasure play' or 'mourning play'] and describes those who carry out the representation as '*Schauspieler*' ['players': literally
'show-players']. The unreality of the writer's imaginative world, however, has very important consequences for the technique of his art; for many things which, if they were

real, could give no enjoyment, can do so in the play of phantasy, and many excitements which, in themselves, are actually distressing, can become a source of pleasure for the hearers and spectators at the performance of a writer's work.

There is another consideration for the sake of which we will dwell a moment 5 longer on this contrast between reality and play. When the child has grown up and has ceased to play, and after he has been labouring for decades to envisage the realities of life with proper seriousness, he may one day find himself in a mental situation which once more undoes the contrast between play and reality. As an adult he can look back on the intense seriousness with which he once carried on his games in childhood; and, by equating his ostensibly serious occupations of to-day with his childhood games, he can throw off the too heavy burden imposed on him by life and win the high yield of pleasure afforded by *humour*.

As people grow up, then, they cease to play, and they seem to give up the yield 6 of pleasure which they gained from playing. But whoever understands the human mind knows that hardly anything is harder for a man than to give up a pleasure which he has once experienced. Actually, we can never give anything up; we only exchange one thing for another. What appears to be a renunciation is really the formation of a substitute or surrogate. In the same way, the growing child, when he stops playing, gives up nothing but the link with real objects; instead of *playing,* he now *phantasies.* He builds castles in the air and creates what are called *daydreams.* I believe that most people construct phantasies at times in their lives. This is a fact which has long been overlooked and whose importance has therefore not been sufficiently appreciated.

People's phantasies are less easy to observe than the play of children. The child, 7 it is true, plays by himself or forms a closed psychical system with other children for the purposes of a game; but even though he may not play his game in front of the grown-ups, he does not, on the other hand, conceal it from them. The adult, on the contrary, is ashamed of his phantasies and hides them from other people. He cherishes his phantasies as his most intimate possessions, and as a rule he would rather confess his misdeeds than tell anyone his phantasies. It may come about that for that reason he believes he is the only person who invents such phantasies and has no idea that creations of this kind are widespread among other people. This difference in the behaviour of a person who plays and a person who phantasies is accounted for by the motives of these two activities, which are nevertheless adjuncts to each other.

A child's play is determined by wishes: in point of fact by a single wish—one 8 that helps in his upbringing—the wish to be big and grown up. He is always playing at being 'grown up', and in his games he imitates what he knows about the lives of his elders. He has no reason to conceal this wish. With the adult, the case is different. On the one hand, he knows that he is expected not to go on playing or phantasying any longer, but to act in the real world; on the other hand, some of the wishes which give rise to his phantasies are of a kind which it is essential to conceal. Thus he is ashamed of his phantasies as being childish and as being unpermissible.

But, you will ask, if people make such a mystery of their phantasying, how is 9 it that we know such a lot about it? Well, there is a class of human beings upon whom, not a god, indeed, but a stern goddess—Necessity—has allotted the task of telling what they suffer and what things give them happiness. These are the victims of nervous illness, who are obliged to tell their phantasies, among other things, to the doctor by whom they expect to be cured by mental treatment. This is our best source of knowledge, and we have since found good reason to suppose that our patients tell us nothing that we might not also hear from healthy people.

Let us now make ourselves acquainted with a few of the characteristics of 10 phantasying. We may lay it down that a happy person never phantasies, only an unsatisfied one. The motive forces of phantasies are unsatisfied wishes, and every single phantasy is the fulfilment of a wish, a correction of unsatisfying reality. These motivating wishes vary according to the sex, character and circumstances of the person who is having the phantasy; but they fall naturally into two main groups. They are either ambitious wishes, which serve to elevate the subject's personality; or they are erotic ones. In young women the erotic wishes predominate almost exclusively, for their ambition is as a rule absorbed by erotic trends. In young men egoistic and ambitious wishes come to the fore clearly enough alongside of erotic ones. But we will not lay stress on the opposition between the two trends; we would rather emphasize the fact that they are often united. Just as, in many altar-pieces, the portrait of the donor is to be seen in a corner of the picture, so, in the majority of ambitious phantasies, we can discover in some corner or other the lady for whom the creator of the phantasy performs all his heroic deeds and at whose feet all his triumphs are laid. Here, as you see, there are strong enough motives for concealment; the well-brought-up young woman is only allowed a minimum of erotic desire, and the young man has to learn to suppress the excess of self-regard which he brings with him from the spoilt days of his childhood, so that he may find his place in a society which is full of other individuals making equally strong demands.

We must not suppose that the products of this imaginative activity—the vari- 11 ous phantasies, castles in the air and daydreams—are stereotyped or unalterable. On the contrary, they fit themselves in to the subject's shifting impressions of life, change with every change in his situation, and receive from every fresh active impression what might be called a 'date-mark'. The relation of a phantasy to time is in general very important. We may say that it hovers, as it were, between three times—the three moments of time which our ideation involves. Mental work is linked to some current impression, some provoking occasion in the present which has been able to arouse one of the subject's major wishes. From there it harks back to a memory of an earlier experience (usually an infantile one) in which this wish was fulfilled; and it now creates a situation relating to the future which represents a fulfilment of the wish. What it thus creates is a day-dream or phantasy, which carries about it traces of its origin from the occasion which provoked it and from the memory. Thus past, present and future are strung together, as it were, on the thread of the wish that runs through them.

A very ordinary example may serve to make what I have said clear. Let us take 12 the case of a poor orphan boy to whom you have given the address of some employer where he may perhaps find a job. On his way there he may indulge in a day-dream appropriate to the situation from which it arises. The content of his phantasy will perhaps be something like this. He is given a job, finds favour with his new employer, makes himself indispensable in the business, is taken into his employer's family, marries the charming young daughter of the house, and then himself becomes a director of the business, first as his employer's partner and then as his successor. In this phantasy, the dreamer has regained what he possessed in his happy childhood—the protecting house, the loving parents and the first objects of his affectionate feelings. You will see from this example the way in which the wish makes use of an occasion in the present to construct, on the pattern of the past, a picture of the future.

There is a great deal more that could be said about phantasies; but I will only 13 allude as briefly as possible to certain points. If phantasies become over-luxuriant and over-powerful, the conditions are laid for an onset of neurosis or psychosis. Phantasies, moreover, are the immediate mental precursors of the distressing symptoms complained of by our patients. Here a broad by-path branches off into pathology.

I cannot pass over the relation of phantasies to dreams. Our dreams at night 14 are nothing else than phantasies like these, as we can demonstrate from the interpretation of dreams. Language, in its unrivalled wisdom, long ago decided the question of the essential nature of dreams by giving the name of 'day-dreams' to the airy creations of phantasy. If the meaning of our dreams usually remains obscure to us in spite of this pointer, it is because of the circumstance that at night there also arise in us wishes of which we are ashamed; these we must conceal from ourselves, and they have consequently been repressed, pushed into the unconscious. Repressed wishes of this sort and their derivatives are only allowed to come to expression in a very distorted form. When scientific work had succeeded in elucidating this factor of *dream-distortion,* it was no longer difficult to recognize that night-dreams are wish-fulfilments in just the same way as day-dreams—the phantasies which we all know so well.

So much for phantasies. And now for the creative writer. May we really attempt 15 to compare the imaginative writer with the 'dreamer in broad daylight', and his creations with day-dreams? Here we must begin by making an initial distinction. We must separate writers who, like the ancient authors of epics and tragedies, take over their material ready-made, from writers who seem to originate their own material. We will keep to the latter kind, and, for the purposes of our comparison, we will choose not the writers most highly esteemed by the critics, but the less pretentious authors of novels, romances and short stories, who nevertheless have the widest and most eager circle of readers of both sexes. One feature above all cannot fail to strike us about the creations of these story-writers: each of them has a hero who is the centre of interest, for whom the writer tries to win our sympathy by every possible means and whom he seems to place under the protection of a special Providence. If, at the end of one chapter of my story, I leave the hero unconscious and bleeding from severe wounds, I am sure to find him at the beginning of the next being carefully nursed and on the way to recovery; and if the first volume closes with the ship he is in going down in a storm at sea, I am certain, at the opening of the second volume, to read of his miraculous rescue—a rescue without which the story could not proceed. The feeling of security with which I follow the hero through his perilous adventures is the same as the feeling with which a hero in real life throws himself into the water to save a drowning man or exposes himself to the enemy's fire in order to storm a battery. It is the true heroic feeling, which one of our best writers has expressed in an inimitable phrase: 'Nothing can happen to *me!*' It seems to me, however, that through this revealing characteristic of invulnerability we can immediately recognize His Majesty the Ego, the hero alike of every day-dream and of every story.

Other typical features of these egocentric stories point to the same kinship. The 16 fact that all the women in the novel invariably fall in love with the hero can hardly be looked on as a portrayal of reality, but it is easily understood as a necessary constituent of a day-dream. The same is true of the fact that the other characters in the story are sharply divided into good and bad, in defiance of the variety of human characters that are to be observed in real life. The 'good' ones are the helpers, while the 'bad' ones are the enemies and rivals, of the ego which has become the hero of the story.

We are perfectly aware that very many imaginative writings are far removed 17 from the model of the naïve day-dream; and yet I cannot suppress the suspicion that even the most extreme deviations from that model could be linked with it through an uninterrupted series of transitional cases. It has struck me that in many of what are known as 'psychological' novels only one person—once again the hero—is described from within. The author sits inside his mind, as it were, and looks at the other characters from outside. The psychological novel in general no doubt owes its special nature to the inclination of the modern writer to split up his ego, by self-observation, into many part-egos, and, in consequence, to personify the conflicting currents of his own mental life in several heroes. Certain novels, which might be described as 'eccentric', seem to stand in quite special contrast to the type of the day-dream. In these, the person who is introduced as the hero plays only a very small active part; he sees the actions and sufferings of other people pass before him like a spectator. Many of Zola's later works belong to this category.* But I must point out that the psychological analysis of individuals who are not creative writers, and who diverge in some respects from the so-called norm, has shown us analogous variations of the day-dream, in which the ego contents itself with the role of spectator.

If our comparison of the imaginative writer with the day-dreamer, and of poeti- 18 cal creation with the day-dream, is to be of any value, it must, above all, show itself in some way or other fruitful. Let us, for instance, try to apply to these authors' works the thesis we laid down earlier concerning the relation between phantasy and the three periods of time and the wish which runs through them; and, with its help, let us try to study the connections that exist between the life of the writer and his works. No one has known, as a rule, what expectations to frame in approaching this problem; and often the connection has been thought of in much too simple terms. In the light of the insight we have gained from phantasies, we ought to expect the following state of affairs. A strong experience in the present awakens in the creative writer a memory of an earlier experience (usually belonging to his childhood) from which there now proceeds a wish which finds its fulfilment in the creative work. The work itself exhibits elements of the recent provoking occasion as well as of the old memory.

Do not be alarmed at the complexity of this formula. I suspect that in fact it will 19 prove to be too exiguous a pattern. Nevertheless, it may contain a first approach to the true state of affairs; and, from some experiments I have made, I am inclined to think that this way of looking at creative writings may turn out not unfruitful. You will not forget that the stress it lays on childhood memories in the writer's life—a stress which may perhaps seem puzzling—is ultimately derived from the assumption that a piece of creative writing, like a day-dream, is a continuation of, and a substitute for, what was once the play of childhood.

---

*The French novelist Emile Zola (1840–1902), whose fiction describes working-class life, urban poverty, vice, and crime.

We must not neglect, however, to go back to the kind of imaginative works 20 which we have to recognize, not as original creations, but as the re-fashioning of ready-made and familiar material. Even here, the writer keeps a certain amount of independence, which can express itself in the choice of material and in changes in it which are often quite extensive. In so far as the material is already at hand, however, it is derived from the popular treasure-house of myths, legends and fairy tales. The study of constructions of folk-psychology such as these is far from being complete, but it is extremely probable that myths, for instance, are distorted vestiges of the wishful phantasies of whole nations, the *secular dreams* of youthful humanity.

You will say that, although I have put the creative writer first in the title of my 21 paper, I have told you far less about him than about phantasies. I am aware of that, and I must try to excuse it by pointing to the present state of our knowledge. All I have been able to do is to throw out some encouragements and suggestions which, starting from the study of phantasies, lead on to the problem of the writer's choice of his literary material. As for the other problem—by what means the creative writer achieves the emotional effects in us that are aroused by his creations—we have as yet not touched on it at all. But I should like at least to point out to you the path that leads from our discussion of phantasies to the problems of poetical effects.

You will remember how I have said that the day-dreamer carefully conceals his 22 phantasies from other people because he feels he has reasons for being ashamed of them. I should now add that even if he were to communicate them to us he could give us no pleasure by his disclosures. Such phantasies, when we learn them, repel us or at least leave us cold. But when a creative writer presents his plays to us or tells us what we are inclined to take to be his personal daydreams, we experience a great pleasure, and one which probably arises from the confluence of many sources. How the writer accomplishes this is his innermost secret; the essential *ars poetica* lies in the technique of overcoming the feeling of repulsion in us which is undoubtedly connected with the barriers that rise between each single ego and the others. We can guess two of the methods used by this technique. The writer softens the character of his egoistic daydreams by altering and disguising it, and he bribes us by the purely formal—that is, aesthetic—yield of pleasure which he offers us in the presentation of his phantasies. We give the name of an *incentive bonus*, or a *fore-pleasure*, to a yield of pleasure such as this, which is offered to us so as to make possible the release of still greater pleasure arising from deeper psychical sources. In my opinion, all the aesthetic pleasure which a creative writer affords us has the character of a fore-pleasure of this kind, and our actual enjoyment of an imaginative work proceeds from a liberation of tensions in our minds. It may even be that not a little of this effect is due to the writer's enabling us thenceforward to enjoy our own day-dreams without self-reproach or shame. This brings us to the threshold of new, interesting and complicated enquiries; but also, at least for the moment, to the end of our discussion.

Questions

1. How is the artist both similar to the child at play and different? How does this difference help Freud to define the dream and the work of art?

2. What is a phantasy? Is it the same thing as a daydream? Or is the daydream only one kind of phantasizing?
3. Does Freud say or imply that all art originates in phantasy? Does he claim to state all possible motives of the artist in shaping a work of art?
4. What is the *ars poetica* or art of poetry, according to Freud? Why is it essential to communication between poet or artist and reader?
5. How would Freud answer the charge of Plato that the artist arouses the emotions that should be repressed and therefore should be banished from the ideal state? What would be the role of the artist in Freud's ideal society?

Suggestions for Writing

1. Use your answers to the above questions to summarize the differences between Freud and Plato on the nature of the artist and the purposes of art in a healthy society. Then state which of the two viewpoints is closest to your own and explain why. Support your ideas from your own experiences and observations.
2. Analyze a frightening story or movie to suggest how the writer generates a feeling of repulsion and then overcomes it to encourage you to finish the story. Freud refers to the "purely formal" or "aesthetic" source of pleasure of the frightening story. Discuss the extent to which the shaping of the story and other formal features keep you interested enough to function as a "bribe."
3. Analyze a joke to discover why it amuses you and other people. Is the joke a euphoric one that gives pleasure merely in the telling of it, or does it arouse tensions that the punch line relieves or deflates?

Additional Reading

Freud, Sigmund. *Jokes and Their Relation to the Unconscious.* Trans. Alan Tyson. New York: Norton, 1963.

———. *Leonardo da Vinci: A Study in Psychosexuality.* Trans. Alan Tyson. New York: Norton, 1965.

———. *On Creativity and the Unconscious: Papers on the Psychology of Art, Literature, Love, Religion.* New York: Harper and Row, 1958.

Jones, Ernest. *The Life and Work of Sigmund Freud.* 3 vols. New York: Basic Books, 1953–57.

Lesser, Simon O. *Fiction and the Unconscious.* Boston: Beacon Press, 1957.

Rickman, John, ed. *A General Selection from the Works of Sigmund Freud.* New York: Anchor-Doubleday, 1957.

Rieff, Philip. *Freud: The Mind of the Moralist.* New York: Viking, 1959.

Ruitenbeek, Hendrik M., ed. *The Creative Imagination: Psychoanalysis and the Genius of Inspiration.* Chicago: Quadrangle, 1965.

Spector, Jack J. *The Aesthetics of Freud: A Study in Psychoanalysis and Art.* New York: Praeger, 1972.

Sulloway, Frank J. *Freud, Biologist of the Mind: Beyond the Psychoanalytic Legend.* New York: Basic Books, 1983.

Wollheim, Richard. *Sigmund Freud.* New York: Viking, 1971.

Nobel Lecture*

Alexander Solzhenitsyn

"To reach this chair from which the Nobel Lecture is delivered," the contemporary Russian novelist Alexander Solzhenitsyn wrote in 1970 on receiving the Nobel Prize for Literature, ". . . I have mounted not three or four temporary steps but hundreds or even thousands, fixed, steep, covered with ice, out of the dark and the cold where I was fated to survive, but others, perhaps more talented, stronger than I perished." However, Solzhenitsyn was not to deliver these words in Sweden; he was not to appear in Stockholm to acknowledge the prize until 1974, the year of his deportation from the Soviet Union. Solzhenitsyn is referring to his eight years as a political prisoner in the Soviet Gulag—the prison camps he tells us of in The Gulag Archipelago, *his great memoir and history of the Stalinist prisons that extended like a chain of islands throughout the Soviet Union.*

Born in 1918, Solzhenitsyn grew up in Rostov-on-Don in southeast Russia and later studied physics and mathematics at Rostov University, graduating in 1941. He married his first wife in 1939. During the Second World War he served as a battery commander in the Red Army. In 1945, he was arrested while on duty in eastern Germany and sentenced to the Gulag for a derogatory reference to Stalin in a letter he wrote to a friend. Solzhenitsyn describes the circumstances of this arrest, his arraignment in Moscow, and the sentence in the opening chapters of The Gulag. *In the eight years that followed, he experienced several types of imprisonment, including a term in a scientific research institute outside of Moscow and a term in a camp described in his most famous novel,* One Day in the Life of Ivan Denisovitch. *Toward the end of his imprisonment he was treated for cancer. On his release from the Gulag in 1953, he lived in exile in central Asia, taught school, and worked intensively on books he had secretly begun to write during his imprisonment. Following his rehabilitation in 1956, he returned to western Russia and continued teaching and writing. Solzhenitsyn had divorced his first wife while in prison and after his release he remarried her; following a second divorce in 1973, he married his secretary and advisor Natalia Svetlova.*

Solzhenitsyn won immediate fame as a writer with the publication of One Day in the Life of Ivan Denisovich *in 1962. The novel, published in the leading literary periodical with the approval of the ruler of the Soviet Union, Nikita Khrushchev, created a sensation; three of his other stories also appeared during this brief political thaw. But Solzhenitsyn was not to see any of his other works published in the Soviet Union. In trouble with the authorities who succeeded Khrushchev, he smuggled his autobiographical novels* The First Circle *and* The Cancer Ward *and later other writings out of the Soviet Union; they were published in the West in Russian, English, and other languages. When the secret police seized his papers in 1965, Solzhenitsyn con-*

---

*Translated by F. D. Reeve.

cealed the manuscript of his memoir and history of the Gulag. He eventually agreed to its publication in the West in 1973, when the KGB secured a copy, and the woman who had hidden it committed suicide following her arrest and torture.

Solzhenitsyn's long struggle with the Soviet authorities led to his expulsion from the Writer's Union in 1969. The climax was reached when, summoned to appear at the public prosecutor's office in February of 1974, Solzhenitsyn refused:

> In the circumstances created by the universal and unrelieved illegality enthroned for many years past in our country . . . I refuse to acknowledge the legality of your summons and shall not report for questioning to any agency of the state. Before requiring citizens to observe the law, you must learn to carry it out yourselves. Free the innocent people now in prison. Punish those responsible for mass extermination, and the false informers. Punish the administrators and the special squads who carried out the policy (the deportation of *whole peoples*). Deprive the local and departmental satraps of their unlimited power over citizens, their arbitrary use of courts and psychiatrists *today*. Satisfy the *millions* of lawful but suppressed complaints.

A second imprisonment seemed now inevitable, but the Soviet government chose to send Solzhenitsyn into exile instead. Arrested by the KGB, he was deported from the Soviet Union on February 13, 1974; his second wife and his children soon followed him into exile in Europe, where they lived for a time before coming to the United States. He has been writing a series of novels, begun in the Soviet Union, on the events leading to the Bolshevik Revolution of 1918 and the people and conditions that produced it.

These facts have important bearing on the ideas of the Nobel lecture. Solzhenitsyn is referring to life in the Soviet Union, which he describes briefly but graphically. He refers to the fate of artists and dissidents, though he is not specific about the dissident movement of which he, with the physicist Andrei Sakharov, became a leader. He gives no details about his personal life; he refers only to the circumstances of his nomination for the Nobel Prize. Solzhenitsyn instead deals with the nature of art and the responsibilities of the writer and artist, particularly in an age of crisis. The central question for Solzhenitsyn in the address is the role of artists in their own society and the world.

As the savage, who in bewilderment has picked up a strange sea-leaving, a thing   1
hidden in the sand, or an incomprehensible something fallen out of the sky—something intricately curved, sometimes shimmering dully, sometimes shining in a bright ray of light—turns it this way and that, turns it looking for a way to use it, for some ordinary use to which he can put it, without suspecting an extraordinary one . . .

So we, holding Art in our hands, self-confidently consider ourselves its owners, 2
brashly give it aim, renovate it, re-form it, make manifestoes of it, sell it for cash, play
up to the powerful with it, and turn it around at times for entertainment, even in vaude-
ville songs and in nightclubs, and at times—using stopper or stick, whichever comes
first—for transitory political or limited social needs. But Art is not profaned by our attempts, does not because of them lose touch with its source. Each time and by each use
it yields us a part of its mysterious inner light.

But will we comprehend *all* that light? Who will dare say that he has DEFINED 3
art? That he has tabulated all its facets? Perhaps someone in ages past did understand
and named them for us, but we could not hold still; we listened; we were scornful; we
discarded them at once, always in a hurry to replace even the best with anything new!
And when the old truth is told us again, we do not remember that we once possessed
it.

One kind of artist imagines himself the creator of an independent spiritual 4
world and shoulders the act of creating that world and the people in it, assuming total
responsibility for it—but he collapses, for no mortal genius is able to hold up under
such a load. Just as man, who once declared himself the center of existence, has not
been able to create a stable spiritual system. When failure overwhelms him, he blames
it on the age-old discord of the world, on the complexity of the fragmented and torn
modern soul, or on the public's lack of understanding.

Another artist acknowledges a higher power above him and joyfully works as a 5
common apprentice under God's heaven, although his responsibility for all that he
writes down or depicts, and for those who understand him, is all the greater. On the
other hand, he did not create the world, it is not given direction by him, it is a world
about whose foundations he has no doubt. The task of the artist is to sense more keenly
than others the harmony of the world, the beauty and the outrage of what man has done
to it, and poignantly to let people know. In failure as well as in the lower depths—in
poverty, in prison, in illness—the consciousness of a stable harmony will never leave
him.

All the irrationality of art, however, its blinding sudden turns, its unpredictable 6
discoveries, its profound impact on people, are too magical to be exhausted by the artist's view of the world, by his overall design, or by the work of his unworthy hands.

Archaeologists have uncovered no early stages of human existence so primitive 7
that they were without art. Even before the dawn of civilization we had received this gift
from Hands we were not quick enough to discern. And we were not quick enough to ask:
WHAT is this gift FOR? What are we to do with it?

All who predict that art is disintegrating, that it has outgrown its forms, and 8
that it is dying are wrong and will be wrong. We will die, but art will remain. Will we,
before we go under, ever understand all its facets and all its ends?

Not everything has a name. Some things lead us into a realm beyond words. Art 9
warms even an icy and depressed heart, opening it to lofty spiritual experience. By
means of art we are sometimes sent—dimly, briefly—revelations unattainable by reason.

Like that little mirror in the fairy tales—look into it, and you will see not your- 10
self but, for a moment, that which passeth understanding, a realm to which no man can
ride or fly. And for which the soul begins to ache . . .

2

Dostoevsky once enigmatically let drop the phrase: "Beauty will save the 11 world." What does this mean? For a long time I thought it merely a phrase. Was such a thing possible? When in our bloodthirsty history did beauty ever save anyone from anything? Ennobled, elevated, yes; but whom has it saved?

There is, however, something special in the essence of beauty, a special quality 12 in art: the conviction carried by a genuine work of art is absolute and subdues even a resistant heart. A political speech, hasty newspaper comment, a social program, a philo- sophical system can, as far as appearances are concerned, be built smoothly and consis- tently on an error or a lie; and what is concealed and distorted will not be immediately clear. But then to counteract it comes a contradictory speech, commentary, program, or differently constructed philosophy—and again everything seems smooth and grace- ful, and again hangs together. That is why they inspire trust—and distrust.

There is no point asserting and reasserting what the heart cannot believe.   13

A work of art contains its verification in itself: artificial, strained concepts do 14 not withstand the test of being turned into images; they fall to pieces, turn out to be sickly and pale, convince no one. Works which draw on truth and present it to us in live and concentrated form grip us, compellingly involve us, and no one ever, not even ages hence, will come forth to refute them.

Perhaps then the old trinity of Truth, Goodness, and Beauty is not simply the 15 dressed-up, worn-out formula we thought it in our presumptuous, materialistic youth? If the crowns of these three trees meet, as scholars have asserted, and if the too obvious, too straight sprouts of Truth and Goodness have been knocked down, cut off, not let grow, perhaps the whimsical, unpredictable, unexpected branches of Beauty will work their way through, rise up TO THAT VERY PLACE, and thus complete the work of all three?

Then what Dostoevsky wrote—"Beauty will save the world"—is not a slip of the 16 tongue but a prophecy. After all, *he* had the gift of seeing much, a man wondrously filled with light.

And in that case could not art and literature, in fact, help the modern world? 17

What little I have managed to learn about this over the years I will try to set 18 forth here today.

3

To reach this chair from which the Nobel Lecture is delivered—a chair by no 19 means offered to every writer and offered only once in a lifetime—I have mounted not three or four temporary steps but hundreds or even thousands, fixed, steep, covered with ice, out of the dark and the cold where I was fated to survive, but others, perhaps more talented, stronger than I, perished. I myself met but few of them in the Gulag Ar- chipelago,[1] a multitude of scattered island fragments. Indeed, under the millstone of surveillance and mistrust, I did not talk to just any man; of some I only heard; and of

---

[1]The chain of Soviet prisons and labor camps extending from the western borders to the Pacific. Gulag is the acronym in Russian for Chief Administration of Corrective Labor Camps.

others I only guessed. Those with a name in literature who vanished into that abyss are, at least, known; but how many were unrecognized, never once publicly mentioned? And so very few, almost no one ever managed to return. A whole national literature is there, buried without a coffin, without even underwear, naked, a number tagged on its toe. Not for a moment did Russian literature cease, yet from outside it seemed a wasteland. Where a harmonious forest could have grown, there were left, after all the cutting, two or three trees accidentally overlooked.

And today how am I, accompanied by the shades of the fallen, my head bowed 20 to let pass forward to this platform others worthy long before me, today how am I to guess and to express what *they* would have wished to say?

This obligation has long lain on us, and we have understood it. In Vladimir 21 Solovyov's words:

> But even chained, we must ourselves complete
> That circle which the gods have preordained.

In agonizing moments in camp, in columns of prisoners at night, in the freez- 22 ing darkness through which the little chains of lanterns shone, there often rose in our throats something we wanted to shout out to the whole world, if only the world could have heard one of us. Then it seemed very clear what our lucky messenger would say and how immediately and positively the whole world would respond. Our field of vision was filled with physical objects and spiritual forces, and in that clearly focused world nothing seemed to outbalance them. Such ideas came not from books and were not borrowed for the sake of harmony or coherence; they were formulated in prison cells and around forest campfires, in conversations with persons now dead, were hardened by *that* life, developed *out of there.*

When the outside pressures were reduced, my outlook and our outlook wid- 23 ened, and gradually, although through a tiny crack, that "whole world" outside came in sight and was recognized. Startlingly for us, the "whole world" turned out to be not at all what we had hoped: it was a world leading "not up there" but exclaiming at the sight of a dismal swamp, "What an enchanting meadow!" or at a set of prisoner's concrete stocks, "What an exquisite necklace!"—a world in which, while flowing tears rolled down the cheeks of some, others danced to the carefree tunes of a musical.

How did this come about? Why did such an abyss open? Were we unfeeling, or 24 was the world? Or was it because of a difference in language? Why are people not capable of grasping each other's every clear and distinct speech? Words die away and flow off like water—leaving no taste, no color, no smell. Not a trace.

Insofar as I understand it, the structure, import, and tone of speech possible for 25 me—of my speech here today—have changed with the years.

It now scarcely resembles the speech which I first conceived on those freezing 26 nights in prison camp.

4

For ages, such has been man's nature that his view of the world (when not in- 27 duced by hypnosis), his motivation and scale of values, his actions and his intentions have been determined by his own personal and group experiences of life. As the Russian proverb puts it, "Don't trust your brother, trust your own bad eye." This is the soundest basis for understanding one's environment and one's behavior in it. During the long eras when our world was obscurely and bewilderingly fragmented, before a unified communications system had transformed it and it had turned into a single, convulsively beating lump, men were unerringly guided by practical experience in their own local area, then in their own community, in their own society, and finally in their own national territory. The possibility then existed for an individual to see with his own eyes and to accept a common scale of values—what was considered average, what improbable; what was cruel, what beyond all bounds of evil; what was honesty, what deceit. Even though widely scattered peoples lived differently and their scales of social values might be strikingly dissimilar, like their systems of weights and measures, these differences surprised none but the occasional tourist, were written up as heathen wonders, and in no way threatened the rest of not yet united mankind.

In recent decades, however, mankind has imperceptibly, suddenly, become 28 one, united in a way which offers both hope and danger, for shock and infection in one part are almost instantaneously transmitted to others, which often have no immunity. Mankind has become one, but not in the way the community or even the nation used to be stably united, not through accumulated practical experience, not through its own, good-naturedly so-called bad *eye,* not even through its own well-understood, native tongue, but, leaping over all barriers, through the international press and radio. A wave of events washes over us and, in a moment, half the world hears the splash, but the standards for measuring these things and for evaluating them, according to the laws of those parts of the world about which we know nothing, are not and cannot be broadcast through the ether or reduced to newsprint. These standards have too long and too specifically been accepted by and incorporated in too special a way into the lives of various lands and societies to be communicated in thin air. In various parts of the world, men apply to events a scale of values achieved by their own long suffering, and they uncompromisingly, self-reliantly judge only by their own scale, and by no one else's.

If there are not a multitude of such scales in the world, nevertheless there are 29 at least several: a scale for local events, a scale for things far away; for old societies, and for new; for the prosperous, and for the disadvantaged. The points and markings on the scale glaringly do not coincide; they confuse us, hurt our eyes, and so, to avoid pain, we brush aside all scales not our own, as if they were follies or delusions, and confidently judge the whole world according to our own domestic values. Therefore, what seems to us more important, more painful, and more unendurable is really not what is more important, more painful, and more unendurable but merely that which is closer to home. Everything distant which, for all its moans and muffled cries, its ruined lives and, even, millions of victims, does not threaten to come rolling up to our threshold today we consider, in general, endurable and of tolerable dimensions.

On one side, persecuted no less than under the old Romans, hundreds of thou- 30 sands of mute Christians give up their lives for their belief in God. On the other side of the world, a madman (and probably he is not the only one) roars across the ocean in order to FREE us from religion with a blow of steel at the Pontiff! Using his own personal scale, he has decided things for everyone.

What on one scale seems, from far off, to be enviable and prosperous freedom, 31 on another, close up, is felt to be irritating coercion calling for the overturning of buses.

What in one country seems a dream of improbable prosperity in another arouses indignation as savage exploitation calling for an immediate strike. Scales of values differ even for natural calamities: a flood with two hundred thousand victims matters less than a local traffic accident. Scales differ for personal insults: at times, merely a sardonic smile or a dismissive gesture is humiliating, whereas, at others, cruel beatings are regarded as a bad joke. Scales differ for punishments and for wrongdoing. On one scale, a month's arrest, or exile to the country, or "solitary confinement" on white bread and milk rocks the imagination and fills the newspaper columns with outrage. On another, both accepted and excused are prison terms of twenty-five years, solitary confinement in cells with ice-covered walls and prisoners stripped to their underclothing, insane asylums for healthy men, and border shootings of countless foolish people who, for some reason, keep trying to escape. The heart is especially at ease with regard to that exotic land about which nothing is known, from which no events ever reach us except the belated and trivial conjectures of a few correspondents.

For such ambivalence, for such thickheaded lack of understanding of someone 32 else's far-off grief, however, mankind is not at fault: that is how man is made. But for mankind as a whole, squeezed into one lump, such mutual lack of understanding carries the threat of imminent and violent destruction. Given six, four, or even two scales of values, there cannot be one world, one single humanity: the difference in rhythms, in oscillations, will tear mankind asunder. We will not survive together on one Earth, just as a man with two hearts is not meant for this world.

5

Who will coordinate these scales of values, and how? Who will give mankind 33 one single system for reading its instruments, both for wrongdoing and for doing good, for the intolerable and the tolerable as they are distinguished from each other today? Who will make clear for mankind what is really oppressive and unbearable and what, for being so near, rubs us raw—and thus direct our anger against what is in fact terrible and not merely near at hand? Who is capable of extending such an understanding across the boundaries of his own personal experience? Who has the skill to make a narrow, obstinate human being aware of others' far-off grief and joy, to make him understand dimensions and delusions he himself has never lived through? Propaganda, coercion, and scientific proofs are all powerless. But, happily, in our world there is a way. It is art, and it is literature.

There is a miracle which they can work: they can overcome man's unfortunate 34 trait of learning only through his own experience, unaffected by that of others. From man to man, compensating for his brief time on earth, art communicates whole the burden of another's long life experience with all its hardships, colors, and vitality, recreating in the flesh what another has experienced, and allowing it to be acquired as one's own.

More important, much more important: countries and whole continents belat- 35 edly repeat each other's mistakes, sometimes after centuries when, it would seem, everything should be so clear! No: what some nations have gone through, thought through, and rejected, suddenly seems to be the latest word in other nations. Here too the only substitute for what we ourselves have not experienced is art and literature.

They have the marvelous capacity of transmitting from one nation to another—despite differences in language, customs, and social structure—practical experience, the harsh national experience of many decades never tasted by the other nation. Sometimes this may save a whole nation from what is a dangerous or mistaken or plainly disastrous path, thus lessening the twists and turns of human history.

Today, from this Nobel lecture platform, I should like to emphasize this great, 36 beneficent attribute of art.

Literature transmits condensed and irrefutable human experience in still an- 37 other priceless way: from generation to generation. It thus becomes the living memory of a nation. What has faded into history it thus keeps warm and preserves in a form that defies distortion and falsehood. Thus literature, together with language, preserves and protects a nation's soul.

(It has become fashionable in recent times to talk of the leveling of nations, and 38 of various peoples disappearing into the melting pot of contemporary civilization. I disagree with this, but that is another matter; all that should be said here is that the disappearance of whole nations would impoverish us no less than if all people were to become identical, with the same character and the same face. Nations are the wealth of humanity, its generalized personalities. The least among them has its own special colors, and harbors within itself a special aspect of God's design.)

But woe to the nation whose literature is cut off by the interposition of force. 39 That is not simply a violation of "freedom of the press"; it is stopping up the nation's heart, carving out the nation's memory. The nation loses its memory; it loses its spiritual unity—and, despite their supposedly common language, fellow countrymen suddenly cease understanding each other. Speechless generations are born and die, having recounted nothing of themselves either to their own times or to their descendants. That such masters as Akhmatova and Zamyatin were buried behind four walls for their whole lives and condemned even to the grave to create in silence, without hearing one reverberation of what they wrote, is not only their own personal misfortune but a tragedy for the whole nation—and, too, a real threat to all nationalities.

In certain cases, it is a danger for all mankind as well: when HISTORY as a whole 40 ceases to be understood because of that silence.

6

At various times in various places people have argued hotly, angrily, and ele- 41 gantly about whether art and the artist should have a life of their own or whether they should always keep in mind their duty to society and serve it, even though in an unbiased way. For me there is no problem here, but I will not again go into this argument. One of the most brilliant speeches on this subject was Albert Camus's Nobel lecture, the conclusions of which I happily support. Indeed, for decades Russian literature has leaned in that direction—not spending too much time in self-admiration, not flitting about too frivolously—and I am not ashamed to continue in that tradition as best I can. From way back, ingrained in Russian literature has been the notion that a writer can do much among his own people—and that he must.

We will not trample on the artist's RIGHT to express exclusively personal experi- 42 ences and observations, ignoring everything that happens in the rest of the world. We will not DEMAND anything of the artist, but we will be permitted to reproach him, to make requests, to appeal to him and to coax him. After all, he himself only partially develops his talent, the greater portion of which is breathed into him, ready-made, at birth and along with it, responsibility for his free will. Even granting that the artist DOES NOT OWE anybody anything, it is painful to see how, retreating into a world of his own creation or into the vast spaces of subjective fancies, he CAN deliver the real world into the hands of self-seeking, insignificant, or even insane people.

Our twentieth century has turned out to be more cruel than those preceding [43] it, and all that is terrible in it did not come to an end with the first half. The same old caveman feelings—greed, envy, violence, and mutual hate, which along the way assumed respectable pseudonyms like class struggle, racial struggle, mass struggle, labor-union struggle—are tearing our world to pieces. The caveman refusal to accept compromise has been turned into a theoretical principle and is considered to be a virtue of orthodoxy. It demands millions of victims in endless civil wars; it packs our hearts with the notion that there are no fixed universal human concepts called good and justice, that they are fluid, changing, and that therefore one must always do what will benefit one's party. Any and every professional group, as soon as it finds a convenient moment TO RIP OFF A PIECE, unearned or not, extra or not, immediately rips it off, let all of society come crashing down if it will. As seen from outside, the mass of waste in Western society is approaching the limit beyond which the system will become metastable and must collapse. Violence, less and less restricted by the framework of age-old legality, brazenly and victoriously strides throughout the world, unconcerned that its futility has been demonstrated and exposed by history many times. It is not simply naked force that triumphs but its trumpeted justification: the whole world overflows with the brazen conviction that force can do everything and justice nothing. Dostoevsky's DEMONS,[2] a provincial nightmare of the last century, one would have thought, are, before our very eyes, crawling over the whole world into countries where they were unimaginable, and by the hijacking of planes, by seizing HOSTAGES, by the bomb explosions, and by the fires of recent years signal their determination to shake civilization apart and to annihilate it! And they may very well succeed. Young people, being at an age when they have no experience except sexual, when they have as yet no years of personal suffering and personal wisdom behind them, enthusiastically repeat our discredited Russian lessons of the nineteenth century and think that they are discovering something new. They take as a splendid example the Chinese Red Guard's degradation of people into nonentities. A superficial lack of understanding of the timeless essence of humanity, a naïve smugness on the part of their inexperienced hearts—We'll kick out *those* fierce, greedy oppressors, those governors, and the rest (we!), we'll then lay down our grenades and machine guns, and become just and compassionate. Oh, of course! Of those who have lived their lives and have come to understand, who could refute the young, many DO NOT DARE argue against them; on the contrary, they flatter them in order not to seem "conservative," again a Russian phenomenon of the nineteenth century, something which Dostoevsky called SLAVERY TO HALF-COOKED PROGRESSIVE IDEAS.

The spirit of Munich has by no means retreated into the past; it was not a brief [44] episode. I even venture to say that the spirit of Munich is dominant in the twentieth

---

[2]A novel by Fyodor Dostoevsky, also known as *The Possessed*.

century. The intimidated civilized world has found nothing to oppose the onslaught of a suddenly resurgent fang-baring barbarism, except concessions and smiles. The spirit of Munich is a disease of the will of prosperous people; it is the daily state of those who have given themselves over to a craving for prosperity in every way, to material well-being as the chief goal of life on earth. Such people—and there are many of them in the world today—choose passivity and retreat, anything if only the life to which they are accustomed might go on, anything so as not to have to cross over to rough terrain today, because tomorrow, see, everything will be all right. (But it never will! The reckoning for cowardice will only be more cruel. Courage and the power to overcome will be ours only when we dare to make sacrifices.)

We are also threatened by the catastrophe that the physically squeezed, constrained world is not allowed to become one spiritually; molecules of knowledge and compassion are not allowed to move across from one half of the world to the other. This is a grave danger: THE STOPPAGE OF INFORMATION between the parts of the planet. Contemporary science knows that such stoppage is the way of entropy, of universal destruction. Stoppage of information makes international signatures and treaties unreal: within the zone of STUNNED SILENCE any treaty can easily be reinterpreted at will or, more simply, covered up, as if it had never existed (Orwell understood this beautifully). Within the zone of stunned silence lives—seemingly not Earth's inhabitants at all—a Martian expeditionary force, knowing nothing whatever about the rest of the Earth and ready to trample it flat in the holy conviction that they are "liberating" it. 45

A quarter of a century ago, with the great hopes of mankind, the United Nations was born. Alas, in the immoral world it, too, became immoral. It is not a United Nations but a United Governments, in which those freely elected and those imposed by force and those which seized power by arms are all on a par. Through the mercenary bias of the majority, the UN jealously worries about the freedom of some peoples and pays no attention to the freedom of others. By an officious vote it rejected the review of PRIVATE COMPLAINTS—the groans, shouts, and pleadings of individual, common PLAIN PEOPLE—insects too small for such a great organization. The UN never tried to make BINDING on governments, a CONDITION of their membership, the Declaration of Human Rights, the outstanding document of its twenty-five years—and thus the UN betrayed the common people to the will of governments they had not chosen. 46

One might think that the shape of the modern world is entirely in the hands of scientists, that they determine mankind's technological steps. One might think that what will happen to the world depends not on politicians but specifically on the international cooperation of scientists. Especially because the example of individuals shows how much could be accomplished by moving together. But no; scientists have made no clear effort to become an important, independently active force of mankind. Whole congresses at a time, they back away from the suffering of others; it is more comfortable to stay within the bounds of science. That same spirit of Munich has spread its debilitating wings over them. 47

In this cruel, dynamic, explosive world on the edge of its ten destructions, what is the place and role of the writer? We send off no rockets, do not even push the lowliest handcart, are scorned by those who respect only material power. Would it not be natural for us, too, to retreat, to lose our faith in the steadfastness of good, in the indivisibility 48 of truth, and merely to let the world have our bitter observations, as of a bystander, about how hopelessly corrupted mankind is, how petty men have become, and how difficult it is for lonely, sensitive, beautiful souls today?

We do not have even this way out. Once pledged to the WORD, there is no get- 49 ting away from it: a writer is no sideline judge of his fellow countrymen and contemporaries; he is equally guilty of all the evil done in his country or by his people. If his country's tanks spill blood on the streets of some alien capital, the brown stains are splashed forever on the writer's face. If, some fatal night, his trusting friend is choked to death while sleeping, the bruises from the rope are on the writer's hands. If his young fellow citizens in their easygoing way declare the superiority of debauchery over frugal labor, abandon themselves to drugs or seize HOSTAGES, the stink of it mixes with the writer's breathing.

Will we have the impudence to announce that we are not responsible for the 50 sores of the world today?

7

I am, however, encouraged by a keen sense of WORLD LITERATURE as the one 51 great heart that beats for the cares and misfortunes of our world, even though each corner sees and experiences them in a different way.

In past times, also, besides age-old national literatures there existed a concept 52 of world literature as the link between the summits of national literatures and as the aggregate of reciprocal literary influences. But there was a time lag; readers and writers came to know foreign writers only belatedly, sometimes centuries later, so that mutual influences were delayed and the network of national literary high points was visible not to contemporaries but to later generations.

Today, between writers of one country and the readers and writers of another, 53 there is an almost instantaneous reciprocity, as I myself know. My books, unpublished, alas, in my own country, despite hasty and often bad translations have quickly found a responsive world readership. Critical analysis of them has been undertaken by such leading Western writers as Heinrich Böll. During all these recent years, when both my work and my freedom did not collapse, when against the laws of gravity they held on seemingly in thin air, seemingly ON NOTHING, on the invisible, mute surface tension of sympathetic people, with warm gratitude I learned, to my complete surprise, of the support of the world's writing fraternity. On my fiftieth birthday I was astounded to receive greetings from well-known European writers. No pressure put on me now passed unnoticed. During the dangerous weeks when I was being expelled from the Writers' Union, THE PROTECTIVE WALL put forward by prominent writers of the world saved me from worse persecution, and Norwegian writers and artists hospitably prepared shelter for me in the event that I was exiled from my country. Finally, my being nominated for a Nobel Prize was originated not in the land where I live and write but by Francois Mauriac and his colleagues. Afterward, national writers' organizations expressed unanimous support for me.

As I have understood it and experienced it myself, world literature is no longer 54 an abstraction or a generalized concept invented by literary critics, but a common body and common spirit, a living, heartfelt unity reflecting the growing spiritual unity of mankind. State borders still turn crimson, heated red-hot by electric fences and machine-gun fire; some ministries of internal affairs still suppose that literature is "an internal affair" of the countries under their jurisdiction; and newspaper headlines still herald, "They have no right to interfere in our internal affairs!" Meanwhile, no such thing as INTERNAL AFFAIRS remains on our crowded Earth. Mankind's salvation lies exclusively in everyone's making everything his business, in the people of the East being anything but indifferent to what is thought in the West, and in the people of the West being anything but indifferent to what happens in the East. Literature, one of the most sensitive and responsive tools of human existence, has been the first to pick up, adopt, and assimilate this sense of the growing unity of mankind. I therefore confidently turn to the world literature of the present, to hundreds of friends whom I have not met face to face and perhaps never will see.

My friends! Let us try to be helpful, if we are worth anything. In our own coun- 55 tries, torn by differences among parties, movements, castes, and groups, who for ages past has been not the dividing but the uniting force? This, essentially, is the position of writers, spokesmen of a national language, of the chief tie binding the nation, the very soil which the people inhabit, and, in fortunate circumstances, the nation's spirit too.

I think that world literature has the power in these frightening times to help 56 mankind see itself accurately despite what is advocated by partisans and by parties. It has the power to transmit the condensed experience of one region to another, so that different scales of values are combined, and so that one people accurately and concisely knows the true history of another with a power of recognition and acute awareness as if it had lived through that history itself—and could thus be spared repeating old mistakes. At the same time, perhaps we ourselves may succeed in developing our own WORLD-WIDE VIEW, like any man, with the center of the eye seeing what is nearby but the periphery of vision taking in what is happening in the rest of the world. We will make correlations and maintain world-wide standards.

Who, if not writers, are to condemn their own unsuccessful governments (in 57 some states this is the easiest way to make a living; everyone who is not too lazy does it) as well as society itself, whether for its cowardly humiliation or for its self-satisfied weakness, or the lightheaded escapades of the young, or the youthful pirates brandishing knives?

We will be told: What can literature do against the pitiless onslaught of naked 58 violence? Let us not forget that violence does not and cannot flourish by itself; it is inevitably intertwined with LYING. Between them there is the closest, the most profound and natural bond: nothing screens violence except lies, and the only way lies can hold out is by violence. Whoever has once announced violence as his METHOD must inexorably choose lying as his PRINCIPLE. At birth, violence behaves openly and even proudly. But as soon as it becomes stronger and firmly established, it senses the thinning of the air around it and cannot go on without befogging itself in lies, coating itself with lying's sugary oratory. It does not always or necessarily go straight for the gullet; usually it demands of its victims only allegiance to the lie, only complicity in the lie.

The simple act of an ordinary courageous man is not to take part, not to sup- 59 port lies! Let *that* come into the world and even reign over it, but not through me. Writers and artists can do more: they can VANQUISH LIES! In the struggle against lies, art has always won and always will. Conspicuously, incontestably for everyone. Lies can stand up against much in the world, but not against art.

Once lies have been dispelled, the repulsive nakedness of violence will be 60 exposed—and hollow violence will collapse.

That, my friends, is why I think we can help the world in its red-hot hour: not 61 by the nay-saying of having no armaments, not by abandoning oneself to the carefree life, but by going into battle!

In Russian, proverbs about TRUTH are favorites. They persistently express the 62 considerable, bitter, grim experience of the people, often astonishingly:

ONE WORD OF TRUTH OUTWEIGHS THE WORLD.

On such a seemingly fantastic violation of the law of the conservation of mass 63 and energy are based both my own activities and my appeal to the writers of the whole world.

Questions

1. Solzhenitsyn refers to the different scales of values by which the people of the world live. Does he illustrate these different values, or does he assume his readers and listeners know what they are?
2. How can art bridge differences in people's values to achieve a single scale? How is art different from other kinds of communication—from the print media and the radio, for example?
3. Is the artist or writer a person different in temperament or mental capacity from other people? Does Solzhenitsyn suggest or imply that the artist has a gift of prophecy or a special source of truth?
4. What should be the role of artists and writers in their society and in the whole world? Is that role a special one in the twentieth century, or does Solzhenitsyn suggest or imply that the role of the artist and writer has always been the same?
5. What things in the life of people and in the institutions and technology of the twentieth century unite people? Does Solzhenitsyn believe that artists have a better chance of achieving the purpose of art in the twentieth century than in earlier centuries?
6. How persuasive do you find the address? What ideas do you find most or least convincing, and why? Do you believe that art can succeed where politicians have failed?
7. To what extent does Solzhenitsyn agree with Plato on the role of the artist and writer and of art in general?

Suggestions for Writing

1. Characterize Solzhenitsyn as a person and a man on the basis of his lecture. Cite and analyze passages that reveal special personal qualities as well as qualities of the mind and character.
2. Compare Solzhenitsyn's conception of the writer and artist and of art with that of Plato. Base your comparison on key passages in the two essays.

3. Solzhenitsyn gives the details of his arrest and conviction in the opening chapters of the first volume of *The Gulag Archipelago.* Discuss the personal qualities of Solzhenitsyn that are most apparent in this account.

4. Solzhenitsyn describes his life in the prison camps and the period following his release in the second and third volumes of *The Gulag.* Analyze one of the chapters in these volumes to show how Solzhenitsyn introduces and develops a thesis.

5. Compare the depiction of life in the camps in *The Gulag* with comparable scenes in *One Day in the Life of Ivan Denisovich* to show the various means Solzhenitsyn uses in both works to describe Soviet political prisons.

6. *The First Circle,* a novel that stands with the greatest in Russian and world literature, describes Solzhenitsyn's experiences in a scientific institute during his imprisonment. *The Cancer Ward,* describing the period immediately following Stalin's death in 1953, is based on his experiences in a central Asian hospital before his release. Discuss how Solzhenitsyn uses satire to expose and criticize an evil in one of the chapters of these novels. Identify the target of his satire and the means Solzhenitsyn chooses to expose the evil.

7. In the autobiographical *The Oak and the Calf,* Solzhenitsyn describes his remaining years in the Soviet Union, focusing on his unsuccessful efforts to get his writings published, his harassment by the KGB, his activities in the dissident movement, and the events leading to his deportation. Discuss how this exposure of the regime of the late 1960s illuminates the Nobel lecture.

8. The conditions in Soviet prison camps have been described in numerous memoirs of prisoners and survivors. Two of the best are those of the widow of the great Russian writer and victim of Stalin, Osip Mandelstam—Nadezhda Mandelstam's *Hope against Hope* and *Hope Abandoned.* Compare a chapter from one of these memoirs or a chapter of another memoir—for example, Anatoly Marchenko's *My Testimony*—with a comparable chapter in *The Gulag* to develop a thesis about literature on political prisons.

9. Investigate the lives of Anna Akhmatova and Yevgeny Zamyatin. Then explain the reference to them in paragraph 3.

Additional Reading

Scammell, Michael. *Solzhenitsyn: A Biography.* New York: Norton, 1984.

Solzhenitsyn, Alexander. *The Cancer Ward.* Trans. Nicholas Bethell and David Burg. New York: Farrar, Straus and Giroux, 1969.

———. *The First Circle.* Trans. Thomas P. Whitney. New York: Harper and Row, 1968.

———. *The Gulag Archipelago, 1918–1956: An Experiment in Literary Investigation.* Trans. Thomas P. Whitney (vols. 1 and 2) and Harry Willetts (vol. 3). New York: Harper and Row, 1974–78.

———. *The Oak and the Calf: A Memoir.* New York: Harper and Row, 1980.

———. *One Day in the Life of Ivan Denisovich.* Trans. Gillon Aitken. New York: Farrar, Straus and Giroux, 1963.

———. *Stories and Prose Poems.* Trans. Michael Glenny. New York: Farrar, Straus and Giroux, 1971.

Musée des Beaux Arts

W. H. Auden

W. H. Auden (1907–1973) was one of the younger British poets in the 1930s for whom literature was a vehicle of social action. In 1937 Auden visited Spain, then in a state of civil war, and wrote an influential poem favoring the Loyalists. His visit to China the following year produced his Journey to War. *Numerous other poems deal with the 1930s. The poem "September 1, 1939," omitted by Auden from later collections, describes the 1930s as a "low, dishonest decade." Auden says of himself in the poem, "All I have is a voice/ To undo the folded lie." In other poems, notably his elegy on the death of the Irish poet W. B. Yeats in 1939, he explores the role of poets and poetry in a particular age. His elegy of Sigmund Freud, who died in the same year, continues this exploration in questioning the value of understanding and analysis in an irrational and violent age. The body of Auden's work is a commentary on political and moral changes in the West from the time of Hitler to the world of the late 1960s.*

"Musée des Beaux Arts," published in 1940, describes several paintings of the sixteenth-century Flemish artist Pieter Breughel— Icarus, The Numbering at Bethlehem, *and* The Massacre of the Innocents. *Auden alludes to the latter paintings and refers directly to* Icarus. *The question explored in the poem suggests some of the concerns of Solzhenitsyn in his Nobel lecture.*

About suffering they were never wrong,
The Old Masters: how well they understood
Its human position; how it takes place
While someone else is eating or opening a window or just walk-
    ing dully along;
How, when the aged are reverently, passionately waiting   5
For the miraculous birth, there always must be
Children who did not specially want it to happen, skating
On a pond at the edge of the wood:
They never forgot
That even the dreadful martyrdom must run its course   10
Anyhow in a corner, some untidy spot
Where the dogs go on with their doggy life and the torturer's
    horse
Scratches its innocent behind on a tree.

In Brueghel's *Icarus,* for instance: how everything turns away
Quite leisurely from the disaster; the ploughman may   15
Have heard the splash, the forsaken cry,
But for him it was not an important failure; the sun shone
As it had to on the white legs disappearing into the green
Water; and the expensive delicate ship that must have seen
Something amazing, a boy falling out of the sky,   20
Had somewhere to get to and sailed calmly on.

Questions

1. What kinds of suffering do the details of the paintings in lines 3–13 depict?
2. What do these details tell us about the "human position" of suffering? Why does Auden suggest that the Old Masters were never wrong?
3. Do the details of Breughel's *Icarus* depict the same kind of suffering and "human position," or is Auden depicting a new kind and making a new point about it?
4. Does Auden suggest or imply what the value of such paintings may be? Does the poem suggest that art generally has the power to change people? If it does have this power, how does Auden account for it? If art cannot change people, why does it lack this power?
5. Do the allusions to Jesus and to biblical events (the "miraculous birth," the massacre of the innocents) convey hope or despair, or does the speaker present them without expressing or implying an attitude?

Suggestions for Writing

1. Write an interpretation of "Musée des Beaux Arts," focusing on the images and the point that Auden is making through them. If you believe Auden is developing a number of themes, distinguish them and explain how he organizes them.

2. Discuss how one of the following other poems by Auden illuminates "Musée des Beaux Arts" or develops a similar or a different attitude toward artists and writers:
a. "In Memory of W. B. Yeats"
b. "Voltaire at Ferney"
c. "Rimbaud"
d. "Matthew Arnold"
e. "In Memory of Sigmund Freud"

Additional Reading

Auden, W. H. *Collected Poems.* Ed. Edward Mendelson. New York: Random House, 1976.

———. *The Dyer's Hand and Other Essays.* New York: Random House, 1962.

Blair, John G. *The Poetic Art of W. H. Auden.* Princeton: Princeton University Press, 1965.

Greenberg, Herbert. *Quest for the Necessary: W. H. Auden and the Dilemma of Divided Consciousness.* Cambridge: Harvard University Press, 1968.

Spears, Monroe K. *The Poetry of W. H. Auden: The Disenchanted Island.* New York: Oxford University Press, 1963.

AIMS OF LIVING

*A*s Plato and Solzhenitsyn suggest, what we value depends on our aims or goals in living. If we were asked to state these goals, probably all of us could name a few immediately. We do so even though we may not have thought about our goals or deliberately chosen them in the course of growing up. Family, school, church, the prevailing culture—these and other groups and institutions give our lives direction and influence how we think and behave. We are aware of some of the goals set for us by those groups, and these we can state readily.

Solzhenitsyn considers the values by which we live today and the values of people who lived in the past. He states in his Nobel lecture that in the past "men were unerringly guided by practical experience in their own local area, then in their own community, in their own society, and finally in their own national territory." People in the past made judgments based on their personal experience: "The possibility then existed for an individual to see with his own eyes and to accept a common scale of values—what was considered average, what improbable; what was cruel, what beyond all bounds of evil; what was honesty, what deceit." An important question for Solzhenitsyn is whether individuals can hold to values confirmed by practical experience and accumulated wisdom in societies where values are imposed upon individuals and mass opinion is engineered and managed by governments and media. In such societies, imposition of values creates a disparity between professed beliefs and behavior. In his essay "Life without Principle," Thoreau states, "Thus men will lie on their backs, talking about the fall of man, and never make an effort to get up."

Such disparity is the subject of the five essays and two stories in this section. Each writer is concerned directly or indirectly with how we discover goals and values and act upon them. Sometimes the writer states the assumptions that support the inquiry into values or, in the two stories, the actions of the principal characters. However, the reader needs to search for other assumptions that may not be stated directly.

Self-Reliance

Ralph Waldo Emerson

The son of a Unitarian minister, Ralph Waldo Emerson (1803–1882) was born in Boston, graduated from Harvard College in 1821, and afterwards taught school. He studied for the ministry and from 1829 to 1832 served as assistant pastor in a Unitarian church in Boston, resigning because of religious doubts and depressed by the death of his wife the year before. Following a trip to Europe, Emerson settled in Concord, Massachusetts, remarried, and made his living as an occasional preacher, lecturer, and writer. In these years he developed a philosophy akin to that of European Romantic writers and philosophers of the early nineteenth century.

In 1838 Emerson scandalized the Harvard Divinity School with an address criticizing "historical Christianity"—which, Emerson stated, "destroys the power of preaching, by withdrawing it from the exploration of the moral nature of man; where the sublime is, where are the resources of astonishment and power." Drawing upon notebooks he began at college, Emerson worked out his ideas in a series of essays collected in 1841 and in successive volumes. He became associated with the Transcendentalist writers of the Boston area, helping to publish their journal The Dial *but disagreeing with some of their social ideas. His later writings show a turning away from the Transcendental idealism of his early writings. Emerson was to become an overseer of Harvard, where he had created a scandal years earlier; he ended his life in a gradual intellectual decline.*

Emerson typifies the turn of many in the nineteenth century from orthodox religious ideas. With the Romantic writers and philosophers and American Transcendentalists, Emerson believed that, in the words of his 1836 essay Nature, *"the mind is a part of the nature of things; the world is a divine dream, from which we may presently awake to the glories and certainties of day." If they choose to do, people can use their intuitive powers to discover God in nature. Emerson states in the same essay, "Idealism sees the world in God." Because nature is continuously changing, the discovery of God in nature is a continuous revelation—each person revealing an aspect of God through personal experience and testimony. Conduct is central for Emerson. "Build therefore your own world," he writes in the conclusion of* Nature. *"As fast as you conform your life to the pure idea in your mind, that will unfold its great proportions."*

How is the person to distinguish ordinary perception from a "pure idea," a revelation of the divine? Emerson answers this question in the essay "The Over-Soul":

> We distinguish the announcements of the soul, its manifestations of its own nature, by the term *Revelation*. These are always attended by the emotion of the sublime. For this communication is an influx of the Divine mind into

our mind. It is an ebb of the individual rivulet before the flowing surges of the sea of life. Every distinct apprehension of this central commandment agitates men with awe and delight.

To know what is true and false, right and wrong, is to listen to the heart. "Speak to his heart," Emerson states in the same essay, "and the man becomes suddenly virtuous." It is our character that disposes us to both revelation and virtue, Emerson points out in his essays. "Self-Reliance," published in 1841, is the central statement of this belief.

Ne te quæsiveris extra.[1]

"Man is his own star; and the soul that can
Render an honest and a perfect man
Commands all light, all influence, all fate;
Nothing to him falls early or too late.
Our acts our angels are, or good or ill.
Our fatal shadows that walk by us still."
—epilogue to Beaumont and
Fletcher's *Honest Man's Fortune*

Cast the bantling on the rocks,
Suckle him with the she-wolf's teat,
Wintered with the hawk and fox,
Power and speed be hands and feet.

I read the other day some verses written by an eminent painter which were original and not conventional. The soul always hears an admonition in such lines, let the subject be what it may. The sentiment they instil is of more value than any thought they may contain. To believe your own thought, to believe that what is true for you in your private heart is true for all men,—that is genius. Speak your latent conviction, and it shall be the universal sense; for the inmost in due time becomes the outmost,—and our first thought is rendered back to us by the trumpets of the Last Judgment. Familiar as the voice of the mind is to each, the highest merit we ascribe to Moses, Plato, and Milton is that they set at naught books and traditions, and spoke not what men, but what they thought. A man should learn to detect and watch that gleam of light which flashes across his mind from within, more than the lustre of the firmament of bards and sages. Yet he dismisses without notice his thought, because it is his. In every work of genius we recognize our own rejected thoughts: they come back to us with a certain alienated majesty. Great works of art have no more affecting lesson for us than this. They teach us to abide by our spontaneous impression with good-humored inflexibility then most when the whole cry of voices is on the other side. Else, to-morrow a stranger will say with masterly good sense precisely what we have thought and felt all the time, and we shall be forced to take with shame our own opinion from another.

---

[1]"Do not quest outside yourself."

There is a time in every man's education when he arrives at the conviction that 2
envy is ignorance; that imitation is suicide; that he must take himself for better for
worse as his portion; that though the wide universe is full of good, no kernel of nourishing corn can come to him but through his toil bestowed on that plot of ground which
is given to him to till. The power which resides in him is new in nature, and none but
he knows what that is which he can do, nor does he know until he has tried. Not for
nothing one face, one character, one fact, makes much impression on him, and another
none. This sculpture in the memory is not without preëstablished harmony. The eye
was placed where one ray should fall, that it might testify of that particular ray. We but
half express ourselves, and are ashamed of that divine idea which each of us represents.
It may be safely trusted as proportionate and of good issues, so it be faithfully imparted,
but God will not have his work made manifest by cowards. A man is relieved and gay
when he has put his heart into his work and done his best; but what he has said or done
otherwise shall give him no peace. It is a deliverance which does not deliver. In the attempt his genius deserts him; no muse befriends; no invention, no hope.

Trust thyself: every heart vibrates to that iron string. Accept the place the di- 3
vine providence has found for you, the society of your contemporaries, the connection
of events. Great men have always done so, and confided themselves childlike to the genius of their age, betraying their perception that the absolutely trustworthy was seated
at their heart, working through their hands, predominating in all their being. And we
are now men, and must accept in the highest mind the same transcendent destiny; and
not minors and invalids in a protected corner, not cowards fleeing before a revolution,
but guides, redeemers, and benefactors, obeying the Almighty effort, and advancing on
Chaos and the Dark.[2]

What pretty oracles nature yields us on this text, in the face and behaviour of 4
children, babes, and even brutes! That divided and rebel mind, that distrust of a sentiment because our arithmetic has computed the strength and means opposed to our purpose, these have not. Their mind being whole, their eye is as yet unconquered, and
when we look in their faces, we are disconcerted. Infancy conforms to nobody: all conform to it, so that one babe commonly makes four or five out of the adults who prattle
and play to it. So God has armed youth and puberty and manhood no less with its own
piquancy and charm, and made it enviable and gracious and its claims not to be put by,
if it will stand by itself. Do not think the youth has no force, because he cannot speak
to you and me. Hark! in the next room his voice is sufficiently clear and emphatic. It
seems he knows how to speak to his contemporaries. Bashful or bold, then, he will know
how to make us seniors very unnecessary.

The nonchalance of boys who are sure of a dinner, and would disdain as much 5
as a lord to do or say aught to conciliate one, is the healthy attitude of human nature.
A boy is in the parlour what the pit is in the playhouse; independent, irresponsible, looking out from his corner on such people and facts as pass by, he tries and sentences them
on their merits, in the swift, summary ways of boys, as good, bad, interesting, silly, eloquent, troublesome. He cumbers himself never about consequences, about interests: he
gives an independent, genuine verdict. You must court him: he does not court you. But
the man is, as it were, clapped into jail by his consciousness. As soon as he has once

---

[2]Personifications in Book 1 of Milton's *Paradise Lost*.

acted or spoken with éclat, he is à committed person, watched by the sympathy or the hatred of hundreds; whose affections must now enter into his account. There is no Lethe[3] for this. Ah, that he could pass again into his neutrality! Who can thus avoid all pledges, and having observed, observe again from the same unaffected, unbiased, unbribable, unaffrighted innocence, must always be formidable. He would utter opinions on all passing affairs, which being seen to be not private, but necessary, would sink like darts into the ear of men, and put them in fear.

These are the voices which we hear in solitude, but they grow faint and inaudi- 6 ble as we enter into the world. Society everywhere is in conspiracy against the manhood of every one of its members. Society is a joint-stock company, in which the members agree, for the better securing of his bread to each shareholder, to surrender the liberty and culture of the eater. The virtue in most request is conformity. Self-reliance is its aversion. It loves not realities and creators, but names and customs.

Whoso would be a man, must be a nonconformist. He who would gather im- 7 mortal palms must not be hindered by the name of goodness, but must explore if it be goodness. Nothing is at last sacred but the integrity of your own mind. Absolve you to yourself, and you shall have the suffrage of the world. I remember an answer which when quite young I was prompted to make to a valued adviser, who was wont to importune me with the dear old doctrines of the church. On my saying, What have I to do with the sacredness of traditions, if I live wholly from within? my friend suggested,—"But these impulses may be from below, not from above." I replied, "They do not seem to me to be such; but if I am the Devil's child, I will live then from the Devil." No law can be sacred to me but that of my nature. Good and bad are but names very readily transferable to that or this; the only right is what is after my constitution, the only wrong what is against it. A man is to carry himself in the presence of all opposition as if everything were titular and ephemeral but he. I am ashamed to think how easily we capitulate to badges and names, to large societies and dead institutions. Every decent and well-spoken individual affects and sways me more than is right. I ought to go upright and vital, and speak the rude truth in all ways. If malice and vanity wear the coat of philanthropy, shall that pass? If an angry bigot assumes this bountiful cause of Abolition, and comes to me with his last news from Barbadoes[4] why should I not say to him, "Go love thy infant; love thy wood-chopper; be good-natured and modest: have that grace; and never varnish your hard, uncharitable ambition with this incredible tenderness for black folk a thousand miles off. Thy love afar is spite at home." Rough and graceless would be such greeting, but truth is handsomer than the affectation of love. Your goodness must have some edge to it,—else it is none. The doctrine of hatred must be preached as the counteraction of the doctrine of love when that pules and whines. I shun father and mother and wife and brother, when my genius calls me. I would write on the lintels of the door-post, *Whim.* I hope it is somewhat better than whim at last, but we cannot spend the day in explanation. Expect me not to show cause why I seek or why I exclude company. Then, again, do not tell me, as a good man did to-day, of my obligation to put all poor men in good situations. Are they *my* poor? I tell thee, thou foolish philanthropist, that I grudge the dollar, the dime, the cent I give to such men

---

[3]River in Hades, the Greek underworld; those who drank from the river forgot the past.
[4]Slavery in the West Indies was ended by the British in 1833.

as do not belong to me and to whom I do not belong. There is a class of persons to whom by all spiritual affinity I am bought and sold; for them I will go to prison, if need be; but your miscellaneous popular charities; the education at college of fools; the building of meeting-houses to the vain end to which many now stand; alms to sots; and the thousandfold Relief Societies;—though I confess with shame I sometimes succumb and give the dollar, it is a wicked dollar, which by and by I shall have the manhood to withhold.

Virtues are, in the popular estimate, rather the exception than the rule. There 8 is the man *and* his virtues. Men do what is called a good action, as some piece of courage or charity, much as they would pay a fine in expiation of daily nonappearance on parade. Their works are done as an apology or extenuation of their living in the world,—as invalids and the insane pay a high board. Their virtues are penances. I do not wish to expiate, but to live. My life is for itself and not for a spectacle. I much prefer that it should be of a lower strain, so it be genuine and equal, than that it should be glittering and unsteady. I wish it to be sound and sweet, and not to need diet and bleeding. I ask primary evidence that you are a man, and refuse this appeal from the man to his actions. I know that for myself it makes no difference whether I do or forbear those actions which are reckoned excellent. I cannot consent to pay for a privilege where I have intrinsic right. Few and mean as my gifts may be, I actually am, and do not need for my own assurance or the assurance of my fellows any secondary testimony.

What I must do is all that concerns me, not what the people think. This rule, 9 equally arduous in actual and in intellectual life, may serve for the whole distinction between greatness and meanness. It is the harder, because you will always find those who think they know what is your duty better than you know it. It is easy in the world to live after the world's opinion; it is easy in solitude to live after our own; but the great man is he who in the midst of the crowd keeps with perfect sweetness the independence of solitude.

The objection to conforming to usages that have become dead to you is, that 10 it scatters your force. It loses your time and blurs the impression of your character. If you maintain a dead church, contribute to a dead Bible-society, vote with a great party either for the government or against it, spread your table like base housekeepers,— under all these screens I have difficulty to detect the precise man you are. And, of course, so much force is withdrawn from all your proper life. But do your work, and I shall know you. Do your work, and you shall reinforce yourself. A man must consider what a blind man's-buff is this game of conformity. If I know your sect, I anticipate your argument. I hear a preacher announce for his text and topic the expendiency of one of the institutions of his church. Do I not know beforehand that not possibly can he say a new and spontaneous word? Do I not know that, with all this ostentation of examining the grounds of the institution, he will do no such thing? Do I not know that he is pledged to himself not to look but at one side,—the permitted side, not as a man, but as a parish minister? He is a retained attorney, and these airs of the bench are the emptiest affectation. Well, most men have bound their eyes with one or another handkerchief, and attached themselves to some one of these communities of opinion. This conformity makes them not false in a few particulars, authors of a few lies, but false in all particulars. Their every truth is not quite true. Their two is not the real two, their four not the real four; so that every word they say chagrins us, and we know not where to begin to set them right. Meantime nature is not slow to equip us in the prison-uniform of the party to which we adhere. We come to wear one cut of face and figure, and acquire by degrees the gentlest asinine expression. There is a mortifying experience in particular, which does not fail to wreak itself also in the general history; I mean "the foolish face of praise,"[5] the forced smile which we put on in company where we do not feel at ease in answer to conversation which does not interest us. The muscles, not spontaneously moved, but moved by a low usurping wilfulness, grow tight about the outline of the face, with the most disagreeable sensation.

For nonconformity the world whips you with its displeasure. And therefore a 11 man must know how to estimate a sour face. The bystanders look askance on him in the public street or in the friend's parlour. If this aversion had its origin in contempt and resistance like his own, he might well go home with a sad countenance; but the sour faces of the multitude, like their sweet faces, have no deep cause, but are put on and off as the wind blows and a newspaper directs. Yet is the discontent of the multitude more formidable than that of the senate and the college. It is easy enough for a firm man who knows the world to brook the rage of the cultivated classes. Their rage is decorous and prudent, for they are timid as being very vulnerable themselves. But when to their feminine rage the indignation of the people is added, when the ignorant and the poor are aroused, when the unintelligent brute force that lies at the bottom of society is made to growl and mow,[6] it needs the habit of magnanimity and religion to treat it godlike as a trifle of no concernment.

The other terror that scares us from self-trust is our consistency; a reverence 12 for our past act or word, because the eyes of others have no other data for computing our orbit than our past acts, and we are loth to disappoint them.

But why should you keep your head over your shoulder? Why drag about this 13 corpse of your memory, lest you contradict somewhat you have stated in this or that public place? Suppose you should contradict yourself; what then? It seems to be a rule of wisdom never to rely on your memory alone, scarcely even in acts of pure memory, but to bring the past for judgment into the thousand-eyed present, and live ever in a new day. In your metaphysics you have denied personality to the Deity: yet when the devout motions of the soul come, yield to them heart and life, though they should clothe God with shape and color. Leave your theory, as Joseph his coat in the hand of the harlot,[7] and flee.

A foolish consistency is the hobgoblin of little minds, adored by little statesmen 14 and philosophers and divines. With consistency a great soul has simply nothing to do. He may as well concern himself with his shadow on the wall. Speak what you think now in hard words, and to-morrow speak what to-morrow thinks in hard words again, though it contradict every thing you said to-day.—"Ah, so you shall be sure to be misunderstood."—Is it so bad, then, to be misunderstood? Pythagoras[8] was misunderstood, and Socrates, and Jesus, and Luther, and Copernicus, and Galileo, and Newton,

---

[5]Alexander Pope, in his poem "Epistle to Dr. Arbuthnot," refers to wits and students of law who put on "a foolish face of praise," pretending to admire a writer they are trying to understand.

[6]To mow is to grimace with pain.

[7]Potiphar's wife, in the Old Testament.

[8]Greek philosopher of the sixth century B.C., who believed that number was the first principle of the universe and discovered that the earth turns on its axis.

and every pure and wise spirit that ever took flesh. To be great is to be misunderstood.

I suppose no man can violate his nature. All the sallies of his will are rounded 15 in by the law of his being, as the inequalities of Andes and Himmaleh are insignificant in the curve of the sphere. Nor does it matter how you gauge and try him. A character is like an acrostic or Alexandrian stanza;—read it forward, backward, or across, it still spells the same thing. In this pleasing, contrite wood-life which God allows me, let me record day by day my honest thought without prospect or retrospect, and, I cannot doubt, it will be found symmetrical, though I mean it not, and see it not. My book should smell of pines and resound with the hum of insects. The swallow over my window should interweave that thread or straw he carries in his bill into my web also. We pass for what we are. Character teaches above our wills. Men imagine that they communicate their virtue or vice only by overt actions, and do not see that virtue or vice emit a breath every moment.

There will be an agreement in whatever variety of actions, so they be each honest and natural in their hour. For of one will, the actions will be harmonious, however 16 unlike they seem. These varieties are lost sight of at a little distance, at a little height of thought. One tendency unites them all. The voyage of the best ship is a zigzag line of a hundred tacks.[9] See the line from a sufficient distance, and it straightens itself to the average tendency. Your genuine action will explain itself, and will explain your other genuine actions. Your conformity explains nothing. Act singly, and what you have already done singly will justify you now. Greatness appeals to the future. If I can be firm enough to-day to do right, and scorn eyes, I must have done so much right before as to defend me now. Be it how it will, do right now. Always scorn appearances, and you always may. The force of character is cumulative. All the foregone days of virtue work their health into this. What makes the majesty of the heroes of the senate and the field, which so fills the imagination? The consciousness of a train of great days and victories behind. They shed a united light on the advancing actor. He is attended as by a visible escort of angels. That is it which throws thunder into Chatham's[10] voice, and dignity into Washington's port, and America into Adams's eye. Honor is venerable to us because it is no ephemera. It is always ancient virtue. We worship it to-day because it is not of to-day. We love it and pay it homage, because it is not a trap for our love and homage, but is self-dependent, self-derived, and therefore of an old immaculate pedigree, even if shown in a young person.

I hope in these days we have heard the last of conformity and consistency. Let 17 the words be gazetted and ridiculous henceforward. Instead of the gong for dinner, let us hear a whistle from the Spartan fife. Let us never bow and apologize more. A great man is coming to eat at my house. I do not wish to please him; I wish that he should wish to please me. I will stand here for humanity, and though I would make it kind, I would make it true. Let us affront and reprimand the smooth mediocrity and squalid contentment of the times, and hurl in the face of custom, and trade, and office, the fact which is the upshot of all history, that there is a great responsible Thinker and Actor

---

[9]Turns of the bow of a sailing ship to the wind.
[10]William Pitt, Earl of Chatham (1708–1778), who opposed taxation of the American colonists in debate in Parliament but later opposed withdrawing British forces from America.

working wherever a man works; that a true man belongs to no other time or place, but is the centre of things. Where he is, there is nature. He measures you, and all men, and all events. Ordinarily, every body in society reminds us of somewhat else, or of some other person. Character, reality, reminds you of nothing else; it takes place of the whole creation. The man must be so much, that he must make all circumstances indifferent. Every true man is a cause, a country, and an age; requires infinite spaces and numbers and time fully to accomplish his design;—and posterity seem to follow his steps as a train of clients. A man Caesar is born, and for ages after we have a Roman Empire. Christ is born, and millions of minds so grow and cleave to his genius that he is confounded with virtue and the possible of man. An institution is the lengthened shadow of one man; as, Monachism, of the Hermit Antony;[11] the Reformation, of Luther; Quakerism, of Fox; Methodism, of Wesley; Abolition, of Clarkson. Scipio, Milton called "the height of Rome;"[12] and all history resolves itself very easily into the biography of a few stout and earnest persons.

Let a man then know his worth, and keep things under his feet. Let him not 18 peep or steal, or skulk up and down with the air of a charity-boy, a bastard, or an interloper, in the world which exists for him. But the man in the street, finding no worth in himself which corresponds to the force which built a tower or sculptured a marble god, feels poor when he looks on these. To him a palace, a statue, or a costly book have an alien and forbidding air, much like a gay equipage, and seem to say like that, "Who are you, Sir?" Yet they all are his, suitors for his notice, petitioners to his faculties that they will come out and take possession. The picture waits for my verdict: it is not to command me, but I am to settle its claims to praise. That popular fable of the sot who was picked up dead drunk in the street, carried to the duke's house, washed and dressed and laid in the duke's bed, and, on his waking, treated with all obsequious ceremony like the duke, and assured that he had been insane, owes its popularity to the fact, that it symbolizes so well the state of man, who is in the world a sort of sot, but now and then wakes up, exercises his reason and finds himself a true prince.

Our reading is mendicant and sycophantic. In history, our imagination plays us 19 false. Kingdom and lordship, power and estate, are a gaudier vocabulary than private John and Edward in a small house and common day's work; but the things of life are the same to both; the sum total of both is the same. Why all this deference to Alfred, and Scanderbeg, and Gustavus?[13] Suppose they were virtuous; did they wear out virtue? As great a stake depends on your private act to-day, as followed their public and renowned steps. When private men shall act with original views, the lustre will be transferred from the actions of kings to those of gentlemen.

The world has been instructed by its kings, who have so magnetized the eyes 20 of nations. It has been taught by this colossal symbol the mutual reverence that is due from man to man. The joyful loyalty with which men have everywhere suffered the king,

---

[11]St. Anthony of Egypt (d. 350), founder of Christian monasticism.

[12]George Fox (1624–1691), founder of the Society of Friends, or Quakers. Thomas Clarkson (1760–1846), a British opponent of slavery. Scipio Africanus (d. 183 B.C.), the Roman military leader who defeated the Carthaginian general Hannibal at the decisive battle of Zama in 202.

[13]Alfred the Great (d. 899), king of the West Saxons who defeated the Danes in 897. George Castriota (d. 1468), called Scandebeg, Albanian military hero in the war against the Turks. Probably Gustavus II (1594–1632), Swedish king and military leader.

the noble, or the great proprietor to walk among them by a law of his own, make his own scale of men and things, and reverse theirs, pay for benefits not with money but with honor, and represent the law in his person, was the hieroglyphic by which they obscurely signified their consciousness of their own right and comeliness, the right of every man.

The magnetism which all original action exerts is explained when we inquire 21 the reason of self-trust. Who is the Trustee? What is the aboriginal Self, on which a universal reliance may be grounded? What is the nature and power of that science-baffling star, without parallax, without calculable elements, which shoots a ray of beauty even into trivial and impure actions, if the least mark of independence appear? The inquiry leads us to that source, at once the essence of genius, of virtue, and of life, which we call Spontaneity or Instinct. We denote this primary wisdom as Intuition, whilst all later teachings are tuitions. In that deep force, the last fact behind which analysis cannot go, all things find their common origin. For the sense of being which in calm hours rises, we know not how, in the soul, is not diverse from things, from space, from light, from time, from man, but one with them, and proceeds obviously from the same source whence their life and being also proceed. We first share the life by which things exist, and afterwards see them as appearances in nature, and forget that we have shared their cause. Here is the fountain of action and of thought. Here are the lungs of that inspiration which giveth man wisdom, and which cannot be denied without impiety and atheism. We lie in the lap of immense intelligence, which makes us receivers of its truth and organs of its activity. When we discern justice, when we discern truth, we do nothing of ourselves, but allow a passage to its beams. If we ask whence this comes, if we seek to pry into the soul that causes, all philosophy is at fault. Its presence or its absence is all we can affirm. Every man discriminates between the voluntary acts of his mind, and his involuntary perceptions, and knows that to his involuntary perceptions a perfect faith is due. He may err in the expression of them, but he knows that these things are so, like day and night, not to be disputed. My wilful actions and acquisitions are but roving;—the idlest reverie, the faintest native emotion, command my curiosity and respect. Thoughtless people contradict as readily the statement of perceptions as of opinions, or rather much more readily; for they do not distinguish between perception and notion. They fancy that I choose to see this or that thing. But perception is not whimsical, but fatal. If I see a trait, my children will see it after me, and in course of time, all mankind,—although it may chance that no one has seen it before me. For my perception of it is as much a fact as the sun.

The relations of the soul to the divine spirit are so pure, that it is profane to 22 seek to interpose helps. It must be that when God speaketh he should communicate, not one thing, but all things; should fill the world with his voice; should scatter forth light, nature, time, souls, from the centre of the present thought; and new date and new create the whole. Whenever a mind is simple, and receives a divine wisdom, old things pass away,—means, teachers, texts, temples fall; it lives now, and absorbs past and future into the present hour. All things are made sacred by relation to it,—one as much as another. All things are dissolved to their centre by their cause, and, in the universal miracle, petty and particular miracles disappear. If, therefore, a man claims to know and speak of God, and carries you backward to the phraseology of some old mouldered nation in another country, in another world, believe him not. Is the acorn better than the oak which is its fulness and completion? Is the parent better than the child into whom he has cast his ripened being? Whence, then, this worship of the past? The centuries are conspirators against the sanity and authority of the soul. Time and space are but physiological colors which the eye makes, but the soul is light; where it is, is day; where it was, is night; and history is an impertinence and an injury, if it be anything more than a cheerful apologue or parable of my being and becoming.

Man is timid and apologetic; he is no longer upright; he dares not say "I think," 23 "I am," but quotes some saint or sage. He is ashamed before the blade of grass or the blowing rose. These roses under my window make no reference to former roses or to better ones; they are for what they are; they exist with God to-day. There is no time to them. There is simply the rose; it is perfect in every moment of its existence. Before a leaf-bud has burst, its whole life acts; in the fullblown flower there is no more; in the leafless root there is no less. Its nature is satisfied, and it satisfies nature, in all moments alike. But man postpones or remembers; he does not live in the present, but with reverted eye laments the past, or, heedless of the riches that surround him, stands on tip-toe to foresee the future. He cannot be happy and strong until he too lives with nature in the present, above time.

This should be plain enough. Yet see what strong intellects dare not yet hear 24 God himself, unless he speaks the phraseology of I know not what David, or Jeremiah, or Paul. We shall not always set so great a price on a few texts, on a few lives. We are like children who repeat by rote the sentences of grandames and tutors, and, as they grow older, of the men of talents and character they chance to see,—painfully recollecting the exact words they spoke; afterwards, when they come into the point of view which those had who uttered these sayings, they understand them, and are willing to let the words go; for, at any time, they can use words as good when occasion comes. If we live truly, we shall see truly. It is as easy for the strong man to be strong, as it is for the weak to be weak. When we have new perception, we shall gladly disburden the memory of its hoarded treasures as old rubbish. When a man lives with God, his voice shall be as sweet as the murmur of the brook and the rustle of the corn.

And now at last the highest truth on this subject remains unsaid; probably can- 25 not be said; for all that we say is the far-off remembering of the intuition. That thought, by what I can now nearest approach to say it, is this. When good is near you, when you have life in yourself, it is not by any known or accustomed way; you shall not discern the foot-prints of any other; you shall not see the face of man; you shall not hear any name;—the way, the thought, the good, shall be wholly strange and new. It shall exclude example and experience. You take the way from man, not to man. All persons that ever existed are its forgotten ministers. Fear and hope are alike beneath it. There is somewhat low even in hope. In the hour of vision, there is nothing that can be called gratitude, nor properly joy. The soul raised over passion beholds identity and eternal causation, perceives the self-existence of Truth and Right, and calms itself with knowing that all things go well. Vast spaces of nature, the Atlantic Ocean, the South Sea,—long intervals of time, years, centuries,—are of no account. This which I think and feel underlay every former state of life and circumstances, as it does underlie my present, and what is called life, and what is called death.

Life only avails, not the having lived. Power ceases in the instant of repose; it 26 resides in the moment of transition from a past to a new state, in the shooting of the gulf, in the darting to an aim. This one fact the world hates, that the soul *becomes;* for that forever degrades the past, turns all riches to poverty, all reputation to a shame, confounds the saint with the rogue, shoves Jesus and Judas equally aside. Why, then, do we prate of self-reliance? Inasmuch as the soul is present, there will be power not confident but agent. To talk of reliance is a poor external way of speaking. Speak rather of that which relies, because it works and is. Who has more obedience than I masters me, though he should not raise his finger. Round him I must revolve by the gravitation of spirits. We fancy it rhetoric, when we speak of eminent virtue. We do not yet see that virtue is Height, and that a man or a company of men, plastic and permeable to principles, by the law of nature must overpower and ride all cities, nations, kings, rich men, poets, who are not.

This is the ultimate fact which we so quickly reach on this, as on every topic, 27 the resolution of all into the ever-blessed ONE. Self-existence is the attribute of the Supreme Cause, and it constitutes the measure of good by the degree in which it enters into all lower forms. All things real are so by so much virtue as they contain. Commerce, husbandry, hunting, whaling, war, eloquence, personal weight, are somewhat, and engage my respect as examples of its presence and impure action. I see the same law working in nature for conservation and growth. Power is in nature the essential measure of right. Nature suffers nothing to remain in her kingdoms which cannot help itself. The genesis and maturation of a planet, its poise and orbit, the bended tree recovering itself from the strong wind, the vital resources of every animal and vegetable, are demonstrations of the self-sufficing, and therefore self-relying soul.

Thus all concentrates: let us not rove; let us sit at home with the cause. Let us 28 stun and astonish the intruding rabble of men and books and institutions, by a simple declaration of the divine fact. Bid the invaders take the shoes from off their feet, for God is here within. Let our simplicity judge them, and our docility to our own law demonstrate the poverty of nature and fortune beside our native riches.

But now we are a mob. Man does not stand in awe of man, nor is his genius ad- 29 monished to stay at home, to put itself in communication with the internal ocean, but it goes abroad to beg a cup of water of the urns of other men. We must go alone. I like the silent church before the service begins, better than any preaching. How far off, how cool, how chaste the persons look, begirt each one with a precinct or sanctuary! So let us always sit. Why should we assume the faults of our friends, or wife, or father, or child, because they sit around our hearth, or are said to have the same blood? All men have my blood, and I all men's. Not for that will I adopt their petulance or folly, even to the extent of being ashamed of it. But your isolation must not be mechanical, but spiritual, that is, must be elevation. At times the whole world seems to be in conspiracy to importune you with emphatic trifles. Friend, client, child, sickness, fear, want, charity, all knock at once at thy closet door, and say,—"Come out unto us." But keep thy state; come not into their confusion. The power men possess to annoy me, I give them by a weak curiosity. No man can come near me but through my act. "What we love that we have, but by desire we bereave ourselves of the love."

If we cannot at once rise to the sanctities of obedience and faith, let us at least 30 resist our temptations; let us enter into the state of war, and wake Thor and Woden,[14]

---

[14]The Norse gods of thunder and war.

courage and constancy, in our Saxon breasts. This is to be done in our smooth times by speaking the truth. Check this lying hospitality and lying affection. Live no longer to the expectation of these deceived and deceiving people with whom we converse. Say to them, "O father, O mother, O wife, O brother, O friend, I have lived with you after appearances hitherto. Henceforward I am the truth's. Be it known unto you that henceforward I obey no law less than the eternal law. I will have no covenants but proximities. I shall endeavor to nourish my parents, to support my family, to be the chaste husband of one wife,—but these relations I must fill after a new and unprecedented way. I appeal from your customs. I must be myself. I cannot break myself any longer for you, or you. If you can love me for what I am, we shall be the happier. If you cannot, I will still seek to deserve that you should. I will not hide my tastes or aversions. I will so trust that what is deep is holy, that I will do strongly before the sun and moon whatever inly rejoices me, and the heart appoints. If you are noble, I will love you; if you are not, I will not hurt you and myself by hypocritical attentions. If you are true, but not in the same truth with me, cleave to your companions; I will seek my own. I do this not selfishly but humbly and truly. It is alike your interest, and mine, and all men's, however long we have dwelt in lies, to live in truth. Does this sound harsh to-day? You will soon love what is dictated by your nature as well as mine, and if we follow the truth, it will bring us out safe at last."—But so you may give these friends pain. Yes, but I cannot sell my liberty and my power, to save their sensibility. Besides, all persons have their moments of reason, when they look out into the region of absolute truth; then will they justify me, and do the same thing.

The populace think that your rejection of popular standards is a rejection of all 31 standard, and mere antinomianism;[15] and the bold sensualist will use the name of philosophy to gild his crimes. But the law of consciousness abides. There are two confessionals, in one or the other of which we must be shriven. You may fulfil your round of duties by clearing yourself in the *direct,* or in the *reflex* way. Consider whether you have satisfied your relations to father, mother, cousin, neighbour, town, cat and dog; whether any of these can upbraid you. But I may also neglect this reflex standard, and absolve me to myself. I have my own stern claims and perfect circle. It denies the name of duty to many offices that are called duties. But if I can discharge its debts, it enables me to dispense with the popular code. If any one imagines that this law is lax, let him keep its commandment one day.

And truly it demands something godlike in him who has cast off the common 32 motives of humanity, and has ventured to trust himself for a taskmaster. High be his heart, faithful his will, clear his sight, that he may in good earnest be doctrine, society, law, to himself, that a simple purpose may be to him as strong as iron necessity is to others!

If any man consider the present aspects of what is called by distinction *society,* 33 he will see the need of these ethics. The sinew and heart of man seem to be drawn out, and we are become timorous, desponding whimperers. We are afraid of truth, afraid of fortune, afraid of death, and afraid of each other. Our age yields no great and perfect persons. We want men and women who shall renovate life and our social state, but we

---

[15]The religious doctrine that salvation is possible by faith in God alone, without necessarily obeying moral injunctions.

see that most natures are insolvent, cannot satisfy their own wants, have an ambition out of all proportion to their practical force and do lean and beg day and night continually. Our housekeeping is mendicant, our arts, our occupations, our marriages, our religion, we have not chosen, but society has chosen for us. We are parlour soldiers. We shun the rugged battle of fate, where strength is born.

If our young men miscarry in their first enterprises, they lose all heart. If the 34 young merchant fails, men say he is *ruined.* If the finest genius studies at one of our colleges, and is not installed in an office within one year afterwards in the cities or suburbs of Boston or New York, it seems to his friends and to himself that he is right in being disheartened, and in complaining the rest of his life. A sturdy lad from New Hampshire or Vermont, who in turn tries all the professions, who *teams it, farms it, peddles,* keeps a school, preaches, edits a newspaper, goes to Congress, buys a township, and so forth, in successive years, and always, like a cat, falls on his feet, is worth a hundred of these city dolls. He walks abreast with his days, and feels no shame in not "studying a profession," for he does not postpone his life, but lives already. He has not one chance, but a hundred chances. Let a Stoic[16] open the resources of man, and tell men they are not leaning willows, but can and must detach themselves; that with the exercise of self-trust, new powers shall appear; that a man is the word made flesh, born to shed healing to the nations, that he should be ashamed of our compassion, and that the moment he acts from himself, tossing the laws, the books, idolatries, and customs out of the window, we pity him no more, but thank and revere him,—and that teacher shall restore the life of man to splendor, and make his name dear to all history.

It is easy to see that a greater self-reliance must work a revolution in all the of- 35 fices and relations of men; in their religion; in their education; in their pursuits; their modes of living; their association; in their property; in their speculative views.

1. In what prayers do men allow themselves! That which they call a holy office 36 is not so much as brave and manly. Prayer looks abroad and asks for some foreign addition to come through some foreign virtue, and loses itself in endless mazes of natural and supernatural, and mediatorial and miraculous. Prayer that craves a particular commodity,—anything less than all good,—is vicious. Prayer is the contemplation of the facts of life from the highest point of view. It is the soliloquy of a beholding and jubilant soul. It is the spirit of God pronouncing his works good. But prayer as a means to effect a private end is meanness and theft. It supposes dualism and not unity in nature and consciousness. As soon as the man is at one with God, he will not beg. He will then see prayer in all action. The prayer of the farmer kneeling in his field to weed it, the prayer of the rower kneeling with the stroke of his oar, are true prayers heard throughout nature, though for cheap ends. Caratach, in Fletcher's Bonduca,[17] when admonished to inquire the mind of the god Audate, replies,—

> "His hidden meaning lies in our endeavours;
> Our valors are our best gods."

---

[16]An ancient school of philosophy that believed everything that happens is fated and therefore should be accepted without protest and with the least feeling possible.
[17]The title character in John Fletcher's Elizabethan play.

Another sort of false prayers are our regrets. Discontent is the want of self- 37 reliance: it is infirmity of will. Regret calamities, if you can thereby help the sufferer; if not, attend your own work, and already the evil begins to be repaired. Our sympathy is just as base. We come to them who weep foolishly, and sit down and cry for company, instead of imparting to them truth and health in rough electric shocks, putting them once more in communication with their own reason. The secret of fortune is joy in our hands. Welcome evermore to gods and men is the self-helping man. For him all doors are flung wide: him all tongues greet, all honors crown, all eyes follow with desire. Our love goes out to him and embraces him, because he did not need it. We solicitously and apologetically caress and celebrate him, because he held on his way and scorned our disapprobation. The gods love him because men hated him. "To the persevering mortal," said Zoroaster,[18] the blessed Immortals are swift."

As men's prayers are a disease of the will, so are their creeds a disease of the 38 intellect. They say with those foolish Israelites, "Let not God speak to us, lest we die. Speak thou, speak any man with us, and we will obey."[19] Everywhere I am hindered of meeting God in my brother, because he has shut his own temple doors, and recites fables merely of his brother's, or his brother's brother's God. Every new mind is a new classification. If it prove a mind of uncommon activity and power, a Locke, a Lavoisier, a Hutton, a Bentham, a Fourier,[20] it imposes its classification on other men, and lo! a new system. In proportion to the depth of the thought, and so to the number of the objects it touches and brings within reach of the pupil, is his complacency. But chiefly is this apparent in creeds and churches, which are also classifications of some powerful mind acting on the elemental thought of duty, and man's relation to the Highest. Such is Calvinism, Quakerism, Swedenborgism. The pupil takes the same delight in subordinating every thing to the new terminology, as a girl who has just learned botany in seeing a new earth and new seasons thereby. It will happen for a time, that the pupil will find his intellectual power has grown by the study of his master's mind. But in all unbalanced minds, the classification is idolized, passes for the end, and not for a speedily exhaustible means, so that the walls of the system blend to their eye in the remote horizon with the walls of the universe; the luminaries of heaven seem to them hung on the arch their master built. They cannot imagine how you aliens have any right to see,— how you can see; "It must be somehow that you stole the light from us." They do not yet perceive that light, unsystematic, indomitable, will break into any cabin, even into theirs. Let them chirp awhile and call it their own. If they are honest and do well, presently their neat new pinfold will be too strait and low, will crack, will lean, will rot and vanish, and the immortal light, all young, and joyful, million-orbed, million-colored, will beam over the universe as on the first morning.

---

[18]The ancient Persian religious prophet and founder of the Zoroastrian religion.

[19]The response of the Israelites on receiving the Commandments from Moses, Exodus 20:19.

[20]John Locke (1632–1704), English physician and philosopher who urged religious tolerance and the contractual theory of government; one of the founders of British empiricism. Antoine Laurent Lavoisier (1743–1794), who created modern chemistry through quantitative methods; he established the role of oxygen in combustion. James Hutton (1726–1797), Scottish geologist who proposed an explanation of the earth's crust. Jeremy Bentham (1748–1832), British legal philosopher and founder of the utilitarian philosophy; see p. 87. Francois Marie Charles Fourier (1772–1837), French social scientist who advocated cooperative societies like the Transcendentalist Brook Farm.

2. It is for want of self-culture that the superstition of Travelling, whose idols 39 are Italy, England, Egypt, retains its fascination for all educated Americans. They who made England, Italy, or Greece venerable in the imagination did so by sticking fast where they were, like an axis of the earth. In manly hours, we feel that duty is our place. The soul is no traveller; the wise man stays at home, and when his necessities, his duties, on any occasion call him from his house, or into foreign lands, he is at home still, and shall make men sensible by the expression of his countenance, that he goes the missionary of wisdom and virtue, and visits cities and men like a sovereign, and not like an interloper or a valet.

I have no churlish objection to the circumnavigation of the globe, for the pur- 40 poses of art, of study, and benevolence, so that the man is first domesticated, or does not go abroad with the hope of finding somewhat greater than he knows. He who travels to be amused, or to get somewhat which he does not carry, travels away from himself, and grows old even in youth among old things. In Thebes, in Palmyra, his will and mind have become old and dilapidated as they. He carries ruins to ruins.

Travelling is a fool's paradise. Our first journeys discover to us the indifference 41 of places. At home I dream that at Naples, at Rome, I can be intoxicated with beauty, and lose my sadness. I pack my trunk, embrace my friends, embark on the sea and at last wake up in Naples, and there beside me is the stern fact, the sad self, unrelenting, identical, that I fled from. I seek the Vatican, and the palaces. I affect to be intoxicated with sights and suggestions, but I am not intoxicated. My giant goes with me wherever I go.

3. But the rage of travelling is a symptom of a deeper unsoundness affecting the 42 whole intellectual action. The intellect is vagabond, and our system of education fosters restlessness. Our minds travel when our bodies are forced to stay at home. We imitate; and what is imitation but the travelling of the mind? Our houses are built with foreign taste; our shelves are garnished with foreign ornaments; our opinions, our tastes, our faculties, lean, and follow the Past and the Distant. The soul created the arts wherever they have flourished. It was in his own mind that the artist sought his model. It was an application of his own thought to the thing to be done and the conditions to be observed. And why need we copy the Doric or the Gothic model? Beauty, convenience, grandeur of thought, and quaint expression are as near to us as to any, and if the American artist will study with hope and love the precise thing to be done by him, considering the climate, the soil, the length of the day, the wants of the people, the habit and form of the government, he will create a house in which all these will find themselves fitted, and taste and sentiment will be satisfied also.

Insist on yourself; never imitate. Your own gift you can present every moment 43 with the cumulative force of a whole life's cultivation; but of the adopted talent of another, you have only an extemporaneous, half possession. That which each can do best, none but his Maker can teach him. No man yet knows what it is, nor can, till that person has exhibited it. Where is the master who could have taught Shakespeare? Where is the master who could have instructed Franklin, or Washington, or Bacon, or Newton? Every great man is a unique. The Scipionism of Scipio is precisely that part he could not borrow. Shakespeare will never be made by the study of Shakespeare. Do that which is assigned you, and you cannot hope too much or dare too much. There is at this moment for you an utterance brave and grand as that of the colossal chisel of Phidias,[21] or trowel of the Egyptians, or the pen of Moses, or Dante, but different from all these. Not possibly will the soul, all rich, all eloquent, with thousand-cloven tongue, deign to repeat itself but if you can hear what these patriarchs say, surely you can reply to them in the same pitch of voice; for the ear and the tongue are two organs of one nature. Abide in the simple and noble regions of thy life, obey thy heart, and thou shall reproduce the Foreworld again.

4. As our Religion, our Education, our Art look abroad, so does our spirit of society. All men plume themselves on the improvement of society, and no man improves. 44

Society never advances. It recedes as fast on one side as it gains on the other. 45 It undergoes continual changes; it is barbarous, it is civilized, it is christianized, it is rich, it is scientific; but this change is not amelioration. For every thing that is given, something is taken. Society acquires new arts, and loses old instincts. What a contrast between the well-clad, reading, writing, thinking American, with a watch, a pencil, and a bill of exchange in his pocket, and the naked New Zealander, whose property is a club, a spear, a mat, and an undivided twentieth of a shed to sleep under! But compare the health of the two men, and you shall see that the white man has lost his aboriginal strength. If the traveller tell us truly, strike the savage with a broad-axe and in a day or two the flesh shall unite and heal as if you struck the blow into soft pitch, and the same blow shall send the white to his grave.

The civilized man has built a coach, but has lost the use of his feet. He is sup- 46 ported on crutches, but lacks so much support of muscle. He has a fine Geneva watch, but he fails of the skill to tell the hour by the sun. A Greenwich nautical almanac he has, and so being sure of the information when he wants it, the man in the street does not know a star in the sky. The solstice he does not observe; the equinox he knows as little; and the whole bright calendar of the year is without a dial in his mind. His note-books impair his memory; his libraries overload his wit; the insurance-office increases the number of accidents; and it may be a question whether machinery does not encumber; whether we have not lost by refinement some energy, by a Christianity, entrenched in establishments and forms, some vigor of wild virtue. For every Stoic was a Stoic; but in Christendom where is the Christian?

There is no more deviation in the moral standard than in the standard of height 47 or bulk. No greater men are now than ever were. A singular equality may be observed between the great men of the first and of the last ages; nor can all the science, art, religion, and philosophy of the nineteenth century avail to educate greater men than Plutarch's heroes, three or four and twenty centuries ago. Not in time is the race progressive. Phocion, Socrates, Anaxagoras, Diogenes, are great men, but they leave no class.[22] He who is really of their class will not be called by their name, but will be his own man, and in his turn the founder of a sect. The arts and inventions of each period

---

[21]Greek sculptor of the fifth century B.C.
[22]Plutarch (d. 120), Greek biographer whose *Parallel Lives* studies paired Greek and Roman historical figures. Phocion (d. 317 B.C.), Greek general and statesman, later dictator of Athens. Socrates (d. 399 B.C.), Athenian philosopher and teacher of Plato; see p. 142. Anaxagoras (d. 428 B.C.), Greek philosopher and atomist. Diogenes (d. 323 B.C.), Greek philosopher of the Cynic school.

are only its costume, and do not invigorate men. The harm of the improved machinery may compensate its good. Hudson and Behring accomplished so much in their fishing-boats, as to astonish Parry and Franklin,[23] whose equipment exhausted the resources of science and art. Galileo, with an opera-glass, discovered a more splendid series of celestial phenomena than any one since. Columbus found the New World in an undecked boat. It is curious to see the periodical disuse and perishing of means and machinery, which were introduced with loud laudation a few years or centuries before. The great genius returns to essential man. We reckoned the improvements of the art of war among the triumphs of science, and yet Napoleon conquered Europe by the bivouac, which consisted of falling back on naked valor, and disencumbering it of all aids. The Emperor held it impossible to make a perfect army, says Las Casas,[24] "without abolishing our arms, magazines, commissaries, and carriages, until, in imitation of the Roman custom, the soldier should receive his supply of corn, grind it in his hand-mill, and bake his bread himself."

Society is a wave. The wave moves onward, but the water of which it is com- 48 posed does not. The same particle does not rise from the valley to the ridge. Its unity is only phenomenal. The persons who make up a nation to-day, next year die, and their experience dies with them.

And so the reliance on Property, including the reliance on governments which 49 protect it, is the want of self-reliance. Men have looked away from themselves and at things so long, that they have come to esteem the religious, learned, and civil institutions as guards of property, and they deprecate assaults on these, because they feel them to be assaults on property. They measure their esteem of each other by what each has, and not by what each is. But a cultivated man becomes ashamed of his property, out of new respect for his nature. Especially he hates what he has, if he sees that it is accidental,—came to him by inheritance, or gift, or crime; then he feels that it is not having, it does not belong to him, has no root in him, and merely lies there, because no revolution or no robber takes it away. But that which a man is, does always by necessity acquire, and what the man acquires is living property, which does not wait the beck of rulers, or mobs, or revolutions, or fire, or storm, or bankruptcies, but perpetually renews itself wherever the man breathes. "Thy lot or portion of life," said the Caliph Ali,[25] "is seeking after thee; therefore be at rest from seeking after it." Our dependence on these foreign goods leads us to our slavish respect for numbers. The political parties meet in numerous conventions; the greater the concourse, and with each new uproar of announcement, The delegation from Essex! The Democrats from New Hampshire! The Whigs of Maine! the young patriot feels himself stronger than before by a new thousand of eyes and arms. In like manner the reformers summon conventions, and vote and resolve in multitude. Not so, O friends! will the God deign to enter and inhabit you, but

---

[23]Henry Hudson (d. 1611), British explorer who discovered the Hudson River and reached Hudson Bay. Vitus Bering (Behring) (1680–1741), Danish explorer who explored the sea and strait between Siberia and Alaska that are now named for him. Sir William E. Parry (1790–1855) and Sir John Franklin (1786–1847), Arctic explorers.

[24]Las Casas, Comte Emmanuel Augustin Dieudonne dé (1766–1842), to whom Napoleon Bonaparte dictated his memoirs at St. Helena. Las Casas wrote about Napoleon in his own memoirs of 1818 and his *Memorial of St. Helena* of 1823.

[25]Ali ibn abu Talib (d. 661), son-in-law of the prophet Mohammed.

by a method precisely the reverse. It is only as a man puts off all foreign support, and stands alone, that I see him to be strong and to prevail. He is weaker by every recruit to his banner. Is not a man better than a town? Ask nothing of men, and, in the endless mutation, thou only firm column must presently appear the upholder of all that surrounds thee. He who knows that power is inborn, that he is weak because he has looked for good out of him and elsewhere, and so perceiving, throws himself unhesitatingly on his thought, instantly rights himself, stands in the erect position, commands his limbs, works miracles; just as a man who stands on his feet is stronger than a man who stands on his head.

So use all that is called Fortune. Most men gamble with her, and gain all, and 50 lose all, as her wheel rolls. But do thou leave as unlawful these winnings, and deal with Cause and Effect, the chancellors of God. In the Will work and acquire, and thou hast chained the wheel of Chance, and shalt sit hereafter out of fear from her rotations. A political victory, a rise of rents, the recovery of your sick, or the return of your absent friend, or some other favorable event, raises your spirits, and you think good days are preparing for you. Do not believe it. Nothing can bring you peace but yourself. Nothing can bring you peace but the triumph of principles.

Questions

1. How does Emerson distinguish the ordinary person from the genius (paragraph 1) and the "true man" (paragraph 17)? Does Emerson say or imply that the genius has a special faculty of inspiration or truth? Why does the "true man" influence the course of history?
2. Is Emerson referring to an actual eye in paragraph 2, or is the reference metaphorical? Are the references to the heart in paragraphs 2 and 3 literal or metaphorical?
3. How does Emerson distinguish children from adults in paragraphs 4–6, and how does this distinction develop his central idea? How does he clarify the difference in paragraph 21?
4. According to paragraph 7, how can a person distinguish between good and bad? In general, how do paragraphs 7 and 8 clarify Emerson's conception of virtue? Would he have agreed with Rousseau that the child is naturally virtuous?
5. Emerson states in paragraph 7, "Whoso would be a man, must be a noncomformist." What must a person not conform to, and why?
6. In criticizing the bigot in paragraph 7, is Emerson attacking the abolition of slavery? In criticizing the philanthropist, is Emerson attacking charitable efforts to help the poor?
7. In praising inconsistency in paragraphs 12–14, is Emerson contradicting his statement in paragraph 16, "For of one will, the actions will be harmonious, however unlike they seem"?
8. Emerson states in paragraph 15: "I suppose no man can violate his nature." Why not? How does he define this nature in this paragraph?
9. What is Emerson warning against in the reading of history in paragraph 19? How does this warning lead into the following discussion of "original action"?

10. In what sense should people be as self-reliant as nature? What kind of power is Emerson referring to in paragraph 27, and in what sense do people possess this kind?
11. What conditions or attitudes in society make a philosophy of self-reliance a necessity, according to paragraphs 29–34?
12. According to paragraphs 36–38, what is the difference between prayers and creeds? What is the chief target of Emerson's criticism in these paragraphs?
13. Why does Emerson turn to travel in paragraphs 39–43? Is he attacking a new target?
14. What is Emerson saying about individuals and their society in paragraph 48? Does this paragraph contradict his earlier statement that great individuals create history?
15. What conception of God emerges in the whole essay? What does the final paragraph contribute to your understanding of Emerson's conception?
16. Does the essay show a buildup of ideas, or is the essay a series of loosely connected reflections?

Suggestions for Writing

1. Explain one of the following statements in light of the whole essay:
   a. "I suppose no man can violate his nature" (paragraph 15).
   b. "Life only avails, not the having lived" (paragraph 26).
   c. "Society never advances" (paragraph 45).
   d. "Nothing can bring you peace but the triumph of principles" (paragraph 50).
2. Develop one of Emerson's statements on the basis of your personal experience and observation. Disagree or qualify the statement if necessary. Use your discussion to draw a conclusion of your own.
3. Discuss the extent to which Emerson would agree with Solzhenitsyn on individual and common scales of value in the world.
4. All of Emerson's early essays illuminate the ideas of "Self-Reliance." "The American Scholar," "Divinity School Address," "The Over-Soul," and "The Poet" are of particular interest. The notebooks of Emerson also give insight into the growth of his ideas. Discuss how one of these essays or a passage in one of the notebooks illuminate one or more ideas of "Self-Reliance."

Additional Reading

Emerson, Ralph Waldo. *Essays and Lectures.* Ed. Joel Porte. Library of America. New York: Viking, 1983.
———. *The Journals and Miscellaneous Notebooks of Ralph Waldo Emerson.* Cambridge: Belknap-Harvard University Press, 1960–82.
Paul, Sherman. *Emerson's Angle of Vision: Man and Nature in American Experience.* Cambridge: Harvard University Press, 1952.
Porte, Joel. *Representative Man: Ralph Waldo Emerson in His Time.* New York: Oxford University Press, 1979.
Rusk, Ralph Leslie. *The Life of Ralph Waldo Emerson.* New York: Scribner's, 1949.

Essays

Albert Schweitzer

Albert Schweitzer, his biographer James Brabazon tells us, exhibited the "reverence for life" discussed in these essays in remarkable ways at his hospital at Lambaréné, in French Equatorial Africa (see p. 16):

> He was fond of ants . . . and he used to leave small pieces of food on his desk while he worked so that he could watch them crawl up the leg in a column and return beneath the floorboards with their booty; when the cat began to join in by sitting in wait for them and killing them with its paw, he protected them with a basket. He truly did love creatures simply for being alive, and refused to endanger anything, ants, mosquitoes, rats included, which did him and his hospital no obvious harm.

In the second of these essays, Schweitzer discusses the origins of the philosophy that is summarized in his autobiographical essay (p. 22). His experiences in Africa led him to think through his ideas and put them on paper. A trip from the west coast to the interior in 1915 was particularly decisive, he tells us in one of the essays reprinted here:

> Late on the third day, at the very moment when, at sunset, we were making our way through a herd of hippopotamuses, there flashed upon my mind, unforeseen and unsought, the phrase, "Reverence for Life." The iron door had yielded: the path in the thicket had become visible. Now I had found my way to the idea in which affirmation of the world and ethics are contained side by side!

The popular image of Schweitzer is that of a benign optimist, but his thoughts could be dark, as he admits in a later passage in his autobiography:

> I am pessimistic in that I experience in its full weight what we conceive to be the absence of purpose in the course of world happenings. Only at quite rare moments have I felt really glad to be alive. I could not but feel with a sympathy full of regret all the pain that I saw around me, not only that of men but that of the whole creation. From this community of suffering that I have never tried to withdraw myself.

How to affirm life in the face of human suffering is one of the concerns of the essays that follow. These are reflections that concern a physician who encountered the terrible ravages of poverty and disease in his daily practice.

Riddles of Existence

Science teaching had something peculiarly stimulating for me. I could not get rid of the feeling that it was never made clear to us how little we really understand of the processes of Nature. For the scientific school books I felt a positive hatred. Their confident explanations—carefully shaped and trimmed with a view to being learnt by heart, and, as I soon observed, already somewhat out of date—satisfied me in no respect. It seemed to me laughable that the wind, the rain, the snow, the hail, the formation of clouds, the spontaneous combustion of hay, the tradewinds, the Gulf Stream, thunder and lightning, should all have found their proper explanation. The formation of drops of rain, of snow flakes, and of hailstones had always been a special puzzle to me. It hurt me to think that we never acknowledge the absolutely mysterious character of Nature, but always speak so confidently of explaining her, whereas all that we have really done is to go into fuller and more complicated descriptions, which only make the mysterious more mysterious than ever. Even at that age, it became clear to me that what we label Force of "Life" remains in its own essential nature forever inexplicable.

Thus I fell gradually into a new habit of dreaming about the thousand and one miracles that surround us, though fortunately the new habit did not, like my earlier thoughtless daydreams, prevent me from working properly. The habit, however, is with me still, and gets stronger. If during a meal I catch sight of the light broken up in a glass jug of water into the colors of the spectrum, I can at once become oblivious of everything around me, and unable to withdraw my gaze from the spectacle.

Thus did love for history and love for science go hand in hand, and I gradually recognized that the historical process too is full of riddles, and that we must abandon forever the hope of really understanding the past.

The Will to Live

We may take as the essential element in civilization the ethical perfecting of the individual and of society as well. But at the same time, every spiritual and every material step in advance has a significance for civilization. The will to civilization is then the universal will to progress which is conscious of the ethical as the highest value for all. In spite of the great importance we attach to the triumphs of knowledge and achievement, it is nevertheless obvious that only a humanity which is striving after ethical ends can in full measure share in the blessings brought by material progress and become master of the dangers which accompany it. To the generation which had adopted a belief in an immanent power of progress realizing itself, in some measure, naturally and automatically, and which thought that it no longer needed any ethical ideals but could advance to its goal by means of knowledge and achievement alone, terrible proof was being given by its present position of the error into which it had sunk.

The only possible way out of chaos is for us to come once more under the control of the ideas of true civilization through the adoption of an attitude toward life that contains those ideals.

But what is the nature of the attitude toward life in which the will to general progress and to ethical progress are alike founded and in which they are bound together?

It consists in an ethical affirmation of the world and of life.

What is affirmation of the world and of life?

To us Europeans and to people of European descent everywhere the will to progress is something so natural and so much a matter of course that it never occurs to us to recognize that it is rooted in an attitude toward life and springs from an act of the spirit. But if we look about us in the world, we see at once that what is to us such a matter of course is in reality anything but that. To Indian thought all effort directed to triumphs in knowledge and power and to the improvement of man's outer life and of society as a whole is mere folly. It teaches that the only sensible line of conduct for a man is to withdraw entirely into himself and to concern himself solely with the deepening of his inner life. He has nothing to do with what may become of human society and of mankind. The deepening of one's inner life, as Indian thought interprets it, means that a man surrenders himself to the thought of "no more will to live," and by abstention from action and by every sort of life denial reduces his earthly existence to a condition of being which has no content beyond a waiting for the cessation of being.

The striving for material and spiritual progress, which characterizes the people of modern Europe, has its source in the attitude toward the world to which these people have come. As a result of the Renaissance and the spiritual and religious movements bound up with it, men have entered on a new relation to themselves and to the world, and this has aroused in them a need to create by their own activities spiritual and material values which shall help to a higher development of individuals and of mankind. It is not the case that the man of modern Europe is enthusiastic for progress because he may hope to get some personal advantage from it. He is less concerned about his own condition than about the happiness which he hopes will be the lot of coming generations. Enthusiasm for progress has taken possession of him. Impressed by his great experience of finding the world revealed to him as constituted and maintained by forces which carry out a definite design he himself wills to become an active, purposeful force in the world. He looks with confidence toward new and better times which shall dawn for mankind, and learns by experience that the ideas which are held and acted upon by the mass of people do win power over circumstances and remold them.

It is on his will to material progress, acting in union with the will to ethical progress, that the foundations of modern civilization are being laid.

In modern European thought a tragedy is occurring in that the original bonds uniting the affirmative attitude toward the world with ethics are, by a slow but irresistible process, loosening and finally parting. The result that we are coming to is that European humanity is being guided by a will-to-progress that has become merely external and has lost its bearings.

The affirmative attitude can produce of itself only a partial and imperfect civilization. Only if it becomes inward and ethical can the will-to-progress which results from it possess the requisite insight to distinguish the valuable from the less valuable, and strive after a civilization which does not consist only in achievements of knowledge and power, but before all else will make men, both individually and collectively, more spiritual and more ethical.

But how could it come about that the modern attitude of the world and life changed from its original ethical character and became nonethical?

The only possible explanation is that it was not really founded on thought. The thought out of which it arose was noble and enthusiastic but not deep. The intimate connection of the ethical with the affirmative attitude toward life was for it a matter of feeling and experience rather than of proof. It took the side of life affirmation and of ethics without having penetrated their inner nature and their inward connection.

This noble and valuable view, therefore, being rooted in belief rather than in thinking which penetrated to the real nature of things was bound to wither and lose its power over men's minds. All subsequent thinking about the problems of ethics and man's relation to his world could not but expose the weak points of this view, and thereby help to hasten its decay. Its activity took effect in this direction even when its intention was to give support, for it never succeeded in replacing the inadequate foundation by one that was adequate. Again and again the new foundations and the underpinning masonry which it had taken in hand showed themselves too weak to support the building.

At bottom I am convinced that the inner connection between the affirmative attitude and ethics, declared to be part of the concept of civilization which had hitherto proved impossible to demonstrate fully, had come from a presentiment of the truth. So it was necessary to undertake to grasp as a necessity of thought by fresh, simple, and sincere thinking the truth which had hitherto been only suspected and believed in although so often proclaimed as proved.

In undertaking this I seemed to myself to be like a man who has to build a new and better boat to replace a rotten one in which he can no longer venture to trust himself to the sea, and yet does not know how to begin.

For months on end I lived in a continual state of mental excitement. Without the least success I let my thinking be concentrated, even all through my daily work at the hospital, on the real nature of the affirmative attitude and of ethics, and on the question of what they have in common. I was wandering about in a thicket in which no path was to be found. I was leaning with all my might against an iron door which would not yield.

All that I had learned from philosophy about ethics left me in the lurch. The conceptions of the Good which it had offered were all so lifeless, so unelemental, so narrow, and so destitute of content that it was quite impossible to bring them into union with the affirmative attitude. Moreover, philosophy could be said never to have concerned itself with the problem of the connection between civilization and attitude toward the world. The modern concept of progress had become to it such a matter of course that it had felt no need for coming to clear ideas about it.

To my surprise I had also to recognize the fact that the central province of philosophy, into which meditation on civilization and attitude toward the world had led me, was practically unexplored land. Now from this point, now from that, I tried to penetrate to its interior, but again and again I had to give up the attempt. I was already exhausted and disheartened. I saw, indeed, the conception needed before me, but I could not grasp it and give it expression.

While in this mental condition I had to undertake a longish journey on the river. The only means of conveyance I could find was a small steamer, towing an overladen barge, which was on the point of starting. Slowly we crept upstream, laboriously feeling—it was the dry season—for the channels between the sandbanks. Lost in thought I sat on the deck of the barge, struggling to find the elementary and universal conception of the ethical which I had not discovered in any philosophy. Sheet after sheet I covered with disconnected sentences, merely to keep myself concentrated on the problem. Late on the third day, at the very moment when, at sunset, we were making our way through a herd of hippopotamuses, there flashed upon my mind, unforeseen and unsought, the phrase "Reverence for Life." The iron door had yielded: the path in the thicket had become visible. Now I had found my way to the idea in which affirmation of the world and ethics are contained side by side! Now I knew that the ethical acceptance of the world and of life, together with the ideals of civilization contained in this concept, has a foundation in thought.

What is Reverence for Life, and how does it arise in us?

If man wishes to reach clear notions about himself and his relation to the world, he must ever again and again be looking away from the manifold, which is the product of his thought and knowledge, and reflect upon the first, the most immediate, and the continually given fact of his own consciousness. Only if he starts from this given fact can he achieve a rational view.

Descartes makes thinking start from the sentence "I think; so I must exist" (*Cogito, ergo sum*), and with his beginning thus chosen he finds himself irretrievably on the road to the abstract. Out of this empty, artificial act of thinking there can result, of course, nothing which bears on the relation of man to himself, and to the universe. Yet in reality the most immediate act of consciousness has some content. To think means to think something. The most immediate fact of man's consciousness is the assertion: "I am life which wills to live, in the midst of life which wills to live," and it is as will-to-live in the midst of will-to-live that man conceives himself during every moment that he spends in meditating on himself and the world around him.

As in my will-to-live there is ardent desire for further life and for the mysterious exaltation of the will-to-live which we call pleasure, while there is fear of destruction and of that mysterious depreciation of the will-to-live which we call pain, so too are these in the will-to-live around me, whether it can express itself to me, or remains dumb.

Man has now to decide what his relation to his will-to-live shall be. He can deny it. But if he bids his will-to-live change into will-not-to-live, as is done in Indian and indeed in all pessimistic thought, he involves himself in self-contradiction. He raises to the position of his philosophy of life something unnatural, something which is in itself untrue, and which cannot be carried to completion. Indian thought, and Schopenhauer's also, is full of inconsistencies because it cannot help making concessions time after time to the will-to-live, which persists in spite of all negation of the world, though it will not admit that the concessions are really such. Negation of the will-to-live is self-consistent only if it is really willing actually to put an end to physical existence.

If man affirms his will-to-live, he acts naturally and honestly. He confirms an act which has already been accomplished in his instinctive thought by repeating it in his conscious thought. The beginning of thought, a beginning which continually repeats itself, is that man does not simply accept his existence as something given, but experiences it as something unfathomably mysterious. Affirmation of life is the spiritual act by which man ceases to live unreflectively and begins to devote himself to his life with reverence in order to raise it to its true value. To affirm life is to deepen, to make more inward, and to exalt the will-to-live.

At the same time the man who has become a thinking being feels a compulsion to give to every will-to-live the same reverence for life that he gives to his own. He experiences that other life in his own. He accepts as being good: to preserve life, to promote life, to raise to its highest value life which is capable of development; and as being evil: to destroy life, to injure life, to repress life which is capable of development. This is the absolute, fundamental principle of the moral, and it is a necessity of thought.

The great fault of all ethics hitherto has been that they believed themselves to have to deal only with the relations of man to man. In reality, however, the question is what is his attitude to the world and all life that comes within his reach. A man is ethical only when life, as such, is sacred to him, that of plants and animals as that of his fellow men, and when he devotes himself helpfully to all life that is in need of help. Only the universal ethic of the feeling of responsibility in an ever-widening sphere for all that lives—only that ethic can be founded in thought. The ethic of the relation of man to man is not something apart by itself; it is only a particular relation which results from the universal one.

The ethic of Reverence for Life, therefore, comprehends within itself everything that can be described as love, devotion, and sympathy whether in suffering, joy, or effort.

The world, however, offers us the horrible drama of Will-to-Live divided against itself. One existence holds its own at the cost of another: one destroys another. Only in the thinking man has the Will-to-Live become conscious of other will-to-live, and desirous of solidarity with it. This solidarity, however, he cannot completely bring about, because man is subject to the puzzling and horrible law of being obliged to live at the cost of other life, and to incur again the guilt of destroying and injuring life. But as an ethical being he strives to escape whenever possible from this necessity, and as one who has become enlightened and merciful to put a stop to this disunion (*Selbstentzweiung*) of the Will-to-Live so far as the influence of his own existence reaches. He thirsts to be permitted to preserve his humanity, and to be able to bring to other existences release from their sufferings.

Reverence for Life arising from the Will-to-Live that has become reflective therefore contains affirmation of life and ethics inseparably combined. It aims to create values, and to realize progress of different kinds which shall serve the material, spiritual, and ethical development of men and mankind. While the unthinking modern acceptance of life stumbles about with its ideals of power won by discovery and invention, the acceptance of life based on reason sets up the spiritual and ethical perfecting of mankind as the highest ideal, and an ideal from which alone all other ideals of progress get their real value.

Through ethical acceptance of the world and of life, we reach a power of reflection which enables us to distinguish between what is essential in civilization and what is not. The stupid arrogance of thinking ourselves civilized loses its power over us. We venture to face the truth that with so much progress in knowledge and power true civilization has become not easier but harder. The problem of the mutual relationship between the spiritual and the material dawns upon us. We know that we all have to struggle with circumstances to preserve our humanity, and that we must be anxiously concerned to turn once more toward hope of victory the almost hopeless struggle which many carry on to preserve their humanity amid unfavorable social circumstances.

A deepened, ethical will to progress which springs from thought will lead us back, then, out of uncivilization and its misery to true civilization. Sooner or later there must dawn the true and final Renaissance which will bring peace to the world.

Questions

1. Why is thinking essential to ethical living? Is Schweitzer saying that a good act is always an act we have thought about?
2. What is the measure or definition of a good act for Schweitzer? Does he know it to be good intuitively and in no other way? Does the good man behave in a certain way?
3. Can human beings feel "reverence for life," at the same time that they injure or destroy life in order to live?
4. Does Schweitzer imply that scientific knowledge diminishes our reverence for life, or does his attitude toward science have another explanation?
5. What resemblances do you find between Schweitzer's philosophy and that of Ralph Waldo Emerson? Do you find any differences?

Suggestions for Writing

1. Discuss whether Schweitzer provides a satisfactory answer to the question of how we can maintain "reverence for life" while we are at the same time injuring or destroying life in order to live. State your own views on this question.
2. Some doctors, nurses, lawyers, and teachers argue that medicine, nursing, and law are businesses and not "callings," and therefore do not demand the selfless dedication of clergymen. Relationships with patients and clients are business ones; professional people expect to be paid for their services. Does this statement seem a satisfactory one to you? Ought a medical or nursing or law school admit only those who claim that their main reason for applying is so that they may serve their fellow human beings, not so that they will be able to make a living?

What I Believe

E. M. Forster

> *The English novelist E. M. Forster (1879–1970) is best known for six novels, including* A Room with a View *(1908),* Howards End *(1910), and* A Passage to India *(1924), the backgrounds of which Forster gives in* The Hills of Devi *(1953). The essays collected in* Abinger Harvest *(1936) and* Two Cheers for Democracy *(1951) develop various ideas in "What I Believe."*
>
> *The phrase "Only connect . . ." appears on the title page of* Howards End. *A major theme of Forster's fiction is the failed connections between individuals, classes, and cultures. Perhaps the most significant failure is expressed by Margaret Wilcox, in* Howards End, *who*

senses *"something a little unbalanced in the mind that so readily shreds the visible. The business man who assumes that this life is everything, and the mystic who asserts that it is nothing, fail, on this side and on that, to hit the truth." Forster was not, however, certain what that truth was. Margaret Wilcox probably speaks for Forster in the remainder of her meditation: "No; truth, being alive, was not half-way between anything. It was only to be found by continuous excursions into either realm, and though proportion is the final secret, to espouse it at the outset is to insure sterility." This statement expresses one of Forster's essential beliefs—that life has first to be lived and then the meaning of experience explored. "What I Believe," Forster's personal statement of belief, was written in 1939, with the Nazi menace and the prospect of war in view.*

I do not believe in Belief. But this is an age of faith, and there are so many mili- 1
tant creeds that, in self-defence, one has to formulate a creed of one's own. Tolerance, good temper and sympathy are no longer enough in a world which is rent by religious and racial persecution, in a world where ignorance rules, and science, who ought to have ruled, plays the subservient pimp. Tolerance, good temper and sympathy—they are what matter really, and if the human race is not to collapse they must come to the front before long. But for the moment they are not enough, their action is no stronger than a flower, battered beneath a military jack-boot. They want stiffening, even if the process coarsens them. Faith, to my mind, is a stiffening process, a sort of mental starch, which ought to be applied as sparingly as possible. I dislike the stuff. I do not believe in it, for its own sake, at all. Herein I probably differ from most people, who believe in Belief, and are only sorry they cannot swallow even more than they do. My law-givers are Erasmus and Montaigne, not Moses and St. Paul. My temple stands not upon Mount Moriah but in that Elysian Field where even the immoral are admitted. My motto is: "Lord, I disbelieve—help thou my unbelief."[1]

I have, however, to live in an Age of Faith—the sort of epoch I used to hear 2
praised when I was a boy. It is extremely unpleasant really. It is bloody in every sense of the word. And I have to keep my end up in it. Where do I start?

With personal relationships. Here is something comparatively solid in a world 3
full of violence and cruelty. Not absolutely solid, for Psychology has split and shattered the idea of a "Person," and has shown that there is something incalculable in each of us, which may at any moment rise to the surface and destroy our normal balance. We don't know what we are like. We can't know what other people are like. How, then, can we put any trust in personal relationships, or cling to them in the gathering political storm? In theory we cannot. But in practice we can and do. Though A is not unchangeably A or B unchangeably B, there can still be love and loyalty between the two. For the purpose of living one has to assume that the personality is solid, and the "self" is an entity, and to ignore all contrary evidence. And since to ignore evidence is

---

[1]Desiderius Erasmus (1466?–1536), the Dutch biblical scholar and student of Latin and Greek culture, supported the Reformation at the beginning but later sought to change the Catholic Church from within. He is remembered most for his satire *In Praise of Folly* (1509). Mount Moriah is the hill where Abraham prepared Isaac for sacrifice. Tradition places it in eastern Jerusalem.

one of the characteristics of faith, I certainly can proclaim that I believe in personal relationships.

Starting from them, I get a little order into the contemporary chaos. One must 4 be fond of people and trust them if one is not to make a mess of life, and it is therefore essential that they should not let one down. They often do. The moral of which is that I must, myself, be as reliable as possible, and this I try to be. But reliability is not a matter of contract—that is the main difference between the world of personal relationships and the world of business relationships. It is a matter for the heart, which signs no documents. In other words, reliability is impossible unless there is a natural warmth. Most men possess this warmth, though they often have bad luck and get chilled. Most of them, even when they are politicians, *want* to keep faith. And one can, at all events, show one's own little light here, one's own poor little trembling flame, with the knowledge that it is not the only light that is shining in the darkness, and not the only one which the darkness does not comprehend. Personal relations are despised today. They are regarded as bourgeois luxuries, as products of a time of fair weather which is now past, and we are urged to get rid of them, and to dedicate ourselves to some movement or cause instead. I hate the idea of causes, and if I had to choose between betraying my country and betraying my friend, I hope I should have the guts to betray my country. Such a choice may scandalise the modern reader, and he may stretch out his patriotic hand to the telephone at once and ring up the police. It would not have shocked Dante, though. Dante places Brutus and Cassius in the lowest circle of Hell because they had chosen to betray their friend Julius Caesar rather than their country Rome. Probably one will not be asked to make such an agonising choice. Still, there lies at the back of every creed something terrible and hard for which the worshipper may one day be required to suffer, and there is even a terror and a hardness in this creed of personal relationships, urbane and mild though it sounds. Love and loyalty to an individual can run counter to the claims of the State. When they do—down with the State, say I, which means that the State would down me.

This brings me along to Democracy, "even Love, the Beloved Republic, which 5 feeds upon Freedom and lives." Democracy is not a Beloved Republic really, and never will be. But it is less hateful than other contemporary forms of government, and to that extent it deserves our support. It does start from the assumption that the individual is important, and that all types are needed to make a civilisation. It does not divide its citizens into the bossers and the bossed—as an efficiency-regime tends to do. The people I admire most are those who are sensitive and want to create something or discover something, and do not see life in terms of power, and such people get more of a chance under a democracy than elsewhere. They found religions, great or small, or they produce literature and art, or they do disinterested scientific research, or they may be what is called "ordinary people," who are creative in their private lives, bring up their children decently, for instance, or help their neighbours. All these people need to express themselves; they cannot do so unless society allows them liberty to do so, and the society which allows them most liberty is a democracy.

Democracy has another merit. It allows criticism, and if there is not public 6 criticism there are bound to be hushed-up scandals. That is why I believe in the Press, despite all its lies and vulgarity, and why I believe in Parliament. Parliament is often sneered at because it is a Talking Shop. I believe in it *because* it is a talking shop. I believe in the Private Member who makes himself a nuisance. He gets snubbed and is told that he is cranky or ill-informed, but he does expose abuses which would otherwise never have been mentioned, and very often an abuse gets put right just by being mentioned. Occasionally, too, a well-meaning public official starts losing his head in the cause of efficiency, and thinks himself God Almighty. Such officials are particularly frequent in the Home Office. Well, there will be questions about them in Parliament sooner or later, and then they will have to mind their steps. Whether Parliament is either a representative body or an efficient one is questionable, but I value it because it criticises and talks, and because its chatter gets widely reported.

So Two Cheers for Democracy: one because it admits variety and two because 7 it permits criticism. Two cheers are quite enough: there is no occasion to give three. Only Love the Beloved Republic deserves that.

What about Force, though? While we are trying to be sensitive and advanced 8 and affectionate and tolerant, an unpleasant question pops up: does not all society rest upon force? If a government cannot count upon the police and the army, how can it hope to rule? And if an individual gets knocked on the head or sent to a labour camp, of what significance are his opinions?

This dilemma does not worry me as much as it does some. I realise that all soci- 9 ety rests upon force. But all the great creative actions, all the decent human relations, occur during the intervals when force has not managed to come to the front. These intervals are what matter. I want them to be as frequent and as lengthy as possible, and I call them "civilisation." Some people idealise force and pull it into the foreground and worship it, instead of keeping it in the background as long as possible. I think they make a mistake, and I think that their opposites, the mystics, err even more when they declare that force does not exist. I believe that it exists, and that one of our jobs is to prevent it from getting out of its box. It gets out sooner or later, and then it destroys us and all the lovely things which we have made. But it is not out all the time, for the fortunate reason that the strong are so stupid. Consider their conduct for a moment in the Niebelung's Ring. The giants there have the guns, or in other words the gold; but they do nothing with it, they do not realise that they are all-powerful, with the result that the catastrophe is delayed and the castle of Walhalla, insecure but glorious, fronts the storms. Fafnir, coiled round his hoard, grumbles and grunts; we can hear him under Europe today; the leaves of the wood already tremble, and the Bird calls its warnings uselessly. Fafnir will destroy us, but by a blessed dispensation he is stupid and slow, and creation goes on just outside the poisonous blast of his breath.[2] The Nietzschean[3] would hurry the monster up, the mystic would say he did not exist, but Wotan, wiser than either, hastens to create warriors before doom declares itself. The Valkyries are symbols not only of courage but of intelligence; they represent the human spirit snatching its opportunity while the going is good, and one of them even finds time to love.

---

[2]In Richard Wagner's four-part opera *The Ring of the Nibelungen,* the god Wotan commissions the giants Fafnir and Fasolt to build Walhalla, a castle in which the gods and earthly hero-warriors will live. Wotan pays the giants with a ring he has stolen from the thief, Alberich. Under the ring's curse, Fafnir kills Fasolt and turns himself into a dragon. Brünnhilde is one of the Valkyrie daughters of Wotan. Put into a deep sleep by her father, whom she has disobeyed, she is awakened by the hero Siegfried, who has slain the dragon and recovered the ring. A forest bird leads Siegfried to Brünnhilde.

[3]A follower of the German philosopher Frederick Nietzsche, who extolls the *Übermensch,* "the man who rises above," in *Thus Spoke Zarathustra* (1883).

Brünnhilde's last song hymns the recurrence of love, and since it is the privilege of art to exaggerate, she goes even further, and proclaims the love which is eternally triumphant and feeds upon freedom, and lives.

So that is what I feel about force and violence. It is, alas! the ultimate reality 10 on this earth, but it does not always get to the front. Some people call its absences "decadence"; I call them "civilisation" and find in such interludes the chief justification for the human experiment. I look the other way until fate strikes me. Whether this is due to courage or to cowardice in my own case I cannot be sure. But I know that if men had not looked the other way in the past, nothing of any value would survive. The people I respect most behave as if they were immortal and as if society was eternal. Both assumptions are false: both of them must be accepted as true if we are to go on eating and working and loving, and are to keep open a few breathing holes for the human spirit. No millennium seems likely to descend upon humanity; no better and stronger League of Nations will be instituted; no form of Christianity and no alternative to Christianity will bring peace to the world or integrity to the individual; no "change of heart" will occur. And yet we need not despair, indeed, we cannot despair; the evidence of history shows us that men have always insisted on behaving creatively under the shadow of the sword; that they have done their artistic and scientific and domestic stuff for the sake of doing it, and that we had better follow their example under the shadow of the aeroplanes. Others, with more vision or courage than myself, see the salvation of humanity ahead, and will dismiss my conception of civilisation as paltry, a sort of tip-and-run game. Certainly it is presumptuous to say that we *cannot* improve, and that Man, who has only been in power for a few thousand years, will never learn to make use of his power. All I mean is that, if people continue to kill one another as they do, the world cannot get better than it is, and that since there are more people than formerly, and their means for destroying one another superior, the world may well get worse. What is good in people— and consequently in the world—is their insistence on creation, their belief in friendship and loyalty for their own sakes; and though Violence remains and is, indeed, the major partner in this muddled establishment, I believe that creativeness remains too, and will always assume direction when violence sleeps. So, though I am not an optimist, I cannot agree with Sophocles that it were better never to have been born. And although, like Horace, I see no evidence that each batch of births is superior to the last, I leave the field open for the more complacent view.[4] This is such a difficult moment to live in, one cannot help getting gloomy and also a bit rattled, and perhaps short-sighted.

In search of a refuge, we may perhaps turn to hero-worship. But here we shall 11 get no help, in my opinion. Hero-worship is a dangerous vice, and one of the minor merits of a democracy is that it does not encourage it, or produce that unmanageable type of citizen known as the Great Man. It produces instead different kinds of small men—a much finer achievement. But people who cannot get interested in the variety of life, and cannot make up their own minds, get discontented over this, and they long for a hero to bow down before and to follow blindly. It is significant that a hero is an integral part of the authoritarian stock-in-trade today. An efficiency-regime cannot be

---

[4]The statement appears in *Oedipus at Colonus*, a tragedy written by Sophocles, the fifth-century-B.C. Greek dramatist. Horace, the first-century Roman poet and satirist, wrote in his *Odes*, Book 3, "Our sires' age was worse than our grandsires'. We their sons are more worthless than they. So in our turn we shall give the world a progeny yet more corrupt."

run without a few heroes stuck about it to carry off the dullness—much as plums have
to be put into a bad pudding to make it palatable. One hero at the top and a smaller one
each side of him is a favourite arrangement, and the timid and the bored are comforted
by the trinity, and, bowing down, feel exalted and strengthened.

No, I distrust Great Men. They produce a desert of uniformity around them and 12
often a pool of blood too, and I always feel a little man's pleasure when they come a
cropper. Every now and then one reads in the newspapers some such statement as: "The
coup d'état appears to have failed, and Admiral Toma's whereabouts is at present unknown." Admiral Toma had probably every qualification for being a Great Man—an iron
will, personal magnetism, dash, flair, sexlessness—but fate was against him, so he re-
tires to unknown whereabouts instead of parading history with his peers. He fails with
a completeness which no artist and no lover can experience, because with them the
process of creation is itself an achievement, whereas with him the only possible achievement is success.

I believe in aristocracy, though—if that is the right word, and if a democrat 13
may use it. Not an aristocracy of power, based upon rank and influence, but an aristocracy of the sensitive, the considerate and the plucky. Its members are to be found in all
nations and classes, and all through the ages, and there is a secret understanding between them when they meet. They represent the true human tradition, the one permanent victory of our queer race over cruelty and chaos. Thousands of them perish in
obscurity, a few are great names. They are sensitive for others as well as for themselves,
they are considerate without being fussy, their pluck is not swankiness but the power
to endure, and they can take a joke. I give no examples—it is risky to do that—but the
reader may as well consider whether this is the type of person he would like to meet and
to be, and whether (going farther with me) he would prefer that this type should *not* be
an ascetic one. I am against asceticism myself. I am with the old Scotsman who wanted
less chastity and more delicacy. I do not feel that my aristocrats are a real aristocracy
if they thwart their bodies, since bodies are the instruments through which we register
and enjoy the world. Still, I do not insist. This is not a major point. It is clearly possible
to be sensitive, considerate and plucky and yet be an ascetic too, if anyone possesses the
first three qualities, I will let him in! On they go—an invincible army, yet not a victorious one. The aristocrats, the elect, the chosen, the Best People—all the words that describe them are false, and all attempts to organise them fail. Again and again Authority,
seeing their value, has tried to net them and to utilise them as the Egyptian Priesthood
or the Christian Church or the Chinese Civil Service or the Group Movement, or some
other worthy stunt. But they slip through the net and are gone; when the door is shut,
they are no longer in the room; their temple, as one of them remarked, is the Holiness
of the Heart's Affection, and their kingdom, though they never possess it, is the wide-
open world.

With this type of person knocking about, and constantly crossing one's path if 14
one has eyes to see or hands to feel, the experiment of earthly life cannot be dismissed
as a failure. But it may well be hailed as a tragedy, the tragedy being that no device has
been found by which these private decencies can be transmitted to public affairs. As
soon as people have power they go crooked and sometimes dotty as well, because the
possession of power lifts them into a region where normal honesty never pays. For instance, the man who is selling newspapers outside the Houses of Parliament can safely
leave his papers to go for a drink and his cap beside them: anyone who takes a paper is

sure to drop a copper into the cap. But the men who are inside the Houses of Parliament—they cannot trust one another like that, still less can the Government they compose trust other governments. No caps upon the pavement here, but suspicion, treachery and armaments. The more highly public life is organised the lower does its morality sink; the nations of today behave to each other worse than they ever did in the past, they cheat, rob, bully and bluff, make war without notice, and kill as many women and children as possible; whereas primitive tribes were at all events restrained by taboos. It is a humiliating outlook—though the greater the darkness, the brighter shine the little lights, reassuring one another, signalling: "Well, at all events, I'm still here. I don't like it very much, but how are you?" Unquenchable lights of my aristocracy! Signals of the invincible army! "Come along—anyway, let's have a good time while we can." I think they signal that too.

The Saviour of the future—if ever he comes—will not preach a new Gospel. He 15 will merely utilise my aristocracy, he will make effective the good will and the good temper which are already existing. In other words, he will introduce a new technique. In economics, we are told that if there was a new technique of distribution, there need be no poverty, and people would not starve in one place while crops were being ploughed under in another. A similar change is needed in the sphere of morals and politics. The desire for it is by no means new; it was expressed, for example, in theological terms by Jacopone da Todi over six hundred years ago. "Ordina questo amore, O tu che m'ami," he said; "O thou who lovest me—set this love in order."[5] His prayer was not granted, and I do not myself believe that it ever will be, but here, and not through a change of heart, is our probable route. Not by becoming better, but by ordering and distributing his native goodness, will Man shut up Force into its box, and so gain time to explore the universe and to set his mark upon it worthily. At present he only explores it at odd moments, when Force is looking the other way, and his divine creativeness appears as a trivial byproduct, to be scrapped as soon as the drums beat and the bombers hum.

Such a change, claim the orthodox, can only be made by Christianity, and will 16 be made by it in God's good time: man always has failed and always will fail to organise his own goodness, and it is presumptuous of him to try. This claim—solemn as it is— leaves me cold. I cannot believe that Christianity will ever cope with the present worldwide mess, and I think that such influence as it retains in modern society is due to the money behind it, rather than to its spiritual appeal. It was a spiritual force once, but the indwelling spirit will have to be restated if it is to calm the waters again, and probably restated in a non-Christian form. Naturally a lot of people, and people who are not only good but able and intelligent, will disagree here; they will vehemently deny that Christianity has failed, or they will argue that its failure proceeds from the wickedness of men, and really proves its ultimate success. They have Faith, with a large F. My faith has a very small one, and I only intrude it because these are strenuous and serious days, and one likes to say what one thinks while speech is comparatively free: it may not be free much longer.

The above are the reflections of an individualist and a liberal who has found lib- 17 eralism crumbling beneath him and at first felt ashamed. Then, looking around, he decided there was no special reason for shame, since other people, whatever they felt, were

---

[5]Jacopone da Todi (1230?–1306) was an Italian Franciscan monk, to whom the "Stabat Mater," a hymn describing the sorrows of the Virgin Mary, is attributed.

equally insecure. And as for individualism—there seems no way of getting off this, even if one wanted to. The dictator-hero can grind down his citizens till they are all alike, but he cannot melt them into a single man. That is beyond his power. He can order them to merge, he can incite them to mass-antics, but they are obliged to be born separately, and to die separately, and, owing to these unavoidable termini, will always be running off the totalitarian rails. The memory of birth and the expectation of death always lurk within the human being, making him separate from his fellows and consequently capable of intercourse with them. Naked I came into the world, naked I shall go out of it! And a very good thing too, for it reminds me that I am naked under my shirt, whatever its colour.

Questions

1. If Forster does not "believe in Belief," why is his motto, "Lord, I disbelieve—help thou my unbelief"?
2. Why does Forster believe in "personal relationships"? What in the contemporary world leads him to depend upon them?
3. What does Forster mean by the word *Democracy?* Why does he prefer Democracy to other forms of government?
4. Why does he give only two cheers for Democracy? What can Democracy not provide?
5. What qualities in people prevent "force and violence" from getting "to the front" some of the time? Why does Forster have more faith in Man than in the Great Man? What is the difference?
6. What does Forster mean by *aristocracy* (paragraph 13)? Is he referring to a social or economic class of people? How can a democrat believe in aristocracy?
7. Why is there trust on the street outside Houses of Parliament but no trust inside? How does the discussion of this point in paragraph 14 develop a central idea of the essay?
8. In saying that the "Saviour of the future—if he ever comes—will not preach a new Gospel" (paragraph 15), is Forster suggesting that his creed is the same as the Christian creed or that his creed does not contradict it? What has Christianity not succeeded in doing so far?
9. What does Forster mean in the final paragraph by *individualism?* What does the word not mean?
10. What is Forster's purpose in writing? What audience is he addressing, and how do you know?

Suggestions for Writing

1. Discuss whether your reasons for valuing friendship are the same as Forster's reasons. Use this discussion to define one or two of your own values or beliefs.
2. State whether you would give two cheers for Democracy, or three, and why.
3. Discuss whether you need heroes and, if so, what kind. State your agreement or disagreement with Forster on the matter of hero-worship.

Additional Reading

Forster, E. M. *The Eternal Moment and Other Stories.* New York: Harcourt Brace Jovanovich, 1964.

————. *The Longest Journey.* New York: Knopf, 1953.

————. *A Passage to India.* New York: Harcourt Brace Jovanovich, 1949.

————. *A Room with a View.* New York: Knopf, 1953.

————. *Two Cheers for Democracy.* New York: Harcourt Brace Jovanovich, 1951.

Furbank, P. N. *E. M. Forster: A Life.* New York: Harcourt Brace Jovanovich, 1981.

McConkey, James. *The Novels of E. M. Forster.* Ithaca, N.Y.: Cornell University Press, 1967.

The Lost Dimension in Religion

Paul Tillich

The Protestant theologian Paul Tillich (1886–1965), born and educated in Germany, was ordained an Evangelical minister in 1912. Following army service as a chaplain in World War One, he taught theology at various universities and in 1929 was appointed professor of philosophy at the University of Frankfort. An opponent of the Nazis, Tillich was dismissed from his professorship in 1933; he came to the United States that same year. He taught at the Union Theological Seminary in New York and, after his retirement in 1955, at Harvard University and the University of Chicago.

A major subject of Tillich's numerous books is the nature of faith. He was particularly interested in the difference between religious doubt and skepticism. As his comments on Billy Graham and Norman Vincent Peale suggest, Tillich identified neither with fundamentalist Protestantism nor with the kind that, in Tillich's words, "heals people with the purpose of making them fit again for the demands of the competitive and conformist society in which we are living." His own Protestantism, exemplified by the ideas in this essay, has been described by some as "liberal" and others as "existentialist."

Tillich's reference to existentialism in the essay reprinted here needs explanation. Existentialism is an influential philosophical movement that originated in the nineteenth century and flourished after the Second World War. The central belief of the twentieth-century existentialist is that human beings are aware that they live and suffer—that they exist—before they ask why they exist. In asking why, they express their "concern" about this ultimate question of existence. Tillich suggests that, in expressing concern, the existentialist is seeking the "religious answer" he refers to at the end of the essay.

For many existentialists, concern of this nature may lead to faith. Faith, Tillich states in Dynamics of Faith, *is surrender to a claim that promises "total fulfillment." The promise of fulfillment need not be specific or definite; it may, as in the religions of the world, be expressed in symbols that point to a reality without disclosing it. Tillich departs from religious fundamentalism in rejecting literal interpretation of the Bible in favor of symbolic interpretation. Every act of faith contains what Tillich calls* existential doubt: *"It does not question whether a special proposition is true or false. It does not reject every concrete truth, but it is aware of the element of insecurity in every existential truth." Such doubt requires courage of the believer. It is, for Tillich, a willed act.*

Every observer of our Western civilization is aware of the fact that something   1
has happened to religion. It especially strikes the observer of the American scene. Everywhere he finds symptoms of what one has called religious revival, or more modestly, the revival of interest in religion. He finds them in the churches with their rapidly increasing membership. He finds them in the mushroomlike growth of sects. He finds them on college campuses and in the theological faculties of universities. Most conspicuously, he finds them in the tremendous success of men like Billy Graham and Norman Vincent Peale, who attract masses of people Sunday after Sunday, meeting after meeting. The facts cannot be denied, but how should they be interpreted? It is my intention to show that these facts must be seen as expressions of the predicament of Western man in the second half of the twentieth century. But I would even go a step further. I believe that the predicament of man in our period gives us also an important insight into the predicament of man generally—at all times and in all parts of the earth.

There are many analyses of man and society in our time. Most of them show   2
important traits in the picture, but few of them succeed in giving a general key to our present situation. Although it is not easy to find such a key, I shall attempt it and, in so doing, will make an assertion which may be somewhat mystifying at first hearing. The decisive element in the predicament of Western man in our period is his loss of the dimension of depth. Of course, "dimension of depth" is a metaphor. It is taken from the spatial realm and applied to man's spiritual life. What does it mean?

It means that man has lost an answer to the question: What is the meaning of   3
life? Where do we come from, where do we go to? What shall we do, what should we become in the short stretch between birth and death? Such questions are not answered or even asked if the "dimension of depth" is lost. And this is precisely what has happened to man in our period of history. He has lost the courage to ask such questions with an infinite seriousness—as former generations did—and he has lost the courage to receive answers to these questions, wherever they may come from.

I suggest that we call the dimension of depth the religious dimension in man's   4
nature. Being religious means asking passionately the question of the meaning of our existence and being willing to receive answers, even if the answers hurt. Such an idea of religion makes religion universally human, but it certainly differs from what is usually called religion. It does not describe religion as the belief in the existence of gods or one God, and as a set of activities and institutions for the sake of relating oneself to

these beings in thought, devotion and obedience. No one can deny that the religions which have appeared in history are religions in this sense. Nevertheless, religion in its innermost nature is more than religion in this narrower sense. It is the state of being concerned about one's own being and being universally.

There are many people who are ultimately concerned in this way who feel far   5
removed, however, from religion in the narrower sense, and therefore from every historical religion. It often happens that such people take the question of the meaning of their life infinitely seriously and reject any historical religion just for this reason. They feel that the concrete religions fail to express their profound concern adequately. They are religious while rejecting the religions. It is this experience which forces us to distinguish the meaning of religion as living in the dimension of depth from particular expressions of one's ultimate concern in the symbols and institutions of a concrete religion. If we now turn to the concrete analysis of the religious situation of our time, it is obvious that our key must be the basic meaning of religion and not any particular religion, not even Christianity. What does this key disclose about the predicament of man in our period?

If we define religion as the state of being grasped by an infinite concern we   6
must say: Man in our time has lost such infinite concern. And the resurgence of religion is nothing but a desperate and mostly futile attempt to regain what has been lost.

How did the dimension of depth become lost? Like any important event, it has   7
many causes, but certainly not the one which one hears often mentioned from ministers' pulpits and evangelists' platforms, namely that a widespread impiety of modern man is responsible. Modern man is neither more pious nor more impious than man in any other period. The loss of the dimension of depth is caused by the relation of man to his world and to himself in our period, the period in which nature is being subjected scientifically and technically to the control of man. In this period, life in the dimension of depth is replaced by life in the horizontal dimension. The driving forces of the industrial society of which we are a part go ahead horizontally and not vertically. In popular terms this is expressed in phrases like "better and better," "bigger and bigger," "more and more." One should not disparage the feeling which lies behind such speech. Man is right in feeling that he is able to know and transform the world he encounters without a foreseeable limit. He can go ahead in all directions without a definite boundary.

A most expressive symbol of this attitude of going ahead in the horizontal di-   8
mension is the breaking through of the space which is controlled by the gravitational power of the earth into the world-space. It is interesting that one calls this world-space simply "space" and speaks, for instance, of space travel, as if every trip were not travel into space. Perhaps one feels that the true nature of space has been discovered only through our entering into indefinite world-space. In any case, the predominance of the horizontal dimension over the dimension of depth has been immensely increased by the opening up of the space beyond the space of the earth.

If we now ask what does man do and seek if he goes ahead in the horizontal di-   9
mension, the answer is difficult. Sometimes one is inclined to say that the mere movement ahead without an end, the intoxication with speeding forward without limits, is what satisfies him. But this answer is by no means sufficient. For on his way into space and time man changes the world he encounters. And the changes made by him change

himself. He transforms everything he encounters into a tool; and in doing so he himself becomes a tool. But if he asks, a tool for what, there is no answer.

One does not need to look far beyond everyone's daily experience in order to 10 find examples to describe this predicament. Indeed our daily life in office and home, in cars and airplanes, at parties and conferences, while reading magazines and watching television, while looking at advertisements and hearing radio, are in themselves continuous examples of a life which has lost the dimension of depth. It runs ahead, every moment is filled with something which must be done or seen or said or planned. But no one can experience depth without stopping and becoming aware of himself. Only if he has moments in which he does not care about what comes next can he experience the meaning of this moment here and now and ask himself about the meaning of his life. As long as the preliminary, transitory concerns are not silenced, no matter how interesting and valuable and important they may be, the voice of the ultimate concern cannot be heard. This is the deepest root of the loss of the dimension of depth in our period—the loss of religion in its basic and universal meaning.

If the dimension of depth is lost, the symbols in which life in this dimension 11 has expressed itself must also disappear. I am speaking of the great symbols of the historical religions in our Western world, of Judaism and Christianity. The reason that the religious symbols became lost is not primarily scientific criticism, but it is a complete misunderstanding of their meaning; and only because of this misunderstanding was scientific critique able, and even justified, in attacking them. The first step toward the nonreligion of the Western world was made by religion itself. When it defended its great symbols, not as symbols, but as literal stories, it had already lost the battle. In doing so the theologians (and today many religious laymen) helped to transfer the powerful expressions of the dimension of depth into objects or happenings on the horizontal plane. There the symbols lose their power and meaning and become an easy prey to physical, biological and historical attack.

If the symbol of creation which points to the divine ground of everything is 12 transferred to the horizontal plane, it becomes a story of events in a removed past for which there is no evidence, but which contradicts every piece of scientific evidence. If the symbol of the Fall of Man, which points to the tragic estrangement of man and his world from their true being is transferred to the horizontal plane, it becomes a story of a human couple a few thousand years ago in what is now present-day Iraq. One of the most profound psychological descriptions of the general human predicament becomes an absurdity on the horizontal plane. If the symbols of the Saviour and the salvation through Him which point to the healing power in history and personal life are transferred to the horizontal plane, they become stories of a half-divine being coming from a heavenly place and returning to it. Obviously, in this form, they have no meaning whatsoever for people whose view of the universe is determined by scientific astronomy.

If the idea of God (and the symbols applied to Him) which expresses man's ulti- 13 mate concern is transferred to the horizontal plane, God becomes a being among others whose existence or nonexistence is a matter of inquiry. Nothing, perhaps, is more symptomatic of the loss of the dimension of depth than the permanent discussion about the existence or nonexistence of God—a discussion in which both sides are equally wrong, because the discussion itself is wrong and possible only after the loss of the dimension of depth.

When in this way man has deprived himself of the dimension of depth and the 14 symbols expressing it, he then becomes a part of the horizontal plane. He loses his self and becomes a thing among things. He becomes an element in the process of manipulated production and manipulated consumption. This is now a matter of public knowledge. We have become aware of the degree to which everyone in our social structure is managed, even if one knows it and even if one belongs himself to the managing group. The influence of the gang mentality on adolescents, of the corporation's demands on the executives, of the conditioning of everyone by public communication, by propaganda and advertising under the guidance of motivation research, et cetera, have all been described in many books and articles.

Under these pressures, man can hardly escape the fate of becoming a thing 15 among the things he produces, a bundle of conditioned reflexes without a free, deciding and responsible self. The immense mechanism, set up by man to produce objects for his use, transforms man himself into an object used by the same mechanism of production and consumption.

But man has not ceased to be man. He resists this fate anxiously, desperately, 16 courageously. He asks the question, for what? And he realizes that there is no answer. He becomes aware of the emptiness which is covered by the continuous movement ahead and the production of means for ends which become means again without an ultimate end. Without knowing what has happened to him, he feels that he has lost the meaning of life, the dimension of depth.

Out of this awareness the religious question arises and religious answers are re- 17 ceived or rejected. Therefore, in order to describe the contemporary attitude toward religion, we must first point to the places where the awareness of the predicament of Western man in our period is most sharply expressed. These places are the great art, literature and partly, at least, the philosophy of our time. It is both the subject matter and the style of these creations which show the passionate and often tragic struggle about the meaning of life in a period in which man has lost the dimension of depth. This art, literature, philosophy is not religious in the narrower sense of the word; but it asks the religious question more radically and more profoundly than most directly religious expressions of our time.

It is the religious question which is asked when the novelist describes a man 18 who tries in vain to reach the only place which could solve the problem of his life, or a man who disintegrates under the memory of a guilt which persecutes him, or a man who never had a real self and is pushed by his fate without resistance to death, or a man who experiences a profound disgust of everything he encounters.

It is the religious question which is asked when the poet opens up the horror 19 and the fascination of the demonic regions of his soul, or if he leads us into the deserts and empty places of our being, or if he shows physical and moral mud under the surface of life, or if he sings the song of transitoriness, giving words to the ever-present anxiety of our hearts.

It is the religious question which is asked when the playwright shows the illu- 20 sion of a life in a ridiculous symbol, or if he lets the emptiness of a life's work end in self-destruction, or if he confronts us with the inescapable bondage to mutual hate and guilt, or if he leads us into the dark cellar of lost hopes and slow disintegration.

It is the religious question which is asked when the painter breaks the visible 21 surface into pieces, then reunites them into a great picture which has little similarity with the world at which we normally look, but which expresses our anxiety and our courage to face reality.

It is the religious question which is asked when the architect, in creating office 22 buildings or churches, removes the trimmings taken over from past styles because they cannot be considered an honest expression of our own period. He prefers the seeming poverty of a purpose-determined style to the deceptive richness of imitated styles of the past. He knows that he gives no final answer, but he does give an honest answer.

The philosophy of our time shows the same hiddenly religious traits. It is di- 23 vided into two main schools of thought, the analytic and the existentialist. The former tries to analyze logical and linguistic forms which are always used and which underlie all scientific research. One may compare them with the painters who dissolve the natural forms of bodies into cubes, planes and lines; or with those architects who want the structural "bones" of their buildings to be conspicuously visible and not hidden by covering features. This self-restriction produces the almost monastic poverty and seriousness of this philosophy. It is religious—without any contact with religion in its method—by exercising the humility of "learned ignorance."

In contrast to this school the existentialist philosophers have much to say 24 about the problems of human existence. They bring into rational concepts what the writers and poets, the painters and architects, are expressing in their particular material. What they express is the human predicament in time and space, in anxiety and guilt and the feeling of meaninglessness. From Pascal in the seventeenth century to Heidegger and Sartre in our time, philosophers have emphasized the contrast between human dignity and human misery. And by doing so, they have raised the religious question. Some have tried to answer the question they have asked. But if they did so, they turned back to past traditions and offered to our time that which does not fit our time. Is it possible for our time to receive answers which are born out of our time?

Answers given today are in danger of strengthening the present situation and 25 with it the questions to which they are supposed to be the answers. This refers to some of the previously mentioned major representatives of the so-called resurgence of religion, as for instance the evangelist Billy Graham and the counseling and healing minister, Norman Vincent Peale. Against the validity of the answers given by the former, one must say that, in spite of his personal integrity, his propagandistic methods and his primitive theological fundamentalism fall short of what is needed to give an answer to the religious question of our period. In spite of all his seriousness, he does not take the radical question of our period seriously.

The effect that Norman Peale has on large groups of people is rooted in the fact 26 that he confirms the situation which he is supposed to help overcome. He heals people with the purpose of making them fit again for the demands of the competitive and conformist society in which we are living. He helps them to become adapted to the situation which is characterized by the loss of the dimension of depth. Therefore, his advice is valid on this level; but it is the validity of this level that is the true religious question of our time. And this question he neither raises nor answers.

In many cases the increase of church membership and interest in religious ac- 27 tivities does not mean much more than the religious consecration of a state of things in which the religious dimension has been lost. It is the desire to participate in activities which are socially strongly approved and give internal and a certain amount of external security. This is not necessarily bad, but it certainly is not an answer to the religious question of our period.

Is there an answer? There is always an answer, but the answer may not be avail- 28 able to us. We may be too deeply steeped in the predicament out of which the question arises to be able to answer it. To acknowledge this is certainly a better way toward a real answer than to bar the way to it by deceptive answers. And it may be that in this attitude the real answer (within available limits) is given. The real answer to the question of how to regain the dimension of depth is not given by increased church membership or church attendance, nor by conversion or healing experiences. But it is given by the awareness that we have lost the decisive dimension of life, the dimension of depth, and that there is no easy way of getting it back. Such awareness is in itself a state of being grasped by that which is symbolized in the term, dimension of depth. He who realizes that he is separated from the ultimate source of meaning shows by this realization that he is not only separated but also reunited. And this is just our situation. What we need above all—and partly have—is the radical realization of our predicament, without try- ing to cover it up by secular or religious ideologies. The revival of religious interest would be a creative power in our culture if it would develop into a movement of search for the lost dimension of depth.

This does not mean that the traditional religious symbols should be dismissed. 29 They certainly have lost their meaning in the literalistic form into which they have been distorted, thus producing the critical reaction against them. But they have not lost their genuine meaning, namely, of answering the question which is implied in man's very ex- istence in powerful, revealing and saving symbols. If the resurgence of religion would produce a new understanding of the symbols of the past and their relevance for our situ- ation, instead of premature and deceptive answers, it would become a creative factor in our culture and a saving factor for many who live in estrangement, anxiety and despair. The religious answer has always the character of "in spite of." In spite of the loss of di- mension of depth, its power is present, and most present in those who are aware of the loss and are striving to regain it with ultimate seriousness.

Questions

1. How does Tillich distinguish the "religious dimension" from particular religions like Christianity and Judaism? Can a person who professes no religion be "religious" for Tillich?
2. Is Tillich saying that the whole of the modern world has lost "the dimension of depth," or is he referring only to some people of today?
3. Are the advances of science the cause of this loss, according to Tillich, or one of many causes, or the symptom of an unnamed cause?

4. What are "horizontal" and "vertical" dimensions, and how do these metaphors help Tillich describe the situation of people today? How does his discussion of space explain the distinction?
5. In what sense do Judaism and Christianity speak to us through symbols? In what way is the "Fall of Man" a symbol?
6. How can the modern world recover "the dimension of depth"? Does the recovery require the sacrifice of scientific knowledge?
7. Why does Tillich believe art and literature have special importance in the modern world? What have they displaced?
8. What qualities define the human being for Tillich? How do these qualities give hope for the future?
9. What changes does Tillich suggest may occur in present-day religions? Does he consider these changes inevitable in our world?
10. Is Tillich writing only to describe the religious situation today, or is he urging his readers to change their thinking or behavior? Is he writing to a general audience that includes believers and nonbelievers, or to a special audience of one or the other?

Suggestions for Writing

1. Discuss your own view of what makes a person "religious" and whether a person can be religious without professing a particular religious creed.
2. On the basis of his statements in "The Lost Dimension in Religion," state whether Tillich would agree or disagree with this statement by a major twentieth-century philosopher:

> The existentialists say at once that man is anguish. What that means is this: the man who involves himself and who realizes that he is not only the person he chooses to be, but also a lawmaker who is, at the same time, choosing all mankind as well as himself, cannot help escape the feeling of his total and deep responsibility. Of course, there are many people who are not anxious; but we claim that they are hiding their anxiety, that they are fleeing from it. Certainly, many people believe that when they do something, they themselves are the only ones involved, and when someone says to them, "What if everyone acted that way?" they shrug their shoulders and answer, "Everyone doesn't act that way." But really, one should always ask himself, "What would happen if everybody looked at things that way?" There is no escaping this disturbing thought except by a kind of double dealing. A man who lies and makes excuses for himself by saying "not everybody does that," is someone with an uneasy conscience, because the act of lying implies that a universal value is conferred upon the lie.—Jean-Paul Sartre, "Existentialism"

Additional Reading

Pauck, Wilhelm and Marion Pauck. *Paul Tillich. Volume 1: Life.* New York: Harper and Row, 1976.

Scharlemann, Robert P. *Reflection and Doubt in the Thought of Paul Tillich.* New Haven: Yale University Press, 1969.

Tillich, Paul. *The Courage to Be.* New Haven; Yale University Press, 1952.

————. *The Dynamics of Faith.* New York: Harper and Row, 1957.

————. *Morality and Beyond.* New York: Harper and Row, 1963.

————. *My Search for Absolutes.* New York: Simon and Schuster, 1967.

Wheat, Leonard. *Paul Tillich's Dialectal Humanism: Unmasking the God above God.* Baltimore: Johns Hopkins University Press, 1970.

The Religion of Americans and American Religion

Will Herberg

From 1955 until his death in 1977 Will Herberg taught Judaic Studies and social philosophy at Drew University. His books on Judaism and religion include Judaic and Modern Man *(1951),* The Writings of Martin Buber *(1956), and* Existential Theologians *(1958). In* Catholic–Protestant–Jew *(1956), from which the essay reprinted here is taken, Herberg examines the religious revival that many believed was occurring in America in the 1950s. "It is the thesis of the present work," Herberg states in the opening chapter, "that both the religiousness and the secularism of the American people derive from very much the same sources, and that both become more intelligible when seen against the background of deep-going sociological processes that have transformed the face of American life in the course of the past generation." Herberg's approach is a sociological one, though he warns that such an approach cannot give the whole picture. There is a dimension of religion that "transcends the social and cultural framework in which it is embedded." Although sociological inquiry is limited, particularly in the study of religion, it can reveal much.*

I

What do Americans believe? Most emphatically, they "believe in God": 97 per [1] cent according to one survey, 96 per cent according to another, 95 per cent according to a third.[1] About 75 per cent of them, as we have seen, regard themselves as members of churches, and a sizable proportion attend divine services with some frequency and regularity.[2] They believe in prayer: about 90 per cent say they pray on various occasions.[3] They believe in life after death, even in heaven and hell.[4] They think well of the church and of ministers.[5] They hold the Bible to be an inspired book, the "word of God."[6] By a large majority, they think children should be given religious instruction and raised as church members.[7] By a large majority, too, they hold religion to be of very great importance.[8] In all of these respects their attitudes are as religious as those of any people today, or, for that matter, as those of any Western people in recent history.

Yet these indications are after all relatively superficial; they tell us what Ameri- 2
cans say (and no doubt believe) about themselves and their religious views; they do not
tell us what in actuality these religious views are. Nowhere are surface appearances
more deceptive, nowhere is it more necessary to try to penetrate beyond mere assertions
of belief than in such ultimate matters as religion.

We do penetrate a little deeper, it would seem, when we take note of certain cu- 3
rious discrepancies the surveys reveal in the responses people make to questions about
their religion. Thus, according to one trustworthy source, 73 per cent said they believed
in an afterlife, with God as judge, but "only 5 per cent [had] any fear, not to say expectation, of going [to hell]."[9] Indeed, about 80 per cent, according to another source, admitted that what they were "most serious about" was not the life after death in which they
said they believed, but in trying to live as comfortably in this life as possible.[10] And in
their opinion they were not doing so badly even from the point of view of the divine
judgment: 91 per cent felt that they could honestly say that they were trying to lead a
good life, and 78 per cent felt no hesitation in saying that they more than half measured
up to their own standards of goodness, over 50 per cent asserting that they were in fact
following the rule of loving one's neighbor as oneself "all the way"![11] This amazingly
high valuation that most Americans appear to place on their own virtue would seem to
offer a better insight into the basic religion of the American people than any figures as
to their formal beliefs can provide, however important in themselves these figures may
be.

But perhaps the most significant discrepancy in the assertions Americans make 4
about their religious views is to be found in another area. When asked, "Would you say
your religious beliefs have any effect on your ideas of politics and business?", a majority
of the same Americans who had testified that they regarded religion as something "very
important" answered that their religious beliefs had no real effect on their ideas or conduct in these decisive areas of everyday life; specifically, 54 per cent said no, 39 per cent
said yes, and 7 per cent refused to reply or didn't know.[12] This disconcerting confession
of the irrelevance of religion to business and politics was attributed by those who ap-
praised the results of the survey as pointing to a calamitous divorce between the "private" and the "public" realms in the religious thinking of Americans.[13] There is certainly
a great deal of truth in this opinion, and we shall have occasion to explore it in a
different context, but in the present connection it would seem that another aspect of the
matter is more immediately pertinent. *Some* ideas and standards undeniably govern the
conduct of Americans in their affairs of business and politics; if they are not ideas and
standards associated with the teachings of religion, what are they? It will not do to say
that people just act "selfishly" without reference to moral standards of any kind. All people act "selfishly," of course; but it is no less true of all people, Americans included, that
their "selfishness" is controlled, mitigated, or, at worst, justified by some sort of moral
commitment, by some sort of belief in a system of values beyond immediate self-
interest. The fact that more than half the people openly admit that their religious beliefs
have no effect on their ideas of politics and business would seem to indicate very
strongly that, over and above conventional religion, there is to be found among Americans some sort of faith or belief or set of convictions, not generally designated as religion but definitely operative as such in their lives in the sense of providing them with

some fundamental context of normativity and meaning. What this unacknowledged "religion" of the American people is, and how it manages to coexist with their formal religious affirmations and affiliations, it is now our task to investigate.

II

"Every functioning society," Robin M. Williams, Jr. points out, "has to an important degree a *common* religion. The possession of a common set of ideas, rituals, and symbols can supply an overarching sense of unity even in a society riddled with conflicts."[14] What is this "common religion" of American society, the "common set of ideas, rituals, and symbols" that give it its "overarching sense of unity"? Williams provides us with a further clue when he suggests that "men are always likely to be intolerant of opposition to their central ultimate values."[15] What are these "central ultimate values" about which Americans are "intolerant"? No one who knows anything about the religious situation in this country would be likely to suggest that the things Americans are "intolerant" about are the beliefs, standards, or teachings of the religions they "officially" acknowledge as theirs. Americans are proud of their tolerance in matters of religion: one is expected to "believe in God," but otherwise religion is not supposed to be a ground of "discrimination." This is, no doubt, admirable, but is it not "at least in part, a sign that the crucial values of the system are no longer couched in a religious framework"?[16]

What, then, is the "framework" in which they *are* couched? What, to return to our original question, is the "common religion" of the American people, as it may be inferred not only from their words but also from their behavior?

It seems to me that a realistic appraisal of the values, ideas, and behavior of the American people leads to the conclusion that Americans, by and large, do have their "common religion" and that that "religion" is the system familiarly known as the American Way of Life. It is the American Way of Life that supplies American society with an "overarching sense of unity" amid conflict. It is the American Way of Life about which Americans are admittedly and unashamedly "intolerant." It is the American Way of Life that provides the framework in terms of which the crucial values of American existence are couched. By every realistic criterion the American Way of Life is the operative faith of the American people.

It would be the crudest kind of misunderstanding to dismiss the American Way of Life as no more than a political formula or propagandist slogan, or to regard it as simply an expression of the "materialistic" impulses of the American people. Americans are "materialistic," no doubt, but surely not more so than other people, than the French peasant or petty bourgeois, for example. All such labels are irrelevant, if not meaningless. The American Way of Life is, at bottom, a spiritual structure, a structure of ideas and ideals, of aspirations and values, of beliefs and standards; it synthesizes all that commends itself to the American as the right, the good, and the true in actual life. It embraces such seemingly incongruous elements as sanitary plumbing and freedom of opportunity, Coca-Cola and an intense faith in education—all felt as moral questions relating to the proper way of life.[17] The very expression "way of life" points to its religious essence, for one's ultimate, over-all way of life is one's religion.

The American Way of Life is, of course, conceived as the corporate "way" of the American people, but it has its implications for the American as an individual as well.

It is something really operative in his actual life. When in the *Ladies' Home Journal* poll, Americans were asked "to look within [themselves] and state honestly whether [they] thought [they] really obeyed the law of love under certain special conditions," 90 per cent said yes and 5 per cent no when the one to be "loved" was a person belonging to a different religion; 80 per cent said yes and 12 per cent no when it was the case of a member of a different race; 78 per cent said yes and 10 per cent no when it concerned a business competitor—but only 27 per cent said yes and 57 per cent no in the case of "a member of a political party that you think is dangerous," while 25 per cent said yes and 63 per cent said no when it concerned an enemy of the nation.[18] These figures are most illuminating, first because of the incredible self-assurance they reveal with which the average American believes he fulfills the "impossible" law of love, but also because of the light they cast on the differential impact of the violation of this law on the American conscience. For it is obvious that the figures reflect not so much the actual behavior of the American people—no people on earth ever loved their neighbors as themselves as much as the American people say they do—as how seriously Americans take transgressions against the law of love in various cases. Americans feel they *ought* to love their fellow men despite differences of race or creed or business interest; that is what the American Way of Life emphatically prescribes.[19] But the American Way of Life almost explicitly sanctions hating a member of a "dangerous" political party (Communists and fascists are obviously meant here) or an enemy of one's country, and therefore an overwhelming majority avow their hate. In both situations, while the Jewish-Christian law of love is formally acknowledged, the truly operative factor is the value system embodied in the American Way of Life. Where the American Way of Life approves of love of one's fellow man, most Americans confidently assert that they practice such love; where the American Way of Life disapproves, the great mass of Americans do not hesitate to confess that they do not practice it, and apparently feel very little guilt for their failure. No better pragmatic test as to what the operative religion of the American people actually is could be desired.[20]

It is not suggested here that the ideals Americans feel to be indicated in the American Way of Life are scrupulously observed in the practice of Americans; they are in fact constantly violated, often grossly. But violated or not, they are felt to be normative and relevant to "business and politics" in a way that the formal tenets of "official" religion are not. That is what makes the American Way of Life the "common religion" of American society in the sense here intended.

It should be clear that what is being designated under the American Way of Life is not the so-called "common denominator" religion; it is not a synthetic system composed of beliefs to be found in all or in a group of religions. It is an organic structure of ideas, values, and beliefs that constitutes a faith common to Americans and genuinely operative in their lives, a faith that markedly influences, and is influenced by, the "official" religions of American society. Sociologically, anthropologically, if one pleases, it is the characteristic American religion, undergirding American life and overarching American society despite all indubitable differences of region, section, culture, and class.

Yet qualifications are immediately in order. Not for all Americans is this American religion, this "common religion" of American society, equally operative; some indeed explicitly repudiate it as religion. By and large, it would seem that what is resistive in contemporary American society to the American Way of Life as religion may be understood under three heads. First, there are the churches of immigrant-ethnic background that still cherish their traditional creeds and confessions as a sign of their distinctive origin and are unwilling to let these be dissolved into an over-all "American religion"; certain Lutheran and Reformed churches in this country[21] as well as sections of the Catholic Church would fall into this classification. Then there are groups, not large but increasing, that have an explicit and conscious theological concern, whether it be "orthodox," "neo-orthodox," or "liberal"; in varying degrees, they find their theologies at odds with the implied "theology" of the American Way of Life. Finally, there are the ill-defined, though by all accounts numerous and influential, "religions of the disinherited," the many "holiness," pentecostal, and millenarian sects of the socially and culturally submerged segments of our society;[22] for them, their "peculiar" religion is frequently still too vital and all-absorbing to be easily subordinated to some "common faith." All of these cases, it will be noted, constitute "hold outs" against the sweep of religious Americanism; in each case there is an element of alienation which generates a certain amount of tension in social life.

What is this American Way of Life that we have said constitutes the "common 13 religion" of American society? An adequate description and analysis of what is implied in this phrase still remains to be attempted, and certainly it will not be ventured here; but some indications may not be out of place.

The American Way of Life is the symbol by which Americans define themselves 14 and establish their unity. German unity, it would seem, is felt to be largely racial-folkish, French unity largely cultural; but neither of these ways is open to the American people, the most diverse in racial and cultural origins of any in the world. As American unity has emerged, it has emerged more and more clearly as a unity embodied in, and symbolized by, the complex structure known as the American Way of Life.

If the American Way of Life had to be defined in one word, "democracy" would 15 undoubtedly be the word, but democracy in a peculiarly American sense. On its political side it means the Constitution; on its economic side, "free enterprise"; on its social side, an equalitarianism which is not only compatible with but indeed actually implies vigorous economic competition and high mobility. Spiritually, the American Way of Life is best expressed in a certain kind of "idealism" which has come to be recognized as characteristically American. It is a faith that has its symbols and its rituals, its holidays and its liturgy, its saints and its sancta;[23] and it is a faith that every American, to the degree that he is an American, knows and understands.

The American Way of Life is individualistic, dynamic, pragmatic. It affirms the 16 supreme value and dignity of the individual; it stresses incessant activity on his part, for he is never to rest but is always to be striving to "get ahead"; it defines an ethic of self-reliance, merit, and character, and judges by achievement: "deeds, not creeds" are what count. The American Way of Life is humanitarian, "forward looking," optimistic. Americans are easily the most generous and philanthropic people in the world, in terms of their ready and unstinting response to suffering anywhere on the globe. The American believes in progress, in self-improvement, and quite fanatically in education. But above all, the American is idealistic. Americans cannot go on making money or achieving worldly success simply on its own merits; such "materialistic" things must, in the

American mind, be justified in "higher" terms, in terms of "service" or "stewardship" or "general welfare." Because Americans are so idealistic, they tend to confuse espousing an ideal with fulfilling it and are always tempted to regard themselves as good as the ideals they entertain: hence the amazingly high valuation most Americans quite sincerely place on their own virtue. And because they are so idealistic, Americans tend to be moralistic: they are inclined to see all issues as plain and simple, black and white, issues of morality. Every struggle in which they are seriously engaged becomes a "crusade." To Mr. Eisenhower, who in many ways exemplifies American religion in a particularly representative way, the second world war was a "crusade" (as was the first to Woodrow Wilson); so was his campaign for the presidency ("I am engaged in a crusade . . . to substitute good government for what we most earnestly believe has been bad government"); and so is his administration—a "battle for the republic" against "godless Communism" abroad and against "corruption and materialism" at home. It was Woodrow Wilson who once said, "Sometimes people call me an idealist. Well, that is the way I know I'm an American: America is the most idealistic nation in the world"; Eisenhower was but saying the same thing when he solemnly affirmed: "The things that make us proud to be Americans are of the soul and of the spirit."[24]

The American Way of Life is, of course, anchored in the American's vision of 17 America. The Puritan's dream of a new "Israel" and a new "Promised Land" in the New World, the *"novus ordo seclorum"* on the Great Seal of the United States reflect the perennial American conviction that in the New World a new beginning has been made, a new order of things established, vastly different from and superior to the decadent institutions of the Old World. This conviction, emerging out of the earliest reality of American history, was continuously nourished through the many decades of immigration into the present century by the residual hopes and expectations of the immigrants, for whom the New World had to be really something new if it was to be anything at all. And this conviction still remains pervasive in American life, hardly shaken by the new shape of the world and the challenge of the "new orders" of the twentieth century, Nazism and Communism. It is the secret of what outsiders must take to be the incredible self-righteousness of the American people, who tend to see the world divided into an innocent, virtuous America confronted with a corrupt, devious, and guileful Europe and Asia. The self-righteousness, however, if self-righteousness it be, is by no means simple, if only because virtually all Americans are themselves derived from the foreign parts they so distrust. In any case, this feeling about America as really and truly the "new order" of things at last established is the heart of the outlook defined by the American Way of Life.[25]

In her *Vermont Tradition,* Dorothy Canfield Fisher lists as that tradition's prin- 18 cipal ingredients: individual freedom, personal independence, human dignity, community responsibility, social and political democracy, sincerity, restraint in outward conduct, and thrift.[26] With some amplification—particularly emphasis on the uniqueness of the American "order" and the great importance assigned to religion—this may be taken as a pretty fair summary of some of the "values" embodied in the American Way of Life. It will not escape the reader that this account is essentially an idealized description of the middle-class ethos. And, indeed, that is just what it is. The American Way of Life is a middle-class way, just as the American people in their entire outlook and feeling are a middle-class people.[27] But the American Way of Life as it has come down to us is not merely middle-class; it is emphatically inner-directed. Indeed, it is probably one of the best expressions of inner-direction in history. As such, it now seems to be undergoing some degree of modification—perhaps at certain points disintegration—under the impact of the spread of other-direction in our society. For the foreseeable future, however, we may with some confidence expect the continuance in strength of the American Way of Life as both the tradition and the "common faith" of the American people.[28]

III

The American Way of Life as the "common faith" of American society has coex- 19 isted for some centuries with the historic faiths of the American people, and the two have influenced each other in many profound and subtle ways. The influence has been complex and reciprocal, to the point where causal priority becomes impossible to assign if indeed it does not become altogether meaningless. From the very beginning the American Way of Life was shaped by the contours of American Protestantism; it may, indeed, best be understood as a kind of secularized Puritanism, a Puritanism without transcendence, without sense of sin or judgment. The Puritan's vision of a new "Promised Land" in the wilderness of the New World has become, as we have suggested, the American's deep sense of the newness and uniqueness of things in the Western Hemisphere. The Puritan's sense of vocation and "inner-worldly asceticism" can still be detected in the American's gospel of action and service, and his consciousness of high responsibility before God in the American's "idealism." The Puritan's abiding awareness of the ambiguity of all human motivations and his insight into the corruptions of inordinate power have left their mark not only on the basic structure of our constitutional system but also on the entire social philosophy of the American people.[29] Nor have other strands of early American Protestantism been without their effect. There can be little doubt that Pietism co-operated with frontier revivalism in breaking down the earlier concern with dogma and doctrine, so that the slogan, "deeds, not creeds," soon became the hallmark both of American religion and of the American Way of Life.[30] These are but aspects of an influence that is often easier to see than to define.

The reciprocal action of the American Way of Life in shaping and reshaping the 20 historic faiths of Christianity and Judaism on American soil is perhaps more readily discerned. By and large, we may say that these historic religions have all tended to become "Americanized" under the pervasive influence of the American environment. This "Americanization" has been the product not so much of conscious direction as of a "diffuse convergence" operating spontaneously in the context of the totality of American life. What it has brought, however, is none the less clear: "religious groupings throughout [American] society [have been] stamped with recognizably 'American' qualities,"[31] to an extent indeed where foreign observers sometimes find the various American religions more like each other than they are like their European counterparts.[32]

Under the influence of the American environment the historic Jewish and 21 Christian faiths have tended to become secularized in the sense of becoming integrated as parts within a larger whole defined by the American Way of Life. "There is a marked tendency," Williams writes in his discussion of the relations of religion to other institutions in the United States, "to regard religion as a good because it is useful in furthering other major values—in other words, to reverse the ends-means relation implied in the conception of religion as an ultimate value."[33] In this reversal the Christian and Jewish faiths tend to be prized because they help promote ideals and standards that all Americans are expected to share on a deeper level than merely "official" religion. Insofar as any reference is made to the God in whom all Americans "believe" and of whom the "official" religions speak, it is primarily as sanction and underpinning for the supreme values of the faith embodied in the American Way of Life. Secularization of religion could hardly go further.

As a consequence, in some cases of its own origins, but primarily of the wide- 22 spread influence of the American environment, religion in America has tended toward a marked disparagement of "forms," whether theological or liturgical. Even the highly liturgical and theological churches have felt the effects of this spirit to the degree that they have become thoroughly acculturated. Indeed, the anti-theological, anti-liturgical bias is still pervasive despite the recent upsurge of theological concern and despite the greater interest being shown in liturgy because of its psychological power and "emotional richness."

American religion is (within the limits set by the particular traditions of the 23 churches) non-theological and non-liturgical; it is activistic and occupied with the things of the world to a degree that has become a byword among European churchmen. With this activism has gone a certain "latitudinarianism," associated with the de-emphasis of theology and doctrine: Americans tend to believe that "ethical behavior and a good life, rather than adherence to a specific creed, [will] earn a share in the heavenly kingdom."[34] The activism of American religion has manifested itself in many forms throughout our history: in the Puritan concern for the total life of the community; in the passionate championing of all sorts of reform causes by the evangelical movements of the first half of the nineteenth century; in the "social gospel" of more recent times; in the ill-starred Prohibition "crusade"; in the advanced "progressive" attitudes on social questions taken by the National Council of Churches, the National Catholic Welfare Conference, and the various rabbinical associations; in the strong social emphasis of American Protestant "neo-orthodoxy." This activism, which many Europeans seem to regard as the distinguishing feature of American religion, both reflects the dynamic temper of the American Way of Life and has been a principal factor in its development.

It is hardly necessary to continue this analysis much farther along these gen- 24 eral lines. The optimism, moralism, and idealism of Jewish and Christian faith in America are plain evidence of the profound effect of the American outlook on American religion. Indeed, such evidence is amply provided by any tabulation of the distinctive features of religion in America,[35] and needs no special emphasis at this point.

What is perhaps of crucial importance, and requires a more detailed examina- 25 tion, is the new attitude toward religion and the new conception of the church that have emerged in America.[36]

Americans believe in religion in a way that perhaps no other people do. It may 26 indeed be said that the primary religious affirmation of the American people, in harmony with the American Way of Life, is that religion is a "good thing," a supremely "good thing," for the individual and the community. And "religion" here means not so much any particular religion, but religion as such, religion-in-general. "Our government makes no sense," President Eisenhower recently declared, "unless it is founded in a deeply felt religious faith—*and I don't care what it is"* (emphasis added).[37] In saying this, the President was saying something that almost any American could understand and approve, but which must seem like a deplorable heresy to the European churchman. Every American could understand, first, that Mr. Eisenhower's apparent indifferentism ("and I don't care what it is") was not indifferentism at all, but the expression of the conviction that at bottom the "three great faiths" were really "saying the same thing" in affirming the "spiritual ideals" and "moral values" of the American Way of Life. Every American, moreover, could understand that what Mr. Eisenhower was emphasizing so vehemently was the indispensability of religion as the foundation of society. This is one aspect of what Americans mean when they say that they "believe in religion." The object of devotion of this kind of religion, however, is "not God but 'religion.' . . . The faith is not in God but in faith; we worship not God but our own worshiping."[38] When Americans think of themselves as a profoundly religious people, whose "first allegiance" is "reserved . . . to the kingdom of the spirit,"[39] this is, by and large, what they mean, and not any commitment to the doctrines or traditions of the historic faiths.

      With this view of religion is associated a closely analogous view of the church. 27 For America, the celebrated dichotomy of "church" and "sect,"[40] however pertinent it may be to European conditions, has only a secondary significance. The concept of the church as the nation religiously organized, established socially, if not always legally, has only an oblique relevance to American reality; and though America does know sects in the sense of "fringe" groups of the "disinherited," it does not understand these groups and their relation to the more conventional churches the way Europe does. An entirely new conception of church and church institutions has emerged in America.

      It must be remembered that in America the variety and multiplicity of 28 churches did not, as in Europe, come with the breakdown of a single established national church; in America, taking the nation as a whole, the variety and multiplicity of churches was almost the original condition and coeval with the emergence of the new society. In America religious pluralism is thus not merely a historical and political fact; it is, in the mind of the American, the primordial condition of things, an essential aspect of the American Way of Life, and therefore in itself an aspect of religious belief.[41] Americans, in other words, believe that the plurality of religious groups is a proper and legitimate condition. However much he may be attached to his own church, however dimly he may regard the beliefs and practices of other churches, the American tends to feel rather strongly that total religious uniformity, even with his own church benefiting thereby, would be something undesirable and wrong, indeed scarcely conceivable. Pluralism of religions and churches is something quite axiomatic to the American. This feeling, more than anything else, is the foundation of the American doctrine of the "separation of church and state," for it is the heart of this doctrine that the government may not do anything that implies the pre-eminence of superior legitimacy of one church over another.

      This means that outside the Old World distinction of church and sect America 29 has given birth to a new type of religious structure—the denomination.[42] The denomination as we know it is a stable, settled church, enjoying a legitimate and recognized place in a larger aggregate of churches, each recognizing the proper status of the others.[43] The denomination is the "non-conformist sect" become central and normative. It differs from the church in the European understanding of the term in that it would never dream of claiming to be *the* national ecclesiastical institution; it differs from the sect in that it is socially established, thoroughly institutionalized, and nuclear to the society in which it is found. The European dichotomy becomes meaningless, and instead we have the nuclear denomination on the one side, and the peripheral sect on the way to becoming a denomination on the other. So firmly entrenched is this denominational idea in the mind of the American that even American Catholics have come to think in such terms; theologically the Catholic Church of course continues to regard itself as the one true church, but in their actual social attitudes American Catholics, hardly less than American Protestants or Jews, tend to think of their church as a denomination existing side by side with other denominations in a pluralistic harmony that is felt to be somehow of the texture of American life.[44]

Denominational pluralism, as the American idea of the church may be called, 30 obviously implies that no church can look to the state for its members or support. Voluntarism and evangelism are thus the immediate consequences of the American idea: for their maintenance, for their very existence, churches must depend on the voluntary adherence of their members, and they are therefore moved to pursue a vigorous evangelistic work to win people to their ranks. The accommodation of the church to American reality extends even to its inner polity. "As the polity of the Roman church followed the pattern of the Roman empire," H. Richard Niebuhr points out, "so the American churches incline to organize themselves [along representative lines] in conformity with the system of state and national legislatures and executives."[45] Even the Roman Catholic Church, with its fixed hierarchical structure, has not been totally immune to American influence of this kind.[46]

The denominational idea is fundamental to American thinking about religion, 31 but it is not the last word. Americans think of their various churches as denominations, but they also feel that somehow the denominations fall into larger wholes which we have called religious communities. This kind of denominational aggregation is, of course, something that pertains primarily to Protestantism and to a lesser degree to Judaism; both have more or less organized denominations which, taken together, form the religious communities. Catholicism, on the other hand, has no such overt inner divisions, but American Catholics readily understand the phenomenon when they see it among Protestants and Jews. Denominations are felt to be somehow a matter of individual preference, and movement between denominations is not uncommon; the religious community, on the other hand, is taken as something more objective and given, something in which, by and large, one is born, lives, and dies, something that (to recall our earlier analysis) identifies and defines one's position in American society.[47] Since the religious community in its present form is a recent social emergent, its relations to the denominations properly so-called are still relatively fluid and undefined but the main lines of development would seem to be fairly clear.

When the plurality of denominations comprehended in religious communities 32 is seen from the standpoint of the "common faith" of American society, what emerges is the conception of the three "communions"—Protestantism, Catholicism, Judaism—as three diverse, but equally legitimate, equally American, expressions of an over-all American religion, standing for essentially the same "moral ideals" and "spiritual values." This conception, whatever may be thought of it theologically, is in fact held, though hardly in explicit form, by many devout and religiously sophisticated Americans.

It would seem to be the obvious meaning of the title, *The Religions of Democracy,* given to a recent authoritative statement of the Protestant, Catholic, and Jewish positions.[48] "Democracy" apparently has its religions which fall under it as species fall under the genus of which they are part. And in this usage "democracy" is obviously a synonym for the American Way of Life.

It is but one more step, though a most fateful one, to proceed from "the reli- 33 gions of democracy" to "democracy as religion" and consciously to erect "democracy" into a super-faith above and embracing the three recognized religions. This step has been taken by a number of thinkers in recent years. Thus, Professor J. Paul Williams has been urging a program of religious reconstruction in which he insists that: "Americans must come to look on the democratic ideal (not necessarily the American practice of it) as the Will of God, or if they please, of Nature. . . . Americans must be brought to the conviction that democracy is the very Law of Life. . . . The state must be brought into the picture; governmental agencies must teach the democratic ideal *as religion* . . . primary responsibility for teaching democracy as religion must be given to the public school, for instance . . ."[49]

Professor Horace M. Kallen reaches very much the same conclusion from an- 34 other direction. "For the communicants of the democratic faith," he writes, "it is the religion *of* and *for* religions. . . . [It is] the religion of religions, all may freely come together in it."[50]

It is not our purpose, at this point, to draw the theological implications of this 35 super-religion of "democracy" as the "religion of religions"; it is only necessary to point out that it marks a radical break with the fundamental presuppositions of both Judaism and Christianity, to which it must appear as a particularly insidious kind of idolatry. What is merely implicit and perhaps never intended in the acceptance of the American Way of Life as the "common religion" of American society is here brought to its logical conclusion and made to reveal its true inner meaning.

By and large, the "common faith" of American society remains implicit and is 36 never carried to the logical conclusion to which a few ideologists have pushed it. By the great mass of the American people the American Way of Life is not avowed as a super-faith above and embracing the historic religions. It operates as a "common faith" at deeper levels, through its pervasive influence on the patterns of American thought and feeling. It makes no pretensions to override or supplant the recognized religions, to which it assigns a place of great eminence and honor in the American scheme of things. But all the implications are there . . .

IV

The "common faith" of American society is not merely a civic religion to cele- 37 brate the values and convictions of the American people as a corporate entity. It has its inner, personal aspects as well; or rather, side by side and in intimate relation with the civic religion of the American Way of Life, there has developed, primarily through a de-vitalization of the historic faiths, an inner, personal religion that promises salvation to the disoriented, tormented souls of a society in crisis.

This inner, personal religion is based on the American's *faith in faith.* We have 38 seen that a primary religious affirmation of the American is his belief in religion. The American believes that religion is something very important for the community; he also believes that "faith," or what we may call religiosity, is a kind of "miracle drug" that can cure all the ailments of the spirit. It is not faith in *anything* that is so powerful, just faith, the "magic of believing." "It was back in those days," a prominent American churchman writes, recalling his early years, "that I formed a habit that I have never broken. I began saying in the morning two words, 'I believe.' Those two words *with nothing added* . . . give me a running start for my day, and for every day" (emphasis not in original).[51]

The cult of faith takes two forms, which we might designate as introvert and 39 extrovert. In its introvert form faith is trusted to bring mental health and "peace of mind," to dissipate anxiety and guilt, and to translate the soul to the blessed land of "normality" and "self-acceptance." In earlier times this cult of faith was quite literally a cult of "faith healing," best expressed in what H. Richard Niebuhr has described as the "man-centered, this-worldly, lift-yourselves-by-your-own-bootstraps doctrine of New Thought and Christian Science."[52] Latterly it has come to vest itself in the fashionable vocabulary of psychoanalysis and is offering a synthesis of religion and psychiatry.[53] But at bottom it is the same cult of faith in faith, the same promise that through "those two words, 'I believe,' with nothing added," all our troubles will be dissipated and inner peace and harmony restored.

The cult of faith has also its extrovert form, and that is known as "positive 40 thinking." "Positive thinking," thinking that is "affirmative" and avoids the corrosions of "negativity" and "skepticism," thinking that "has faith," is recommended as a powerful force in the world of struggle and achievement.[54] Here again it is not so much faith in anything, certainly not the theocentric faith of the historic religions, that is supposed to confer this power—but just faith, the psychological attitude of having faith, so to speak. And here too the cult is largely the product of the inner disintegration and enfeeblement of the historic religions; the familiar words are retained, but the old meaning is voided. "Have faith," "don't lose faith," and the like, were once injunctions to preserve one's unwavering trust in the God from Whom comes both the power to live and the "peace that passeth understanding." Gradually these phrases have come to be an appeal to maintain a "positive" attitude to life and not to lose confidence in oneself and one's activities. "To believe in yourself and in everything you do": such, at bottom, is the meaning of the contemporary cult of faith, whether it is proclaimed by devout men from distinguished pulpits or offered as the "secret of success" by self-styled psychologists who claim to have discovered the "hidden powers" of man.[55] What is important is faith, faith in faith. Even where the classical symbols and formulas are still retained, that is very often what is meant and what is understood.

Such are some major aspects of the social, cultural, and spiritual environment 41 in which religion in America moves and has its being. And religion in America means the three great religious communities, the Protestant, the Catholic, and the Jewish.

NOTES

1. *Belief in God:* 97 per cent—"Do Americans Believe in God?", *The Catholic Digest,* November 1952; 96 per cent—Gallup poll, *Public Opinion News Service,* December 18, 1954; 95 per cent—Lincoln Barnett, "God and the American People," *Ladies' Home Journal,* November

1948, p. 37. According to the *Catholic Digest* poll 89 per cent of Americans believe in the Trinity ("How Many in the U. S. Believe in the Trinity?", *The Catholic Digest,* July 1953) and 80 per cent think of Christ as divine ("What We Americans Think of Our Lord," *The Catholic Digest*, August 1953). [Herberg's notes]

2. *Church membership and attendance:* see above, chap. iv, pp. 47–50 [*Protestant–Catholic– Jew*].
3. *Prayer:* 92 per cent answer yes to the question, "Do you ever pray to God?" ("Americans and Prayer," *The Catholic Digest,* November 1953); 90 per cent say they pray, 56 per cent "frequently"—Barnett, "God and the American People," *Ladies' Home Journal,* November 1948, p. 37.
4. *Life after death:* 77 per cent believe in afterlife, 7 per cent don't, 16 per cent don't know— "What Do Americans Think of Heaven and Hell?", *The Catholic Digest,* March 1953; 76 per cent say yes, 13 per cent no, 11 per cent don't know—Gallup poll, *Public Opinion News Service,* December 11, 1944; 73 per cent say yes, 15 per cent no, 12 per cent no opinion—Barnett, "God and the American People," *Ladies' Home Journal,* November 1948, pp. 230–31; 74 per cent believe in life after death—Gallup poll, *Public Opinion News Service,* April 19, 1957.

    Heaven and Hell: 72 per cent believe in heaven, 58 per cent in hell—*The Catholic Digest,* as above; 52 per cent think that "life after death is divided into heaven and hell," though heaven looms larger in their minds than hell—Barnett, "God and the American People," *Ladies' Home Journal,* November 1948, p. 231; 61 per cent believe there is a devil—Gallup poll, *Public Opinion News Service,* April 19, 1957.
5. *Opinion about church and clergymen:* 75 per cent deny the allegation that the church is too much concerned about money—"Is the Church Too Much Concerned About Money?", *The Catholic Digest,* March 1954; 68 per cent regard clergymen as "very understanding," 21 per cent as "fairly understanding"—"How Understanding Are Clergymen?", *The Catholic Digest,* December 1953; clergymen rank at the top in the scale of those who "do most good"—see above, chap. iv, p. 51.
6. *Bible:* 86 per cent regard it as divinely inspired, the "word of God"—"What Do Americans Think of the Bible?", *The Catholic Digest,* May 1954; a survey conducted by the *British Weekly* gives the figure for Americans who regard the Bible as divinely inspired as 86.5 per cent (see *Information Service* [National Council of Churches of Christ], December 27, 1952).
7. *Religious instruction:* 98 per cent say yes—"Do Americans Want Their Children to Receive Religious Instruction?", *The Catholic Digest,* September 1953. *Children raised as church members:* 72 per cent say yes—"How Important Is Religion to Americans?", *The Catholic Digest,* February 1953.
8. *Importance of religion:* 75 per cent regard it as "very important," 20 per cent as "fairly important"—"How Important Is Religion to Americans?", *The Catholic Digest,* February 1953; 69 per cent think that the influence of religion is increasing and 81 per cent believe that religion can answer "most of today's problems"—Gallup poll, *Public Opinion News Service,* April 21, 1957. The religiosity of the American people appears even more striking when it is contrasted with the much more "skeptical" views held by the British; see the series of comparative surveys conducted by the Gallup organization, *Public Opinion News Service,* April 16, 17, 18, 19, 21, 1957.
9. Barnett, "God and the American People," *Ladies' Home Journal,* November 1948, p. 234.
10. "What the U.S. Thinks of Life Here and Hereafter," *The Catholic Digest,* May 1953.
11. Barnett, "God and the American People," *Ladies' Home Journal,* November 1948, pp. 233, 234, 235.
12. Barnett, "God and the American People," *Ladies' Home Journal,* November 1948, p. 234.
13. See particularly the statement of Father George B. Ford, in Barnett, "God and the American People," *Ladies' Home Journal,* November 1948, p. 237.

14. Robin M. Williams, Jr., *American Society: A Sociological Interpretation* (Knopf, 1951), p. 312.

15. Williams, *American Society,* p. 320 n.

16. Williams, *American Society,* p. 344.

17. When an American tourist comes upon the inadequate sanitary arrangements in certain parts of Europe and discovers what seems to him the careless attitude of the inhabitants in matters of personal hygiene, he is inclined to feel what he experiences not simply as a shortcoming in modern living conveniences but as a *moral defect,* on a par with irreligion, caste rigidity, and the absence of American representative democracy. Cp. the following placard displayed by many restaurants in the midwest: "Sanitation is a way of life. As a way of life, it must be nourished from within and grow as an ideal in human relations."

18. Barnett, "God and the American People," *Ladies' Home Journal,* November 1948, pp. 235–36.

19. Where this "principle" of the American Way of Life is flagrantly violated by local prescription, as in the case of racial attitudes in the south and elsewhere, festering "bad conscience" and a destructive defensive aggressiveness are the result.

20. "Differences in religion make a difference in social conduct" (Williams, *American Society,* p. 311). Investigating belief-systems from this angle would seem to be a good way of discovering what the "religion" of an individual or a group really is.

21. Discussing the European background of such churches, H. Richard Niebuhr writes: "These churches are doctrinal and liturgical in character, regarding conformity to creed and ritual as the essential requirements of Christianity" (*The Social Sources of Denominationalism* [Holt, 1929], p. 126).

22. For a discussion of the "religions of the disinherited," see below, chap. vi, pp. 122–23, chap. ix, pp. 216–19.

23. See the illuminating account of Memorial Day as an "American sacred ceremony" in W. Lloyd Warner, *Structure of American Life* (Edinburgh, 1952), chap. x. Warner writes: "The Memorial Day ceremonies and subsidiary rites, such as those of Armistice Day, of today, yesterday, and tomorrow, are rituals which are a sacred symbol system which functions periodically to integrate the whole community, with its conflicting symbols and its opposing autonomous churches and associations. . . . Memorial Day is a cult of the dead which organizes and integrates the various faiths, ethnic and class groups, into a sacred unity" (p. 214). As to the "saints" of the American Way of Life, Warner quotes a Memorial Day orator: "No character except the Carpenter of Nazareth has ever been honored the way Washington and Lincoln have been in New England. Virtue, freedom from sin, and righteousness were qualities possessed by Washington and Lincoln, and in possessing these qualities both were true Americans, and we would do well to emulate them. Let us first be true Americans" (p. 220). The theological implications of this statement are sensational: Washington and Lincoln, as "true Americans," are credited with the moral and spiritual qualities ("virtue, freedom from sin, and righteousness") traditionally associated with Christ, and we are all urged to "emulate" them!

24. For the quotations, as well as a general account of Mr. Eisenhower's religion, see Paul Hutchinson, "The President's Religious Faith," *The Christian Century,* March 24, 1954. For a sharp critique, see William Lee Miller, "Piety Along the Potomac," *The Reporter,* August 17, 1954.

25. For a penetrating examination of the sources and expressions of the American conviction of a "new order of things" in the New World, see Reinhold Niebuhr, *The Irony of American History* (Scribner's, 1952).

26. Dorothy Canfield Fisher, *Vermont Tradition* (Little, Brown, 1953). For a comprehensive survey of American life, see Max Lerner, *America as a Civilization: Life and Thought in the United States Today* (Simon and Schuster, 1957); see also Elting E. Morison, ed., *The American Style: Essays in Value and Performance* (Harper, 1958).

27. "America is a middle-class country, and the middle-class values and styles of perception reach into all levels except perhaps the fringes at the very top and the very bottom" (David Riesman, *Individualism Reconsidered* [Free Press, 1954], p. 499).

28. Riesman sees the immigrant generations as an important source of replenishment of old-line middle-class inner-directedness in American society (*Individualism Reconsidered,* pp. 289, 290).

29. See H. Richard Niebuhr, *The Kingdom of God in America* (Willett, Clark, 1937), pp. 76–83.

30. See F. E. Mayer, *The Religious Bodies of America* (Concordia, 1954), pp. 352–53, 354, 378 n.

31. Williams, *American Society,* p. 319. See also Roy F. Nichols, *Religion and American Democracy* (Louisiana State University Press, 1959) and William Lee Miller, "Religion and the American Way of Life," in *Religion and the Free Society* (Fund for the Republic, 1958).

32. "European visitors are able to detect better than we ourselves the emergence of a 'typically American' form of Christian worship" (Herbert Wallace Schneider, *Religion in 20th Century America* [Harvard, 1952], p. 170). "As many have noticed, the Protestant churches in America, even though brought from Europe, show more qualities in common than any one retains with its European stem. And they feel that in America, the synagogue is no longer an alien. Even the Catholic Church in America acquires a tone unlike Catholicism in Europe" (Perry Miller, "The Location of American Religious Freedom," in *Religion and Freedom of Thought* [Doubleday, 1954], p. 21).

33. Williams, *American Society,* p. 337. Something of the shift involved in this secularization of Jewish-Christian faith is suggested by Ralph Barton Perry in his apologia for Protestant "liberalism": "If it does not stress the love of God, it does at least embrace the love of neighbor. If it neglects the fatherhood of God, it at any rate proclaims the fraternity of men. If it disparages the church along with other corporate entities, it is because it is so insistent on the finality of the human person. The independence of this moral ideal in no way argues *against* theism . . ." (Ralph Barton Perry, *Characteristically American* [Knopf, 1949], p. 117).

34. Oscar Handlin, *The Uprooted* (Little, Brown, 1951), p. 128.

35. See, e.g., the section, "Relatively Distinctive Features of American Religious Institutions," in Williams, *American Society,* pp. 315–51.

36. Two recent studies of contemporary American religion are of major, importance: A. Roy Eckardt, *The Surge of American Piety* (Association Press, 1958) and Martin E. Marty, *The New Shape of American Religion* (Harper, 1959). See also Lerner, *America as a Civilization,* chap. x. sec. 1, "God and the Churches" (pp. 703–17) and William H. Whyte, Jr., *The Organization Man* (Simon and Schuster, 1956), Part VII, chap. 26, "The Church of Suburbia" (pp. 365–81).

37. *The New York Times,* December 23, 1952; see also G. Elson Ruff, *The Dilemma of Church and State* (Muhlenberg, 1954), p. 85. Cp. the very similar sentiment expressed by Robert C. Ruark: "Although I am not a practicing religionist, I have a great respect for organized religion, no matter what shape it takes" ("Scoff-religious," *New York World Telegram,* October 10, 1955).

38. Miller, "Piety Along the Potomac," *The Reporter,* August 17, 1954. Mr. Miller continues: "If the object of devotion is not God but 'religion' . . . then the resulting religiosity may become simply the instrument of more substantial commitments." The most "substantial" commitment of the American people, to which their "religiosity" is instrumental, is the American Way of Life. Once more to quote Mr. Eisenhower: "I am the most intensely religious man I know. Nobody goes through six years of war without faith. A democracy cannot exist without a religious base. I believe in democracy" (*New York Times,* May 4, 1948).

39. Dwight D. Eisenhower, quoted in Paul Hutchinson, "The President's Religious Faith," *The Christian Century,* March 24, 1954.

40. See Ernst Troeltsch, *The Social Teaching of the Christian Churches* (1911; tr. by Olive Wyon, Macmillian, 1931), Vol. I, pp. 331–49, Vol. II, pp. 691–728; also J. Milton Yinger, *Religion in the Struggle for Power* (Duke, 1946), pp. 16–50.

41. Williams speaks of a "value-consensus in which religious differences are subsidiary to the values of religious liberty" (*American Society,* p. 345).

42. "The Mormons, the Orthodox Jews, and a few small religious communities are religiously organized peoples, but almost all other religious bodies in the United States, including the Roman Catholic Church, are neither national churches nor sects; they are commonly known as denominations or 'communions' " (Schneider, *Religion in 20th Century America*, p. 22). Even the groups Schneider mentions as exceptions, insofar as they have become acculturated to American life, would seem to fall into the same pattern.

43. Since most American denominations emerged from earlier sects, denominations have sometimes been defined as "simply sects in an advanced stage of development and adjustment to each other and the secular world" (Leopold von Wiese, *Systematic Sociology,* adapted and amplified by Howard Becker [Wiley, 1932], p. 626). There is, of course, a good deal of truth in this definition; its defect, however, is that it regards the denomination as essentially transitional between sect and church, which is emphatically not the case with denominations in the American sense. American denominations have indeed, by and large, developed out of sects, but they represent the final stage of development, rather than a transitional stage to something else ("church" in the European sense). For a more general discussion, see Joachim Wach, *Types of Religious Experience* (Routledge and Kegan Paul, 1951), chap. ix, "Church, Denomination, and Sect."

44. In a number of European countries (Germany, Holland, Switzerland), Protestant and Catholic churches have reached a kind of balance in which neither can pretend to be "the" national church. But where this is the case, it is simply a social and historical fact, not the proper and normative condition. In America, on the other hand, the plurality of churches is held to be proper and normative; in this the American situation differs fundamentally from the European, even where the latter seems to resemble it most.

45. H. Richard Niebuhr, *The Social Sources of Denominationalism,* p. 207. "The Church in our time, like the Church in any place at any time, is deeply influenced in its institutional forms by the political and economic society with which it lives in conjunction. As the polity of all the churches, whether they are episcopal, presbyterian, or congregational by tradition, has been modified in the direction of the political structure of Canada and the United States, so the institutional status and authority of the ministry are being modified in the direction of the democratic type of political, educational, and economic executive or managerial authority" (H. Richard Niebuhr, *The Purpose of the Church and Its Ministry* [Harper, 1956], p. 90). Cf. the statement of Franklin Clark Fry, president of the United Lutheran Church of America: "The polity of our church as a whole is frankly constructed on a secular model. Its prototype is the government of the United States" (quoted in H.E.F., "Lutherans Centralize," *The Christian Century,* October 27, 1954).

46. Thus McAvoy speaks of the "practical and parochial character of American Catholicism,"; the "parochial" character he relates to the "American tradition of disestablishment," while for the "practical" aspect of American Catholicism, he notes that "some observers have claimed that [it] is the product of the puritanism dominant in American Protestantism" (Thomas T. McAvoy, "The Catholic Church in the United States," in Waldemar Gurian and M. A. Fitzsimons, *The Catholic Church in World Affairs* [Notre Dame, 1954], pp. 361, 364).

47. Despite all the instability of American life, fully 96 per cent of Americans were found in 1955 still belonging to the religious community of their birth (see *Public Opinion News Service,* March 20, 1955).

48. Louis Finkelstein, J. Elliot Ross, and William Adams Brown, *The Religions of Democracy: Judaism, Catholicism, and Protestantism in Creed and Life* (Devin-Adair, 1946). One of the clearest expressions of this conception by a layman was voiced by Admiral William F. Halsey, principal speaker at the fifth annual "four chaplains award dinner." "This picture," Admiral Halsey declared, "is symbolic of our national life. Protestant, Catholic, and Jew, each group has given, when called upon, the full measure of devotion in defense of our [American democratic] way of life" (*The New York Times,* February 6, 1955).

49. J. Paul Williams, *What Americans Believe and How They Worship* (Harper, 1952), pp. 71, 78, 368, 374; see the critical review of this book by J. H. Nichols, *The Christian Century,* September 3, 1952. (A strong tendency toward this kind of "religion of democracy" is to be found in Jewish Reconstructionism; see Ira Eisenstein and Eugene Kohn, *Mordecai M. Kaplan: An Evaluation* [Jewish Reconstructionist Foundation, 1952], p. 259). "The religion of the American majority is democracy. . . . In fact, the religion of public education is a more powerful factor in American life today than that of the churches. The only religion with which the great majority of American youth have ever come in contact is the religion of public education" (Conrad Moehlman, *School and Church: The American Way* [Harper, 1944], pp. ix, x). David Riesman speaks of "new ways of using the school as a kind of community center, as the chapel of a secular religion perhaps" (*Individualism Reconsidered,* p. 211).

50. H. M. Kallen, "Democracy's True Religion," *Saturday Review of Literature,* July 28, 1951.

51. Daniel A. Poling, "A Running Start for Every Day," *Parade: The Sunday Picture Magazine,* September 19, 1954.

52. H. Richard Niebuhr, *The Social Sources of Denominationalism,* p. 104. Niebuhr thus describes this type of religiosity in which the old Puritan spirituality has terminated: "In its final phase, the development of this religious movement exhibits the complete enervation of the once virile force . . . the problem of evil [has been] simplified out of existence, and for the mysterious will of the Sovereign of life and death and sin and salvation [has been substituted] the sweet benevolence of a Father-Mother God for the vague goodness of the All. Here the concern for self has been secularized to its last degree; the conflicts of sick souls have been replaced by the struggles of sick minds and bodies; the Puritan passion for perfection has become a seeking after the kingdom of health and mental peace and its comforts" (p. 105).

53. The most celebrated effort along these lines is undoubtedly Joshua Loth Liebman, *Peace of Mind* (Simon and Schuster, 1946).

54. Norman Vincent Peale, *The Power of Positive Thinking* (Prentice-Hall, 1952). For a careful study of American religious literature reflecting both the "peace of mind" and the "positive thinking" gospels, see Louis Schneider and Sanford M. Dornbusch, *Popular Religion: Inspirational Books in America* (University of Chicago Press, 1958).

55. A salesman writes to Norman Vincent Peale in the latter's regular question page in *Look:* "I have lost my faith and enthusiasm. How can I get them back?" To which Dr. Peale replies: "Every morning, give thanks for the new day and its opportunities. Think outgoingly of every prospect you will call on. . . . Affirm aloud that you are going to have a great day. Flush out all depressing, negative, and tired thoughts. Start thinking faith, enthusiasm and joy . . ." ("Norman Vincent Peale Answers Your Questions," *Look,* August 10, 1954). This may be compared with an advertisement for a quite "secular" self-help book in *The New York Times Magazine* for May 8, 1949:

DON'T WORRY
If you don't acknowledge it,
it isn't so!
Develop the Art of Adaptability

Questions

1. What kinds of evidence does Herberg present for his generalizations about religion in America? What are the methods of his sociological study?
2. What is the difference between a "synthetic system composed of beliefs to be found in all or in a group of religions" and an "organic structure of ideas, values, and beliefs" that forms a common faith (paragraph 11)?
3. What exceptions does Herberg make in paragraph 12 to the "common religion" of Americans? What explanation does he give for these exceptions?
4. If most people everywhere are materialistic, what is special or distinctive about American materialism according to paragraph 16?
5. How do paragraphs 17 and 18 explain the phrase "inner-directed"—Herberg's description of the American Way of Life? Does the phrase mean the same thing as "selfishness," as it is discussed in paragraph 4?
6. What has been the particular contribution of Protestantism to American values and political life?
7. What does the word *secularized* in the phrase "secularized Puritanism" (paragraph 19) mean? How have Judaism and Catholicism been secularized, and why does Herberg conclude in paragraph 21 that "secularization of religion could hardly go further"?
8. Why would President Eisenhower's statement in paragraph 26 seem "a deplorable heresy" to some European churchmen? What point is Herberg making through the views of Eisenhower?
9. What is the American view of a multiplicity of churches, and how does Herberg account for the view? How does his discussion of this view in paragraphs 27–30 develop the thesis of the chapter?
10. What does Herberg mean by "voluntarism" and "evangelism" (paragraph 30), and why are these the "immediate consequences of the American idea?
11. In general, why is religion integral to the idea of American democracy? And what is that idea?
12. What does Herberg mean by the "introvert" and "extrovert" forms of the "cult of faith"? How does his discussion of these forms advance his argument?
13. How early in the essay does Herberg state his thesis? How does he organize the essay to develop this thesis?
14. Is Herberg writing critically of the American Way of Life, or does he make no judgments in the course of his analysis?
15. What different kind of analysis might be made of the attitudes that Herberg discusses? How would it be different from Herberg's sociological analysis?

Suggestions for Writing

1. Herberg wrote this analysis of religion in America in 1955. Discuss the extent to which Herberg describes the attitudes and practices of your own religion today. Distinguish those that have stayed the same and those that have changed.

2. Discuss the extent to which Herberg and Paul Tillich agree on attitudes and goals of most Americans in the 1950s.

Additional Reading

Buber, Martin. *The Prophetic Faith.* New York: Macmillan, 1949.

Ellis, John T. *American Catholicism.* 2nd edition. Ed. Daniel J. Boorstin. Chicago: University of Chicago Press, 1969.

Glazer, Nathan. *American Judaism.* Rev. ed. Chicago; University of Chicago Press, 1972.

Herberg, Will. *Judaism and Modern Man: An Interpretation of Jewish Religion.* New York: Farrar, Straus and Young, 1951.

———. *Protestant, Catholic, Jew: An Essay in American Religious Sociology.* Garden City, N.Y.: Doubleday, 1935.

Hertzberg, Arthur. *Being Jewish in America: The Modern Experience.* New York: Schocken, 1979.

Hudson, Winthrop S. *American Protestantism.* Chicago: University of Chicago Press, 1961.

Marty, Martin E. *A Cry of Absence: Reflections for the Winter of the Heart.* New York: Harper and Row, 1983.

———. *A Nation of Behavers.* Chicago: University of Chicago Press, 1980.

Murray, John Courtney. *Problem of God: Yesterday and Today.* New Haven: Yale University Press, 1964.

Niebuhr, Reinhold. *The Children of Light and the Children of Darkness.* New York: Scribner's, 1944.

———. *Moral Man and Immoral Society: A Study in Ethics and Politics.* New York: Scribner's, 1936.

Novak, Michael. *Confession of a Catholic.* New York: Harper and Row, 1983.

Riesman, David. *The Lonely Crowd.* New Haven: Yale University Press, 1950.

The Last Pope

Graham Greene

The British novelist Graham Greene was born in 1904 and educated at the school where his father taught and later served as headmaster. Greene attended Oxford University, and afterwards worked as a journalist and film critic and wrote novels. During World War Two he worked for the British Foreign Office in Sierra Leone, West Africa—the scene of his most famous novel, The Heart of the Matter. *After the war, he traveled widely;* The Quiet Man, Our Man in Havana, *and* The Comedians *are based on his experiences in French Indochina, pre-Castro Cuba, and Haiti. His later novels, notably* The Human Factor *and the* The Honorary Consul, *focus on issues of character and politics. Greene's two remarkable autobiographies,* A Sort of Life *and* Ways of Escape, *give considerable insight into his ideas. Greene has written screenplays for several movies based on his fiction, the most famous being* The Fallen Idol *and* The Third Man

Greene converted to Roman Catholicism at the age of twenty-two. Much of his fiction turns on religious issues, though in an introduction to one edition of The Heart of the Matter *he states that the religious question of salvation or damnation cannot be an issue in a novel. Many readers have found the expression of religious ideas in that novel as well as in* Brighton Rock, The Power and the Glory, *and* A Burnt-Out Case. *In the essay reprinted here, Greene examines a religious issue directly—the destruction of six million Jews, the murder of millions of people that occurred in a Christian nation in twentieth-century Europe. In 1948, a conference convened by the French novelist Francois Mauriac and Catholics in Brussels, Belgium, considered the question posed by these events, "Is Christian civilization in peril?" The following essay is the address Greene delivered in answer to this question.*

No doubt because he continues an uninterrupted tradition of Christian state of mind, thought, and style, the French novelist seems to move easily among abstractions: they surround his childhood, and the liturgy is as familiar to him as his nursery rhymes. When a door opens in a novel by Mauriac, even before one leaves the shadows to enter the well-lit room where the characters are assembled, one is aware of forces of Good and Evil that slide along the walls and press their fingers against the window-pane ready to crowd in. This awareness is, in general, banished from the English novel. Perhaps it is because we live in a northern island where the sun shines so spasmodically and where we can be cut off from the continent for days at a time by fog or storm, an island to which Christianity came like a stranger from across the sea—perhaps because of this we tend to be more materialistic in our reactions and more concrete in imagination than those who live in sunnier lands who can permit themselves the luxury of shadow. The English novelist has become accustomed to bypass eternity. Evil appears in Dickens's novels only as an economic factor, nothing more. Christianity is a woman serving soup to the poor. How vivid are his images of the still Sunday streets, the dark, mean little courts near the river, the prison buildings, but how barren and dim is the life of the spirit! In Dickens, Evil has lost its supernatural quality, it has become something that the power of money, an amendment to the law, or perhaps simply death can abolish, for when a character dies, the evil dies with him. The English novel always makes us live within time. 1

Is Christian civilization in peril? For each of you these words possess the solidity of statues. You move freely among them like a man making his way past the overpopulated side-chapels of a great cathedral: the Immaculate Conception stretches out its arms of stone to you; the Sacred Heart is there made out of carved and painted wood; the candles burn with a tangible flame. But I feel as though I am surrounded by shadows. Civilization is a thing I learned in books, and Christianity is something that happens somewhere else, beyond my range of vision, perhaps in another country, certainly 2 in another heart. I cannot touch the words unless they are given a human shape. The Apostle Thomas should be the patron saint of people in my country, for we must see the marks of the nails and put our hands in the wounds before we can understand.

So this question, even before I begin to consider it, becomes three questions. 3 First, what is a Christian civilization in terms of human characters, human acts, and the daily commerce of human lives? Second, has this civilization ever existed, and does it exist today in any part of the world? It is only if the reply to this second question is affirmative that it will be necessary to ask whether Christian civilization is in danger.

Naturally, it would be convenient to adopt a rigid and clearly defined attitude, 4 to represent Christian civilization as a corporate arrangement of human life that would permit everyone to follow, without the least hindrance from his fellows, the teaching of the Sermon on the Mount. In that case, without further ado, we could examine our own age, retrace the course of history, and declare that such a civilization has never existed. But in adopting such an attitude—and the enemies of Christianity have often used this kind of argument—we are confusing the city of man and the City of God. The perfect imitation of Christ is impossible here, but our very imperfection is sanctified, for didn't God imitate man, and weren't man's despair and failure expressed by God himself on the cross? So in our definition of a Christian civilization we should not be led astray by the presence of wars, injustice and cruelty, or by the absence of charity. All those things can exist in a Christian state. They are not marks of Christianity, but of man.

But if we give up all thought of achieving or even of pursuing perfection, what 5 clues can we hope to find that will help us distinguish a Christian from a pagan civilization? Perhaps, truthfully, we can count on nothing more than the divided mind, the uneasy conscience, and the sense of personal failure.

Of course this sense of guilt was already present in Greek civilization; it hangs 6 over Greek drama like a heavy cloud. But it is a kind of impersonal guilt that a Christian literature might have produced on the theme of the fall of man if there had been the Revelation without the Incarnation, or if we had experienced personal failure without having had the model. In Greek literature any excess is synonymous with fear—excess of riches, happiness, luck, or power—but this fear is only an abstract fear. The fortunate man believes in justice operating like a pendulum; he follows like all men the swing of the pendulum; he has no sense of an individual failure which differentiates him from other men equally fortunate.

My conviction that the Christian conscience is the only satisfactory sign of a 7 Christian civilization is reinforced by the fact that this trait was completely lacking in the pagan powers that so recently reigned over the world. How the Nazis strutted in their hour of triumph and how they justified themselves in their defeat! How deliberately and explicitly they followed the doctrine which consists in doing evil to achieve good—their own personal good! The totalitarian state contrives, by educating its citizens, to suppress all sense of guilt, all indecision of mind. Let the State assume the responsibility for the crime, I am innocent. My only crime is my loyalty. The parrot voices proclaim with a terrifying pathetic resignation, "My chief gave the order." No soldier makes a cross of sticks to hand his victim.

The years we have just lived through are perhaps not the worst Europe has 8 known. Many times in Christian civilization cities have been sacked and prisoners tortured, but doesn't one always find these tyrants of the past haunted by a sense of guilt?

Let me read you a passage from the Anglo-Saxon Chronicles which describes the situation in England in the twelfth century, in the reign of Stephen.[1] It is a contemporary report. It is at least equal in horror to anything we have seen in Europe in the past few years.

> . . . They sorely burdened the unhappy people of the country with forced labour on the castles; and when the castles were built, they filled them with devils and wicked men. By night and by day they seized those whom they believed to have any wealth, whether they were men or women; and in order to get their gold and silver, they put them into prison and tortured them with unspeakable tortures, for never were martyrs tortured as they were. They hung them up by the feet and smoked them with foul smoke. They strung them up by the thumbs, or by the head, and hung coats of mail on their feet. They tied knotted cords round their heads and twisted it till it entered the brain. They put them in dungeons wherein were adders and snakes and toads, and so destroyed them. Some they put into a "crucethus"; that is to say, into a short, narrow, shallow chest into which they put sharp stones; and they crushed the man in it until they had broken every bone in his body.
>
> . . . Then was corn dear and flesh and cheese and butter, for there was none in the land. The wretched people perished with hunger; some, who had been great men, were driven to beggary, while others fled from the country. Never did a country endure greater misery, and never did the heathen act more vilely than they did.
>
> . . . If two or three men came riding towards a village, all the villagers fled for fear of them, believing that they were robbers. The bishops and the clergy were for ever cursing them, but that was nothing to them, for they were all excommunicated and forsworn and lost.
>
> Wherever the ground was tilled the earth bore no corn, for the land was ruined by such doings; and men said openly that Christ and His saints slept. Such things and others more than we know how to relate we suffered nineteen years for our sins.

I would not refuse the name of Christian civilization to those sombre years. Don't we, in fact, in reading this chronicle get the distinct impression of a bad conscience, of an acute sense of guilt? There were still some who raised voices in protest, the chronicle tells us so. The saints slept, but they were not disowned. Darkness covered the face of the island, but Christianity continued to move in the shadows. The possibility of an enormous repentance counterbalanced the possibility of enormous crimes. Take an example from English history. Our great king Henry II, in his grief, made a deliberate pact with the enemy of God. When he saw his native city burned in Normandy he made this great oath (so Christian even in its denial of Christ): "O God, since you have seen well to take from me the thing I loved most, the city where I was born and bred, I swear that I, too, will take from you that which you love the most in me." How could one class among the enemies of God this saint in reverse who gave us a true saint, Thomas of Canterbury, and who, after the murder of Saint Thomas, demanded to be

---

[1]The Anglo-Saxon Chronicles, written by monks during the Old English period, records the history of Saxon England to the middle of the twelfth century. Stephen of Blois ruled England from 1135 to 1154.

whipped publicly by the monks. Contrition was born at the same time as the crime: twin births of sin and punishment.[2]

Our enemies can call to witness many crimes committed in Christ's name. But in the long run what importance do such crimes have? In all our poetry you can hear a common note, the note of what I have called the divided mind—in the words of Sir Thomas Browne: "There's another man within me that's angry with me."[3]

. . . This is the signature of a Christian civilization. Challenged by our enemies we can admit our crimes because throughout history it is possible to point to our repentance.

If you accept my definition of the distinguishing mark of a Christian civilization, we can now easily answer the second question, "Has such a civilization ever existed?" The answer is "Yes." In a large part of the world man's conscience remains sensitive to moral failure. To cite only one recent example, it was not just political opportunism that determined the liberation of India. Half a century ago it would have seemed absurd to suggest that Christian civilization was in any danger. There have been so many wars and revolutions that a few more or less matter very little in the eyes of history. No new weapon can kill the impetus of Christianity. If that were possible, gunpowder would have finished it off. The atom bomb is powerless against conscience. But in the last twenty years we have witnessed an attempt to kill it by means of a new philosophy designed to persuade men that Lazarus is without importance. Dives, in a fancy dress uniform, receives the acclamations of the crowd in the streets of Berlin or from a balcony in Red Square. Perhaps my countrymen are not entirely wrong to mistrust those abstract words which allowed Dives to become a hero, by replacing Lazarus with "the people" or "the proletariat" or "the working class." In countries that were formerly democratic, and nowadays in countries that are still democratic, we have seen abstractions extend their domain in man's thought and leave their rightful place in philosophy and theology to invade history, economics and politics, subjects which, by their very nature, should be treated in concrete terms. Read any article in the popular press, even if the subject is as matter of fact as the extraction of iron ore, or estimates of this year's crop yield—one seeks in vain for a concrete image. Abstractions have been administered to our democracies like a drug. A phrase like "render unto Caesar" is translated by political journalists into "our responsibilities towards the State." Abstract expressions help dictators to power by troubling the clear waters of thought. William Blake said that whoever wishes to do good to his neighbour should do so on small occasions, for the general good is always invoked by scoundrels, hypocrites and flatterers.

We can no longer take lightly the danger that threatens Christian civilization. Between 1933 and 1945 civilization was almost completely destroyed in Germany. That abscess has been lanced, but the totalitarian poison can still spread to countries which escaped the first infection. It is terrifying to think of the distance Russia has travelled

[2]Henry II of England (1133–1189) appointed his friend Thomas of Becket chancellor of England. Appointed Archbishop of Canterbury in 1162, Thomas defended the church against the claims of the king. Henry ordered the murder of Thomas at Canterbury Cathedral, December 29, 1170.

[3]Sir Thomas Browne (1605–1682) was a physician and the author of the widely read *Religion of a Doctor (Religio Medici)*.

in less than a hundred years. Remember in *The Brothers Karamazov* Aliosha stripping himself of everything for the service of God: "I cannot give up two roubles instead of 'all thou hast' or just go to morning mass instead of 'come and follow me.' " And remember Father Zossima and his all-embracing charity: "Hate not atheists, the teachers of evil, materialists, even the most wicked of them, let alone the good ones among them. . . . Remember them in your prayers thus: 'Save, O Lord, all who have no one to pray for them, and save those, too, who do not want to pray to thee.' " And then think of the Moscow Trials and of Prosecutor Vishinsky and of that inaccessible grey figure in the Kremlin with his skin-deep bonhomie reserved for state banquets and the dark in the depths of his eyes.[4]

And yet it would surely be a sin against faith to exaggerate the danger. We are [14] bound to believe that Christianity cannot die. A hundred years is, after all, a very short time. Perhaps it will turn out that it is Mitya Karamazov who rules in Russia today. You remember his words: "If I am to precipitate myself into the abyss, I shall do so without a moment's reflection, head over heels, and indeed I shall be glad to fall in such a degrading attitude and consider it beautiful for a man like me. And it is at this very moment of shame and disgrace that I suddenly begin to intone this hymn." Perhaps if we were well enough informed we could discern here and there in Russia, too, the signs of an uneasy conscience. For we must not forget that in Germany's darkest days the voice of conscience was heard intermittently, never among the leaders of the state, but among the leaders of the Church—Faulhaber, Galen, Niemöller, and others too obscure or too unimportant to escape death.[5] I remember one of my friends, von Bernstorff. Before Hitler's rise to power he was First Secretary of the German Embassy in London. He resigned in 1933 and was executed in 1944 in Dachau because he belonged to a secret organization that continued to help Jews escape from Germany even during the war. What a strange fate that this heavy, superficial man, who loved the good life and a good laugh, with his aristocratic indolence and his taste for old cognac, should be transformed into a martyr for the cause of charity!

As I have said, we are bound to believe that Faith cannot die. It can suffer re- [15] verses, large parts of the world can be conquered by its enemies, but there will always exist pockets of Christian resistance. In England during the sinister year 1940 we used to say, "But just look at the map of the world," meaning that if our island seemed tiny and desperately imperilled in relation to Europe, all the same, hope was rekindled at the sight of allied territories in Africa, Australia and Canada. Christians, too, should look at the map of the world from time to time. Suppose the whole of Europe should become a totalitarian state; we are not the world.

It is not impossible that we might see the whole world succumb to a totalitar- [16] ian and atheistic regime. Even so, it would still not be the end. In that case we, the spies of God, would have to draw up large-scale maps of every city and every village. There, in such and such a street, behind the café, at the crossroads in the town of X, in the

---

[4]A reference to the Soviet dictator Joseph Stalin (1879–1953), who used the Moscow Purge Trials of 1937–38 to kill political enemies and former rivals. Andrei Vishinsky (1883–1954), a prominent Soviet jurist and later foreign minister, prosecuted Stalin's designated enemies.
[5]German clergymen who spoke out against Hitler in the Nazi era.

fifteenth house on the right, there is a cellar, and in this cellar a child, playing, has traced a clumsy cross on the plaster wall. . . .

Permit me to close with a story which I once intended to write—a fantasy in 17 a melodramatic vein, which takes place in the distant future, say two centuries from now, when the whole world is governed by a single party and organized with an efficiency undreamt of today. The curtain rises on a sordid little hotel in London or New York, it doesn't matter which. It is late at night. An old man, tired, down-hearted, non-descript, wearing a shabby raincoat and carrying a battered suitcase, comes up to the reception desk and asks for a room. He signs the register and disappears wearily up the stairs (the hotel is too poor to have an elevator). The house detective looks at the register and says to the clerk:

"Did you see who that was?"   18

"No."   19

"It's the Pope."   20

"The Pope? Who's that?"   21

Catholicism has been successfully stamped out. Only the Pope survives, elected 22 thirty years before at the last conclave (a secret conclave, its members believed, though in reality monitored by an even more secret police), and doomed to rule over a Church which has virtually ceased to exist. After the conclave the cardinals had met the fate of the rest of the priests: a white wall and a firing squad. But the Pope was authorized to live. He even receives a small pension from the State because he is of use in demonstrating how dead the Church is, and because there is always the possibility that some survivor will betray himself by trying to get in touch with him. But there are no more survivors. Rome, naturally, has been renamed for over a century.

I was going to describe this little man, this little Pope, drifting miserably here 23 and there, purposelessly, driven on by the vague hope that somewhere, some day, he might encounter a sign to show him that the Faith survived after all and he need no longer be haunted by the fear that what he had professed to be eternal might die with him. I won't bore you with the story of his useless wanderings and his deceptions, each duly recorded and filed at the headquarters of the World Police. In the end the World Dictator got tired of the game. He wanted to put an end to it in his own lifetime, for although he was only fifty while the Pope had long since passed seventy, accidents happen to dictators and he did not wish to surrender his place in history as the man who, with his own finger on the trigger of the revolver, had put an end to the Christian myth.

So at the end of this story which I never wrote, the Pope was brought by the 24 police into the Dictator's secret room with its soundproof, bulletproof walls, and there, in the padded silence, the Dictator, after offering the Pope a cigarette, which he refused, and a glass of wine, which he accepted, told him he was going to die on the spot—the last Christian, the last man in the world who still believed. After dismissing the detectives the Dictator took a revolver out of his desk drawer. He granted the Pope a moment to pray (he had read in a book that this was customary), but he didn't listen to the prayer. Then he shot him in the left side of the chest and leaned forward over the body to give the coup de grâce. At that instant, in the second between the pressure on the trigger and the skull cracking, a thought crossed the Dictator's mind: "Is it just possible that what this man believed is true?" Another Christian had been born.

Questions

1. What distinguishes a civilization as Christian for Greene? Is it Christian if the majority of its people profess Christianity? Could a civilization be Christian even if no one
   professed to be so?
2. What does the word *evil* mean to Greene? And what does he mean by *guilt?* Why does
   Greene distinguish between guilt in Greek literature and Christian literature?
3. Can a person be evil and at the same time feel guilt, or does the person cease to be
   evil at the moment he feels guilt?
4. What does Greene mean by a "divided mind"? Does he mean a mind uncertain about
   what is good and evil or a mind uncertain about which to choose?
5. What is the greatest threat to Christian civilization for Greene—totalitarian governments, nationalism, economic depression, technology, human atrocities, human nature, or what? How does he express this threat in the essay?
6. Would Greene agree with Paul Tillich that to be religious "means asking passionately
   the question of the meaning of our existence and being willing to receive answers,
   even if the answers hurt"? Or would Greene seek other qualities?

Suggestions for Writing

1. Greene suggests that Charles Dickens implies an attitude toward evil in his novels:
   "In Dickens, Evil has lost its supernatural quality, it has become something that the
   power of money, an amendment to the law, or perhaps simply death can abolish, for
   when a character dies, the evil dies with him." Analyze "My Kinsman, Major
   Molineux" to define the concept of evil that you find there. Or analyze a novel, story,
   or movie for that purpose.
2. Explain what Greene means by the phrase "divided mind." In the course of your discussion, compare Greene with the views of the Christian in Albert Schweitzer's essays
   and Paul Tillich's essay.

Additional Reading

Greene, Graham. *Collected Essays.* New York: Viking, 1969.
———. *Collected Stories.* New York: Viking, 1973.
———. *The Power and the Glory.* New York: Viking, 1958.
———. *A Sort of Life.* New York: Viking, 1982.
———. *Ways of Escape.* New York: Viking, 1982.
Stratford, Philip, ed. *The Portable Graham Greene.* New York: Viking, 1977. Contains
   the full text of Greene's novel *The Heart of the Matter* as well as other fiction and es-
   says.

The Guest*

Albert Camus

Born in 1913, French novelist and essayist Albert Camus was raised in Algeria, the country he describes in his story "The Guest." Camus worked as a journalist in Algeria, and in 1942 he joined the Resistance to the Nazis in France and wrote for its newsmagazine Combat. *In the same year he wrote his best-known novel,* The Stranger, *and the philosophical essays collected under the title* The Myth of Sisyphus. *After the war he devoted himself entirely to literature. Algerian nationalists engaged in a war with the French in the 1950s to make the colony a separate nation; Camus wrote philosophically about the struggle in* The Rebel: An Essay on Man in Revolt *(1954). This book and his other writings, in particular the novels* The Plague *(1947) and* The Fall *(1956), established Camus as a leading figure in the so-called philosophy of the Absurd, a movement of thought and art related to French Existentialism (see p. 215). In 1957 he received the Nobel Prize for Literature in honor of the insight his writings had given into the problem of conscience in the modern world.*

In his essays, Camus discusses at length ideas that he dramatizes in his fiction. In his stories and novels, he sometimes allows his characters to comment on the meaning of their experience. In "The Guest" he depends on the action and the setting, though he does give us the feelings and thoughts of his central character.

The schoolmaster was watching the two men climb toward him. One was on horseback, the other on foot. They had not yet tackled the abrupt rise leading to the schoolhouse built on the hillside. They were toiling onward, making slow progress in the snow, among the stones, on the vast expanse of the high, deserted plateau. From time to time the horse stumbled. Without hearing anything yet, he could see the breath issuing from the horse's nostrils. One of the men, at least, knew the region. They were following the trail although it had disappeared days ago under a layer of dirty white snow. The schoolmaster calculated that it would take them half an hour to get onto the hill. It was cold; he went back into the school to get a sweater.

He crossed the empty, frigid classroom. On the blackboard the four rivers of France, drawn with four different colored chalks, had been flowing toward their estuaries for the past three days. Snow had suddenly fallen in mid-October after eight months of drought without the transition of rain, and the twenty pupils, more or less, who lived in the villages scattered over the plateau had stopped coming. With fair weather they would return. Daru now heated only the single room that was his lodging, adjoining the classroom and giving also onto the plateau to the east. Like the class windows, his window looked to the south too. On that side the school was a few kilometers from the point

---
*Translated by Justin O'Brien

where the plateau began to slope toward the south. In clear weather could be seen the purple mass of the mountain range where the gap opened onto the desert.

Somewhat warmed, Daru returned to the window from which he had first seen the two men. They were no longer visible. Hence they must have tackled the rise. The sky was not so dark, for the snow had stopped falling during the night. The morning had opened with a dirty light which had scarcely become brighter as the ceiling of clouds lifted. At two in the afternoon it seemed as if the day were merely beginning. But still this was better than those three days when the thick snow was falling amidst unbroken darkness with little gusts of wind that rattled the double door of the classroom. Then Daru had spent long hours in his room, leaving it only to go to the shed and feed the chickens or get some coal. Fortunately the delivery truck from Tadjid, the nearest village to the north, had brought his supplies two days before the blizzard. It would return in forty-eight hours.

Besides, he had enough to resist a siege, for the little room was cluttered with bags of wheat that the administration left as a stock to distribute to those of his pupils whose families had suffered from the drought. Actually they had all been victims because they were all poor. Every day Daru would distribute a ration to the children. They had missed it, he knew, during these bad days. Possibly one of the fathers or big brothers would come this afternoon and he could supply them with grain. It was just a matter of carrying them over to the next harvest. Now shiploads of wheat were arriving from France and the worst was over. But it would be hard to forget that poverty, that army of ragged ghosts wandering in the sunlight, the plateaus burned to a cinder month after month, the earth shriveled up little by little, literally scorched, every stone bursting into dust under one's foot. The sheep had died then by thousands and even a few men, here and there, sometimes without anyone's knowing.

In contrast with such poverty, he who lived almost like a monk in his remote schoolhouse, nonetheless satisfied with the little he had and with the rough life, had felt like a lord with his whitewashed walls, his narrow couch, his unpainted shelves, his well, and his weekly provision of water and food. And suddenly this snow, without warning, without the foretaste of rain. This is the way the region was, cruel to live in, even without men—who didn't help matters either. But Daru had been born here. Everywhere else, he felt exiled.

He stepped out onto the terrace in front of the schoolhouse. The two men were now halfway up the slope. He recognized the horseman as Balducci, the old gendarme[1] he had known for a long time. Balducci was holding on the end of a rope an Arab who was walking behind him with hands bound and head lowered. The gendarme waved a greeting to which Daru did not reply, lost as he was in contemplation of the Arab dressed in a faded blue jellaba,[2] his feet in sandals but covered with socks of heavy raw wool, his head surmounted by a narrow, short *chèche*.[3] They were approaching. Balducci was holding back his horse in order not to hurt the Arab, and the group was advancing slowly.

---

[1] A policeman.
[2] A cloak with hood.
[3] A scarf worn as a headband.

Within earshot, Balducci shouted: "One hour to do the three kilometers from El Ameur!" Daru did not answer. Short and square in his thick sweater, he watched them climb. Not once had the Arab raised his head. "Hello," said Daru when they got up onto the terrace. "Come in and warm up." Balducci painfully got down from his horse without letting go the rope. From under his bristling mustache he smiled at the schoolmaster. His little dark eyes, deepset under a tanned forehead, and his mouth surrounded with wrinkles made him look attentive and studious. Daru took the bridle, led the horse to the shed, and came back to the two men, who were now waiting for him in the school. He led them into his room. "I am going to heat up the classroom," he said. "We'll be more comfortable there." When he entered the room again, Balducci was on the couch. He had undone the rope tying him to the Arab, who had squatted near the stove. His hands still bound, the *chèche* pushed back on his head, he was looking toward the window. At first Daru noticed only his huge lips, fat, smooth, almost Negroid; yet his nose was straight, his eyes were dark and full of fever. The *chèche* revealed an obstinate forehead and, under the weathered skin now rather discolored by the cold, the whole face had a restless and rebellious look that struck Daru when the Arab, turning his face toward him, looked him straight in the eyes. "Go into the other room," said the schoolmaster, "and I'll make you some mint tea." "Thanks," Balducci said. "What a chore! How I long for retirement." And addressing his prisoner in Arabic: "Come on, you." The Arab got up and, slowly, holding his bound wrists in front of him, went into the classroom.

With the tea, Daru brought a chair. But Balducci was already enthroned on the nearest pupil's desk and the Arab had squatted against the teacher's platform facing the stove, which stood between the desk and the window. When he held out the glass of tea to the prisoner, Daru hesitated at the sight of his bound hands. "He might perhaps be untied." "Sure," said Balducci. "That was for the trip." He started to get to his feet. But Daru, setting the glass on the floor, had knelt beside the Arab. Without saying anything, the Arab watched him with his feverish eyes. Once his hands were free, he rubbed his swollen wrists against each other, took the glass of tea, and sucked up the burning liquid in swift little sips.

"Good," said Daru. "And where are you headed?"

Balducci withdrew his mustache from the tea. "Here, son."

"Odd pupils! And you're spending the night?"

"No. I'm going back to El Ameur. And you will deliver this fellow to Tinguit. He is expected at police headquarters."

Balducci was looking at Daru with a friendly little smile.

"What's this story?" asked the schoolmaster. "Are you pulling my leg?"

"No, son. Those are the orders."

"The orders? I'm not . . ." Daru hesitated, not wanting to hurt the old Corsican. "I mean, that's not my job."

"What! What's the meaning of that? In wartime people do all kinds of jobs."

"Then I'll wait for the declaration of war!"

Balducci nodded.

"O.K. But the orders exist and they concern you too. Things are brewing, it appears. There is talk of a forthcoming revolt. We are mobilized, in a way."

Daru still had his obstinate look.

"Listen, son," Balducci said. "I like you and you must understand. There's only a dozen of us at El Ameur to patrol throughout the whole territory of a small department and I must get back in a hurry. I was told to hand this guy over to you and return without delay. He couldn't be kept there. His village was beginning to stir; they wanted to take him back. You must take him to Tinguit tomorrow before the day is over. Twenty kilometers shouldn't faze a husky fellow like you. After that, all will be over. You'll come back to your pupils and your comfortable life."

Behind the wall the horse could be heard snorting and pawing the earth. Daru was looking out the window. Decidedly, the weather was clearing and the light was increasing over the snowy plateau. When all the snow was melted, the sun would take over again and once more would burn the fields of stone. For days, still, the unchanging sky would shed its dry light on the solitary expanse where nothing had any connection with man.

"After all," he said, turning toward Balducci, "what did he do?" And, before the gendarme had opened his mouth, he asked: "Does he speak French?"

"No, not a word. We had been looking for him for a month, but they were hiding him. He killed his cousin."

"Is he against us?"

"I don't think so. But you can never be sure."

"Why did he kill?"

"A family squabble, I think. One owed the other grain, it seems. It's not at all clear. In short, he killed his cousin with a billhook.[4] You know, like a sheep, *kreezk!*"

Balducci made the gesture of drawing a blade across his throat and the Arab, his attention attracted, watched him with a sort of anxiety. Daru felt a sudden wrath against the man, against all men with their rotten spite, their tireless hates, their blood lust.

But the kettle was singing on the stove. He served Balducci more tea, hesitated, then served the Arab again, who, a second time, drank avidly. His raised arms made the jellaba fall open and the schoolmaster saw his thin, muscular chest.

"Thanks, kid," Balducci said. "And now, I'm off."

He got up and went toward the Arab, taking a small rope from his pocket.

"What are you doing?" Daru asked dryly.

Balducci, disconcerted, showed him the rope.

"Don't bother."

The old gendarme hesitated. "It's up to you. Of course, you are armed?"

"I have my shotgun."

"Where?"

"In the trunk."

"You ought to have it near your bed."

"Why? I have nothing to fear."

"You're crazy, son. If there's an uprising, no one is safe, we're all in the same boat."

---

[4] A pruning implement.

"I'll defend myself. I'll have time to see them coming."

Balducci began to laugh, then suddenly the mustache covered the white teeth.

"You'll have time? O.K. That's just what I was saying. You have always been a little cracked. That's why I like you, my son was like that."

At the same time he took out his revolver and put it on the desk.

"Keep it; I don't need two weapons from here to El Ameur."

The revolver shone against the black paint of the table. When the gendarme turned toward him, the schoolmaster caught the smell of leather and horseflesh.

"Listen, Balducci," Daru said suddenly, "every bit of this disgusts me, and first of all your fellow here. But I won't hand him over. Fight, yes, if I have to. But not that."

The old gendarme stood in front of him and looked at him severely.

"You're being a fool," he said slowly. "I don't like it either. You don't get used to putting a rope on a man even after years of it, and you're even ashamed—yes, ashamed. But you can't let them have their way."

"I won't hand him over," Daru said again.

"It's an order, son, and I repeat it."

"That's right. Repeat to them what I've said to you: I won't hand him over."

Balducci made a visible effort to reflect. He looked at the Arab and at Daru. At last he decided.

"No, I won't tell them anything. If you want to drop us, go ahead; I'll not denounce you. I have an order to deliver the prisoner and I'm doing so. And now you'll just sign this paper for me."

"There's no need. I'll not deny that you left him with me."

"Don't be mean with me. I know you'll tell the truth. You're from hereabouts and you are a man. But you must sign, that's the rule."

Daru opened his drawer, took out a little square bottle of purple ink, the red wooden penholder with the "sergeant-major" pen he used for making models of penmanship, and signed. The gendarme carefully folded the paper and put it into his wallet. Then he moved toward the door.

"I'll see you off," Daru said.

"No," said Balducci. "There's no use being polite. You insulted me."

He looked at the Arab, motionless in the same spot, sniffed peevishly, and turned away toward the door. "Good-bye, son," he said. The door shut behind him. Balducci appeared suddenly outside the window and then disappeared. His footsteps were muffled by the snow. The horse stirred on the other side of the wall and several chickens fluttered in fright. A moment later Balducci reappeared outside the window leading the horse by the bridle. He walked toward the little rise without turning around and disappeared from sight with the horse following him. A big stone could be heard bouncing down. Daru walked back toward the prisoner, who, without stirring, never took his eyes off him. "Wait," the schoolmaster said in Arabic and went toward the bedroom. As he was going through the door, he had a second thought, went to the desk, took the revolver, and stuck it in his pocket. Then, without looking back, he went into his room.

For some time he lay on his couch watching the sky gradually close over, listening to the silence. It was this silence that had seemed painful to him during the first days here, after the war. He had requested a post in the little town at the base of the foothills separating the upper plateaus from the desert. There, rocky walls, green and black to the north, pink and lavender to the south, marked the frontier of eternal summer. He had been named to a post farther north, on the plateau itself. In the beginning, the solitude and the silence had been hard for him on these wastelands peopled only by stones. Occasionally, furrows suggested civilization, but they had been dug to uncover a certain kind of stone good for building. The only plowing here was to harvest rocks. Elsewhere a thin layer of soil accumulated in the hollows would be scraped out to enrich paltry village gardens. This is the way it was: bare rock covered three quarters of the region. Towns sprang up, flourished, then disappeared; men came by, loved one another or fought bitterly, then died. No one in this desert, neither he nor his guest, mattered. And yet, outside this desert neither of them, Daru knew, could have really lived.

When he got up, no noise came from the classroom. He was amazed at the unmixed joy he derived from the mere thought that the Arab might have fled and that he would be alone with no decision to make. But the prisoner was there. He had merely stretched out between the stove and the desk. With eyes open, he was staring at the ceiling. In that position, his thick lips were particularly noticeable, giving him a pouting look. "Come," said Daru. The Arab got up and followed him. In the bedroom, the schoolmaster pointed to a chair near the table under the window. The Arab sat down without taking his eyes off Daru.

"Are you hungry?"

"Yes," the prisoner said.

Daru set the table for two. He took flour and oil, shaped a cake in the frying-pan, and lighted the little stove that functioned on bottled gas. While the cake was cooking, he went out to the shed to get cheese, eggs, dates, and condensed milk. When the cake was done he set it on the window sill to cool, heated some condensed milk diluted with water, and beat up the eggs into an omelette. In one of his motions he knocked against the revolver stuck in his right pocket. He set the bowl down, went into the classroom, and put the revolver back in his desk drawer. When he came back to the room, night was falling. He put on the light and served the Arab. "Eat," he said. The Arab took a piece of the cake, lifted it eagerly to his mouth, and stopped short.

"And you?" he asked.

"After you. I'll eat too."

The thick lips opened slightly. The Arab hesitated, then bit into the cake determinedly.

The meal over, the Arab looked at the schoolmaster. "Are you the judge?"

"No, I'm simply keeping you until tomorrow."

"Why do you eat with me?"

"I'm hungry."

The Arab fell silent. Daru got up and went out. He brought back a folding bed from the shed, set it up between the table and the stove, perpendicular to his own bed. From a large suitcase which, upright in a corner, served as a shelf for papers, he took two blankets and arranged them on the camp bed. Then he stopped, felt useless, and sat down on his bed. There was nothing more to do or to get ready. He had to look at this man. He looked at him, therefore, trying to imagine his face bursting with rage. He couldn't do so. He could see nothing but the dark yet shining eyes and the animal mouth.

"Why did you kill him?" he asked in a voice whose hostile tone surprised him.

The Arab looked away.

"He ran away. I ran after him."

He raised his eyes to Daru again and they were full of a sort of woeful interrogation. "Now what will they do to me?"

"Are you afraid?"

He stiffened, turning his eyes away.

"Are you sorry?"

The Arab stared at him openmouthed. Obviously he did not understand. Daru's annoyance was growing. At the same time he felt awkward and self-conscious with his big body wedged between the two beds.

"Lie down there," he said impatiently. "That's your bed."

The Arab didn't move. He called to Daru.

"Tell me!"

The schoolmaster looked at him.

"Is the gendarme coming back tomorrow?"

"I don't know."

"Are you coming with us?"

"I don't know. Why?"

The prisoner got up and stretched out on top of the blankets, his feet toward the window. The light from the electric bulb shone straight into his eyes and he closed them at once.

"Why?" Daru repeated, standing beside the bed.

The Arab opened his eyes under the blinding light and looked at him, trying not to blink.

"Come with us," he said.

In the middle of the night, Daru was still not asleep. He had gone to bed after undressing completely; he generally slept naked. But when he suddenly realized that he had nothing on, he hesitated. He felt vulnerable and the temptation came to him to put his clothes back on. Then he shrugged his shoulders; after all, he wasn't a child, and, if need be, he could break his adversary in two. From his bed he could observe him, lying on his back, still motionless with eyes closed under the harsh light. When Daru turned out the light, the darkness seemed to coagulate all of a sudden. Little by little, the night came back to life in the window where the starless sky was stirring gently. The schoolmaster soon made out the body lying at his feet. The Arab still did not move, but his eyes seemed open. A faint wind was prowling around the schoolhouse. Perhaps it would drive away the clouds and the sun would reappear.

During the night the wind increased. The hens fluttered a little and then were silent. The Arab turned over on his side with his back to Daru, who thought he heard him moan. Then he listened for his guest's breathing, become heavier and more regular. He listened to that breath so close to him and mused without being able to go to sleep. In this room where he had been sleeping alone for a year, this presence bothered him. But it bothered him also by imposing on him a sort of brotherhood he knew well but refused to accept in the present circumstances. Men who share the same rooms, soldiers or prisoners, develop a strange alliance as if, having cast off their armor with their clothing, they fraternized every evening, over and above their differences, in the ancient community of dream and fatigue. But Daru shook himself; he didn't like such musings, and it was essential to sleep.

A little later, however, when the Arab stirred slightly, the schoolmaster was still not asleep. When the prisoner made a second move, he stiffened, on the alert. The Arab was lifting himself slowly on his arms with almost the motion of a sleepwalker. Seated upright in bed, he waited motionless without turning his head toward Daru, as if he were listening attentively. Daru did not stir; it had just occurred to him that the revolver was still in the drawer of his desk. It was better to act at once. Yet he continued to observe the prisoner, who, with the same slithery motion, put his feet on the ground, waited again, then began to stand up slowly. Daru was about to call out to him when the Arab began to walk, in a quite natural but extraordinarily silent way. He was heading toward the door at the end of the room that opened into the shed. He lifted the latch with precaution and went out, pushing the door behind him but without shutting it. Daru had not stirred. "He is running away," he merely thought. "Good riddance!" Yet he listened attentively. The hens were not fluttering; the guest must be on the plateau. A faint sound of water reached him, and he didn't know what it was until the Arab again stood framed in the doorway, closed the door carefully, and came back to bed without a sound. Then Daru turned his back on him and fell asleep. Still later he seemed, from the depths of his sleep, to hear furtive steps around the schoolhouse. "I'm dreaming! I'm dreaming!" he repeated to himself. And he went on sleeping.

When he awoke, the sky was clear; the loose window let in a cold, pure air. The Arab was asleep, hunched up under the blankets now, his mouth open, utterly relaxed. But when Daru shook him, he started dreadfully, staring at Daru with wild eyes as if he had never seen him and such a frightened expression that the schoolmaster stepped back. "Don't be afraid. It's me. You must eat." The Arab nodded his head and said yes. Calm had returned to his face, but his expression was vacant and listless.

The coffee was ready. They drank it seated together on the folding bed as they munched their pieces of the cake. Then Daru led the Arab under the shed and showed him the faucet where he washed. He went back into the room, folded the blankets and the bed, made his own bed and put the room in order. Then he went through the classroom and out onto the terrace. The sun was already rising in the blue sky; a soft, bright light was bathing the deserted plateau. On the ridge the snow was melting in spots. The stones were about to reappear. Crouched on the edge of the plateau, the schoolmaster looked at the deserted expanse. He thought of Balducci. He had hurt him, for he had sent him off in a way as if he didn't want to be associated with him. He could still hear the gendarme's farewell and, without knowing why, he felt strangely empty and vulnerable. At that moment, from the other side of the schoolhouse, the prisoner coughed. Daru listened to him almost despite himself and then, furious, threw a pebble that whistled through the air before sinking into the snow. The man's stupid crime revolted him, but to hand him over was contrary to honor. Merely thinking of it made him smart with humiliation. And he cursed at one and the same time his own people who had sent him this Arab and the Arab too who had dared to kill and not managed to get away. Daru got up, walked in a circle on the terrace, waited motionless, and then went back into the schoolhouse.

The Arab, leaning over the cement floor of the shed, was washing his teeth with two fingers. Daru looked at him and said: "Come." He went back into the room ahead of the prisoner. He slipped a hunting-jacket on over his sweater and put on walking shoes. Standing, he waited until the Arab had put on his *chèche* and sandals. They went into the classroom and the schoolmaster pointed to the exit, saying: "Go ahead." The fellow didn't budge. "I'm coming," said Daru. The Arab went out. Daru went back into the room and made a package of pieces of rusk, dates, and sugar. In the classroom, before going out, he hesitated a second in front of his desk, then crossed the threshold and locked the door. "That's the way," he said. He started toward the east, followed by the prisoner. But, a short distance from the schoolhouse, he thought he heard a slight sound behind them. He retraced his steps and examined the surroundings of the house; there was no one there. The Arab watched him without seeming to understand. "Come on," said Daru.

They walked for an hour and rested beside a sharp peak of limestone. The snow was melting faster and faster and the sun was drinking up the puddles at once, rapidly cleaning the plateau, which gradually dried and vibrated like the air itself. When they resumed walking, the ground rang under their feet. From time to time a bird rent the space in front of them with a joyful cry. Daru breathed in deeply the fresh morning light. He felt a sort of rapture before the vast familiar expanse, now almost entirely yellow under its dome of blue sky. They walked an hour more, descending toward the south. They reached a level height made up of crumbly rocks. From there on, the plateau sloped down, eastward, toward a low plain where there were a few spindly trees and, to the south, toward outcroppings of rock that gave the landscape a chaotic look.

Daru surveyed the two directions. There was nothing but the sky on the horizon. Not a man could be seen. He turned toward the Arab, who was looking at him blankly. Daru held out the package to him. "Take it," he said. "There are dates, bread, and sugar. You can hold out for two days. Here are a thousand francs too." The Arab took the package and the money but kept his full hands at chest level as if he didn't know what to do with what was being given him. "Now look," the schoolmaster said as he pointed in the direction of the east, "there's the way to Tinguit. You have a two-hour walk. At Tinguit you'll find the administration and the police. They are expecting you." The Arab looked toward the east, still holding the package and the money against his chest. Daru took his elbows and turned him rather roughly toward the south. At the foot of the height on which they stood could be seen a faint path. "That's the trail across the plateau. In a day's walk from here you'll find pasturelands and the first nomads. They'll take you in and shelter you according to their law." The Arab had now turned toward Daru and a sort of panic was visible in his expression. "Listen," he said. Daru shook his head: "No, be quiet. Now I'm leaving you." He turned his back on him, took two long steps in the direction of the school, looked hesitantly at the motionless Arab, and started off again. For a few minutes he heard nothing but his own step resounding on the cold ground and did not turn his head. A moment later, however, he turned around. The Arab was still there on the edge of the hill, his arms hanging now, and he was looking at the schoolmaster. Daru felt something rise in his throat. But he swore with impatience, waved vaguely, and started off again. He had already gone some distance when he again stopped and looked. There was no longer anyone on the hill.

Daru hesitated. The sun was now rather high in the sky and was beginning to beat down on his head. The schoolmaster retraced his steps, at first somewhat uncertainly, then with decision. When he reached the little hill, he was bathed in sweat. He climbed it as fast as he could and stopped, out of breath, at the top. The rock-fields to the south stood out sharply against the blue sky, but on the plain to the east a steamy heat was already rising. And in that slight haze, Daru, with heavy heart, made out the Arab walking slowly on the road to prison.

A little later, standing before the window of the classroom, the schoolmaster was watching the clear light bathing the whole surface of the plateau, but he hardly saw it. Behind him on the blackboard, among the winding French rivers, sprawled the clumsily chalked-up words he had just read: "You handed over our brother. You will pay for this." Daru looked at the sky, the plateau, and, beyond, the invisible lands stretching all the way to the sea. In this vast landscape he had loved so much, he was alone.

Questions

1. Is Daru in a state of conflict over the order communicated by Balducci, or is it obvious from the moment he receives the order what he will do?
2. What details reveal the state of the mind of the Arab during his stay in the schoolhouse? Does your understanding of the Arab deepen as the story proceeds, or is he a simple character, without mystery?
3. In what sense is Daru alone at the end of the story? Do you sense that Camus is hinting at a truth about life or people through Daru, or is the implication of the end political or personal to Daru only?
4. What features of the Algerian landscape and sky does Camus emphasize? How do these features contribute to your understanding of Daru as a man and of his state of mind at the beginning of the story and later?
5. Is Daru a symbolic character—a character that embodies an idea or attitude—or is Camus writing about individual character and action only?

Suggestions for Writing

1. Write a character analysis of Daru, explaining what you learn about him through the action and setting as well as through his thoughts and feelings. Focus on the qualities of Daru that develop the central theme or idea of the story.
2. Discuss what setting, action, statements by Daru, and comments of the narrator contribute to your understanding of the character.
3. Post-war French literature deals with themes and ideas similar to those in the fiction and essays of Camus mentioned in the introduction. The novels and plays of Jean-Paul Sartre, the leading Existentialist philosopher in this period, are of particular interest; they include *The Age of Reason* (1945), *Nausea* (1949), *The Flies* (1947), *No*

Exit (1947), and *The Reprieve*. Analyze one of these novels or plays to show how philosophical ideas shape the action and the attitude of the narrator toward one or more of the characters.

Additional Reading

Brée, Germaine. *Camus.* Rev. ed. New Brunswick, N.J.: Rutgers University Press, 1961.

Camus, Albert. *Exile and the Kingdom.* Trans. Justin O'Brien. New York: Knopf, 1958.

————. *The Fall.* Trans. Justin O'Brien. New York: Knopf, 1957.

————. *The Myth of Sisyphus and Other Essays.* Trans. Justin O'Brien. New York: Knopf, 1955.

————. *The Plague.* Trans. Stuart Gilbert. New York: Knopf, 1948.

————. *The Rebel: An Essay on Man in Revolt.* Trans. Anthony Bower. New York: Knopf, 1957.

————. *The Stranger.* Trans. Stuart Gilbert. New York: Knopf, 1946.

The Death of Ivan Ilych*

Leo Tolstoy

The Russian novelist Leo Tolstoy (1828–1910) was raised and educated on his family's large estate south of Moscow. His youth was a restless one, given to drink and women. Tolstoy attended Kazan University for a short time, leaving to join the Russian army as an artillery officer. His war experiences provided material for military stories that made him known to readers. During his years in the army, he wrote novels based on his own life. In 1862, Tolstoy married and settled on his family estate; in the early years of his marriage he wrote his most famous novels, War and Peace *(1869) and* Anna Karenina *(1876). His religious writings begin with* What Men Live By *(1881).* Ivan Ilyich *(1886) is a fictional exploration of what gives life meaning.*

As a novelist and short story writer, Tolstoy was influenced by the movement of literary realism then flourishing in France and other European countries. Realists were generally concerned with the details of ordinary life, the sum of which they believed would give an objective, reliable picture of the world. The early-nineteenth-century French novelist Stendhal described the novel as "a mirror in the roadway," and that metaphor suggests that if the novelist looks at the world honestly and reports exactly what the world is, the novel becomes a vehicle of truth. The later French novelist Émile Zola indeed saw the novelist as akin to the scientist in following the inductive sciences—patiently observing the world and recording what the neutral eye sees. At least this was the naive view of what the scientist does.

---

*Translated by Louise and Alymer Maude.

Few novelists followed the analogy to its full conclusions. The realistic novelist is seldom if ever a neutral observer, though the novelist might stand silently behind the work and allow the exact details of the story to make their own points. As Tolstoy does in his great novels War and Peace *and* Anna Karenina *and other fiction, the author might interpret his characters and actions for the reader. Tolstoy is a realistic novelist in giving us a detailed picture of Ivan Ilych's world. He also allows these details to make their own point, and he perhaps makes fewer statements about Ivan through his narrator than the reader expects. But the reader nevertheless is aware of Tolstoy's presence as the story builds to its climax. Tolstoy shapes our view of Ivan Ilych and our response to the events of his life.*

1

During an interval in the Melvinski trial in the large building of the Law Courts the members and public prosecutor met in Ivan Egorovich Shebek's private room, where the conversation turned on the celebrated Krasovski case. Fedor Vasilievich warmly maintained that it was not subject to their jurisdiction, Ivan Egorovich maintained the contrary, while Peter Ivanovich, not having entered into the discussion at the start, took no part in it but looked through the *Gazette* which had just been handed in.

"Gentlemen," he said, "Ivan Ilych has died!"

"You don't say so!"

"Here, read it yourself," replied Peter Ivanovich, handing Fedor Vasilievich the paper still damp from the press. Surrounded by a black border were the words "Praskovya Fedorovna Golovina, with profound sorrow, informs relatives and friends of the demise of her beloved husband Ivan Ilych Golovin, Member of the Court of Justice, which occurred on February the 4th of this year 1882. The funeral will take place on Friday at one o'clock in the afternoon."

Ivan Ilych had been a colleague of the gentlemen present and was liked by them all. He had been ill for some weeks with an illness said to be incurable. His post had been kept open for him, but there had been conjectures that in case of his death Alexeev might receive his appointment, and that either Vinnikov or Shtabel would succeed Alexeev. So on receiving the news of Ivan Ilych's death the first thought of each of the gentlemen in that private room was of the changes and promotions it might occasion among themselves or their acquaintances.

"I shall be sure to get Shtabel's place or Vinnikov's," thought Fedor Vasilievich. "I was promised that long ago, and the promotion means an extra eight hundred rubles a year for me besides the allowance."

"Now I must apply for my brother-in-law's transfer from Kaluga," thought Peter Ivanovich. "My wife will be very glad, and then she won't be able to say that I never do anything for her relations."

"I thought he would never leave his bed again," said Peter Ivanovich aloud. "It's very sad."

"But what really was the matter with him?"

"The doctors couldn't say—at least they could, but each of them said something different. When last I saw him I thought he was getting better."

"And I haven't been to see him since the holidays. I always meant to go."

"Had he any property?"

"I think his wife had a little—but something quite trifling."

"We shall have to go to see her, but they live so terribly far away."

"Far away from you, you mean. Everything's far away from your place."

"You see, he never can forgive my living on the other side of the river," said Peter Ivanovich, smiling at Shebek. Then, still talking of the distances between different parts of the city, they returned to the Court.

Besides considerations as to the possible transfers and promotions likely to result from Ivan Ilych's death, the mere fact of the death of a near acquaintance aroused, as usual, in all who heard of it the complacent feeling that "it is he who is dead and not I."

Each one thought or felt, "Well, he's dead but I'm alive!" But the more intimate of Ivan Ilych's acquaintances, his so-called friends, could not help thinking also that they would now have to fulfill the very tiresome demands of propriety by attending the funeral service and paying a visit of condolence to the widow.

Fedor Vasilievich and Peter Ivanovich had been his nearest acquaintances. Peter Ivanovich had studied law with Ivan Ilych and had considered himself to be under obligations to him.

Having told his wife at dinner-time of Ivan Ilych's death, and of his conjecture that it might be possible to get her brother transferred to their circuit, Peter Ivanovich sacrificed his usual nap, put on his evening clothes, and drove to Ivan Ilych's house.

At the entrance stood a carriage and two cabs. Leaning against the wall in the hall downstairs near the cloak-stand was a coffin-lid covered with cloth of gold, ornamented with gold cord and tassels, that had been polished up with metal powder. Two ladies in black were taking off their fur cloaks. Peter Ivanovich recognized one of them as Ivan Ilych's sister, but the other was a stranger to him. His colleague Schwartz was just coming downstairs, but on seeing Peter Ivanovich enter he stopped and winked at him, as if to say: "Ivan Ilych has made a mess of things—not like you and me."

Schwartz's face with his Piccadilly whiskers, and his slim figure in evening dress, had as usual an air of elegant solemnity which contrasted with the playfulness of his character and had a special piquancy here, or so it seemed to Peter Ivanovich.

Peter Ivanovich allowed the ladies to precede him and slowly followed them upstairs. Schwartz did not come down but remained where he was, and Peter Ivanovich understood that he wanted to arrange where they should play bridge that evening. The ladies went upstairs to the widow's room, and Schwartz with seriously compressed lips but a playful look in his eyes, indicated by a twist of his eye-brows the room to the right where the body lay.

Peter Ivanovich, like everyone else on such occasions, entered feeling uncertain what he would have to do. All he knew was that at such times it is always safe to cross oneself. But he was not quite sure whether one should make obeisances while doing so. He therefore adopted a middle course. On entering the room he began crossing himself and made a slight movement resembling a bow. At the same time, as far as the motion of his head and arm allowed, he surveyed the room. Two young men—apparently nephews, one of whom was a high school pupil—were leaving the room, crossing themselves as they did so. An old woman was standing motionless, and a lady with strangely arched eyebrows was saying something to her in a whisper. A vigorous, resolute Church Reader, in a frock-coat, was reading something in a loud voice with an expression that precluded any contradiction. The butler's assistant, Gerasim, stepping lightly in front of Peter Ivanovich, was strewing something on the floor. Noticing this, Peter Ivanovich was immediately aware of a faint odour of a decomposing body.

The last time he had called on Ivan Ilych, Peter Ivanovich had seen Gerasim in the study. Ivan Ilych had been particularly fond of him and he was performing the duty of a sick nurse.

Peter Ivanovich continued to make the sign of the cross slightly inclining his head in an intermediate direction between the coffin, the Reader, and the icons on the table in a corner of the room. Afterwards, when it seemed to him that this movement of his arm in crossing himself had gone on too long, he stopped and began to look at the corpse.

The dead man lay, as dead men always lie, in a specially heavy way, his rigid limbs sunk in the soft cushions of the coffin, with the head forever bowed on the pillow. His yellow waxen brow with bald patches over his sunken temples was thrust up in the way peculiar to the dead, the protruding nose seeming to press on the upper lip. He was much changed and had grown even thinner since Peter Ivanovich had last seen him, but, as is always the case with the dead, his face was handsomer and above all more dignified than when he was alive. The expression on the face said that what was necessary had been accomplished, and accomplished rightly. Besides this there was in that expression a reproach and a warning to the living. This warning seemed to Peter Ivanovich out of place, or at least not applicable to him. He felt a certain discomfort and so he hurriedly crossed himself once more and turned and went out of the door—too hurriedly and too regardless of propriety, as he himself was aware.

Schwartz was waiting for him in the adjoining room with legs spread wide apart and both hands toying with his top-hat behind his back. The mere sight of that playful, well-groomed, and elegant figure refreshed Peter Ivanovich. He felt that Schwartz was above all these happenings and would not surrender to any depressing influences. His very look said that this incident of a church service for Ivan Ilych could not be a sufficient reason for infringing the order of the session—in other words, that it would certainly not prevent his unwrapping a new pack of cards and shuffling them that evening while a footman placed four fresh candles on the table: in fact, there was no reason for supposing that this incident would hinder their spending the evening agreeably. Indeed he said this in a whisper as Peter Ivanovich passed him, proposing that they should meet for a game at Fedor Vasilievich's. But apparently Peter Ivanovich was not destined to play bridge that evening. Praskovya Fedorovna (a short, fat woman who despite all efforts to the contrary had continued to broaden steadily from her shoulders downwards and who had the same extraordinarily arched eyebrows as the lady who had been standing by the coffin), dressed all in black, her head covered with lace, came out of her own room with some other ladies, conducted them to the room where the dead body lay, and said: "The service will begin immediately. Please go in."

Schwartz, making an indefinite bow, stood still, evidently neither accepting nor declining this invitation. Praskovya Fedorovna recognizing Peter Ivanovich, sighed, went close up to him, took his hand, and said: "I know you were a true friend to Ivan Ilych . . ." and looked at him awaiting some suitable response. And Peter Ivanovich knew that, just as it had been the right thing to cross himself in that room, so what he had to do here was to press her hand, sigh, and say, "Believe me . . ." So he did all this and as he did it felt that the desired result had been achieved: that both he and she were touched.

"Come with me. I want to speak to you before it begins," said the widow. "Give me your arm."

Peter Ivanovich gave her his arm and they went to the inner rooms, passing Schwartz who winked at Peter Ivanovich compassionately.

"That does for our bridge! Don't object if we find another player. Perhaps you can cut in when you do escape," said his playful look.

Peter Ivanovich sighed still more deeply and despondently, and Praskovya Fedorovna pressed his arm gratefully. When they reached the drawing-room, uphol-stered in pink cretonne and lighted by a dim lamp, they sat down at the table—she on a sofa and Peter Ivanovich on a low pouffe, the springs of which yielded spasmodically under his weight. Praskovya Fedorovna had been on the point of warning him to take another seat, but felt that such a warning was out of keeping with her present condition and so changed her mind. As he sat down on the pouffe Peter Ivanovich recalled how Ivan Ilych had arranged this room and had consulted him regarding this pink cretonne with green leaves. The whole room was full of furniture and knick-knacks, and on her way to the sofa the lace of the widow's black shawl caught on the carved edge of the table. Peter Ivanovich rose to detach it, and the springs of the pouffe, relieved of his weight, rose also and gave him a push. The widow began detaching her shawl herself, and Peter Ivanovich again sat down, suppressing the rebellious springs of the pouffe under him. But the widow had not quite freed herself and Peter Ivanovich got up again, and again the pouffe rebelled and even creaked. When this was all over she took out a clean cambric handkerchief and began to weep. The episode with the shawl and the struggle with the pouffe had cooled Peter Ivanovich's emotions and he sat there with a sullen look on his face. This awkward situation was interrupted by Sokolov, Ivan Ilych's butler, who came to report that the plot in the cemetery that Praskovya Fedorovna had chosen would cost two hundred rubles. She stopped weeping and, looking at Peter Ivanovich with the air of a victim, remarked in French that it was very hard for her. Peter Ivanovich made a silent gesture signifying his full conviction that it must in-deed be so.

"Please smoke," she said in a magnanimous yet crushed voice, and turned to discuss with Sokolov the price of the plot for the grave.

Peter Ivanovich while lighting his cigarette heard her inquiring very circum-stantially into the price of different plots in the cemetery and finally decide which she would take. When that was done she gave instructions about engaging the choir. Sokolov then left the room.

"I look after everything myself," she told Peter Ivanovich, shifting the albums that lay on the table; and noticing that the table was endangered by his cigarette-ash, she immediately passed him an ashtray, saying as she did so: "I consider it an affectation to say that my grief prevents my attending to practical affairs. On the contrary, if anything can—I won't say console me, but—distract me, it is seeing to everything concerning him." She again took out her handkerchief as if preparing to cry, but suddenly, as if mastering her feeling, she shook herself and began to speak calmly. "But there is something I want to talk to you about."

Peter Ivanovich bowed, keeping control of the springs of the pouffe, which immediatley began quivering under him.

"He suffered terribly the last few days."

"Did he?" said Peter Ivanovich.

"Oh, terribly! He screamed unceasingly, not for minutes but for hours. For the last three days he screamed incessantly. It was unendurable. I cannot understand how I bore it; you could hear him three rooms off. Oh, what I have suffered!"

"Is it possible that he was conscious all that time?" asked Peter Ivanovich.

"Yes," she whispered. "To the last moment. He took leave of us a quarter of an hour before he died, and asked us to take Volodya away."

The thought of the sufferings of this man he had known so intimately, first as a merry little boy, then as a school-mate, and later as a grown-up colleague, suddenly struck Peter Ivanovich with horror, despite an unpleasant consciousness of his own and this woman's dissimulation. He again saw that brow, and that nose pressing down on the lip, and felt afraid for himself.

"Three days of frightful suffering and then death! Why, that might suddenly, at any time, happen to me," he thought, and for a moment felt terrified. But—he did not himself know how—the customary reflection at once occurred to him that this had happened to Ivan Ilych and not to him, and that it should not and could not happen to him, and that to think that it could would be yielding to depression which he ought not to do, as Schwartz's expression plainly showed. After which reflection Peter Ivanovich felt reassured, and began to ask with interest about the details of Ivan Ilych's death, as though death was an accident natural to Ivan Ilych but certainly not to himself.

After many details of the really dreadful physical sufferings Ivan Ilych had endured (which details he learnt only from the effect those sufferings had produced on Praskovya Fedorovna's nerves) the widow apparently found it necessary to get to business.

"Oh, Peter Ivanovich, how hard it is! How terribly, terribly hard!" and she again began to weep.

Peter Ivanovich sighed and waited for her to finish blowing her nose. When she had done so he said, "Believe me . . ." and she again began talking and brought out what was evidently her chief concern with him—namely, to question him as to how she could obtain a grant of money from the government on the occasion of her husband's death. She made it appear that she was asking Peter Ivanovich's advice about her pension, but he soon saw that she already knew about that to the minutest detail, more even than he did himself. She knew how much could be got out of the government in consequence of her husband's death, but wanted to find out whether she could not possibly extract something more. Peter Ivanovich tried to think of some means of doing so, but after reflecting for a while and, out of propriety, condemning the government for its niggardliness, he said he thought that nothing more could be got. Then she sighed and evidently began to devise means of getting rid of her visitor. Noticing this, he put out his cigarette, rose, pressed her hand, and went out into the anteroom.

In the dining-room where the clock stood that Ivan Ilych had liked so much and had bought at an antique shop, Peter Ivanovich met a priest and a few acquaintances who had come to attend the service, and he recognized Ivan Ilych's daughter, a handsome young woman. She was in black and her slim figure appeared slimmer than ever. She had a gloomy, determined, almost angry expression, and bowed to Peter Ivanovich as though he were in some way to blame. Behind her, with the same offended look, stood a wealthy young man, an examining magistrate, whom Peter Ivanovich also knew and who was her fiancé, as he had heard. He bowed mournfully to them and was about to pass into the death-chamber, when from under the stairs appeared the figure of Ivan Ilych's schoolboy son, who was extremely like his father. He seemed a little Ivan Ilych, such as Peter Ivanovich remembered when they studied law together. His tear-stained eyes had in them the look that is seen in the eyes of boys of thirteen or fourteen who are not pure-minded. When he saw Peter Ivanovich he scowled morosely and shame-facedly. Peter Ivanovich nodded to him and entered the death-chamber. The service began: candles, groans, incense, tears, and sobs. Peter Ivanovich stood looking gloomily down at his feet. He did not look once at the dead man, did not yield to any depressing influence, and was one of the first to leave the room. There was no one in the anteroom, but Gerasim darted out of the dead man's room, rummaged with his strong hands among the fur coats to find Peter Ivanovich's and helped him on with it.

"Well, friend Gerasim," said Peter Ivanovich, so as to say something. "It's a sad affair, isn't it?"

"It's God's will. We shall all come to it some day," said Gerasim, displaying his teeth—the even, white teeth of a healthy peasant—and, like a man in the thick of urgent work, he briskly opened the front door, called the coachman, helped Peter Ivanovich into the sledge, and sprang back to the porch as if in readiness for what he had to do next.

Peter Ivanovich found the fresh air particularly pleasant after the smell of incense, the dead body, and carbolic acid.

"Where to, sir?" asked the coachman.

"It's not too late even now . . . I'll call around on Fedor Vasilievich."

He accordingly drove there and found them just finishing the first rubber, so that it was quite convenient for him to cut in.

2

Ivan Ilych's life had been most simple and most ordinary and therefore most terrible.

He had been a member of the Court of Justice, and died at the age of forty-five. His father had been an official who after serving in various ministries and departments of Petersburg had made the sort of career which brings men to positions from which by reason of their long service they cannot be dismissed, though they are obviously unfit to hold any responsible position, and for whom therefore posts are specially created, which though fictitious carry salaries of from six to ten thousand rubles that are not fictitious, and in receipt of which they live on to a great age.

Such was the Privy Councillor and superfluous member of various superfluous institutions, Ilya Epimovich Golovin.

He had three sons, of whom Ivan Ilych was the second. The eldest son was following in his father's footsteps only in another department, and was already approaching that stage in the service at which a similar sinecure would be reached. The third son was a failure. He had ruined his prospects in a number of positions and was now serving in the railway department. His father and brothers, and still more their wives, not merely disliked meeting him, but avoided remembering his existence unless compelled to do so. His sister had married Baron Greff, a Petersburg official of her father's type. Ivan Ilych was *le phénix de la famille* as people said. He was neither as cold and formal as his elder brother nor as wild as the younger, but was a happy mean between them— an intelligent, polished, lively and agreeable man. He had studied with his younger brother at the School of Law, but the latter had failed to complete the course and was expelled when he was in the fifth class. Ivan Ilych finished the course well. Even when he was at the School of Law he was just what he remained for the rest of his life: a capable, cheerful, good-natured, and sociable man, though strict in the fulfilment of what he considered to be his duty: and he considered his duty to be what was so considered by those in authority. Neither as a boy nor as a man was he a toady, but from early youth was by nature attracted to people of high station as a fly is drawn to the light, assimilating their ways and views of life and establishing friendly relations with them. All the enthusiasms of childhood and youth passed without leaving much trace on him; he succumbed to sensuality, to vanity, and latterly among the highest classes to liberalism, but always within limits which his instinct unfailingly indicated to him as correct.

At school he had done things which had formerly seemed to him very horrid and made him feel disgusted with himself when he did them; but when later on he saw that such actions were done by people of good position and that they did not regard them as wrong, he was able not exactly to regard them as right, but to forget about them entirely or not be at all troubled at remembering them.

Having graduated from the School of Law and qualified for the tenth rank of civil service, and having received money from his father for his equipment, Ivan Ilych ordered himself clothes at Scharmer's, the fashionable tailor, hung a medallion inscribed *respice finem* on his watch-chain, took leave of his professor and the prince who was patron of the school, had a farewell dinner with his comrades at Donon's first-class restaurant, and with his new and fashionable portmanteau, linen, clothes, shaving and other toilet appliances, and a travelling rug, all purchased at the best shops, he set off for one of the provinces where, through his father's influence, he had been attached to the Governor as an official for special service.

In the province Ivan Ilych soon arranged as easy and agreeable a position for himself as he had had at the School of Law. He performed his official tasks, made his career, and at the same time amused himself pleasantly and decorously. Occasionally he paid official visits to country districts, where he behaved with dignity both to his superiors and inferiors, and performed the duties entrusted to him, which related chiefly to the sectarians, with an exactness and incorruptible honesty of which he could not but feel proud.

In official matters, despite his youth and taste for frivolous gaiety, he was exceedingly reserved, punctilious, and even severe; but in society he was often amusing and witty, and always good-natured, correct in his manner, and *bon enfant,* as the governor and his wife—with whom he was like one of the family—used to say of him.

In the provinces he had an affair with a lady who made advances to the elegant young lawyer, and there was also a milliner; and there were carousals with aides-de-camp who visited the district, and after-supper visits to a certain outlying street of doubtful reputation; and there was too some obsequiousness to his chief and even to his chief's wife, but all this was done with such a tone of good breeding that no hard names could be applied to it. It all came under the heading of the French saying: "Il faut que jeunesse se passe." It was all done with clean hands, in clean linen, with French phrases, and above all among people of the best society and consequently with the approval of people of rank.

So Ivan Ilych served for five years and then came a change in his official life. The new and reformed judicial institutions were introduced, and new men were needed. Ivan Ilych became such a new man. He was offered the post of Examining Magistrate, and he accepted it though the post was in another province and obliged him to give up the connexions he had formed and to make new ones. His friends met to give him a send-off; they had a group-photograph taken and presented him with a silver cigarette-case, and he set off to his new post.

As examining magistrate Ivan Ilych was just as *comme il faut* and decorous a man, inspiring general respect and capable of separating his official duties from his private life, as he had been when acting as an official on special service. His duties now as examining magistrate were far more interesting and attractive than before. In his former position it had been pleasant to wear an undress uniform made by Scharmer, and to pass through the crowd of petitioners and officials who were timorously awaiting an audience with the governor, and who envied him as with free and easy gait he went straight into his chief's private room to have a cup of tea and a cigarette with him. But not many people had then been directly dependent on him—only police officials and the sectarians when he went on special missions—and he liked to treat them politely, almost as comrades, as if he were letting them feel that he who had the power to crush them was treating them in this simple, friendly way. There were then but few such people. But now, as an examining magistrate, Ivan Ilych felt that everyone without exception, even the most important and self-satisfied, was in his power, and that he need only write a few words on a sheet of paper with a certain heading, and this or that important, self-satisfied person would be brought before him in the role of an accused person or a witness, and if he did not choose to allow him to sit down, would have to stand before him and answer his questions. Ivan Ilych never abused his power; he tried on the contrary to soften its expression, but the consciousness of it and of the possibility of softening its effect, supplied the chief interest and attraction of his office. In his work itself, especially in his examinations, he very soon acquired a method of eliminating all considerations irrelevant to the legal aspect of the case, and reducing even the most complicated case to a form in which it would be presented on paper only in its externals, completely excluding his personal opinion of the matter, while above all observing every prescribed formality. The work was new and Ivan Ilych was one of the first men to apply the new Code of 1864.

On taking up the post of examining magistrate in a new town, he made new acquaintances and connexions, placed himself on a new footing, and assumed a somewhat different tone. He took up an attitude of rather dignified aloofness towards the provincial authorities, but picked out the best circle of legal gentlemen and wealthy gentry living in the town and assumed a tone of slight dissatisfaction with the government, of moderate liberalism, and of enlightened citizenship. At the same time, without at all altering the elegance of his toilet, he ceased shaving his chin and allowed his beard to grow as it pleased.

Ivan Ilych settled down very pleasantly in this new town. The society there, which inclined towards opposition to the Governor, was friendly, his salary was larger, and he began to play *vint,* which he found added not a little to the pleasure of life, for he had a capacity for cards, played good-humouredly, and calculated rapidly and astutely, so that he usually won.

After living there for two years he met his future wife, Praskovya Fedorovna Mikhel, who was the most attractive, clever, and brilliant girl of the set in which he moved, and among other amusements and relaxations from his labours as examining magistrate, Ivan Ilych established light and playful relations with her.

While he had been an official on special service he had been accustomed to dance, but now as an examining magistrate it was exceptional for him to do so. If he danced now, he did it as if to show that though he served under the reformed order of things, and had reached the fifth official rank, yet when it came to dancing he could do it better than most people. So at the end of an evening he sometimes danced with Praskovya Fedorovna, and it was chiefly during these dances that he captivated her. She fell in love with him. Ivan Ilych had at first no definite intention of marrying, but when the girl fell in love with him he said to himself: "Really, why shouldn't I marry?"

Praskovya Fedorovna came of a good family, was not bad looking and had some little property. Ivan Ilych might have aspired to a more brilliant match, but even this was good. He had his salary, and she, he hoped, would have an equal income. She was well connected, and was a sweet, pretty, and thoroughly correct young woman. To say that Ivan Ilych married because he fell in love with Praskovya Fedorovna and found that she sympathized with his views of life would be as incorrect as to say that he married because his social circle approved of the match. He was swayed by both these considerations: the marriage gave him personal satisfaction, and at the same time it was considered the right thing by the most highly placed of his associates.

So Ivan Ilych got married.

The preparations for marriage and the beginning of married life, with its conjugal caresses, the new furniture, new crockery, and new linen, were very pleasant until his wife became pregnant—so that Ivan Ilych had begun to think that marriage would not impair the easy, agreeable, gay and always decorous character of his life, approved of by society and regarded by himself as natural, but would even improve it. But from the first months of his wife's pregnancy, something new, unpleasant, depressing, and unseemly, and from which there was no way of escape, unexpectedly showed itself.

His wife, without any reason—*de gaieté de coeur* as Ivan Ilych expressed it to himself—began to disturb the pleasure and propriety of their life. She began to be jealous without any cause, expected him to devote his whole attention to her, found fault with everything, and made coarse and ill-mannered scenes.

At first Ivan Ilych hoped to escape from the unpleasantness of this state of affairs by the same easy and decorous relation to life that had served him heretofore: he tried to ignore his wife's disagreeable moods, continued to live in his usual easy and pleasant way, invited friends to his house for a game of cards, and also tried going out to his club or spending his evenings with friends. But one day his wife began upbraiding him so vigorously, using such coarse words, and continued to abuse him every time he did not fulfil her demands, so resolutely and with such evident determination not to give way till he submitted—that is, till he stayed at home and was bored just as she was—that he became alarmed. He now realized that matrimony—at any rate with Praskovya Fedorovna—was not always conducive to the pleasures and amenities of life but on the contrary often infringed both comfort and propriety, and that he must therefore entrench himself against such infringement. And Ivan Ilych began to seek for means of doing so. His official duties were the one thing that imposed upon Praskovya Fedorovna, and by means of his official work and the duties attached to it he began struggling with his wife to secure his own independence.

With the birth of their child, the attempts to feed it and the various failures in doing so, and with the real and imaginary illnesses of mother and child, in which Ivan Ilych's sympathy was demanded but about which he understood nothing, the need of securing for himself an existence outside his family life became still more imperative.

As his wife grew more irritable and exacting and Ivan Ilych transferred the centre of gravity of his life more and more to his official work, so did he grow to like his work better and became more ambitious than before.

Very soon, within a year of his wedding, Ivan Ilych had realized that marriage, though it may add some comforts to life, is in fact a very intricate and difficult affair towards which in order to perform one's duty, that is, to lead a decorous life approved of by society, one must adopt a definite attitude just as towards one's official duties.

And Ivan Ilych evolved such an attitude towards married life. He only required of it those conveniences—dinner at home, housewife, and bed—which it could give him, and above all that propriety of external forms required by public opinion. For the rest he looked for light-hearted pleasure and propriety, and was very thankful when he found them, but if he met with antagonism and querulousness he at once retired into his separate fenced-off world of official duties, where he found satisfaction.

Ivan Ilych was esteemed a good official, and after three years was made Assistant Public Prosecutor. His new duties, their importance, the possibility of indicting and imprisoning anyone he chose, the publicity his speeches received, and the success he had in all these things, made his work still more attractive.

More children came. His wife became more and more querulous and ill tempered, but the attitude Ivan Ilych had adopted towards his home life rendered him almost impervious to her grumbling.

After seven years' service in that town he was transferred to another province as Public Prosecutor. They moved, but were short of money and his wife did not like the place they moved to. Though the salary was higher the cost of living was greater, besides which two of their children died and family life became still more unpleasant for him.

Praskovya Fedorovna blamed her husband for every inconvenience they encountered in their new home. Most of the conversations between husband and wife, especially as to the children's education, led to topics which recalled former disputes, and those disputes were apt to flare up again at any moment. There remained only those rare periods of amorousness which still came to them at times but did not last long. These were islets at which they anchored for a while and then again set out upon that ocean of veiled hostility which showed itself in their aloofness from one another. This aloofness might have grieved Ivan Ilych had he considered that it ought not to exist, but he now regarded the position as normal, and even made it the goal at which he aimed in family life. His aim was to free himself more and more from those unpleasantnesses and to give them a semblance of harmlessness and propriety. He attained this by spending less and less time with his family, and when obliged to be at home he tried to safeguard his position by the presence of outsiders. The chief thing however was that he had his official duties. The whole interest of his life now centered in the official world and that interest absorbed him. The consciousness of his power, being able to ruin anybody he wished to ruin, the importance, even the external dignity of his entry into court, or meetings with his subordinates, his success with superiors and inferiors, and above all his masterly handling of cases, of which he was conscious—all this gave him pleasure and filled his life, together with chats with his colleagues, dinners, and bridge. So that on the whole Ivan Ilych's life continued to flow as he considered it should do—pleasantly and properly.

So things continued for another seven years. His eldest daughter was already sixteen, another child had died, and only one son was left, a schoolboy and a subject of dissension. Ivan Ilych wanted to put him in the School of Law, but to spite him Praskovya Fedorovna entered him at the High School. The daughter had been educated at home and had turned out well: the boy did not learn badly either.

3

So Ivan Ilych lived for seventeen years after his marriage. He was already a Public Prosecutor of long standing, and had declined several proposed transfers while awaiting a more desirable post, when an unanticipated and unpleasant occurrence quite upset the peaceful course of his life. He was expecting to be offered the post of presiding judge in a University town, but Happe somehow came to the front and obtained the appointment instead. Ivan Ilych became irritable, reproached Happe, and quarrelled both with him and with his immediate superiors—who became colder to him and again passed him over when other appointments were made.

This was in 1880, the hardest year of Ivan Ilych's life. It was then that it became evident on the one hand that his salary was insufficient for them to live on, and on the other that he had been forgotten, and not only this, but that what was for him the greatest and most cruel injustice appeared to others a quite ordinary occurrence. Even his father did not consider it his duty to help him. Ivan Ilych felt himself abandoned by everyone, and that they regarded his position with a salary of 3,500 rubles as quite normal and even fortunate. He alone knew that with the consciousness of the injustices done him, with his wife's incessant nagging, and with the debts he had contracted by living beyond his means, his position was far from normal.

In order to save money that summer he obtained leave of absence and went with his wife to live in the country at her brother's place.

In the country, without his work, he experienced *ennui* for the first time in his life, and not only *ennui* but intolerable depression, and he decided that it was impossible to go on living like that, and that it was necessary to take energetic measures.

Having passed a sleepless night pacing up and down the veranda, he decided to go to Petersburg and bestir himself, in order to punish those who had failed to appreciate him and to get transferred to another ministry.

Next day, despite many protests from his wife and her brother, he started for Petersburg with the sole object of obtaining a post with a salary of five thousand rubles a year. He was no longer bent on any particular department, or tendency, or kind of activity. All he now wanted was an appointment to another post with a salary of five thousand rubles, either in the administration, in the banks, with the railways, in one of the Empress Marya's Institutions, or even in the customs—but it had to carry with it a salary of five thousand rubles and be in a ministry other than that in which they had failed to appreciate him.

And this quest of Ivan Ilych's was crowned with remarkable and unexpected success. At Kursk an acquaintance of his, F. I. Ilyin, got into the first-class carriage, sat down beside Ivan Ilych, and told him of a telegram just received by the Governor of Kursk announcing that a change was about to take place in the ministry: Peter Ivanovich was to be superseded by Ivan Semenovich.

The proposed change, apart from its significance for Russia, had a special significance for Ivan Ilych, because by bringing forward a new man, Peter Petrovich, and consequently his friend Zachar Ivanovich, it was highly favourable for Ivan Ilych, since Zachar Ivanovich was a friend and colleague of his.

In Moscow this news was confirmed, and on reaching Petersburg Ivan Ilych found Zachar Ivanovich and received a definite promise of an appointment in his former Department of Justice.

A week later he telegraphed to his wife: "Zachar in Miller's place. I shall receive appointment on presentation of report."

Thanks to this change of personnel, Ivan Ilych had unexpectedly obtained an appointment in his former ministry which placed him two stages above his former colleagues besides giving him five thousand rubles salary and three thousand five hundred rubles for expenses connected with his removal. All his ill humour towards his former enemies and the whole department vanished, and Ivan Ilych was completely happy.

He returned to the country more cheerful and contented than he had been for a long time. Praskovya Fedorovna also cheered up and a truce was arranged between them. Ivan Ilych told of how he had been feted by everybody in Petersburg, how all those who had been his enemies were put to shame and now fawned on him, how envious they were of his appointment, and how much everybody in Petersburg had liked him.

Praskovya Fedorovna listened to all this and appeared to believe it. She did not contradict anything, but only made plans for their life in the town to which they were going. Ivan Ilych saw with delight that these plans were his plans, that he and his wife agreed, and that, after a stumble, his life was regaining its due and natural character of pleasant lightheartedness and decorum.

Ivan Ilych had come back for a short time only, for he had to take up his new duties on the 10th of September. Moreover, he needed time to settle into the new place, to move all his belongings from the province, and to buy and order many additional things: in a word, to make such arrangements as he had resolved on, which were almost exactly what Praskovya Fedorovna too had decided on.

Now that everything had happened so fortunately, and that he and his wife were at one in their aims and moreover saw so little of one another, they got on together better than they had done since the first years of marriage. Ivan Ilych had thought of taking his family away with him at once, but the insistence of his wife's brother and her sister-in-law, who had suddenly become particularly amiable and friendly to him and his family, induced him to depart alone.

So he departed, and the cheerful state of mind induced by his success and by the harmony between his wife and himself, the one intensifying the other, did not leave him. He found a delightful house, just the thing both he and his wife had dreamt of. Spacious, lofty reception rooms in the old style, a convenient and dignified study, rooms for his wife and daughter, a study for his son—it might have been specially built for them. Ivan Ilych himself superintended the arrangement, chose the wall-papers, supplemented the furniture (preferably with antiques which he considered particularly *comme il faut*), and supervised the upholstering. Everything progressed and progressed and approached the ideal he had set himself: even when things were only half completed they exceeded his expectations. He saw what a refined and elegant character, free from vulgarity, it would all have when it was ready. On falling asleep he pictured to himself how the reception-room would look. Looking at the yet unfinished drawing-room he could see the fireplace, the screen, the what-not, the little chairs dotted her and there, the dishes and plates on the walls, and the bronzes, as they would be when everything was in place. He was pleased by the thought of how his wife and daughter, who shared his taste in this matter, would be impressed by it. They were certainly not expecting as much. He had been particularly successful in finding, and buying cheaply, antiques which gave a particularly aristocratic character to the whole place. But in his letters he intentionally understated everything in order to be able to surprise them. All this so absorbed him that his new duties—though he liked his official work—interested him less than he had expected. Sometimes he even had moments of absentmindedness during the Court Sessions, and would consider whether he should have straight or curved cornices for his curtains. He was so interested in it all that he often did things himself, rearranging the furniture, or rehanging the curtains. Once when mounting a step-ladder to show the upholsterer, who did not understand, how he wanted the hangings draped, he made a false step and slipped, but being a strong and agile man he clung on and only knocked his side against the knob of the window frame. The bruised place was painful but the pain soon passed, and he felt particularly bright and well just then. He wrote: "I feel fifteen years younger." He thought he would have everything ready by September, but it dragged on till mid-October. But the result was charming not only in his eyes but to everyone who saw it.

In reality it was just what is usually seen in the houses of people of moderate means who want to appear rich, and therefore succeed only in resembling others like themselves: there were damasks, dark wood, plants, rugs, and dull and polished bronzes—all the things people of a certain class have in order to resemble other people of that class. His house was so like the others that it would never have been noticed, but to him it all seemed to be quite exceptional. He was very happy when he met his family at the station and brought them to the newly furnished house all lit up, where a footman in a white tie opened the door into the hall decorated with plants, and when they went on into the drawing-room and the study uttering exclamations of delight. He conducted them everywhere, drank in their praises eagerly, and beamed with pleasure. At tea that evening, when Praskovya Fedorovna among other things asked him about his fall, he laughed, and showed them how he had gone flying and had frightened the upholsterer.

"It's a good thing I'm a bit of an athlete. Another man might have been killed, but I merely knocked myself, just here; it hurts when it's touched, but it's passing off already—it's only a bruise."

So they began living in their new home—in which, as always happens, when they got thoroughly settled in they found they were just one room short—and with the increased income, which as always was just a little (some five hundred rubles) too little, but it was all very nice.

Things went particularly well at first, before everything was finally arranged and while something had still to be done: this thing bought, that thing ordered, another thing moved, and something else adjusted. Though there were some disputes between husband and wife, they were both so well satisfied and had so much to do that it all passed off without any serious quarrels. When nothing was left to arrange it became rather dull and something seemed to be lacking, but they were then making acquaintances, forming habits, and life was growing fuller.

Ivan Ilych spent his mornings at the law court and came home to dinner, and at first he was generally in a good humor, though he occasionally became irritable just on account of his house. (Every spot on the tablecloth or the upholstery, and every broken window-blind string, irritated him. He had devoted so much trouble to arranging it all that every disturbance of it distressed him.) But on the whole his life ran its course as he believed life should do: easily, pleasantly, and decorously.

He got up at nine, drank his coffee, read the paper, and then put on his undress uniform and went to the law courts. There the harness in which he worked had already been stretched to fit him and he donned it without a hitch: petitioners, inquiries at the chancery, the chancery itself, and the sittings public and administrative. In all this the thing was to exclude everything fresh and vital, which always disturbs the regular course of official business, and to admit only official relations with people, and then only on official grounds. A man would come, for instance, wanting some information. Ivan Ilych, as one in whose sphere the matter did not lie, would have nothing to do with him: but if the man had some business with him in his official capacity, something that could be expressed on officially stamped paper, he would do everything, positively everything he could within the limits of such relations, and in doing so would maintain the semblance of friendly human relations, that is, would observe the courtesies of life. As soon as the official relations ended, so did everything else. Ivan Ilych possessed this capacity to separate his real life from the official side of affairs and not mix the two, in the highest degree, and by long practice and natural aptitude had brought it to such a pitch that sometimes, in the manner of a virtuoso, he would even allow himself to let the human and official relations mingle. He let himself do this just because he felt that he could at

any time he chose resume the strictly official attitude again and drop the human relation. And he did it all easily, pleasantly, correctly, and even artistically. In the intervals
between the sessions he smoked, drank tea, chatted a little about politics, a little about
general topics, a little about cards, but most of all about official appointments. Tired,
but with the feelings of a virtuoso—one of the first violins who has played his part in
an orchestra with precision—he would return home to find that his wife and daughter
had been out paying calls, or had a visitor, and that his son had been to school, had done
his homework with his tutor, and was duly learning what is taught at High Schools.
Everything was as it should be. After dinner, if they had no visitors, Ivan Ilych sometimes read a book that was being much discussed at the time, and in the evening settled
down to work, that is, read official papers, compared the depositions of witnesses, and
noted paragraphs of the Code applying to them. This was neither dull nor amusing. It
was dull when he might have been playing bridge, but if no bridge was available it was
at any rate better than doing nothing or sitting with his wife. Ivan Ilych's chief pleasure
was giving little dinners to which he invited men and women of good social position,
and just as his drawing-room resembled all other drawing-rooms so did his enjoyable
little parties resemble all other such parties.

Once they even gave a dance. Ivan Ilych enjoyed it and everything went off well,
except that it led to a violent quarrel with his wife about the cakes and sweets. Praskovya
Fedorovna had made her own plans, but Ivan Ilych insisted on getting everything from
an expensive confectioner and ordered too many cakes, and the quarrel occurred because some of those cakes were left over and the confectioner's bill came to forty-five
rubles. It was a great and disagreeable quarrel. Praskovya Fedorovna called him "a fool
and an imbecile," and he clutched at his head and made angry allusions to divorce.

But the dance itself had been enjoyable. The best people were there, and Ivan
Ilych had danced with Princess Trufonova, a sister of the distinguished founder of the
Society "Bear my Burden."

The pleasures connected with his work were pleasures of ambition; his social
pleasures were those of vanity; but Ivan Ilych's greatest pleasure was playing bridge. He
acknowledged that whatever disagreeable incident happened in his life, the pleasure
that beamed like a ray of light above everything else was to sit down to bridge with good
players, not noisy partners, and of course to four-handed bridge (with five players it was
annoying to have to stand out, though one pretended not to mind), to play a clever and
serious game (when the cards allowed it) and then to have supper and drink a glass of
wine. After a game of bridge, especially if he had won a little (to win a large sum was
unpleasant), Ivan Ilych went to bed in specially good humour.

So they lived. They formed a circle of acquaintances among the best people and
were visited by people of importance and by young folk. In their views as to their acquaintances, husband, wife and daughter were entirely agreed, and tacitly and unanimously kept at arm's length and shook off the various shabby friends and relations who,
with much show of affection, gushed into the drawing-room with its Japanese plates on
the walls. Soon these shabby friends ceased to obtrude themselves and only the best
people remained in the Golovins' set.

Young men made up to Lisa, and Petrishchev, an examining magistrate and
Dmitri Ivanovich Petrishchev's son and sole heir, began to be so attentive to her that

Ivan Ilych had already spoken to Praskovya Fedorovna about it, and considered whether they should not arrange a party for them or get up some private theatricals.

So they lived, and all went well, without change, and life flowed pleasantly.

4

They were all in good health. It could not be called ill health if Ivan Ilych some-times said that he had a queer taste in his mouth and felt some discomfort in his left side.

But this discomfort increased and, though not exactly painful, grew into a sense of pressure in his side accompanied by ill humour. And his irritability became worse and worse and began to mar the agreeable, easy, and correct life that had estab-lished itself in the Golovin family. Quarrels between husband and wife became more and more frequent, and soon the ease and amenity disappeared and even the decorum was barely maintained. Scenes again became frequent, and very few of those islets remained on which husband and wife could meet without an explosion. Praskovya Fedorovna now had good reason to say that her husband's temper was trying. With characteristic exag-geration she said he had always had a dreadful temper, and that it had needed all her good nature to put up with it for twenty years. It was true that now the quarrels were started by him. His bursts of temper always came just before dinner, often just as he began to eat his soup. Sometimes he noticed that a plate or dish was chipped, or the food was not right, or his son put his elbow on the table, or his daughter's hair was not done as he liked it, and for all this he blamed Praskovya Fedorovna. At first she retorted and said disagreeable things to him, but once or twice he fell into such a rage at the be-ginning of dinner that she realized it was due to some physical derangement brought on by taking food, and so she restrained herself and did not answer, but only hurried to get the dinner over. She regarded this self-restraint as highly praiseworthy. Having come to the conclusion that her husband had a dreadful temper and made her life mis-erable, she began to feel sorry for herself, and the more she pitied herself the more she hated her husband. She began to wish he would die; yet she did not want him to die be-cause then his salary would cease. And this irritated her against him still more. She con-sidered herself dreadfully unhappy just because not even his death could save her, and though she concealed her exasperation, that hidden exasperation of hers increased his irritation also.

After one scene in which Ivan Ilych had been particularly unfair and after which he had said in explanation that he certainly was irritable but that it was due to his not being well, she said that if he was ill it should be attended to, and insisted on his going to see a celebrated doctor.

He went. Everything took place as he had expected and as it always does. There was the usual waiting and the important air assumed by the doctor, with which he was so familiar (resembling that which he himself assumed in court), and the sounding and listening, and the questions which called for answers that were forgone conclusions and were evidently unnecessary, and the look of importance which implied that "if only you put yourself in our hands we will arrange everything—we know indubitably how it has to be done, always in the same way for everybody alike." It was all just as it was in the law courts. The doctor put on just the same air towards him as he himself put on towards an accused person.

The doctor said that so-and-so indicated that there was so-and-so inside the patient, but if the investigation of so-and-so did not confirm this, then he must assume that and that. If he assumed that and that, then . . . and so on. To Ivan Ilych only one question was important: was his case serious or not? But the doctor ignored that inappropriate question. From his point of view it was not the one under consideration, the real question was to decide between a floating kidney, chronic catarrh, or appendicitis. It was not a question of Ivan Ilych's life or death, but one between a floating kidney and appendicitis. And that question the doctor solved brilliantly, as it seemed to Ivan Ilych, in favour of the appendix, with the reservation that should an examination of the urine give fresh indications the matter would be reconsidered. All this was just what Ivan Ilych had himself brilliantly accomplished a thousand times in dealing with men on trial. The doctor summed up just as brilliantly, looking over his spectacles triumphantly and even gaily at the accused. From the doctor's summing up Ivan Ilych concluded that things were bad, but that for the doctor, and perhaps for everybody else, it was a matter of indifference, though for him it was bad. And this conclusion struck him painfully, arousing in him a great feeling of pity for himself and of bitterness towards the doctor's indifference to a matter of such importance.

He said nothing of this, but rose, placed the doctor's fee on the table, and remarked with a sigh: "We sick people probably often put inappropriate questions. But tell me, in general, is this complaint dangerous, or not? . . ."

The doctor looked at him sternly over his spectacles with one eye, as if to say: "Prisoner, if you will not keep to the questions put to you, I shall be obliged to have you removed from the court."

"I have already told you what I consider necessary and proper. The analysis may show something more." And the doctor bowed.

Ivan Ilych went out slowly, seated himself disconsolately in his sledge, and drove home. All the way home he was going over what the doctor had said, trying to translate those complicated, obscure, scientific phrases into plain language and find in them an answer to the question: "Is my condition bad? Is it very bad? Or is there as yet nothing much wrong?" And it seemed to him that the meaning of what the doctor had said was that it was very bad. Everything in the streets seemed depressing. The cabmen, the houses, the passers-by, and the shops, were dismal. His ache, this dull gnawing ache that never ceased for a moment, seemed to have acquired a new and more serious significance from the doctor's dubious remarks. Ivan Ilych now watched it with a new and oppressive feeling.

He reached home and began to tell his wife about it. She listened, but in the middle of his account his daughter came in with her hat on, ready to go out with her mother. She sat down reluctantly to listen to this tedious story, but could not stand it long, and her mother too did not hear him to the end.

"Well, I am very glad," she said. "Mind now to take your medicine regularly. Give me the prescription and I'll send Gerasim to the chemist's." And she went to get ready to go out.

While she was in the room Ivan Ilych had hardly taken time to breathe, but he sighed deeply when she left it.

"Well," he thought, "perhaps it isn't so bad after all."

He began taking his medicine and following the doctor's directions, which had been altered after the examination of the urine. But then it happened that there was a contradiction between the indications drawn from the examination of the urine and the symptoms that showed themselves. It turned out that what was happening differed from what the doctor had told him, and that he had either forgotten, or blundered, or hidden something from him. He could not, however, be blamed for that, and Ivan Ilych still obeyed his orders implicitly and at first derived some comfort from doing so.

From the time of his visit to the doctor, Ivan Ilych's chief occupation was the exact fulfilment of the doctor's instructions regarding hygiene and the taking of medicine, and the observation of his pain and his excretions. His chief interests came to be people's ailments and people's health. When sickness, deaths, or recoveries were mentioned in his presence, especially when the illness resembled his own, he listened with agitation which he tried to hide, asked questions, and applied what he heard to his own case.

The pain did not grow less, but Ivan Ilych made efforts to force himself to think that he was better. And he could do this so long as nothing agitated him. But as soon as he had any unpleasantness with his wife, any lack of success in his official work, or held bad cards at bridge, he was at once acutely sensible of his disease. He had formerly borne such mischances, hoping soon to adjust what was wrong, to master it and attain success, or make a grand slam. But now every mischance upset him and plunged him into despair. He would say to himself: "There now, just as I was beginning to get better and the medicine had begun to take effect, comes this accursed misfortune, or unpleasantness . . ." And he was furious with the mishap, or with the people who were causing the unpleasantness and killing him, for he felt that this fury was killing him but could not restrain it. One would have thought that it should have been clear to him that this exasperation with circumstances and people aggravated his illness, and that he ought therefore to ignore unpleasant occurrences. But he drew the very opposite conclusion: he said that he needed peace, and he watched for everything that might disturb it and became irritable at the slightest infringement of it. His condition was rendered worse by the fact that he read medical books and consulted doctors. The progress of his disease was so gradual that he could deceive himself when comparing one day with another—the difference was so slight. But when he consulted the doctors it seemed to him that he was getting worse, and even very rapidly. Yet despite this he was continually consulting them.

That month he went to see another celebrity, who told him almost the same as the first had done but put his questions rather differently, and the interview with this celebrity only increased Ivan Ilych's doubts and fears. A friend of a friend of his, a very good doctor, diagnosed his illness again quite differently from the others, and though he predicted recovery, his questions and suppositions bewildered Ivan Ilych still more and increased his doubts. A homoeopathist diagnosed the disease in yet another way, and prescribed medicine which Ivan Ilych took secretly for a week. But after a week, not feeling any improvement and having lost confidence both in the former doctor's treatment and in this one's, he became still more despondent. One day a lady acquaintance mentioned a cure effected by a wonder-working icon. Ivan Ilych caught himself listening attentively and beginning to believe that it had occurred. This incident alarmed him. "Has my mind really weakened to such an extent?" he asked himself. "Nonsense! It's all rubbish. I mustn't give way to nervous fears but having chosen a doctor must keep strictly to his treatment. That is what I will do. Now it's all settled. I won't think about it, but will follow the treatment seriously till summer, and then we shall see. From now there must be no more of this wavering!" This was easy to say but impossible to carry out. The pain in his side oppressed him and seemed to grow worse and more incessant, while the taste in his mouth grew stranger and stranger. It seemed to him that his breath had a disgusting smell, and he was conscious of a loss of appetite and strength. There was no deceiving himself: something terrible, new, and more important than anything before in his life, was taking place within him of which he alone was aware. Those about him did not understand or would not understand it, but thought everything in the world was going on as usual. That tormented Ivan Ilych more than anything. He saw that his household, especially his wife and daughter who were in a perfect whirl of visiting, did not understand anything of it and were annoyed that he was so depressed and so exacting, as if he were to blame for it. Though they tried to disguise it he saw that he was an obstacle in their path, and that his wife had adopted a definite line in regard to his illness and kept to it regardless of anything he said or did. Her attitude was this: "You know," she would say to her friends, "Ivan Ilych can't do as other people do, and keep to the treatment prescribed for him. One day he'll take his drops and keep strictly to his diet and go to bed in good time, but the next day unless I watch him he'll suddenly forget his medicine, eat sturgeon—which is forbidden—and sit up playing cards till one o'clock in the morning."

"Oh, come, when was that?" Ivan Ilych would ask in vexation. "Only once at Peter Ivanovich's."

"And yesterday with Shebek."

"Well, even if I hadn't stayed up, this pain would have kept me awake."

"Be that as it may you'll never get well like that, but will always make us wretched."

Praskovya Fedorovna's attitude to Ivan Ilych's illness, as she expressed it both to others and to him, was that it was his own fault and was another of the annoyances he caused her. Ivan Ilych felt that this opinion escaped her involuntarily—but that did not make it easier for him.

At the law courts too, Ivan Ilych noticed, or thought he noticed, a strange attitude towards himself. It sometimes seemed to him that people were watching him inquisitively as a man whose place might soon be vacant. Then again, his friends would suddenly begin to chaff him in a friendly way about his low spirits, as if the awful, horrible, and unheard-of thing that was going on within him, incessantly gnawing at him and irresistibly drawing him away, was a very agreeable subject for jests. Schwartz in particular irritated him by his jocularity, vivacity, and *savoir-faire,* which reminded him of what he himself had been ten years ago.

Friends came to make up a set and they sat down to cards. They dealt, bending the new cards to soften them, and he sorted the diamonds in his hand and found he had seven. His partner said "No trumps" and supported him with two diamonds. What more could be wished for? It ought to be jolly and lively. They would make a grand slam. But suddenly Ivan Ilych was conscious of that gnawing pain, that taste in his mouth, and it seemed ridiculous that in such circumstances he should be pleased to make a grand slam.

He looked at his partner Mikhail Mikhaylovich, who rapped the table with his strong hand and instead of snatching up the tricks pushed the cards courteously and indulgently towards Ivan Ilych that he might have the pleasure of gathering them up without the trouble of stretching out his hand for them. "Does he think I am too weak to stretch out my arm?" thought Ivan Ilych, and forgetting what he was doing he overtrumped his partner, missing the grand slam by three tricks. And what was most awful of all was that he saw how upset Mikhail Mikhaylovich was about it but did not himself care. And it was dreadful to realize why he did not care.

They all saw that he was suffering, and said: "We can stop if you are tired. Take a rest." Lie down? No, he was not at all tired, and he finished the rubber. All were gloomy and silent. Ivan Ilych felt that he diffused this gloom over them and could not dispel it. They had supper and went away, and Ivan Ilych was left alone with the consciousness that his life was poisoned and was poisoning the lives of others, and that this poison did not weaken but penetrated more and more deeply into his whole being.

With this consciousness, and with physical pain besides the terror, he must go to bed, often to lie awake the greater part of the night. Next morning he had to get up again, dress, go to the law courts, speak, and write; or if he did not go out, spend at home those twenty-four hours a day each of which was a torture. And he had to live thus all alone on the brink of an abyss, with no one who understood or pitied him.

5

So one month passed and then another. Just before the New Year his brother-in-law came to town and stayed at their house. Ivan Ilych was at the law courts and Praskovya Fedorovna had gone shopping. When Ivan Ilych came home and entered his study he found his brother-in-law there—a healthy, florid man—unpacking his portmanteau himself. He raised his head on hearing Ivan Ilych's footsteps and looked up at him for a moment without a word. That stare told Ivan Ilych everything. His brother-in-law opened his mouth to utter an exclamation of surprise but checked himself, and that action confirmed it all.

"I have changed, eh?"

"Yes, there is a change."

And after that, try as he would to get his brother-in-law to return to the subject of his looks, the latter would say nothing about it. Praskovya Fedorovna came home and her brother went out to her. Ivan Ilych locked the door and began to examine himself in the glass, first full face, then in profile. He took up a portrait of himself taken with his wife, and compared it with what he saw in the glass. The change in him was immense. Then he bared his arms to the elbow, looked at them, drew the sleeves down again, sat down on an ottoman, and grew blacker than night.

"No, no, this won't do!" he said to himself, and jumped up, went to the table, took up some law papers and began to read them, but could not continue. He unlocked the door and went into the reception-room. The door leading to the drawing-room was shut. He approached it on tiptoe and listened.

"No, you are exaggerating!" Praskovya Fedorovna was saying.

"Exaggerating! Don't you see it? Why, he's a dead man! Look at his eyes—there's no light in them. But what is it that is wrong with him?"

"No one knows. Nikolaevich (that was another doctor) said something, but I don't know what. And Leshchetitsky (this was the celebrated specialist) said quite the contrary . . ."

Ivan Ilych walked away, went to his own room, lay down, and began musing: "The kidney, a floating kidney." He recalled all the doctors had told him of how it detached itself and swayed about. And by an effort of imagination he tried to catch that kidney and arrest it and support it. So little was needed for this, it seemed to him. "No, I'll go to see Peter Ivanovich again." (That was the friend whose friend was a doctor.) He rang, ordered the carriage, and got ready to go.

"Where are you going, Jean?" asked his wife, with a specially sad and exceptionally kind look.

This exceptionally kind look irritated him. He looked morosely at her.

"I must go to see Peter Ivanovich."

He went to see Peter Ivanovich, and together they went to see his friend, the doctor. He was in, and Ivan Ilych had a long talk with him.

Reviewing the anatomical and physiological details of what in the doctor's opinion was going on inside him, he understood it all.

There was something, a small thing, in the vermiform appendix. It might all come right. Only stimulate the energy of one organ and check the activity of another, then absorption would take place and everything would come right. He got home rather late for dinner, ate his dinner, and conversed cheerfully, but could not for a long time bring himself to go back to work in his room. At last, however, he went to his study and did what was necessary, but the consciousness that he had put something aside—an important, intimate matter which he would revert to when his work was done—never left him. When he had finished his work he remembered that this intimate matter was the thought of his vermiform appendix. But he did not give himself up to it, and went to the drawing-room for tea. There were callers there, including the examining magistrate who was a desirable match for his daughter, and they were conversing, playing the piano and singing. Ivan Ilych, as Praskovya Fedorovna remarked, spent that evening more cheerfully than usual, but he never for a moment forgot that he had postponed the important matter of the appendix. At eleven o'clock he said good-night and went to his bedroom. Since his illness he had slept alone in a small room next to his study. He undressed and took up a novel by Zola, but instead of reading it he fell into thought, and in his imagination that desired improvement in the vermiform appendix occurred. There was the absorption and evacuation and the reestablishment of normal activity. "Yes, that's it!" he said to himself. "One need only assist nature, that's all." He remembered his medicine, rose, took it, and lay down on his back watching for the beneficent action of the medicine and for it to lessen the pain. "I need only take it regularly and avoid all injurious influences. I am already feeling better, much better." He began touching his side: it was not painful to the touch. "There, I really don't feel it. It's much better already." He put out the light and turned on his side . . . "The appendix is getting better, absorption is occurring." Suddenly he felt the old, familiar, dull, gnawing pain, stubborn and serious. There was the same familiar loathsome taste in his mouth. His heart sank and he felt dazed. "My God! My God!" he muttered. "Again, again! And it will never cease." And suddenly the matter presented itself in a quite different aspect. "Vermiform appendix! Kidney!" he said to himself. "It's not a question of appendix or kidney, but of life and . . . death. Yes, life was there and now it is going, going and I cannot stop it. Yes. Why deceive myself? Isn't it obvious to everyone but me that I'm dying, and that it's only a question of weeks, days . . . it may happen this moment. There was light and now there is darkness. I was here and now I'm going there! Where?" A chill came over him, his breathing ceased, and he felt only the throbbing of his heart.

"When I am not, what will there be? There will be nothing. Then where shall I be when I am no more? Can this be dying? No, I don't want to!" He jumped up and tried to light the candle, felt for it with trembling hands, dropped candle and candlestick on the floor, and fell back on his pillow.

"What's the use? It makes no difference," he said to himself, staring with wide-open eyes into the darkness. "Death. Yes, death. And none of them know or wish to know it, and they have no pity for me. Now they are playing." (He heard through the door the distant sound of a song and its accompaniment.) "It's all the same to them, but they will die too! Fools! I first, and they later, but it will be the same for them. And now they are merry . . . the beasts!"

Anger choked him and he was agonizingly, unbearably miserable. "It is impossible that all men have been doomed to suffer this awful horror!" He raised himself.

"Something must be wrong. I must calm myself—must think it all over from the beginning." And he again began thinking. "Yes, the beginning of my illness: I knocked my side, but I was still quite well that day and the next. It hurt a little, then rather more. I saw the doctors, then followed despondency and anguish, more doctors, and I drew nearer to the abyss. My strength grew less and I kept coming nearer and nearer, and now I have wasted away and there is no light in my eyes. I think of the appendix—but this is death! I think of mending the appendix, and all the while here is death! Can it really be death?" Again terror seized him and he gasped for breath. He leant down and began feeling for the matches, pressing with his elbow on the stand beside the bed. It was in his way and hurt him, he grew furious with it, pressed on it still harder, and upset it. Breathless and in despair he fell on his back, expecting death to come immediately.

Meanwhile the visitors were leaving. Praskovya Fedorovna was seeing them off. She heard something fall and came in.

"What has happened?"

"Nothing. I knocked it over accidentally."

She went out and returned with a candle. He lay there panting heavily, like a man who has run a thousand yards, and stared upwards at her with a fixed look.

"What is it, Jean?"

"No . . . o . . . thing. I upset it." ("Why speak of it? She won't understand," he thought.)

And in truth she did not understand. She picked up the stand, lit his candle, and hurried away to see another visitor off. When she came back he still lay on his back, looking upwards.

"What is it? Do you feel worse?"

"Yes."

She shook her head and sat down.

"Do you know, Jean, I think we must ask Leshchetitsky to come and see you here."

This meant calling in the famous specialist, regardless of expense. He smiled malignantly and said "No." She remained a little longer and then went up to him and kissed his forehead.

While she was kissing him he hated her from the bottom of his soul and with difficulty refrained from pushing her away.

"Good-night. Please God you'll sleep."

"Yes."

6

Ivan Ilych saw that he was dying, and he was in continual despair.

In the depth of his heart he knew he was dying, but not only was he not accustomed to the thought, he simply did not and could not grasp it.

The syllogism he had learnt from Kiezewetter's Logic: "Caius is a man, men are mortal, therefore Caius is mortal," had always seemed to him correct as applied to Caius, but certainly not as applied to himself. That Caius—man in the abstract—was mortal, was perfectly correct, but he was not Caius, not an abstract man, but a creature quite, quite separate from all others. He had been little Vanya, with a mamma and a papa; with Mitya and Volodya, and the toys, a coachman and a nurse, afterwards with Katenka and with all the joys, griefs, and delights of childhood, boyhood, and youth. What did Caius know of the smell of that striped leather ball Vanya had been so fond of? Had Caius kissed his mother's hand like that, and did the silk of her dress rustle so for Caius? Had he rioted like that at school when the pastry was bad? Had Caius been in love like that? Could Caius preside at a session as he did? "Caius really was mortal, and it was right for him to die; but for me, little Vanya, Ivan Ilych, with all my thoughts and emotions, it's altogether a different matter. It cannot be that I ought to die. That would be too terrible."

Such was his feeling.

"If I had to die like Caius I should have known it was so. An inner voice would have told me so, but there was nothing of the sort in me and I and all my friends felt that our case was quite different from that of Caius. And now here it is!" he said to himself. "It can't be. It's impossible! But here it is. How is this? How is one to understand it?"

He could not understand it, and tried to drive this false, incorrect, morbid thought away and to replace it by other proper and healthy thoughts. But that thought and not the thought only but the reality itself, seemed to come and confront him.

And to replace that thought he called up a succession of others, hoping to find in them some support. He tried to get back into the former current of thoughts that had once screened the thought of death from him. But strange to say, all that had formerly shut off, hidden, and destroyed, his consciousness of death, no longer had that effect. Ivan Ilych now spent most of his time in attempting to re-establish that old current. He would say to himself: "I will take up my duties again—after all I used to live by them." And banishing all doubts he would go to the law courts, enter into conversation with his colleagues, and sit carelessly as was his wont, scanning the crowd with a thoughtful look and leaning both his emaciated arms on the arms of his oak chair; bending over as usual to a colleague and drawing his papers nearer he would interchange whispers with him, and then suddenly raising his eyes and sitting erect would pronounce certain words and open the proceedings. But suddenly in the midst of those proceedings the pain in his side, regardless of the stage the proceedings had reached, would begin its own gnawing work. Ivan Ilych would turn his attention to it and try to drive the thought of it away, but without success. *It* would come and stand before him and look at him, and he would be petrified and the light would die out of his eyes, and he would again begin asking himself whether *It* alone was true. And his colleagues and subordinates would see with surprise and distress that he, the brilliant and subtle judge, was becoming confused and making mistakes. He would shake himself, try to pull himself together, manage somehow to bring the sitting to a close, and return home with the sorrowful consciousness that his judicial labours could not as formerly hide from him what he wanted them to hide, and could not deliver him from *It*. And what was worst of all was that *It* drew his attention to itself not in order to make him take some action but only that he should look at *It,* look it straight in the face: look at it and without doing anything, suffer inexpressibly.

And to save himself from this condition Ivan Ilych looked for consolations—new screens—and new screens were found and for a while seemed to save him, but then they immediately fell to pieces or rather became transparent, as if *It* penetrated them and nothing could veil *It*.

In these latter days he would go into the drawing-room he had arranged—that drawing-room where he had fallen and for the sake of which (how bitterly ridiculous it seemed) he had sacrificed his life—for he knew that his illness originated with that knock. He would enter and see that something had scratched the polished table. He would look for the cause of this and find that it was the bronze ornamentation of an album, that had got bent. He would take up the expensive album which he had lovingly arranged, and feel vexed with his daughter and her friends for their untidiness—for the album was torn here and there and some of the photographs turned upside down. He would put it carefully in order and bend the ornamentation back into position. Then it would occur to him to place all those things in another corner of the room, near the plants. He could call the footman, but his daughter or wife would come to help him. They would not agree, and his wife would contradict him, and he would dispute and grow angry. But that was all right, for then he did not think about *It*. It was invisible.

But then, when he was moving something himself, his wife would say: "Let the servants do it. You will hurt yourself again." And suddenly *It* would flash through the screen and he would see it. It was just a flash, and he hoped it would disappear, but he would involuntarily pay attention to his side. "It sits there as before, gnawing just the same!" And he could no longer forget *It,* but could distinctly see it looking at him from behind the flowers. "What is it all for?"

"It really is so! I lost my life over that curtain as I might have done when storming a fort. Is that possible? How terrible and how stupid. It can't be true! It can't, but it is!"

He would go to his study, lie down, and again be alone with *It:* face to face with *It*. And nothing could be done with *It* except to look at it and shudder.

7

How it happened it is impossible to say because it came about step by step, unnoticed, but in the third month of Ivan Ilych's illness, his wife, his daughter, his son, his acquaintances, the doctors, the servants, and above all he himself, were aware that the whole interest he had for other people was whether he would soon vacate his place, and at last release the living from the discomfort caused by his presence and be himself released from his sufferings.

He slept less and less. He was given opium and hypodermic injections of morphine, but this did not relieve him. The dull depression he experienced in a somnolent condition at first gave him a little relief, but only as something new, afterwards it became as distressing as the pain itself or even more so.

Special foods were prepared for him by the doctors' orders, but all those foods became increasingly distasteful and disgusting to him.

For his excretions also special arrangements had to be made, and this was a torment to him every time—a torment from the uncleanliness, the unseemliness, and the smell, and from knowing that another person had to take part in it.

But just through this most unpleasant matter Ivan Ilych obtained comfort. Gerasim, the butler's young assistant, always came in to carry the things out. Gerasim was a clean, fresh peasant lad, grown stout on town food and always cheerful and bright. At first the sight of him, in his clean Russian peasant costume, engaged on that disgusting task embarrassed Ivan Ilych.

Once when he got up from the commode too weak to draw up his trousers, he dropped into a soft armchair and looked with horror at his bare, enfeebled thighs with the muscles so sharply marked on them.

Gerasim with a firm light tread, his heavy boots emitting a pleasant smell of tar and fresh winter air, came in wearing a clean Hessian apron, the sleeves of his print shirt tucked up over his strong bare young arms; and refraining from looking at his sick master out of consideration for his feelings, and restraining the joy of life that beamed from his face, went up to the commode.

"Gerasim!" said Ivan Ilych in a weak voice.

Gerasim started, evidently afraid he might have committed some blunder, and with a rapid movement turned his fresh, kind, simple young face which just showed the first downy signs of a beard.

"Yes, sir?"

"That must be very unpleasant for you. You must forgive me. I am helpless."

"Oh, why, sir," and Gerasim's eyes beamed and he showed his glistening white teeth, "what's a little trouble? It's a case of illness with you, sir."

And his deft strong hands did their accustomed task, and he went out of the room stepping lightly. Five minutes later he as lightly returned.

Ivan Ilych was still sitting in the same position in the armchair.

"Gerasim," he said when the latter had replaced the freshly-washed utensil. "Please come here and help me." Gerasim went up to him. "Lift me up. It is hard for me to get up, and I have sent Dmitri away."

Gerasim went up to him, grasped his master with his strong arms deftly but gently, in the same way that he stepped—lifted him, supported him with one hand, and with the other drew up his trousers and would have set him down again, but Ivan Ilych asked to be led to the sofa. Gerasim, without an effort and without apparent pressure, led him, almost lifting him, to the sofa and placed him on it.

"Thank you. How easily and well you do it all!"

Gerasim smiled again and turned to leave the room. But Ivan Ilych felt his presence such a comfort that he did not want to let him go.

"One thing more, please move up that chair. No, the other one—under my feet. It is easier for me when my feet are raised."

Gerasim brought the chair, set it down gently in place, and raised Ivan Ilych's legs on to it. It seemed to Ivan Ilych that he felt better while Gerasim was holding up his legs.

"It's better when my legs are higher," he said. "Place that cushion under them."

Gerasim did so. He again lifted the legs and placed them, and again Ivan Ilych felt better while Gerasim held his legs. When he set them down Ivan Ilych fancied he felt worse.

"Gerasim," he said. "Are you busy now?"

"Not at all, sir," said Gerasim, who had learnt from the townsfolk how to speak to gentlefolk.

"What have you still to do?"

"What have I to do? I've done everything except chopping the logs for tomorrow."

"Then hold my legs up a bit higher, can you?"

"Of course I can. Why not?" And Gerasim raised his master's legs higher and Ivan Ilych thought that in that position he did not feel any pain at all.

"And how about the logs?"

"Don't trouble about that, sir. There's plenty of time."

Ivan Ilych told Gerasim to sit down and hold his legs, and began to talk to him. And strange to say it seemed to him that he felt better while Gerasim held his legs up.

After that Ivan Ilych would sometimes call Gerasim and get him to hold his legs on his shoulders, and he liked talking to him. Gerasim did it all easily, willingly, simply, and with a good nature that touched Ivan Ilych. Health, strength, and vitality in other people were offensive to him, but Gerasim's strength and vitality did not mortify but soothed him.

What tormented Ivan Ilych most was the deception, the lie, which for some reason they all accepted, that he was not dying but was simply ill, and that he only need keep quiet and undergo a treatment and then something very good would result. He however knew that do what they would nothing would come of it, only still more agonizing suffering and death. This deception tortured him—their not wishing to admit what they all knew and what he knew, but wanting to lie to him concerning his terrible condition, and wishing and forcing him to participate in that lie. Those lies—lies enacted over him on the eve of his death and destined to degrade this awful, solemn act to the level of their visitings, their curtains, their sturgeon for dinner—were a terrible agony for Ivan Ilych. And strangely enough, many times when they were going through their antics over him he had been within a hairbreadth of calling out to them: "Stop lying! You know and I know that I am dying. Then at least stop lying about it!" But he had never had the spirit to do it. The awful, terrible act of his dying was, he could see, reduced by those about him to the level of a casual, unpleasant, and almost indecorous incident (as if someone entered a drawing-room diffusing an unpleasant odour) and this was done by that very decorum which he had served all his life long. He saw that no one felt for him, because no one even wished to grasp his position. Only Gerasim recognized it and pitied him. And so Ivan Ilych felt at ease only with him. He felt comforted when Gerasim supported his legs (sometimes all night long) and refused to go to bed, saying: "Don't you worry, Ivan Ilych. I'll get sleep enough later on," or when he suddenly became familiar and exclaimed: "If you weren't sick it would be another matter, but as it is, why should I grudge a little trouble?" Gerasim alone did not lie; everything showed that he alone understood the facts of the case and did not consider it necessary to disguise them, but simply felt sorry for his emaciated and enfeebled master. Once when Ivan Ilych was sending him away he even said straight out: "We shall all of us die, so why should I grudge a little trouble?"—expressing the fact that he did not think his work burdensome, because he was doing it for a dying man and hoped someone would do the same for him when his time came.

Apart from this lying, or because of it, what most tormented Ivan Ilych was that no one pitied him as he wished to be pitied. At certain moments after prolonged suffering he wished most of all (though he would have been ashamed to confess it) for someone to pity him as a sick child is pitied. He longed to be petted and comforted. He knew he was an important functionary, that he had a beard turning grey, and that therefore what he longed for was impossible, but still he longed for it. And in Gerasim's attitude towards him there was something akin to what he wished for, and so that attitude comforted him. Ivan Ilych wanted to weep, wanted to be petted and cried over, and then his colleague Shebek would come, and instead of weeping and being petted, Ivan Ilych would assume a serious, severe, and profound air, and by force of habit would express his opinion on a decision of the Court of Cassation and would stubbornly insist on that view. This falsity around him and within him did more than anything else to poison his last days.

8

It was morning. He knew it was morning because Gerasim had gone, and Peter the footman had come and put out the candles, drawn back one of the curtains, and begun quietly to tidy up. Whether it was morning or evening, Friday or Sunday, made no difference, it was all just the same: the gnawing, unmitigated, agonizing pain, never ceasing for an instant, the consciousness of life inexorably waning but not yet extinguished, that approach of that ever dreaded and hateful Death which was the only reality, and always the same falsity. What were days, weeks, hours, in such a case?

"Will you have some tea, sir?"

"He wants things to be regular, and wishes the gentlefolk to drink tea in the morning," thought Ivan Ilych, and only said "No."

"Wouldn't you like to move onto the sofa, sir?"

"He wants to tidy up the room, and I'm in the way. I am uncleanliness and disorder," he thought, and said only:

"No, leave me alone."

The man went on bustling about. Ivan Ilych stretched out his hand. Peter came up, ready to help.

"What is it, sir?"

"My watch."

Peter took the watch which was close at hand and gave it to his master.

"Half-past eight. Are they up?"

"No sir, except Vladimir Ivanich" (the son) "who has gone to school. Praskovya Fedorovna ordered me to wake her if you asked for her. Shall I do so?"

"No, there's no need to." "Perhaps I'd better have some tea," he thought, and added aloud: "Yes, bring me some tea."

Peter went to the door but Ivan Ilych dreaded being left alone. "How can I keep him here? Oh yes, my medicine." "Peter, give me my medicine." "Why not? Perhaps it may still do me some good." He took a spoonful and swallowed it. "No, it won't help. It's all tomfoolery, all deception," he decided as soon as he became aware of the familiar, sickly, hopeless taste. "No, I can't believe in it any longer. But the pain, why this pain? If it would only cease just for a moment!" And he moaned. Peter turned towards him. "It's all right. Go and fetch me some tea."

Peter went out. Left alone Ivan Ilych groaned not so much with pain, terrible though that was, as from mental anguish. Always and for ever the same, always these endless days and nights. If only it would come quicker! If only *what* would come quicker? Death, darkness? . . . No, no! Anything rather than death!

When Peter returned with the tea on a tray, Ivan Ilych stared at him for a time in perplexity, not realizing who and what he was. Peter was disconcerted by that look and his embarrassment brought Ivan Ilych to himself.

"Oh, tea! All right, put it down. Only help me to wash and put on a clean shirt."

And Ivan Ilych began to wash. With pauses for rest, he washed his hands and then his face, cleaned his teeth, brushed his hair, and looked in the glass. He was terrified by what he saw, especially by the limp way in which his hair clung to his pallid forehead.

While his shirt was being changed he knew that he would be still more frightened at the sight of his body, so he avoided looking at it. Finally he was ready. He drew on a dressing-gown, wrapped himself in a plaid, and sat down in the armchair to take his tea. For a moment he felt refreshed, but as soon as he began to drink the tea he was again aware of the same taste, and the pain also returned. He finished it with an effort, and then lay down stretching out his legs, and dismissed Peter.

Always the same. Now a spark of hope flashes up, then a sea of despair rages, and always pain; always pain, always despair, and always the same. When alone he had a dreadful and distressing desire to call someone, but he knew beforehand that with others present it would be still worse. "Another dose of morphine—to lose consciousness. I will tell him, the doctor, that he must think of something else. It's impossible, impossible, to go on like this."

An hour and another pass like that. But now there is a ring at the door bell. Perhaps it's the doctor? It is. He comes in fresh, hearty, plump, and cheerful, with that look on his face that seems to say: "There now, you're in a panic about something, but we'll arrange it all for you directly!" The doctor knows this expression is out of place here, but he has put it on once for all and can't take it off—like a man who has put on a frock-coat in the morning to pay a round of calls.

The doctor rubs his hands vigorously and reassuringly.

"Brr! How cold it is! There's such a sharp frost; just let me warm myself!" he says, as if it were only a matter of waiting till he was warm, and then he would put everything right.

"Well now, how are you?"

Ivan Ilych feels that the doctor would like to say: "Well, how are our affairs?" but that even he feels that this would not do, and says instead: "What sort of a night have you had?"

Ivan Ilych looks at him as much as to say: "Are you really never ashamed of lying?" But the doctor does not wish to understand this question, and Ivan Ilych says: "Just as terrible as ever. The pain never leaves me and never subsides. If only something . . ."

"Yes, you sick people are always like that . . . There, now I think I am warm enough. Even Praskovya Fedorovna, who is so particular, could find no fault with my temperature. Well, now I can say good-morning," and the doctor presses his patient's hand.

Then, dropping his former playfulness, he begins with a most serious face to examine the patient, feeling his pulse and taking his temperature, and then begins the sounding and auscultation.

Ivan Ilych knows quite well and definitely that all this is nonsense and pure deception, but when the doctor, getting down on his knee, leans over him, putting his ear first higher then lower, and performs various gymnastic movements over him with a significant expression on his face, Ivan Ilych submits to it all as he used to submit to the speeches of the lawyers, though he knew very well that they were all lying and why they were lying.

The doctor, kneeling on the sofa, is still sounding him when Praskovya Fedorovna's silk dress rustles at the door and she is heard scolding Peter for not having let her know of the doctor's arrival.

She comes in, kisses her husband, and at once proceeds to prove that she has been up a long time already, and only owing to a misunderstanding failed to be there when the doctor arrived.

Ivan Ilych looks at her, scans her all over, sets against her the whiteness and plumpness and cleanness of her hands and neck, the gloss of her hair, and the sparkle of her vivacious eye. He hates her with his whole soul. And the thrill of hatred he feels for her makes him suffer from her touch.

Her attitude towards him and his disease is still the same. Just as the doctor had adopted a certain relation to his patient which he could not abandon, so had she formed one towards him—that he was not doing something he ought to do and was himself to blame, and that she reproached him lovingly for this—and she could not now change that attitude.

"You see he doesn't listen to me and doesn't take his medicine at the proper time. And above all he lies in a position that is no doubt bad for him—with his legs up."

She described how he made Gerasim hold his legs up.

The doctor smiled with a contemptuous affability that said: "What's to be done? These sick people do have foolish fancies of that kind, but we must forgive them."

When the examination was over the doctor looked at his watch, and then Praskovya Fedorovna announced to Ivan Ilych that it was of course as he pleased, but she had sent to-day for a celebrated specialist who would examine him and have a consultation with Michael Danilovich (their regular doctor).

"Please don't raise any objections. I am doing this for my own sake," she said ironically, letting it be felt that she was doing it all for his sake and only said that to leave him no right to refuse. He remained silent, knitting his brows. He felt that he was so surrounded and involved in a mesh of falsity that it was hard to unravel anything.

Everything she did for him was entirely for her own sake, and she told him she was doing for herself what she actually was doing for herself, as if that was so incredible that he must understand the opposite.

At half-past eleven the celebrated specialist arrived. Again the sounding began and the significant conversations in his presence and in another room, about the kidneys and the appendix, and the questions and answers, with such an air of importance that again, instead of the real question of life and death which now alone confronted him, the question arose of the kidney and appendix which were not behaving as they ought to and would now be attacked by Michael Danilovich and the specialist and forced to amend their ways.

The celebrated specialist took leave of him with a serious though not hopeless look, and in reply to the timid question Ivan Ilych, with eyes glistening with fear and hope, put to him as to whether there was a chance of recovery, said that he could not vouch for it but there was a possibility. The look of hope with which Ivan Ilych watched the doctor out was so pathetic that Praskovya Fedorovna, seeing it, even wept as she left the room to hand the doctor his fee.

The gleam of hope kindled by the doctor's encouragement did not last long. The same room, the same pictures, curtains, wall-paper, medicine bottles, were all there, and the same aching suffering body, and Ivan Ilych began to moan. They gave him a subcutaneous injection and he sank into oblivion.

It was twilight when he came to. They brought him his dinner and he swallowed some beef tea with difficulty, and then everything was the same again and night was coming on.

After dinner, at seven o'clock, Praskovya Fedorovna came into the room in evening dress, her full bosom pushed up by her corset, and with traces of powder on her face. She had reminded him in the morning that they were going to the theatre. Sarah Bernhardt was visiting the town and they had a box, which he had insisted on their taking. Now he had forgotten about it and her toilet offended him, but he concealed his vexation when he remembered that he had himself insisted on their securing a box and going because it would be an instructive and aesthetic pleasure for the children.

Praskovya Fedorovna came in, self-satisfied but yet with a rather guilty air. She sat down and asked how he was but, as he saw, only for the sake of asking and not in order to learn about it, knowing that there was nothing to learn—and then went on to what she really wanted to say: that she would not on any account have gone but that the box had been taken and Helen and their daughter were going, as well as Petrishchev (the examining magistrate, their daughter's fiancé) and that it was out of the question to let them go alone; but that she would have much preferred to sit with him for a while; and he must be sure to follow the doctor's orders while she was away.

"Oh and Fedor Petrovich" (the fiancé) "would like to come in. May he? And Lisa?"

"All right."

Their daughter came in in full evening dress, her fresh young flesh exposed (making a show of that very flesh which in his own case caused so much suffering), strong, healthy, evidently in love, and impatient with illness, suffering, and death, because they interfered with her happiness.

Fedor Petrovich came in too, in evening dress, his hair curled *à la Capoul*, a tight stiff collar round his long sinewy neck, an enormous white shirt-front and narrow black trousers tightly stretched over his strong thighs. He had one white glove tightly drawn on, and was holding his opera hat in his hand.

Following him the schoolboy crept in unnoticed, in a new uniform, poor little fellow, and wearing gloves. Terribly dark shadows showed under his eyes, the meaning of which Ivan Ilych knew well.

His son had always seemed pathetic to him, and now it was dreadful to see the boy's frightened look of pity. It seemed to Ivan Ilych that Vasya was the only one besides Gerasim who understood and pitied him.

They all sat down and again asked how he was. A silence followed. Lisa asked her mother about the opera-glasses, and there was an altercation between mother and daughter as to who had taken them and where they had been put. This occasioned some unpleasantness.

Fedor Petrovich inquired of Ivan Ilych whether he had ever seen Sarah Bernhardt. Ivan Ilych did not at first catch the question, but then replied: "No, have you seen her before?"

"Yes, in *Adrienne Lecouvreur.*"

Praskovya Fedorovna mentioned some roles in which Sarah Bernhardt was particularly good. Her daughter disagreed. Conversation sprang up as to the elegance and realism of her acting—the sort of conversation that is always repeated and is always the same.

In the midst of the conversation Fedor Petrovich glanced at Ivan Ilych and became silent. The other also looked at him and grew silent. Ivan Ilych was staring with glittering eyes straight before him, evidently indignant with them. This had to be rectified, but it was impossible to do so. The silence had to be broken, but for a time no one dared to break it and they all became afraid that the conventional deception would suddenly become obvious and the truth become plain to all. Lisa was the first to pluck up courage and break that silence, but by trying to hide what everybody was feeling, she betrayed it.

"Well, if we are going it's time to start," she said, looking at her watch, a present from her father, and with a faint and significant smile at Fedor Petrovich relating to something known only to them. She got up with a rustle of her dress.

They all rose, said good-night, and went away.

When they had gone it seemed to Ivan Ilych that he felt better; the falsity had gone with them. But the pain remained—that same pain and that same fear that made everything monotonously alike, nothing harder and nothing easier. Everything was worse.

Again minute followed minute and hour followed hour. Everything remained the same and there was no cessation. And the inevitable end of it all became more and more terrible.

"Yes, send Gerasim here," he replied to a question Peter asked.

9

His wife returned late at night. She came in on tiptoe, but he heard her, opened his eyes, and made haste to close them again. She wished to send Gerasim away and to sit with him herself, but he opened his eyes and said: "No, go away."

"Are you in great pain?"

"Always the same."

"Take some opium."

He agreed and took some. She went away.

Till about three in the morning he was in a state of stupefied misery. It seemed to him that he and pain were being thrust into a narrow, deep black sack, but though they were pushed further and further in they could not be pushed to the bottom. And this, terrible enough in itself, was accompanied by suffering. He was frightened yet wanted to fall through the sack, he struggled but yet co-operated. And suddenly he broke through, fell, and regained consciousness. Gerasim was sitting at the foot of the bed dozing quietly and patiently, while he himself lay with his emaciated stockinged legs resting on Gerasim's shoulders; the same shaded candle was there and the same unceasing pain.

"Go away, Gerasim." he whispered.

"It's all right, sir. I'll stay a while."

"No. Go away."

He removed his legs from Gerasim's shoulders, turned sideways onto his arm, and felt sorry for himself. He only waited till Gerasim had gone into the next room and then restrained himself no longer but wept like a child. He wept on account of his helplessness, his terrible loneliness, the cruelty of man, the cruelty of God, and the absence of God.

"Why hast Thou done all this? Why hast Thou brought me here? Why, why dost Thou torment me so terribly?"

He did not expect an answer and yet wept because there was no answer and could be none. The pain again grew more acute, but he did not stir and did not call. He said to himself: "Go on! Strike me! But what is it for? What have I done to Thee? What is it for?"

Then he grew quiet and not only ceased weeping but even held his breath and became all attention. It was as though he were listening not to an audible voice but to the voice of his soul, to the current of thoughts arising within him.

"What is it you want?" was the first clear conception capable of expression in words, that he heard.

"What do you want? What do you want?" he repeated to himself.

"What do I want? To live and not to suffer," he answered.

And again he listened with such concentrated attention that even his pain did not distract him.

"To live? How?" asked his inner voice.

"Why, to live as I used to—well and pleasantly."

"As you lived before, well and pleasantly?" the voice repeated.

And in imagination he began to recall the best moments of his pleasant life. But strange to say none of these best moments of his pleasant life now seemed at all what they had then seemed—none of them except the first recollections of childhood. There, in childhood, there had been something really pleasant with which it would be possible to live if it could return. But the child who had experienced that happiness existed no longer, it was like a reminiscense of somebody else.

As soon as the period began which had produced the present Ivan Ilych, all that had then seemed joys now melted before his sight and turned into something trivial and often nasty.

And the further he departed from childhood and the nearer he came to the present the more worthless and doubtful were the joys. This began with the School of Law. A little that was really good was still found there—there was light-heartedness, friendship, and hope. But in the upper classes there had already been fewer of such good moments. Then during the first years of his official career, when he was in the service of the Governor, some pleasant moments again occurred: they were the memories of love for a woman. Then all became confused and there was still less of what was good; later on again there was still less that was good, and the further he went the less there was. His marriage, a mere accident, then the disenchantment that followed it, his wife's bad breath and the sensuality and hypocrisy: then that deadly official life and those preoccupations about money, a year of it, and two, and ten, and twenty, and always the same thing. And the longer it lasted the more deadly it became. "It is as if I had been going downhill while I imagined I was going up. And that is really what it was. I was going up in public opinion, but to the same extent life was ebbing away from me. And now it is all done and there is only death."

"Then what does it mean? Why? It can't be that life is so senseless and horrible. But if it really has been so horrible and senseless, why must I die and die in agony? There is something wrong!"

Maybe I did not live as I ought to have done," it suddenly occurred to him. "But how could that be, when I did everything properly?" he replied, and immediately dismissed from his mind this, the sole solution of all the riddles of life and death, as something quite impossible.

"Then what do you want now? To live? Live how? Live as you lived in the law courts when the usher proclaimed 'The judge is coming!' " "The judge is coming, the judge!" he repeated to himself. "Here he is, the judge. But I am not guilty!" he exclaimed angrily. "What is it for?" And he ceased crying, but turning his face to the wall continued to ponder on the same question: Why, and for what purpose, is there all this horror? But however much he pondered he found no answer. And whenever the thought occurred to him, as often as it often did, that it all resulted from his not having lived as he ought to have done, he at once recalled the correctness of his whole life and dismissed so strange an idea.

10

Another fortnight passed. Ivan Ilych now no longer left his sofa. He would not lie in bed but lay on the sofa, facing the wall nearly all the time. He suffered ever the same unceasing agonies and in his loneliness pondered always on the same insoluble question: "What is this? Can it be that it is Death?" And the inner voice answered: "Yes, it is Death."

"Why these sufferings?" And the voice answered, "For no reason—they just are so." Beyond and besides this there was nothing.

From the very beginning of his illness, ever since he had first been to see the doctor, Ivan Ilych's life had been divided between two contrary and alternating moods: now it was despair and the expectation of this uncomprehended and terrible death, and now hope and intently interested observation of the functioning of his organs. Now before his eyes there was only a kidney or an intestine that temporarily evaded its duty, and now only that incomprehensible and dreadful from which it was impossible to escape.

These two states of mind had alternated from the very beginning of his illness, but the further it progressed the more doubtful and fantastic became the conception of the kidney, and the more real the sense of impending death.

He had but to call to mind what he had been three months before and what he was now, to call to mind with what regularity he had been going downhill, for every possibility of hope to be shattered.

Latterly during that loneliness in which he found himself as he lay facing the back of the sofa, a loneliness in the midst of a populous town and surrounded by numerous acquaintances and relations but that yet could not have been more complete anywhere—either at the bottom of the sea or under the earth—during that terrible loneliness Ivan Ilych had lived only in memories of the past. Pictures of his past rose before him one after another. They always began with what was nearest in time and then went back to what was more remote—to his childhood—and rested there. If he thought of the stewed prunes that had been offered him that day, his mind went back to the raw shrivelled French plums of his childhood, their peculiar flavour and the flow of saliva when he sucked their stones, and along with the memory of that taste came a whole series of memories of those days: his nurse, his brother, and their toys. "No, I mustn't think of that. . . . It is too painful," Ivan Ilych said to himself, and brought himself back to the present—to the bottom of the back of the sofa and the creases in its morocco. "Morocco is expensive, but it does not wear well: There had been a quarrel about it. It was a different kind of quarrel and a different kind of morocco that time when we tore father's portfolio and were punished, and mama brought us some tarts. . . . " And again his thoughts dwelt on his childhood, and again it was painful and he tried to banish them and fix his mind on something else.

Then again together with that chain of memories another series passed through his mind—of how his illness had progressed and grown worse. There also the further back he looked the more life there had been. There had been more of what was good in life and more of life itself. The two merged together. "Just as the pain went on getting worse and worse so my life grew worse and worse," he thought. "There is one bright spot there at the back, at the beginning of life, and afterwards all becomes blacker and blacker and proceeds more and more rapidly—in inverse ratio to the square of the distance from death," thought Ivan Ilych. And the example of a stone falling downwards with increasing velocity entered his mind. Life, a series of increasing sufferings, flies, further and further towards its end—the most terrible suffering. "I am flying. . . . " He shuddered, shifted himself, and tried to resist, but was already aware that resistance was impossible, and again with eyes weary of gazing but unable to cease seeing what was before them, he stared at the back of the sofa and waited—awaiting the dreadful fall and shock and destruction.

"Resistance is impossible!" he said to himself. "If I could only understand what it is all for! But that too is impossible. An explanation would be possible if it could be said that I have not lived as I ought to. But it is impossible to say that," and he remembered all the legality, correctitude, and propriety of his life. "That at any rate can certainly not be admitted," he thought, and his lips smiled ironically as if someone could see that smile and be taken in by it. "There is no explanation! agony, death. . . . What for?"

11

Another two weeks went by in this way and during that fortnight an event occurred that Ivan Ilych and his wife had desired. Petrishchev formally proposed. It happened in the evening. The next day Praskovya Fedorovna came into her husband's room considering how best to inform him of it, but that very night there had been a fresh change for the worse in his condition. She found him still lying on the sofa but in a different position. He lay on his back, groaning and staring fixedly straight in front of him.

She began to remind him of his medicines, but he turned his eyes towards her with such a look that she did not finish what she was saying; so great an animosity, to her in particular, did that look express.

"For Christ's sake, let me die in peace!" he said.

She would have gone away, but just then their daughter came in and went up to say good morning. He looked at her as he had done at his wife, and in reply to her inquiry about his health said dryly that he would soon free them all of himself. They were both silent and after sitting with him for a while went away.

"Is it our fault?" Lisa said to her mother. "It's as if we were to blame! I am sorry for papa, but why should we be tortured?"

The doctor came at his usual time. Ivan Ilych answered "Yes" and "No," never taking his angry eyes from him, and at last said: "You know you can do nothing for me, so leave me alone."

"We can ease your sufferings."

"You can't even do that. Let me be."

The doctor went into the drawing-room and told Praskovya Fedorovna that the case was very serious and that the only resource left was opium to allay her husband's sufferings, which must be terrible.

It was true, as the doctor said, that Ivan Ilych's physical sufferings were terrible, but worse than the physical sufferings were his mental sufferings which were his chief torture.

His mental sufferings were due to the fact that that night, as he looked at Gerasim's sleepy, good-natured face with its prominent cheek-bones, the question suddenly occurred to him: "What if my whole life has really been wrong?"

It occurred to him that what had appeared perfectly impossible before, namely that he had not spent his life as he could have done, might after all be true. It occurred to him that his scarcely perceptible attempts to struggle against what was considered good by the most highly placed people, those scarcely noticeable impulses which he had immediately suppressed, might have been the real thing, and all the rest false. And his professional duties and the whole arrangement of his life and of his family, and all his social and official interests, might all have been false. He tried to defend all those things to himself and suddenly felt the weakness of what he was defending. There was nothing to defend.

"But if that is so," he said to himself, "and I am leaving this life with the consciousness that I have lost all that was given me and it is impossible to rectify it—what then?"

He lay on his back and began to pass his life in review in quite a new way. In the morning when he saw first his footman, then his wife, then his daughter, and then the doctor, their every word and movement confirmed to him the awful truth that had been revealed to him during the night. In them he saw himself—all that for which he had lived—and saw clearly that it was not real at all, but a terrible and huge deception which had hidden both life and death. This consciousness intensified his physical suffering tenfold. He groaned and tossed about, and pulled at his clothing which choked and stifled him. And he hated them on that account.

He was given a large dose of opium and became unconscious, but at noon his sufferings began again. He drove everybody away and tossed from side to side.

His wife came to him and said:

"Jean, my dear, do this for me. It can't do any harm and often helps. Healthy people often do it."

He opened his eyes wide.

"What? Take communion? Why? It's unnecessary! However. . . . "

She began to cry.

"Yes, do, my dear. I'll send for our priest. He is such a nice man."

"All right. Very well," he muttered.

When the priest came and heard his confession, Ivan Ilych was softened and seemed to feel a relief from his doubts and consequently from his sufferings, and for a moment there came a ray of hope. He again began to think of the vermiform appendix and the possibility of correcting it. He received the sacrament with tears in his eyes.

When they laid him down again afterwards he felt a moment's ease, and the hope that he might live awoke him again. He began to think of the operation that had been suggested to him. "To live! I want to live!" he said to himself.

His wife came in to congratulate him after his communion, and when uttering the usual conventional words she added:

"You feel better, don't you?"

Without looking at her he said "Yes."

Her dress, her figure, the expression of her face, the tone of her voice, all revealed the same thing. "This is wrong, it is not as it should be. All you have lived for and still live for is falsehood and deception, hiding life and death from you." And as soon as he admitted that thought, his hatred and his agonizing physical suffering again sprang up, and with that suffering a consciousness of the unavoidable, approaching end. And to this was added a new sensation of grinding shooting pain and a feeling of suffocation.

The expression of his face when he uttered that "yes" was dreadful. Having uttered it, he looked her straight in the eyes, turned on his face with a rapidity extraordinary in his weak state and shouted:

"Go away! go away and leave me alone!"

12

From that moment the screaming began that continued for three days, and was so terrible that one could not hear it through two closed doors without horror. At the moment he answered his wife he realized that he was lost, that there was no return, that the end had come, the very end, and his doubts were still unsolved and remained doubts.

"Oh! Oh! Oh!" he cried in various intonations. He had begun by screaming "I won't!" and continued screaming on the letter "o."

For three whole days, during which time did not exist for him, he struggled in that black sack into which he was being thrust by an invisible, resistless force. He struggled as a man condemned to death struggles in the hands of the executioner, knowing that he cannot save himself. And every moment he felt that despite all his efforts he was drawing nearer and nearer to what terrified him. He felt that his agony was due to his being thrust into that black hole and still more to his not being able to get right into it. He was hindered from getting into it by his conviction that his life had been a good one. That very justification of his life held him fast and prevented his moving forward, and it caused him most torment of all.

Suddenly some force struck him in the chest and side, making it still harder to breathe, and he fell through the hole and there at the bottom was a light. What had happened to him was like the sensation one sometimes experiences in a railway carriage when one thinks one is going backwards while one is really going forwards and suddenly becomes aware of the real direction.

"Yes, it was all not the right thing," he said to himself, "but that's no matter. It can be done. But what *is* the right thing?" he asked himself, and suddenly grew quiet.

This occurred at the end of the third day, two hours before his death. Just then his schoolboy son had crept softly in and gone up to the bedside. The dying man was still screaming desperately and waving his arms. His hand fell on the boy's head, and the boy caught it, pressed it to his lips, and began to cry.

At that very moment Ivan Ilych fell through and caught sight of the light, and it was revealed to him that though his life had not been what it should have been, this could still be rectified. He asked himself, "What *is* the right thing?" and grew still, listening. Then he felt that someone was kissing his hand. He opened his eyes, looked at his son, and felt sorry for him. His wife came up to him and he glanced at her. She was gazing at him open-mouthed, with undried tears on her nose and cheek and a despairing look on her face. He felt sorry for her too.

"Yes, I am making them wretched," he thought. "They are sorry, but it will be better for them when I die." He wished to say this but had not the strength to utter it. "Besides, why speak? I must act," he thought. With a look at his wife he indicated his son and said: Take him away . . . sorry for him . . . sorry for you too. . . . " He tried to add, "forgive me," but said "forego" and waved his hand, knowing that He whose understanding mattered would understand.

And suddenly it grew clear to him that what had been oppressing him and would not leave him was all dropping away at once from two sides, from ten sides, and from all sides. He was sorry for them, he must act so as not to hurt them: release them and free himself from these sufferings. "How good and how simple!" he thought. "And the pain?" he asked himself. "What has become of it? Where are you, pain?"

He turned his attention to it.

"Yes, here it is. Well, what of it? Let the pain be."

"And death . . . where is it?"

He sought his former accustomed fear of death and did not find it. "Where is it? What death?" There was no fear because there was no death.

In place of death there was light.

"So that's what it is!" he suddenly exclaimed aloud. "What joy!"

To him all this happened in a single instant, and the meaning of that instant did not change. For those present his agony continued for another two hours. Something rattled in his throat, his emaciated body twitched, then the gasping and rattle became less and less frequent.

"It is finished!" said someone near him.

He heard these words and repeated them in his soul.

"Death is finished," he said to himself. "It is no more!"

He drew in a breath, stopped in the midst of a sigh, stretched out, and died.

Questions

1. How does the opening section of the story shape your view of Ivan Ilych? Why does Tolstoy show us how Ivan's colleagues and family react to his death?
2. What qualities does Tolstoy stress in Peter Ivanovich? What do Peter's thoughts and acts in Ivan Ilych's house tell you about him? How different would the opening section be if Tolstoy had omitted Peter Ivanovich?
3. Would the story be different in its effect or its meaning if Tolstoy had omitted the opening section?
4. What qualities of Ivan Ilych's life does Tolstoy show to have been "ordinary" in his life up to his marriage?
5. Why is Ivan's marriage unhappy before his coming to St. Petersburg? Does Ivan's marriage change his character or outlook? What changes do we see in Ivan after his appointment to a position in the Department of Justice?
6. What does Ivan have in common with the doctor who first examines him? What point is Tolstoy making in noting this resemblance?

7. To what qualities and attitudes in others does Ivan become sensitive at the beginning of his illness? Is Tolstoy suggesting in these scenes that Ivan is becoming a better person than he was? Or is Ivan the same person?
8. What effect does the illness have upon Ivan in its later stages? Does Ivan become more perceptive or thoughtful or sympathetic toward his wife, family, and servants? Or is Ivan only absorbed in his illness?
9. Why does it matter to Ivan that everyone except Gerasim lies to him and refuses to acknowledge that he is dying? Does Gerasim make Ivan less self-absorbed and give him insight into his character?
10. Why does Ivan's dialogue with "the voice of his soul" not end his pain? When does the pain disappear?
11. What is the light that Ivan finds before he dies? Has he found the answer to the questions that tortured him earlier? Is there a change of character in these final moments?
12. What is the meaning of Ivan's life and death? Is Tolstoy making a statement about people through a character symbolic of all people, or is he telling the story about a single person whose life was merely ordinary?

Suggestions for Writing

1. Discuss how you discover Tolstoy's attitude toward Ivan and his world in the course of the story.
2. Discuss how you discover Tolstoy's values—how he viewed his world, what he believes people should live for.
3. Discuss what the story suggests about Tolstoy's view of doctors and lawyers.

Additional Reading

Crankshaw, Edward. *Tolstoy: The Making of the Novelist.* New York: Viking, 1974.

Simmons, Ernest J. *Leo Tolstoy.* Boston: Little, Brown, 1946.

Tolstoy, Leo. *Anna Karenina.* Trans. Louise and Aylmer Maude. London: Oxford University Press, 1973.

———. *The Death of Ivan Ilych and Other Stories.* Trans. Michael Scammell. New York: McGraw-Hill, 1964.

———. *Resurrection.* Trans. Rosemary Edmonds. Baltimore: Penguin, 1966.

———. *War and Peace.* Trans. Louise and Aylmer Maude. London: Oxford University Press, 1922–23.

Troyat, Henri. *Tolstoy.* Garden City, N.Y.: Doubleday, 1967.

Wasiolek, Edward. *Tolstoy's Major Fiction.* Chicago: University of Chicago Press, 1978.

PEOPLE AND STEREOTYPES

*T*he sacredness of the individual is an idea that we prize; it is considered integral to American democracy. It is also an idea that has had particular importance in recent social and political controversies. The Holocaust of the Second World War and other recent horrors have shown the consequences of thinking of people collectively as members of religious, ethnic, or racial groups—sometimes thought dangerous enough to segregate or exterminate.

At the same time, our consciousness of stereotypes is inconstant and highly selective. Blacks and other minorities remind us that stereotypes existed before this century, and that they killed the mind and spirit as well as the body then as they do today. Many Americans still know few if any of the facts of slavery in the United States, of the legal restrictions that governed women until recent times, of the conditions under which the Irish and other immigrants lived in past years, and of the discrimination that Hispanics and other recent immigrants suffer today in the United States. Today many people see and treat Jews or blacks or women or Hispanics as persons, but other people do not.

The essays and stories in this section explore from very different perspectives the causes and the consequences of stereotyping people. The readings begin with Mary Wollstonecraft, who wrote about the education of women at the end of the eighteenth century. Stephen Jay Gould writes about racial classifications from the perspective of twentieth-century physical anthropology. Martin Luther King, Jr., addresses the issue of segregation in the South of the early 1960s. Eudora Welty and Wright Morris write fictionally about the end of segregation and continuing racial conflict in the South and the Middle West. This section focuses on three minorities only—women, blacks, and white southerners in a Northern city. But the issues raised affect other minorities equally, as the suggested readings show.

A Vindication of the Rights of Woman, Chapter 3

Mary Wollstonecraft

An early feminist and writer on education and women's rights, Mary Wollstonecraft (1759–1797) as a young woman supported herself by running a school. Later she worked as a governess to children of a nobleman and for a London publisher. In 1792, she left England to live in France, then at the height of revolution; Louis XVI and his wife, Marie Antoinette, would be guillotined during the Reign of Terror the following year. Wollstonecraft lived in Paris from 1793 to 1795 with an American, Gilbert Imlay, and a daughter was born to them in 1795. When Imlay proved to be unfaithful, Mary failed in an attempt at suicide and returned to London. She became a friend of Thomas Paine, William Blake, William Godwin, and other political and philosophical radicals of the time. She married Godwin, dying shortly after the birth of their daughter, Mary—the future wife of the poet Percy Bysshe Shelley and the author of the novel Frankenstein.

In A Vindication of the Rights of Woman, *written in 1792, Wollstonecraft argues for equality of education and attacks stereotypes of women. In an early chapter, she attacks the argument (repeated in Milton's* Paradise Lost) *that God created women as inferior in character and ability to men:*

> For if it be allowed that women were destined by Providence to acquire human virtues, and by the exercise of their understandings, that stability of character which is the firmest ground to rest our future hopes upon, they must be permitted to turn to the fountain of light, and not forced to shape their course by the twinkling of a mere satellite.

Later in the same chapter, she states her agreement with Rousseau on education, but with an important qualification:

> [T]he most perfect education, in my opinion, is such an exercise of the understanding as is best calculated to strengthen the body and form the heart. Or, in other words, to enable the individual to attain such habits of virtue as will render it independent. In fact, it is a farce to call any being virtuous whose virtues do not result from the exercise of its own reason. This was Rousseau's opinion respecting men: I extend it to women, and confidently assert that they have been drawn out of their sphere by false refinement, and not by an endeavor to acquire masculine qualities.

In the remainder of the chapter, Wollstonecraft examines the relations of men and women, and in the succeeding chapter—reprinted here— considers the effect on women of traditional stereotypes.

Bodily strength from being the distinction of heroes is now sunk into such un- 1
merited contempt that men, as well as women, seem to think it unnecessary; the latter,
as it takes from their feminine graces, and from that lovely weakness, the source of their
undue power; and the former, because it appears inimical to the character of a gentleman.

That they have both, by departing from one extreme run into another, may easily be proved; but first it may be proper to observe that a vulgar error has obtained a degree of credit, which has given force to a false conclusion, in which an effect has been
mistaken for a cause.

People of genius have very frequently impaired their constitutions by study or 2
careless inattention to their health, and the violence of their passions bearing a proportion to the vigour of their intellects, the sword's destroying the scabbard has become almost proverbial, and superficial observers have inferred from thence that men of genius
have commonly weak, or, to use a more fashionable phrase, delicate constitutions. Yet
the contrary, I believe, will appear to be the fact; for, on diligent inquiry, I find that
strength of mind has in most cases been accompanied by superior strength of body,—
natural soundness of constitution,—not that robust tone of nerves and vigour of muscles, which arise from bodily labour, when the mind is quiescent, or only directs the
hands.

Dr. Priestley has remarked, in the preface to his biographical chart, that the 3
majority of great men have lived beyond forty-five. And considering the thoughtless
manner in which they have lavished their strength when investigating a favourite science, they have wasted the lamp of life, forgetful of the midnight hour; or, when lost in
poetic dreams, fancy has peopled the scene, and the soul has been disturbed, till it shook
the constitution by the passions that meditation had raised,—whose objects, the base-
less fabric of a vision, faded before the exhausted eye,—they must have had iron frames.
Shakespeare never grasped the airy dagger with a nerveless hand, nor did Milton tremble when he led Satan far from the confines of his dreary prison. These were not the
ravings of imbecility, the sickly effusions of distempered brains, but the exuberance of
fancy, that "in a fine frenzy" wandering, was not continually reminded of its material
shackles.

I am aware that this argument would carry me further than it may be supposed 4
I wish to go; but I follow truth, and still adhering to my first position, I will allow that
bodily strength seems to give man a natural superiority over woman; and this is the only
solid basis on which the superiority of the sex can be built. But I still insist that not only
the virtue but the *knowledge* of the two sexes should be the same in nature, if not in
degree, and that women, considered not only as moral but rational creatures, ought to
endeavour to acquire human virtues (or perfections) by the *same* means as men, instead
of being educated like a fanciful kind of *half* being—one of Rousseau's wild chi-
meras.[1]

---

[1]"Researches into abstract and speculative truths, the principles and axioms of sciences,—in short, everything
which tends to generalise our ideas,—is not the proper province of women; their studies should be relative
to points of practice; it belongs to them to apply those principles which men have discovered; and it is their
part to make observations which direct men to the establishment of general principles. All the ideas of
women, which have not the immediate tendency to points of duty, should be directed to the study of men,

But if strength of body be with some show of reason the boast of men, why are women so infatuated as to be proud of a defect? Rousseau has furnished them with a plausible excuse, which could only have occurred to a man whose imagination had been allowed to run wild, and refine on the impressions made by exquisite senses; that they might forsooth have a pretext for yielding to a natural appetite without violating a romantic species of modesty, which gratifies the pride and libertinism of man.

Women, deluded by these sentiments, sometimes boast of their weakness, cunningly obtaining power by playing on the *weakness* of men; and they may well glory in their illicit sway, for like Turkish bashaws, they have more real power than their masters; but virtue is sacrificed to temporary gratifications, and the respectability of life to the triumph of an hour.

Women, as well as despots, have now perhaps more power than they would have if the world, divided and subdivided into kingdoms and families, were governed by laws deduced from the exercise of reason; but in obtaining it, to carry on the comparison, their character is degraded, and licentiousness spread through the whole aggregate of society. The many become pedestal to the few. I, therefore, will venture to assert that till women are more rationally educated, the progress of human virtue and improvement in knowledge must receive continual checks. And if it be granted that woman was not created merely to gratify the appetite of man, or to be the upper servant, who provides his meals and takes care of his linen, it must follow that the first care of those mothers or fathers who really attend to the education of females should be, if not to strengthen the body, at least not to destroy the constitution by mistaken notions of beauty and female excellence; nor should girls ever be allowed to imbibe the pernicious notion that a defect can, by any chemical process of reasoning, become an excellence. In this respect I am happy to find that the author of one of the most instructive books that our

and to the attainment of those agreeable accomplishments which have taste for their object; for as to works of genius, they are beyond their capacity; neither have they sufficient precision or power of attention to succeed in sciences which require accuracy; and as to physical knowledge, it belongs to those only who are most active, most inquisitive, who comprehend the greatest variety of objects; in short, it belongs to those who have the strongest powers, and who exercise them most, to judge the relations between sensible beings and the laws of nature. A woman who is naturally weak, and does not carry her ideas to any great extent, knows how to judge and make a proper estimate of those movements which she sets to work, in order to aid her weakness; and these movements are the passions of men. The mechanism she employs is much more powerful than ours, for all her levers move the human heart. She must have the skill to incline us to do everything which her sex will not enable her to do herself, and which is necessary or agreeable to her; therefore she ought to study the mind of man thoroughly, not the mind of man in general, abstractedly, but the dispositions of those men to whom she is subject either by the laws of her country or by the force of opinion. She should learn to penetrate into their real sentiments from their conversation, their actions, their looks and gestures. She should also have the art, by her own conversation, action, looks, and gestures, to communicate those sentiments which are agreeable to them, without seeming to intend it. Men will argue more philosophically about the human heart; but women will read the heart of men better than they. It belongs to women—if I may be allowed the expression—to form an experimental morality, and to reduce the study of man to a system. Women have most wit, men have most genius; women observe, men reason. From the concurrence of both we derive the clearest light and the most perfect knowledge which the human mind is of itself capable of attaining. In one word, from hence we acquire the most intimate acquaintance, both with ourselves and others, of which our nature is capable; and it is thus that art has a constant tendency to perfect those endowments which nature has bestowed. The world is the book of women."—ROUSSEAU's *Emilius.*

I hope my readers still remember the comparison which I have brought forward between women and officers. [Notes throughout are Wollstonecraft's] country has produced for children, coincides with me in opinion. I shall quote his pertinent remarks to give the force of his respectable authority to reason.[2]

But should it be proved that woman is naturally weaker than man, whence does 8 it follow that it is natural for her to labour to become still weaker than nature intended her to be? Arguments of this cast are an insult to common sense, and savour of passion. The *divine right* of husbands, like the divine right of kings, may, it is to be hoped, in this enlightened age, be contested without danger; and though conviction may not silence many boisterous disputants, yet, when any prevailing prejudice is attacked, the wise will consider, and leave the narrow-minded to rail with thoughtless vehemence at innovation.

The mother who wishes to give true dignity of character to her daughter must, 9 regardless of the sneers of ignorance, proceed on a plan diametrically opposite to that which Rousseau has recommended with all the deluding charms of eloquence and philosophical sophistry, for his eloquence renders absurdities plausible, and his dogmatic conclusions puzzle, without convincing, those who have not ability to refute them.

Throughout the whole animal kingdom every young creature requires almost 10 continual exercise, and the infancy of children, conformable to this intimation, should be passed in harmless gambols that exercise the feet and hands, without requiring very minute direction from the head, or the constant attention of a nurse. In fact, the care necessary for self-preservation is the first natural exercise of the understanding as little inventions to amuse the present moment unfold the imagination. But these wise designs of nature are counteracted by mistaken fondness or blind zeal. The child is not left a moment to its own direction—particularly a girl—and thus rendered dependent. Dependence is called natural.

To preserve personal beauty—woman's glory—the limbs and faculties are 11 cramped with worse than Chinese bands, and the sedentary life which they are condemned to live, whilst boys frolic in the open air, weakens the muscles and relaxes the

---

[2]"A respectable old man gives the following sensible account of the method he pursued when educating his daughter: 'I endeavoured to give both to her mind and body a degree of vigour which is seldom found in the female sex. As soon as she was sufficiently advanced in strength to be capable of the lighter labours of husbandry and gardening, I employed her as my constant companion. Selene—for that was her name—soon acquired a dexterity in all these rustic employments which I considered with equal pleasure and admiration. If women are in general feeble both in body and mind, it arises less from nature than from education. We encourage a vicious indolence and inactivity, which we falsely call delicacy. Instead of hardening their minds by the severer principles of reason and philosophy, we breed them to useless arts, which terminate in vanity and sensuality. In most of the countries which I had visited they are taught nothing of an higher nature than a few modulations of the voice, or useless postures of the body; their time is consumed in sloth or trifles, and trifles become the only pursuits capable of interesting them. We seem to forget that it is upon the qualities of the female sex that our own domestic comforts and the education of our children must depend. And what are the comforts or the education which a race of beings, corrupted from their infancy, and unacquainted with all the duties of life, are fitted to bestow? To touch a musical instrument with useless skill, to exhibit their natural or affected graces to the eyes of indolent and debauched young men, to dissipate their husband's patrimony in riotous and unnecessary expenses, these are the only arts cultivated by women in most of the polished nations I had seen. And the consequences are uniformly such as may be expected to proceed from such polluted sources—private misery and public servitude.

" 'But Selene's education was regulated by different views, and conducted upon severer principles—if that can be called severity which opens the mind to a sense of moral and religious duties, and most effectually arms it against the inevitable evils of life.' "—Mr. Day's *Sandford and Merton*, vol. iii.

nerves. As for Rousseau's remarks, which have since been echoed by several writers, that they have naturally, that is, from their birth, independent of education, a fondness for dolls, dressing, and talking, they are so puerile as not to merit a serious refutation. That a girl, condemned to sit for hours together listening to the idle chat of weak nurses, or to attend at her mother's toilet, will endeavor to join the conversation, is, indeed, very natural; and that she will imitate her mother or aunts, and amuse herself by adorning her lifeless doll, as they do in dressing her, poor innocent babe! is undoubtedly a most natural consequence. For men of the greatest abilities have seldom had sufficient strength to rise above the surrounding atmosphere; and if the pages of genius have always been blurred by the prejudices of the age, some allowance should be made for a sex, who, like kings, always sees things through a false medium.

Purposing these reflections, the fondness for dress, conspicuous in woman, 12 may be easily accounted for, without supposing it the result of a desire to please the sex on which they are dependent. The absurdity, in short, of supposing that a girl is naturally a coquette, and that a desire connected with the impulse of nature to propagate the species, should appear even before an improper education has, by heating the imagination, called it forth prematurely, is so unphilosophical, that such a sagacious observer as Rousseau would not have adopted it, if he had not been accustomed to make reason to give way to his desire of singularity, and truth to a favourite paradox.

Yet thus to give a sex to mind was not very consistent with the principles of a 13 man who argued so warmly, and so well, for the immortality of the soul. But what a weak barrier is truth when it stands in the way of an hypothesis! Rousseau respected—almost adored virtue—and yet he allowed himself to love with sensual fondness. His imagination constantly prepared inflammable fuel for his inflammable senses; but, in order to reconcile his respect for self-denial, fortitude, and those heroic virtues, which a mind like his could not cooly admire, he labours to invert the law of nature, and broaches a doctrine pregnant with mischief, and derogatory to the character of supreme wisdom.

His ridiculous stories, which tend to prove that girls are *naturally* attentive to 14 their persons, without laying any stress on daily example, are below contempt. And that a little miss should have such a correct taste as to neglect the pleasing amusement of making O's, merely because she perceived that it was an ungraceful attitude, should be selected with the anecdotes of the learned pig.[3]

I have, probably, had an opportunity of observing more girls in their infancy 15 than J. J. Rousseau. I can recollect my own feelings, and I have looked steadily around me; yet, so far from coinciding with him in opinion respecting the first dawn of the female character, I will venture to affirm, that a girl, whose spirits have not been damped by inactivity, or innocence tainted by false shame, will always be a romp, and the doll will never excite attention unless confinement allows her no alternative. Girls and boys,

---

[3]"I once knew a young person who learned to write before she learned to read, and began to write with her needle before she could use a pen. At first, indeed, she took it into her head to make no letter than the O: this letter she was constantly making of all sizes, and always the wrong way. Unluckily, one day, as she was intent on this employment, she happened to see herself in the looking-glass; when, taking a dislike to the constrained attitude in which she sat while writing, she threw away her pen, like another Pallas, and determined against making the O any more. Her brother was also equally averse to writing; it was the confinement however, and not the constrained attitude, that most disgusted him."—ROUSSEAU'S *Emilius.*

in short, would play harmlessly together, if the distinction of sex was not inculcated long before nature makes any difference. I will go further, and affirm, as an indisputable fact, that most of the women, in the circle of my observation, who have acted like rational creatures, or shown any vigour of intellect, have accidentally been allowed to run wild, as some of the elegant formers of the fair sex would insinuate.

The baneful consequences which flow from inattention to health during in- 16 fancy and youth, extend further than is supposed—dependence of body naturally produces dependence of mind; and how can she be a good wife or mother, the greater part of whose time is employed to guard against or endure sickness? Nor can it be expected that a woman will resolutely endeavour to strengthen her constitution and abstain from enervating indulgences, if artificial notions of beauty, and false descriptions of sensibility, have been early entangled with her motives of action. Most men are sometimes obliged to bear with bodily inconveniences, and to endure, occasionally, the inclemency of the elements; but genteel women are, literally speaking, slaves to their bodies, and glory in their subjection.

I once knew a weak woman of fashion, who was more than commonly proud 17 of her delicacy and sensibility. She thought a distinguishing taste and puny appetite the height of all human perfection, and acted accordingly. I have seen this weak sophisticated being neglect all the duties of life, yet recline with self-complacency on a sofa, and boast of her want of appetite as a proof of delicacy that extended to, or, perhaps, arose from, her exquisite sensibility; for it is difficult to render intelligible such ridiculous jargon. Yet, at the moment, I have seen her insult a worthy old gentlewoman, whom unexpected misfortunes had made dependent on her ostentatious bounty, and who, in better days, had claims on her gratitude. Is it possible that a human creature could have become such a weak and depraved being, if, like the Sybarites, dissolved in luxury, everything like virtue had not been worn away, or never impressed by precept, a poor substitute, it is true, for cultivation of mind, though it serves as a fence against vice?

Such a woman is not a more irrational monster than some of the Roman em- 18 perors, who were depraved by lawless power. Yet, since kings have been more under the restraint of law, and the curb, however weak, of honour, the records of history are not filled with such unnatural instances of folly and cruelty, nor does the despotism that kills virtue and genius in the bud, hover over Europe with that destructive blast which desolates Turkey, and renders the men, as well as the soil, unfruitful.

Women are everywhere in this deplorable state; for, in order to preserve their 19 innocence, as ignorance is courteously termed, truth is hidden from them, and they are made to assume an artificial character before their faculties have acquired any strength. Taught from their infancy that beauty is woman's sceptre, the mind shapes itself to the body, and roaming round its gilt cage, only seeks to adore its prison. Men have various employments and pursuits which engage their attention, and give a character to the opening mind; but women, confined to one, and having their thoughts constantly directed to the most insignificant part of themselves, seldom extend their views beyond the triumph of the hour. But were their understanding once emancipated from the slavery to which the pride and sensuality of man and their short-sighted desire, like that of dominion in tyrants, of present sway, has subjected them, we should probably read of their weaknesses with surprise. I must be allowed to pursue the argument a little further.

Perhaps, if the existence of an evil being were allowed, who, in the allegorical 20 language of Scripture, went about seeking whom he should devour, he could not more effectually degrade the human character, than by giving a man absolute power.

This argument branches into various ramifications. Birth, riches, and every ex- 21 trinsic advantage that exalt a man above his fellows, without any mental exertion, sink him in reality below them. In proportion to his weakness, he is played upon by design- ing men, till the bloated monster has lost all traces of humanity. And that tribes of men, like flocks of sheep, should quietly follow such a leader, is a solecism that only a desire of present enjoyment and narrowness of understanding can solve. Educated in slavish dependence, and enervated by luxury and sloth, where shall we find men who will stand forth to assert the rights of man, or claim the privilege of moral beings, who should have but one road to excellence? Slavery to monarchs and ministers, which the world will be long in freeing itself from, and whose deadly grasp stops the progress of the human mind, is not yet abolished.

Let not men then in the pride of power, use the same arguments that tyrannic 22 kings and venal ministers have used, and fallaciously assert that woman ought to be subjected because she has always been so. But, when man, governed by reasonable laws, enjoys his natural freedom, let him despise woman, if she do not share it with him; and, till that glorious period arrives, in descanting on the folly of the sex, let him not over- look his own.

Women, it is true, obtaining power by unjust means, by practising or fostering 23 vice, evidently lose the rank which reason would assign them, and they become either abject slaves or capricious tyrants. They lose all simplicity, all dignity of mind, in ac- quiring power, and act as men are observed to act when they have been exalted by the same means.

It is time to effect a revolution in female manners—time to restore to them 24 their lost dignity—and make them, as a part of the human species, labour by reforming themselves to reform the world. It is time to separate unchangeable morals from local manners. If men be demi-gods, why let us serve them! And if the dignity of the female soul be as disputable as that of animals—if their reason does not afford sufficient light to direct their conduct whilst unerring instinct is denied—they are surely of all crea- tures the most miserable! and, bent beneath the iron hand of destiny, must submit to be a *fair defect* in creation. But to justify the ways of Providence respecting them, by pointing out some irrefragable reason for thus making such a large portion of mankind accountable and not accountable, would puzzle the subtilest casuist.

The only solid foundation for morality appears to be the character of the Su- 25 preme Being; the harmony of which arises from a balance of attributes;—and, to speak with reverence, one attribute seems to imply the *necessity* of another. He must be just, because He is wise; He must be good, because He is omnipotent. For to exalt one attrib- ute at the expense of another equally noble and necessary, bears the stamp of the warped reason of man—the homage of passion. Man, accustomed to bow down to power in his savage state, can seldom divest himself of this barbarous prejudice, even when civilisa- tion determines how much superior mental is to bodily strength; and his reason is clouded by these crude opinions, even when he thinks of the Deity. His omnipotence is made to swallow up, or preside over His other attributes, and those mortals are sup- posed to limit His power irreverently, who think that it must be regulated by His wis- dom.

I disclaim that specious humility which, after investigating nature, stops at the 26 Author. The High and Lofty One, who inhabiteth eternity, doubtless possesses many attributes of which we can form no conception; but Reason tells me that they cannot clash with those I adore—and I am compelled to listen to her voice.

It seems natural for man to search for excellence, and either to trace it in the 27 object that he worships, or blindly to invest it with perfection, as a garment. But what good effect can the latter mode of worship have on the moral conduct of a rational being? He bends to power; he adores a dark cloud, which may open a bright prospect to him, to burst in angry, lawless fury, on his devoted head—he knows not why. And, supposing that the Deity acts from the vague impulse of an undirected will, man must also follow his own, or act according to rules, deduced from principles which he disclaims as irreverent. Into this dilemma have both enthusiasts and cooler thinkers fallen, when they laboured to free men from the wholesome restraints which a just conception of the character of God imposes.

It is not impious thus to scan the attributes of the Almighty: in fact, who can 28 avoid it that exercises his faculties? For to love God as the fountain of wisdom, goodness, and power, appears to be the only worship useful to a being who wishes to acquire either virtue or knowledge. A blind unsettled affection may, like human passions, occupy the mind and warm the heart, whilst, to do justice, love mercy, and walk humbly with our God, is forgotten. I shall pursue this subject still further, when I consider religion in a light opposite to that recommended by Dr. Gregory, who treats it as a matter of sentiment or taste.

To return from this apparent digression. It were to be wished that women 29 would cherish an affection for their husbands, founded on the same principle that devotion ought to rest upon. No other firm base is there under heaven—for let them beware of the fallacious light of sentiment; too often used as a softer phrase for sensuality. It follows then, I think, that from their infancy women should either be shut up like Eastern princes, or educated in such a manner as to be able to think and act for themselves.

Why do men halt between two opinions, and expect impossibilities? Why do 30 they expect virtue from a slave, from a being whom the constitution of civil society has rendered weak, if not vicious?

Still I know that it will require a considerable length of time to eradicate the 31 firmly rooted prejudices which sensualists have planted; it will also require some time to convince women that they act contrary to their real interest on an enlarged scale, when they cherish or affect weakness under the name of delicacy, and to convince the world that the poisoned source of female vices and follies, if it be necessary, in compliance with custom, to use synonymous terms in a lax sense, has been the sensual homage paid to beauty:—to beauty of features; for it has been shrewdly observed by a German writer, that a pretty woman, as an object of desire, is generally allowed to be so by men of all descriptions; whilst a fine woman, who inspires more sublime emotions by displaying intellectual beauty, may be overlooked or observed with indifference, by those men who find their happiness in their gratification of their appetites. I foresee an obvious retort—whilst man remains such an imperfect being as he appears hitherto to have been, he will, more or less, be the slave of his appetites; and those women obtaining most power who gratify a predominant one, the sex is degraded by a physical, if not by a moral necessity.

This objection has, I grant, some force; but while such a sublime precept exists, 32 as, "Be pure as your heavenly Father is pure"; it would seem that the virtues of man are not limited by the Being who alone could limit them; and that he may press forward without considering whether he steps out of his sphere by indulging such a noble ambition. To the wild billows it has been said, "Thus far shalt thou go, and no farther; and here shall thy proud waves be stayed." Vainly then do they beat and foam, restrained by the power that confines the struggling planets in their orbits, matter yields to the great governing Spirit. But an immortal soul, not restrained by mechanical laws and struggling to free itself from the shackles of matter, contributes to, instead of disturbing, the order of creation, when, co-operating with the Father of spirits, it tries to govern itself by the invariable rule that, in a degree, before which our imagination faints, regulates the universe.

Besides, if women be educated for dependence, that is, to act according to the 33 will of another fallible being, and submit, right or wrong, to power, where are we to stop? Are they to be considered as vicegerents allowed to reign over a small domain, and answerable for their conduct to a higher tribunal, liable to error?

It will not be difficult to prove that such delegates will act like men subjected 34 by fear, and make their children and servants endure their tyrannical oppression. As they submit without reason, they will, having no fixed rules to square their conduct by, be kind, or cruel, just as the whim of the moment directs; and we ought not to wonder if sometimes, galled by their heavy yoke, they take a malignant pleasure in resting it on weaker shoulders.

But, supposing a woman, trained up to obedience, be married to a sensible 35 man, who directs her judgment without making her feel the servility of her subjection, to act with as much propriety by this reflected light as can be expected when reason is taken at secondhand, yet she cannot ensure the life of her protector; he may die and leave her with a large family.

A double duty devolves on her; to educate them in the character of both father 36 and mother; to form their principles and secure their property. But, alas! she has never thought, much less acted for herself. She has only learned to please[4] men, to depend

---

[4]"In the union of the sexes, both pursue one common object, but not in the same manner. From their diversity in this particular, arises the first determinate difference between the moral relations of each. The one should be active and strong, the other passive and weak; it is necessary the one should have both the power and the will, and that the other should make little resistance.

"This principle being established, it follows that woman is expressly formed to please the man: if the obligation be reciprocal also, and the man ought to please in his turn, it is not so immediately necessary: his great merit is in his power, and he pleases merely because he is strong. This, I must confess, is not one of the refined maxims of love; it is, however, one of the laws of nature, prior to love itself.

"If woman be formed to please and be subjected to man, it is her place, doubtless, to render herself agreeable to him, instead of challenging his passion. The violence of his desires depends on her charms; it is by means of these she should urge him to the exertion of those powers which nature hath given him. The most successful method of exciting them, is, to render such exertion necessary by resistance; as, in that case, self-love is added to desire, and the one triumphs in the victory which the other is obliged to acquire. Hence arise the various modes of attack and defense between the sexes; the boldness of one sex and the timidity of the other; and, in a word, that bashfulness and modesty with which nature hath armed the weak in order to subdue the strong."—Rousseau's *Emilius*.

I shall make no other comment on this ingenious passage than just to observe that it is the philosophy of lasciviousness.

gracefully on them; yet, encumbered with children, how is she to obtain another protector—a husband to supply the place of reason? A rational man, for we are not treading on romantic ground, though he may think her a pleasing docile creature, will not choose to marry a *family* for love, when the world contains many more pretty creatures. What is then to become of her? She either falls an easy prey to some mean fortune-hunter, who defrauds her children of their paternal inheritance, and renders her miserable; or becomes the victim of discontent and blind indulgence. Unable to educate her sons, or impress them with respect,—for it is not a play on words to assert, that people are never respected, though filling an important station, who are not respectable,—she pines under the anguish of unavailing impotent regret. The serpent's tooth enters into her very soul, and the vices of licentious youth bring her with sorrow, if not with poverty also, to the grave.

This is not an overcharged picture; on the contrary, it is a very possible case, 37 and something similar must have fallen under every attentive eye.

I have, however, taken it for granted, that she was well disposed, though expe- 38 rience shows, that the blind may as easily be led into a ditch as along the beaten road. But supposing, no very improbable conjecture, that a being only taught to please must still find her happiness in pleasing; what an example of folly, not to say vice, will she be to her innocent daughters! The mother will be lost in the coquette, and, instead of making friends of her daughters, view them with eyes askance, for they are rivals—rivals more cruel than any other, because they invite a comparison, and drive her from the throne of beauty, who has never thought of a seat on the bench of reason.

It does not require a lively pencil, or the discriminating outline of a caricature, 39 to sketch the domestic miseries and petty vices which such a mistress of a family diffuses. Still she only acts as a woman ought to act, brought up according to Rousseau's system. She can never be reproached for being masculine, or turning out of her sphere; nay, she may observe another of his grand rules, and, cautiously preserving her reputation free from spot, be reckoned a good kind of woman. Yet in what respect can she be termed good? She abstains, it is true, without any great struggle, from committing gross crimes; but how does she fulfil her duties? Duties! in truth she has enough to think of to adorn her body and nurse a weak constitution.

With respect to religion, she never presumed to judge for herself; but con- 40 formed, as a dependent creature should, to the ceremonies of the Church which she was brought up in, piously believing that wiser heads than her own have settled that business; and not to doubt is her point of perfection. She therefore pays her tithe of mint and cumin—and thanks her God that she is not as other women are. These are the blessed effects of a good education! These are virtues of man's helpmate![5]

I must relieve myself by drawing a different picture.   41

Let fancy now present a woman with a tolerable understanding, for I do not 42 wish to leave the line of mediocrity, whose constitution, strengthened by exercise, has

---

[5]"O how lovely," exclaims Rousseau, speaking of Sophia, "is her ignorance! Happy is he who is destined to instruct her! She will never pretend to be the tutor of her husband, but will be content to be his pupil. Far from attempting to subject him to her taste, she will accommodate herself to his. She will be more estimable to him, than if she was learned, he will have a pleasure in instructing her."—Rousseau's *Emilius*.

I shall content myself with simply asking, how friendship can subsist when love expires, between the master and his pupil.

allowed her body to acquire its full vigour; her mind, at the same time, gradually expanding itself to comprehend the moral duties of life, and in what human virtue and dignity consist.

Formed thus by the discharge of the relative duties of her station, she marries 43 from affection, without losing sight of prudence, and looking beyond matrimonial felicity, she secures her husband's respect before it is necessary to exert mean arts to please him and feed a dying flame, which nature doomed to expire when the object became familiar, when friendship and forbearance take place of a more ardent affection. This is the natural death of love, and domestic peace is not destroyed by struggles to prevent its extinction. I also suppose the husband to be virtuous; or she is still more in want of independent principles.

Fate, however, breaks this tie. She is left a widow, perhaps, without a sufficient 44 provision; but she is not desolate! The pang of nature is felt; but after time has softened sorrow into melancholy resignation, her heart turns to her children with redoubled fondness, and anxious to provide from them, affection gives a sacred heroic cast to her maternal duties. She thinks that not only the eye sees her virtuous efforts from whom all her comfort now must flow, and whose approbation is life; but her imagination, a little abstracted and exalted by grief, dwells on the fond hope that the eyes which her trembling hand closed, may still see how she subdues every wayward passion to fulfil the double duty of being the father as well as the mother of her children. Raised to heroism by misfortunes, she represses the first faint dawning of a natural inclination, before it ripens into love, and in the bloom of life forgets her sex—forgets the pleasure of an awakening passion, which might again have been inspired and returned. She no longer thinks of pleasing, and conscious dignity prevents her from priding herself on account of the praise which her conduct demands. Her children have her love, and her brightest hopes are beyond the grave, where her imagination often strays.

I think I see her surrounded by her children, reaping the reward of her care. 45 The intelligent eye meets hers, whilst health and innocence smile on their chubby cheeks, and as they grow up the cares of life are lessened by their grateful attention. She lives to see the virtues which she endeavoured to plant on principles, fixed into habits, to see her children attain a strength of character sufficient to enable them to endure adversity without forgetting their mother's example.

The task of life thus fulfilled, she calmly waits for the sleep of death, and rising 46 from the grave, may say—"Behold, Thou gavest me a talent, and here are five talents."

I wish to sum up what I have said in a few words, for I here throw down my 47 gauntlet, and deny the existence of sexual virtues, not excepting modesty. For man and woman, truth, if I understand the meaning of the word, must be the same; yet the fanciful female character, so prettily drawn by poets and novelists, demanding the sacrifice of truth and sincerity, virtue becomes a relative idea, having no other foundation than utility, and of that utility men pretend arbitrarily to judge, shaping it to their own convenience.

Women, I allow, may have different duties to fulfil; but they are *human* duties, 48 and the principles that should regulate the discharge of them, I sturdily maintain, must be the same.

To become respectable, the exercise of their understanding is necessary, there 49 is no other foundation for independence of character; I mean explicitly to say that they must only bow to the authority of reason, instead of being the *modest* slaves of opinion.

In the superior ranks of life how seldom do we meet with a man of superior 50 abilities, or even common acquirements? The reason appears to me clear, the state they are born in was an unnatural one. The human character has ever been formed by the employments the individual, or class, pursues; and if the faculties are not sharpened by necessity, they must remain obtuse. The argument may fairly be extended to women; for, seldom occupied by serious business, the pursuit of pleasure gives that insignificancy to their character which renders the society of the *great* so insipid. The same want of firmness, produced by a similar cause, forces them both to fly from themselves to noisy pleasures, and artificial passions, till vanity takes place of every social affection, and the characteristics of humanity can scarcely be discerned. Such are the blessings of civil governments, as they are at present organized, that wealth and female softness equally tend to debase mankind, and are produced by the same cause; but allowing women to be rational creatures, they should be incited to acquire virtues which they may call their own, for how can a rational being be ennobled by anything that is not obtained by its *own* exertions?

Questions

1. Wollstonecraft states in paragraph 6 that women "sometimes boast of their weakness, cunningly obtaining power by playing on the *weakness* of men. . . ." What kind of weakness in women is she referring to? What kind of weakness in men? What has been the result of the possession of this power by women?
2. What in women's education does Wollstonecraft blame for this situation in paragraphs 10–12 and 19, and what changes does she recommend?
3. How does the opening discussion of physical strength in men and women support the argument of paragraphs 7–12?
4. What opinions of Rousseau concerning women does Wollstonecraft attack in paragraphs 9, 13–15, 36, and 40–42? How does she account in paragraphs 16–17 for the faults she concedes that women in her time possess?
5. What other dependency does "dependence on body" lead to in women, according to paragraph 17? How does Wollstonecraft illustrate the consequences of this dependency?
6. According to paragraphs 20–23, what attitudes in men encourage this dependency? How does Wollstonecraft account for these attitudes?
7. In attacking the argument in paragraph 24 that the ways of God "justify" the idea that women are inferior, Wollstonecraft is alluding to the opening lines of Milton's *Paradise Lost* ("and justify the ways of God to Men") and to Milton's later statement that God created man for "contemplation" and "absolute rule" and woman for "softness," "sweet attractive grace," and "subjection." How does Wollstonecraft account for this male view of God in paragraphs 26–28?
8. How does Wollstonecraft use this discussion of God in defining the ideal relationship between man and woman in paragraphs 30–32? How does she answer the "retort" presented in paragraph 31?
9. What other arguments against educating women for dependence does Wollstonecraft present in paragraphs 34–48?

10. To what audience is the argument directed? To women only? To women and men? Does Wollstonecraft speak directly to her audience, or does she avoid personal address?

11. How effective do you find the rhetoric of the essay—the means of persuasion Wollstonecraft uses? How convincing do you find her argument? Does the rhetoric of the essay strengthen or weaken the argument?

Suggestions for Writing

1. Use your personal experience or observation to discuss the extent to which the education of women in schools today resembles the education criticized by Wollstonecraft. In schools you attended, were expectations different for boys and girls in physical and mental education? Were "delicacy" and "dependence" assumed or stated to be desirable qualities in girls? Or does the education of women today have the same goals as the education of men?

2. Discuss the extent to which Wollstonecraft states your beliefs on the proper role and education of men and women. Focus on one of these beliefs later in your essay, defending it through personal experiences, observations, or other evidence that leads you to hold it.

3. Discuss the ways in which Wollstonecraft's ideas on education resemble those of Rousseau. Note any differences, stated or implied, that you find.

Additional Reading

Flexner, Eleanor. *Mary Wollstonecraft.* New York: Coward, McCann, and Geoghegan, 1972.

James, H. R. *Mary Wollstonecraft: A Sketch.* London: Oxford University Press, 1932.

Wardle, Ralph M. *Mary Wollstonecraft: A Critical Biography.* Lawrence: University of Kansas Press, 1951.

Wollstonecraft, Mary. *Mary: A Fiction* and *The Wrongs of Woman.* Ed. Gary Kelly. New York: Oxford University Press, 1976.

———. *A Vindication of the Rights of Woman* (1792). London: Dent, 1929.

Human Equality Is a Contingent Fact of History

Stephen Jay Gould

Stephen Jay Gould has taught geology, biology, and the history of science at Harvard University since 1967. He is well known today for his contributions to evolutionist theory, his active part in the current debate over creationism, and his writings on human intelli-

gence. Gould is also known for his column in Natural History *magazine. His essays have been collected in several books. "I follow one cardinal rule in writing these essays—no compromises," Gould states in the prologue to his collection of essays,* The Flamingo's Smile. *"I will make language accessible by defining or eliminating jargon; I will not simplify concepts."*

Gould is concerned with the issue of social and racial classification in this essay. It focuses on the use of supposedly scientific evidence in attempts to prove that blacks and other minorities are inferior by reason of their race. In the course of the essay, Gould alludes to the issues of apartheid in South Africa. Writing in 1984, Gould discusses this same idea from the viewpoint of recent findings in biology and genetics. In The Mismeasure of Man, *published in 1981, Gould considers the controversial use of intelligence tests as a measure of racial characteristics.*

PRETORIA, AUGUST 5, 1984

ersatz=) replacement, substitution

History's most famous airplane, Lindbergh's *Spirit of St. Louis,* hangs from the 1 ceiling of Washington's Air and Space Museum, imperceptible in its majesty to certain visitors. Several years ago, a delegation of blind men and women met with the museum's director to discuss problems of limited access. Should we build, he asked, an accurate scale model of Lindbergh's plane, freely available for touch and examination? Would such a replica solve the problem? The delegation reflected together and gave an answer that moved me deeply for its striking recognition of universal needs. Yes, they said, such a model would be acceptable, but only on one condition—that it be placed directly beneath the invisible original.

Authenticity exerts a strange fascination over us; our world does contain sacred 2 objects and places. Their impact cannot be simply aesthetic, for an ersatz absolutely indistinguishable from the real McCoy evokes no comparable awe. The jolt is direct and emotional—as powerful a feeling as anything I know. Yet the impetus is purely intellectual—a visceral disproof of romantic nonsense that abstract knowledge cannot engender deep emotion.

Last night, I watched the sun set over the South African savanna—the original 3 location and habitat of our australopithecine ancestors. The air became chill; sounds of the night began, the incessant repetition of toad and insect, laced with an occasional and startling mammalian growl; the Southern Cross appeared in the sky, with Jupiter, Mars, and Saturn ranged in a line above the arms of Scorpio. I sensed the awe, fear, and mystery of the night. I am tempted to say (describing emotions, not making any inferences about realities, higher or lower) that I felt close to the origin of religion as a historical phenomenon of the human psyche. I also felt kinship in that moment with our most distant human past—for an *Australopithecus africanus* may once have stood, nearly three million years ago, on the same spot in similar circumstances, juggling (for all I know) that same mixture of awe and fear.

I was then rudely extricated from that sublime, if fleeting, sentiment of unity 4 with all humans past and present. I remembered my immediate location—South Africa, 1984 (during a respite in Kruger Park from a lecture tour on the history of racism). I also understood, in a more direct way than ever before, the particular tragedy of the history of biological views about human races. This history is largely a tale of division—an account of barriers and ranks erected to maintain the power and hegemony of those on top. The greatest irony of all presses upon me: I am a visitor in the nation most committed to myths of inequality—yet the savannas of this land staged an evolutionary story of opposite import.

My visceral perception of brotherhood harmonizes with our best modern biological knowledge. Such union of feeling and fact may be quite rare, for one offers no guide to the other (more romantic twaddle aside). Many people think (or fear) that equality of human races represents a hope of liberal sentimentality probably squashed by the hard realities of history. They are wrong.

This essay can be summarized in a single phrase, a motto if you will: *Human equality is a contingent fact of history.* Equality is not true by definition; it is neither an ethical principle (though equal treatment may be) nor a statement about norms of social action. It just worked out that way. A hundred different and plausible scenarios for human history would have yielded other results (and moral dilemmas of enormous magnitude). They didn't happen.

The history of Western views on race is a tale of denial—a long series of progressive retreats from initial claims for strict separation and ranking by intrinsic worth toward an admission of the trivial differences revealed by our contingent history. In this essay, I shall discuss just two main stages of retreat for each of two major themes: genealogy, or separation among races as a function of their geological age; and geography, or our place of origin. I shall then summarize the three major arguments from modern biology for the surprisingly small extent of human racial differences.

Genealogy, the First Argument

Before evolutionary theory redefined the issue irrevocably, early to mid-nineteenth-century anthropology conducted a fierce debate between schools of monogeny and polygeny. Monogenists advocated a common origin for all people in the primeval couple, Adam and Eve (lower races, they then argued, had degenerated further from original perfection). Polygenists held that Adam and Eve were ancestors of white folks only, and that other—and lower—races had been separately created. Either argument could fuel a social doctrine of inequality, but polygeny surely held the edge as a compelling justification for slavery and domination at home and colonialism abroad. "The benevolent mind," wrote Samuel George Morton (a leading American polygenist) in 1839, "may regret the inaptitude of the Indian for civilization. . . . The structure of his mind appears to be different from that of the white man. . . . They are not only averse to the restraints of education, but for the most part are incapable of a continued process of reasoning on abstract subjects."

Genealogy, the Second Argument

Evolutionary theory required a common origin for human races, but many post-Darwinian anthropologists found a way to preserve the spirit of polygeny. They argued, in a minimal retreat from permanent separation, that the division of our lineage into modern races had occurred so long ago that differences, accumulating slowly through time, have now built unbridgeable chasms. Though once alike in an apish dawn, human races are now separate and unequal.

We cannot understand much of the history of late nineteenth- and early 10 twentieth-century anthropology, with its plethora of taxonomic names proposed for nearly every scrap of fossil bone, unless we appreciate its obsession with the identification and ranking of races. For many schemes of classification sought to tag the various fossils as ancestors of modern races and to use their relative age and apishness as a criterion for racial superiority. Piltdown, for example, continued to fool generations of professionals partly because it fit so comfortably with ideas of white superiority. After all, this "ancient" man with a brain as big as ours (the product, we now know, of a hoax constructed with a modern cranium) lived in England—an obvious ancestor for whites—while such apish (and genuine) fossils as *Homo erectus* inhabited Java and China as putative sources for Orientals and other peoples of color.

This theory of ancient separation received its last prominent defense in 1962, 11 when Carleton Coon published his *Origin of Races*. Coon divided humanity into five major races—caucasoids, mongoloids, australoids, and, among African blacks, congoids and capoids. He claimed that these five groups had already become distinct subspecies during the reign of our ancestor, *Homo erectus. H. erectus* then evolved toward *H. sapiens* in five parallel streams, each traversing the same path toward increased consciousness. But whites and yellows, who "occupied the most favorable of the earth's zoological regions," crossed the threshold to *H. sapiens* first, while dark peoples lagged behind and have paid for their sluggishness ever since. Black inferiority, Coon argues, is nobody's fault, just an accident of evolution in less challenging environments:

> Caucasoids and Mongoloids . . . did not rise to their present population levels
> and positions of cultural dominance by accident . . . Any other subspecies that
> had evolved in these regions would probably have been just as successful.

Leading evolutionists throughout the world reacted to Coon's thesis with in- 12 credulity. Could modern races really be identified at the level of *H. erectus?* I shall always be grateful to W. E. Le Gros Clark, England's greatest anatomist at the time. I was spending an undergraduate year in England, an absolute nobody in a strange land. Yet he spent an afternoon with me, patiently answering my questions about race and evolution. Asked about Coon's thesis, this splendidly modest man simply replied that he, at least, could not identify a modern race in the bones of an ancient species.

More generally, parallel evolution of such precision in so many lineages seems 13 almost impossible on grounds of mathematical probability alone. Could five separate subspecies undergo such substantial changes and yet remain so similar at the end that all can still interbreed freely, as modern races so plainly do? In the light of these empirical weaknesses and theoretical implausibilities, we must view Coon's thesis more as the last gasp of a dying tradition than a credible synthesis of available evidence.

Genealogy, the Modern View

Human races are not separate species (the first argument) or ancient divisions 14 within an evolving plexus (the second argument). They are recent, poorly differentiated subpopulations of our modern species. *Homo sapiens,* separated at most by tens or hundreds of thousands of years, and marked by remarkably small genetic differences.

Geography, the First Argument

When Raymond Dart found the first australopithecine in South Africa sixty 15 years ago, scientists throughout the world rejected this oldest ancestor, this loveliest of intermediate forms, because it hailed from the wrong place. Darwin, without a shred of fossil evidence but with a good criterion for inference, had correctly surmised that humans evolved in Africa. Our closest living relatives, he argued, are chimps and gorillas—and both species live only in Africa, the probable home, therefore, of our common ancestor as well.

But few scientists accepted Darwin's cogent inference because hope, tradition, 16 and racism conspired to locate our ancestral abode on the plains of central Asia. Notions of Aryan supremacy led anthropologists to assume that the vast "challenging" reaches of Asia, not the soporific tropics of Africa, had prompted our ancestors to abandon an apish past and rise toward the roots of Indo-European culture. The diversity of colored people in the world's tropics could only record the secondary migrations and subsequent degenerations of this original stock. The great Gobi Desert expedition, sponsored by the American Museum of Natural History just a few years before Dart's discovery, was dispatched primarily to find the ancestry of man in Asia. We remember this expedition for success in discovering dinosaurs and their eggs; we forget that its major quest ended in utter failure because Darwin's simple inference was correct.

Geography, the Second Argument

By the 1950's, further anatomical study and the sheer magnitude of continuing 17 discovery forced the general admission that our roots lay with the australopithecines, and that Africa had been our original home. But the subtle hold of unacknowledged prejudice still conspired (with other, more reasonable bases of uncertainty) to deny Africa its continuing role as the cradle of what really matters to us—the origin of human consciousness. In a stance of intermediate retreat, most scientists now argued that Africa had kindled our origin but not our mental emergence. Human ancestors migrated out, again to mother Asia, and there crossed the threshold to consciousness as *Homo erectus* (or so-called Java and Peking man). We emerged from the apes in Africa; we evolved our intelligence in Asia. Carleton Coon wrote in his 1962 book: "If Africa was the cradle of mankind, it was only an indifferent kindergarten. Europe and Asia were our principal schools."

Geography, the Modern View

The tempo of African discovery has accelerated since Coon constructed his 18 metaphor of the educational hierarchy. *Homo erectus* apparently evolved in Africa as well, where fossils dating to nearly two million years have been found, while the Asian sites may be younger than previously imagined. One might, of course, take yet another step in retreat and argue that *H. sapiens,* at least, evolved later from an Asian stock of *H. erectus.* But the migration of *H. erectus* into Europe and Asia does not guarantee (or even suggest) any further branching from these mobile lineages. For *H. erectus* continued to live in Africa as well. Evidence is not yet conclusive, but the latest hints may be pointing toward an African origin for *H. sapiens* as well. Ironically then (with respect to previous expectations), every human species may have evolved first in Africa and only then—for the two latest species of *Homo*—spread elsewhere.

I have, so far, only presented the negative evidence for my thesis that human 19 equality is a contingent fact of history. I have argued that the old bases for inequality have evaporated. I must now summarize the positive arguments (primarily three in number) and, equally important, explain how easily history might have happened in other ways.

The Positive (and Formal, or Taxonomic) Argument from Racial Definition

[handwritten margin note: Taxonomic => classification according to their natural relationships esp animals and plants]

We recognize only one formal category for divisions within species—the sub- 20 species. Races, if formally defined, are therefore subspecies. Subspecies are populations inhabiting a definite geographic subsection of a species' range and sufficiently distinct in any set of traits for taxonomic recognition. Subspecies differ from all other levels of the taxonomic hierarchy in two crucial ways. First, they are categories of convenience only and need never be designated. Each organism must belong to a species, a genus, a family, and to all higher levels of the hierarchy; but a species need not be formally divided. Subspecies represent a taxonomist's personal decision about the best way to report geographic variation. Second, the subspecies of any species cannot be distinct and discrete. Since all belong to a single species, their members can, by definition, interbreed. Modern quantitative methods have permitted taxonomists to describe geographic variation more precisely in numerical terms; we need no longer construct names to describe differences that are, by definition, fleeting and changeable. Therefore, the practice of naming subspecies has largely fallen into disfavor, and few taxonomists use the category any more. Human variation exists; the formal designation of races is passé.

Some species are divided into tolerably distinct geographic races. Consider, for 21 example, an immobile species separated on drifting continental blocks. Since these subpopulations never meet, they may evolve substantial differences. We might still choose to name subspecies for such discrete geographic variants. But humans move about and maintain the most notorious habits of extensive interbreeding. We are not well enough divided into distinct geographic groups, and the naming of human subspecies makes little sense.

Our variation displays all the difficulties that make taxonomists shudder (or 22 delight in complexity) and avoid the naming of subspecies. Consider just three points. First, discordance of characters. We might make a reasonable division on skin color, only to discover that blood groups imply different alliances. When so many good characters exhibit such discordant patterns of variation, no valid criterion can be established for unambiguous definition of subspecies. Second, fluidity and gradations. We interbreed wherever we move, breaking down barriers and creating new groups. Shall the Cape Colored, a vigorous people more than two million strong and the offspring of unions between Africans and white settlers (the ancestors, ironically, of the authors of apartheid and its antimiscegenation laws), be designated a new subspecies or simply the living disproof that white and black are very distinct? Third, convergences. Similar characters evolve independently again and again; they confound any attempt to base subspecies on definite traits. Most indigenous tropical people, for example, have evolved dark skin.

The arguments against naming human races are strong, but our variation still 23 exists and could, conceivably, still serve as a basis for invidious comparisons. Therefore, we must add the second and third arguments as well.

The Positive Argument from Recency of Division

As I argued in the first part of this essay (and need only state in repetition now), 24 the division of humans into modern "racial" groups happened yesterday, in geological terms. This differentiation does not predate the origin of our own species, *Homo sapiens,* and probably occurred during the last few tens (or at most hundreds) of thousands of years.

The Positive Argument from Genetic Separation

Mendel's work was rediscovered in 1900 and the science of genetics spans our 25 entire century. Yet, until twenty years ago, a fundamental question in evolutionary genetics could not be answered for a curious reason. We were not able to calculate the average amount of genetic difference between organisms because we had devised no method for taking a random sample of genes. In the classical Mendelian analysis of pedigrees, a gene cannot be identified until it varies among individuals. For example, if absolutely every *Drosophila* in the world had red eyes, we would rightly suspect that some genetic information coded this universal feature, but we would not be able to identify a gene for red eyes by analyzing pedigrees, because all flies would look the same. But as soon as we find a few white-eyed flies, we can mate white with red, trace pedigrees through generations of off-spring, and make proper inferences about the genetic basis of eye color.

To measure the average genetic differences among races, we must be able to 26 sample genes at random—and this unbiased selection can't be done if we can only identify variable genes. Ninety percent of human genes might be held in common by all people, and an analysis confined to varying genes would grossly overestimate the total difference.

In the late 1960s, several geneticists harnessed the common laboratory tech- 27 nique of electrophoresis to solve this old dilemma. Genes code for proteins, and varying proteins may behave differently when subjected in solution to an electric field. Any protein could be sampled, independent of prior knowledge about whether it varied or not. (Electrophoresis can only give us a minimal estimate because some varying proteins may exhibit the same electrical mobility but be different in other ways.) Thus, with electrophoresis we could finally ask the key question: How much genetic difference exists among human races?

The answer, surprising for many people, soon emerged without ambiguity: 28 damned little. Intense studies for more than a decade have detected not a single "race gene"—that is, a gene present in all members of one group and none of another. Frequencies vary, often considerably, among groups, but all human races are much of a muchness. We can measure so much variation among individuals *within* any race that we encounter very little new variation by adding another race to the sample. In other words, the great preponderance of human variation occurs within groups, not in the differences between them. My colleague Richard Lewontin (see bibliography), who did much of the original electrophoretic work on human variation, puts it dramatically: If, God forbid, the holocaust occurs "and only the Xhosa people of the southern tip of Africa survived, the human species would still retain 80 percent of its genetic variation."

As long as most scientists accepted the ancient division of races, they expected 29 important genetic differences. But the recent origin of races (second positive argument) affirms the minor genetic differences now measured. Human groups do vary strikingly in a few highly visible characters (skin color, hair form)—and these external differences may fool us into thinking that overall divergence must be great. But we now know that our usual metaphor of superficiality—skin deep—is literally accurate.

In thus completing my précis, I trust that one essential point will not be mis- 30 construed: I am, emphatically, not talking about ethical precepts but about information in our best current assessment. It would be poor logic and worse strategy to hinge a moral or political argument for equal treatment or equal opportunity upon any factual statement about human biology. For if our empirical conclusions need revision—and all facts are tentative in science—then we might be forced to justify prejudice and apartheid (directed, perhaps, against ourselves, since who knows who would turn up on the bottom). I am no ethical philosopher, but I can only view equality of opportunity as inalienable, universal, and unrelated to the biological status of individuals. Our races may vary little in average characters, but our individuals differ greatly—and I cannot imagine a decent world that does not treat the most profoundly retarded person as a full human being in all respects, despite his evident and pervasive limitations.

I am, instead, making a smaller point, but one that tickles my fancy because 31 most people find it surprising. The conclusion is evident once articulated, but we rarely pose the issue in a manner that lets such a statement emerge. I have called equality among races a *contingent* fact. So far I have only argued for the fact; what about the contingency? In other words, how might history have been different? Most of us can grasp and accept the equality; few have considered the easy plausibility of alternatives that didn't happen.

My creationist incubi, in one of their most deliciously ridiculous arguments, 32 often imagine that they can sweep evolution away in the following unanswerable riposte: "Awright," they exclaim, "you say that humans evolved from apes, right?" "Right," I reply. "Awright, if humans evolved from apes, why are apes still around? Answer that one!" If evolution proceeded by this caricature—like a ladder of progress, each rung disappearing as it transforms bodily to the next stage—then I suppose this argument would merit attention. But evolution is a bush, and ancestral groups usually survive after their descendants branch off. Apes come in many shapes and sizes; only one line led to modern humans.

Most of us know about bushes, but we rarely consider the implications. We 33 know that australopithecines were our ancestors and that their bush included several species. But we view them as forebears, and subtly assume that since we are here, they must be gone. It is so indeed, but it ain't *necessarily* so. One population of one line of australopithecines became *Homo habilis;* several others survived. One species, *Austra-*

lopithecus robustus, died less than a million years ago and lived in Africa as a contemporary of *H. erectus* for a million years. We do not know why *A. robustus* disappeared. It might well have survived and presented us today with all the ethical dilemmas of a human species truly and markedly inferior in intelligence (with its cranial capacity only one-third our own). Would we have built zoos, established reserves, promoted slavery, committed genocide, or perhaps even practiced kindness? Human equality is a contingent fact of history.

Other plausible scenarios might also have produced marked inequality. *Homo* 34 *sapiens* is a young species, its division into races even more recent. This historical context has not provided enough time for the evolution of substantial differences. But many species are millions of years old, and their geographic divisions may be marked and deep. *H. sapiens* might have evolved along such a scale of time and produced races of great age and large accumulated differences—but we didn't. Human equality is a contingent fact of history.

A few well-placed mottoes might serve as excellent antidotes against deeply in- 35 grained habits of Western thought that so constrain us because we do not recognize their influence—so long as these mottoes become epitomes of real understanding, not the vulgar distortions that promote "all is relative" as a précis of Einstein.

I have three favorite mottoes, short in statement but long in implication. The 36 first, the epitome of punctuated equilibrium, reminds us that gradual change is not the only reality in evolution: other things count as well; "stasis is data." The second confutes the bias of progress and affirms that evolution is not an inevitable sequence of ascent: "mammals evolved at the same time as dinosaurs." The third is the theme of this essay, a fundamental statement about human variation. Say it five times before breakfast tomorrow; more important, understand it as the center of a network of implication: "Human equality is a contingent fact of history."

Questions

1. How do the arguments summarized in paragraphs 8–13 support the idea of racial inequality? What were the schools of monogeny and polygeny? What does Gould show to be the consequences of these arguments?
2. How has the modern genealogical view, summarized in paragraph 14, been disputed by geographical arguments? How does Gould explain the popularity of these arguments and defend the modern geographical view?
3. Why does Gould call the evidence of paragraphs 8–18 "negative evidence"? How is the evidence that follows "positive evidence"? What is a "formal" or "taxonomic" argument?
4. Why does the word *race* require no definition? What other positive arguments does Gould present for the equality of the races?
5. What does the word *equality* mean, and what is a "contingent fact"? What is a "contingent history"? And what does Gould mean by the statement, "Human equality is a contingent fact of history"?
6. What do the three mottoes discussed in the final paragraph mean?
7. What technical matters does Gould not discuss in detail? Why does he not do so?

Suggestions for Writing

Philistine=> antagonistic to PROSAIC ?
those of artistic or poetic, Learning

1. Write a summary of the argument Gould makes for the equality of the races. Include his rebuttal of arguments of the past.
2. Examine the definitions of the word *race* in the *Oxford English Dictionary*—a historical dictionary that gives the various meanings of a word and examples of usage from the past to the present. Compare these definitions with that of *race* in your college dictionary. Trace the changes that have occurred in the use of the word, and note meanings that are no longer current.

Additional Reading

Gould, Stephen Jay. *Ever since Darwin: Reflections in Natural History.* New York: Norton, 1977.

———. *Hen's Teeth and Horse's Toes: Further Reflections in Natural History.* New York: Norton, 1983.

———. *The Mismeasure of Man.* New York: Norton, 1981.

———. *The Panda's Thumb: More Reflections in Natural History.* New York: Norton, 1980.

Lewontin, R. C. *Human Diversity.* New York. Scientific American Library, 1982.

Those Proud and Set Faces

Robert Coles

> *Robert Coles received his M.D. from Columbia University in 1954, and he later worked on the psychiatric staff of Harvard Medical School and as a research psychiatrist at Harvard University. He has been Professor of Psychiatry and Humanities at Harvard since 1977. Coles has devoted most of his career to the study of children of various classes and cultures in America. His studies have appeared in numerous books, including the multivolumed* Children of Crisis, *the first volume of which appeared in 1967.* Migrants, Sharecroppers, and Mountaineers *(1972) and* The South Goes North *(1972) in this series were awarded the Pulitzer Prize. With Jane Hallowell Coles he has written a series of books titled* Women in Crisis, *and he has also written several books on American and British writers.*
>
> *The essay reprinted here is a section of* The South Goes North. *Coles states in the foreword:*

>> If one wants to learn some of the reasons America's cities are now struggling so hard with certain problems, one place to find out is "back there," back on the American earth, the farmland and hill territory from which came so many of our nation's present-day urban poor. Men and

women and children come North in pursuit of bread and work and freedom and dignity; but they arrive with more than their needs and hopes. They arrive as particular individuals with ways of seeing things and doing things, with their own ideas about the world and God and man, with their beliefs and values, their rhythms of speech and habits of cooking and preferences in music. These people carry with them a history: memories of the past, diseases and lacks and wants that linger in the form of scars and wounds and hurts and injuries, but also recollections of good times—real triumphs, or simply remembered moments of delight and contentment.

Coles is concerned in this section of The South Goes North *with the very different stereotypes held by social workers of white and black Southern immigrants to cities of the North.*

I don't know how many times I have used the word "proud" to describe the   1 mountaineers of Appalachia and their city cousins, even as I have heard it used again and again by others: "They pride themselves on their independence and ability to get on, no matter how difficult their lives may be." I suppose that some would want to say that pride is only a cover, that underneath a proud man can be a worried, frightened man, particularly if he is hungry. The fact is, however, that some deeply troubled and poverty-stricken people demonstrate pride, even as they struggle desperately to stay alive, while others, similarly afflicted, appear more openly apathetic or apprehensive or sad. Do we get very far by turning every coin over and saying that "really" this is that, and what seems to be one thing is "secretly" or "deep down" something else? Everyone's behavior masks something; even the insistent desire to pin psychological labels on people can itself be shown to be the product of something other than scientific curiosity or therapeutic zeal. Perhaps the apparent pride of the mountaineers can for once be looked upon as evidence of deep-seated pride.

Yet, it is only natural for a harassed and earnest welfare worker to be a little   2 skeptical about the pride mountaineers up North show in the face of the hard lives so many of them live. She knows about their disasters, their hardships, their illnesses and periods of joblessness, and she wonders how it is possible for people to contend with such a fate and still be so tight-lipped and defiant and long-suffering—so proud. Since *she* is unnerved by the stories she hears, the situations she meets up with, she wonders why "they" seem to be so stolid and quiet and controlled and (sometimes even) so able to smile and demonstrate a light touch. Maybe, she wonders, there is something wrong with "them." Maybe they are "depressed," badly so, and therefore they only *seem* proud or resolute or unyielding. Underneath, underneath where everything *really* important *really* is, there must be another story, far different from what usually meets the eye. In her words: "Underneath I believe they are anything but proud. They are probably terrified."

I tell her yes; I tell her I am sure "they" are terrified—though I think they are   3 quite aware of the terror they feel. But she tells me no; she tells me that there is something almost startling and certainly inappropriate about "those proud and set faces."

How *can* they be so proud, she asks, she exclaims almost, in view of the hurt and pain they have had for so long and *must* realize they will continue to know just about indefinitely? I reply that I am puzzled, even as she is. I reply that like her I see the proud and set faces she talks about. I reply that people, particular people, develop their own special ways of dealing with the world's turmoil and injustice—which is hardly a very original idea. And in reply she talks about her daily experiences, which in fact may contain answers that both of us seek. For her those experiences are exhausting and confusing and at times quite maddening. Yet, she can recognize that she is not as hopelessly bewildered as she sometimes feels: "I go to homes, poor homes, and I want to help, I want to help so badly. The people need help, too. A minister may have called me to suggest I go see a family. And there they are: the tall, quiet, shy man, and the gracious wife, and their lovely children—lovely to look at and sad to look at. It's an American stereotype, I guess, that blond, blue-eyed children are supposed to be neat and clean and healthy and perky and in the best of spirits. Some of the children look lovely, and they try to be nice and pleasant, but I can see how sick they are; I can see what living up a Kentucky hollow in extreme poverty has done to them and to their parents.

"Every time I go to a home I try to figure out a way to help the people. I find 4 myself wanting to tell the father that if he would just go away, or pretend to go away, things would be so much easier, so far as relief goes. But I could never say that, not to families that have come here from Appalachia. It even turns out often that a family doesn't really want help from the city. The city is trying to be flexible; I am allowed to go out and take a look at 'problem families' whenever a minister or a policeman or someone like that calls us up. Yet, time and again I'll go and meet the people and decide they need emergency help and all kinds of medical services and help in a job-training program or whatever—only to be told that no charity is wanted, none at all. They are not beggars, they say, and when I reply that I know that, they really watch me, to make sure I really mean what I say. If they detect an ounce of pity in me, they gently show me to the door.

"I've finally begun to realize that the very fact they can be gentle and polite in 5 showing me the door proves they are genuinely, honestly, through-and-through proud. If they were putting on an act, if they thought they could get more by pretending to be self-reliant and denying their need for assistance until I pressed them hard, if they wanted our help but didn't quite know how to come out and ask for it, or if they were afraid to ask for it, but were hoping eventually they would get up the nerve—well, I think they would be disappointed if I somehow let them down, showed pity for them but failed to 'force' money or food on them. Then they would get rid of me fast, or turn sullen and crabby or completely silent. Instead, they treat me as a guest. They are obviously sorry they can't be even more hospitable. They offer me tea or coffee. If it's hot weather, they offer me water. And I leave feeling as rotten and guilty and amazed as a welfare worker can be!

"I'm supposed to be watching out for con artists, for people who want welfare 6 but shouldn't be getting it. Instead, I find people who don't want what a lot of them call 'free money.' They want medical care for their children, yes. They'll take food, especially free hot lunches for their children at school. They'll sign up for job-training programs. But welfare checks, those pose another problem. They want work, that's what they want. They don't want 'a lot of everything in exchange for doing nothing.' That's how welfare was described to me by a man from West Virginia.

"Some of them *do* want welfare, of course. I don't mean to paint a total picture, 7 with every Appalachian family alike. Some of the men do in fact desert their families; they become drunks, serious alcoholics, broken and wasted men—'hillbilly lushes,' I've heard them called. And some families will take, take, take—the way you read in the conservative editorials welfare families are supposed to do. But I'd like to bring along with me the most niggling critics of our welfare program and have them meet some of the families I meet. I do believe in a short while those critics would be as troubled as I can get; they might feel like begging those parents to take money, just a little money, for themselves and their children.

"I don't know how to explain such things. Is it a special kind of honesty in 8 them, almost perverse honesty? After all, they really are entitled to as much help as we can arrange for them, within the letter, if not the spirit, of the law. Is it that pride we keep on talking about? What kind of pride encourages parents who need money for their children to turn their backs on that money, or at any rate put obstacles in the way of getting the money? Are we talking about *shame,* the shame that people feel when they have to ask for something and take something? Are they *angry,* so angry they can't accept help? I've thought of that often—that the proud look on their faces actually is a way of expressing hostility. They must resent people who have more than them, but they are quite inhibited by their culture, and so they don't feel free to express their resentments. And just when I'm ready to consign all the Appalachian families I know in this city to one big 'group therapy' meeting, I remind myself how lovely and genuinely hospitable they are, those people I call hostile and resentful and about a dozen other names. Then, I begin to wonder if it's not *me* who's hostile and resentful, because 'the poor' don't come running to me and begging for everything they can get. It's a hard job, this one— making sense of the people I meet and making sense out of my own reactions to them."

She has had some psychiatric treatment. She prides herself on her ability to 9 look inward and say what is on her mind. She finds herself uncomfortable with people who prefer to keep silent, watch rather than pour forth ideas and feelings. When she gets nervous she starts analyzing herself, describing her behavior, categorizing what bothers her and what bothers others. When she meets people and they do not immediately fit into one or another psychological scheme she has learned (and learned to use in her various "relationships") she starts out with the words: they are "defensive," or they are "overreacting," or they are "really" trying to say not what they mean but something different. God, it can be a bore to hear such a mind wordily grind human beings up—and yet, I have to remind myself that the young woman is a sincere and hardworking person, perhaps hindered by a lot of stupid and fanciful jargon, a lot of terminological drivel, but also utterly intent on doing what she can to bring money and food to people who badly need both.

Those men and women and children she meets seem to have more patience 10 than Job even could have had. They seem to be stubborn to a degree no mule could ever match. They have the resignation, it almost seems, that Kierkegaard wrote about and envied and singled out as man's highest task and least common achievement. Since, over the decades, they have challenged and confused any number of people and held fast to certain distinctive customs and habits, no wonder various efforts to understand mountaineers have been made, among them resort to biblical allusions and allegorical stories and philosophical formulations, not to mention psychological and psychiatric ones. Because so many mountaineers are themselves very devout Christians, and because they look eligible, given the right clothes and environmental background, for a photograph aimed at expanding the consumption of Coca-Cola or family-size station wagons or outdoor cooking gadgets, an observer or a welfare worker feels in contact with two strands of American life: the tradition of religious piety, which until recently was very much present, especially in the South and Midwest, and the secular, materialist tradition, which clothed itself in advertising stereotypes, such as the clean-cut blond family, with the eyes staring right at the reader or television-watcher. Yet, mountain people are not just formally religious; they are dead serious about God and His presence among us. Nor do they behave like the "typical" Americans they so often appear to be— all of which confuses people like that welfare worker and me, strangers to a region and its traditions.

Here is the welfare worker again, struggling hard to see clearly what it is that 11 unsettles her so: "I worked with black families for a while, and despite all the talk about how hard it is for white workers like me and black people in the ghetto to trust one another and speak frankly, I found that work far easier than the work I'm now doing. The blacks came up North to get away from southern sheriffs, and to get money either by working or through welfare. They want help; they need it and they ask for it. They would welcome me—so long as I behaved myself and didn't start pushing them with a lot of insulting questions. They would laugh and joke with me, and they made me feel I was doing a lot of good: I helped hundreds of children eat better food and wear better clothes. I would hear 'thank you' all day and if some people laughed behind my back and snickered at 'the dumb welfare lady,' as I accidentally heard myself called once, I didn't mind. I knew I was being conned sometimes. Why *shouldn't* they con me, I thought. I was on their side, and I knew just what their side was. They have been cheated for generations in this country, sold into slavery, then treated like animals; if they now try to squeeze their due from a tightfisted, regulation-crazy welfare department, that's just fine, I felt.

"One day I was told the department needed a real good worker to try making 12 contact with Appalachian families up here, and even though they kept on telling me the work was very difficult, I thought the supervisors must be kidding either themselves or me—because I believed that nothing could be tougher than working in the ghetto. I was tired, and I felt the need for a change, and I was curious, too; I'd never been to West Virginia or Kentucky, so I thought I'd have an interesting time meeting new people and learning about their way of life—you know, all we're told we're supposed to do when we're in social-work school. I was always the rebellious student, who wasn't going to be an ordinary social worker, who wanted to go out into the community and visit homes rather than stay in a clinic or a hospital. So, I became a welfare worker, not a social worker, and I decided to try visiting Appalachian families rather than the black families most people like me work with.

"At first, I expected to have an easy time, because the people seemed so easy- 13 going and so *familiar*—you know, very American-looking. They didn't speak my kind of English, but I could understand them better than I could a black woman from rural Mississippi or Alabama. And to be blunt: they were white, and I wasn't always worried about the race thing, the race barrier, the race problem. I'm white, and my parents weren't rich, and I'm from the Midwest, so I thought I wouldn't have too much trouble making good contact with families originally from Kentucky or West Virginia. I should have known better, though. My supervisor told me that there were 'serious problems,' but the people concerned tended to deny their difficulties. I asked her why we were going out and *looking* for new clients. If people don't want help, then what can we do? I asked her that. She said there had been complaints from ministers and community organizers and political pressures as a result of newspaper stories. What's more, some people in the state administration believe that it will help the welfare program and the blacks if welfare payments weren't so heavily going to blacks in so many cities and towns.

"I started by going to talk first with a minister, and then a reporter who origi- 14 nally came from Kentucky. I got the names of families from the minister, and I started visiting them alone. I didn't want any previous introductions. I told them the truth! I told them I knew they had serious money problems, and we in the welfare department want to do the best we can to help people in need. I told them that sometimes people don't know about us, or don't have a way to get to see us—so I was coming around to talk with some people the Reverend so-and-so suggested I go visit. They always smiled and asked me in and offered me coffee mostly, tea sometimes. They would often tell me right away that things are bad, yes, but they are managing, and they hope to keep on managing. I would ask them if they perhaps need some emergency food, and they would say no. In fact, often the mother would get angry when I mentioned food—as if I was accusing her of some crime. They don't go and fling open their refrigerators and show me how little they have. They don't tell me what they've been eating—so little their stomach hurts and they feel weak and all the rest. Instead they look hurt and tell me that they're doing fine, just fine, and they don't want to be taking, always taking.

"All they want is work. That's what I heard when I first started, and that's what 15 I still hear. All they want is a chance to be independent and make their own way through the world. I tell you, after hearing that for a year, I can almost recite the words by heart. I've almost come to think that way myself. It got so bad that I went on 'rounds' with a friend of mine; she works among the blacks, and we'd go into a house, and I'd hear a complaint about how inadequate the welfare payments are—and they *are* inadequate— but instead of nodding in agreement I could feel my face tightening up, and I could just hear those voices inside my head, saying: all I want is a chance to work, and I don't want money I haven't worked for, and I'll as soon die as take what's not become mine by the sweat of my brow. It's interesting, though: they will let the church help them. I think it's because to them God and His church are friends, whereas city or state agencies are like the county officials back in Appalachia—the enemy."

Perhaps one reason black families don't feel the way she describes mountain- 16 eers feeling is this: blacks have had no land of their own, no hollows and creeks of their own to defend and live on and cultivate with gardens and in general fall back on for survival. Blacks have always had to depend upon the hated and feared and envied enemy. In contrast, the poor in Appalachia have had sanctuaries of their own that no authority would dare approach. Within those sanctuaries people hunted, fished, grew vegetables, took care of chickens and goats, and maintained their sense of themselves as aloof, self-protected, defiant, ingenious, inventive people—as proud people who will survive, come what may, with God's help. It must be remembered that for a long time after mountaineers recognize they will have to leave for the cities, they hesitate and stay put. They never really have had to "go asking," as they say it, or "go begging," or "go on hands and knees for anything." Proudly and with set faces they have, rather, withdrawn and worked hard on their own and learned how to fend for themselves. The price they paid was a stiff one, but they had no real alternative. Their county agencies are hated and distrusted, and in a poor region they have only so much to give, even to friends and allies. And the strip-mining companies, what have they done for mountaineers? The moral, then, is to be wary of outsiders, and perhaps especially those bearing gifts—like the strip miners. The moral, then, is to stand on one's mountain territory, however bleak and unpromising it may seem, and guard it, and not suffer entry into it lightly.

No wonder the welfare worker talks this way about those who have left that 17 mountain country for the city: "They are in those apartments, and they don't want to move. They're not always shifting from one place to another, like poor blacks do when they get into the city. Instead, they almost burrow in and help each other out as best they can. If one man gets a job, he tries to find a job for his neighbor, often his kin. They have their emissaries—the men who work, and the women who get to know a minister or a worker up here from one of the Appalachian organizations. I've never been up a hollow, but one child told me the apartment building was a hollow, too. He was joking, the way children joke when they want to say something very important!"

I told her I had heard that remark, too—from several children. I told her one 18 child even let me know that his parents had always been the highest up the hollow back home, and now were happy to be living on the top floor of a building in which their kinfolk predominated. And it was important to the child's parents that the front door of that apartment house be kept locked. Poor as they all were, and old and broken-down as the building was, the fact remained that the families were living together, felt together, felt as one, and they wanted no outsider, ostensibly friendly or obviously on the prowl, coming up those stairs and asking questions or trying to suggest something or sell something—or "talk a fast line and end up fleecing us." I will in another chapter let that child describe at greater length how he and his parents look at the building they now live in—at the world they once lived in and the world they now inhabit. Here I can only emphasize that before we name such people "passive" or "masochistic" or "suspicious" or more ominously, "paranoid," we had better understand their historical fate in Kentucky or West Virginia, their economic and political experience over the generations with respect to an assortment of powers and principalities, their social customs and their religious beliefs, their long-standing and intensely shared values, ideals and habits. I believe that both the welfare worker and I have quite similarly had to learn, learn thoroughly and not forget, what I have just written. Unfortunately, to this day there are moments when I do forget, when my eyes narrow, my brow wrinkles, my ears perk up, and my mind gets ready to take note of yet additional evidence of the mountaineer's "psychopathology." But then a child will casually remark upon how he did this back home, or heard that up in the hollow, or was told something a year or two ago by his uncle or his grandmother—and I find myself saying to myself: slow down, wait, hear more, and above all, keep your psychiatric mouth shut.

Questions

1. What stereotype does the Northern social worker hold of the Appalachian mountaineer?
2. How accurately does this stereotype reflect the characters and lives of any of the mountaineers encountered by the social worker?

3. How does Coles characterize the social worker? What qualities in the mountaineer does she misunderstand or fail to recognize?
4. How does the social worker's image of blacks on welfare differ from that of whites on welfare? Does Coles suggest that her view of blacks is also a stereotype?
5. What differences does Coles point out in the history of the black and the white people he discusses with the social worker? Is he correcting her view of blacks through his explanation in paragraph 17, or is he affirming that view?
6. Is Coles critical of the social worker as a person? Is she deficient in experience or sympathy? Does he consider her "psychiatric treatment" an indication of deficient intelligence or character? Or is his account of her opinions neutral and uncritical?
7. Why does Coles stress the statement of the Appalachian child that the Northern apartment building is a hollow (paragraph 18)? What do paragraph 18 and other paragraphs tell you about the hollows in Southern communities?
8. What lesson does Coles draw about how we look at Southern whites and at people in general?

Suggestions for Writing

1. State fully and honestly your general view of a racial, ethnic, or professional class of people. Then discuss what experiences or influences helped to shape this view.
2. Discuss the extent to which actual experiences with people of this class confirm the view or stereotype you hold of them.
3. Discuss the extent to which a stereotype of a group or class to which you belong has influenced your view of yourself and of others in the same group or class and how it has also influenced your behavior.
4. In his notes to *The South Goes North,* Coles cites numerous books that influenced his own work. These include two books by E. Franklin Frazier, *The Negro in the United States* (1957) and *The Negro Family in the United States* (1966), Talcott Parsons and Kenneth B. Clark's book *The Negro American* (1966), St. Clair Drake and Horace Cayton's *Black Metropolis* (1970), and Elliot Liebow's *Talley's Corner: A Study of Negro Street Corner Men* (1966). Books on white classes include Oscar Handlin's *The Uprooted* (1951) and *Children of the Uprooted* (1966), Lillian Smith's *Killers of the Dream* (1961), Herbert Gans's *The Urban Villagers* (1962), and I. A. Newby's *Anti-Negro Thought in America* (1965), Leon Litwack's *North of Slavery* (1961), and Todd Gitlin and Nanci Hollander's *Uptown: Poor Whites in Chicago* (1970). Use these and other books and articles to write a documented paper on one of the following topics:
   a. problems of adjusting to Northern urban life
   b. the effect of stereotypes on Southern children in Northern cities
   c. holding on to old values in a new environment
   d. the indignities of the welfare system
   e. the realities of urban poverty
      These are general topics. As your reading progresses, try to limit the topic to a specific one of most interest to you. Let the thesis of your documented paper develop from your analysis of the evidence, and state an important discovery you make.

Additional Reading

Coles, Robert. *Children of Crisis, Vol. 1: A Study of Courage and Fear.* Boston: Little, Brown–Atlantic Monthly Press, 1967.
———. *Children of Crisis, Vol. 2: Migrants, Sharecroppers, Mountaineers.* Boston: Little, Brown–Atlantic Monthly Press, 1972.
———. *Children of Crisis, Vol. 3: The South Goes North.* Boston: Little, Brown–Atlantic Monthly Press, 1972.
———. *Uprooted Children: The Early Life of Migrant Farm Workers.* Pittsburgh: University of Pittsburgh Press, 1970.
Coles, Robert, and Jane H. Coles. *Women of Crisis: Lives of Struggle and Hope.* New York: Delacorte, 1978.
———. *Women of Crisis 2: Lives of Work and Dreams.* New York: Delacorte, 1980.

Letter from Birmingham Jail

Martin Luther King, Jr.

Martin Luther King, Jr., was the leader of the black Civil Rights Movement in the United States and a leader in the world human rights movement. Born in 1929, King chose to follow the career of his father, a Protestant minister in Atlanta, Georgia. Ordained in 1947, he graduated from Morehouse College in Atlanta, and in 1953 received his Ph.D. in theology from Boston University. King participated in the Montgomery, Alabama, bus boycott in 1955—begun when a black woman, Rosa Parks, refused to observe the segregation law governing city buses. King quickly rose to leadership in the civil rights movement that sought an end to segregation throughout the South. He was active in protests throughout the United States in the years that followed. Shortly before his assassination in Memphis, Tennessee, on April 4, 1968, King led the Civil Rights March in Washington, D.C., one of the significant events in the movement. In 1964 he received the Nobel Peace Prize.

"From my Christian background I gained my ideals, and from Gandhi my technique," King said. The most famous statement of his philosophy of nonviolent resistance occurs in a letter he wrote from the Birmingham, Alabama, jail on April 16, 1963. King had been jailed for attempting to desegregate eating establishments in Birmingham— the larger issue was segregation of all public facilities. During the protests that engaged blacks and the Birmingham police, eight Alabama clergymen issued a statement criticizing King for promoting public unrest through an "unwise and untimely" challenge to the city authorities. The clergymen stated that change was occurring gradually in Birmingham, and that confrontation with authority would impede it. King was responding to that argument in his letter. He later stated:

"Begun on the margins of the newspaper in which the statement appeared while I was in jail, the letter was continued on scraps of writing paper supplied by a friendly Negro trusty, and concluded on a pad my attorneys were eventually permitted to leave me. Although the text remains in substance unaltered, I have indulged in the author's prerogative of polishing it for publication."

Birmingham City Jail
April 16, 1963

Bishop C. C. J. CARPENTER
Bishop JOSEPH A. DURICK
Rabbi MILTON L. GRAFMAN
Bishop PAUL HARDIN
Bishop NOLAN B. HARMON
The Rev. GEORGE M. MURRAY
The Rev. EDWARD V. RAMAGE
The Rev. EARL STALLINGS

My dear Fellow Clergymen,

While confined here in the Birmingham City Jail, I came across your recent 1
statement calling our present activities "unwise and untimely." Seldom, if ever, do I pause to answer criticism of my work and ideas. If I sought to answer all of the criticisms that cross my desk, my secretaries would be engaged in little else in the course of the day and I would have no time for constructive work. But since I feel that you are men of genuine good will and your criticisms are sincerely set forth, I would like to answer your statement in what I hope will be patient and reasonable terms.

I think I should give the reason for my being in Birmingham, since you have 2
been influenced by the argument of "outsiders coming in." I have the honor of serving as president of the Southern Christian Leadership Conference, an organization operating in every Southern state with headquarters in Atlanta, Georgia. We have some eighty-five affiliate organizations all across the South—one being the Alabama Christian Movement for Human Rights. Whenever necessary and possible we share staff, educational, and financial resources with our affiliates. Several months ago our local affiliate here in Birmingham invited us to be on call to engage in a nonviolent direct action program if such were deemed necessary. We readily consented and when the hour came we lived up to our promises. So I am here, along with several members of my staff, because we were invited here. I am here because I have basic organizational ties here. Beyond this, I am in Birmingham because injustice is here. Just as the eighth century prophets left their little villages and carried their "thus saith the Lord" far beyond the boundaries of their home town, and just as the Apostle Paul left his little village of Tarsus and carried the gospel of Jesus Christ to practically every hamlet and city of the Graeco-Roman world, I too am compelled to carry the gospel of freedom beyond my particular home town. Like Paul, I must constantly respond to the Macedonian call for aid.

Moreover, I am cognizant of the interrelatedness of all communities and states. 3
I cannot sit idly by in Atlanta and not be concerned about what happens in Birmingham.

Injustice anywhere is a threat to justice everywhere. We are caught in an inescapable network of mutuality tied in a single garment of destiny. Whatever affects one directly affects all indirectly. Never again can we afford to live with the narrow, provincial "outside agitator" idea. Anyone who lives inside the United States can never be considered an outsider anywhere in this country.

You deplore the demonstrations that are presently taking place in Birming- 4
ham. But I am sorry that your statement did not express a similar concern for the conditions that brought the demonstrations into being. I am sure that each of you would want to go beyond the superficial social analyst who looks merely at effects, and does not grapple with underlying causes. I would not hesitate to say that it is unfortunate that so-called demonstrations are taking place in Birmingham at this time, but I would say in more emphatic terms that it is even more unfortunate that the white power structure of this city left the Negro community with no other alternative.

In any nonviolent campaign there are four basic steps: (1) collection of the 5
facts to determine whether injustices are alive; (2) negotiation; (3) self-purification; and (4) direct action. We have gone through all of these steps in Birmingham. There can be no gainsaying of the fact that racial injustice engulfs this community. Birmingham is probably the most thoroughly segregated city in the United States. Its ugly record of police brutality is known in every section of this country. Its unjust treatment of Negroes in the courts is a notorious reality. There have been more unsolved bombings of Negro homes and churches in Birmingham than any city in this nation. These are the hard, brutal, and unbelievable facts. On the basis of these conditions Negro leaders sought to negotiate with the city fathers. But the political leaders consistently refused to engage in good faith negotiation.

Then came the opportunity last September to talk with some of the leaders of 6
the economic community. In these negotiating sessions certain promises were made by the merchants—such as the promise to remove the humiliating racial signs from the stores. On the basis of these promises Rev. Shuttlesworth[1] and the leaders of the Alabama Christian Movement for Human Rights agreed to call a moratorium on any type of demonstrations. As the weeks and months unfolded we realized that we were the victims of a broken promise. The signs remained. As in so many experiences of the past we were confronted with blasted hopes, and the dark shadow of a deep disappointment settled upon us. So we had no alternative except that of preparing for direct action, whereby we would present our very bodies as a means of laying our case before the conscience of the local and national community. We were not unmindful of the difficulties involved. So we decided to go through a process of self-purification. We started having workshops on nonviolence and repeatedly asked ourselves the questions, "Are you able to accept blows without retaliating?" "Are you able to endure the ordeals of jail?"

We decided to set our direct action program around the Easter season, realiz- 7
ing that with the exception of Christmas, this was the largest shopping period of the year. Knowing that a strong economic withdrawal program would be the by-product of direct action, we felt that this was the best time to bring pressure on the merchants for the needed changes. Then it occurred to us that the March election was ahead, and so we speedily decided to postpone action until after election day. When we discovered that

---

[1]Rev. Fred L. Shuttlesworth, Alabama civil rights leader and aide to King.

Mr. Connor[2] was in the run-off, we decided again to postpone so that the demonstrations could not be used to cloud the issues. At this time we agreed to begin our nonviolent witness the day after the run-off.

This reveals that we did not move irresponsibly into direct action. We too 8 wanted to see Mr. Connor defeated; so we went through postponement after postponement to aid in this community need. After this we felt that direct action could be delayed no longer.

You may well ask, "Why direct action? Why sit-ins, marches, etc.? Isn't negoti- 9 ation a better path?" You are exactly right in your call for negotiation. Indeed, this is the purpose of direct action. Nonviolent direct action seeks to create such a crisis and establish such creative tension that a community that has constantly refused to negotiate is forced to confront the issue. It seeks so to dramatize the issue that it can no longer be ignored. I just referred to the creation of tension as a part of the work of the nonviolent resister. This may sound rather shocking. But I must confess that I am not afraid of the word tension. I have earnestly worked and preached against violent tension, but there is a type of constructive nonviolent tension that is necessary for growth. Just as Socrates felt that it was necessary to create a tension in the mind so that individuals could rise from the bondage of myths and half-truths to the unfettered realm of creative analysis and objective appraisal, we must see the need of having nonviolent gadflies to create the kind of tension in society that will help men rise from the dark depths of prejudice and racism to the majestic heights of understanding and brotherhood. So the purpose of the direct action is to create a situation so crisis-packed that it will inevitably open the door to negotiation. We, therefore, concur with you in your call for negotiation. Too long has our beloved Southland been bogged down in the tragic attempt to live in monologue rather than dialogue.

One of the basic points in your statement is that our acts are untimely. Some 10 have asked, "Why didn't you give the new administration time to act?" The only answer that I can give to this inquiry is that the new administration must be prodded about as much as the outgoing one before it acts. We will be sadly mistaken if we feel that the election of Mr. Boutwell will bring the millennium to Birmingham. While Mr. Boutwell is much more articulate and gentle than Mr. Connor, they are both segregationists dedicated to the task of maintaining the status quo. The hope I see in Mr. Boutwell is that he will be reasonable enough to see the futility of massive resistance to desegregation. But he will not see this without pressure from the devotees of civil rights. My friends, I must say to you that we have not made a single gain in civil rights without determined legal and nonviolent pressure. History is the long and tragic story of the fact that privileged groups seldom give up their privileges voluntarily. Individuals may see the moral light and voluntarily give up their unjust posture; but as Reinhold Niebuhr has reminded us, groups are more immoral than individuals.

We know through painful experience that freedom is never voluntarily given by 11 the oppressor; it must be demanded by the oppressed. Frankly I have never yet engaged in a direct action movement that was "well timed," according to the timetable of those who have not suffered unduly from the disease of segregation. For years now I have

---

[2]The police chief of Birmingham, Eugene "Bull" Connor, obtained a writ of injunction against a mass march. The march took place on April 12, 1963.

heard the word "Wait!" It rings in the ear of every Negro with a piercing familiarity. This "wait" has almost always meant "never." It has been a tranquilizing thalidomide, relieving the emotional stress for a moment, only to give birth to an ill-formed infant of frustration. We must come to see with the distinguished jurist of yesterday that "justice too long delayed is justice denied." We have waited for more than three hundred and forty years for our constitutional and God-given rights. The nations of Asia and Africa are moving with jet-like speed toward the goal of political independence, and we still creep at horse and buggy pace toward the gaining of a cup of coffee at a lunch counter.

I guess it is easy for those who have never felt the stinging darts of segregation 12 to say wait. But when you have seen vicious mobs lynch your mothers and fathers at will and drown your sisters and brothers at whim; when you have seen hate filled policemen curse, kick, brutalize, and even kill your black brothers and sisters with impunity; when you see the vast majority of your twenty million Negro brothers smothering in an air-tight cage of poverty in the midst of an affluent society; when you suddenly find your tongue twisted and your speech stammering as you seek to explain to your six-year-old daughter why she can't go to the public amusement park that has just been advertised on television, and see tears welling up in her little eyes when she is told that Funtown is closed to colored children, and see the depressing clouds of inferiority begin to form in her little mental sky, and see her begin to distort her little personality by unconsciously developing a bitterness toward white people; when you have to concoct an answer for a five-year-old son asking in agonizing pathos: "Daddy, why do white people treat colored people so mean?"; when you take a cross country drive and find it necessary to sleep night after night in the uncomfortable corners of your automobile because no motel will accept you; when you are humiliated day in and day out by nagging signs reading "white" men and "colored"; when your first name becomes "nigger" and your middle name becomes "boy" (however old you are) and your last name becomes "John," and when your wife and mother are never given the respected title "Mrs."; when you are harried by day and haunted by night by the fact that you are a Negro, living constantly at tip-toe stance never quite knowing what to expect next, and plagued with inner fears and outer resentments; when you are forever fighting a degenerating sense of "nobodiness";—then you will understand why we find it difficult to wait. There comes a time when the cup of endurance runs over, and men are no longer willing to be plunged into an abyss of injustice where they experience the bleakness of corroding despair. I hope, sirs, you can understand our legitimate and unavoidable impatience.

You express a great deal of anxiety over our willingness to break laws. This is 13 certainly a legitimate concern. Since we so diligently urge people to obey the Supreme Court's decision of 1954 outlawing segregation in public schools, it is rather strange and paradoxical to find us consciously breaking laws.[3] One may well ask, "How can you advocate breaking some laws and obeying others?" The answer is found in the fact that there are two types of laws. There are *just* laws and there are *unjust* laws. I would be the first to advocate obeying just laws. One has not only a legal but moral responsibility to obey just laws. Conversely, one has a moral responsibility to disobey unjust laws. I would agree with Saint Augustine that "An unjust law is no law at all."

---

[3]*Brown vs. Board of Education,* the 1954 Supreme Court decision that declared public school segregation unconstitutional.

Now what is the difference between the two? How does one determine when a 14 law is just or unjust? A just law is a man-made code that squares with the moral law or the law of God. An unjust law is a code that is out of harmony with the moral law. To put it in the terms of Saint Thomas Aquinas, an unjust law is a human law that is not rooted in eternal and natural law. Any law that uplifts human personality is just. Any law that degrades human personality is unjust. All segregation statutes are unjust because segregation distorts the soul and damages the personality. It gives the segregator a false sense of superiority and the segregated a false sense of inferiority. To use the words of Martin Buber, the great Jewish philosopher, segregation substitutes an "I–it" relationship for the "I–thou" relationship, and ends up relegating persons to the status of things. So segregation is not only politically, economically, and sociologically unsound, but it is morally wrong and sinful. Paul Tillich has said that sin is separation. Isn't segregation an existential expression of man's tragic separation, an expression of his awful estrangement, his terrible sinfulness? So I can urge men to obey the 1954 decision of the Supreme Court because it is morally right, and I can urge them to disobey segregation ordinances because they are morally wrong.

Let us turn to a more concrete example of just and unjust laws. An unjust law is a code that a majority inflicts on a minority that is not binding on itself. This is *difference* made legal. On the other hand a just law is a code that a majority compels a minority to follow that it is willing to follow itself. This is *sameness* made legal.

Let me give another explanation. An unjust law is a code inflicted upon a mi- 16 nority which that minority had no part in enacting or creating because they did not have the unhampered right to vote. Who can say the legislature of Alabama which set up the segregation laws was democratically elected? Throughout the state of Alabama all types of conniving methods are used to prevent Negroes from becoming registered voters and there are some counties without a single Negro registered to vote despite the fact that the Negro constitutes a majority of the population. Can any law set up in such a state be considered democratically structured?

These are just a few examples of unjust and just laws. There are some instances 17 when a law is just on its face but unjust in its application. For instance, I was arrested Friday on a charge of parading without a permit. Now there is nothing wrong with an ordinance which requires a permit for a parade, but when the ordinance is used to preserve segregation and to deny citizens the First Amendment privilege of peaceful assembly and peaceful protest, then it becomes unjust.

I hope you can see the distinction I am trying to point out. In no sense do I ad- 18 vocate evading or defying the law as the rabid segregationist would do. This would lead to anarchy. One who breaks an unjust law must do it *openly*, *lovingly* (not hatefully as the white mothers did in New Orleans when they were seen on television screaming "nigger, nigger, nigger") and with a willingness to accept the penalty. I submit that an individual who breaks a law that conscience tells him is unjust, and willingly accepts the penalty by staying in jail to arouse the conscience of the community over its injustice, is in reality expressing the very highest respect for law.

Of course there is nothing new about this kind of civil disobedience. It was seen 19 sublimely in the refusal of Shadrach, Meshach, and Abednego to obey the laws of Nebuchadnezzar because a higher moral law was involved. It was practiced superbly by the early Christians who were willing to face hungry lions and the excruciating pain of chopping blocks, before submitting to certain unjust laws of the Roman Empire. To a degree academic freedom is a reality today because Socrates practiced civil disobedience.

We can never forget that everything Hitler did in Germany was "legal" and 20 everything the Hungarian freedom fighters did in Hungary was "illegal." It was "illegal" to aid and comfort a Jew in Hitler's Germany. But I am sure that, if I had lived in Germany during that time, I would have aided and comforted my Jewish brothers even though it was illegal. If I lived in a communist country today where certain principles dear to the Christian faith are suppressed, I believe I would openly advocate disobeying those antireligious laws.

I must make two honest confessions to you, my Christian and Jewish brothers. 21 First I must confess that over the last few years I have been gravely disappointed with the white moderate. I have almost reached the regrettable conclusion that the Negroes' great stumbling block in the stride toward freedom is not the White Citizens' "Counciler" or the Ku Klux Klanner, but the white moderate who is more devoted to "order" than to justice; who prefers a negative peace which is the absence of tension to a positive peace which is the presence of justice; who constantly says "I agree with you in the goal you seek, but I can't agree with your methods of direct action"; who paternalistically feels that he can set the timetable for another man's freedom; who lives by the myth of time and who constantly advises the Negro to wait until a "more convenient season." Shallow understanding from people of good will is more frustrating than absolute misunderstanding from people of ill will. Lukewarm acceptance is much more bewildering than outright rejection.

I had hoped that the white moderate would understand that law and order exist 22 for the purpose of establishing justice, and that when they fail to do this they become the dangerously structured dams that block the flow of social progress. I had hoped that the white moderate would understand that the present tension in the South is merely a necessary phase of the transition from an obnoxious negative peace, where the Negro passively accepted his unjust plight, to a substance-filled positive peace, where all men will respect the dignity and worth of human personality. Actually, we who engage in nonviolent direct action are not the creators of tension. We merely bring to the surface the hidden tension that is already alive. We bring it out in the open where it can be seen and dealt with. Like a boil that can never be cured as long as it is covered up but must be opened with all its pus-flowing ugliness to the natural medicines of air and light, injustice must likewise be exposed, with all of the tension its exposing creates, to the light of human conscience and the air of national opinion before it can be cured.

In your statement you asserted that our actions, even though peaceful, must be 23 condemned because they precipitate violence. But can this assertion be logically made? Isn't this like condemning the robbed man because his possession of money precipitated the evil act of robbery? Isn't this like condemning Socrates because his unswerving commitment to truth and his philosophical delvings precipitated the misguided popular mind to make him drink the hemlock? Isn't this like condemning Jesus because His unique God consciousness and never-ceasing devotion to His will precipitated the evil act of crucifixion? We must come to see, as federal courts have consistently affirmed, that it is immoral to urge an individual to withdraw his efforts to gain his basic constitutional rights because the quest precipitates violence. Society must protect the robbed and punish the robber.

I had also hoped that the white moderate would reject the myth of time. I re- 24 ceived a letter this morning from a white brother in Texas which said: "All Christians know that the colored people will receive equal rights eventually, but is it possible that you are in too great of a religious hurry? It has taken Christianity almost 2000 years to accomplish what it has. The teachings of Christ take time to come to earth." All that is said here grows out of a tragic misconception of time. It is the strangely irrational notion that there is something in the very flow of time that will inevitably cure all ills. Actually time is neutral. It can be used either destructively or constructively. I am coming to feel that the people of ill will have used time much more effectively than the people of good will. We will have to repent in this generation not merely for the vitriolic words and actions of the bad people, but for the appalling silence of the good people. We must come to see that human progress never rolls in on wheels of inevitability. It comes through the tireless efforts and persistent work of men willing to be co-workers with God, and without this hard work time itself becomes an ally of the forces of social stagnation.

We must use time creatively, and forever realize that the time is always ripe to 25 do right. Now is the time to make real the promise of democracy, and transform our pending national elegy into a creative psalm of brotherhood. Now is the time to lift our national policy from the quicksand of racial injustice to the solid rock of human dignity.

You spoke of our activity in Birmingham as extreme. At first I was rather disap- 26 pointed that fellow clergymen would see my nonviolent efforts as those of the extremist. I started thinking about the fact that I stand in the middle of two opposing forces in the Negro community. One is a force of complacency made up of Negroes who, as a result of long years of oppression, have been so completely drained of self-respect and a sense of "somebodiness" that they have adjusted to segregation, and of a few Negroes in the middle class who, because of a degree of academic and economic security, and because at points they profit by segregation, have unconsciously become insensitive to the problems of the masses. The other force is one of bitterness and hatred and comes perilously close to advocating violence. It is expressed in the various black nationalist groups that are springing up over the nation, the largest and best known being Elijah Muhammad's Muslim movement. This movement is nourished by the contemporary frustration over the continued existence of racial discrimination. It is made up of people who have lost faith in America, who have absolutely repudiated Christianity, and who have concluded that the white man is an incurable "devil." I have tried to stand between these two forces saying that we need not follow the "do-nothingism" of the complacent or the hatred and despair of the black nationalist. There is the more excellent way of love and nonviolent protest. I'm grateful to God that, through the Negro church, the dimension of nonviolence entered our struggle. If this philosophy had not emerged I am convinced that by now many streets of the South would be flowing with floods of blood. And I am further convinced that if our white brothers dismiss us as "rabble rousers" and "outside agitators"—those of us who are working through the channels of nonviolent direct action—and refuse to support our nonviolent efforts, millions of Negroes, out of frustration and despair, will seek solace and security in black nationalist ideologies, a development that will lead inevitably to a frightening racial nightmare.

Oppressed people cannot remain oppressed forever. The urge for freedom will 27 eventually come. This is what has happened to the American Negro. Something within has reminded him of his birthright of freedom; something without has reminded him that he can gain it. Consciously and unconsciously, he has been swept in by what the Germans call the *Zeitgeist,* and with his black brothers of Africa, and his brown and yellow brothers of Asia, South America, and the Caribbean, he is moving with a sense of cosmic urgency toward the promised land of racial justice. Recognizing this vital urge that has engulfed the Negro community, one should readily understand public demonstrations. The Negro has many pent-up resentments and latent frustrations. He has to get them out. So let him march sometime; let him have his prayer pilgrimages to the city hall; understand why he must have sit-ins and freedom rides. If his repressed emotions do not come out in these nonviolent ways, they will come out in ominous expressions of violence. This is not a threat; it is a fact of history. So I have not said to my people, "Get rid of your discontent." But I have tried to say that this normal and healthy discontent can be channeled through the creative outlet of nonviolent direct action. Now this approach is being dismissed as extremist. I must admit that I was initially disappointed in being so categorized.

But as I continued to think about the matter I gradually gained a bit of satisfac- 28 tion from being considered an extremist. Was not Jesus an extremist in love? "Love your enemies, bless them that curse you, pray for them that despitefully use you." Was not Amos an extremist for justice—"Let justice roll down like waters and righteousness like a mighty stream." Was not Paul an extremist for the gospel of Jesus Christ—"I bear in my body the marks of the Lord Jesus." Was not Martin Luther an extremist—"Here I stand; I can do none other so help me God." Was not John Bunyan an extremist—"I will stay in jail to the end of my days before I make a butchery of my conscience."[4] Was not Abraham Lincoln an extremist—"This nation cannot survive half slave and half free." Was not Thomas Jefferson an extremist—"We hold these truths to be self evident that all men are created equal." So the question is not whether we will be extremist but what kind of extremist will we be. Will we be extremists for hate or will we be extremists for love? Will we be extremists for the preservation of injustice—or will we be extremists for the cause of justice? In that dramatic scene on Calvary's hill three men were crucified. We must never forget that all three were crucified for the same crime—the crime of extremism. Two were extremists for immorality, and thus fell below their environment. The other, Jesus Christ, was an extremist for love, truth, and goodness, and thereby rose above His environment. So, after all, maybe the South, the nation, and the world are in dire need of creative extremists.

I had hoped that the white moderate would see this. Maybe I was too optimis- 29 tic. Maybe I expected too much. I guess I should have realized that few members of a race that has oppressed another race can understand or appreciate the deep groans and passionate yearnings of those that have been oppressed, and still fewer have the vision

---

[4]John Bunyan (1628–1688): Puritan preacher and writer, imprisoned for illegal preaching; author of *Pilgrim's Progress.*

to see that injustice must be rooted out by strong, persistent, and determined action. I am thankful, however, that some of our white brothers have grasped the meaning of this social revolution and committed themselves to it. They are still all too small in quantity, but they are big in quality. Some like Ralph McGill, Lillian Smith, Harry Golden, and James Dabbs have written about our struggle in eloquent, prophetic, and understanding terms.[5] Others have marched with us down nameless streets of the South. They have languished in filthy, roach-infested jails, suffering the abuse and brutality of angry policemen who see them as "dirty nigger lovers." They, unlike so many of their moderate brothers and sisters, have recognized the urgency of the moment and sensed the need for powerful "action" antidotes to combat the disease of segregation.

Let me rush on to mention my other disappointment. I have been so greatly 30 disappointed with the white Church and its leadership. Of course there are some notable exceptions. I am not unmindful of the fact that each of you has taken some significant stands on this issue. I commend you, Rev. Stallings, for your Christian stand on this past Sunday, in welcoming Negroes to your worship service on a nonsegregated basis. I commend the Catholic leaders of this state for integrating Springhill College several years ago.

But despite these notable exceptions I must honestly reiterate that I have been 31 disappointed with the Church. I do not say that as one of those negative critics who can always find something wrong with the Church. I say it as a minister of the gospel, who loves the Church; who was nurtured in its bosom; who has been sustained by its spiritual blessings and who will remain true to it as long as the cord of life shall lengthen.

I had the strange feeling when I was suddenly catapulted into the leadership of 32 the bus protest in Montgomery several years ago that we would have the support of the white Church. I felt that the white ministers, priests, and rabbis of the South would be some of our strongest allies. Instead, some have been outright opponents, refusing to understand the freedom movement and misrepresenting its leaders; all too many others have been more cautious than courageous and have remained silent behind the anesthetizing security of stained glass windows.

In spite of my shattered dreams of the past, I came to Birmingham with the 33 hope that the white religious leadership of the community would see the justice of our cause and, with deep moral concern, serve as the channel through which our just grievances could get to the power structure. I had hoped that each of you would understand. But again I have been disappointed.

I have heard numerous religious leaders of the South call upon their worship- 34 pers to comply with a desegregation decision because it is the law, but I have longed to hear white ministers say follow this decree because integration is morally right and the Negro is your brother. In the midst of blatant injustices inflicted upon the Negro, I have watched white churches stand on the sideline and merely mouth pious irrelevancies and sanctimonious trivialities. In the midst of a mighty struggle to rid our nation of racial and economic injustice, I have heard so many ministers say, "Those are social issues with which the Gospel has no real concern," and I have watched so many churches commit themselves to a completely otherworldly religion which made a strange distinction between body and soul, the sacred and the secular.

---

[5]Southern writers and editors who protested the treatment of blacks in the segregated South.

So here we are moving toward the exit of the twentieth century with a religious 35 community largely adjusted to the status quo, standing as a tail light behind other community agencies rather than a headlight leading men to higher levels of justice.

I have travelled the length and breadth of Alabama, Mississippi, and all the 36 other Southern states. On sweltering summer days and crisp autumn mornings I have looked at her beautiful churches with their spires pointing heavenward. I have beheld the impressive outlay of her massive religious education buildings. Over and over again I have found myself asking: "Who worships here? Who is their God? Where were their voices when the lips of Governor Barnett dripped with words of interposition and nullification? Where were they when Governor Wallace gave the clarion call for defiance and hatred? Where were their voices of support when tired, bruised, and weary Negro men and women decided to rise from the dark dungeons of complacency to the bright hills of creative protest?"

Yes, these questions are still in my mind. In deep disappointment, I have wept 37 over the laxity of the Church. But be assured that my tears have been tears of love. There can be no deep disappointment where there is not deep love. Yes, I love the Church; I love her sacred walls. How could I do otherwise? I am in the rather unique position of being the son, the grandson, and the great grandson of preachers. Yes, I see the Church as the body of Christ. But, oh! How we have blemished and scarred that body through social neglect and fear of being nonconformists.

There was a time when the Church was very powerful. It was during that period 38 when the early Christians rejoiced when they were deemed worthy to suffer for what they believed. In those days the Church was not merely a thermometer that recorded the ideas and principles of popular opinion; it was a thermostat that transformed the mores of society. Wherever the early Christians entered a town the power structure got disturbed and immediately sought to convict them for being "disturbers of the peace" and "outside agitators." But they went on with the conviction that they were a "colony of heaven" and had to obey God rather than man. They were small in number but big in commitment. They were too God-intoxicated to be "astronomically intimidated." They brought an end to such ancient evils as infanticide and gladiatorial contest.

Things are different now. The contemporary Church is so often a weak, ineffec- 39 tual voice with an uncertain sound. It is so often the archsupporter of the status quo. Far from being disturbed by the presence of the Church, the power structure of the average community is consoled by the Church's silent and often vocal sanction of things as they are.

But the judgment of God is upon the Church as never before. If the Church of 40 today does not recapture the sacrificial spirit of the early Church, it will lose its authentic ring, forfeit the loyalty of millions, and be dismissed as an irrelevant social club with no meaning for the twentieth century. I am meeting young people every day whose disappointment with the Church has risen to outright disgust.

Maybe again I have been too optimistic. Is organized religion too inextricably 41 bound to the status quo to save our nation and the world? Maybe I must turn my faith to the inner spiritual Church, the church within the Church, as the true *ecclesia* and the hope of the world. But again I am thankful to God that some noble souls from the ranks of organized religion have broken loose from the paralyzing chains of conformity and joined us as active partners in the struggle for freedom. They have left their secure congregations and walked the streets of Albany, Georgia, with us. They have gone through the highways of the South on torturous rides for freedom. Yes, they have gone to jail with us. Some have been kicked out of their churches and lost the support of their bishops and fellow ministers. But they have gone with the faith that right defeated is stronger than evil triumphant. These men have been the leaven in the lump of the race. Their witness has been the spiritual salt that has preserved the true meaning of the Gospel in these troubled times. They have carved a tunnel of hope through the dark mountain of disappointment.

I hope the Church as a whole will meet the challenge of this decisive hour. But 42 even if the Church does not come to the aid of justice, I have no despair about the future. I have no fear about the outcome of our struggle in Birmingham, even if our motives are presently misunderstood. We will reach the goal of freedom in Birmingham and all over the nation, because the goal of America is freedom. Abused and scorned though we may be, our destiny is tied up with the destiny of America. Before the pilgrims landed at Plymouth, we were here. Before the pen of Jefferson etched across the pages of history the majestic words of the Declaration of Independence, we were here. For more than two centuries our foreparents labored in this country without wages; they made cotton "king"; and they built the homes of their masters in the midst of brutal injustice and shameful humiliation—and yet out of a bottomless vitality they continued to thrive and develop. If the inexpressible cruelties of slavery could not stop us, the opposition we now face will surely fail. We will win our freedom because the sacred heritage of our nation and the external will of God are embodied in our echoing demands.

I must close now. But before closing I am impelled to mention one other point 43 in your statement that troubled me profoundly. You warmly commended the Birmingham police force for keeping "order" and "preventing violence." I don't believe you would have so warmly commended the police force if you had seen its angry violent dogs literally biting six unarmed, nonviolent Negroes. I don't believe you would so quickly commend the policemen if you would observe their ugly and inhuman treatment of Negroes here in the city jail; if you would watch them push and curse old Negro women and young Negro girls; if you would see them slap and kick old Negro men and young Negro boys; if you will observe them, as they did on two occasions, refuse to give us food because we wanted to sing our grace together. I'm sorry that I can't join you in your praise for the police department.

It is true that they have been rather disciplined in their public handling of the 44 demonstrators. In this sense they have been rather publicly "nonviolent." But for what purpose? To preserve the evil system of segregation. Over the last few years I have consistently preached that nonviolence demands that the means we use must be as pure as the ends we seek. So I have tried to make it clear that it is wrong to use immoral means to attain moral ends. But now I must affirm that it is just as wrong, or even more so, to use moral means to preserve immoral ends. Maybe Mr. Connor and his policemen have been rather publicly nonviolent, as Chief Prichett was in Albany, Georgia, but they have used the moral means of nonviolence to maintain the immoral end of flagrant racial injustice. T. S. Eliot has said that there is no greater treason than to do the right deed for the wrong reason.[6]

---

[6]Thomas of Becket makes this statement in Eliot's verse play *Murder in the Cathedral.*

I wish you had commended the Negro sit-inners and demonstrators of Bir- 45 mingham for their sublime courage, their willingness to suffer, and their amazing discipline in the midst of the most inhuman provocation. One day the South will recognize its real heroes. They will be the James Merediths, courageously and with a majestic sense of purpose, facing jeering and hostile mobs and the agonizing loneliness that characterizes the life of the pioneer. They will be old, oppressed, battered Negro women, symbolized in a seventy-two year old woman of Montgomery, Alabama, who rose up with a sense of dignity and with her people decided not to ride the segregated buses, and responded to one who inquired about her tiredness with ungrammatical profundity: "My feets is tired, but my soul is rested." They will be young high school and college students, young ministers of the gospel and a host of the elders, courageously and nonviolently sitting in at lunch counters and willingly going to jail for conscience sake. One day the South will know that when these disinherited children of God sat down at lunch counters they were in reality standing up for the best in the American dream and the most sacred values in our Judeo-Christian heritage, and thus carrying our whole nation back to great wells of democracy which were dug deep by the founding fathers in the formulation of the Constitution and the Declaration of Independence.

Never before have I written a letter this long (or should I say a book?). I'm 46 afraid that it is much too long to take your precious time. I can assure you that it would have been much shorter if I had been writing from a comfortable desk, but what else is there to do when you are alone for days in the dull monotony of a narrow jail cell other than write long letters, think strange thoughts, and pray long prayers?

If I have said anything in this letter that is an overstatement of the truth and 47 is indicative of an unreasonable impatience, I beg you to forgive me. If I have said anything in this letter that is an understatement of the truth and is indicative of my having a patience that makes me patient with anything less than brotherhood, I beg God to forgive me.

I hope this letter finds you strong in the faith. I also hope that circumstances 48 will soon make it possible for me to meet each of you, not as an integrationist or a civil rights leader, but as a fellow clergyman and a Christian brother. Let us all hope that the dark clouds of racial prejudice will soon pass away and the deep fog of misunderstanding will be lifted from our fear-drenched communities and in some not too distant tomorrow the radiant stars of love and brotherhood will shine over our great nation with all of their scintillating beauty.

Yours for the cause of
Peace and Brotherhood

MARTIN LUTHER KING, JR.

Questions

1. What is King's purpose in the introduction to his letter? What is his stated attitude toward the clergymen in the opening paragraph?
2. How does King establish the fact that he came to Birmingham on a religious mission? Does he defend this mission?
3. What is the basic argument King will develop? How does he make the details of this argument pertinent to events in Birmingham prior to his arrival?

4. How does King respond to the charges that sit-ins and marches create "tension" and are "untimely"? How does he redefine these words to show that the clergymen need to be reminded of history?
5. On the basis of what philosophy does King defend civil disobedience in paragraphs 15–19? How does he distinguish his own disobedience from that of the "rabid segregationist"?
6. In his rebuttal or answer to objections in paragraphs 19–20, why does King reject the argument that civil disobedience is "illegal"?
7. What assumptions of the clergymen does King attack in paragraph 24? How does this attack build upon King's earlier defense of civil disobedience?
8. How does King answer the charge that he is an extremist? How does his answer resemble his earlier answers to charges by his opponents that his actions create tension, are untimely, are illegal, and are extremist?
9. How does the argument of paragraphs 32–42 build upon his earlier defense of civil disobedience?
10. Why does King close with the statement about the clergymen's commendation of the Birmingham police? Is his statement central to his defense of civil disobedience?
11. Does King write in a single tone, or does his tone shift from paragraph to paragraph or from one argument to another?
12. How successful do you believe the letter is in achieving its purpose? Is King more conciliatory than you would have been? Should he have attacked the clergymen and the Birmingham authorities in stronger language?

Suggestions for Writing

1. King states that a person has the right to disobey an unjust law. First explain what he means by *unjust*. Then discuss whether a student should not only protest a school regulation but should disobey it. Use your discussion to explain your agreement or disagreement with King on the issue of disobedience.
2. King states in paragraph 30: "So the question is not whether we will be extremist but what kind of extremist will we be." What is your own definition of a social or political extremist? Do you agree with King that some kinds of extremism are justified?
3. King refers to the ideas of Martin Buber and Paul Tillich. The "I–Thou" philosophy of Buber is the subject of his book *Between Man and Man* (1965). Tillich discusses the nature of sin in his book *Dynamics of Faith*. Mahatma Gandhi's philosophy of civil disobedience is developed in his autobiography *My Life* and *Selected Writings of Mahatma Gandhi* (1951), edited by Ronald Duncan, and in other collections. Use the writings of one or more of these authors to illuminate one or more ideas in King's letter.

Additional Reading

King, Coretta Scott. *My Life with Martin Luther King, Jr.* New York: Holt, 1969.
King, Martin Luther, Jr. *Stride toward Freedom: The Montgomery Story.* New York: Harper and Row, 1958.

————. *Why We Can't Wait.* New York: Harper and Row, 1964.

————. *Where Do We Go from Here: Chaos or Community.* New York: Harper and Row, 1967.

————. *The Trumpet of Conscience.* New York: Harper and Row, 1968.

Where Is the Voice Coming From?

Eudora Welty

Born in Jackson, Mississippi, in 1909, Eudora Welty attended Mississippi State College for Women and later the University of Wisconsin and Columbia University. She worked in advertising before returning to Jackson to work for the government as a publicist. Living in Jackson, she began publishing stories about Southern life. The first collection of her stories, A Curtain of Green *(1941), immediately established her as an important writer.*

Her story "Where Is the Voice Coming From?" was first published in The New Yorker *magazine following racial disturbances in Mississippi and the shooting of a Mississippi civil rights leader, Medgar Evers, on June 13, 1963. Welty said of the story in 1972: "I tried to write from the interior of my own South and that's why I dared to put it in the first person. . . . At the time I wrote it—it was overnight—no one knew who the murderer was . . . ."*

I says to my wife, "You can reach and turn it off. You don't have to set and look at a black nigger face no longer than you want to, or listen to what you don't want to hear. It's still a free country."

I reckon that's how I give myself the idea.

I says, I could find right exactly where in Thermopylae that nigger's living that's asking for equal time. And without a bit of trouble to me.

And I ain't saying it might not be because that's pretty close to where *I* live. The other hand, there could be reasons you might have yourself for knowing how to get there in the dark. It's where you all go for the thing you want when you want it the most. Ain't that right?

The Branch Bank sign tells you in lights, all night long even, what time it is and how hot. When it was quarter to four, and 92, that was me going by in my brother-in-law's truck. He don't deliver nothing at that hour of the morning.

So you leave Four Corners and head west on Nathan B. Forrest Road, past the Surplus & Salvage, not much beyond the Kum Back Drive-In and Trailer Camp, not as far as where the signs starts saying "Live Bait," "Used Parts," "Fireworks," "Peaches," and "Sister Peebles Reader and Adviser." Turn before you hit the city limits and duck back towards the I. C. tracks. And his street's been paved.

And there was his light on, waiting for me. In his garage, if you please. His car's gone. He's out planning still some other ways to do what we tell 'em they can't. I *thought* I'd beat him home. All I had to do was pick my tree and walk in close behind it.

I didn't come expecting not to wait. But it was so hot, all I did was hope and pray one or the other of us wouldn't melt before it was over.

Now, it wasn't no bargain I'd struck.

I've heard what you've heard about Goat Dykeman, in Mississippi. Sure, everybody knows about Goat Dykeman. Goat he got word to the Governor's Mansion he'd go up yonder and shoot that nigger Meredith clean out of school, if he's let out of the pen to do it. Old Ross turned *that* over in his mind before saying him nay, it stands to reason.

I ain't no Goat Dykeman, I ain't in no pen, and I ain't ask no Governor Barnett to give me one thing. Unless he wants to give me a pat on the back for the trouble I took this morning. But he don't have to if he don't want to. I done what I done for my own pure-D satisfaction.

As soon as I heard wheels, I knowed who was coming. That was him and bound to be him. It was the right nigger heading in a new white car up his driveway towards his garage with the light shining, but stopping before he got there, maybe not to wake 'em. That was him. I knowed it when he cut off the car lights and put his foot out and I knowed him standing dark against the light. I knowed him then like I know me now. I knowed him even by his still, listening back.

Never seen him before, never seen him since, never seen anything of his black face but his picture, never seen his face alive, any time at all, or anywheres, and didn't want to, need to, never hope to see that face and never will. As long as there was no question in my mind.

He had to be the one. He stood right still and waited against the light, his back was fixed, fixed on me like a preacher's eyeballs when he's yelling "Are you saved?" He's the one.

I'd already brought up my rifle, I'd already taken my sights. And I'd already got him, because it was too late then for him or me to turn by one hair.

Something darker than him, like the wings of a bird, spread on his back and pulled him down. He climbed up once, like a man under bad claws, and like just blood could weigh a ton he walked with it on his back to better light. Didn't get no further than his door. And fell to stay.

He was down. He was down, and a ton load of bricks on his back wouldn't have laid any heavier. There on his paved driveway, yes sir.

And it wasn't till the minute before, that the mockingbird had quit singing. He'd been singing up my sassafras tree. Either he was up early, or he hadn't never gone to bed, he was like me. And the mocker he'd stayed right with me, filling the air till come the crack, till I turned loose of my load. I was like him. I was on top of the world myself. For once.

I stepped to the edge of his light there, where he's laying flat. I says, "Roland? There was one way left, for me to be ahead of you and stay ahead of you, by Dad, and I just taken it. Now I'm alive and you ain't. We ain't never now, never going to be equals and you know why? One of us is dead. What about that, Roland?" I said. "Well, you seen to it, didn't you?"

I stood a minute—just to see would somebody inside come out long enough to pick him up. And there she comes, the woman. I doubt she'd been to sleep. Because it seemed to me she'd been in there keeping awake all along.

It was mighty green where I skint over the yard getting back. That nigger wife of his, she wanted nice grass! I bet my wife would hate to pay her water bill. And for burning her electricity. And there's my brother-in-law's truck, still waiting with the door open. "No Riders"—that didn't mean me.

There wasn't a thing I been able to think of since would have made it to go any nicer. Except a chair to my back while I was putting in my waiting. But going home, I seen what little time it takes after all to get a thing done like you really want it. It was 4:34, and while I was looking it moved to 35. And the temperature stuck where it was. All that night I guarantee you it had stood without dropping, a good 92.

My wife says, "What? Didn't the skeeters bite you?" She said, "Well, they been asking that—why somebody didn't trouble to load a rifle and get some of these agitators out of Thermopylae. Didn't the fella keep drumming it in, what a good idea? The one that writes a column ever' day?"

I says to my wife, "Find *some* way I don't get the credit."

"He says do it for Thermopylae," she says. "Don't you ever skim the paper?"

I says, "Thermopylae never done nothing for me. And I don't owe nothing to Thermopylae. Didn't do it for you. Hell, any more'n I'd do something or other for them Kennedys! I done it for my own pure-D satisfaction."

"It's going to get him right back on TV," says my wife. "You watch for the funeral."

I says, "You didn't even leave a light burning when you went to bed. So how was I supposed to even get me home or pull Buddy's truck up safe in our front yard?"

"Well, hear another good joke on you," my wife says next. "Didn't you hear the news? The N. double A.C.P. is fixing to send somebody to Thermopylae. Why couldn't you waited? You might could have got you somebody better. Listen and hear 'em say so."

I ain't but one. I reckon you have to tell *somebody*.

"Where's the gun, then?" my wife says. "What did you do with our pro-tection?"

I says, "It was scorching! It was scorching!" I told her, "It's laying out on the ground in rank weeds, trying to cool off, that's what it's doing now."

"You dropped it," she says. "Back there."

And I told her, "Because I'm so tired of ever'thing in the world being just that hot to the touch! The keys to the truck, the doorknob, the bedsheet, ever'thing, it's all like a stove lid. There just ain't much going that's worth holding on to it no more," I says, "when it's a hundred and two in the shade by day and by night not too much differ-ence. I wish *you'd* laid *your* finger to that gun."

"Trust you to come off and leave it," my wife says.

"Is that how no-'count I am?" she makes me ask. *"You* want to go back and get it?"

"You're the one they'll catch. I say it's so hot that even if you get to sleep you wake up feeling like you cried all night!" says my wife. "Cheer up, here's one more joke before time to get up. Heard what *Caroline* said? Caroline said, 'Daddy, I just can't wait to grow up big, so I can marry *James Meredith.*' I heard that where I work. One rich-bitch to another one, to make her cackle."

"At least I kept some dern teen-ager from North Thermopylae getting there and doing it first," I says. "Driving his own car."

On TV and in the paper, they don't know but half of it. They know who Roland Summers was without knowing who I am. His face was in front of the public before I got rid of him, and after I got rid of him there it is again—the same picture. And none of me. I ain't ever had one made. Not ever! The best that newspaper could do for me was offer a five-hundred-dollar reward for finding out who I am. For as long as they don't know who that is, whoever shot Roland is worth a good deal more right now than Roland is.

But by the time I was moving around uptown, it was hotter still. That pavement in the middle of Main Street was so hot to my feet I might've been walking the barrel of my gun. If the whole world could've just felt Main Street this morning through the soles of my shoes, maybe it would've helped some.

Then the first thing I heard "em say was the N. double A.C.P. done it themselves, killed Roland Summers, and proved it by saying the shooting was done by a expert (I hope to tell you it was!) and at just the right hour and minute to get the whites in trouble.

You can't win.

"They'll never find him," the old man trying to sell roasted peanuts tells me to my face.

And it's so hot.

It looks like the town's on fire already, whichever ways you turn, ever' street you strike, because there's those trees hanging them pones of bloom like split watermelon. And a thousand cops crowding ever'where you go, half of 'em too young to start shaving, but all streaming sweat alike. I'm getting tired of 'em.

I was already tired of seeing a hundred cops getting us white people nowheres. Back at the beginning, I stood on the corner and I watched them new babyface cops loading nothing but nigger children into the paddy wagon and they come marching out of a little parade and into the paddy wagon singing. And they got in and sat down without providing a speck of trouble, and their hands held little new American flags, and all the cops could do was knock them flagsticks a-loose from their hands, and not let 'em pick 'em up, that was all, and give 'em a free ride. And children can just get 'em more flags.

Everybody: It don't get you nowhere to take nothing from nobody unless you make sure it's for keeps, for good and all, for ever and amen.

I won't be sorry to see them brickbats hail down on us for a change. Pop bottles too, they can come flying whenever they want to. Hundreds, all to smash, like Birmingham. I'm waiting on 'em to bring out them switchblade knives, like Harlem and Chicago. Watch TV long enough and you'll see it all to happen on Deacon Street in Thermopylae. What's holding it back, that's all?—Because it's *in* 'em.

I'm ready myself for that funeral.

Oh, they may find me. May catch me one day in spite of 'emselves. (But I grew up in the country.) May try to railroad me into the electric chair, and what that amounts to is something hotter than yesterday and today put together.

But I advise 'em to go careful. Ain't it about time us taxpayers starts to calling the moves? Starts to telling the teachers *and* the preachers *and* the judges of our so-called courts how far they can go?

Even the President so far, he can't walk in my house without being invited, like he's my daddy, just to say whoa. Not yet!

Once, I run away from my home. And there was a ad for me, come to be printed in our county weekly. My mother paid for it. It was from her. It says: "SON: You are not being hunted for anything but to find you." That time, I come on back home.

But people are dead now.

And it's so hot. Without it even being August yet.

Anyways, I seen him fall. I was evermore the one.

So I reach me down my old guitar off the nail in the wall. 'Cause I've got my guitar, what I've held on to from way back when, and I never dropped that, never lost or forgot it, never hocked it but to get it again, never give it away, and I set in my chair, with nobody home but me, and I start to play, and sing a-Down. And sing a-down, down, down, down. Sing a-down, down, down, down. Down.

Questions

1. What general grievances against black people does the speaker express in the course of the story? Does he express a particular grievance against the black man and his wife? Do you have the sense of unexpressed grievances or hidden motives?
2. What exactly does he fear from black people and the government? Would you say that fear is the chief motive of his act?
3. Why does he leave the rifle at the house of the black man? What does this act reveal about his state of mind or motive?
4. Why does he tell us what happened when he ran away from home as a boy?
5. The speaker says toward the end: "I won't be sorry to see them brickbats hail down on us for a change." What does he mean?
6. What is the implication of the refrain he sings at the end of the story?
7. What does Eudora Welty gain in having the speaker tell his own story? Does he provide facts that an impersonal narrator could not have presented? Would there be a gain or a loss in having a narrator analyze the character and the motives of the speaker in the course of the story?
8. Is the story a character study, a picture of a time or a society, or a political statement? Or is it some or all of these? Is it necessary to the purpose of the story to know the motives of the speaker fully?

Suggestions for Writing

1. Characterize Eudora Welty's values as fully as you can, and explain how you discover them in the story.
2. Characterize the speaker of the story and explain how you discover his qualities. Discuss significant statements and details.

Additional Reading

Welty, Eudora. *The Collected Stories.* New York: Harcourt Brace Jovanovich, 1980.
———. *Delta Wedding.* New York: Harcourt Brace Jovanovich, 1946.
———. *The Eye of the Story: Selected Essays and Reviews.* New York: Random House, 1978.
———. *Losing Battles.* New York: Harcourt Brace Jovanovich, 1970.
———. *The Optimist's Daughter.* New York: Harcourt Brace Jovanovich, 1972.
———. *The Ponder Heart.* New York: Harcourt Brace Jovanovich, 1954.

A Fight between a White Boy and a Black Boy in the Dusk of a Fall Afternoon in Omaha, Nebraska

Wright Morris

Wright Morris was born in Central City, Nebraska, in 1910, and he has written much about Nebraska and the Middle West in his fiction and his several volumes of autobiography, including A Life *(1973). He has written more than eighteen novels.* The Field of Vision *earned him the National Book Award in 1957, and* Plains Song, *the American Book Award in 1980. Morris also has several books of photographs with text, including* The Home Place *(1948) and* God's Country and My People *(1968), and several collections of essays.*

In a book on the writing of fiction, Morris gives us insight into his intention as a writer: "The fiction writer is not so confined as the lion, nor is he as free as the eagle or the falcon, but he is now in a position to see that the corridor of man's history is narrow, and that men stand at both ends of it, blocking the light. We yearn to be different, but we prefer to be as we are." Eudora Welty says of Morris in a review of one of his novels: "Laying sure hands on the daily *is Wright Morris's forte. What the rest of us may have accepted too casually he sets upon with his own highly specialized focus."*

How did it start? If there is room for speculation, it lies in how to end it. Neither the white boy nor the black boy gives it further thought. They stand, braced off, in the cinder-covered schoolyard, in the shadow of the darkened red-brick building. Eight or ten smaller boys circle the fighters, forming sides. A white boy observes the fight upside down as he hangs by his knees from the iron rail of the fence. A black girl pasting cutouts of pumpkins in the windows of the annex seems unconcerned. Fights are not so unusual. Halloween and pumpkins come but once a year.

At the start of the fight there was considerable jeering and exchange of formidable curses. The black boy was much better at this part of the quarrel and jeered the feebleness of his opponent's remarks. The white boy lacked even the words. His experience with taunts and scalding invective proved to be remarkably shallow. Twice the black boy dropped his arms as if they were useless against such a potato-mouthed, stupid adversary. Once he laughed, showing the coral roof of his mouth. In the shadow of the school little else stood out clearly for the white boy to strike at. The black boy did not have large whites to his eyes, or pearly white teeth. In the late afternoon light he made a poor target except for the shirt that stood out against the fence that closed in the school. He had rolled up the sleeves and opened the collar so that he could breathe easier and fight better. His black bare feet are the exact color of the cinder yard.

The white boy is a big, hulking fellow, large for his age. It is not clear what it might be, since he has been in the same grade for three years. The bottom board has been taken from the drawer of his desk to allow for his knees. Something said about that may have started the quarrel, or the way he likes to suck on toy train wheels. (He blows softly and wetly through the hole, the wheel at the front of his mouth.) But none of that is clear; all that is known is that he stands like a boxer, his head ducked low, his huge fists doubled before his face. He stands more frontally than sidewise, as if uncertain which fist to lead with. As a rule he wrestles. He would much rather wrestle than fight with his fists. Perhaps he refused to wrestle with a black boy, and *that* could be the problem. One never knows. Who ever knows for sure what starts a fight?

The black boy's age hardly matters and it doesn't show. All that shows clearly` is his shirt and the way he stands. His head looks small because his shoulders are so wide. He has seen pictures of famous boxers and stands with his left arm stretched out before him as if approaching something in the darkness. His right arm, cocked, he holds as if his chest pained him. Both boys are hungry, scared, and waiting for the other one to give up.

The white boy is afraid of the other one's blackness, and the black boy hates and fears whiteness. Something of their mutual fear is now shared by those who are watching. One of the small black boys hoots like an Indian and takes off. One of the white boys has a pocketful of marbles he dips his hand into and rattles. This was distracting when the fight first started, and he was asked to take his hands out of his pockets. Now it eases the strain of the silence.

The need to take sides has also dwindled, and the watchers have gathered with the light behind them, out of their eyes. They say "Come on!" the way you say "Sic 'em," not caring which dog. A pattern has emerged which the two fighters know, but it is not yet known to the watchers. Nobody is going to win. The dilemma is how nobody is going to lose. It has early been established that the black boy will hit the white boy on the head with a sound like splitting a melon—but it's the white boy who moves forward, the black boy who moves back. It isn't clear if the white boy, or any of the watchers, perceives the method in this tactic. Each step backward the black boy takes he is closer to home, and nearer to darkness.

In time they cross the cinder-covered yard to the narrow steps going down to the sidewalk. There the fight is delayed while a passing adult, a woman with a baby sitting up in its carriage, tells them to stop acting like children, and asks their names to inform their teachers. The black boy's name is Eustace Beecher. The white boy's name is Emil Hrdlic, or something like that. He's a real saphead, and not at all certain how it is spelled. When the woman leaves, they return to their fighting and go along the fronts of darkened houses. Dogs bark. Little dogs, especially, enjoy a good fight.

The black boy has changed his style of fighting so that his bleeding nose doesn't drip on his shirt. The white boy has switched around to give his cramped, cocked arm a rest. The black boy picks up support from the fact that he doesn't take advantage of this situation. One reason might be that his left eye is almost closed. When he stops to draw a shirtsleeve across his face, the white boy does not leap forward and strike him. It's a good fight. They have learned what they can do and what they can't do.

At the corner lit up by the bug-filled streetlamp they lose about half of their seven spectators. It's getting late and dark. You can smell the bread baking on the bakery draft. The light is better for the fighters now than the watchers, who see the two figures only in profile. It's not so easy anymore to see which one is black and which one is white. Sometimes the black boy, out of habit, takes a step backward, then has to hop forward to his proper position. The hand he thrusts out before him is limp at the wrist, as if he had just dropped something unpleasant. The white boy's shirt, once blue in color, shines like a slicker on his sweaty back. The untied laces of his shoes are broken from the way he is always stepping on them. He is the first to turn his head and check the time on the bakery clock.

Behind the black boy the street enters the Negro section. Down there, for two long blocks, there is no light. A gas streetlamp can be seen far at the end, the halo around it swimming with insects. One of the two remaining fight watchers whistles shrilly, then enters the bakery to buy penny candy. There's a gum-ball machine that sometimes returns your penny, but it takes time, and you have to shake it.

The one spectator left to watch this fight stands revealed in the glow of the bakery window. One pocket is weighted with marbles; the buckles of his britches are below his knees. He watches the fighters edge into the darkness where the white shirt of the black boy is like an object levitated at a séance. Nothing else can be seen. Black boy and white boy are swallowed up. For a moment one can hear the shuffling feet of the white boy; then that, too, dissolves into darkness. The street is a tunnel with a lantern gleaming far at its end. The last fight watcher stands as if paralyzed until the rumble of a passing car can be felt through the soles of his shoes, tingling the blood in his feet. Behind him the glow of the sunset reddens the sky. He goes toward it on the run, a racket of marbles, his eyes fixed on the FORD sign beyond the school building, where there is a hollow with a shack used by ice skaters under which he can crawl and peer out like a cat. When the streetlights cast more light he will go home.

Somewhere, still running, there is a white boy who saw all of this and will swear to it; otherwise, nothing of what he saw remains. The Negro section, the bakery on the corner, the red-brick school with one second-floor window (the one that opens out on the fire escape) outlined by the chalk dust where they slapped the erasers—all of that is gone, the earth leveled and displaced to accommodate the ramps of the new freeway. The cloverleaf approaches look great from the air. It saves the driving time of those headed east or west. Omaha is no longer the gateway to the West, but the plains remain, according to one traveler, a place where his wife still sleeps in the seat while he drives through the night.

Questions

1. What in the dress and appearance of the two boys does the narrator stress? What details of the fight? What details of the setting?
2. Does the narrator suggest that the event is a recent one? Is it important to know whether it is recent?

3. Is the narrator one of the spectators? Or is the narrator an adult watching and imagining the fight?
4. Why does the narrator stress that the spectators drift away?
5. Does the narrator find meaning or a lesson in the fight, or does he merely describe what happens? Is the fact that the fight is between a white boy and a black boy incidental, or is their color central to the issue or theme of the story?
6. The narrator states: "A pattern has emerged which the two fighters know, but it is not yet known to the watchers. Nobody is going to win. The dilemma is how nobody is going to lose." What does the narrator mean?
7. How does the narrator shape your response to the episode? What response does the narrator want to generate?

Suggestions for Writing

1. Organize your answers to the above questions into an interpretation of the story. Include a discussion of how you discover the intention of the author and the meaning of the story.
2. Discuss how different the narrative might be if it were presented from the point of view of one of the boys.
3. Each of the following stories concerns a stereotype of men or women, a race, an ethnic group, a region, or a nation. Identify the stereotype and then discuss the use the author makes of it in the story:
   a. Sherwood Anderson, "I Want to Know Why"
   b. Stephen Crane, "The Blue Hotel" or "The Bride Comes to Yellow Sky"
   c. F. Scott Fitzgerald, "The Rich Boy"
   d. William Faulkner, "Dry September"
   e. Nadine Gordimer, "The Train from Rhodesia"
   f. Dorothy Parker, "Big Blonde"
   g. Philip Roth, "The Defenders of the Faith"
   h. Isaac Bashevis Singer, "Gimpel the Fool"
   i. Alice Walker, "The Flowers"
   j. Richard Wright, "The Man Who Was Almost a Man"

Additional Readings

Morris, Wright. *A Bill of Rites, A Bill of Wrongs, A Bill of Goods.* Lincoln: University of Nebraska Press, 1980.

———. *Ceremony in Lone Tree.* Lincoln: University of Nebraska Press, 1973.

———. *Collected Stories: 1948–1986.* New York: Harper and Row, 1986.

———. *The Field of Vision.* New York: Harcourt Brace Jovanovich, 1956.

———. *Fire Sermon.* New York: Harper and Row, 1971.

———. *In Orbit.* New York: New American Library, 1967.

———. *A Life.* New York: Harper and Row, 1973.

———. *One Day.* New York: Atheneum, 1965.

———. *Real Losses, Imaginary Gains.* New York; Harper and Row, 1976.

———. *Wright Morris: A Reader.* Ed. Granville Hicks. New York: Harper and Row, 1970.

PEOPLE AND SOCIETY

*I*ndividual and social responsibility are of concern to the six writers in this section. The perspectives and approaches are again different. Writing as a citizen opposed to a war in progress, Henry David Thoreau asks whether government has an independent will and purpose and can enforce the participation of those who consider the war unjust. His perspective is that of the philosopher who seeks a definition of the ideal state and ideal citizen and uses this definition to reach an ethical judgment. Writing as a political scientist, Hannah Arendt defines the complex of social and political circumstances that guide individuals in a particular society. Concerned with the same philosophical problem as Thoreau, she asks a somewhat different question: whether the individual has responsibility for acts he performs in the name of a despotic government. A journalist who knew India well, George Orwell explores a related question: the impact of a charismatic individual on a society. His perspective is best defined as that of the political scientist, though Orwell does not approach Gandhi in the systematic and clinical way that Arendt approaches Eichmann. The social psychologist Stanley Milgram is concerned not with philosophical definition but rather with empirical evidence of how individuals make decisions when they are asked to perform acts that violate conscience. The South African novelist Nadine Gordimer and the American poet Irving Feldman approach similar issues through the medium of art.

These essays, story, and poem also consider issues of previous sections. Hannah Arendt, Nadine Gordimer, and Irving Feldman are indirectly concerned with how stereotypes of people influence thought and behavior. All six writers are concerned with how individuals choose or discover their goals and values.

Resistance to Civil Government

Henry David Thoreau

Henry David Thoreau was born in 1817 and lived most of his life in Concord, Massachusetts. Following his graduation from Harvard College, he taught school for two years and did surveying for Concord. He lived in the household of Ralph Waldo Emerson at various times. At Walden Pond near Concord, Thoreau built a cabin on land owned by Emerson and lived there from July 4, 1845 to September 6, 1847; his experiences there are the basis of his famous book, Walden; or Life in the Woods, *published in 1856. From 1849 until his death in 1862, he lived with his father, assisting him in the business of pencil manufacture. He was strongly influenced by Emerson's philosophy, was a member of the Transcendental Club, and wrote essays and poetry for its magazine* The Dial. *Long ill with tuberculosis, Thoreau died in 1862. Emerson wrote in a memorial essay: "His robust common sense, armed with stout hands, keen perceptions, and strong will, cannot yet account for the superiority which shone in his simple and hidden life. . . . [T]here was excellent wisdom in him, proper to a rare class of men, which showed him the material world as a means and symbol."*

Published in 1849 under the title "Resistance to Civil Government," the essay later titled "Civil Disobedience" expresses Thoreau's contempt for the support of the Mexican War (1846–48) by Massachusetts congressmen. During his stay at Walden Pond, Thoreau refused to pay the poll tax as a protest against the war and was jailed overnight; he was released when, unknown to him, his aunt paid the tax. In the view of Northern abolitionists, the war promoted slavery in seeking to acquire slave-owning Texas. An abolitionist, Thoreau opposed the fugitive slave laws enforced by the administration of James K. Polk (1845–49). The year after "Resistance to Civil Government" was published, the Compromise of 1850 led to new laws and increased resistance by reformers and abolitionists in the North. Though it was not widely known in Thoreau's time, the essay later became highly influential. Mohandas Gandhi acknowledged the contribution of Thoreau to his philosophy of passive resistance called satyagraha.

I heartily accept the motto,—"That government is best which governs least;"   1
and I should like to see it acted up to more rapidly and systematically. Carried out, it finally amounts to this, which also I believe,—"That government is best which governs not at all;" and when men are prepared for it, that will be the kind of government which they will have. Government is at best but an expedient; but most governments are usually, and all governments are sometimes, inexpedient. The objections which have been brought against a standing army, and they are many and weighty, and deserve to prevail, may also at last be brought against a standing government. The standing army is only an arm of the standing government. The government itself, which is only the mode which the people have chosen to execute their will, is equally liable to be abused and

perverted before the people can act through it. Witness the present Mexican war, the work of comparatively a few individuals using the standing government as their tool; for, in the outset, the people would not have consented to this measure.[1]

This American government,—what is it but a tradition, though a recent one, 2 endeavoring to transmit itself unimpaired to posterity, but each instant losing some of its integrity? It has not the vitality and force of a single living man; for a single man can bend it to his will. It is a sort of wooden gun to the people themselves; and, if ever they should use it in earnest as a real one against each other, it will surely split. But it is not the less necessary for this; for the people must have some complicated machinery or other, and hear its din, to satisfy that idea of government which they have. Governments show thus how successfully men can be imposed on, even impose on themselves, for their own advantage. It is excellent, we must all allow; yet this government never of itself furthered any enterprise, but by the alacrity with which it got out of its way. *It* does not keep the country free. *It* does not settle the West. *It* does not educate. The character inherent in the American people has done all that has been accomplished; and it would have done somewhat more, if the government had not sometimes got in its way. For government is an expedient by which men would fain succeed in letting one another alone; and, as has been said, when it is most expedient, the governed are most let alone by it. Trade and commerce, if they were not made of India rubber, would never manage to bounce over the obstacles which legislators are continually putting in their way; and, if one were to judge these men wholly by the effects of their actions, and not partly by their intentions, they would deserve to be classed and punished with those mischievous persons who put obstructions on the railroads.

But, to speak practically and as a citizen, unlike those who call themselves no- 3 government men, I ask for, not at once no government, but *at once* a better government. Let every man make known what kind of government would command his respect, and that will be one step toward obtaining it.

After all, the practical reason why, when the power is once in the hands of the 4 people, a majority are permitted, and for a long period continue, to rule, is not because they are most likely to be in the right, nor because this seems fairest to the minority, but because they are physically the strongest. But a government in which the majority rule in all cases cannot be based on justice, even as far as men understand it. Can there not be a government in which majorities do not virtually decide right and wrong, but conscience?—in which majorities decide only those questions to which the rule of expediency is applicable? Must the citizen ever for a moment, or in the least degree, resign his conscience to the legislator? Why has every man a conscience, then? I think that we should be men first, and subjects afterward. It is not desirable to cultivate a respect for the law, so much as for the right. The only obligation which I have a right to assume, is to do at any time what I think right. It is truly enough said, that a corporation has no conscience; but a corporation of conscientious men is a corporation *with* a conscience. Law never made men a whit more just; and, by means of their respect for it, even the well-disposed are daily made the agents of injustice. A common and natural result of an undue respect for law is, that you may see a file of soldiers, colonel, captain,

---

[1]The Mexican War (1846–1848), following the resistance of Mexico to the U.S. annexation of Texas. Opponents to the war charged that the purpose of the war was to enlarge slave territory.

corporal, privates, powder-monkeys and all, marching in admirable order over hill and dale to the wars, against their wills, aye, against their common sense and consciences, which makes it very steep marching indeed, and produces a palpitation of the heart. They have no doubt that it is a damnable business in which they are concerned; they are all peaceably inclined. Now, what are they? Men at all? or small moveable forts and magazines, at the service of some unscrupulous man in power? Visit the Navy Yard, and behold a marine, such a man as an American government can make, or such as it can make a man with its black arts, a mere shadow and reminiscence of humanity, a man laid out alive and standing, and already, as one may say, buried under arms with funeral accompaniments, though it may be

"Not a drum was heard, not a funeral note,
As his corse to the rampart we hurried;
Not a soldier discharged his farewell shot
O'er the grave where our hero we buried."[2]

The mass of men serve the State thus, not as men mainly, but as machines, with their bodies. They are the standing army, and the militia, jailers, constables, *posse comitatus,*[3] &c. In most cases there is no free exercise whatever of the judgment or of the moral sense; but they put themselves on a level with wood and earth and stones, and wooden men can perhaps be manufactured that will serve the purpose as well. Such command no more respect than men of straw, or a lump of dirt. They have the same sort of worth only as horses and dogs. Yet such as these even are commonly esteemed good citizens. Others, as most legislators, politicians, lawyers, ministers, and officeholders, serve the State chiefly with their heads; and, as they rarely make any moral distinctions, they are as likely to serve the devil, without intending it, as God. A very few, as heroes, patriots, martyrs, reformers in the great sense, and *men,* serve the State with their consciences also, and so necessarily resist it for the most part; and they are commonly treated by it as enemies. A wise man will only be useful as a man, and will not submit to be "clay," and "stop a hole to keep the wind away," but leave that office to his dust at least:—

"I am too high-born to be propertied,
To be a secondary at control,
Or useful serving-man and instrument
To any sovereign state throughout the world."[4]

He who gives himself entirely to his fellow-men appears to them useless and selfish; but he who gives himself partially to them is pronounced a benefactor and philanthropist.

How does it become a man to behave toward this American government to-day? I answer that he cannot without disgrace be associated with it. I cannot for an instant recognize that political organization as *my* government which is the *slave's* government also.

---

[2]Opening lines of a poem by Charles Wolfe, "Burial of Sir John Moore at Corunna" (1817).
[3]Armed band organized by a sheriff to assist in a search.
[4]Shakespeare, *King John,* V, 2.

All men recognize the right of revolution; that is, the right to refuse allegiance 8
to and to resist the government, when its tyranny or its inefficiency are great and unendurable. But almost all say that such is not the case now. But such was the case, they
think, in the Revolution of '75. If one were to tell me that this was a bad government
because it taxed certain foreign commodities brought to its ports, it is most probable
that I should not make an ado about it, for I can do without them: all machines have
their friction; and possibly this does enough good to counter-balance the evil. At any
rate, it is a great evil to make a stir about it. But when the friction comes to have its
machine, and oppression and robbery are organized, I say, let us not have such a machine any longer. In other words, when a sixth of the population of a nation which has
undertaken to be the refuge of liberty are slaves, and a whole country is unjustly overrun and conquered by a foreign army, and subjected to military law, I think that it is
not too soon for honest men to rebel and revolutionize. What makes this duty the more
urgent is the fact, that the country so overrun is not our own, but ours is the invad-
ing army.

Paley, a common authority with many on moral questions, in his chapter on 9
the "Duty of Submission to Civil Government,"[5] resolves all civil obligation into expediency; and he proceeds to say, "that so long as the interest of the whole society requires
it, that is, so long as the established government cannot be resisted or changed without
public inconveniency, it is the will of God that the established government be obeyed,
and no longer.". . . "This principle being admitted, the justice of every particular case
of resistance is reduced to a computation of the quantity of the danger and grievance on
the one side, and of the probability and expense of redressing it on the other." Of this,
he says, every man shall judge for himself. But Paley appears never to have contemplated those cases to which the rule of expediency does not apply, in which a people, as
well as an individual, must do justice, cost what it may. If I have unjustly wrested a
plank from a drowning man, I must restore it to him though I drown myself. This, according to Paley, would be inconvenient. But he that would save his life, in such a case,
shall lose it. This people must cease to hold slaves, and to make war on Mexico, though
it cost them their existence as a people.

In their practice, nations agree with Paley; but does any one think that Massa- 10
chusetts does exactly what is right at the present crisis?

> "A drab of state, a cloth-o'-silver slut,
> To have her train borne up, and her soul trail in the dirt."

Practically speaking, the opponents to a reform in Massachusetts are not a hundred
thousand politicians at the South, but a hundred thousand merchants and farmers here,
who are more interested in commerce and agriculture than they are in humanity, and
are not prepared to do justice to the slave and to Mexico, *cost what it may.* I quarrel not
with far-off foes, but with those who, near at home, co-operate with, and do the bidding
of those far away, and without whom the latter would be harmless. We are accustomed
to say, that the mass of men are unprepared; but improvement is slow, because the few
are not materially wiser or better than the many. It is not so important that many
should be as good as you, as that there be some absolute goodness somewhere; for that

---

[5]William Paley (1743–1805): a utilitarian philosopher and theologian.

will leaven the whole lump. There are thousands who are *in opinion* opposed to slavery and to the war, who yet in effect do nothing to put an end to them; who, esteeming themselves children of Washington and Franklin, sit down with their hands in their pockets, and say that they know not what to do, and do nothing; who even postpone the question of freedom to the question of free-trade, and quietly read the prices-current along with the latest advices from Mexico, after dinner, and, it may be, fall asleep over them both. What is the price-current of an honest man and patriot to-day? They hesitate, and they regret, and sometimes they petition; but they do nothing in earnest and with effect. They will wait, well-disposed, for others to remedy the evil, that they may no longer have it to regret. At most, they give only a cheap vote, and a feeble countenance and God-speed, to the right, as it goes by them. There are nine hundred and ninety-nine patrons of virtue to one virtuous man; but it is easier to deal with the real possessor of a thing than with the temporary guardian of it.

All voting is a sort of gaming, like chequers or backgammon, with a slight 11 moral tinge to it, a playing with right and wrong, with moral questions; and betting naturally accompanies it. The character of the voters is not staked. I cast my vote, perchance, as I think right; but I am not vitally concerned that that right should prevail. I am willing to leave it to the majority. Its obligation, therefore, never exceeds that of expediency. Even voting *for the right* is *doing* nothing for it. It is only expressing to men feebly your desire that it should prevail. A wise man will not leave the right to the mercy of chance, nor wish it to prevail through the power of the majority. There is but little virtue in the action of masses of men. When the majority shall at length vote for the abolition of slavery, it will be because they are indifferent to slavery, or because there is but little slavery left to be abolished by their vote. *They* will then be the only slaves. Only *his* vote can hasten the abolition of slavery who asserts his own freedom by his vote.

I hear of a convention to be held at Baltimore, or elsewhere, for the selection 12 of a candidate for the Presidency, made up chiefly of editors, and men who are politicians by profession; but I think, what is it to any independent, intelligent, and respectable man what decision they may come to, shall we not have the advantage of his wisdom and honesty, nevertheless? Can we not count upon some independent votes? Are there not many individuals in the country who do not attend conventions? But no: I find that the respectable man, so called, has immediately drifted from his position, and despairs of his country, when his country has more reason to despair of him. He forthwith adopts one of the candidates thus selected as the only *available* one, thus proving that he is himself *available* for any purposes of the demagogue. His vote is of no more worth than that of any unprincipled foreigner or hireling native, who may have been bought. Oh for a man who is a *man,* and, as my neighbor says, has a bone in his back which you cannot pass your hand through! Our statistics are at fault: the population has been returned too large. How many *men* are there to a square thousand miles in this country? Hardly one. Does not America offer any inducement for men to settle here? The American has dwindled into an Odd Fellow,—one who may be known by the development of his organ of gregariousness, and a manifest lack of intellect and cheerful self-reliance; whose first and chief concern, on coming into the world, is to see that the alms-houses are in good repair; and, before yet he has lawfully donned the virile garb,[6] to collect a fund for the support of the widows and orphans that may be; who, in short,

---

[6]The toga, donned by Roman boys of fourteen.

ventures to live only by the aid of the mutual insurance company, which has promised to bury him decently.

It is not a man's duty, as a matter of course, to devote himself to the eradica- 13 tion of any, even the most enormous wrong; he may still properly have other concerns to engage him; but it is his duty, at least, to wash his hands of it, and, if he gives it no thought longer, not to give it practically his support. If I devote myself to other pursuits and contemplations, I must first see, at least, that I do not pursue them sitting upon another man's shoulders. I must get off him first, that he may pursue his contemplations too. See what gross inconsistency is tolerated. I have heard some of my townsmen say, "I should like to have them order me out to help put down an insurrection of the slaves, or to march to Mexico,—see if I would go;" and yet these very men have each, directly by their allegiance, and so indirectly, at least, by their money, furnished a substitute. The soldier is applauded who refuses to serve in an unjust war by those who do not refuse to sustain the unjust government which makes the war; is applauded by those whose own act and authority he disregards and sets at nought; as if the State were penitent to that degree that it hired one to scourge it while it sinned, but not to that degree that it left off sinning for a moment. Thus, under the name of order and civil government, we are all made at last to pay homage to and support our own meanness. After the first blush of sin, comes its indifference: and from immoral it becomes, as it were, *un*moral, and not quite unnecessary to that life which we have made.

The broadest and most prevalent error requires the most disinterested virtue to 14 sustain it. The slight reproach to which the virtue of patriotism is commonly liable, the noble are most likely to incur. Those who, while they disapprove of the character and measures of a government, yield to it their allegiance and support, are undoubtedly its most conscientious supporters, and so frequently the most serious obstacles to reform. Some are petitioning the State to dissolve the Union, to disregard the requisitions of the President. Why do they not dissolve it themselves,—the union between themselves and the State,—and refuse to pay their quota into its treasury? Do not they stand in the same relation to the State, that the State does to the Union? And have not the same reasons prevented the State from resisting the Union, which have prevented them from resisting the State?

How can a man be satisfied to entertain an opinion merely, and enjoy *it?* Is 15 there any enjoyment in it, if his opinion is that he is aggrieved? If you are cheated out of a single dollar by your neighbor, you do not rest satisfied with knowing that you are cheated, or with saying that you are cheated, or even with petitioning him to pay you your due; but you take effectual steps at once to obtain the full amount, and see that you are never cheated again. Action from principle,—the perception and the performance of right,—changes things and relations; it is essentially revolutionary, and does not consist wholly with any thing which was. It not only divides states and churches, it divides families; aye, it divides the *individual,* separating the diabolical in him from the divine.

Unjust laws exist: shall we be content to obey them, or shall we endeavor to 16 amend them, and obey them until we have succeeded, or shall we transgress them at once? Men generally, under such a government as this, think that they ought to wait until they have persuaded the majority to alter them. They think that, if they should resist, the remedy would be worse than the evil. But it is the fault of the government itself that the remedy *is* worse than the evil. *It* makes it worse. Why is it not more apt to anticipate and provide for reform? Why does it not cherish its wise minority? Why does it cry and resist before it is hurt? Why does it not encourage its citizens to be on the alert to point out its faults, and *do* better than it would have them? Why does it always crucify Christ, and excommunicate Copernicus and Luther, and pronounce Washington and Franklin rebels?

One would think, that a deliberate and practical denial of its authority was the 17 only offence never contemplated by government; else, why has it not assigned its definite, its suitable and proportionate penalty? If a man who has no property refuses but once to earn nine shillings for the State, he is put in prison for a period unlimited by any law that I know, and determined only by the discretion of those who placed him there; but if he should steal ninety times nine shillings from the State, he is soon permitted to go at large again.

If the injustice is part of the necessary friction of the machine of government, 18 let it go, let it go: perchance it will wear smooth,—certainly the machine will wear out. If the injustice has a spring, or a pulley, or a rope, or a crank, exclusively for itself, then perhaps you may consider whether the remedy will not be worse than the evil; but if it is of such a nature that it requires you to be the agent of injustice to another, then, I say, break the law. Let your life be a counter friction to stop the machine. What I have to do is to see, at any rate, that I do not lend myself to the wrong which I condemn.

As for adopting the ways which the State has provided for remedying the evil, 19 I know not of such ways. They take too much time, and a man's life will be gone. I have other affairs to attend to. I came into this world, not chiefly to make this a good place to live in, but to live in it, be it good or bad. A man has not every thing to do, but something; and because he cannot do *every thing,* it is not necessary that he should do *something* wrong. It is not my business to be petitioning the governor or the legislature any more than it is theirs to petition me; and, if they should not hear my petition, what should I do then? But in this case the State has provided no way: its very Constitution is the evil. This may seem to be harsh and stubborn and unconciliatory; but it is to treat with the utmost kindness and consideration the only spirit that can appreciate or deserves it. So is all change for the better, like birth and death which convulse the body.

I do not hesitate to say, that those who call themselves abolitionists should at 20 once effectually withdraw their support, both in person and property, from the government of Massachusetts, and not wait till they constitute a majority of one, before they suffer the right to prevail through them. I think that it is enough if they have God on their side, without waiting for that other one. Moreover, any man more right than his neighbors, constitutes a majority of one already.

I meet this American government, or its representative the State government, 21 directly, and face to face, once a year, no more, in the person of its tax-gatherer; this is the only mode in which a man situated as I am necessarily meets it; and it then says distinctly, Recognize me; and the simplest, the most effectual, and, in the present posture of affairs, the indispensablest mode of treating with it on this head, of expressing your little satisfaction with and love for it, is to deny it then. My civil neighbor, the tax-gatherer, is the very man I have to deal with,—for it is, after all, with men and not with parchment that I quarrel,—and he has voluntarily chosen to be an agent of the government. How shall he ever know well what he is and does as an officer of the government, or as a man, until he is obliged to consider whether he shall treat me, his neighbor, for whom he has respect, as a neighbor and well-disposed man, or as a maniac and disturber of the peace, and see if he can get over this obstruction to his neighborliness without a ruder and more impetuous thought or speech corresponding with his action? I know this well, that if one thousand, if one hundred, if ten men whom I could name,— if ten *honest* men only,—aye, if *one* HONEST man, in this State of Massachusetts, *ceasing to hold slaves,* were actually to withdraw from this copartnership, and be locked up in the county jail therefor, it would be the abolition of slavery in America. For it matters not how small the beginning may seem to be: what is once well done is done for ever. But we love better to talk about it: that we say is our mission. Reform keeps many scores of newspapers in its service, but not one man. If my esteemed neighbor,[7] the State's ambassador, who will devote his days to the settlement of the question of human rights in the Council Chamber, instead of being threatened with the prisons of Carolina, were to sit down the prisoner of Massachusetts, that State which is so anxious to foist the sin of slavery upon her sister,—though at present she can discover only an act of inhospitality to be the ground of a quarrel with her,—the Legislature would not wholly waive the subject the following winter.

Under a government which imprisons any unjustly, the true place for a just 22 man is also a prison. The proper place to-day, the only place which Massachusetts has provided for her freer and less desponding spirits, is in her prisons, to be put out and locked out of the State by her own act, as they have already put themselves out by their principles. It is there that the fugitive slave, and the Mexican prisoner on parole, and the Indian come to plead the wrongs of his race, should find them; on that separate, but more free and honorable ground, where the State places those who are not *with* her but *against* her,—the only house in a slave-state in which a free man can abide with honor. If any think that their influence would be lost there, and their voices no longer afflict the ear of the State, that they would not be as an enemy within its walls, they do not know by how much truth is stronger than error, nor how much more eloquently and effectively he can combat injustice who has experienced a little in his own person. Cast your whole vote, not a strip of paper merely, but your whole influence. A minority is powerless while it conforms to the majority; it is not even a minority then; but it is irresistible when it clogs by its whole weight. If the alternative is to keep all just men in prison, or give up war and slavery, the State will not hesitate which to choose. If a thousand men were not to pay their tax-bills this year, that would not be a violent and bloody measure, as it would be to pay them, and enable the State to commit violence and shed innocent blood. This is, in fact, the definition of a peaceable revolution, if any such is possible. If the tax-gatherer, or any other public officer, asks me, as one has done, "But what shall I do?" my answer is, "If you really wish to do any thing, resign your office." When the subject has refused allegiance, and the officer has resigned his office, then the revolution is accomplished. But even suppose blood should flow. Is there not a sort of blood shed when the conscience is wounded? Through this wound a man's real manhood and immortality flow out, and he bleeds to an everlasting death. I see this blood flowing now.

I have contemplated the imprisonment of the offender, rather than the seizure 23 of his goods,—though both will serve the same purpose,—because they who assert the

---

[7]Massachusetts Congressman Samuel Hoar (1778–1856) was sent to South Carolina to investigate laws that threatened the enslavement of black crewmen on Massachusetts boats entering port.

purest right, and consequently are most dangerous to a corrupt State, commonly have not spent much time in accumulating property. To such the State renders comparatively small service, and a slight tax is wont to appear exorbitant, particularly if they are obliged to earn it by special labor with their hands.[8] If there were one who lived wholly without the use of money, the State itself would hesitate to demand it of him. But the rich man—not to make any invidious comparison—is always sold to the institution which makes him rich. Absolutely speaking, the more money, the less virtue; for money comes between a man and his objects, and obtains them for him; and it was certainly no great virtue to obtain it. It puts to rest many questions which he would otherwise be taxed to answer; while the only new question which it puts is the hard but superfluous one, how to spend it. Thus his moral ground is taken from under his feet. The opportunities of living are diminished in proportion as what are called the "means" are increased. The best thing a man can do for his culture when he is rich is to endeavour to carry out those schemes which he entertained when he was poor. Christ answered the Herodians according to their condition. "Show me the tribute-money," said he;—and one took a penny out of his pocket;—If you use money which has the image of Cæsar on it, and which he has made current and valuable, that is, *if you are men of the State,* and gladly enjoy the advantages of Cæsar's government, then pay him back some of his own when he demands it; "Render therefore to Cæsar that which is Cæsar's, and to God those things which are God's,"—leaving them no wiser than before as to which was which; for they did not wish to know.

When I converse with the freest of my neighbors, I perceive that, whatever they may say about the magnitude and seriousness of the question, and their regard for the public tranquillity, the long and the short of the matter is, that they cannot spare the protection of the existing government, and they dread the consequences of disobedience to it to their property and families. For my own part, I should not like to think that I ever rely on the protection of the State. But, if I deny the authority of the State when it presents its tax-bill, it will soon take and waste all my property, and so harass me and my children without end. This is hard. This makes it impossible for a man to live honestly and at the same time comfortably in outward respects. It will not be worth the while to accumulate property; that would be sure to go again. You must hire or squat somewhere, and raise but a small crop, and eat that soon. You must live within yourself, and depend upon yourself, always tucked up and ready for a start, and not have many affairs. A man may grow rich in Turkey even, if he will be in all respects a good subject of the Turkish government. Confucius said,—"If a State is governed by the principles of reason, poverty and misery are subjects of shame; if a State is not governed by the principles of reason, riches and honors are the subjects of shame."[9] No: until I want the protection of Massachusetts to be extended to me in some distant southern port, where my liberty is endangered, or until I am bent solely on building up an estate at home by peaceful enterprise, I can afford to refuse allegiance to Massachusetts, and her right to

---

[8]Massachusetts levied a church tax and a poll tax on male citizens. Thoreau resisted paying these taxes mainly because the state government supported slavery.

[9]Confucius (c. 551–479 B.C.): Chinese philosopher and author of the wisdom book, *The Analects.*

my property and life. It costs me less in every sense to incur the penalty of disobedience to the State, than it would to obey. I should feel as if I were worth less in that case.

Some years ago, the State met me in behalf of the church, and commanded me 25 to pay a certain sum toward the support of a clergyman whose preaching my father attended, but never I myself. "Pay it," it said, "or be locked up in the jail." I declined to pay. But, unfortunately, another man saw fit to pay it. I did not see why the schoolmaster should be taxed to support the priest, and not the priest the schoolmaster; for I was not the State's schoolmaster, but I supported myself by voluntary subscription. I did not see why the lyceum should not present its tax-bill, and have the State to back its demand, as well as the church. However, at the request of the selectmen, I condescended to make some such statement as this in writing:—"Know all men by these presents, that I, Henry Thoreau, do not wish to be regarded as a member of any incorporated society which I have not joined." This I gave to the town-clerk; and he has it. The State, having thus learned that I did not wish to be regarded as a member of that church, has never made a like demand on me since; though it said that it must adhere to its original presumption that time. If I had known how to name them, I should then have signed off in detail from all the societies which I never signed on to; but I did not know where to find a complete list.

I have paid no poll-tax for six years. I was put into a jail once on this account, 26 for one night; and, as I stood considering the walls of solid stone, two or three feet thick, the door of wood and iron, a foot thick, and the iron grating which strained the light, I could not help being struck with the foolishness of that institution which treated me as if I were mere flesh and blood and bones, to be locked up. I wondered that it should have concluded at length that this was the best use it could put me to, and had never thought to avail itself of my services in some way. I saw that, if there was a wall of stone between me and my townsmen, there was a still more difficult one to climb or break through, before they could get to be as free as I was. I did not for a moment feel confined, and the walls seemed a great waste of stone and mortar. I felt as if I alone of all my townsmen had paid my tax. They plainly did not know how to treat me, but behaved like persons who are underbred. In every threat and in every compliment there was a blunder; for they thought that my chief desire was to stand the other side of that stone wall. I could not but smile to see how industriously they locked the door on my meditations, which followed them out again without let or hinderance, and *they* were really all that was dangerous. As they could not reach me, they had resolved to punish my body; just as boys, if they cannot come at some person against whom they have a spite, will abuse his dog. I saw that the State was half-witted, that it was timid as a lone woman with her silver spoons, and that it did not know its friends from its foes, and I lost all my remaining respect for it, and pitied it.

Thus the State never intentionally confronts a man's sense, intellectual or 27 moral, but only his body, his senses. It is not armed with superior wit or honesty, but with superior physical strength. I was not born to be forced. I will breathe after my own fashion. Let us see who is the strongest. What force has a multitude? They only can force me who obey a higher law than I. They force me to become like themselves. I do not hear of *men* being *forced* to live this way or that by masses of men. What sort of life were that to live? When I meet a government which says to me, "Your money or your life," why should I be in haste to give it my money? It may be in a great strait, and not know what to do: I cannot help that. It must help itself; do as I do. It is not worth the while to snivel about it. I am not responsible for the successful working of the machinery of society. I am not the son of the engineer. I perceive that, when an acorn and a chestnut fall side by side, the one does not remain inert to make way for the other, but both obey their own laws, and spring and grow and flourish as best they can, till one, perchance, overshadows and destroys the other. If a plant cannot live according to its nature, it dies; and so a man.

The night in prison was novel and interesting enough. The prisoners in their 28 shirt-sleeves were enjoying a chat and the evening air in the door-way, when I entered. But the jailer said, "Come, boys, it is time to lock up;" and so they dispersed, and I heard the sound of their steps returning into the hollow apartments. My roommate was introduced to me by the jailer, as "a first-rate fellow and a clever man." When the door was locked, he showed me where to hang my hat, and how he managed matters there. The rooms were whitewashed once a month; and this one, at least, was the whitest, most simply furnished, and probably the neatest apartment in the town. He naturally wanted to know where I came from, and what brought me there; and, when I had told him, I asked him in my turn how he came there, presuming him to be an honest man, of course; and, as the world goes, I believe he was. "Why," said he, "they accuse me of burning a barn; but I never did it." As near as I could discover, he had probably gone to bed in a barn when drunk, and smoked his pipe there; and so a barn was burnt. He had the reputation of being a clever man, had been there some three months waiting for his trial to come on, and would have to wait as much longer; but he was quite domesticated and contented, since he got his board for nothing, and thought that he was well treated.

He occupied one window, and I the other; and I saw, that, if one stayed there 29 long, his principal business would be to look out the window. I had soon read all the tracts that were left there, and examined where former prisoners had broken out, and where a grate had been sawed off, and heard the history of the various occupants of that room; for I found that even here there was a history and a gossip which never circulated beyond the walls of the jail. Probably this is the only house in the town where verses are composed, which are afterward printed in a circular form, but not published. I was shown quite a long list of verses which were composed by some young men who had been detected in an attempt to escape, who avenged themselves by singing them.

I pumped my fellow-prisoner as dry as I could, for fear I should never see him 30 again; but at length he showed me which was my bed, and left me to blow out the lamp.

It was like travelling into a far country, such as I had never expected to behold, 31 to lie there for one night. It seemed to me that I never had heard the town-clock strike before, nor the evening sounds of the village; for we slept with the windows open, which were inside the grating. It was to see my native village in the light of the middle ages, and our Concord was turned into a Rhine stream, and visions of knights and castles passed before me. They were the voices of old burghers that I heard in the streets. I was an involuntary spectator and auditor of whatever was done and said in the kitchen of the adjacent village-inn,—a wholly new and rare experience to me. It was a closer view of my native town. I was fairly inside of it. I never had seen its institutions before. This is one of its peculiar institutions; for it is a shire town. I began to comprehend what its inhabitants were about.

In the morning, our breakfasts were put through the hole in the door, in small 32 oblong-square tin pans, made to fit, and holding a pint of chocolate, with brown bread, and an iron spoon. When they called for the vessels again, I was green enough to return what bread I had left; but my comrade seized it, and said that I should lay that up for lunch or dinner. Soon after, he was let out to work at haying in a neighboring field, whither he went every day, and would not be back till noon; so he bade me good-day, saying that he doubted if he should see me again.

When I came out of prison,—for some one interfered, and paid the tax,—I did 33 not perceive that great changes had taken place on the common, such as he observed who went in a youth, and emerged a tottering and grayheaded man; and yet a change had to my eyes come over the scene,—the town, and State, and country,—greater than any that mere time could effect. I saw yet more distinctly the State in which I lived. I saw to what extent the people among whom I lived could be trusted as good neighbors and friends; that their friendship was for summer weather only; that they did not greatly purpose to do right; that they were a distinct race from me by their prejudices and superstitions, as the Chinamen and Malays are; that, in their sacrifices to humanity, they ran no risks, not even to their property; that, after all, they were not so noble but they treated the thief as he had treated them, and hoped, by a certain outward observance and a few prayers, and by walking in a particular straight though useless path from time to time, to save their souls. This may be to judge my neighbors harshly; for I believe that most of them are not aware that they have such an institution as the jail in their village.

It was formerly the custom in our village, when a poor debtor came out of jail, 34 for his acquaintances to salute him, looking through their fingers, which were crossed to represent the grating of a jail window, "How do ye do?" My neighbors did not thus salute me, but first looked at me, and then at one another, as if I had returned from a long journey. I was put into jail as I was going to the shoemaker's to get a shoe which was mended. When I was let out the next morning, I proceeded to finish my errand, and, having put on my mended shoe, joined a huckleberry party, who were impatient to put themselves under my conduct; and in half an hour,—for the horse was soon tackled,— was in the midst of a huckleberry field, on one of our highest hills, two miles off; and then the State was nowhere to be seen.

This is the whole history of "My Prisons."[10]   35

I have never declined paying the highway tax, because I am as desirous of being 36 a good neighbor as I am of being a bad subject; and, as for supporting schools, I am doing my part to educate my fellow-countrymen now. It is for no particular item in the tax-bill that I refuse to pay it. I simply wish to refuse allegiance to the State, to withdraw and stand aloof from it effectually. I do not care to trace the course of my dollar, if I could, till it buys a man, or a musket to shoot one with,—the dollar is innocent,—but I am concerned to trace the effects of my allegiance. In fact, I quietly declare war with

---

[10]A reference to an 1832 book on imprisonment by Silvio Pellico, an Italian patriot.

the State, after my fashion, though I will still make what use and get what advantage of her I can, as is usual in such cases.

If others pay the tax which is demanded of me, from a sympathy with the State, 37 they do but what they have already done in their own case, or rather they abet injustice to a greater extent than the State requires. If they pay the tax from a mistaken interest in the individual taxed, to save his property or prevent his going to jail, it is because they have not considered wisely how far they let their private feelings interfere with the public good.

This, then, is my position at present. But one cannot be too much on his guard 38 in such a case, lest his action be biassed by obstinacy, or an undue regard for the opinions of men. Let him see that he does only what belongs to himself and to the hour.

I think sometimes, Why, this people mean well; they are only ignorant; they 39 would do better if they knew how: why give your neighbors this pain to treat you as they are not inclined to? But I think, again, this is no reason why I should do as they do, or permit others to suffer much greater pain of a different kind. Again, I sometimes say to myself, When many millions of men, without heat, without ill-will, without personal feeling of any kind, demand of you a few shillings only, without the possibility, such is their constitution, of retracting or altering their present demand, and without the possibility, on your side, of appeal to any other millions, why expose yourself to this overwhelming brute force? You do not resist cold and hunger, the winds and the waves, thus obstinately; you quietly submit to a thousand similar necessities. You do not put your head into the fire. But just in proportion as I regard this as not wholly a brute force, but partly a human force, and consider that I have relations to those millions as to so many millions of men, and not of mere brute or inanimate things, I see that appeal is possible, first and instantaneously, from them to the Maker of them, and, secondly, from them to themselves. But, if I put my head deliberately into the fire, there is no appeal to fire or to the Maker of fire, and I have only myself to blame. If I could convince myself that I have any right to be satisfied with men as they are, and to treat them accordingly, and not according, in some respects, to my requisitions and expectations of what they and I ought to be, then, like a good Mussulman and fatalist, I should endeavor to be satisfied with things as they are, and say it is the will of God. And, above all, there is this difference between resisting this and a purely brute or natural force, that I can resist this with some effect; but I cannot expect, like Orpheus, to change the nature of the rocks and trees and beasts.[11]

I do not wish to quarrel with any man or nation. I do not wish to split hairs, 40 to make fine distinctions, or set myself up as better than my neighbors. I seek rather, I may say, even an excuse for conforming to the laws of the land. I am but too ready to conform to them. Indeed I have reason to suspect myself on this head; and each year, as the tax-gatherer comes round, I find myself disposed to review the acts and position of the general and state governments, and the spirit of the people, to discover a pretext for conformity. I believe that the State will soon be able to take all my work of this sort out of my hands, and then I shall be no better a patriot than my fellow-countrymen. Seen from a lower point of view, the Constitution, with all its faults, is very good; the

---

[11]Orpheus: the mythic Greek singer who charmed animals with his lute.

law and the courts are very respectable; even this State and this American government are, in many respects, very admirable and rare things, to be thankful for, such as a great many have described them; but seen from a point of view a little higher, they are what I have described them; seen from a higher still, and the highest, who shall say what they are, or that they are worth looking at or thinking of at all?

However, the government does not concern me much, and I shall bestow the 41 fewest possible thoughts on it. It is not many moments that I live under a government, even in this world. If a man is thought-free, fancy-free, imagination-free, that which *is not* never for a long time appearing *to be* to him, unwise rulers or reformers cannot fatally interrupt him.

I know that most men think differently from myself; but those whose lives are 42 by profession devoted to the study of these or kindred subjects, content me as little as any. Statesmen and legislators, standing so completely within the institution, never distinctly and nakedly behold it. They speak of moving society, but have no resting-place without it. They may be men of a certain experience and discrimination, and have no doubt invented ingenious and even useful systems, for which we sincerely thank them; but all their wit and usefulness lie within certain not very wide limits. They are wont to forget that the world is not governed by policy and expediency. Webster never goes behind government, and so cannot speak with authority about it.[12] His words are wisdom to those legislators who contemplate no essential reform in the existing government; but for thinkers, and those who legislate for all time, he never once glances at the subject. I know of those whose serene and wise speculations on this theme would soon reveal the limits of his mind's range and hospitality. Yet, compared with the cheap professions of most reformers, and the still cheaper wisdom and eloquence of politicians in general, his are almost the only sensible and valuable words, and we thank Heaven for him. Comparatively, he is always strong, original, and, above all, practical. Still his quality is not wisdom, but prudence. The lawyer's truth is not Truth, but consistency, or a consistent expediency. Truth is always in harmony with herself, and is not concerned chiefly to reveal the justice that may consist with wrong-doing. He well deserves to be called, as he has been called, the Defender of the Constitution. There are really no blows to be given by him but defensive ones. He is not a leader, but a follower. His leaders are the men of '87. "I have never made an effort," he says, "and never propose to make an effort; I have never countenanced an effort, and never mean to countenance an effort, to disturb the arrangement as originally made, by which the various States came into the Union." Still thinking of the sanction which the Constitution gives to slavery, he says, "Because it was a part of the original compact,—let it stand." Notwithstanding his special acuteness and ability, he is unable to take a fact out of its merely political relations, and behold it as it lies absolutely to be disposed of by the intellect,—what, for instance, it behoves a man to do here in America to-day with regard to slavery,—but ventures, or is driven, to make some such desperate answer as the following, while professing to speak absolutely, and as a private man,—from which what new and singular

---

[12]Daniel Webster (1782–1852), senator from Massachusetts at the time Thoreau was writing, opposed the Mexican War but supported proposed compromise legislation on slavery on constitutional grounds. Webster's leaders, Thoreau states, are the men who framed the U.S. Constitution in 1787.

code of social duties might be inferred?—"The manner," says he, "in which the governments of those States where slavery exists are to regulate it, is for their own consideration, under their responsibility to their constituents, to the general laws of propriety,
humanity, and justice, and to God. Associations formed elsewhere, springing from a
feeling of humanity, or any other cause, have nothing whatever to do with it. They have
never received any encouragement from me, and they never will."*

They who know of no purer sources of truth, who have traced up its stream no 43
higher, stand, and wisely stand, by the Bible and the Constitution, and drink at it there
with reverence and humility; but they who behold where it comes trickling into this
lake or that pool, gird up their loins once more, and continue their pilgrimage toward
its fountain-head.

No man with a genius for legislation has appeared in America. They are rare in 44
the history of the world. There are orators, politicians, and eloquent men, by the thousand; but the speaker has not yet opened his mouth to speak, who is capable of settling
the much-vexed questions of the day. We love eloquence for its own sake, and not for
any truth which it may utter, or any heroism it may inspire. Our legislators have not
yet learned the comparative value of free-trade and of freedom, of union, and of recti-
tude, to a nation. They have no genius or talent for comparatively humble questions of
taxation and finance, commerce and manufactures and agriculture. If we were left solely
to the wordy wit of legislators in Congress for our guidance, uncorrected by the seasonable experience and the effectual complaints of the people, America would not long
retain her rank among the nations. For eighteen hundred years, though perchance I
have no right to say it, the New Testament has been written; yet where is the legislator
who has wisdom and practical talent enough to avail himself of the light which it sheds
on the science of legislation?

The authority of government, even such as I am willing to submit to,—for I 45
will cheerfully obey those who know and can do better than I, and in many things even
those who neither know nor can do so well,—is still an impure one: to be strictly just,
it must have the sanction and consent of the governed. It can have no pure right over
my person and property but what I concede to it. The progress from an absolute to a
limited monarchy, from a limited monarchy to a democracy, is a progress toward a true
respect for the individual. Is a democracy, such as we know it, the last improvement
possible in government? Is it not possible to take a step further towards recognizing and
organizing the rights of man? There will never be a really free and enlightened State,
until the State comes to recognize the individual as a higher and independent power,
from which all its own power and authority are derived, and treats him accordingly. I
please myself with imagining a State at last which can afford to be just to all men, and
to treat the individual with respect as a neighbor; which even would not think it inconsistent with its own repose, if a few were to live aloof from it, not meddling with it, nor
embraced by it, who fulfilled all the duties of neighbors and fellow-men. A State which
bore this kind of fruit, and suffered it to drop off as fast as it ripened, would prepare the
way for a still more perfect and glorious State, which also I have imagined, but not yet
anywhere seen.

*These extracts have been inserted since the lecture was read. [Thoreau]

Questions

1. What kind of government would Thoreau consider an improvement over the one in office in 1849? Why does he reject the idea that a citizen has an obligation to obey the government even if it represents the majority of citizens?
2. Why, according to paragraph 11, is a vote not necessarily an expression of the will of the voters? If the vote did express the will of the voters, would Thoreau then agree that the government takes precedence over the will of a minority?
3. What does Thoreau mean by *expediency* in paragraph 9? What word would express the opposite kind of conduct?
4. In saying that "the American has dwindled into an Odd Fellow" (paragraph 12), is Thoreau suggesting that American government has fostered mediocrity and conformity? What is the target of his criticism if the government is not the cause?
5. What does Thoreau mean by "disinterested virtue" in paragraph 14? How can virtue sustain error?
6. Is Thoreau contradicting earlier statements when he argues in paragraph 18 that injustice should be tolerated if it is "part of the necessary friction of the machine of government"? Why is it enough that people withdraw their support, "both in person and property," and tend to their own business? Is his statement of this position in paragraphs 39–41 consistent and credible?
7. Why does the State intentionally confront only a person's body, according to paragraphs 26–27? How does this fact suggest a way to deal with the demands of the state?
8. How does Thoreau defend his payment of the highway tax but not the poll tax, in paragraphs 35–36? Do you find this a consistent or credible argument?
9. How credible do you find Thoreau's argument as a whole? Is it one that an individual could seriously consider and adopt in the 1980s?

Suggestions for Writing

1. Write a summary of Thoreau's argument. You need not present his ideas in the order he presents them. Give as full an account as you can of Thoreau's ideal of government.
2. Explain your reasons for agreeing or disagreeing with one of the ideas in Thoreau's essay. If you disagree with Thoreau, suggest an alternative belief or course of action.
3. Write your own definition of patriotism. Then discuss why Thoreau would agree or disagree with this definition.

Additional Reading

Harding, Walter. *The Days of Henry Thoreau.* New York: Knopf, 1965.

Porte, Joel. *Emerson and Thoreau: Transcendentalists in Conflict.* Middletown, Conn.: Wesleyan University Press, 1966.

Thoreau, Henry David. *Prose Works.* Ed. Robert F. Sayre. The Library of America. New York: Viking, 1985.

————. *The Portable Thoreau.* Ed. Carl Bode. New York: Viking, 1977.

————. *Selected Journals of Henry David Thoreau.* Ed. Carl Bode. Carbondale: Southern Illinois Press, 1971.

————. *The Writings of Henry D. Thoreau.* 4 vols. Princeton: Princeton University Press, 1971–73.

Reflections on Gandhi

George Orwell

George Orwell was the pseudonym of the British journalist and novelist Eric Blair. Born in India in 1903 to English parents, he was educated in England at a preparatory school and later at Eton. Orwell wrote his review of Gandhi's autobiography from first-hand knowledge, having worked as a British policeman in Burma from 1922 to 1927 and closely observing the British colonial establishment in the East. Returning to Europe, he lived an impoverished life in Paris and London, working at various jobs until he was able to sustain himself as a journalist and writer of fiction. The first of several early novels, Burmese Days, *appeared in 1934. His memoir* Homage to Catalonia *(1938) describes his experiences in Spain, where he participated in the Civil War on the Republican side. Most of Orwell's numerous essays appeared as columns and reviews in British periodicals; many were collected in* Inside the Whale *(1940) and other books. Orwell's reputation was finally established with his novels on totalitarian regimes,* Animal Farm *(1945) and* Nineteen Eighty-Four *(1949)—published a year before his death in 1950.*

Mohandas K. Gandhi was born in India in 1869 and trained as a lawyer in England. While he was pursuing a legal career in South Africa, he became a leader of the Indian community in its protest against discrimination. During these early years, Gandhi developed the doctrine of satyagraha *("firmness in the truth"), popularly known as "passive resistance." He was strongly influenced by Leo Tolstoy's religious writings and other Western and Indian writings, in particular the Bhagavad Gita and other Hindu sacred books. The means to self-realization for Gandhi was "renunciation of fruits of action" though not the cessation of work—an ascetic philosophy that Gandhi lived to the end of his life. "Every moment of our life should be filled with activity, but that activity should be* sattvika, *tending to Truth."*

Gandhi characterized his famous philosophy of nonviolent resistance—an idea that would influence Martin Luther King, Jr., and others in the West—in these words:

> A non-cooperationist strives to compel attention and to set an example not by his violence, but by his unobtrusive humility. He allows his solid action to speak for his

creed. His strength lies in his reliance upon the correctness of his position. And the conviction of it grows most in his opponent when he least interposes his speech between his action and his opponent.

Nonviolence was for Gandhi "a goal towards which all mankind moves naturally though unconsciously." This belief is the basis of conciliation:

We must try patiently to convert our opponents. If we wish to evolve the spirit of democracy out of slavery, we must be scrupulously exact in our dealings with opponents.

As leader of the Indian National Congress Party, Gandhi made satyagraha *the chief political means by which India was to achieve nationhood. Imprisoned by the British, his reputation increased throughout the colony and, as Orwell shows in his essay, made Gandhi a living saint in the eyes of Indians and many Westerners—a* mahatma *or person of great wisdom and soul. When the partition of India and the formation of the Moslem nation of Pakistan led to massacres of Hindus and Moslems during mass migrations between the north and south, Gandhi began a hunger strike—one of several he conducted during his life. He was assassinated in New Delhi at the beginning of 1948 by a young Hindu fanatic.*

Gandhi's later autobiography My Life Story: The Later Years, 1920–1948 *is a continuation of* My Experiments with Truth *(often reprinted under the title* Autobiography*). In his review of* The Story of My Experiments with Truth, *George Orwell explores both Gandhi's character and the nature of his achievement. The essay is a model book review—an account of the book's main ideas and an estimate of these ideas and of the author. Orwell clearly identifies his own Western attitudes and beliefs and so qualifies his judgments.*

Saints should always be judged guilty until they are proved innocent, but the tests that have to be applied to them are not, of course, the same in all cases. In Gandhi's case the questions one feels inclined to ask are: to what extent was Gandhi moved by vanity—by the consciousness of himself as a humble, naked old man, sitting on a praying-mat and shaking empires by sheer spiritual power—and to what extent did he compromise his own principles by entering into politics, which of their nature are inseparable from coercion and fraud? To give a definite answer one would have to study Gandhi's acts and writings in immense detail, for his whole life was a sort of pilgrimage in which every act was significant. But this partial autobiography, which ends in the nineteen-twenties, is strong evidence in his favour, all the more because it covers what he would have called the unregenerate part of his life and reminds one that inside the saint, or near-saint, there was a very shrewd, able person who could, if he had chosen, have been a brilliant success as a lawyer, an administrator or perhaps even a businessman.

At about the time when the autobiography[1] first appeared I remember reading 2 its opening chapters in the ill-printed pages of some Indian newspaper. They made a good impression on me, which Gandhi himself, at that time, did not. The things that one associated with him—homespun cloth, "soul forces" and vegetarianism—were unappealing, and his medievalist program was obviously not viable in a backward, starving, overpopulated country. It was also apparent that the British were making use of him, or thought they were making use of him. Strictly speaking, as a Nationalist, he was an enemy, but since in every crisis he would exert himself to prevent violence—which, from the British point of view, meant preventing any effective action whatever—he could be regarded as "our man." In private this was sometimes cynically admitted. The attitude of the Indian millionaires was similar. Gandhi called upon them to repent, and naturally they preferred him to the Socialists and Communists who, given the chance, would actually have taken their money away. How reliable such calculations are in the long run is doubtful; as Gandhi himself says, "in the end deceivers deceive only themselves"; but at any rate the gentleness with which he was nearly always handled was due partly to the feeling that he was useful. The British Conservatives only became really angry with him when, as in 1942, he was in effect turning his non-violence against a different conqueror.

But I could see even then that the British officials who spoke of him with a mixture of amusement and disapproval also genuinely liked and admired him, after a fashion. Nobody ever suggested that he was corrupt, or ambitious in any vulgar way, or that anything he did was actuated by fear or malice. In judging a man like Gandhi one seems instinctively to apply high standards, so that some of his virtues have passed almost unnoticed. For instance, it is clear even from the autobiography that his natural physical courage was quite outstanding: the manner of his death was a later illustration of this, for a public man who attached any value to his own skin would have been more adequately guarded. Again, he seems to have been quite free from that maniacal suspiciousness which, as E. M. Forster rightly says in *A Passage to India,* is the besetting Indian vice, as hypocrisy is the British vice. Although no doubt he was shrewd enough in detecting dishonesty, he seems wherever possible to have believed that other people were acting in good faith and had a better nature through which they could be approached. And though he came of a poor middle-class family, started life rather unfavourably, and was probably of unimpressive physical appearance, he was not afflicted by envy or by the feeling of inferiority. Colour feeling, when he first met it in its worst form in South Africa, seems rather to have astonished him. Even when he was fighting what was in effect a colour war he did not think of people in terms of race or status. The governor of a province, a cotton millionaire, a half-starved Dravidian coolie, a British private soldier, were all equally human beings, to be approached in much the same way. It is noticeable that even in the worst possible circumstances, as in South Africa, when he was making himself unpopular as the champion of the Indian community, he did not lack European friends.

Written in short lengths for newspaper serialisation, the autobiography is not 4 a literary masterpiece, but it is the more impressive because of the commonplaceness

---

[1]*The Story of my Experiments with Truth* by M. K. Gandhi, translated from the Gujarati by Mahadev Desai.

of much of its material. It is well to be reminded that Gandhi started out with the normal ambitions of a young Indian student and only adopted his extremist opinions by degrees and, in some cases, rather unwillingly. There was a time, it is interesting to learn, when he wore a top-hat, took dancing lessons, studied French and Latin, went up the Eiffel Tower, and even tried to learn the violin—all this with the idea of assimilating European civilisation as thoroughly as possible. He was not one of those saints who are marked out by their phenomenal piety from childhood onwards, nor one of the other kind who forsake the world after sensational debaucheries. He makes full confession of the misdeeds of his youth, but in fact there is not much to confess. As a frontispiece to the book there is a photograph of Gandhi's possessions at the time of his death. The whole outfit could be purchased for about £5, and Gandhi's sins, at least his fleshly sins, would make the same sort of appearance if placed all in one heap. A few cigarettes, a few mouthfuls of meat, a few annas pilfered in childhood from the maidservant, two visits to a brothel (on each occasion he got away without "doing anything"), one narrowly escaped lapse with his landlady in Plymouth, one outburst of temper—that is about the whole collection. Almost from childhood onwards he had a deep earnestness, an attitude ethical rather than religious, but, until he was about thirty, no very definite sense of direction. His first entry into anything describable as public life was made by way of vegetarianism. Underneath his less ordinary qualities one feels all the time the solid middle-class businessmen who were his ancestors. One feels that even after he had abandoned personal ambition he must have been a resourceful, energetic lawyer and a hard-headed political organiser, careful in keeping down expenses, an adroit handler of committees and an indefatigable chaser of subscriptions. His character was an extraordinarily mixed one, but there was almost nothing in it that you can put your finger on and call bad, and I believe that even Gandhi's worst enemies would admit that he was an interesting and unusual man who enriched the world simply by being alive. Whether he was also a lovable man, and whether his teachings can have much value for those who do not accept the religious beliefs on which they are founded, I have never felt fully certain.

Of late years it has been the fashion to talk about Gandhi as though he were not only sympathetic to the western left-wing movement, but were even integrally part of it. Anarchists and pacifists, in particular, have claimed him for their own, noticing only that he was opposed to centralism and State violence and ignoring the other-worldly, anti-humanist tendency of his doctrines. But one should, I think, realise that Gandhi's teachings cannot be squared with the belief that Man is the measure of all things, and that our job is to make life worth living on this earth, which is the only earth we have. They make sense only on the assumption that God exists and that the world of solid objects is an illusion to be escaped from. It is worth considering the disciplines which Gandhi imposed on himself and which—though he might not insist on every one of his followers observing every detail—he considered indispensable if one wanted to serve either God or humanity. First of all, no meat eating, and if possible no animal food in any form. (Gandhi himself, for the sake of his health, had to compromise on milk, but seems to have felt this to be a backsliding.) No alcohol or tobacco, and no spices or condiments, even of a vegetable kind, since food should be taken not for its own sake, but solely in order to preserve one's strength. Secondly, if possible, no sexual intercourse.

If sexual intercourse must happen, then it should be for the sole purpose of begetting children and presumably at long intervals. Gandhi himself, in his middle thirties, took the vow of *bramahcharya,* which means not only complete chastity but the elimination of sexual desire. This condition, it seems, is difficult to attain without a special diet and frequent fasting. One of the dangers of milk drinking is that it is apt to arouse sexual desire. And finally—this is the cardinal point—for the seeker after goodness there must be no close friendships and no exclusive loves whatever.

Close friendships, Gandhi says, are dangerous, because "friends react on one [6] another" and through loyalty to a friend one can be led into wrong-doing. This is un-questionably true. Moreover, if one is to love God, or to love humanity as a whole, one cannot give one's preference to any individual person. This again is true, and it marks the point at which the humanistic and the religious attitudes cease to be reconcilable. To an ordinary human being, love means nothing if it does not mean loving some peo-ple more than others. The autobiography leaves it uncertain whether Gandhi behaved in an inconsiderate way to his wife and children, but at any rate it makes clear that on three occasions he was willing to let his wife or a child die rather than administer the animal food prescribed by the doctor. It is true that the threatened death never actually occurred, and also that Gandhi—with, one gathers, a good deal of moral pressure in the opposite direction—always gave the patient the choice of staying alive at the price of committing a sin: still, if the decision had been solely his own, he would have forbidden the animal food, whatever the risks might be. There must, he says, be some limit to what we will do in order to remain alive, and the limit is well on this side of chicken broth. This attitude is perhaps a noble one, but, in the sense which—I think—most peo-ple would give to the word, it is inhuman. The essence of being human is that one does not seek perfection, that one *is* sometimes willing to commit sins for the sake of loyalty, that one does not push asceticism to the point where it makes friendly intercourse im-possible, and that one is prepared in the end to be defeated and broken up by life, which is the inevitable price of fastening one's love upon other human individuals. No doubt alcohol, tobacco and so forth are things that a saint must avoid, but sainthood is also a thing that human beings must avoid. There is an obvious retort to this, but one should be wary about making it. In this yogi-ridden age, it is too readily assumed that "non-attachment" is not only better than a full acceptance of earthly life, but that the ordinary man only rejects it because it is too difficult: in other words, that the average human being is a failed saint. It is doubtful whether this is true. Many people genuinely do not wish to be saints, and it is probable that some who achieve or aspire to sainthood have never felt much temptation to be human beings. If one could follow it to its psy-chological roots, one would, I believe, find that the main motive for "non-attachment" is a desire to escape from the pain of living, and above all from love, which, sexual or non-sexual, is hard work. But it is not necessary here to argue whether the other-worldly or the humanistic ideal is "higher". The point is that they are incompatible. One must choose between God and Man, and all "radicals" and "progressives", from the mildest Liberal to the most extreme Anarchist, have in effect chosen Man.

However, Gandhi's pacifism can be separated to some extent from his other [7] teachings. Its motive was religious, but he claimed also for it that it was a definite tech-nique, a method, capable of producing desired political results. Gandhi's attitude was not that of most western pacifists. *Satyagraha,* first evolved in South Africa, was a sort of non-violent warfare, a way of defeating the enemy without hurting him and without feeling or arousing hatred. It entailed such things as civil disobedience, strikes, lying down in front of railway trains, enduring police charges without running away and without hitting back, and the like. Gandhi objected to "passive resistance" as a translation of *Satyagraha:* in Gujarati, it seems, the word means "firmness in the truth". In his early days Gandhi served as a stretcher-bearer on the British side in the Boer war, and he was prepared to do the same again in the war of 1914–18. Even after he had completely abjured violence he was honest enough to see that in war it is usually necessary to take sides. He did not—indeed, since his whole political life centred round a struggle for national independence, he could not—take the sterile and dishonest line of pretending that in every war both sides are exactly the same and it makes no difference who wins. Nor did he, like most western pacifists, specialise in avoiding awkward questions. In relation to the late war, one question that every pacifist had a clear obligation to answer was: "What about the Jews? Are you prepared to see them exterminated? If not, how do you propose to save them without resorting to war?" I must say that I have never heard, from any western pacifist, an honest answer to this question, though I have heard plenty of evasions, usually of the "you're another" type. But it so happens that Gandhi was asked a somewhat similar question in 1938 and that his answer is on record in Mr Louis Fischer's *Gandhi and Stalin.* According to Mr Fischer Gandhi's view was that the German Jews ought to commit collective suicide, which "would have aroused the world and the people of Germany to Hitler's violence". After the war he justified himself: the Jews had been killed anyway, and might as well have died significantly. One has the impression that this attitude staggered even so warm an admirer as Mr Fischer, but Gandhi was merely being honest. If you are not prepared to take life, you must often be prepared for lives to be lost in some other way. When, in 1942, he urged non-violent resistance against a Japanese invasion, he was ready to admit that it might cost several million deaths.

At the same time there is reason to think that Gandhi, who after all was born 8 in 1869, did not understand the nature of totalitarianism and saw everything in terms of his own struggle against the British Government. The important point here is not so much that the British treated him forbearingly as that he was always able to command publicity. As can be seen from the phrase quoted above, he believed in "arousing the world", which is only possible if the world gets a chance to hear what you are doing. It is difficult to see how Gandhi's methods could be applied in a country where opponents of the régime disappear in the middle of the night and are never heard of again. Without a free press and the right of assembly, it is impossible not merely to appeal to outside opinion, but to bring a mass movement into being, or even to make your intentions known to your adversary. Is there a Gandhi in Russia at this moment? And if there is, what is he accomplishing? The Russian masses could only practise civil disobedience if the same idea happened to occur to all of them simultaneously, and even then, to judge by the history of the Ukraine famine, it would make no difference. But let it be granted that non-violent resistance can be effective against one's own government, or against an occupying power: even so, how does one put it into practice internationally? Gandhi's various conflicting statements on the late war seem to show that he felt the difficulty of this. Applied to foreign politics, pacifism either stops being pacifist or becomes appeasement. Moreover the assumption, which served Gandhi so well in dealing with individuals, that all human beings are more or less approachable and will respond to a generous gesture, needs to be seriously questioned. It is not necessarily true, for example, when you are dealing with lunatics. Then the question becomes: Who is sane? Was Hitler sane? And is it not possible for one whole culture to be insane by the standards of another? And, so far as one can gauge the feelings of whole nations, is there any apparent connection between a generous deed and a friendly response? Is gratitude a factor in international politics?

These and kindred questions need discussion, and need it urgently, in the few 9 years left to us before somebody presses the button and the rockets begin to fly. It seems doubtful whether civilisation can stand another major war, and it is at least thinkable that the way out lies through non-violence. It is Gandhi's virtue that he would have been ready to give honest consideration to the kind of question that I have raised above; and, indeed, he probably did discuss most of these questions somewhere or other in his innumerable newspaper articles. One feels of him that there was much that he did not understand, but not that there was anything that he was frightened of saying or thinking. I have never been able to feel much liking for Gandhi, but I do not feel sure that as a political thinker he was wrong in the main, nor do I believe that his life was a failure. It is curious that when he was assassinated, many of his warmest admirers exclaimed sorrowfully that he had lived just long enough to see his life work in ruins, because India was engaged in a civil war which had always been foreseen as one of the by-products of the transfer of power. But it was not in trying to smooth down Hindu-Moslem rivalry that Gandhi had spent his life. His main political objective, the peaceful ending of British rule, had after all been attained. As usual, the relevant facts cut across one another. On the one hand, the British did get out of India without fighting, an event which very few observers indeed would have predicted until about a year before it happened. On the other hand, this was done by a Labour Government, and it is certain that a Conservative Government, especially a government headed by Churchill, would have acted differently. But if, by 1945, there had grown up in Britain a large body of opinion sympathetic to Indian independence, how far was this due to Gandhi's personal influence? And if, as may happen, India and Britain finally settle down into a decent and friendly relationship, will this be partly because Gandhi, by keeping up his struggle obstinately and without hatred, disinfected the political air? That one even thinks of asking such questions indicates his stature. One may feel, as I do, a sort of aesthetic distaste for Gandhi, one may reject the claims of sainthood made on his behalf (he never made any such claim himself, by the way), one may also reject sainthood as an ideal and therefore feel that Gandhi's basic aims were anti-human and reactionary: but regarded simply as a politician, and compared with the other leading political figures of our time, how clean a smell he has managed to leave behind!

Questions

1. In arguing that "saints should always be judged guilty until they are proved innocent," what tests does Orwell apply to Gandhi? Is he chiefly concerned with Gandhi's character or with the effect of his ideas?

2. What are Orwell's assumptions in stating that Gandhi's "medievalist program was obviously not viable in a backward, starving, overpopulated country" (paragraph 2)? Why was Gandhi's basic aim "antihuman"? Does Orwell consider Gandhi's influence on India to have been wholly negative?
3. Does Orwell reject Gandhi's belief that "all human beings are more or less approachable and will respond to a generous gesture" (paragraph 8)?
4. What conclusion does Orwell reach about Gandhi as a saint? Why does he not consider his life a failure?
5. What is the purpose of Orwell's review of Gandhi's autobiography? Does he assess the book as an autobiography, or is he concerned with the ideas of the book and its revelations about Gandhi?

Suggestions for Writing

1. Discuss what the essay reveals about Orwell's values and ideas about people and society—in particular, what he respects in individuals and political leaders. Cite evidence from the essay to support your judgments.
2. Write your own review of a recent autobiography—using striking statements and episodes to evaluate the character of the author. Explain your criteria or the bases of your judgments, as Orwell does in his review.
3. Among the many collections of Gandhi's writings are *All Men Are Brothers* and Louis Fischer's *Essential Gandhi*. Some of his numerous writings on nonviolent resistance are in print. A first-hand account of Gandhi and his ideas occurs in the collected writings of Jawaharlal Nehru, Gandhi's colleague and the first prime minister of India. Use these sources to give a full account of Gandhi's philosophy of *satyagraha*. In the course of your account, compare this philosophy with that of Martin Luther King's *Letter from Birmingham Jail* or Thoreau's "Resistance to Civil Government."

Additional Reading

Abrahams, William, and Peter Stansky. *The Unknown Orwell*. New York: Knopf, 1972.
Crick, Bernard. *George Orwell: A Life*. Boston: Little, Brown, 1981.
Orwell, George. *Animal Farm*. New York: Harcourt Brace Jovanovich, 1946.
———. *Burmese Days*. New York: Harcourt Brace Jovanovich, 1950.
———. *Collected Essays, Journalism and Letters of George Orwell*. 4 vols. Ed. Sonia Orwell and Ian Angus. New York: Harcourt Brace Jovanovich, 1968.
———. *Nineteen Eighty-Four*. New York: Harcourt Brace Jovanovich, 1949.
———. *The Orwell Reader: Fiction, Essays, and Reportage*. New York: Harcourt Brace Jovanovich, 1956.

Duties of a Law-Abiding Citizen

Hannah Arendt

The political scientist and philosopher Hannah Arendt was born in Hanover, Germany, in 1906, and educated at various German universities, receiving her Ph.D. from the University of Heidelberg. She left Germany in 1933, shortly after Adolf Hitler's coming to power, and worked with refugee children in France until her departure for the United States in 1941. Arendt taught political science at the University of Chicago and other universities, and she was University Professor at the New School for Social Research in New York. Her book The Origins of Totalitarianism *(1951) is the classic study of Nazi Germany and its origins. Equally influential has been her philosophical book* The Human Condition *(1970). In 1961 Arendt reported the trial of Adolf Eichmann in Jerusalem for* The New Yorker *magazine, her articles forming the original version of* Eichmann in Jerusalem *(1963).*

Adolf Eichmann was born in Germany in 1906. His mother died when he was four years old and he was taken to Linz, Austria. The inflation of the 1920s ruined his father financially and ended Eichmann's schooling. He began attending Nazi Party meetings and in 1932 joined the Austrian Nazi Party and the S. S., Heinrich Himmler's black-shirted elite guard—the organization that later ran the concentration camps. After military training and service in Bavarian S.S. camps, Eichmann found employment in the S.D. or Reich Security Service, under Reinhard Heydrich. Eichmann saw an opportunity for advancement in claiming to be an expert on Jews. "Some of my early work was with the Nuremberg Laws, in force since 1935," he told a journalist after the war. "Under the formula adopted at that time for 'Final Solution of the Jewish Question,' the laws were intended to drive Jews out of all phases of German life." Eichmann was referring to laws enacted by the Nazis to deprive Jews of citizenship, which was limited to those of "German or related blood." The laws also forbade marriage and sexual intercourse between Germans and Jews and imposed other restrictions. With the seizure of Austria in 1938, Eichmann was put in charge of the expulsion of Austrian Jews from the country.

At the Wannsee Conference in Berlin in January 1942, Heydrich outlined what was to be called the "Final Solution," the extermination of the nine million Jews of Europe at death camps established at Auschwitz and Treblinka in Eastern Poland and elsewhere. Eichmann was appointed chief of the deportations to these camps. Approximately six million Jews had perished by the end of the war, many from starvation and torture in the concentration camps established in 1933, but most of them in the gas chambers of the death camps— corpses and half-alive people were cremated in ovens. In western Russia death squads shot or buried thousands alive. "Nature is cruel, therefore we, too, may be cruel," Hitler said to one of his followers. "If I don't mind sending the pick of the German people into the hell of war

*without regret for the shedding of valuable German blood, then I have
naturally the right to destroy millions of men of inferior races who increase like vermin."*

    *With the defeat of the Reich and Hitler's suicide in the spring
of 1945, Eichmann succeeded in fleeing Germany and Europe. He was
captured in Argentina by Israelis and brought to Jerusalem for trial.
Following his conviction, he was hanged on May 31, 1962. In the words
of the judges who passed sentence, "[T]he idea of the Final Solution
would never have assumed the infernal forms of the flayed skin and
tortured flesh of millions of Jews without the fanatical zeal and the unquenchable blood thirst of the appellant and his accomplices."*

    So Eichmann's opportunities for feeling like Pontius Pilate were many, and as 1
the months and the years went by, he lost the need to feel anything at all. This was the
way things were, this was the new law of the land, based on the Führer's[1] order; whatever he did he did, as far as he could see, as a law-abiding citizen. He did his *duty,* as
he told the police and the court over and over again; he not only obeyed *orders,* he also
obeyed the *law.* Eichmann had a muddled inkling that this could be an important distinction, but neither the defense nor the judges ever took him up on it. The well-worn
coins of "superior orders" versus "acts of state" were handed back and forth; they had
governed the whole discussion of these matters during the Nuremberg Trials,[2] for no
other reason than that they gave the illusion that the altogether unprecedented could
be judged according to precedents and the standards that went with them. Eichmann,
with his rather modest mental gifts, was certainly the last man in the courtroom to be
expected to challenge these notions and to strike out on his own. Since, in addition to
performing what he conceived to be the duties of a law-abiding citizen, he had also acted
upon orders—always so careful to be "covered"—he became completely muddled, and
ended by stressing alternately the virtues and the vices of blind obedience, or the "obedience of corpses," *Kadavergehorsam,* as he himself called it.

    The first indication of Eichmann's vague notion that there was more involved 2
in this whole business than the question of the soldier's carrying out orders that are
clearly criminal in nature and intent appeared during the police examination, when he
suddenly declared with great emphasis that he had lived his whole life according to
Kant's moral precepts, and especially according to a Kantian definition of duty.[3] This
was outrageous, on the face of it, and also incomprehensible, since Kant's moral philosophy is so closely bound up with man's faculty of judgment, which rules out blind obedience. The examining officer did not press the point, but Judge Raveh, either out of curiosity or out of indignation at Eichmann's having dared to invoke Kant's name in
connection with his crimes, decided to question the accused. And, to the surprise of
everybody, Eichmann came up with an approximately correct definition of the categori-

---

[1]Führer, or "Leader," the title assumed by Adolf Hitler as head of the Nazi Party and dictator of Germany from
  1933 to 1945.

[2]The United States and its allies conducted trials of Nazi officials in Nuremberg, Germany, in 1945–46.

[3]Immanuel Kant (1724–1804): German philosopher who argued that humans can reason what is good and
  then will to act upon their reason. Kant defines duty as the free decision to obey laws that reason determines
  are good.

cal imperative: "I meant by my remark about Kant that the principle of my will must always be such that it can become the principle of general laws" (which is not the case with theft or murder, for instance, because the thief or the murderer cannot conceivably wish to live under a legal system that would give others the right to rob or murder him). Upon further questioning, he added that he had read Kant's *Critique of Practical Reason.* He then proceeded to explain that from the moment he was charged with carrying out the Final Solution he had ceased to live according to Kantian principles, that he had known it, and that he had consoled himself with the thought that he no longer "was master of his own deeds," that he was unable "to change anything." What he failed to point out in court was that in this "period of crimes legalized by the state," as he himself now called it, he had not simply dismissed the Kantian formula as no longer applicable, he had distorted it to read: Act as if the principle of your actions were the same as that of the legislator or of the law of the land—or, in Hans Frank's formulation of "the categorical imperative in the Third Reich," which Eichmann might have known: "Act in such a way that the Führer, if he knew your action, would approve it" *(Die Technik des Staates,* 1942, pp. 15–16). Kant, to be sure, had never intended to say anything of the sort; on the contrary, to him every man was a legislator the moment he started to act: by using his "practical reason" man found the principles that could and should be the principles of law. But it is true that Eichmann's unconscious distortion agrees with what he himself called the version of Kant "for the household use of the little man." In this household use, all that is left of Kant's spirit is the demand that a man do more than obey the law, that he go beyond the mere call of obedience and identify his own will with the principle behind the law—the source from which the law sprang. In Kant's philosophy, that source was practical reason; in Eichmann's household use of him, it was the will of the Führer. Much of the horribly painstaking thoroughness in the execution of the Final Solution—a thoroughness that usually strikes the observer as typically German, or else as characteristic of the perfect bureaucrat—can be traced to the odd notion, indeed very common in Germany, that to be law-abiding means not merely to obey the laws but to act as though one were the legislator of the laws that one obeys. Hence the conviction that nothing less than going beyond the call of duty will do.

Whatever Kant's role in the formation of "the little man's" mentality in Germany may have been, there is not the slightest doubt that in one respect Eichmann did indeed follow Kant's precepts: a law was a law, there could be no exceptions. In Jerusalem, he admitted only two such exceptions during the time when "eighty million Germans" had each had "his decent Jew": he had helped a half-Jewish cousin, and a Jewish couple in Vienna for whom his uncle had intervened. This inconsistency still made him feel somewhat uncomfortable, and when he was questioned about it during cross-examination, he became openly apologetic: he had "confessed his sins" to his superiors. This uncompromising attitude toward the performance of his murderous duties damned him in the eyes of the judges more than anything else, which was comprehensible, but in his own eyes it was precisely what justified him, as it had once silenced whatever conscience he might have had left. No exceptions—this was the proof that he had always acted against his "inclinations," whether they were sentimental or inspired by interest, that he had always done his "duty." 3

Doing his "duty" finally brought him into open conflict with orders from his superiors. During the last year of the war, more than two years after the Wannsee Con- 4 ference,[4] he experienced his last crisis of conscience. As the defeat approached, he was confronted by men from his own ranks who fought more and more insistently for exceptions and, eventually, for the cessation of the Final Solution. That was the moment when his caution broke down and he began, once more, taking initiatives—for instance, he organized the foot marches of Jews from Budapest to the Austrian border after Allied bombing had knocked out the transportation system. It now was the fall of 1944, and Eichmann knew that Himmler had ordered the dismantling of the extermination facilities in Auschwitz and that the game was up. Around this time, Eichmann had one of his very few personal interviews with Himmler, in the course of which the latter allegedly shouted at him, "If up to now you have been busy liquidating Jews, you will from now on, since I order it, take good care of Jews, act as their nursemaid. I remind you that it was I—and neither Gruppenführer Müller nor you—who founded the R.S.H.A. in 1933; I am the one who gives orders here!" Sole witness to substantiate these words was the very dubious Mr. Kurt Becher; Eichmann denied that Himmler had shouted at him, but he did not deny that such an interview had taken place. Himmler cannot have spoken in precisely these words, he surely knew that the R.S.H.A. was founded in 1939, not in 1933, and not simply by himself but by Heydrich, with his endorsement. Still, something of the sort must have occurred, Himmler was then giving orders right and left that the Jews be treated well—they were his "soundest investment"—and it must have been a shattering experience for Eichmann.

Eichmann's last crisis of conscience began with his missions to Hungary in March, 1944, when the Red Army was moving through the Carpathian Mountains toward the Hungarian border. Hungary had joined the war on Hitler's side in 1941, for no other reason than to receive some additional territory from her neighbors, Slovakia, Rumania, and Yugoslavia. The Hungarian government had been outspokenly anti-Semitic even before that, and now it began to deport all stateless Jews from the newly acquired territories. (In nearly all countries, anti-Jewish action started with stateless persons.) This was quite outside the Final Solution, and, as a matter of fact, didn't fit in with the elaborate plans then in preparation under which Europe would be "combed from West to East," so that Hungary had a rather low priority in the order of operations. The stateless Jews had been shoved by the Hungarian police into the nearest part of Russia, and the German occupation authorities on the spot had protested their arrival; the Hungarians had taken back some thousands of able-bodied men and had let the others be shot by Hungarian troops under the guidance of German police units. Admiral Horthy, the country's Fascist ruler, had not wanted to go any further, however—probably due to the restraining influence of Mussolini and Italian Fascism—and in the intervening years Hungary, not unlike Italy, had become a haven for Jews, to which even refugees from Poland and Slovakia could sometimes still escape. The annexation of territory and the trickle of incoming refugees had increased the number of Jews in Hungary from about

---

[4]The Wannsee Conference, convened on January 20, 1942, in a Berlin suburb, to plan the "final solution"—the extermination of European Jews at death camps like Auschwitz and Treblinka in eastern Poland. The R.S.H.A. was the "head office for reich security" of the SS (*Schutzstaffel* or "elite guard"), which took control of various state police and intelligence agencies in 1939.

five hundred thousand before the war to approximately eight hundred thousand in 1944, when Eichmann moved in.

As we know today, the safety of these three hundred thousand Jews newly ac-   6 quired by Hungary was due to the Germans' reluctance to start a separate action for a limited number, rather than to the Hungarians' eagerness to offer asylum. In 1942, under pressure from the German Foreign Office (which never failed to make it clear to Germany's allies that the touchstone of their trustworthiness was their helpfulness not in winning the war but in "solving the Jewish question"), Hungary had offered to hand over all Jewish refugees. The Foreign Office had been willing to accept this as a step in the right direction, but Eichmann had objected: for technical reasons, he thought it "preferable to defer this action until Hungary is ready to include the Hungarian Jews"; it would be too costly "to set in motion the whole machinery of evacuation" for only one category, and hence "without making any progress in the solution of the Jewish problem in Hungary." Now, in 1944, Hungary was "ready," because on the nineteenth of March two divisions of the German Army had occupied the country. With them had arrived the new Reich Plenipotentiary, S.S. Standartenführer Dr. Edmund Veesenmayer, Himmler's agent in the Foreign Office, and S.S. Obergruppenführer Otto Winkelmann, a member of the Higher S.S. and Police Leader Corps and therefore under the direct command of Himmler. The third S.S. official to arrive in the country was Eichmann, the expert on Jewish evacuation and deportation, who was under the command of Müller and Kaltenbrunner of the R.S.H.A. Hitler himself had left no doubt what the arrival of the three gentlemen meant; in a famous interview, prior to the occupation of the country, he had told Horthy that "Hungary had not yet introduced the steps necessary to settle the Jewish question," and had charged him with "not having permitted the Jews to be massacred" (Hilberg).

Eichmann's assignment was clear. His whole office was moved to Budapest (in   7 terms of his career, this was a "gliding down"), to enable him to see to it that all "necessary steps" were taken. He had no foreboding of what was to happen; his worst fear concerned possible resistance on the part of the Hungarians, which he would have been unable to cope with, because he lacked manpower and also lacked knowledge of local conditions. These fears proved quite unfounded. The Hungarian *gendarmerie* was more than eager to do all that was necessary, and the new State Secretary in Charge of Political (Jewish) Affairs in the Hungarian Ministry of the Interior, László Endre, was a man "well versed in the Jewish problem," and became an intimate friend, with whom Eichmann could spend a good deal of his free time. Everything went "like a dream," as he repeated whenever he recalled this episode; there were no difficulties whatsoever. Unless, of course, one calls difficulties a few minor differences between his orders and the wishes of his new friends; for instance, probably because of the approach of the Red Army from the East, his orders stipulated that the country was to be "combed from East to West," which meant that Budapest Jews would not be evacuated during the first weeks or months—a matter for great grief among the Hungarians, who wanted their capital to take the lead in becoming *judenrein*. (Eichmann's "dream" was an incredible nightmare for the Jews: nowhere else were so many people deported and exterminated in such a brief span of time. In less than two months, 147 trains, carrying 434,351 people in sealed freight cars, a hundred persons to a car, left the country, and the gas chambers of Auschwitz were hardly able to cope with this multitude.)

The difficulties arose from another quarter. Not one man but three had orders 8 specifying that they were to help in "the solution of the Jewish problem"; each of them belonged to a different outfit and stood in a different chain of command. Technically, Winkelmann was Eichmann's superior, but the Higher S.S. and Police Leaders were not under the command of the R.S.H.A., to which Eichmann belonged. And Veesenmayer, of the Foreign Office, was independent of both. At any rate, Eichmann refused to take orders from either of the others, and resented their presence. But the worst trouble came from a fourth man, whom Himmler had charged with a "special mission" in the only country in Europe that still harbored not only a sizable number of Jews but Jews who were still in an important economic position. (Of a total of a hundred and ten thousand commercial stores and industrial enterprises in Hungary, forty thousand were reported to be in Jewish hands.) This man was Obersturmbannführer, later Standartenführer, Kurt Becher.

Becher, an old enemy of Eichmann who is today a prosperous merchant in 9 Bremen, was called, strangely enough, as a witness for the defense. He could not come to Jerusalem, for obvious reasons, and he was examined in his German home town. His testimony had to be dismissed, since he had been shown, well ahead of time, the questions he was later called on to answer under oath. It was a great pity that Eichmann and Becher could not have been confronted with each other, and this not merely for juridical reasons. Such a confrontation would have revealed another part of the "general picture," which, even legally, was far from irrelevant. According to his own account, the reason Becher joined the S.S. was that "from 1932 to the present day he had been actively engaged in horseback riding." Thirty years ago, this was a sport engaged in only by Europe's upper classes. In 1934, his instructor had persuaded him to enter the S.S. cavalry regiment, which at that moment was the very thing for a man to do if he wished to join the "movement" and at the same time maintain a proper regard for his social standing. (A possible reason Becher in his testimony stressed horseback riding was never mentioned: the Nuremberg Tribunal had excluded the *Reiter-S.S.* from its list of criminal organizations.) The war saw Becher on active duty at the front, as a member not of the Army but of the Armed S.S., in which he was a liaison officer with the Army commanders. He soon left the front to become the principal buyer of horses for the S.S. personnel department, a job that earned him nearly all the decorations that were then available.

Becher claimed that he had been sent to Hungary only in order to buy twenty 10 thousand horses for the S.S.; this is unlikely, since immediately upon his arrival he began a series of very successful negotiations with the heads of big Jewish business concerns. His relations with Himmler were excellent, he could see him whenever he wished. His "special mission" was clear enough. He was to obtain control of major Jewish business concerns behind the backs of the Hungarian government, and, in return, to give the owners free passage out of the country, plus a sizable amount of money in foreign currency. His most important transaction was with the Manfred Weiss steel combine, a mammoth enterprise, with thirty thousand workers, which produced everything from airplanes, trucks, and bicycles to tinned goods, pins, and needles. The result was that forty-five members of the Weiss family emigrated to Portugal while Mr. Becher became head of their business. When Eichmann heard of this *Schweinerei,* he was outraged; the deal threatened to compromise his good relations with the Hungarians, who naturally expected to take possession of Jewish property confiscated on their own soil. He had some reason for his indignation, since these deals were contrary to the regular Nazi policy, which had been quite generous. For their help in solving the Jewish question in any country, the Germans had demanded no part of the Jews' property, only the costs of their deportation and extermination, and these costs had varied widely from country to country—the Slovaks had been supposed to pay between three hundred and five hundred Reichsmarks per Jew, the Croats only thirty, the French seven hundred, and the Belgians two hundred and fifty. (It seems that no one ever paid except the Croats.) In Hungary, at this late stage of the war, the Germans were demanding payment in goods—shipments of food to the Reich, in quantities determined by the amount of food the deported Jews would have consumed.

The Weiss affair was only the beginning, and things were to get considerably 11 worse, from Eichmann's point of view. Becher was a born businessman, and where Eichmann saw only enormous tasks of organization and administration, he saw almost unlimited possibilities for making money. The one thing that stood in his way was the narrow-mindedness of subordinate creatures like Eichmann, who took their jobs seriously. Obersturmbannführer Becher's projects soon led him to cooperate closely in the rescue efforts of Dr. Rudolf Kastner. (It was to Kastner's testimony on his behalf that Becher later, at Nuremberg, owed his freedom. Being an old Zionist, Kastner had moved to Israel after the war, where he held a high position until a journalist published a story about his collaboration with the S.S.—whereupon Kastner sued him for libel. His testimony at Nuremberg weighed heavily against him, and when the case came before the Jerusalem District Court, Judge Halevi, one of the three judges in the Eichmann trial, told Kastner that he "had sold his soul to the devil." In March, 1957, shortly before his case was to be appealed before the Israeli Supreme Court, Kastner was murdered; none of the murderers, it seems, came from Hungary. In the hearing that followed the verdict of the lower court was repealed and Kastner was fully rehabilitated.) The deals Becher made through Kastner were much simpler than the complicated negotiations with the business magnates; they consisted in fixing a price for the life of each Jew to be rescued. There was considerable haggling over prices, and at one point, it seems, Eichmann also got involved in some of the preliminary discussions. Characteristically, his price was the lowest, a mere two hundred dollars per Jew—not, of course, because he wished to save more Jews but simply because he was not used to thinking big. The price finally arrived at was a thousand dollars, and one group, consisting of 1,684 Jews, and including Dr. Kastner's family, actually left Hungary for the exchange camp at Bergen-Belsen, from which they eventually reached Switzerland. A similar deal, through which Becher and Himmler hoped to obtain twenty million Swiss francs from the American Joint Distribution Committee, for the purchase of merchandise of all sorts, kept everybody busy until the Russians liberated Hungary, but nothing came of it.

There is no doubt that Becher's activities had the full approval of Himmler and 12 stood in the sharpest possible opposition to the old "radical" orders, which still reached Eichmann through Müller and Kaltenbrunner, his immediate superiors in the R.S. H.A. In Eichmann's view, people like Becher were corrupt, but corruption could not very well have caused his crisis of conscience, for although he was apparently not susceptible to this kind of temptation, he must by this time have been surrounded by corruption for many years. It is difficult to imagine that he did not know that his friend and subordinate Hauptsturmführer Dieter Wisliceny had, as early as 1942, accepted fifty

thousand dollars from the Jewish Relief Committee in Bratislava for delaying the deportations from Slovakia, though it is not altogether impossible; but he cannot have been
ignorant of the fact that Himmler, in the fall of 1942, had tried to sell exit permits to
the Slovakian Jews in exchange for enough foreign currency to pay for the recruitment
of a new S.S. division. Now, however, in 1944, in Hungary, it was different, not because
Himmler was involved in "business," but because business had now become official policy; it was no longer mere corruption.

At the beginning, Eichmann tried to enter the game and play it according to 13
the new rules; that was when he got involved in the fantastic "blood-for-wares"
negotiations—one million Jews for ten thousand trucks for the crumbling German
Army—which certainly were not initiated by him. The way he explained his role in this
matter, in Jerusalem, showed clearly how he had once justified it to himself: as a military necessity that would bring him the additional benefit of an important new role in
the emigration business. What he probably never admitted to himself was that the
mounting difficulties on all sides made it every day more likely that he would soon be
without a job (indeed, this happened, a few months later) unless he succeeded in finding
some foothold amid the new jockeying for power that was going on all around him.
When the exchange project met with its predictable failure, it was already common
knowledge that Himmler, despite his constant vacillations, chiefly due to his justified
physical fear of Hitler, had decided to put an end to the whole Final Solution—
regardless of business, regardless of military necessity, and without anything to show
for it except the illusions he had concocted about his future role as the bringer of peace
to Germany. It was at this time that a "moderate wing" of the S.S. came into existence,
consisting of those who were stupid enough to believe that a murderer who could prove
he had not killed as many people as he could have killed would have a marvelous alibi,
and those who were clever enough to foresee a return to "normal conditions," when
money and good connections would again be of paramount importance.

Eichmann never joined this "moderate wing," and it is questionable whether 14
he would have been admitted if he had tried to. Not only was he too deeply compromised
and, because of his constant contact with Jewish functionaries, too well known; he was
too primitive for these well-educated upper-middle-class "gentlemen," against whom he
harbored the most violent resentment up to the very end. He was quite capable of sending millions of people to their death, but he was not capable of talking about it in the
appropriate manner without being given his "language rule." In Jerusalem, without any
rules, he spoke freely of "killing" and of "murder," of "crimes legalized by the state";
he called a spade a spade, in contrast to counsel for the defense, whose feeling of social
superiority to Eichmann was more than once in evidence. (Servatius' assistant Dr. Dieter Wechtenbruch—a disciple of Carl Schmitt who attended the first few weeks of the
trial, then was sent to Germany to question witnesses for the defense, and reappeared
for the last week in August—was readily available to reporters out of court; he seemed
to be shocked less by Eichmann's crimes than by his lack of taste and education. "Small
fry," he said; "we must see how we get him over the hurdles"—*wie wir das Würstchen
über die Runden bringen.* Servatius himself had declared, even prior to the trial, that
his client's personality was that of "a common mailman.")

When Himmler became "moderate," Eichmann sabotaged his orders as much 15
as he dared, to the extent at least that he felt he was "covered" by his immediate superiors. "How does Eichmann dare to sabotage Himmler's orders?"—in this case, to stop

the foot marches, in the fall of 1944—Kastner once asked Wisliceny. And the answer was: "He can probably show some telegram. Müller and Kaltenbrunner must have covered him." It is quite possible that Eichmann had some confused plan for liquidating Theresienstadt before the arrival of the Red Army, although we know this only through the dubious testimony of Dieter Wisliceny (who months, and perhaps years, before the end began carefully preparing an alibi for himself at the expense of Eichmann, to which he then treated the court at Nuremberg, where he was a witness for the prosecution; it did him no good, for he was extradited to Czechoslovakia, prosecuted and executed in Prague, where he had no connections and where money was of no help to him). Other witnesses claimed that it was Rolf Günther, one of Eichmann's men, who planned this, and that there existed, on the contrary, a written order from Eichmann that the ghetto be left intact. In any event, there is no doubt that even in April, 1945, when practically everybody had become quite "moderate," Eichmann took advantage of a visit that M. Paul Dunand, of the Swiss Red Cross, paid to Theresienstadt to put it on record that he himself did not approve of Himmler's new line in regard to the Jews.

That Eichmann had at all times done his best to make the Final Solution final 16 was therefore not in dispute. The question was only whether this was indeed proof of his fanaticism, his boundless hatred of Jews, and whether he had lied to the police and committed perjury in court when he claimed he had always obeyed orders. No other explanation ever occurred to the judges, who tried so hard to understand the accused, and treated him with a consideration and an authentic, shining humanity such as he had probably never encountered before in his whole life. (Dr. Wechtenbruch told reporters that Eichmann had "great confidence in Judge Landau," as though Landau would be able to sort things out, and ascribed this confidence to Eichmann's need for authority. Whatever its basis, the confidence was apparent throughout the trial, and it may have been the reason the judgment caused Eichmann such great "disappointment"; he had mistaken humanity for softness.) That they never did come to understand him may be proof of the "goodness" of the three men, of their untroubled and slightly old-fashioned faith in the moral foundations of their profession. For the sad and very uncomfortable truth of the matter probably was that it was not his fanaticism but his very conscience that prompted Eichmann to adopt his uncompromising attitude during the last year of the war, as it had prompted him to move in the opposite direction for a short time three years before. Eichmann knew that Himmler's orders ran directly counter to the Führer's order. For this, he needed to know no factual details, though such details would have backed him up: as the prosecution underlined in the proceedings before the Supreme Court, when Hitler heard, through Kaltenbrunner, of negotiations to exchange Jews for trucks, "Himmler's position in Hitler's eyes was completely undermined." And only a few weeks before Himmler stopped the extermination at Auschwitz, Hitler, obviously unaware of Himmler's newest moves, had sent an ultimatum to Horthy, telling him he "expected that the measures against Jews in Budapest would now be taken without any further delay by the Hungarian government." When Himmler's order to stop the evacuation of Hungarian Jews arrived in Budapest, Eichmann threatened, according to a telegram from Veesenmayer, "to seek a new decision from the Führer," and this telegram the judgment found "more damning than a hundred witnesses could be."

Eichmann lost his fight against the "moderate wing," headed by the 17 Reichsführer S.S. and Chief of the German Police. The first indication of his defeat came in January, 1945, when Obersturmbannführer Kurt Becher was promoted to *Standartenführer,* the very rank Eichmann had been dreaming about all during the war. (His story, that no higher rank was open to him in his outfit, was a half-truth; he could have been made chief of Department IV-B, instead of occupying the desk of IV-B-4, and would then have been automatically promoted. The truth probably was that people like Eichmann, who had risen from the ranks, were never permitted to advance beyond a lieutenant colonelcy except at the front.) That same month Hungary was liberated, and Eichmann was called back to Berlin. There, Himmler had appointed his enemy Becher *Reichssonderkommissar* in charge of all concentration camps, and Eichmann was transferred from the desk concerned with "Jewish Affairs" to the utterly insignificant one concerned with the "Fight Against the Churches," of which, moreover, he knew nothing. The rapidity of his decline during the last months of the war is a most telling sign of the extent to which Hitler was right when he declared, in his Berlin bunker, in April, 1945, that the S.S. were no longer reliable.

In Jerusalem, confronted with documentary proof of his extraordinary loyalty 18 to Hitler and the Führer's order, Eichmann tried a number of times to explain that during the Third Reich "the Führer's words had the force of law" *(Führerworte haben Gesetzeskraft),* which meant, among other things, that if the order came directly from Hitler it did not have to be in writing. He tried to explain that this was why he had never asked for a written order from Hitler (no such document relating to the Final Solution has ever been found; probably it never existed), but had demanded to see a written order from Himmler. To be sure, this was a fantastic state of affairs, and whole libraries of very "learned" juridical comment have been written, all demonstrating that the Führer's *words,* his oral pronouncements, were the basic law of the land. Within this "legal" framework, every order contrary in letter or spirit to a word spoken by Hitler was, by definition, unlawful. Eichmann's position, therefore, showed a most unpleasant resemblance to that of the often-cited soldier who, acting in a normal legal framework, refuses to carry out orders that run counter to his ordinary experience of lawfulness and hence can be recognized by him as criminal. The extensive literature on the subject usually supports its case with the common equivocal meaning of the word "law," which in this context means sometimes the law of the land—that is, posited, positive law—and sometimes the law that supposedly speaks in all men's hearts with an identical voice. Practically speaking, however, orders to be disobeyed must be "manifestly unlawful" and unlawfulness must "fly like a black flag above [them] as a warning reading: 'Prohibited!'"—as the judgment pointed out. And in a criminal regime this "black flag" with its "warning sign" flies as "manifestly" above what normally is a lawful order—for instance, not to kill innocent people just because they happen to be Jews—as it flies above a criminal order under normal circumstances. To fall back on an unequivocal voice of conscience—or, in the even vaguer language of the jurists, on a "general sentiment of humanity" (Oppenheim–Lauterpacht in *International Law,* 1952)—not only begs the question, it signifies a deliberate refusal to take notice of the central moral, legal, and political phenomena of our century.

To be sure, it was not merely Eichmann's conviction that Himmler was now 19 giving "criminal" orders that determined his actions. But the personal element undoubtedly involved was not fanaticism, it was his genuine, "boundless and immoderate admiration for Hitler" (as one of the defense witnesses called it)—for the man who had made it "from lance corporal to Chancellor of the Reich." It would be idle to try to figure out which was stronger in him, his admiration for Hitler or his determination to remain a law-abiding citizen of the Third Reich when Germany was already in ruins. Both motives came into play once more during the last days of the war, when he was in Berlin and saw with violent indignation how everybody around him was sensibly enough getting himself fixed up with forged papers before the arrival of the Russians or the Americans. A few weeks later, Eichmann, too, began to travel under an assumed name, but by then Hitler was dead, and the "law of the land" was no longer in existence, and he, as he pointed out, was no longer bound by his oath. For the oath taken by the members of the S.S. differed from the military oath sworn by the soldiers in that it bound them only to Hitler, not to Germany.

The case of the conscience of Adolf Eichmann, which is admittedly complicated 20 but is by no means unique, is scarcely comparable to the case of the German generals, one of whom, when asked at Nuremberg, "How was it possible that all you honorable generals could continue to serve a murderer with such unquestioning loyalty?," replied that it was "not the task of a soldier to act as judge over his supreme commander. Let history do that or God in heaven." (Thus General Alfred Jodl, hanged at Nuremberg.) Eichmann, much less intelligent and without any education to speak of, at least dimly realized that it was not an order but a law which had turned them all into criminals. The distinction between an order and the Führer's word was that the latter's validity was not limited in time and space, which is the outstanding characteristic of the former. This is also the true reason why the Führer's order for the Final Solution was followed by a huge shower of regulations and directives, all drafted by expert lawyers and legal advisers, not by mere administrators; this order, in contrast to ordinary orders, was treated as a law. Needless to add, the resulting legal paraphernalia, far from being a mere symptom of German pedantry or thoroughness, served most effectively to give the whole business its outward appearance of legality.

And just as the law in civilized countries assumes that the voice of conscience 21 tells everybody "Thou shalt not kill," even though man's natural desires and inclinations may at times be murderous, so the law of Hitler's land demanded that the voice of conscience tell everybody: "Thou shalt kill," although the organizers of the massacres knew full well that murder is against the normal desires and inclinations of most people. Evil in the Third Reich had lost the quality by which most people recognize it—the quality of temptation. Many Germans and many Nazis, probably an overwhelming majority of them, must have been tempted *not* to murder, *not* to rob, *not* to let their neighbors go off to their doom (for that the Jews were transported to their doom they knew, of course, even though many of them may not have known the gruesome details), and not to become accomplices in all these crimes by benefiting from them. But, God knows, they had learned how to resist temptation.

Questions

1. Referring to Immanuel Kant's moral precepts, Arendt states that Eichmann showed awareness "that there was more involved in this whole business than the question of the soldier's carrying out orders that are clearly criminal in nature and intent . . ." (paragraph 2). What more did Eichmann think was involved?

2. How does Arendt reconcile Eichmann's "thoroughness in the execution of the Final Solution," in paragraphs 2 and 3, with the crises of conscience discussed in paragraphs 3 and 4?
3. How do Eichmann's actions in Hungary illustrate Arendt's earlier characterization of him? What difference does she stress between Eichmann and Kurt Becher in paragraphs 9–12?
4. What do his later effort "to enter the game and play it according to the new rules" (paragraph 13) and his subsequent refusal to join the "moderate wing" of the S.S. show? Is Arendt suggesting different characters or motivations in Eichmann and Himmler?
5. What did Eichmann's judges fail to understand about his state of mind? What point does Arendt make about this state of mind in paragraph 18? What point is Arendt making about his resemblance to the soldier cited in the paragraph?
6. How does Arendt characterize the quality of evil in the Third Reich?

Suggestions for Writing

1. Discuss the lessons Arendt wishes the reader to draw from her characterization of Eichmann and his behavior and that of other Nazis.
2. Arendt notes that by the end of World War Two the technology of war had made all warfare criminal according to the prevailing Hague Convention definition of war crimes: "Hence, it was felt that under these new conditions war crimes were only those outside all military necessities, where a deliberate inhuman purpose could be demonstrated." A war crime thus became an act of "gratuitous brutality." Does this definition seem adequate to you? Under what circumstances should a person be considered a war criminal rather than a soldier?
3. One of the best general accounts of the Nazi era is William L. Shirer's *The Rise and Fall of the Third Reich* (1960). The concentration camps and the death camps are the subject of Bruno Bettelheim's *The Informed Heart: Autonomy in a Mass Age* (1960), Terrence Des Pres, *The Survivor: An Anatomy of Life in the Death Camps* (1976), Eugen Kogon's *The Theory and Practice of Hell: The Concentration Camps and the System behind Them* (1950), Ota Kraus and Erich Kulka's *The Death Factory: Documents on Auschwitz* (1966), Gerald Reitlinger's *The Final Solution: The Attempt to Exterminate the Jews of Europe* (1961), and George H. Stein's *The Waffen SS* (1966). *Commandant of Auschwitz: The Autobiography of Rudolf Hoess* (1960) is indispensable. Studies of Hitler include Alan Bullock's *Hitler: A Study in Tyranny* (1964) and Joachim C. Fest's *Hitler* (1975). The destruction of European Jews is documented in Lucy S. Dawidowicz's *The War against the Jews: 1933–1945* (1975), Martin Gilbert's *The Holocaust: A History of the Jews of Europe during the Second World War* (1986), Raul Hilberg's *The Destruction of the European Jews,* revised edition (1984), and Nora Levin's *The Holocaust: The Destruction of European Jewry, 1933–1945* (1968). Hannah Arendt's indispensable books are cited above. Use these and other reliable sources to write a documented paper on one of the following:
   a. the purposes of the Nazi concentration camps and death camps—a comparison
   b. the organization of the concentration camps

c. the effect of the concentration camps on prisoners
d. the organization of the death camps
e. the system of transportation to the death camps
f. Hitler's racial theories and antisemitism

Additional Reading

Arendt, Hannah. *Eichmann in Jerusalem: A Report on the Banality of Evil.* Rev. ed.
     New York: Viking, 1964.
————. *The Human Condition.* Chicago: University of Chicago Press, 1958.
————. *On Violence.* New York: Harcourt Brace Jovanovich, 1970.
————. *The Origins of Totalitarianism.* New ed. New York: Harcourt Brace Jovanovich,
     1966.
Bullock, Alan. *Hitler—A Study in Tyranny.* Rev. ed. New York: Harper and Row, 1964.
Dicks, H. V. *Licensed Mass Murder: A Socio-Psychological Study of Some S.S. Killers.*
     New York: Basic Books, 1972.
Shirer, William L. *The Rise and Fall of the Third Reich.* New York: Simon and Schuster,
     1960.
Stein, George H. *Waffen S.S.: Hitler's Elite Guard at War, 1939–1945.* Ithaca, N.Y.:
     Cornell University Press, 1984.

Obedience and Disobedience to Authority

Stanley Milgram

Stanley Milgram taught social psychology at Yale and Harvard universities before becoming a professor of psychology at the City
University of New York in 1967. Milgram studied the effects of television violence for CBS from 1969 to 1972. He is the author of Obedience
to Authority (1974)—a book that expands upon his much-discussed article, reprinted here, which was first published in the journal Human
Relations.
     Milgram's essay describes a controversial experiment he and
his associates conducted at Yale to discover how people behave when
they are asked to perform a morally repulsive act. As Milgram's notes
to the essay show, a similar study had been performed in 1961 to study
aggression; the experiment differed from Milgram's in its measure of
the conduct of the people studied. Milgram's findings led to widespread
discussion of an issue explored by Hannah Arendt in her essay on Adolf
Eichmann. The essay illustrates the investigative techniques of an important social science as well as a common method of reporting the
findings.

The situation in which one agent commands another to hurt a third turns up 1
time and again as a significant theme in human relations.[1] It is powerfully expressed in
the story of Abraham, who is commanded by God to kill his son. It is no accident that
Kierkegaard,[2] seeking to orient his thought to the central themes of human experience,
chose Abraham's conflict as the springboard to his philosophy.

War too moves forward on the triad of an authority which commands a person 2
to destroy the enemy, and perhaps all organized hostility may be viewed as a theme and
variation on the three elements of authority, executant, and victim.[3] We describe an experimental program, recently concluded at Yale University, in which a particular expression of this conflict is studied by experimental means.

In its most general form the problem may be defined thus: if X tells Y to hurt 3
Z, under what conditions will Y carry out the command of X and under what conditions
will he refuse. In the more limited form possible in laboratory research, the question becomes: If an experimenter tells a subject to hurt another person, under what conditions
will the subject go along with this instruction, and under what conditions will he refuse
to obey. The laboratory problem is not so much a dilution of the general statement as
one concrete expression of the many particular forms this question may assume.

One aim of the research was to study behavior in a strong situation of deep con- 4
sequence to the participants, for the psychological forces operative in powerful and life-
like forms of the conflict may not be brought into play under diluted conditions.

This approach meant, first, that we had a special obligation to protect the wel- 5
fare and dignity of the persons who took part in the study; subjects were, of necessity,
placed in a difficult predicament, and steps had to be taken to ensure their wellbeing before they were discharged from the laboratory. Toward this end, a careful, post-
experimental treatment was devised and has been carried through for subjects in all
conditions.[4]

---

[1]This research was supported by two grants from the National Science Foundation: NSF G-17916 and NSF
G-24152. Exploratory studies carried out in 1960 were financed by a grant from the Higgins Funds of Yale
University. I am grateful to John T. Williams, James J. McDonough, and Emil Elges for the important part
they played in the project. Thanks are due also to Alan Elms, James Miller, Taketo Murata, and Stephen Stier
for their aid as graduate assistants. My wife, Sasha, performed many valuable services. Finally, I owe a profound debt to the many persons in New Haven and Bridgeport who served as subjects. [Milgram's notes
throughout, unless cited as the editor's.]
[2]Soren Kierkegaard: nineteenth-century Danish philosopher and theologian. [Ed.]
[3]Consider, for example, J. P. Scott's analysis of war in his monograph on aggression:
  ". . . while the actions of key individuals in a war may be explained in terms of direct stimulation
to aggression, vast numbers of other people are involved simply by being part of an organized society.
  . . . For example, at the beginning of World War I an Austrian archduke was assassinated in Sara-
jevo. A few days later soldiers from all over Europe were marching toward each other, not because they were
stimulated by the archduke's misfortune, but because they had been trained to obey orders." (Slightly rear-
ranged from Scott (1958), *Aggression,* p. 103.)
[4]It consisted of an extended discussion with the experimenter and, of equal importance, a friendly reconciliation with the victim. It is made clear that the victim did *not* receive painful electric shocks. After the completion of the experimental series, subjects were sent a detailed report of the results and full purposes of the experimental program. A formal assessment of this procedure points to its overall effectiveness. Of the subjects,
83.7 percent indicated that they were glad to have taken part in the study; 15.1 percent reported neutral
feelings; and 1.3 percent stated that they were sorry to have participated. A large number of subjects spontaneously requested that they be used in further experimentation. Four-fifths of the subjects felt that more ex-

Terminology

If Y follows the command of X we shall say that he has obeyed X; if he fails to 6 carry out the command of X, we shall say that he has disobeyed X. The terms to *obey* and to *disobey,* as used here, refer to the subject's overt action only, and carry no implication for the motive or experiential states accompanying the action.[5]

To be sure, the everyday use of the word *obedience* is not entirely free from 7 complexities. It refers to action within widely varying situations, and connotes diverse motives within those situations: a child's obedience differs from a soldier's obedience, or the love, honor, and *obey* of the marriage vow. However, a consistent behavioral relationship is indicated in most uses of the term: in the act of obeying, a person does what another person tells him to do. Y obeys X if he carries out the prescription for action which X has addressed to him; the term suggests, moreover, that some form of dominance-subordination, or hierarchical element, is part of the situation in which the transaction between X and Y occurs.

A subject who complies with the entire series of experimental commands will 8 be termed an *obedient* subject; one who at any point in the command series defies the experimenter will be called a *disobedient* or *defiant* subject. As used in this report the terms refer only to the subject's performance in the experiment, and do not necessarily imply a general personality disposition to submit to or reject authority.

---

periments of this sort should be carried out, and 74 percent indicated that they had learned something of personal importance as a result of being in the study. Furthermore, a university psychiatrist, experienced in outpatient treatment, interviewed a sample of experimental subjects with the aim of uncovering possible injurious effects resulting from participation. No such effects were in evidence. Indeed, subjects typically felt that their participation was instructive and enriching. A more detailed discussion of this question can be found in Milgram (1964).

[5]To *obey* and to *disobey* are not the only terms one could use in describing the critical action of Y. One could say that Y is cooperating with X, or displays conformity with regard to X's commands. However, *cooperation* suggests that X agrees with Y's ends, and understands the relationship between his own behavior and the attainment of those ends. (But the experimental procedure, and, in particular, the experimenter's command that the subject shock the victim even in the absence of a response from the victim, preclude such understanding.) Moreover, cooperation implies status parity for the co-acting agents, and neglects the asymmetrical, dominance-subordination element prominent in the laboratory relationship between experimenter and subject. *Conformity* has been used in other important contexts in social psychology, and most frequently refers to imitating the judgments or actions of others when no explicit requirement for imitation has been made. Furthermore, in the present study there are two sources of social pressure; pressure from the experimenter issuing the commands, and pressure from the victim to stop the punishment. It is the pitting of a common man (the victim) against an authority (the experimenter) that is the distinctive feature of the conflict. At a point in the experiment the victim demands that he be let free. The experimenter insists that the subject continue to administer shocks. Which act of the subject can be interpreted as conformity? The subject may conform to the wishes of his peer or to the wishes of the experimenter, and conformity in one direction means the absence of conformity in the other. Thus the word has no useful reference in this setting, for the dual and conflicting social pressures cancel out its meaning.

In the final analysis, the linguistic symbol representing the subject's action must take its meaning from the concrete context in which that action occurs; and there is probably no word in everyday language that covers the experimental situation exactly, without omissions or irrelevant connotations. It is partly for convenience, therefore, that the terms *obey* and *disobey* are used to describe the subject's actions. At the same time, our use of the words is highly congruent with dictionary meaning.

Subject Population

The subjects used in all experimental conditions were male adults, residing in [9] the greater New Haven and Bridgeport areas, aged 20 to 50 years, and engaged in a wide variety of occupations. Each experimental condition described in this report employed 40 fresh subjects and was carefully balanced for age and occupational types. The occupational composition for each experiment was: workers, skilled and unskilled: 40 percent; white collar, sales, business: 40 percent; professionals: 20 percent. The occupations were intersected with three age categories (subjects in 20's, 30's, and 40's, assigned to each condition in the proportions of 20, 40, and 40 percent, respectively).

The General Laboratory Procedure[6]

The focus of the study concerns the amount of electric shock a subject is will- [10] ing to administer to another person when ordered by an experimenter to give the "victim" increasingly more severe punishment. The act of administering shock is set in the context of a learning experiment, ostensibly designed to study the effect of punishment on memory. Aside from the experimenter, one naïve subject and one accomplice perform in each session. On arrival each subject is paid $4.50. After a general talk by the experimenter, telling how little scientists know about the effect of punishment on memory, subjects are informed that one member of the pair will serve as teacher and one as learner. A rigged drawing is held so that the naïve subject is always the teacher, and the accomplice becomes the learner. The learner is taken to an adjacent room and strapped into an "electric chair."

The naïve subject is told that it is his task to teach the learner a list of paired [11] associates, to test him on the list, and to administer punishment whenever the learner errs in the test. Punishment takes the form of electric shock, delivered to the learner by means of a shock generator controlled by the naïve subject. The teacher is instructed to increase the intensity of electric shock one step on the generator on each error. The learner, according to plan, provides many wrong answers, so that before long the naïve subject must give him the strongest shock on the generator. Increases in shock level are met by increasingly insistent demands from the learner that the experiment be stopped because of the growing discomfort to him. However, in clear terms the experimenter orders the teacher to continue with the procedure in disregard of the learner's protests. *Thus, the naïve subject must resolve a conflict between two mutually incompatible demands from the social field. He may continue to follow the orders of the experimenter and shock the learner with increasing severity, or he may refuse to follow the orders of the experimenter and heed the learner's pleas. The experimenter's authority operates not in a free field, but against ever-mounting countervailing pressure from the person being punished.*

---

[6]A more detailed account of the laboratory procedure can be found in Milgram (1963). A similar and independently evolved experimental procedure, employing a shock generator, victim, and learning task, was reported by Buss (1961). Buss used the technique for studying aggression, not obedience, and did not make use of the fundamental measure employed in the present study: breakoff points.

A few technical points need to be considered before the findings of the study are 12 described. For the purpose of delivering shock, a simulated shock generator is used, with 30 clearly marked voltage levels that range from 15 to 450 volts. (Each level is activated by one of 30 individual lever switches set in a horizontal line.) The naïve subject is given a sample shock of 45 volts to convince him of the authenticity of the instrument. The generator bears verbal designations that range from "Slight Shock" to "Danger: Severe Shock."

The responses of the victim are standardized on tape, and each protest is coor- 13 dinated to a particular voltage level on the shock generator. Starting with 75 volts the learner begins to grunt and moan. At 150 volts he demands to be let out of the experiment. At 180 volts he cries out that he can no longer stand the pain. At 300 volts he refuses to provide any more answers to the memory test, insisting that he is no longer a participant in the experiment and must be freed. In response to this last tactic, the experimenter instructs the naïve subject to treat the absence of an answer as equivalent to a wrong answer, and to follow the usual shock procedure. The experimenter reinforces his demand with the statement: "You have no other choice, you must go on!" (This imperative is used whenever the naïve subject tries to break off the experiment.) If the subject refuses to give the next higher level of shock, the experiment is considered at an end. A quantitative value is assigned to the subject's performance based on the maximum-intensity shock he administered before breaking off. Thus any subject's score may range from zero (for a subject unwilling to administer the first shock level) to 30 (for a subject who proceeds to the highest voltage level on the board). For any particular subject and for any particular experimental condition, the degree to which participants have followed the experimenter's orders may be specified with a numerical value, corresponding to the metric on the shock generator.

This laboratory situation gives us a framework in which to study the subject's 14 reactions to the principal conflict of the experiment. Again, this conflict is between the experimenter's demands that he continue to administer the electric shock, and the learner's demands, which become increasingly more insistent, that the experiment be stopped. The crux of the study is to vary systematically the factors believed to alter the degree of obedience to the experimental commands, to learn under what conditions submission to authority is most probable and under what conditions defiance is brought to the fore.

Pilot Studies

Pilot studies for the present research were completed in the winter of 1960; 15 they differed from the regular experiments in a few details: for one, the victim was placed behind a silvered glass, with the light balance on the glass such that the victim could be dimly perceived by the subject (Milgram, 1961).

Though essentially qualitative in treatment, these studies pointed to several 16 significant features of the experimental situation. At first no vocal feedback was used from the victim. It was thought that the verbal and voltage designations on the control panel would create sufficient pressure to curtail the subject's obedience. However, this was not the case. In the absence of protests from the learner, virtually all subjects, once commanded, went blithely to the end of the board, seemingly indifferent to the verbal designations ("Extreme Shock" and "Danger: Severe Shock"). This deprived us of an adequate basis for scaling obedient tendencies. A force had to be introduced that would strengthen the subject's resistance to the experimenter's commands, and reveal individual differences in terms of a distribution of break-off points.

This force took the form of protests from the victim. Initially, mild protests 17 were used, but proved inadequate. Subsequently, more vehement protests were inserted into the experimental procedure. To our consternation, even the strongest protests from the victim did not prevent all subjects from administering the harshest punishment ordered by the experimenter; but the protests did lower the mean maximum shock somewhat and created some spread in the subject's performance; therefore, the victim's cries were standardized on tape and incorporated into the regular experimental procedure.

The situation did more than highlight the technical difficulties of finding a 18 *workable experimental procedure: It indicated that subjects would obey authority to a greater extent than we had supposed.* It also pointed to the importance of feedback from the victim in controlling the subject's behavior.

One further aspect of the pilot study was that subjects frequently averted their 19 eyes from the person they were shocking, often turning their heads in an awkward and conspicuous manner. One subject explained: "I didn't want to see the consequences of what I had done." Observers wrote:

> . . . subjects showed a reluctance to look at the victim, whom they could see through the glass in front of them. When this fact was brought to their attention they indicated that it caused them discomfort to see the victim in agony. We note, however, that although the subject refuses to look at the victim, he continues to administer shocks.

This suggested that the salience of the victim may have, in some degree, regu- 20 lated the subject's performance. If, in obeying the experimenter, the subject found it necessary to avoid scrutiny of the victim, would the converse be true? If the victim were rendered increasingly more salient to the subject, would obedience diminish? The first set of regular experiments was designed to answer this question.

Immediacy of the Victim

This series consisted of four experimental conditions. In each condition the 21 victim was brought "psychologically" closer to the subject giving him shocks.

In the first condition (Remote Feedback) the victim was placed in another 22 room and could not be heard or seen by the subject, except that, at 300 volts, he pounded on the wall in protest. After 315 volts he no longer answered or was heard from.

The second condition (Voice Feedback) was identical to the first except that 23 voice protests were introduced. As in the first condition the victim was placed in an adjacent room, but his complaints could be heard clearly through a door left slightly ajar and through the walls of the laboratory.[7]

The third experimental condition (Proximity) was similar to the second, except 24 that the victim was now placed in the same room as the subject, and 1½ feet from him. Thus he was visible as well as audible, and voice cues were provided.

The fourth, and final, condition of this series (Touch-Proximity) was identical 25 to the third, with this exception: The victim received a shock only when his hand rested on a shockplate. At the 150-volt level the victim again demanded to be let free and, in this condition, refused to place his hand on the shockplate. The experimenter ordered the naïve subject to force the victim's hand onto the plate. Thus obedience in this condition required that the subject have physical contact with the victim in order to give him punishment beyond the 150-volt level.

Forty adult subjects were studied in each condition. The data revealed that obe- 26 dience was significantly reduced as the victim was rendered more immediate to the subject. The mean maximum shock for the conditions is shown in Figure 1.

Expressed in terms of the proportion of obedient to defiant subjects, the 27 findings are that 34 percent of the subjects defied the experimenter in the Remote condition, 37.5 percent in Voice Feedback, 60 percent in Proximity, and 70 percent in Touch-Proximity.

How are we to account for this effect? A first conjecture might be that as the 28 victim was brought closer the subject became more aware of the intensity of his suffering and regulated his behavior accordingly. This makes sense, but our evidence does not

---

[7]It is difficult to convey on the printed page the full tenor of the victim's responses, for we have no adequate notation for vocal intensity, timing, and general qualities of delivery. Yet these features are crucial to producing the effect of an increasingly severe reaction to mounting voltage levels. (They can be communicated fully only by sending interested parties the recorded tapes.) In general terms, however, the victim indicates no discomfort until the 75-volt shock is administered, at which time there is a light grunt in response to the punishment. Similar reactions follow the 90- and 105-volt shocks, and at 120 volts the victim shouts to the experimenter that the shocks are becoming painful. Painful groans are heard on administration of the 135-volt shock, and at 150 volts the victim cries out, 'Experimenter, get me out of here! I won't be in the experiment any more! I refuse to go on!' Cries of this type continue with generally rising intensity, so that at 180 volts the victim cries out, 'I can't stand the pain,' and by 270 volts his response to the shock is definitely an agonized scream. Throughout, he insists that he be let out of the experiment. At 300 volts the victim shouts in desperation that he will no longer provide answers to the memory test; and at 315 volts, after a violent scream, he reaffirms with vehemence that he is no longer a participant. From this point on, he provides no answers, but shrieks in agony whenever a shock is administered; this continues through 450 volts. Of course, many subjects will have broken off before this point.

A revised and stronger set of protests was used in all experiments outside the Proximity series. Naturally, new baseline measures were established for all comparisons using the new set of protests.

There is overwhelming evidence that the great majority of subjects, both obedient and defiant, accepted the victims' reactions as genuine. The evidence takes the form of: (a) tension created in the subjects (see discussion of tension); (b) scores on "estimated-pain" scales filled out by the subjects immediately after the experiment; (c) subjects' accounts of their feelings in post-experimental interviews; and (d) quantifiable responses to questionnaires distributed to subjects several months after their participation in the experiments. This matter will be treated fully in a forthcoming monograph.

(The procedure in all experimental conditions was to have the naïve subject announce the voltage level before administering each shock, so that—independently of the victim's responses—he was continually reminded of delivering punishment of ever-increasing severity.)

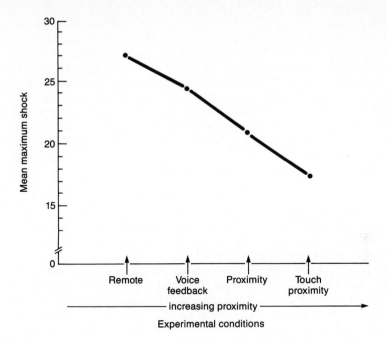

FIGURE 1. Mean maxima in proximity series.

support the interpretation. There are no consistent differences in the attributed level of pain across the four conditions (i.e., the amount of pain experienced by the victim as estimated by the subject and expressed on a 14-point scale). But it is easy to speculate about alternative mechanisms:

Empathic cues. In the Remote and to a lesser extent the Voice Feedback conditions, the victim's suffering possesses an abstract, remote quality for the subject. He is aware, but only in a conceptual sense, that his actions cause pain to another person; the fact is apprehended, but not felt. The phenomenon is common enough. The bombardier can reasonably suppose that his weapons will inflict suffering and death, yet this knowledge is divested of affect and does not move him to a felt, emotional response to the suffering resulting from his actions. Similar observations have been made in wartime. It is possible that the visual cues associated with the victim's suffering trigger empathic responses in the subject and provide him with a more complete grasp of the victim's experience. Or it is possible that the empathic responses are themselves unpleasant, possessing drive properties which cause the subject to terminate the arousal situation. Diminishing obedience, then, would be explained by the enrichment of empathic cues in the successive experimental conditions.

Denial and narrowing of the cognitive field. The Remote condition allows a narrowing of the cognitive field so that the victim is put out of mind. The subject no longer considers the act of depressing a lever relevant to moral judg-

30

ment, for it is no longer associated with the victim's suffering. When the victim is close it is more difficult to exclude him phenomenologically. He necessarily intrudes on the subject's awareness since he is continuously visible. In the Remote condition his existence and reactions are made known only after the shock has been administered. The auditory feedback is sporadic and discontinuous. In the Proximity conditions his inclusion in the immediate visual field renders him a continuously salient element for the subject. The mechanism of denial can no longer be brought into play. One subject in the Remote condition said: "It's funny how you really begin to forget that there's a guy out there, even though you can hear him. For a long time I just concentrated on pressing the switches and reading the words."

Reciprocal fields. If in the Proximity condition the subject is in an improved   31
position to observe the victim, the reverse is also true. The actions of the subject now come under proximal scrutiny by the victim. Possibly, it is easier to harm a person when he is unable to observe our actions than when he can see what we are doing. His surveillance of the action directed against him may give rise to shame, or guilt, which may then serve to curtail the action. Many expressions of language refer to the discomfort or inhibitions that arise in face-to-face confrontation. It is often said that it is easier to criticize a man "behind his back" than to "attack him to his face." If we are in the process of lying to a person it is reputedly difficult to "stare him in the eye." We "turn away from others in shame" or in "embarrassment" and this action serves to reduce our discomfort. The manifest function of allowing the victim of a firing squad to be blindfolded is to make the occasion less stressful for him, but it may also serve a latent function of reducing the stress of the executioner. In short, in the Proximity conditions, the subject may sense that he has become more salient in the victim's field of awareness. Possibly he becomes more self-conscious, embarrassed, and inhibited in his punishment of the victim.

Phenomenal unity of act. In the Remote condition it is more difficult for the   32
subject to gain a sense of *relatedness* between his own actions and the consequences of these actions for the victim. There is a physical and spatial separation of the act and its consequences. The subject depresses a lever in one room, and protests and cries are heard from another. The two events are in correlation, yet they lack a compelling phenomenological unity. The structure of a meaningful act—*I am hurting a man*—breaks down because of the spatial arrangements, in a manner somewhat analogous to the disappearance of phi phenomena[8] when the blinking lights are spaced too far apart. The unity is more fully achieved in the Proximity condition as the victim is brought closer to the action that causes him pain. It is rendered complete in Touch-Proximity.

Incipient group formation. Placing the victim in another room not only takes   33
him further from the subject, but the subject and the experimenter are drawn relatively closer. There is incipient group formation between the experimenter

---

[8]phi phenomena: the sense that fixed objects shown steadily are moving [Ed.]

and the subject, from which the victim is excluded. The wall between the victim and the others deprives him of an intimacy which the experimenter and subject feel. In the Remote condition, the victim is truly an outsider, who stands alone, physically and psychologically.

When the victim is placed close to the subject, it becomes easier to form an alliance with him against the experimenter. Subjects no longer have to face the experimenter alone. They have an ally who is close at hand and eager to collaborate in a revolt against the experimenter. Thus, the changing set of spatial relations leads to a potentially shifting set of alliances over the several experimental conditions.

Acquired behavior dispositions. It is commonly observed that laboratory mice will rarely fight with their litter mates. Scott (1958) explains this in terms of passive inhibition. He writes: "By doing nothing under . . . circumstances [the animal] learns to do nothing, and this may be spoken of as passive inhibition . . . this principle has great importance in teaching an individual to be peaceful, for it means that he can learn not to fight simply by not fighting." Similarly, we may learn not to harm others simply by not harming them in everyday life. Yet this learning occurs in a context of proximal relations with others, and may not be generalized to that situation in which the person is physically removed from us. Or possibly, in the past, aggressive actions against others who were physically close resulted in retaliatory punishment which extinguished the original form of response. In contrast, aggression against others at a distance may have only sporadically led to retaliation. Thus the organism learns that it is safer to be aggressive toward others at a distance, and precarious to be so when the parties are within arm's reach. Through a pattern of rewards and punishments, he acquires a disposition to avoid aggression at close quarters, a disposition which does not extend to harming others at a distance. And this may account for experimental findings in the remote and proximal experiments.

Proximity as a variable in psychological research has received far less attention than it deserves. If men were sessile it would be easy to understand this neglect. But we move about; our spatial relations shift from one situation to the next, and the fact that we are near or remote may have a powerful effect on the psychological processes that mediate our behavior toward others. In the present situation, as the victim is brought closer to the subject ordered to give him shocks, increasing numbers of subjects break off the experiment, refusing to obey. The concrete, visible, and proximal presence of the victim acts in an important way to counteract the experimenter's power to generate disobedience.[9]

---

[9]Admittedly, the terms *proximity, immediacy, closeness,* and *salience-of-the-victim* are used in a loose sense, and the experiments themselves represent a very coarse treatment of the variable. Further experiments are needed to refine the notion and tease out such diverse factors as spatial distance, visibility, audibility, barrier interposition, etc.

The Proximity and Touch-Proximity experiments were the only conditions where we were unable to use taped feedback from the victim. Instead, the victim was trained to respond in these conditions as he had in Experiment 2 (which employed taped feedback). Some improvement is possible here, for it should be technically feasible to do a proximity series using taped feedback.

Closeness of Authority

If the spatial relationship of the subject and victim is relevant to the degree of 37 obedience, would not the relationship of subject to experimenter also play a part?

There are reasons to feel that, on arrival, the subject is oriented primarily to 38 the experimenter rather than to the victim. He has come to the laboratory to fit into the structure that the experimenter—not the victim—would provide. He has come less to understand his behavior than to *reveal* that behavior to a competent scientist, and he is willing to display himself as the scientist's purposes require. Most subjects seem quite concerned about the appearance they are making before the experimenter, and one could argue that this preoccupation in a relatively new and strange setting makes the subject somewhat insensitive to the triadic nature of the social situation. In other words, the subject is so concerned about the show he is putting on for the experimenter that influences from other parts of the social field do not receive as much weight as they ordinarily would. This overdetermined orientation to the experimenter would account for the relative insensitivity of the subject to the victim, and would also lead us to believe that alterations in the relationship between subject and experimenter would have important consequences for obedience.

In a series of experiments we varied the physical closeness and degree of sur- 39 veillance of the experimenter. In one condition the experimenter sat just a few feet away from the subject. In a second condition, after giving initial instructions, the experimenter left the laboratory and gave his orders by telephone. In still a third condition the experimenter was never seen, providing instructions by means of a tape recording activated when the subjects entered the laboratory.

Obedience dropped sharply as the experimenter was physically removed from 40 the laboratory. The number of obedient subjects in the first condition (Experimenter Present) was almost three times as great as in the second, where the experimenter gave his orders by telephone. Twenty-six subjects were fully obedient in the first condition, and only nine in the second (Chi square obedient *vs.* defiant in the two conditions, df = 14.7; $p < 0.001$). Subjects seemed able to take a far stronger stand against the experimenter when they did not have to encounter him face to face, and the experimenter's power over the subject was severely curtailed.[10]

Moreover, when the experimenter was absent, subjects displayed an interesting 41 form of behavior that had not occurred under his surveillance. Though continuing with the experiment, several subjects administered lower shocks than were required and never informed the experimenter of their deviation from the correct procedure. (Unknown to the subjects, shock levels were automatically recorded by an Esterline-Angus event recorder wired directly into the shock generator; the instrument provided us with an objective record of the subjects' performance.) Indeed, in telephone conversations some subjects specifically assured the experimenter that they were raising the shock level according to instruction, whereas in fact they were repeatedly using the lowest shock on the board. This form of behavior is particularly interesting: although these subjects acted in a way that clearly undermined the avowed purposes of the experiment,

---

[10]The third condition also led to significantly lower obedience than this first situation in which the experimenter was present, but it contains technical difficulties that require extensive discussion.

they found it easier to handle the conflict in this manner than to precipitate an open break with authority.

Other conditions were completed in which the experimenter was absent during 42 the first segment of the experiment, but reappeared at the point that the subject definitely refused to give higher shocks when commanded by telephone. Although he had exhausted his power via telephone, the experimenter could frequently force further obedience when he reappeared in the laboratory.

Experiments in this series show that the *physical presence* of an authority is an 43 important force contributing to the subject's obedience or defiance. Taken together with the first experimental series on the proximity of the victim, it would appear that something akin to fields of force, diminishing in effectiveness with increasing psychological distance from their source, have a controlling effect on the subject's performance. As the victim is brought closer, the subject finds it harder to administer shocks to him. When the victim's position is held constant relative to the subject, and the authority is made more remote, the subject finds it easier to break off the experiment. This effect is substantial in both cases, but manipulation of the experimenter's position yielded the more powerful results. Obedience to destructive commands is highly dependent on the proximal relations between authority and subject.

Tensions

The description of final scores does not fully convey the character of the sub- 44 jects' performance, and it would be useful to interrupt our reporting of quantitative relationships to remark on the subjects' general reaction to the situation.

One might suppose that a subject would simply break off or continue as his 45 conscience and temperament dictated. Yet this is very far from what happened. There were powerful reactions of tension and emotional strain in a substantial proportion of the participants. Persons were observed to sweat, tremble, stutter, bite their lips, and groan as they found themselves increasingly implicated in the experimental conflict. Some sense of the subjects' mood can be found in a transcript of their remarks at break-off point. Here are the remarks of two defiant subjects:

> Is he banging? . . . Is he hurt out there? Well, I don't want to be responsible for anything that happens to him. No, I can't go on with it. I don't know whether he's all right or not. I mean he may have a heart condition or something; I wouldn't feel right doing it. He's banging for help. He's evidently in trouble or he wouldn't bang . . . I don't see any sense to this—to knocking him out or something. I just can't see it.
> [*Subject refuses to administer shocks*]   [*Subject 0108*]

> The man is banging. He wants to get out . . . I'm sorry. If the man wants to get out I'd just as soon stop . . . I don't want to administer any more [extremely excited] . . . I will gladly refund the check, but I will not harm this man . . . I'm sorry, I will not give him any more if he obviously wants to get out. There is no money in the world that will make me hurt another individual.   [*Subject 010X*]

And here is a transcript from an obedient subject. He began the experiment 46 calmly, but became increasingly tense as the experiment proceeded. After administering the 150-volt shock, he began to address the experimenter in agitated tones:

> *150 volts delivered.* You want me to keep going?
> *165 volts delivered.* That guy is hollering in there. There's a lot of them here. He's liable to have heart condition. You want me to go?
> *180 volts delivered.* He can't stand it! I'm not going to kill that man in there! You hear him hollering? He's hollering. He can't stand it. What if something happens to him? . . . I'm not going to get that man sick in there. He's hollering in there. You know what I mean? I mean I refuse to take responsibility. He's getting hurt in there. He's in there hollering. Too many left here. Geez, if he gets them wrong. There's too many of them left. I mean who is going to take responsibility if anything happens to that gentleman?
> *[The experimenter accepts responsibility.]* All right.
> *195 volts delivered.* You see he's hollering. Hear that. Gee, I don't know.
> *[The experimenter says: 'The experiment requires that you go on.']*—I know it does, sir, but I mean—hugh—he don't know what he's in for. He's up to 195 volts.
> *210 volts delivered.*
> *225 volts delivered.*
> *240 volts delivered.* Aw, no. You mean I've got to keep going up with the scale? No sir. I'm not going to kill that man! I'm not going to give him 450 volts! *[The experimenter says: 'The experiment requires that you go on.']*—I know it does, but that man is hollering there, sir . . .

Despite his numerous, agitated objections, which were constant accompaniments to his actions, the subject unfailingly obeyed the experimenter, proceeding to the highest shock level on the generator. He displayed a curious dissociation between word and action. Although at the verbal level he had resolved not to go on, his actions were fully in accord with the experimenter's commands. This subject did not want to shock the victim, and he found it an extremely disagreeable task, but he was unable to invent a response that would free him from *E's* authority. Many subjects cannot find the specific verbal formula that would enable them to reject the role assigned to them by the experimenter. Perhaps our culture does not provide adequate models for disobedience.

One puzzling sign of tension was the regular occurrence of nervous laughing 47 fits. In the first four conditions 71 of the 160 subjects showed definite signs of nervous laughter and smiling. The laughter seemed entirely out of place, even bizarre. Full-blown, uncontrollable seizures were observed for 15 of these subjects. On one occasion we observed a seizure so violently convulsive that it was necessary to call a halt to the experiment. In the post-experimental interviews subjects took pains to point out that they were not sadistic types and that the laughter did not mean they enjoyed shocking the victim.

In the interview following the experiment subjects were asked to indicate on a 48 14-point scale just how nervous or tense they felt at the point of maximum tension (Figure 2). The scale ranged from "not at all tense and nervous" to "extremely tense and nervous." Self-reports of this sort are of limited precision and at best provide only a

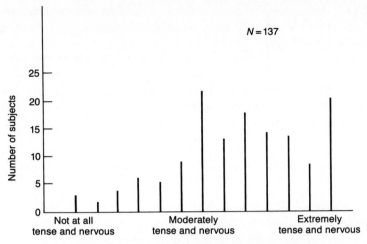

FIGURE 2. Level of tension and nervousness: the self-reports on "tension and nervousness" for 137 subjects in the Proximity experiments. Subjects were given a scale with 14 values ranging from "not at all tense and nervous" to "extremely tense and nervous." They were instructed: "Thinking back to that point in the experiment when you felt the most tense and nervous, indicate just how you felt by placing an X at the appropriate point on the scale." The results are shown in terms of midpoint values.

rough indication of the subject's emotional response. Still, taking the reports for what they are worth, it can be seen that the distribution of responses spans the entire range of the scale, with the majority of subjects concentrated at the center and upper extreme. A further breakdown showed that obedient subjects reported themselves as having been slightly more tense and nervous than the defiant subjects at the point of maximum tension.

　　　　How is the occurrence of tension to be interpreted? First, it points to the presence of conflict. If a tendency to comply with authority were the only psychological force operating in the situation, all subjects would have continued to the end and there would have been no tension. Tension, it is assumed, results from the simultaneous presence of two or more incompatible response tendencies (Miller, 1944). If sympathetic concern for the victim were the exclusive force, all subjects would have calmly defied the experimenter. Instead, there were both obedient and defiant outcomes, frequently accompanied by extreme tension. A conflict develops between the deeply ingrained disposition not to harm others and the equally compelling tendency to obey others who are in authority. The subject is quickly drawn into a dilemma of a deeply dynamic character, and the presence of high tension points to the considerable strength of each of the antagonistic vectors.

　　　　Moreover, tension defines the strength of the aversive state from which the subject is unable to escape through disobedience. When a person is uncomfortable, tense, or stressed, he tries to take some action that will allow him to terminate this unpleasant state. Thus tension may serve as a drive that leads to escape behavior. But in the present situation, even where tension is extreme, many subjects are unable to perform the response that will bring about relief. Therefore there must be a competing drive, tendency, or inhibition that precludes activation of the disobedient response. The strength of this inhibiting factor must be of greater magnitude than the stress experienced, or else the terminating act would occur. Every evidence of extreme tension is at the same time an indication of the strength of the forces that keep the subject in the situation.

Finally, tension may be taken as evidence of the reality of the situations for the subjects. Normal subjects do not tremble and sweat unless they are implicated in a deep and genuinely felt predicament. 51

Background Authority

In psychophysics, animal learning, and other branches of psychology, the fact that measures are obtained at one institution rather than another is irrelevant to the interpretation of the findings, so long as the technical facilities for measurement are adequate and the operations are carried out with competence. 52

But it cannot be assumed that this holds true for the present study. The effectiveness of the experimenter's commands may depend in an important way on the larger institutional context in which they are issued. The experiments described thus far were conducted at Yale University, an organization which most subjects regarded with respect and sometimes awe. In post-experimental interviews several participants remarked that the locale and sponsorship of the study gave them confidence in the integrity, competence, and benign purposes of the personnel; many indicated that they would not have shocked the learner if the experiments had been done elsewhere. 53

This issue of background authority seemed to us important for an interpretation of the results that had been obtained thus far; moreover it is highly relevant to any comprehensive theory of human obedience. Consider, for example, how closely our compliance with the imperatives of others is tied to particular institutions and locales in our day-to-day activities. On request, we expose our throats to a man with a razor blade in the barber shop, but would not do so in a shoe store; in the latter setting we willingly follow the clerk's request to stand in our stockinged feet, but resist the command in a bank. In the laboratory of a great university, subjects may comply with a set of commands that would be resisted if given elsewhere. *One must always question the relationship of obedience to a person's sense of the context in which he is operating.* 54

To explore the problem we moved our apparatus to an office building in industrial Bridgeport and replicated experimental conditions, without any visible tie to the university. 55

Bridgeport subjects were invited to the experiment through a mail circular similar to the one used in the Yale study, with appropriate changes in letterhead, etc. As in the earlier study, subjects were paid $4.50 for coming to the laboratory. The same age and occupational distributions used at Yale and the identical personnel were employed. 56

The purpose in relocating in Bridgeport was to assure a complete dissociation from Yale, and in this regard we were fully successful. On the surface, the study appeared to be conducted by Research Associates of Bridgeport, an organization of unknown character (the title had been concocted exclusively for use in this study). 57

The experiments were conducted in a three-room office suite in a somewhat 58 run-down commercial building located in the downtown shopping area. The laboratory was sparsely furnished, though clean, and marginally respectable in appearance. When subjects inquired about professional affiliations, they were informed only that we were a private firm conducting research for industry.

Some subjects displayed skepticism concerning the motives of the Bridgeport 59 experimenter. One gentleman gave us a written account of the thoughts he experienced at the control board:

> . . . Should I quit this damn test? Maybe he passed out? What dopes we were not to check up on this deal. How do we know that these guys are legit? No furniture, bare walls, no telephone. We could of called the Police up or the Better Business Bureau. I learned a lesson tonight. How do I know that Mr. Williams [the experimenter] is telling the truth . . . I wish I knew how many volts a person could take before lapsing into unconsciousness . . .
> [*Subject 2414*]

Another subject stated:

> I questioned on my arrival my own judgment [about coming]. I had doubts as to the legitimacy of the operation and the consequences of participation. I felt it was a heartless way to conduct memory or learning processes on human beings and certainly dangerous without the presence of a medical doctor.
> [*Subject 2440V*]

There was no noticeable reduction in tension for the Bridgeport subjects. And 60 the subjects' estimation of the amount of pain felt by the victim was slightly, though not significantly, higher than in the Yale study.

A failure to obtain complete obedience in Bridgeport would indicate that the 61 extreme compliance found in New Haven subjects was tied closely to the background authority of Yale University; if a large proportion of the subjects remained fully obedient, very different conclusions would be called for.

As it turned out, the level of obedience in Bridgeport, although somewhat re- 62 duced, was not significantly lower than that obtained at Yale. A large proportion of the Bridgeport subjects were fully obedient to the experimenter's commands (48 percent of the Bridgeport subjects delivered the maximum shock versus 65 percent in the corresponding condition at Yale).

How are these findings to be interpreted? It is possible that if commands of a 63 potentially harmful or destructive sort are to be perceived as legitimate they must occur within some sort of institutional structure. But it is clear from the study that it need not be a particularly reputable or distinguished institution. The Bridgeport experiments were conducted by an unimpressive firm lacking any credentials; the laboratory was set up in a respectable office building with title listed in the building directory. Beyond that, there was no evidence of benevolence or competence. It is possible that the *category* of institution, judged according to its professed function, rather than its qualitative position within that category, wins our compliance. Persons deposit money in elegant, but also in seedy-looking banks, without giving much thought to the differences in security they offer. Similarly, our subjects may consider one laboratory to be as competent as another, so long as it is a scientific laboratory.

It would be valuable to study the subjects' performance in other contexts which 64
go even further than the Bridgeport study in denying institutional support to the experimenter. It is possible that, beyond a certain point, obedience disappears completely. But
that point had not been reached in the Bridgeport office: almost half the subjects obeyed
the experimenter fully.

Further Experiments

We may mention briefly some additional experiments undertaken in the Yale 65
series. A considerable amount of obedience and defiance in everyday life occurs in connection with groups. And we had reason to feel in light of the many group studies already done in psychology that group forces would have a profound effect on reactions
to authority. A series of experiments was run to examine these effects. In all cases only
one naïve subject was studied per hour, but he performed in the midst of actors who,
unknown to him, were employed by the experimenter. In one experiment (Groups for
Disobedience) two actors broke off in the middle of the experiment. When this happened
90 percent of the subjects followed suit and defied the experimenter. In another condition the actors followed the orders obediently; this strengthened the experimenter's
power only slightly. In still a third experiment the job of pushing the switch to shock
the learner was given to one of the actors, while the naïve subject performed a subsidiary act. We wanted to see how the teacher would respond if he were involved in the situation but did not actually give the shocks. In this situation only three subjects out of
forty broke off. In a final group experiment the subjects themselves determined the
shock level they were going to use. Two actors suggested higher and higher shock levels; some subjects insisted, despite group pressure, that the shock level be kept low; others followed along with the group.

Further experiments were completed using women as subjects, as well as a set 66
dealing with the effects of dual, unsanctioned, and conflicting authority. A final experiment concerned the personal relationship between victim and subject. These will have
to be described elsewhere, lest the present report be extended to monographic length.

It goes without saying that future research can proceed in many different direc- 67
tions. What kinds of response from the victim are most effective in causing disobedience
in the subject? Perhaps passive resistance is more effective than vehement protest. What
conditions of entry into an authority system lead to greater or lesser obedience? What
is the effect of anonymity and masking on the subject's behavior? What conditions lead
to the subject's perception of responsibility for his own actions? Each of these could be
a major research topic in itself, and can readily be incorporated into the general experimental procedure described here.

Levels of Obedience and Defiance

One general finding that merits attention is the high level of obedience mani- 68
fested in the experimental situation. Subjects often expressed deep disapproval of shocking a man in the face of his objections, and others denounced it as senseless and stupid.

Yet many subjects complied even while they protested. The proportion of obedient subjects greatly exceeded the expectations of the experimenter and his colleagues. At the outset, we had conjectured that subjects would not, in general, go above the level of "Strong Shock." In practice, many subjects were willing to administer the most extreme shocks available when commanded by the experimenter. For some subjects the experiment provided an occasion for aggressive release. And for others it demonstrated the extent to which obedient dispositions are deeply ingrained and engaged, irrespective of their consequences for others. Yet this is not the whole story. Somehow, the subject becomes implicated in a situation from which he cannot disengage himself.

The departure of the experimental results from intelligent expectation, to some 69 extent, has been formalized. The procedure was to describe the experimental situation in concrete detail to a group of competent persons, and to ask them to predict the performance of 100 hypothetical subjects. For purposes of indicating the distribution of break-off points, judges were provided with a diagram of the shock generator and recorded their predictions before being informed of the actual results. Judges typically underestimated the amount of obedience demonstrated by subjects.

In Figure 3, we compare the predictions of forty psychiatrists at a leading medi- 70 cal school with the actual performance of subjects in the experiment. The psychiatrists predicted that most subjects would not go beyond the tenth shock level (150 volts; at this point the victim makes his first explicit demand to be freed). They further predicted that by the twentieth shock level (300 volts; the victim refuses to answer) 3.73 percent of the subjects would still be obedient; and that only a little over one-tenth of one percent of the subjects would administer the highest shock on the board. But, as the graph

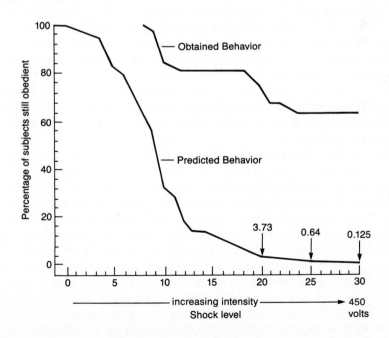

FIGURE 3. Predicted and obtained behavior in voice feedback.

indicates, the obtained behavior was very different. Sixty-two percent of the subjects obeyed the experimenter's commands fully. Between expectation and occurrence there is a whopping discrepancy.

Why did the psychiatrists underestimate the level of obedience? Possibly, be- 71 cause their predictions were based on an inadequate conception of the determinants of human action, a conception that focuses on motives in *vacuo*. This orientation may be entirely adequate for the repair of bruised impulses as revealed on the psychiatrist's couch, but as soon as our interest turns to action in larger settings, attention must be paid to the situations in which motives are expressed. A situation exerts an important press on the individual. It exercises constraints and may provide push. In certain circumstances it is not so much the kind of person a man is, as the kind of situation in which he is placed, that determines his actions.

Many people, not knowing much about the experiment, claim that subjects 72 who go to the end of the board are sadistic. Nothing could be more foolish than an overall characterization of these persons. It is like saying that a person thrown into a swift-flowing stream is necessarily a fast swimmer, or that he has great stamina because he moves so rapidly relative to the bank. The context of action must always be considered. The individual, upon entering the laboratory, becomes integrated into a situation that carries its own momentum. The subject's problem then is how to become disengaged from a situation which is moving in an altogether ugly direction.

The fact that disengagement is so difficult testifies to the potency of the forces 73 that keep the subject at the control board. Are these forces to be conceptualized as individual motives and expressed in the language of personality dynamics, or are they to be seen as the effects of social structure and pressures arising from the situational field?

A full understanding of the subject's action will, I feel, require that both per- 74 spectives be adopted. The person brings to the laboratory enduring dispositions toward authority and aggression, and at the same time he becomes enmeshed in a social structure that is no less an objective fact of the case. From the standpoint of personality theory one may ask: What mechanisms of personality enable a person to transfer responsibility to authority? What are the motives underlying obedient and disobedient performance? Does orientation to authority lead to a short-circuiting of the shame-guilt system? What cognitive and emotional defenses are brought into play in the case of obedient and defiant subjects?

The present experiments are not, however, directed toward an exploration of 75 the motives engaged when the subject obeys the experimenter's commands. Instead, they examine the situational variables responsible for the elicitation of obedience. Elsewhere, we have attempted to spell out some of the structural properties of the experimental situation that account for high obedience, and this analysis need not be repeated here (Milgram, 1963). The experimental variations themselves represent our attempt to probe that structure, by systematically changing it and noting the consequences for behavior. It is clear that some situations produce greater compliance with the experimenter's commands than others. However, this does not necessarily imply an increase or decrease in the strength of any single definable motive. Situations producing the greatest obedience could do so by triggering the most powerful, yet perhaps the most idiosyncratic, of motives in each subject confronted by the setting. Or they may simply recruit a greater number and variety of motives in their service. But whatever the motives involved—and it is far from certain that they can ever be known—action may be studied as a direct function of the situation in which it occurs. This has been the approach of the present study, where we sought to plot behavioral regularities against manipulated properties of the social field. Ultimately, social psychology would like to have a compelling *theory of situations* which will, first, present a language in terms of which situations can be defined; proceed to a typology of situations; and then point to the manner in which definable properties of situations are transformed into psychological forces in the individual.[11]

Postscript

Almost a thousand adults were individually studied in the obedience research, 76 and there were many specific conclusions regarding the variables that control obedience and disobedience to authority. Some of these have been discussed briefly in the preceding sections, and more detailed reports will be released subsequently.

There are now some other generalizations I should like to make, which do not 77 derive in any strictly logical fashion from the experiments as carried out, but which, I feel, ought to be made. They are formulations of an intuitive sort that have been forced on me by observation of many subjects responding to the pressures of authority. The assertions represent a painful alteration in my own thinking; and since they were acquired only under the repeated impact of direct observation, I have no illusion that they will be generally accepted by persons who have not had the same experience.

With numbing regularity good people were seen to knuckle under the demands 78 of authority and perform actions that were callous and severe. Men who are in everyday life responsible and decent were seduced by the trappings of authority, by the control of their perceptions, and by the uncritical acceptance of the experimenter's definition of the situation, into performing harsh acts.

What is the limit of such obedience? At many points we attempted to establish 79 a boundary. Cries from the victim were inserted; not good enough. The victim claimed heart trouble; subjects still shocked him on command. The victim pleaded that he be let free, and his answers no longer registered on the signal box; subjects continued to shock him. At the outset we had not conceived that such drastic procedures would be needed to generate disobedience, and each step was added only as the ineffectiveness of the earlier techniques became clear. The final effort to establish a limit was the Touch-Proximity condition. But the very first subject in this condition subdued the victim on command, and proceeded to the highest shock level. A quarter of the subjects in this condition performed similarly.

The results, as seen and felt in the laboratory, are to this author disturbing. 80 They raise the possibility that human nature or, more specifically, the kind of character produced in American democratic society cannot be counted on to insulate its citizens from brutality and inhumane treatment at the direction of malevolent authority. A substantial proportion of people do what they are told to do, irrespective of the content of the act and without limitations of conscience, so long as they perceive that the command comes from a legitimate authority. If in this study an anonymous experimenter

---

[11]My thanks to Professor Howard Leventhal of Yale for strengthening the writing in this paragraph.

could successfully command adults to subdue a fifty-year-old man and force on him painful electric shocks against his protests, one can only wonder what government, with its vastly greater authority and prestige, can command of its subjects. There is, of course, the extremely important question of whether malevolent political institutions could or would arise in American society. The present research contributes nothing to this issue.

In an article titled "The Danger of Obedience," Harold J. Laski wrote: 81

> . . . civilization means, above all, an unwillingness to inflict unnecessary pain. Within the ambit of that definition, those of us who heedlessly accept the commands of authority cannot yet claim to be civilized men.
>
> . . . Our business, if we desire to live a life, not utterly devoid of meaning and significance, is to accept nothing which contradicts our basic experience merely because it comes to us from tradition or convention or authority. It may well be that we shall be wrong; but our self-expression is thwarted at the root unless the certainties we are asked to accept coincide with the certainties we experience. That is why the condition of freedom in any state is always a widespread and consistent skepticism of the canons upon which power insists.

References

Buss, Arnold   1961. *The Psychology of Aggression.* New York and London: John Wiley.

Kierkegaard, S.   1843. *Fear and Trembling.* English edition, Princeton: Princeton University Press, 1941.

Laski, Harold J.   1929. "The dangers of obedience." *Harper's Monthly Magazine,* 15 June 1–10.

Miligram, S.   1961. "Dynamics of obedience: experiments in social psychology." Mimeographed report, *National Science Foundation,* January 25.

_____   1963. "Behavioral study of obedience." *J. Abnorm. Soc. Psychol.* 67, 371–378.

_____   1964. "Issues in the study of obedience: a reply to Baumrind." *Amer. Psychol.* 1. 848–852.

Miller, N.E.   1944. "Experimental studies of conflict." In J. McV. Hunt (ed.), *Personality and the Behavior Disorders.* New York: Ronald Press.

Scott, J. P.   1958. *Aggression.* Chicago: University of Chicago Press.

Questions

1. What precautions did the researchers set in designing the experiment, and why were these necessary?
2. What "complexities" of the word *obedience* does Milgram discuss in paragraph 7? How does the definition stated in paragraph 8 take into account or overcome these complexities? Why does Milgram discuss other terms for *obey* and *disobey* in the note to paragraph 6?
3. How did the pilot studies discussed in paragraphs 15–20 shape the experiment?
4. How did Milgram seek to verify that the subjects accepted the responses of the victims as genuine? Why might the subjects have pretended to do so?

5. What are "empathic cues" (paragraph 29)? What is the difference between a sympathetic and an empathic response? Why are empathic cues not a full explanation for the behavior of the subjects?
6. What are "reciprocal fields" (paragraph 31), and what alternative explanation do they provide for the evidence? What alternative explanations for the evidence do the "mechanics" discussed in paragraphs 29–35 provide?
7. Does Milgram present closeness or proximity of authority as an alternative explanation or as a complementary explanation?
8. How does Milgram interpret the tension of the subject? What is the "aversive state from which the subject is unable to escape through disobedience" (paragraph 50)? What is the "inhibiting factor" that prevents the subject from disobeying?
9. Why did the general laboratory procedure described in paragraphs 10–14 test "mutually incompatible demands from the social field" rather than social and personal demands such as conscience?
10. How does Milgram show that the responses of a subject cannot be measured in a vacuum?
11. What additional research does Milgram propose, and why is this research needed?

Suggestions for Writing

1. Discuss the influence of "background authority" on your own behavior in the classroom, in the library, or in a similar environment. Use your discussion to test Milgram's conclusions in paragraph 54.
2. Discuss the extent to which authority shaped one of your decisions concerning school or work. Give sufficient details of the episode and draw a conclusion from it.

Additional Reading

Bettelheim, Bruno. *The Informed Heart: Autonomy in a Mass Age*. New York: The Free Press, 1960.
Fromm, Erich. *Escape from Freedom*. New York: Farrar and Rinehart, 1941.
Milgram, Stanley. *Obedience to Authority: An Experimental View*. New York: Harper and Row, 1974.
Sennett, Richard. *Authority*. New York: Knopf, 1980.

The Smell of Death and Flowers

Nadine Gordimer

Born in 1923, Nadine Gordimer has lived most of her life in South Africa—the setting of most of her fiction. Her numerous stories have been collected in The Soft Voice of the Serpent *(1953),* Six Feet of the Country *(1956),* Friday's Footprint *(1960), and other volumes. Her many novels include* A Guest of Honor *(1971), which was awarded the* James Black Tait Memorial Prize in Great Britain, The Conservationist *(1974), which was awarded the Booker Prize, and* Burger's Daughter *(1979). A major theme of Gordimer's fiction is the effect on black and white people of apartheid in South Africa, the government policy of segregating nonwhites that was established in 1947. The localities to which Gordimer refers are all-black towns, most of them close to Johannesburg, Port Elizabeth, Capetown, and other South African cities. The homelands of the people are all-black territorial entities, recognized by the South African government as independent political states in which black people hold citizenship—they do not hold citizenship in South Africa.*

Written in the early 1950s and first published in The New Yorker *magazine, "The Smell of Death and Flowers" describes the effect of apartheid on a white South African young woman.*

The party was an unusual one for Johannesburg. A young man called Derek Ross—out of sight behind the "bar" at the moment—had white friends and black friends, Indian friends and friends of mixed blood, and sometimes he liked to invite them to his flat all at once. Most of them belonged to the minority that, through bohemianism, godliness, politics, or a particularly sharp sense of human dignity, did not care about the difference in one another's skins. But there were always one or two— white ones—who came, like tourists, to see the sight, and to show that they did not care, and one or two black or brown or Indian ones who found themselves paralyzed by the very ease with which the white guests accepted them.

One of the several groups that huddled to talk, like people sheltering beneath a cliff, on divans and hard borrowed chairs in the shadow of the dancers, was dominated by a man in a gray suit, Malcolm Barker. "Why not pay the fine and have done with it, then?" he was saying.

The two people to whom he was talking were silent a moment, so that the haphazard noisiness of the room and the organized wail of the gramophone suddenly burst in irrelevantly upon the conversation. The pretty brunette said, in her quick, officious voice, "Well, it wouldn't be the same for Jessica Malherbe. It's not quite the same thing, you see . . ." Her stiff, mascaraed lashes flickered an appeal—for confirmation, and for sympathy because of the impossibility of explaining—at a man whose gingerish whiskers and flattened, low-set ears made him look like an angry tomcat.

"It's a matter of principle," he said to Malcolm Barker.

"Oh, quite, I see," Malcolm conceded. "For someone like this Malherbe woman, paying the fine's one thing; sitting in prison for three weeks is another."

The brunette rapidly crossed and then uncrossed her legs. "It's not even quite that," she said. "Not the unpleasantness of being in prison. Not a sort of martyrdom on Jessica's part. Just the *principle.*" At that moment a black hand came out from the crush of dancers bumping round and pulled the woman to her feet; she went off, and as she danced she talked with staccato animation to her African partner, who kept his lids half lowered over his eyes while she followed his gentle shuffle. The ginger-whiskered man got up without a word and went swiftly through the dancers to the "bar," a kitchen table covered with beer and gin bottles, at the other end of the small room.

"*Satyagraha*," said Malcolm Barker, like the infidel pronouncing with satisfaction the holy word that the believers hesitate to defile.

A very large and plain African woman sitting next to him smiled at him hugely and eagerly out of shyness, not having the slightest idea what he had said.

He smiled back at her for a moment, as if to hypnotize the onrush of some frightening animal. Then, suddenly, he leaned over and asked in a special, loud, slow voice, "What do you do? Are you a teacher?"

Before the woman could answer, Malcolm Barker's young sister-in-law, a girl who had been sitting silent, pink and cold as a porcelain figurine, on the window sill behind his back, leaned her hand for balance on his chair and said urgently, near his ear, "Has Jessica Malherbe really been in prison?"

"Yes, in Port Elizabeth. And in Durban, they tell me. And now she's one of the civil-disobedience people—defiance campaign leaders who're going to walk into some native location forbidden to Europeans. Next Tuesday. So she'll land herself in prison again. For Christ's sake, Joyce, what are you drinking that stuff for? I've told you that punch is the cheapest muck possible—"

But the girl was not listening to him any longer. Balanced delicately on her rather full, long neck, her fragile-looking face with the eyes and the fine, short line of nose of a Marie Laurenceçin painting was looking across the room with the intensity peculiar to the blank-faced. Hers was an essentially two-dimensional prettiness: flat, dazzlingly pastel-colored, as if the mask of make-up on the unlined skin *were* the face; if one had turned her around, one would scarcely have been surprised to discover canvas. All her life she had suffered from this impression she made of not being quite real.

"She *looks* so nice," she said now, her eyes still fixed on some point near the door. "I mean she uses good perfume, and everything. You can't imagine it."

Her brother-in-law made as if to take the tumbler of alcohol out of the girl's hand, impatiently, the way one might take a pair of scissors from a child, but, without looking at him or at her hands, she changed the glass from one hand to the other, out of his reach. "At least the brandy's in a bottle with a recognizable label," he said peevishly. "I don't know why you don't stick to that."

"I wonder if she had to eat the same food as the others," said the girl.

"You'll feel like death tomorrow morning," he said, "and Madeline'll blame me. You are an obstinate little devil."

A tall, untidy young man, whose blond head outtopped all others like a tousled palm tree, approached with a slow, drunken smile and, with exaggerated courtesy, asked Joyce to dance. She unhurriedly drank down what was left in her glass, put the glass carefully on the window sill, and went off with him, her narrow waist upright and correct in his long arm. Her brother-in-law followed her with his eyes, irritatedly, for a moment, then closed them suddenly, whether in boredom or in weariness one could not tell.

The young man was saying to the girl as they danced, "You haven't left the side of your husband—or whatever he is—all night. What's the idea?"

"My brother-in-law," she said. "My sister couldn't come because the child's got a temperature."

He squeezed her waist; it remained quite firm, like the crisp stem of a flower. "Do I know your sister?" he asked. Every now and then his drunkenness came over him in a delightful swoon, so that his eyelids dropped heavily and he pretended that he was narrowing them shrewdly.

"Maybe. Madeline McCoy—Madeline Barker now. She's the painter. She's the one who started that arts-and-crafts school for Africans."

"Oh, yes. Yes, I know," he said. Suddenly, he swung her away from him with one hand, executed a few loose-limbed steps around her, lost her in a collision with another couple, caught her to him again, and, with an affectionate squeeze, brought her up short against the barrier of people who were packed tight as a Rugby scrum around the kitchen table, where the drinks were. He pushed her through the crowd to the table.

"What d'you want, Roy, my boy?" said a little, very blackfaced African, gleaming up at them.

"Barberton'll do for me." The young man pressed a hand on the African's head, grinning.

"Ah, that stuff's no good. Sugar-water. Let me give you a dash of Pineapple. Just like mother makes."

For a moment, the girl wondered if any of the bottles really did contain Pineapple or Barberton, two infamous brews invented by African natives living in the segregated slums that are called locations. Pineapple, she knew, was made out of the fermented fruit and was supposed to be extraordinarily intoxicating; she had once read a newspaper report of a shebeen raid in which the Barberton still contained a lopped-off human foot—whether for additional flavor or the spice of witchcraft, it was not known.

But she was reassured at once. "Don't worry," said a good-looking blonde, made up to look heavily sun-tanned, who was standing at the bar. "No shebeen ever produced anything much more poisonous than this gin-punch thing of Derek's." The host was attending to the needs of his guests at the bar, and she waved at him a glass containing the mixture that the girl had been drinking over at the window.

"Not gin. It's arak—lovely," said Derek. "What'll you have, Joyce?"

"Joyce," said the gangling young man with whom she had been dancing. "Joyce. That's a nice name for her. Now tell her mine."

"Roy Wilson. But you seem to know each other quite adequately without names," said Derek. "This is Joyce McCoy, Roy—and, Joyce, these are Matt Shabalala, Brenda Shotley, Mahinder Singh, Martin Mathlongo."

They smiled at the girl: the shiny-faced African, on a level with her shoulder; the blond woman with the caked powder cracking on her cheeks; the handsome, scholarly-looking Indian with the high, bald dome; the ugly light-colored man, just light enough for freckles to show thickly on his fleshy face.

She said to her host, "I'll have the same again, Derek. Your punch." And even before she had sipped the stuff, she felt a warmth expand and soften inside her, and she said the names over silently to herself—Matt Sha-ba-lala, Martin Math-longo, Mahinder Singh. Out of the corner of her eye, as she stood there, she could just see Jessica Malherbe, a short, plump white woman in an elegant black frock, her hair glossy, like a bird's wing, as she turned her head under the light while she talked.

Then it happened, just when the girl was most ready for it, just when the time had come. The little African named Matt said, "This is Miss Joyce McCoy—Eddie Ntwala," and stood looking on with a smile while her hand went into the slim hand of a tall, light-skinned African with the tired, appraising, cynical eyes of a man who drinks too much in order to deaden the pain of his intelligence. She could tell from the way little Shabalala presented the man that he must be someone important and admired, a leader of some sort, whose every idiosyncrasy—the broken remains of handsome, smoke-darkened teeth when he smiled, the wrinkled tie hanging askew—bespoke to those who knew him his distinction in a thousand different situations. She smiled as if to say, "Of course, Eddie Ntwala himself, I knew it," and their hands parted and dropped.

The man did not seem to be looking at her—did not seem to be looking at the crowd or at Shabalala, either. There was a slight smile around his mouth, a public smile that would do for anybody. "Dance?" he said, tapping her lightly on the shoulder. They turned to the floor together.

Eddie Ntwala danced well and unthinkingly, if without much variation. Joyce's right hand was in his left, his right hand on the concavity of her back, just as if—well, just as if he were anyone else. And it was the first time—the first time in all her twenty-two years. Her head came just to the point of his lapel, and she could smell the faint odor of cigarette smoke in the cloth. When he turned his head and her head was in the path of his breath, there was the familiar smell of wine or brandy breathed down upon her by men at dances. He looked, of course, apart from his eyes—eyes that she had seen in other faces and wondered if she would ever be old enough to understand—exactly like an errand "boy" or house "boy." He had the same close-cut wool on his head, the same smooth brown skin, the same rather nice high cheekbones, the same broadnostriled small nose. Only, he had his arm around her and her hand in his and he was leading her through the conventional arabesques of polite dancing. She would not let herself formulate the words in her brain: I am dancing with a black man. But she allowed herself to question, with the careful detachment of scientific inquiry, quietly inside herself: "Do I feel anything? What do I feel?" The man began to hum a snatch of the tune to which they were dancing, the way a person will do when he suddenly hears music out of some forgotten phase of his youth; while the hum reverberated through his chest, she slid her eyes almost painfully to the right, not moving her head, to see his very well-shaped hand—an almost feminine hand compared to the hands of most white men—dark brown against her own white one, the dark thumb and the pale one crossed, the dark fingers and the pale ones folded together. "Is this exactly how I always dance?" she asked herself closely. "Do I always hold my back exactly like this, do I relax just this much, hold myself in reserve to just this degree?"

She found she was dancing as she always danced.

I feel nothing, she thought. *I feel nothing.*

And all at once a relief, a mild elation, took possession of her, so that she could begin to talk to the man with whom she was dancing. In any case, she was not a girl who had much small talk; she knew that at least half the young men who, attracted by her exceptional prettiness, flocked to ask her to dance at parties never asked her again because they could not stand her vast minutes of silence. But now she said in her flat, small voice the few things she could say—remarks about the music and the pleasantness of the rainy night outside. He smiled at her with bored tolerance, plainly not listening to what she said. Then he said, as if to compensate for his inattention, "You from England?"

She said, "Yes. But I'm not English. I'm South African, but I've spent the last five years in England. I've only been back in South Africa since December. I used to know Derek when I was a little girl," she added, feeling that she was obliged to explain her presence in what she suddenly felt was a group conscious of some distinction or privilege.

"England," he said, smiling down past her rather than at her. "Never been so happy anywhere."

"London?" she said.

He nodded. "Oh, I agree," she said. "I feel the same about it."

"No, you don't, McCoy," he said very slowly, smiling at her now. "No, you don't."

She was silenced at what instantly seemed her temerity.

He said, as they danced around again, "The way you speak. Really English. Whites in S.A. can't speak that way."

For a moment, one of the old, blank, impassively pretty-faced silences threatened to settle upon her, but the second glass of arak punch broke through it, and, almost animated, she answered lightly, "Oh, I find I'm like a parrot. I pick up the accent of the people among whom I live in a matter of hours."

He threw back his head and laughed, showing the gaps in his teeth. "How will you speak tomorrow, McCoy?" he said, holding her back from him and shaking with laughter, his eyes swimming. "Oh, how will you speak tomorrow, I wonder?"

She said, immensely daring, though it came out in her usual small, unassertive feminine voice, a voice gently toned for the utterance of banal pleasantries, "Like you."

"Let's have a drink," he said, as if he had known her a long time—as if she were someone like Jessica Malherbe. And he took her back to the bar, leading her by the hand; she walked with her hand loosely swinging in his, just as she had done with young men at country-club dances. "I promised to have one with Rajati," he was saying, "Where.has he got to?"

"Is that the one I met?" said the girl. "The one with the high, bald head?"

"An Indian?" he said. "No, you mean Mahinder. This one's his cousin, Jessica Malherbe's husband."

"She's married to an Indian?" The girl stopped dead in the middle of the dancers. "Is she?" The idea went through her like a thrill. She felt startled as if by a sudden piece of good news about someone who was important to her. Jessica Malherbe—the name, the idea—seemed to have been circling about her life since before she left England. Even there, she had read about her in the papers: the daughter of a humble Afrikaner farmer, who had disowned her in the name of a stern Calvinist God for her antinationalism and her radical views; a girl from a back-veld farm—such a farm as Joyce herself could remember seeing from a car window as a child—who had worked in a factory and educated herself and been sent by her trade union to study labor problems all over the world; a girl who negotiated with ministers of state; who, Joyce had learned that evening, had gone to prison for her principles. Jessica Malherbe, who was almost the first person the girl had met when she came in to the party this evening, and who turned out to look like any well-groomed English woman you might see in a London restaurant, wearing a pearl necklace and smelling of expensive perfume. An Indian! It was the final gesture. Magnificent. A world toppled with it—Jessica Malherbe's father's world. An Indian!

"Old Rajati," Ntwala was saying. But they could not find him. The girl thought of the handsome, scholarly-looking Indian with the domed head, and suddenly she remembered that once, in Durban, she had talked across the counter of a shop with an Indian boy. She had been down in the Indian quarter with her sister, and they had entered a shop to buy a piece of silk. She had been the spokeswoman, and she had murmured across the counter to the boy and he had said, in a voice as low and gentle as her own, no, he was sorry, that length of silk was for a sari, and could not be cut. The boy had very beautiful, unseeing eyes, and it was as if they spoke to each other in a dream. The shop was small and deep-set. It smelled strongly of incense, the smell of the village church in which her grandfather had lain in state before his funeral, the scent of her mother's garden on a summer night—the smell of death and flowers, compounded, as the incident itself came to be, of ugliness and beauty, of attraction and repulsion. For just after she and her sister had left the little shop, they had found themselves being followed by an unpleasant man, whose presence first made them uneasily hold tightly to their handbags but who later, when they entered a busy shop in an attempt to get rid of him, crowded up against them and made an obscene advance. He had had a vaguely Eurasian face, they believed, but they could not have said whether or not he was an Indian; in their disgust, he had scarcely seemed human to them at all.

She tried now, in the swarming noise of Derek's room, to hear again in her head the voice of the boy saying the words she remembered so exactly: "No, I am sorry, that length of silk is for a sari, it cannot be cut." But the tingle of the alcohol that she had been feeling in her hands for quite a long time became a kind of sizzling singing in her ears, like the sound of bubbles rising in aerated water, and all that she could convey to herself was the curious finality of the phrase: *can-not-be-cut, can-not-be-cut.*

She danced the next dance with Derek. "You look sweet tonight, old thing," he said, putting wet lips to her ear. "Sweet."

She said, "Derek, which is Rajati?"

He let go her waist. "Over there," he said, but in an instant he clutched her again and was whirling her around and she saw only Mahinder Singh and Martin Mathlongo, the big, freckled colored man, and the back of some man's dark neck with a businessman's thick roll of fat above the collar.

"Which?" she said, but this time he gestured toward a group in which there were white men only, and so she gave up.

The dance was cut short with a sudden wailing screech as someone lifted the needle of the gramophone in the middle of the record, and it appeared that a man was about to speak. It turned out that it was to be a song and not a speech, for Martin Mathlongo, little Shabalala, two colored women, and a huge African woman with cork-soled green shoes grouped themselves with their arms hanging about one another's necks. When the room had quieted down, they sang. They sang with extraordinary beauty, the men's voices deep and tender, the women's high and passionate. They sang in some Bantu language, and when the song was done, the girl asked Eddie Ntwala, next to whom she found herself standing, what they had been singing about. He said as simply as a peasant, as if he had never danced with her, exchanging sophisticated banter, "It's about a young man who passes and sees a girl working in her father's field."

Roy Wilson giggled and gave him a comradely punch on the arm. "Eddie's never seen a field in his life. Born and bred in Apex Location."

Then Martin Mathlongo, with his spotted bow tie under his big, loose-mouthed, strong face, suddenly stood forward and began to sing "Ol' Man River." There was something insulting, defiant, yet shamefully supplicating in the way he sang the melodramatic, servile words, the way he kneeled and put out his big hands with their upturned pinkish palms. The dark faces in the room watched him, grinning as if at the antics of a monkey. The white faces looked drunk and withdrawn.

Joyce McCoy saw that, for the first time since she had been introduced to her that evening, she was near Jessica Malherbe. The girl was feeling a strong distress at the sight of the colored man singing the blackface song, and when she saw Jessica Malherbe, she put—with a look, as it were—all this burden at the woman's feet. She put it all upon her, as if *she* could make it right, for on the woman's broad, neatly made-up face there was neither the sullen embarrassment of the other white faces nor the leering self-laceration of the black.

The girl felt the way she usually felt when she was about to cry, but this time it was the prelude to something different. She made her way with difficulty, for her legs were the drunkest part of her, murmuring politely, "Excuse me," as she had been taught to do for twenty-two years, past all the people who stood, in their liquor daze, stolid as cows in a stream. She went up to the trade-union leader, the veteran of political imprisonment, the glossy-haired woman who used good perfume. "Miss Malherbe," she said, and her blank, exquisite face might have been requesting an invitation to a garden party. "Please, Miss Malherbe, I want to go with you next week. I want to march into the location."

Next day, when Joyce was sober, she still wanted to go. As her brother-in-law had predicted, she felt sick from Derek's punch, and every time she inclined her head, a great, heavy ball seemed to roll slowly from one side to the other inside her skull. The presence of this ball, which sometimes felt as if it were her brain itself, shrunken and hardened, rattling like a dried nut in its shell, made it difficult to concentrate, yet the thought that she would march into the location the following week was perfectly clear. As a matter of fact, it was almost obsessively clear.

She went to see Miss Malherbe at the headquarters of the Civil Disobedience Campaign, in order to say again what she had said the night before. Miss Malherbe did again just what *she* had done the night before—listened politely, was interested and sympathetic, thanked the girl, and then gently explained that the movement could not allow anyone but bonafide members to take part in such actions. "Then I'll become a member now," said Joyce. She wore today a linen dress as pale as her own skin, and on the square of bare, matching flesh at her neck hung a little necklace of small pearls— the sort of necklace that is given to a girl child and added to, pearl by pearl, a new one on every birthday. Well, said Miss Malherbe, she could join the movement, by all means—and would not that be enough? Her support would be much appreciated. But no, Joyce wanted to *do* something; she wanted to march with the others into the location. And before she left the office, she was formally enrolled.

When she had been a member for two days, she went to the headquarters to see Jessica Malherbe again. This time, there were other people present; they smiled at her when she came in, as if they already had heard about her. Miss Malherbe explained to her the gravity of what she wanted to do. Did she realize that she might have to go to prison? Did she understand that it was the policy of the passive resisters to serve their prison sentences rather than to pay fines? Even if she did not mind for herself, what about her parents, her relatives? The girl said that she was over twenty-one; her only parent, her mother, was in England; she was responsible to no one.

She told her sister Madeline and her brother-in-law nothing. When Tuesday morning came, it was damp and cool. Joyce dressed with the consciousness of the performance of the ordinary that marks extraordinary days. Her stomach felt hollow; her hands were cold. She rode into town with her brother-in-law, and all the way his car popped the fallen jacaranda flowers, which were as thick on the street beneath the tires as they were on the trees. After lunch, she took a tram to Fordsburg, a quarter where Indians and people of mixed blood, debarred from living anywhere better, lived alongside poor whites, and where, it had been decided, the defiers were to forgather. She had never been to this part of Johannesburg before, and she had the address of the house to which she was to go written in her tartan-silk-covered notebook in her minute, backward-sloping hand. She carried her white angora jacket over her arm and she had put on sensible flat sandals. *I don't know why I keep thinking of this as if it were a lengthy expedition, requiring some sort of special equipment,* she thought; *actually it'll be all over in half an hour. Jessica Malherbe said we'd pay bail and be back in town by four-thirty.*

The girl sat in the tram and did not look at the other passengers, and they did not look at her, although the contrast between her and them was startling. They were thin, yellow-limbed children with enormous sooty eyes; bleary-eyed, shuffling men, whom degeneracy had enfeebled into an appearance of indeterminate old age; heavy women with swollen legs, who were carrying newspaper parcels; young, almost white factory girls whose dull, kinky hair was pinned up into a decent simulation of fashionable style, and on whose proud, pert faces rouge and lipstick had drawn a white girl's face. Sitting among them, Joyce looked—quite apart from the social difference apparent in her clothes—so different, so other, that there were only two possible things to think about her, and which one thought depended upon one's attitude: either she was a kind of fairy—ideal, exquisite, an Ariel among Calibans—or she was something too tender, something unfinished, and beautiful only in the way the skin of the unborn lamb, taken from the belly of the mother, is beautiful, because it is a thing as yet unready for this world.

She got off at the stop she had been told to and went slowly up the street, watching the numbers. It was difficult to find out how far she would have to walk, or even, for the first few minutes, whether she was walking in the right direction, because the numbers on the doorways were half obliterated, or ill-painted, or sometimes missing entirely. As in most poor quarters, houses and stores were mixed, and, in fact, some houses were being used as business premises, and some stores had rooms above, in which, obviously, the storekeepers and their families lived. The street had a flower name, but there were no trees and no gardens. Most of the shops had Indian firm names amateurishly written on homemade wooden signboards or curlicued and flourished in signwriter's yellow and red across the lintel: Moonsammy Dadoo, Hardware, Ladies Smart Outfitting & General; K. P. Patel & Sons, Fruit Merchants; Vallabhir's Bargain Store. A shoemaker had enclosed the veranda of his small house as a workshop, and had hung outside a huge black tin shoe, of a style worn in the twenties.

The gutters smelled of rotting fruit. Thin *café-au-lait* children trailed smaller brothers and sisters; on the veranda of one of the little semidetached houses a lean light-colored man in shirt sleeves was shouting, in Afrikaans, at a fat woman who sat on the steps. An Indian woman in a sari and high-heeled European shoes was knocking at the door of the other half of the house. Farther on, a very small house, almost eclipsed by the tentacles of voracious-looking creepers, bore a polished brass plate with the name and consulting hours of a well-known Indian doctor.

The street was quiet enough; it had the dead, listless air of all places where people are making some sort of living in a small way. And so Joyce started when a sudden shriek of drunken laughter came from behind a rusty corrugated-iron wall that seemed to enclose a yard. Outside the wall, someone was sitting on a patch of the tough, gritty grass that sometimes scrabbles a hold for itself on worn city pavements; as the girl passed, she saw that the person was one of the white women tramps whom she occasionally saw in the city crossing a street with the peculiar glassy purposefulness of the outcast.

She felt neither pity nor distaste at the sight. It was as if, dating from this day, her involvement in action against social injustice had purged her of sentimentality; she did not have to avert her gaze. She looked quite calmly at the woman's bare legs, which were tanned, with dirt and exposure, to the color of leather. She felt only, in a detached way, a prim, angry sympathy for the young pale-brown girl who stood nursing a baby at the gate of the house just beyond, because she had to live next door to what was almost certainly a shebeen.

Then, ahead of her in the next block, she saw three cars parked outside a house and knew that that must be the place. She walked a little faster, but quite evenly, and when she reached it—No. 260, as she had been told—she found that it was a small house of purplish brick, with four steps leading from the pavement to the narrow veranda. A sword fern in a paraffin tin, painted green, stood on each side of the front door, which had been left ajar, as the front door sometimes is in a house where there is a party. She went up the steps firmly, over the dusty imprints of other feet, and, leaning into the doorway a little, knocked on the fancy glass panel of the upper part of the door. She found herself looking straight down a passage that had a worn flowered linoleum on the floor. The head of a small Indian girl—low forehead and great eyes—appeared in a curtained archway halfway down the passage and disappeared again instantly.

Joyce McCoy knocked again. She could hear voices, and, above all the others, the tone of protest in a woman's voice.

A bald white man with thick glasses crossed the passage with quick, nervous steps and did not, she thought, see her. But he might have, because, prompted perhaps by his entry into the room from which the voices came, the pretty brunette woman with the efficient manner, whom the girl remembered from the party, appeared suddenly with her hand outstretched, and said enthusiastically, "Come *in*, my dear. Come inside. Such a racket in there! You could have been knocking all day."

The girl saw that the woman wore flimsy sandals and no stockings, and that her toenails were painted like the toes of the languid girls in *Vogue*. The girl did not know why details such as these intrigued her so much, or seemed so remarkable. She smiled in greeting and followed the woman into the house.

Now she was really there; she heard her own footsteps taking her down the passage of a house in Fordsburg. There was a faintly spicy smell about the passage; on the wall she caught a glimpse of what appeared to be a photograph of an Indian girl in Euro-pean bridal dress, the picture framed with fretted gold paper, like a cake frill. And then they were in a room where everyone smiled at her quickly but took no notice of her. Jessica Malherbe was there, in a blue linen suit, smoking a cigarette and saying some-thing to the tall, tousle-headed Roy Wilson, who was writing down what she said. The bald man was talking low and earnestly to a slim woman who wore a man's wrist watch and had the hands of a man. The tiny African, Shabalala, wearing a pair of spectacles with thin tortoise-shell rims, was ticking a penciled list. Three or four others, black and white, sat talking. The room was as brisk with chatter as a birds' cage.

Joyce lowered herself gingerly onto a dining-room chair whose legs were loose and swayed a little. And as she tried to conceal herself and sink into the composition of the room, she noticed a group sitting a little apart, near the windows, in the shadow of the heavy curtains, and, from the arresting sight of them, saw the whole room as it was beneath the overlay of people. The group was made up of an old Indian woman, and a slim Indian boy and another Indian child, who were obviously her grandchildren. The woman sat with her feet apart, so that her lap, under the voluminous swathings of her sari, was broad, and in one nostril a ruby twinkled. Her hands were little and beringed—a fat woman's hands. Her forehead was low beneath the coarse black hair and the line of tinsel along the sari, and she looked out through the company of white men and women, Indian men in business suits, Africans in clerkly neatness, as if she were deaf or could not see. Yet when Joyce saw her eyes move, as cold and as lacking in inter-est as the eyes of a tortoise, and her foot stir, asserting an inert force of life, like the twitch in a muscle of some supine creature on a mudbank, the girl knew it was not deaf-ness or blindness that kept the woman oblivious of the company but simply the knowl-edge that this house, this room, was her place. She was here before the visitors came; she would not move for them; she would be here when they had gone. And the children clung with their grandmother, knowing that she was the kind who could never be ban-ished to the kitchen or some other backwater.

From the assertion of this silent group the girl became aware of the whole room (*their* room), of its furnishings: the hideous "suite" upholstered in imitation vel-vet with a stamped design of triangles and sickles; the yellow varnished table with the pink silk mat and the brass vase of paper roses; the easy chairs with circular apertures in the arms where colored glass ash trays were balanced; the crudely colored photo-graphs; the barbola vase; the green ruched-silk cushions; the standard lamp with more platforms for more colored glass ash trays; the gilded plaster dog that stood at the door. An Indian went over and said something to the old woman with the proprietary, apolo-getic, irritated air of a son who wishes his mother would keep out of the way; as he turned his head, the girl saw something familiar in the angle and recognized him as the man the back of whose neck she had seen when she was trying to identify Jessica Malherbe's husband at the party. Now he came over to her, a squat, pleasant man, with a great deal of that shiny black Indian hair making his head look too big for his body. He said, "My congratulations. My wife, Jessica, tells me you have insisted on identifying yourself with today's defiance. Well, how do you feel about it?"

She smiled at him with great difficulty; she really did not know why it was so difficult. She said, "I'm sorry. We didn't meet that night. Just your cousin—I believe it is?—Mr. Singh." He was such a remarkably commonplace-looking Indian, Jessica Malherbe's husband, but Jessica Malherbe's husband after all—the man with the roll of fat at the back of his neck.

She said, "You don't resemble Mr. Singh in the least," feeling that it was herself so offended by the obvious thought behind the comparison, and not this fat, amiable middle-aged man, who needed only to be in his shirt sleeves to look like any well-to-do Indian merchant, or in a grubby white coat, and unshaven, to look like a fruit-and-vegetable hawker. He sat down beside her (she could see the head of the old woman just beyond his ear), and as he began to talk to her in his Cambridge-modulated voice, she began to notice something that she had not noticed before. It was curious, because surely it must have been there all the time; then again it might not have been—it might have been released by some movement of the group of the grandmother, the slender boy, and the child, perhaps from their clothes—but quite suddenly she began to be aware of the odor of incense. Sweet and dry and smoky, like the odor of burning leaves—she began to smell it. Then she thought, It must be in the furniture, the curtains; the old woman burns it and it permeates the house and all the gewgaws from Birmingham, and Denver, Colorado, and American-occupied Japan. Then it did not remind her of burning leaves any longer. It was incense, strong and sweet. The smell of death and flowers. She remembered it with such immediacy that it came back literally, absolutely, the way a memory of words or vision never can.

"Are you all right, Miss McCoy?" said the kindly Indian, interrupting himself because he saw that she was not listening and that her pretty, pale, impassive face was so white and withdrawn that she looked as if she might faint.

She stood up with a start that was like an inarticulate apology and went quickly from the room. She ran down the passage and opened a door and closed it behind her, but the odor was there, too, stronger than ever, in somebody's bedroom, where a big double bed had an orange silk cover. She leaned with her back against the door, breathing it in and trembling with fear and with the terrible desire to be safe: to be safe from one of the kindly women who would come, any moment now, to see what was wrong; to be safe from the gathering up of her own nerve to face the journey in the car to the location, and the faces of her companions, who were not afraid, and the walk up the location street.

The very conventions of the life which, she felt, had insulated her in softness against the sharp, joyful brush of real life in action came up to save her now. If she was afraid, she was also polite. She had been polite so long that the colorless formula of good manners, which had stifled so much spontaneity in her, could also serve to stifle fear.

It would be so *terribly rude* simply to run away out of the house, and go home, now.

That was the thought that saved her—the code of a well-brought-up child at a party—and it came to her again and again, slowing down her thudding heart, uncurling her clenched hands. *It would be terribly rude to run away now.* She knew with distress, somewhere at the back of her mind, that this was the wrong reason for staying, but it worked. Her manners had been with her longer and were stronger than her fear. Slowly the room ceased to sing so loudly about her, the bedspread stopped dancing up and down before her eyes, and she went slowly over to the mirror in the door of the wardrobe and straightened the belt of her dress, not meeting her own eyes. Then she opened the door and went down the passage and back again into the room where the others were gathered, and sat down in the chair she had left. It was only then that she noticed that the others were standing—had risen, ready to go.

"What about your jacket, my dear. Would you like to leave it?" the pretty brunette said, noticing her.

Jessica Malherbe was on her way to the door. She smiled at Joyce and said, "I'd leave it, if I were you."

"Yes, I think so, thank you." She heard her own voice as if it were someone else's.

Outside, there was the mild confusion of deciding who should go with whom and in which car. The girl found herself in the back of the car in which Jessica Malherbe sat beside the driver. The slim, mannish woman got in; little Shabalala got in but was summoned to another car by an urgently waving hand. He got out again, and then came back and jumped in just as they were off. He was the only one who seemed excited. He sat forward, with his hands on his knees. Smiling widely at the girl, he said, "Now we really are taking you for a ride, Miss McCoy."

The cars drove through Fordsburg and skirted the city. Then they went out one of the main roads that connect the goldmining towns of the Witwatersrand with each other and with Johannesburg. They passed mine dumps, pale gray and yellow; clusters of neat, ugly houses, provided for white mineworkers; patches of veld, where the rain of the night before glittered thinly in low places; a brickfield; a foundry; a little poultry farm. And then they turned in to a muddy road, along which they followed a native bus that swayed under its load of passengers, exhaust pipe sputtering black smoke, canvas flaps over the windows wildly agitated. The bus thundered ahead through the location gates, but the three cars stopped outside. Jessica Malherbe got out first, and stood, pushing back the cuticles of the nails of her left hand as she talked in a businesslike fashion to Roy Wilson. "Of course, don't give the statement to the papers unless they ask for it. It would be more interesting to see *their* version first, and come along with our own afterward. But they *may* ask—"

"There's a press car," Shabalala said, hurrying up. "There."

"Looks like Brand, from the *Post*."

"Can't be Dick Brand; he's transferred to Bloemfontein," said the tall, mannish woman.

"Come here, Miss McCoy, you're the baby," said Shabalala, straightening his tie and twitching his shoulders, in case there was going to be a photograph. Obediently, the girl moved to the front.

But the press photographer waved his flash bulb in protest. "No, I want you walking."

"Well, you better get us before we enter the gates or you'll find yourself arrested, too," said Jessica Malherbe, unconcerned. "Look at that," she added to the mannish woman, lifting her foot to show the heel of her white shoe, muddy already.

Lagersdorp Location, which they were entering and which Joyce McCoy had never seen before, was much like all such places. A high barbed-wire fence—more a symbol than a means of confinement, since, except for the part near the gates, it had comfortable gaps in many places—enclosed almost a square mile of dreary little dwellings, to which the African population of the nearby town came home to sleep at night. There were mean houses and squalid tin shelters and, near the gates where the administrative offices were, one or two decent cottages, which had been built by the white housing authorities "experimentally" and never duplicated; they were occupied by the favorite African clerks of the white location superintendent. There were very few shops, since every license granted to a native shop in a location takes business away from the white stores in the town, and there were a great many churches, some built of mud and tin, some neo-Gothic and built of brick, representing a great many sects.

They began to walk, the seven men and women, toward the location gates. Jessica Malherbe and Roy Wilson were a little ahead, and the girl found herself between Shabalala and the bald white man with thick glasses. The flash bulb made its brief sensation, and the two or three picannins who were playing with tin hoops on the roadside looked up, astonished. A fat native woman selling oranges and roast mealies shouted speculatively to a passer-by in ragged trousers.

At the gateway, a fat black policeman sat on a soapbox and gossiped. He raised his hand to his cap as they passed. In Joyce McCoy, the numbness that had followed her nervous crisis began to be replaced by a calm embarrassment; as a child she had often wondered, seeing a circle of Salvation Army people playing a hymn out of tune on a street corner, how it would feel to stand there with them. Now she felt she knew. Little Shabalala ran a finger around the inside of his collar, and the girl thought, with a start of warmth, that he was feeling as she was; she did not know that he was thinking what he had promised himself he would not think about during this walk—that very likely the walk would cost him his job. People did not want to employ Africans who "made trouble." His wife, who was immensely proud of his education and his cleverness, had said nothing when she learned that he was going—had only gone, with studied consciousness, about her cooking. But, after all, Shabalala, like the girl—though neither he nor she could know it—was also saved by convention. In his case, it was a bold convention—that he was an amusing little man. He said to her as they began to walk up the road, inside the gateway, "Feel the bump?"

"I beg your pardon?" she said, polite and conspiratorial.

A group of ragged children, their eyes alight with the tenacious beggarliness associated with the East rather than with Africa, were jumping and running around the white members of the party, which they thought was some committee come to judge a competition for the cleanest house, or a baby show. "Penny, *missus,* penny, penny, *baas!*" they whined. Shabalala growled something at them playfully in their own language before he answered, with his delightful grin, wide as a slice of melon. "The bump over the color bar."

Apart from the children, who dropped away desultorily, like flying fish behind a boat, no one took much notice of the defiers. The African women, carrying on their heads food they had bought in town, or bundles of white people's washing, scarcely looked at them. African men on bicycles rode past, preoccupied. But when the party came up parallel with the administration offices—built of red brick, and, along with the experimental cottages at the gate and the clinic next door, the only buildings of European standard in the location—a middle-aged white man in a suit worn shiny on the seat and the elbows (his slightly stooping body seemed to carry the shape of his office chair and desk) came out and stopped Jessica Malherbe. Obediently, the whole group stopped; there was an air of quiet obstinacy about them. The man, who was the location superintendent himself, evidently knew Jessica Malherbe, and was awkward with the necessity of making this an official and not a personal encounter. "You know that I must tell you it is prohibited for Europeans to enter Lagersdorp Location," he said. The girl noticed that he carried his glasses in his left hand, dangling by one earpiece, as if he had been waiting for the arrival of the party and had jumped up from his desk nervously at last.

Jessica Malherbe smiled, and there was in her smile something of the easy, informal amusement with which Afrikaners discount pomposity. "Mr. Dougal, good afternoon. Yes, of course, we know you have to give us official warning. How far do you think we'll get?"

The man's face relaxed. He shrugged and said, "They're waiting for you."

And suddenly the girl, Joyce McCoy, felt this—the sense of something lying in wait for them. The neat, stereotyped faces of African clerks appeared at the windows of the administrative offices. As the party approached the clinic, the European doctor, in his white coat, looked out; two white nurses and an African nurse came out onto the veranda. And all the patient African women who were sitting about in the sun outside, suckling their babies and gossiping, sat silent while the party walked by—sat silent, and had in their eyes something of the look of the Indian grandmother, waiting at home in Fordsburg.

The party walked on up the street, and on either side, in the little houses, which had homemade verandas flanking the strip of worn, unpaved earth that was the sidewalk, or whose front doors opened straight out onto a foot or two of fenced garden, where hens ran and pumpkins had been put to ripen, doors were open, and men and women stood, their children gathered in around them, as if they sensed the approach of a storm. Yet the sun was hot on the heads of the party, walking slowly up the street. And they were silent, and the watchers were silent, or spoke to one another only in whispers, each bending his head to another's ear but keeping his eyes on the group passing up the street. Someone laughed, but it was only a drunk—a wizened little old man—returning from some shebeen. And ahead, at the corner of a crossroad, stood the police car, a black car, with the aerial from its radio-communication equipment a shining lash against all the shabbiness of the street. The rear doors opened, and two heavy, smartly dressed policemen got out and slammed the doors behind them. They approached the party slowly, not hurrying themselves. When they drew abreast, one said, as if in reflex, "Ah—good afternoon." But the other cut in, in an emotionless official voice, "You are all under arrest for illegal entry into Lagersdorp Location. If you'll just give us your names . . ."

Joyce stood waiting her turn, and her heart beat slowly and evenly. She thought again, as she had once before—how long ago was that party?—I feel *nothing*. It's all right. I feel *nothing*.

But as the policeman came to her, and she spelled out her name for him, she looked up and saw the faces of the African onlookers who stood nearest her. Two men, a small boy, and a woman, dressed in ill-matched castoffs of European clothing, which hung upon them without meaning, like coats spread on bushes, were looking at her. When she looked back, they met her gaze. And she felt, suddenly, not *nothing* but what they were feeling, at the sight of her, a white girl, taken—incomprehensibly, as they themselves were used to being taken—under the force of white men's wills, which dispensed and withdrew life, which imprisoned and set free, fed or starved, like God himself.

Questions

1. What are Joyce's thoughts about the black people at the party—in particular, Eddie Ntwala? What feelings do her thoughts awaken about the shop in which she talked across the counter to an Indian boy?
2. Why is Joyce curious about Jessica Malherbe? Do her feelings toward Jessica change in the course of the party? Why does she say that she wants to walk into the location?
3. Why does the memory of the Indian shop recur in the house in the Indian district? Do her feelings about the march change as she waits for a ride to the location? Does Jessica know why she has come?
4. What in the people and in the location is Joyce most aware of? How do her perceptions help us understand her state of mind and feelings as she approaches the gate?
5. What point is Gordimer making through the details of the inhabitants of the location? Are these people interested in the march as a political protest, or are they only curious?
6. What are Joyce's thoughts and feelings as she waits to give her name to the policeman? Is she a different person from the young woman who attended the party?
7. What idea or truth is the author developing? How do the plot, the characters, and the setting help her to develop it?

Suggestions for Writing

1. Write an interpretation of Joyce's character and the decision that she makes. Discuss the point the author is making about Joyce's changing thoughts and feelings.
2. Discuss what the author is saying about South Africa in the 1950s through the details of the party.

Additional Reading

Gordimer, Nadine. *Burger's Daughter*. New York: Viking, 1979.
———. *July's People*. New York: Viking, 1981.
———. *Selected Stories*. New York: Viking, 1975.
———. *Something Out There*. New York: Viking, 1984.
———. *A Sport of Nature*. New York: Knopf, 1987.

The Pripet Marshes

Irving Feldman

Born in Brooklyn, New York, in 1928, Irving Feldman has taught in Puerto Rico and France, and at Kenyon College and the State University of New York at Buffalo. His collections of poems include Works and Day *(1961),* The Pripet Marshes *(1965),* Magic Papers *(1970),* Leaping Clear *(1976), and* Teach Me, Dear Sister *(1983).*

The Pripet Marshes are in the southwestern Soviet Union, in the northwest of the Ukraine—once the site of numerous Jewish villages or shtetls. In czarist Russia, Jews had been confined to an area of the country called the Pale of Settlement, and it was through the villages and towns there that Nazi murder squads (the Einsatzgruppen) *swept. At the postwar Nuremberg Trials, one commander of a death squad gave this account of a killing:*

> Usually, the smaller units were led by a member of the S.D., the Gestapo or the criminal police. The unit selected for this task would enter a village or city and order the prominent Jewish citizens to call together all Jews for the purpose of resettlement. They were requested to hand over their valuables to the leaders of the unit, and shortly before the execution, to surrender their outer clothing. The men, women and children were led to a place of execution which in most cases was located next to a more deeply excavated antitank ditch. Then they were shot, kneeling or standing, and the corpses thrown into the ditch. I never permitted the shooting by individuals in the group D, but ordered that several of the men should shoot at the same time in order to avoid direct personal responsibility. The leaders of the unit or specially designated persons, however, had to fire the last bullet against those victims that were not dead immediately. I learned from conversations with other group leaders that some of them demanded that the victims lie down flat on the ground to be shot through the nape of the neck. I did not approve of these methods. —quoted by Nora Levin, *The Holocaust*

Often I think of my Jewish friends and seize them as they are and transport them in my mind to the *shtetlach* and ghettos,

And set them walking the streets, visiting, praying in *shul,* feasting and dancing. The men I set to arguing, because I love dialectic and song—my ears tingle when I hear their voices—and the girls and women I set to promenading or to cooking in the kitchens, for the sake of their tiny feet and clever hands.

And put kerchiefs and long dresses on them, and some of the men I dress in black and reward with beards. And all of them I set among the mists of the Pripet Marshes, which I have never seen, among wooden buildings that loom up suddenly one at a time, because I have only heard of them in stories, and that long ago.

It is the moment before the Germans will arrive.

Maury is there, uncomfortable, and pigeon-toed, his voice is rapid and slurred, and he is brilliant;

And Frank who is goodhearted and has the hair and yellow skin of a Tartar and is like a flame turned low;

And blonde Lottie who is coarse and miserable, her full mouth is turning down with a self-contempt she can never hide, while the steamroller of her voice flattens every delicacy;

And Marian, her long body, her face pale under her bewildered black hair and of the purest oval of those Greek signets she loves; her head tilts now like the heads of the birds she draws;

And Adele who is sullen and an orphan and so like a beaten creature she trusts no one, and who doesn't know what to do with herself, lurching with her magnificent body like a despoiled tigress;

And Munji, moping melancholy clown, arms too short for his barrel chest, his penny-whistle nose, and mocking nearsighted eyes that want to be straightforward and good;

And Abbie who, when I listen closely, is speaking to me, beautiful with her large nose and witty mouth, her coloring that always wants lavender, her vitality that body and mind can't quite master;

And my mother whose gray eyes are touched with yellow, and who is as merry as a young girl;

And my brown-eyed son who is glowing like a messenger impatient to be gone and who may stand for me.

I cannot breathe when I think of him there.

And my red-haired sisters, and all my family, our embarrassed love bantering our tenderness away.

Others, others, in crowds filling the town on a day I have made sunny for them; the streets are warm and they are at their ease.

How clearly I see them all now, how miraculously we are linked! And sometimes I make them speak Yiddish in timbres whose unfamiliarity thrills me.

But in a moment the Germans will come.

What, will Maury die? Will Marian die?

Not a one of them who is not transfigured then!

The brilliant in mind have bodies that glimmer with a total dialectic;
The stupid suffer an inward illumination; their stupidity is a subtle tenderness that glows in and around them;
The sullen are surrounded with great tortured shadows raging with pain, against whom they struggle like titans;
In Frank's low flame I discover an enormous perspectiveless depth;
The gray of my mother's eyes dazzles me with our love;
No one is more beautiful than my red-haired sisters.
And always I imagine the least among them last, one I did not love, who was almost a stranger to me.
I can barely see her blond hair under the kerchief; her cheeks are large and faintly pitted, her raucous laugh is tinged with shame as it subsides; her bravado forces her into still another lie;
But her vulgarity is touched with a humanity I cannot exhaust, her wretched self-hatred is as radiant as the faith of Abraham, or indistinguishable from that faith.
I can never believe my eyes when this happens, and I want to kiss her hand, to exchange a blessing

In the moment when the Germans are beginning to enter the town.

But there isn't a second to lose, I snatch them all back,
For, when I want to, I can be a God.
No, the Germans won't have one of them!
This is my people, they are mine!

And I flee with them, crowd out with them; I hide myself in a pillow-case stuffed with clothing, in a woman's knotted handkerchief, in a shoebox.

And one by one I cover them in mist, I take them out.
The German motorcycles zoom through the town,
They break their fists on the hollow doors.
But I can't hold out any longer. My mind clouds over.
I sink down as though drunk or beaten.

Questions

1. Is the speaker in the poem imagining a shtetl he has never seen and people he has never met, or is he describing a place and people he knew before the Second World War?
2. In what sense are the speaker and the people of the shtetl "miraculously linked"?
3. Why does he always imagine "the least among them last, one I did not love"? In what ways is the woman the "least among them"?
4. What do we discover is the speaker's reason for imagining the village and people?
5. Why can't the speaker "hold out any longer"? Why does he "sink down"?

Suggestions for Writing

1. Discuss the emotional effect of the poem and explain how the writer achieves this effect.
2. Compare the development of the central theme of "The Pripet Marshes" with that of one of the following poems. Discuss similarities and differences in both theme and development.
   a. Robert Lowell, "The Dead in Europe"
   b. Edwin Muir, "The Refugees"
   c. Wilfred Owen, "Anthem for Doomed Youth"
   d. Karl Shapiro, "Elegy for a Dead Soldier"
   e. Stephen Spender, "Ultima Ratio Regum"
   f. Jon Stallworthy, "A Letter from Berlin"

Additional Reading

Dawidowicz, Lucy S. *The War against the Jews: 1933–1945.* New York: Holt, Rinehart and Winston, 1975.

Feldman, Irving. *New and Selected Poems.* New York: Viking, 1979.

————. *The Pripet Marshes.* New York: Viking, 1965.

————. *Teach Me, Dear Sister.* New York: Viking, 1983.

Gilbert, Martin. *The Holocaust: A History of the Jews of Europe during the Second World War.* New York: Holt, 1986.

Levin, Nora. *The Holocaust: The Destruction of European Jewry.* New York: Crowell, 1968.

PART TWO

PERSPECTIVES ON CONTEMPORARY ISSUES

RESPONSIBILITIES OF THE SCIENTIST

---

*T*his section and the following sections of Part Two open with essays that define or state an opinion on a current issue or give an overview of the current debate. One or more of the essays in each section discuss the same issue. Other essays in the sections discuss issues related to the general topic.

The general topic of this section is the responsibilities of the scientist. All of the essays that follow deal with an issue of much concern to scientists and others today—the ethics of genetic engineering, the modifying of genes that became possible with the discovery and description of the DNA molecule. These essays do not represent all current opinions and attitudes. Rather they present important considerations of the issues and, as with Thomas H. Murray's essay on genetic engineering, general ethical approaches. The reader will notice that some of the essays raise issues suggested in the essays, stories, and poems of Part One. Individual responsibility is the concern of the writers in the previous section, People and Society. The essays of the following section deal with the responsibilities of the doctor.

Ethical Issues in Genetic Engineering

Thomas H. Murray

Genetic engineering, the popular name for the science of re-combinant DNA, originated with the discovery that genes of different species can be spliced to create a new organism. In a later article in this section, Elliot S. Gershon gives the details of this discovery and the controversy it produced. DNA, deoxyribonucleic acids in cell nuclei, is responsible for heredity. In 1953 James Watson and Francis Crick described the DNA molecule as a double helix, and that achievement has generated great advances in molecular biology.

Watson and Crick's discovery was the outcome of work by many earlier geneticists and biochemists as well as scientists, in particular the crystallographer Rosalind Franklin, who were seeking to describe the DNA molecule at the same time. The science of genetics had its beginnings in the nineteenth century. In 1865 the Austrian monk Gregor Mendel, after years of experimenting with garden peas in his monastery garden, published his findings in the journal of the local natural history society. In his writings on evolution of species, Charles Darwin referred to the "strong principle of inheritance," but he had no knowledge of its physical mechanism. Mendel described the mechanism in his paper—and in effect, founded the science of heredity. Mendel's findings became known, but they were not understood immediately. In 1900 the Dutch botanist Hugo DeVries publicized Mendel's findings and, along with other scientists, sought to verify them. DeVries eventually established that what Darwin had described as the mechanism of natural selection was best understood through the mutations of genes—substances in the germ plasm that transmit hereditary characteristics. DeVries and other transmission geneticists studied the functions of the gene—not only its ability to mutate, but also its ability to combine with other genes in the process called recombination. The discovery by biochemists that genes interact with enzymes led to further discoveries in the new science of biochemical genetics. The work of Watson and Crick culminated efforts to discover the nature of the gene itself. Further discoveries, including that of protein synthesis, eventually produced the achievements that gave birth to genetic engineering.

In the essay that follows, Thomas H. Murray examines the ethical issues that have arisen with this new science. Of central importance to Murray are consequential *and* deontological *considerations in ethics—those based narrowly on usefulness and those based on broader moral criteria, respectively. These two approaches to the ethics of recombinant DNA represent very different values, and Murray is careful to distinguish them. His essay and those that follow show how scientists in a particular field define ethical questions and deal with them. The notes throughout are Murray's.*

The scientific study of recombinant DNA—known colloquially as "genetic engineering"—has shown a singular talent for attracting public approbation as well as exciting public fears. Why this should be so is difficult to say, though several factors probably make significant contributions. First, genetic engineering deals with nothing less than the elementary language of life, the letters and words by which cells translate their genetic code, inherited from their predecessors, into the daily biochemical business of life. They will pass that same message on to their own inheritors. Genetic engineering allows us to peek at the letters themselves, which we now know well. We are beginning to have a better understanding of how the letters form into words—sequences of amino acids commonly known as proteins. Our knowledge is considerably spottier when it comes to knowing what makes a cell speak a particular word at a particular time—the problems of gene expression and regulation.

But it is not our increasing though still primitive ability to read the genetic language that stirs public hopes and fears; it is rather our new-found skill at editing. In the past decade, we have developed the capacity to identify genetic words—specific genes—and then to slice them out of a cell, either to leave the cell without them or to insert them into another cell, possibly even the cell of another species.

That is the fearsome wizardry of genetic engineering—editing the genetic information in cells. Its practical implications may take many forms. Commercial production of human insulin, for example, involved isolating, spelling out, and copying the human gene that produces insulin and then inserting it into a microorganism. Finally, that microorganism had to be taught to "speak" insulin—to express the gene product. All this has been accomplished, and human sufferers from diabetes may no longer have to rely on animal insulin, which is slightly different from human insulin although biologically active in humans. Another tactic is to genetically alter the function of a microorganism, in one case a bacterium with the disconcerting habit of acting as a nucleus for the formation of ice crystals in the leaves of potato plants. The result often is frost damage to potato crops. Scientists were able to snip out the offending gene and grow the altered bacteria, now dubbed "ice-minus." The plan is to spread the engineered organisms over a potato field, in the hope that they will elbow out their ice-forming cousins. Perhaps the most controversial of all uses of genetic engineering is to alter human cells in the hope of affecting living human beings, an effort known as human gene therapy.

There have been other controversies as well. Initially, there were concerns about the accidental creation of organisms that would bring new diseases or drastically alter the earth's ecology. Later came worries about the impact of the commercial value of genetic engineering on scientists, the university, and society. At this writing, biological warfare research also looms as an important issue.

It may be useful to group the ethical issues raised by genetic engineering into three subsets. First are worries about the risks to public health and environmental integrity now and in the future, among them fears of Andromeda-like strains of microbes, agricultural releases of deliberately redesigned organisms, and biological warfare. Second are concerns about the privatization and commercialization of genetic engineering, including problems of justice, the autonomy of the university, and the ownership of life forms. Third are the issues surrounding the use of gene therapy in humans.

At least two broad disjunctions underlie the variety of controversies. The first is the source of our uncertainty and disquiet. In some cases, we are animated by a concern that we are in too great ignorance of nature; that nature is unpredictable and therefore ought not be tampered with lightly. But in other cases, our suspicions focus on our fellow humans and their possibly tainted motives and inadequate wisdom. These two foci—nature's incomprehensibility and humankind's all too predictable foibles— call for different forms of redress. Enhancing our knowledge about nature's ways is a reasonable response to worries of the first sort. An increase in scientific knowledge, or at least the representation of scientists expert in ecology and properly in awe of nature's complexities on those bodies reviewing and controlling decisions with potentially great impact, offers some security against ignorant and unwarranted assaults. But science alone cannot placate those worried about human stupidity and misconduct; other means must be found. All such worries are exacerbated by secrecy, and so it should be no surprise that some of the greatest fears are focused on corporate actions undertaken in secrecy and on the possibility of genetic engineering for biological warfare.

The second disjunction, familiar to moral philosophers, is between those ethi-   7 cal theories or judgments concentrating exclusively on the *consequences* of actions or policies and those that insist that certain things could be wrong in themselves, despite the consequences. The first, or *consequentialist,* theories have as their most familiar representative utilitarianism, or the principle that one should judge things according to whether they realize the greatest good for the greatest number. On the other hand, *deontological* theories maintain that consequences do not always tell the whole story, morally speaking, and that other considerations must be included.[1]

While most of the debates over the ethics of genetic engineering focus on con-   8 sequences of one kind or another, occasional deontological whispers are heard. Each approach has its problems. Consequentialist ethics require some reasonable accounting of pluses and minuses. If we are unable to estimate the consequences of a particular course of action, then a consequentialist ethics is essentially mute; it cannot speak of what it knoweth not.[2] In many of the ethical issues raised by genetic engineering, we are able to do no more than list many possible kinds of consequences, with no idea how likely any one of them may be. For example, consequentialist ethics are unhelpful when trying to balance the possibility of a highly unlikely but potentially catastrophic event (like an Andromeda strain or an ecological disaster) against a more predictable but mundane gain. A familiarity with strategic thinking or other means of estimating—actually guessing at—the probability of unprecedented, improbable, but awful consequences should illustrate the difficulties of doing so and the limitations of a consequentialist approach to problems with those characteristics.

Unfortunately, deontological ethics has its own problems, especially in a plur-   9 alistic society. With a few exceptions, political and moral debate in the United States seems to be carried on within the conceptual framework laid down by welfare economics, by the politics of interest groups, and by the calculation of advantages obtained and opportunities forgone. When we stray from that vocabulary into the language of principles, we seem so easily to engage in a cacophony of incompatible claims about rights. The abortion debate, cast in terms of a "right to life" and a "right to choose," is a prime example of this phenomenon. And while there are undoubtedly those who believe in the deontological character of rights, it is also true that in other mouths the appeal to rights is simply a strategic battle cry, a way to gain attention for what are, at base, arguments over consequences again, the mere simulacra of a deontological conception of rights. Nonetheless, deontological ideas appear in the debates over genetic engineering, and despite their inability to achieve complete acceptance they often capture truths with deep moral resonance. They deserve to be considered, along with consequences, as far as we can apprehend them.

---

[1]William K. Frankena, *Ethics,* 2d ed. (Englewood Cliffs, N.J.: Prentice-Hall, 1973).
[2]Ruth Macklin, "On the Ethics of *Not* Doing Scientific Research," *Hastings Center Report 7,* no. 6 (1977): 11–13.

Worries about Risks to Public Health and to the Future

July 26, 1974, was a significant day in the history of the public accountability [10] of science. On that day a prestigious committee of molecular biologists published a letter in the journal *Science* acknowledging their concern "that some of these artificial recombinant DNA molecules could prove biologically hazardous." They recommended that further research on recombinant DNA be deferred until the social and ethical issues could be aired more fully.[3] The fear was that science might be heading down a path the consequences of which for human well-being were highly uncertain and possibly momentous. At a conference the following year in Asilomar, California, the moratorium was lifted and research continued cautiously, under guidelines developed by the National Institutes of Health, establishing standards for physical containment (the use of mutated microbes unable to survive outside of special laboratory conditions).[4]
tainment (four degrees of laboratory security from accidental exposure or release) and biological containment (the use of mutated microbes unable to survive outside of special laboratory conditions).[4]

The principal concern seemed to be the fear of a public health disaster should [11] some genetically superpowered microorganism be accidentally released onto an unsuspecting public. The city of Cambridge went so far as to pass an ordinance regulating recombinant DNA research within its boundaries (encompassing the laboratories of Harvard University and MIT). The debate between scientist-proponents of recombinant DNA research and its opponents, a mix of people in politics and science, was often acrimonious. It appears that people thought more was at stake than a simple difference in estimates of the probability of a superbug wreaking havoc on the public. Concerns about the general propriety of tinkering with genes, whatever the consequences, may also have been a part of the debate, however inchoately.

With time, the fears of new epidemics have faded, largely because a decade of [12] research has been accomplished in comparative safety. Safety constraints have been gradually loosened, although research with pathogens remains fairly tightly controlled. The principal fears have shifted from human epidemics to ecological upheavals.

It now appears that some of the most important commercial applications of ge- [13] netic engineering will come in agriculture, in the release of deliberately redesigned microorganisms. The first such release may well be the "ice-minus" bacteria mentioned before. Opponents of such field trials maintain that they may have grossly destructive ecological consequences on the order of the introduction of such novel plants as kudzu or hydrilla, which clog southern landscapes and water bodies respectively, or the familiar pests the gypsy moth and Japanese beetle. One coalition has successfully blocked the "ice-minus" field trial by filing a suit demanding a full "environmental impact statement."[5]

---

[3]Paul Berg and others, "Letter," *Science,* July 26, 1974, p. 303.

[4]For a recent restatement of the full guidelines, see Department of Health and Human Services, National Institute of Health, "Guidelines for Research Involving Recombinant DNA Molecules," *Federal Register* 48 (June 1, 1983): 24556–87.

[5]Jeffrey I. Fox and Colin Norman, "Agricultural Genetics Goes to Court," *Science* 221 (Sept. 30, 1983): 1355. See also Winston J. Brill, "Safety Concerns and Genetic Engineering in Agriculture," *Science* 227 (Jan. 25, 1985): 381–384.

The suit points out that the body charged with reviewing such proposals, the 14 Recombinant DNA Advisory Committee of NIH—RAC for short—does not contain the relevant expertise to do environmental assessments. The ultimate effect of all this maneuvering remains to be seen. It appears to be animated almost completely by concerns about consequences and to focus on our uncertainty about natural processes rather than mistrust of human motives.

The latest fear to emerge is focused on biological warfare research, which may 15 involve recombinant DNA. Almost since the beginnings of genetic engineering research, one of the most horrible possibilities imagined was the deliberate creation of disease-causing organisms or the melding of disease-causing genes with a previously benign microbe. What if, for example, we could insert the gene for botulinus toxin into an omnipresent bacteria like escherichia coli? Scientists dismissed those fears, saying that no one would ever want to do such a thing. But the concern remained that, should the powerful techniques of genetic engineering be turned to biological warfare, they could result in the purposeful—not accidental—creation of an Andromeda-strain-like organism.

Against that background, in August 1984, the U.S. Army requested a realloca- 16 tion of funds for a number of minor projects, including a heated parking garage, troop housing, and an aerosol test facility. This is a common procedure, utilized to transfer funds from where they are not needed to minor and uncontroversial projects. The request requires approval only by the chair and ranking minority member of the House and Senate subcommittees responsible for military construction. Only later did it emerge that the "aerosol test facility" was in fact a P-4 laboratory, capable of handling the most dangerous experiments with recombinant DNA and unequivocally devoted to biological warfare research, at the moment one of the most controversial items in the defense budget. Only four P-4 laboratories exist in the country, and no other is dedicated exclusively to nonmedical research.[6]

Defenders of the laboratory argue that it is needed to match vaguely described 17 efforts at biological warfare research in the U.S.S.R. They assert that it would do only defensive research and not engage in developing offensive biological weapons. Critics offer several arguments. U.S. Senator James Sasser argues that construction of the laboratory would allow the testing of offensive biological weapons, which would be a violation of a 1972 treaty. Scientists opposed to the laboratory claim that doing "defensive" research on biological weapons requires doing work on "offensive" weapons as well. If the Army suspects that the Soviet Union is developing biological weapons of a certain kind, it may do the same in order to test the new biological weapon against various defenses. But in that instance, it has done, or at least replicated, the research on the offensive biological weapon. Other scientists argue that if the genuine intention is to develop defensive capabilities, the research can be carried out in less secure laboratories. Matthew Meselson, a biochemist and molecular biologist at Harvard, suggests that virtually all the information needed can be obtained by simulating pathogens with far less hazardous organisms and that there may even be gains in efficiency by using the simulants rather than the pathogens themselves.[7]

---

[6]R. Jeffrey Smith. "New Army Biowarfare Lab Raises Concerns," *Science* 226 (Dec. 7, 1984): 1116–18.
[7]*Ibid.*, p. 1117.

Perhaps the most disturbing part of the entire episode is the cloak of secrecy, 18 and even dishonesty, over the effort to obtain funding for the laboratory. By employing a procedure for obtaining congressional approval without debate or formal vote, the Army has created suspicion about its motives and about the respect, or lack of it, in which it holds congressional approval and public opinion. At this time, as well, there are no provisions for review of the laboratory's work. A number of eminent scientists are calling for the creation of a panel of experts to oversee all work done there, including classified research. The proposed use of genetic engineering for biological warfare research evokes consequentialist concerns of two kinds: fear of what may happen when we concentrate on developing disease-bearing organisms and mistrust of the motives and wisdom of those doing the research. These fears are compounded by the aura of surreptitiousness and secrecy.

Privatization and Commercialization

Quite apart from fears of catastrophe are a number of issues surrounding the 19 commercialization of genetic engineering and the general move toward private control of recombinant DNA research. While the objections are usually framed in terms of the unfavorable consequences of privatization and commercialization, at times issues of justice are raised, along with suggestions of deontological problems pertaining to the nature of the human relationship to the natural world. Without question, discussions of these issues have been influenced by the swiftness with which commercialization has progressed and by the enormous enthusiasm with which financiers have greeted companies dedicated to genetic engineering. There is also the remarkable phenomenon of scientists discovering almost overnight that a fortune rests among their test tubes and petri dishes.

Perhaps the most celebrated issue associated with genetic engineering is the 20 matter of patenting life. Ironically, the first microorganism for which a patent was sought and granted was developed without any resort to recombinant DNA techniques. Ananda Chakrabarty developed his oil-eating *Pseudomonas aeruginosa* with conventional methods of inducing random mutations and selecting those with the desired properties. Yet the timing of the case and the U.S. Supreme Court decision on June 16, 1980, caused the issue to be carried along with the crest of public interest and concern with genetic engineering.

Opinion remains divided on the wisdom of permitting patenting of life forms 21 themselves rather than of the processes by which they are developed, which has been less controversial. Key Dismukes points out the continuity between what Chakrabarty, or for that matter a genetic engineer, does and natural processes of genetic change. He claims that "[t]he argument that the bacterium is Chakrabarty's handiwork and not nature's wildly exaggerates human power and displays the same hubris and ignorance of biology that have had such devastating impact on the ecology of our planet."[8] On the other hand, people such as Harold P. Green argue that the issue should be understood narrowly as the question of how society may regulate and encourage the development of technologies.[9] From that perspective, patenting is merely one device among several

---

[8] Key Dismukes, "Life Is Patently Not Human-Made," *Hastings Center Report* 10, no. 5 (1980): 11–12, at 12.
[9] Harold P. Green, "Chakrabarty: Tempest in a Test Tube," *Hastings Center Report* 10, no. 5 (1980): 12–13.

that a society may employ to spur research and development. For someone who holds a view like Green's, patenting in itself is ethically neutral; the question is one of relative effectiveness with respect to the desired consequences.

The specifics of patenting aside though, what remains to be explained is the 22 hold that issue exerts on the public consciousness. It may be that two quite distinct considerations merge to create the impression that, by permitting life forms to be patented, something that is importantly "public" is being made "private."[10] The first aspect is an ordinarily inchoate sense that there is something different about the animate so that, while it would be acceptable to own individual animals, owning an entire "type" is trespassing on the commons, which can belong to no one. This is usually expressed more as a moral sentiment than a careful argument, though it should not be dismissed too easily; often enough, moral sentiments are expressions of important, deeply held, and valid moral beliefs. Clearly, this type of argument does not rely solely on consequences but is closer to a deontological principle about humankind's relationship with natural kinds. In a brilliant article, the historian Lynn White has traced the origin of the more prevalent attitude holding that nature is a proper object of humankind's exploitation to its roots in Western cultural traditions.[11] White argues that the exploitative stance is dangerous and not the only one available, even in Western thought.

The second aspect of public discomfort at patenting life may be a perception 23 that it is, in some circumstances, also unjust. Without question, the public has supported genetic engineering through decades of corporate indifference. Public funds have supported research, trained scientists, and paid for equipment. It may be that people see this largesse as a gift. If it is a gift, then, while there is no requirement that it be reciprocated, a failure to show some measure of gratitude could result in resentment on the part of the giver and poison future relationships. It is difficult to prove that this is in fact what is behind the public's disquiet, and more difficult still to know what would constitute a proper expression of gratitude. But if the thesis is correct, and people regard commercial genetic engineering as monopolizing a corner of creation with skills and tools developed at public expense, then industry had best be willing to temper the unalloyed pursuit of profit with some concern for public well-being.

A specific example of the conflict between private profit and public welfare is 24 the delayed development of a vaccine against malaria, a disease that kills 2 million people a year, almost all in less-developed nations. The World Health Organization supported research at New York University leading to the development of an early form of a vaccine, one which, with proper development, could probably be made into an effective vaccine against malaria in humans. WHO negotiated with one of the leading biotechnology firms. Genentech, to pursue the production of the vaccine. Genentech insisted on having exclusive right to exploit the vaccine commercially, once it paid a royalty to NYU. WHO balked, possibly at the thought of objections by the nations who supported the research with government funds, or those nations, some of the earth's poorest, who would have to buy the vaccine from Genentech. The company withdrew from negotiations, and the vaccine's development languished, while the death toll from malaria mounts.[12]

---

[10]Thomas H. Murray, "Societal Objections to Patenting of Recombinant Life Forms," *Genetic Engineering News,* April 1984, pp. 19, 30.

[11]Lynn White, Jr., "The Historical Roots of Our Ecological Crisis," *Science* 155 (1967): 1203.

[12]John Maddox, "Malaria: What Price Progress?" *London Times,* Apr. 9, 1983.

Another field of conflict for the commercialization of genetic engineering has 25 been the academy itself. Biotechnology has spawned a host of formal industry-university relationships, giving birth at the same time to questions about academic freedom, the problems of serving two masters, and possibly distorted priorities within the university itself. For the most part, university administrators have welcomed funding and formal agreements with industry as a substitute for uncertain and possibly shrinking government funding of research. The president of Stanford University, a leader in discussions of industry-science relations, argues that private funds fill an important need in the contemporary university.[13] He argues that modern science has become more capital intensive. (He defines "Big Science" as when "[t]he capital cost of the equipment and special facilities . . . become[s] larger than the capital value of the endowment necessary to yield the faculty member's salary.") At the same time, government funding for science has not shown a comparable willingness to pay for capital expenses. Industry is ready and willing to step into the breach, in selected areas of science.

In contrast to administrators such as Donald Kennedy are academicians who 26 advance a number of concerns about the links being forged and the consequent dependency on industry. Some academicians show a visceral distaste for corporations, but there are other, more carefully considered objections. There are concerns about the value of openness within the university and how proprietary research may be incompatible with that norm. There are worries about graduate students in the sciences being exploited for profit-making ends. Some objections, though, focus not on specific instances but on the general and long-term impact of industry-university connections. Nicholas A. Ashford, for example, identifies a number of forces that might prompt a shift in research priorities away from issues to which industry is indifferent or hostile and toward topics likely to be useful to industry. He sees the problem as one of "opportunity cost"—the use of scientific resources and talent for corporate ends siphoning off resources from problems perhaps more valuable to the public but without well-heeled interests behind them.[14]

Acknowledging that universities are unlikely to refuse private funds as long as 27 public funds are insufficient, Charles C. Caldart argues that the greatest danger comes from subtle, long-term effects. He writes: "Closer contact between academia and industry will bring about subtle changes in attitude that could affect the basic policies and direction of the university. Indeed, the fabric of academic research could be slowly rewoven on industry's loom."[15] He suggests that the most reasonable response to the threat is to avoid piecemeal collaboration by constructing general policies designed to protect the autonomy of the university and its faculty and students.

We cannot leave the issue of privatization without mentioning two ironic direc- 28 tions it has recently taken. The first concerns the claim by a number of nations, principally in the Third World, that the genetic resources of plants native to their countries

---

[13]Donald Kennedy, "Government Policies and the Costs of Doing Research," *Science* 227 (Feb. 1, 1985): 480–484.

[14]Nicholas A. Ashford, "A Framework for Examining the Effects of Industrial Funding on Academic Freedom and the Integrity of the University," *Science, Technology and Human Values* 8, no. 2 (1983): 16–23.

[15]Charles C. Caldart, "Industry Investment in University Research," *Science, Technology and Human Values* 8, no. 2 (1983): 24–32, at 30.

have been appropriated by other countries and their profit-making corporations, only to be sold back to the nation of origin in highly bred and high-priced plant seeds. In one case, wheat genes originally taken from Libya and Afghanistan have been withheld from those countries. The plant genes no longer exist there.[16]

The second curious incident is a suit filed on behalf of John Moore, formerly 29 a leukemia patient at UCLA. Moore's attorney alleges that scientists used cells taken from his spleen as the basis of a cell line that produces a number of biologically active and important substances, including a type of interferon. Two scientists have patented that cell line, called Mo (after Moore). Moore claims a share of profits from the patented cells.[17] Privatization and commercialization have more facets than at first appeared. Once we permit the commercial control and exploitation of cell lines, microorganisms and the like, questions about what belongs to whom are likely to proliferate like cancer cells.

Gene Therapy in Humans

Between two and three thousand human diseases are caused by genetic abnor- 30 malities. Some are prevalent, like sickle-cell disease and another red-blood-cell condition known as glucose-6-phosphate-dehydrogenase or G-6-PD. Others are well known, although less common—for example, phenylketone urea (PKU) and cystic fibrosis. Others are rarer still. Three of the rarest are candidates for the first gene therapy in humans. They are Lesch-Nyhan, a disorder in very young children resulting in self-mutilation among other symptoms, and two deficiencies of the immune system, purine necleoside phosphorylase (PNP) and adenosine deaminase (ADA).[18] What makes these prime candidates is a combination of factors. First, the untreated disease is invariably fatal and, in the case of Lesch-Nyhan, horrible as well. Second, there are no effective treatments at present. Third, the normal gene corresponding to the diseased one has been cloned and is therefore available for addition to diseased cells. Fourth, a method for placing the normal gene inside diseased cells is available. It consists of removing bone marrow cells from the patient's own body, culturing them in vitro, mixing them with a suitably modified virus, and replacing them in the person's body at the appropriate tissue site. The virus has been deprived of its ability to reproduce but retains its capacity to invade a human cell. A copy of the healthy human gene has been added to the virus's own genetic material, so it, in essence, "infects" the child's defective cell with a human gene that will perform the function the child's own genetic material cannot.[19]

Much of the debate about human gene therapy has centered on the question of 31 whether deliberately altering a person's genes constitutes a morally forbidden tampering with life. This was commonly expressed as a charge that scientists were "playing God." Separately and in concert, a number of religious leaders and theologians ex-

---

[16]Debora MacKenzie, "UN Takes Control of World's Food Genes." *New Scientist,* Nov. 24, 1983, p. 558.

[17]Barbara J. Culliton, "Mo Cell Case Has Its First Court Hearing," *Science* 226 (Nov. 16, 1984): 813–814.

[18]W. French Anderson. "Prospects for Human Gene Therapy," *Science* 226 (Oct. 26, 1984): 401–409.

[19]U.S. Congress, Office of Technology Assessment, "Human Gene Therapy—A Background Paper." Washington, D.C. OTA-BP-BA-32. December 1984.

pressed concerns about the genetic manipulation of human beings.[20] The "playing God" accusation was clearly a deontological argument that there are certain things people should not do no matter how morally good the consequences. But where do we draw the line? And what principle guides us in knowing when we are making acceptable interventions and when we have crossed into forbidden territory? Eventually, most participants in the debate came to an agreement about two things. First, they made the factual distinction between *somatic* cells, or all those cells of the human body *not* involved in reproduction, and *germ* cells, or those cells that are now or are destined to become sperm or ova. Any alterations made in a person's somatic cells will die with that individual; they cannot be passed on to one's children. In that sense, gene therapy is like other medical therapies designed to aid the particular patient. Altering germ cells, however, means that any changes induced may be passed on indefinitely, through uncountable generations of descendants.

This was a new wrinkle. Although it is true that other medical therapies may 32 affect germ cells, especially the powerful drugs and radiation used to treat cancers, the effects are random and unknowable. (For that matter, a person's germ cells may be affected also by occupational or environmental exposures to numerous mutagenic chemicals.) Nevertheless, it became clear that systematically altering germ cells was ethically distinctive from gene therapy on somatic cells.

The second area of agreement was moral—that somatic cell therapy was mor- 33 ally acceptable, under certain conditions, and that germ cell therapy was morally problematic. Why is germ cell alteration more of an ethical problem? Because its impact is not limited to the person under study or treatment and its effects may be propagated for generations, germ cell alteration entails a projection of intentional human action far beyond the scope of somatic cell therapy. In that respect it is discontinuous with usual medical therapies. Since its effects are passed on to subsequent generations, and since those persons yet unborn have no possible say in whether to participate in the research, it may constitute a form of "experimentation" on unconsenting future generations. Finally, it is the prospect of making inheritable changes in genes that leads many to feel that we have indeed crossed the barrier separating the permissible imitation of the divine with the usurpation of God's prerogatives.

There is also an argument from consequences: that widespread gene therapy 34 would substantially alter the gene pool of the human population. Short of gene therapy on an almost unimaginable scale, the mathematics of the problem do not support the critics. It would take millennia of intensive gene therapy to make a noticeable impact on gene frequencies in the human population.[21]

Not all commentators agree that germ cell therapy should be categorically pro- 35 hibited. The recent report of a presidential commission argued that, under the proper

---

[20]Two documents are especially important. One is a letter written to President Jimmy Carter on June 20, 1980, and signed by the general secretaries of the National Council of Churches, the Synagogue Council of America, and the U.S. Catholic Conference. The other is a resolution circulated by Jeremy Rifkin and signed by sixty-one religious leaders, activists, authors, theologians, and scientists. It and a commentary appended later by Rifkin were released on June 8, 1983, by the Foundation on Economic Trends.

[21]U.S. Congress, Office of Technology Assessment, "Human Gene Therapy," p. 32.

circumstances, if germ cell therapy were available it would be justifiable to use it.[22] The argument is that it would be a greater wrong to allow people to die from a disease like Huntington's than to do germ cell line therapy to correct the disorder, even or *especially* because the corrected gene would be passed on to offspring.

Practically, though, germ cell therapy is not likely in the near future because 36 of the scientific difficulties it would entail and because of an informal ban on research with human embryos, which makes development of the techniques difficult.

One of the most cogent warnings about gene therapy is not particular to it, but 37 rather speaks to a general problem with medical intervention. It is the difficulty in maintaining the distinction between intervening with a therapy in order to treat a disease and intervening in order to effect some other change in a person who has no disease. A graphic example appeared when it was discovered that large numbers of Olympic athletes were using massive doses of anabolic steroids—potent and possibly dangerous drugs—in the belief that the drugs improved their athletic performances.[23] A connection with genetic engineering appeared when it was learned that human growth hormone (HGH), which had been available in very limited quantities harvested from human cadaver pituitary glands, was being used in an attempt to increase the adult height of young children. HGH is somewhat effective in treating a variety of dwarfism, and that was the reason for collecting it. Since it was in chronic short supply, it was essentially unavailable for other, more questionable uses.

Genetic engineers, however, have inserted the gene for HGH into a microbe, 38 and are able to produce it in quantities significantly greater than the harvest of cadavers could ever generate. Now, experiments are under way to see if HGH will also increase the growth rate and adult height of children who are not physiologically deficient in the hormone, but who have something called "familial short stature."[24] The "disease," in other words, is being short like your parents. It is not surprising in a society that apparently values height, and where taller people generally fare better, that being much shorter than average is regarded as justification for medical intervention, while being much taller than average (absent more generally agreed upon diseases) is a blessing.

The worry expressed about genetic engineering more generally is that there is 39 no natural line that can be drawn between using gene therapy to "cure" a "disease" and using it to enhance a desirable trait that is not a disease. It is a concern about our wisdom, or rather our lack of it. It seems to be a well-founded concern, given our recent history with other medical tools. But the alternative is even less palatable. Should we give up our effort to treat disease because we sometimes put the tools we develop to questionable uses? Should we forgo beneficial inventions because there is some chance they may be misused? I believe the answer to both questions is no, and that the sensible course is to proceed continuously with the development of genetic engineering, always

---

[22]President's Commission for the Study of Ethical Problems in Medicine and Biomedical and Behavioral Research, *Splicing Life: The Social and Ethical Issues of Genetic Engineering with Human Beings* (Washington, D.C.: U.S. Government Printing Office, 1982).

[23]Thomas H. Murray, "The Coercive Power of Drugs in Sports," *Hastings Center Report* 13, no. 4 (1983): 24–30.

[24]Ad Hoc Committee on Growth Hormone Usage, The Lawson Wilkins Pediatric Endocrine Society, and Committee on Drugs, "Growth Hormone in the Treatment of Children with Short Stature," *Pediatrics* 72, no. 6 (1983): 891–894.

alert to the ever-present potential for misuse of every technology, whatever its genesis. We must also not underestimate the need for many forms of social oversight and many forums for social discussions of the possible uses—and misuses—of genetic engineering.

      An important part of the discussions that should take place is consideration of 40 ethical issues. So far, the debate on the ethics of genetic engineering has been vigorous and reasonably well informed. I have tried to indicate here the importance of both consequentialist and deontological considerations while stressing as well their limitations: for consequentialist ethics, a reliance on empirical predictions that may be unreliable or impossible; for deontological ethics, the limited force of moral claims without reference to consequences in a morally and culturally pluralistic society.

Questions

1. How do consequential considerations in ethics differ from deontological ones? Why are some questions difficult to discuss consequentially or deontologically?
2. Is the debate over abortion described in paragraph 9 consequential or deontological? What kind is the debate over biological warfare (paragraphs 14–17)?
3. Does Murray discuss the issues of patents and commercialization consequentially, deontologically, or both ways?
4. What physical possibility has complicated the discussion of gene therapy? Does Murray discuss the issue consequentially or deontologically?
5. Does Murray only state his opinions about the issues, or does he defend his opinion through a weighing of evidence or argument?
6. Under what circumstances should companies be permitted to patent medical procedures and substances? Should public support of the research that produced these be a consideration in the awarding of patents?
7. Do you believe that John Moore is entitled to a share of the profits from substances like interferon that are parented from cells taken from his spleen? On what personal beliefs do you base your opinion?
8. Do you believe the benefits of gene therapy—the prevention of Huntington's Chorea, for example—warrant the risks discussed by Murray?

Suggestions for Writing

1. Defend your own beliefs on one of the issues discussed by Murray—patents and commercialization, gene therapy, and the like. State and defend assumptions that support your beliefs.
2. Show how a current issue of concern to you might be discussed consequentially or deontologically. Then briefly develop an argument on the issue in one of these ways.

Additional Reading

Cherfas, Jeremy. *Man-Made Life: An Overview of the Science, Technology, and Commerce of Genetic Engineering.* New York: Pantheon, 1982.

Cooke, Robert. *Improving on Nature: the Brave New World of Genetic Engineering.* New York: Quadrangle–New York Times, 1977.

Sylvester, Edward J., and Lynn C. Klotz. *The Gene Age: Genetic Engineering and the Next Industrial Revolutions.* New York: Scribner's, 1983.

Creating the Efficient Gene

Jeremy Rifkin

Jeremy Rifkin has written on a wide range of subjects, including environmentalism, the changing world economy, and biological experimentation; his books include Entropy: A New World View *(1980),* Algeny *(1983), and* Declaration of a Heretic *(1985), from which the following essay on genetic engineering is reprinted. Rifkin has sought to end biological experiments by the U.S. Government and private industry. In 1984 he filed a challenge in federal court against experiments of the University of California, Berkeley, with genetically engineered bacteria to control potato damage from frost. On May 16, 1984, Judge John J. Sirica ordered the United States government to delay approval of field experiments with genetically modified bacteria and plants. On February 11, 1987, the Environmental Protection Agency gave approval to a California biotechnological company to conduct these experiments—the first experiments with pesticides created by recombinant DNA.*

In the first essay of this section, Thomas H. Murray discusses the proposed use of ice-minus P-syringae to increase potato production. Jeremy Rifkin discusses P-syringae at length in this essay opposing genetic engineering. Rifkin summarizes the chief arguments in opposition, but he also explores the assumptions underlying the technology itself, and in doing so, he states his own assumptions.

The great underlying myth of the Biotechnical Revolution is that it is possible 1 to accelerate the production of more efficient living utilities without ever running out. This grand illusion will not be easy to dismiss or shunt aside. It has gained widespread currency over the past few decades because of the unfortunate choice of words we have come to use in distinguishing between fossil fuels and biological resources. We often refer to the former as non-renewable and to the latter as renewable. Therein lies the nub of the problem. In actuality, living resources are as depletable and finite as fossil fuels. Somewhere down the road, however, we have managed to confuse the idea of reproducible resources with the idea of perpetually inexhaustible resources. They are not the same. Living resources reproduce, but the life support systems that nourish them do not.

The genetic engineers refuse to come to grips with this underlying reality. In- 2 stead they continue to talk of the ever accelerating production of living things firmly convinced that the information coded in the genetic instructions provides the key to un-limited output. To illustrate this point, consider the possibility of genetically engineer-ing new plants that could absorb greater sunlight and increase the rate of photosynthe-sis. While the benefit of such a procedure seems apparent, at first glance, a closer examination reveals the price that would have to be paid to achieve the desired results.

Increased photosynthesis would require a greater use of soil nutrients, thus 3 threatening the further depletion and erosion of an already endangered agricultural soil base. Soil depletion and erosion is one of the major problems in agriculture today. Up to one-third of some of our prime agricultural top-soil has been depleted in the past three decades, largely as a result of the accelerated production tempo of green revolu-tion farming. Attempts to genetically engineer increases in speed of maturation and gross productivity will place additional burdens on an already over-taxed soil structure, thus posing the very real danger of inadequate nutrient reserves for sustaining future agricultural crops.

Genetic engineering will unquestionably result in the short term acceleration 4 of biological materials into useful economic products, but at the expense of depleting the reservoir of life-support materials that are essential for maintaining the reproduc-tive viability of living organisms in the future. In nature, there is no such thing as a free lunch. All biological and physical phenomena are subject to entropy and the Second Law of Thermodynamics.* Being able to store and program the genetic instructions for living things is of little help if the biotic environment is bereft of the nutrients to sustain life.

All great technological revolutions secure the present by mortgaging the fu- 5 ture. In this respect, genetic engineering represents the ultimate lien on the future. Ge-netic engineering raises the interest rates that will have to be paid by future generations beyond anything we've ever experienced in the long history of our attempts to control the forces of nature.

Everytime we choose to introduce a new genetically modified organism into 6 the environment the ecological interest rate moves up a point. That's because every ge-netically engineered product presents a potential threat to the ecosystem it is released in. To appreciate why this is so, we need to be able to understand some of the defining characteristics of engineered organisms. The best way to do that is to contrast biotechnical products with petro-chemical products.

Genetically engineered products differ from petro-chemical products in several important ways. Because they are alive, genetically engineered products are inherently more unpredictable than petro-chemicals in the way they interact with other living things in the environment. Consequently, it is much more difficult to assess all of the potential impacts that a biotechnical product might have on the earth's ecosystems.

Genetically engineered products also reproduce. They grow and they migrate. 8 Unlike petro-chemical products, it is impossible to constrain them within a given geo-graphical locale. Finally, once released, it is virtually impossible to recall living products back to the laboratory, especially those products that are microscopic in nature. For all

---

*Entropy: the measure of decreasing energy in a thermodynamic system. Second law of thermodynamics: The amount of energy available for work is constantly diminishing. [Ed.]

these reasons, genetically engineered products pose far greater long-term potential risks to the environment than petro-chemical substances.

Exactly how dangerous are genetically engineered products? Environmental scientists tell us that the risks in releasing biotechnical products into the biosphere are comparable to those we've encountered in introducing exotic organisms into the North American habitat. Over the past several hundred years thousands of non-native organisms have been brought to America from other regions of the globe. While most of these creatures have adapted to the ecosystem without severe dislocations, a small percentage of them have run wild, wreaking havoc on the flora and fauna of the continent. Gypsy moth, Kudzu vine, Dutch elm disease, chestnut blight, starlings, Mediterranean fruit flies come easily to mind. Each year the American continent is ravaged by these non-native organisms, with destruction to plant and animal life running into the tens of billions of dollars. 9

Whenever a genetically engineered organism is released there is always a small chance that it too will run amok because, like exotic organisms, it is not a naturally occurring life form. It has been artificially introduced into a complex environment that has developed a web of highly synchronized relationships over millions of years. Each new synthetic introduction is tantamount to playing ecological roulette. That is, while there is only a small chance of it triggering an environmental explosion, if it does, the consequences can be thunderous and irreversible. 10

For example, consider the first set of experiments in the US to release a genetically engineered organism into the open environment. Researchers at the University of California have modified a bacteria called P-syringae. This particular bacteria is found in its naturally occurring state in temperate regions all over the world. Its most unique attribute is its ability to nucleate ice crystals. In other words, it helps facilitate the formation of frost or ice. Using recombinant DNA technology, University of California researchers have found a way to delete the genetic instructions for making ice from the bacteria. This new genetically modified P-syringae microbe is called ice-minus. 11

Scientists are excited about the long-term commercial possibilities of ice-minus in agriculture. Frost damage has long been a major problem for American farmers. The chief culprit has been P-syringae which attaches itself to the plants, creating ice crystals. The American corporation financing this research hopes that by spraying massive concentrations of ice-minus P-syringae on agricultural crops, the naturally occurring P-syringae will be edged out, providing a protective blanket against frost damage. The benefits in introducing this genetically engineered organism appear impressive. It's only when one looks at the long-term ecological costs that problems begin to surface. 12

To begin with, the first question a good environmental scientist would ask is what role does the naturally occurring P-syringae play in nature? The experts that have studied this particular organism say that its ice-making capacity helps shape worldwide precipitation patterns and is a key determinant in establishing climatic conditions on the planet. The experts also contend that the P-syringae bacteria has played an important evolutionary role in enhancing the viability of frost resistant plants and insects in the northern areas of the globe. 13

Many of our agricultural crops, however, are tropical in origin and frost sensitive like citrus, corn, beans and tomatoes. Now consider the prospect of spraying ice-minus bacteria on millions of acres of frost-sensitive crops over several decades. While 14 the crops will be protected against frost, the local flora and fauna will be at a disadvantage as the naturally occurring ice-nucleating bacteria which they have relied on for millions of years will have been edged out. Blanketing millions of acres of agricultural land with ice-minus also provides a protective coat of warmth allowing tropical based insects to begin migrating into colder regions. Then too, what will be the long-term effect on worldwide precipitation patterns and climate if ice-minus replaces the ice-making bacteria over millions of acres of land for a sustained period of time?

Introducing just this one genetically engineered product into the environment 15 raises disturbing ecological questions. Yet, in the coming decades, industry is expected to introduce thousands of new genetically engineered products into the environment each year, just as industry introduced thousands of petro-chemical products into the environment each year. While many of these genetically engineered organisms will prove to be benign, sheer statistical probability suggests that a small percentage will prove to be dangerous and highly destructive to the environment.

For example, scientists are considering the possibility of producing a geneti- 16 cally engineered enzyme that could destroy lignin, an organic substance that makes wood rigid. They believe there might be great commercial advantage in using this genetically modified organism to clean up the effluent from paper mills or for decomposing biological material for energy. But if the enzyme were to migrate offsite and spread through forest land, it could well end up destroying millions of acres of woodland by eating away at the substance that provides trees with their rigidity.

Several years ago, General Electric developed and patented a micro-organism 17 that eats up oil spills. This new microscopic creation has never been let out, probably for the reason that there is no way to guarantee that it won't get loose, reproduce in mass volumes and begin eating up oil reserves in gasoline storage tanks all over the planet. Environmental scientists also warn that new micro-organisms designed to consume toxic materials might develop an appetite for more valuable resources.

In fact, the long-term cumulative impact of thousands upon thousands of in- 18 troductions of genetically modified organisms could well eclipse by a magnitude the damage that has resulted from the wholesale release of petro-chemical products into the earth's ecosystems. With these new biological based products, however, the damage is not containable, the destructive effects continue to reproduce, and the organisms can not be recalled, making the process irreversible.

Many people labor under the misguided assumption that genetic engineering 19 has a good side and a bad side, and that steps can be taken to regulate potential abuses, assuring that only the beneficial aspects of the technology are employed. They fail to understand that it is the built-in assumptions of the technology, the inherent logic of the process, that creates the problem regardless of the good or bad intention of those using it. This can be seen quite clearly when looking at genetic engineering in agriculture and animal husbandry. The objective of genetic engineering technology is to improve the efficiency and productive output of plants and domestic animals. Efficiency and productivity, however, are cultural values not ecological rules.

Engineering efficiency and productivity into plants and animals means engi- 20 neering sustainability out. Every breeder knows that attempts to streamline the productive efficiency of plants and animals results in more lucrative but less fit strains and breeds. It has long been acknowledged that over-breeding and over-hybridization result in monoculturing and loss of genetic variability. Reliance on a few super strains or breeds has proven to be very unwise, because it increases vulnerability to specific diseases or radical changes in the environment. Genetic diversity assures that each species will have enough variety to effectively adapt to changing environments. By eliminating all of the so called unprofitable strains and breeds, we undermine the adaptive capacity of each species. Farmers have witnessed, first hand, the problem that can arise from monoculturing. Not long ago the corn farmers were hit with a devastating blight. The corn strain they were all using was particularly vulnerable to the disease, resulting in massive losses. Had they planted a variety of corns, some of the strains would have been hardy enough to ward off the pest.

Animal breeding has posed similar problems. For example, many dairy farmers 21 have chosen to breed only Holsteins because of their superior milk yield. Other less lucrative breeds have all but disappeared. The Holstein, while more lucrative, is less fit. It relies on specialized feeds, an array of technological support systems and continual monitoring, and cannot survive in pasture land over winter like other breeds.

Genetic engineering technology will dramatically accelerate the problems of 22 monoculturing and loss of gene diversity. This technology allows scientists to more effectively increase short-term productivity by engineering efficiency directly into the genetic code of a species. At the same time, non-useful traits can be deleted directly from the hereditary blueprint further to increase productive output. There is even talk about introducing cloning techniques on a large scale in agriculture and animal husbandry over the next several decades. By reproducing millions of identical copies of a single superior strain or breed, agriculturists hope to increase efficiency and output dramatically. This kind of pure monoculturing is going to result in the almost complete loss of minor strains or breeds, as they will be considered uneconomical and uncompetitive in the open marketplace. The long-term environmental consequences could be profound. Imagine millions of exact cloned replicas of a particular cow being used throughout the country and the world. The spread of one disease to which that particular genotype is not immune could result in the wholesale destruction of entire herds and the collapse of much of the dairy industry. It could take years to search for any remaining minor breeds as replacements, and decades more to rebreed new herds from them.

Cloning livestock only begins to touch on the possibilities that lie ahead. Even 23 more ambitious are current experiments being conducted by the US Department of Agriculture to insert human growth hormone genes into the permanent hereditary make-up of pigs, sheep and other domestic animals. Some scientists predict that within a very few years barnyard animals will double in size and develop to maturity in half the normal time. It is possible, say the experts, that with genetic engineering technology, they could produce a cow the size of a small elephant, producing over 45,000 pounds of milk products per year.

By transferring genes from one species into the biological codes of another spe- 24 cies it is possible to change the essential character of domestic animals. These changes will not only revolutionize the business of animal husbandry, but also our concept of nature as well. As already mentioned, in accepting the notion of transferring genes from one species into another, we begin the process of eliminating species' borders from our thinking. Already researchers in the field of molecular biology are arguing that there is nothing particularly sacred about the concept of a species. As they see it, the important unit of life is no longer the organism, but rather the gene. They increasingly view life from the vantage point of the chemical composition at the genetic level. From this reductionist perspective, life is merely the aggregate representation of the chemicals that give rise to it and therefore they see no ethical problem whatsoever in transferring one, five or a hundred genes from one species into the hereditary blueprint of another species. For they truly believe that they are only transferring chemicals coded in the genes and not anything unique to a specific animal. By this kind of reasoning, all of life becomes desacralized. All of life becomes reduced to a chemical level and becomes available for manipulation.

Some ethicists and professional observers of science say they are not concerned 25 about these first few experiments, but would be concerned with the transfer of more sophisticated genetic traits. Unfortunately, they fail to see that the blurring of species' borders begins the first moment a human gene is permanently implanted into the hereditary make-up of a mouse, pig or sheep. It is the first experiment that legitimizes the process. After all, if there is nothing particularly sacred about the human growth hormone gene, as researchers contend, then they might just as well argue that there is nothing particularly unique or special about all of the thousands of other individual genes that make-up the human gene pool. When it comes to more complex human traits (polygenic) that influence behavior and intellectual capacity, researchers will undoubtedly argue that they are not unique either, since they are merely a composite of the chemicals coded in the individual genes that make them up.

What, then, is unique about the human gene pool, or any other mammalian 26 gene pool? Nothing, if you view each species as merely the sum total of the chemicals coded in the individual genes that make it up. It is this radical new concept of life that legitimizes the idea of crossing all species' barriers, and undermines the inviolability of discrete, recognizable species in nature.

Many scientists contend that it would be wrong to discontinue these kinds of 27 experiments, because they broaden our field of knowledge. They rely on the rather clichéd argument that to halt such research would constitute a form of censorship. This is nonsense. Just because something can be done is no longer adequate justification for arguing that it should be done. The point is, it is a bit foolish to argue that every scientific experiment is worth pursuing. If certain types of scientific activity undermine the ethical principles and canons of civilization, we have an obligation to ourselves and future generations to be willing to say no. That doesn't make us guilty of stifling freedom of inquiry or "progress." It simply makes us responsible human beings.

Other proponents of this research argue that species have evolved, one from 28 the other over the long period of history and, as such, the process of genetic transfer is merely a speed up of evolutionary development. On the other hand, it is also true that since Homo sapiens have populated the earth, we have never once recorded an event where one species has mutated into another species. Even accepting that these occurrences have taken place before human eyes could have ever recorded the events, we know little or nothing about how or why such changes might have occurred. In contrast, with the new genetic technologies we have the tools to "evolve" our own concept of life in a dramatically short span of historical time. Should we allow the cultural biases of a particular moment in human history to dictate basic changes in the biological blueprint of animals and humans? Should social criteria like efficiency, profits, productivity and national security determine which traits should be transferred between species?

These are profound questions deserving long and prudent public debate. The time to discuss these questions is before the process unfolds, not after the technology has run its course.

Questions

1. How does Rifkin illustrate the statement that "living resources reproduce, but the life support systems that nourish them do not" (paragraph 1)?
2. Explain entropy and the Second Law of Thermodynamics. How do they support the same principle?
3. How do genetically engineered products differ from petrochemical ones? Why does Rifkin use petrochemical substances for his comparison? Why not hybrid foods?
4. How does ice-minus P-syringae illustrate the dangers of genetically engineered products? Does Rifkin only conjecture about possible risks, or does he present evidence of actual risks? Do you find his discussion of P-syringae persuasive?
5. On what evidence does Rifkin predict that a percentage of genetically engineered substances will prove dangerous? Might he have presented other evidence, or was he limited to the evidence that he cites?
6. How does Rifkin illustrate the "built-in assumptions" of genetic engineering?
7. Is Rifkin making a consequential or a deontological ethical argument (see Murray, p. 436) in opposing genetic engineering, or is he not concerned with the ethical implications of genetic engineering in this essay?
8. How does Rifkin respond to the arguments for research presented in paragraphs 27–28? What advantage does he gain by ending the essay with these responses? Would there be an advantage in responding earlier in the essay?

Suggestions for Writing

1. Discuss how Rifkin might respond to the argument, "Nothing ventured, nothing gained." Identify his key assumptions and show how you discover them in the essay.
2. Argue your own view on the issue of experimentation—specifically, whether the advantages of introducing ice-minus P-syringae are worth the risks. Defend your assumptions and beliefs.
3. Explain Rifkin's statement: "All great technological revolutions secure the present by mortgaging the future." State why you believe mortgaging the future is justifiable or unjustifiable. Identify your assumptions and defend them.

Additional Reading

Rifkin, Jeremy. *Algeny.* New York: Viking, 1983.
———. *Declaration of a Heretic.* Boston: Routledge and Kegan Paul, 1985.

Should Science Be Stopped? The Case of Recombinant DNA Research

Elliot S. Gershon

Elliot S. Gershon received his M.D. in psychiatry from Harvard University in 1965. Since 1969 he has done work in psychogenetics and neurogenetics at the National Institutes of Mental Health in Washington. His books include Impact of Biology on Modern Psychiatry *(1977) and* Genetic Research Strategies for Psychobiology and Psychiatry *(1981).*

In arguing for recombinant DNA and similar scientific research, Gershon gives a history of the controversy that began with the actions of two scientists who helped to isolate a DNA strand. The National Institutes of Health guidelines have been central to the issue, Gershon shows. In his concluding paragraphs, he considers the nature of scientific investigation. Scientists frequently point out that science is a neutral activity, and some of them go on to say that the consequences of scientific research should be the concern of social scientists and humanists, not of scientists. The scientist Glenn Seaborg states that "knowledge is born without moral properties. It is man who applies it according to his acquired patterns of behavior. . . . Man, not knowledge, is the cause of violence." This belief has been challenged anew in the debate over recombinant DNA, as Gershon's discussion of the issue shows. The notes throughout are Gershon's.

In 1970, shortly after the first isolation of a DNA fragment which constituted 1 a single identifiable gene, the young scientists involved in the project decided they would not continue their work on DNA. The reason, they reported, was that such work would eventually be put to evil uses by the large corporations and governments that control science.[1] They also believed it would lead to political oppression and the creation of so-called inferior subclasses of beings based on genetic classification.[2] Dr. James Shapiro, who was 26 at the time, announced he would leave science altogether for a career in radical politics; Dr. Jonathan Beckwith, who was then 33, shifted his work to other areas of genetics and became a leader of Science for the People. This is a radical group which several years later—during the height of the recombinant DNA debate—argued against permitting recombinant DNA research in the United States on the grounds that it was intrinsically dangerous to man and nature, and that this danger had been ignored by scientists concerned only with their immediate, personal advantage. Furthermore, the group argued, as social policy this research would diminish awareness of the social and political causes of health problems, and would allow genetics to be used as a tool

---

[1]R. Reinhold, "Scientists isolate a gene; step in heredity control," *New York Times,* (November 23, 1969); J.K. Glassman, "Harvard genetics researcher quits science for politics," *Science* 167 (1970): 963–964.
[2]J. Beckwith, "Social and political uses of genetics in the United States: Past and present," *Annals of the New York Academy of Sciences* 265 (1976): 46–58.

of social control against "the people." Emphasis on technological solutions to health problems, they declared, results in diversion or distraction from other goals that are essential for real social progress.[3]

Beckwith's and Shapiro's renunciations of their work seem to have had no effect whatever on subsequent developments in molecular genetics, because the dangers they described seemed utterly fantastic to scientists in the field and made no significant impression on public opinion. Only after the discovery of recombinant DNA did concern over genetics research become more widespread, and the political opponents of human genetics then joined forces with those concerned with the environmental and health effects of proposed laboratory experiments. 2

The movement these groups generated to stop recombinant DNA experimentation is a fascinating case of political-scientific controversy—in this instance, over the public perceptions of the imminent hazards of a new scientific or technical development. Among the numerous public health concerns in recent years, this one is important in several respects. For this movement failed to stop the technology, so the predictions of imminent hazard can now be tested against reality, and the intellectual and political agendas of the movement can be distinguished from its valid scientific claims. 3

The Recombinant Revolution

By 1970 the double-helix structure of DNA had been known for eighteen years, as had the fact that DNA stores genetic information in a linear sequence, much like a magnetic tape containing a computer program. Although it was not known in the 1950s, the magnetic tape analogy holds in nearly all respects, including splicing. Like a computer tape, the genetic code is translated into output, and the connection between specific nucleic-acid sequences (code) and specific amino-acid constituents of proteins (which are a principal output) had been discovered in 1961. What was not known in 1970, but was discovered shortly thereafter, was that segments of DNA genetic code can be spliced together precisely from virtually any source. When the splice is between DNA from different species, the result is "recombinant DNA." Copies of one segment of code can be inserted onto other areas of the same "reel"—that is, the same chromosome in the case of higher organisms—or onto different "reels." These processes can occur *in nature*, as well as in the laboratory; this was not demonstrated until 1977, though, after critics had advanced the argument that the production of recombinant DNA was a new evolutionary event, one that would violate natural barriers and result in the production of dangerous new species.[4] The mobility of genes in nature had been one of the hardest concepts for the scientific community, and for intelligent people in general, to appreciate. (Gene rearrangement had actually been demonstrated in maize before the helical structure of DNA was known, but the work had been dismissed.) The growing opinion 4

---

[3]Science for the People, "Biological, social and political issues in genetic engineering," in *The Recombinant DNA Debate*, eds., D.A. Jackson and S.P. Stich (Englewood Cliffs, New Jersey, Prentice-Hall, 1979) pp. 99–126.

[4]S. Chang and S.N. Cohen, "In vivo site-specific genetic recombination promoted by EcoRI restriction endonuclease," *Proceedings of the National Academy of Sciences of the USA* 74 (1977): 4811–4815.

now is that genetic deletions, insertions, duplications, inversions, and other rearrange-
ments and migrations are the major source of genetic change and variation in nature,
and this view has led to a reassessment of evolutionary theories of continuous and gradual change, in favor of those crediting sudden genetic events as major factors in evolution.

The isolation of bacterial enzymes that can splice together DNA from different 5
species was an historic development in molecular genetics. Scientists quickly realized
that these enzymes, called "restriction endonucleases" or "restriction enzymes," could
be used to place a gene in a context in which it could be reproduced and possibly function. (The work of Beckwith and his colleagues had isolated the gene in a form in which
it would not function or reproduce, thereby preventing gene cloning or the expression
of gene products.) The first scientists to use restriction enzymes to form recombinant
DNA from different species considered this a unique and far reaching event; talk of "new
life forms" circulated in the scientific community and in the press.[5] The excitement
generated by these first experiments has endured to this day, fueled by a series of scientific advances that followed the new ability to isolate and clone specific genes, as well as
by numerous Nobel prizes and by the financial community's interest.

But serious concerns followed the same experiments. In 1971, Paul Berg (who 6
later won a Nobel prize for his role in developing recombinant DNA) and a student
planned to produce a hybrid of two viruses, SV40 and lambda. When this plan was announced at a conference, the discussants noted that SV40 is a mammalian tumor virus
and lambda is a virus of E. coli, the common bacteria of the human intestinal tract. The
obvious question was raised: Could not this experiment produce organisms with the potential ability to spread epidemics of cancer? As it happens, the specific experiment as
proposed would have interrupted the reproduction genes of lambda, and so the products
would have constituted no danger; but this was not known at the time, and the concerns
were of a more general nature and had to be considered very seriously.

Self-regulation Begins

There were two kinds of scientific concerns—specific fears of identifiable risks 7
associated with specific experiments, and general fears of cataclysmic dangers if this research were pursued. At a 1973 Gordon Conference, a group of molecular biologists
formed a committee chaired by Berg, and sponsored by the prestigious National Academy of Sciences, to take up the entire question. In a now famous pair of identical letters
to *Science* and *Nature*—famous in part because a Nobel prize seems to have come to
each signer—the committee warned of "potential biohazards of recombinant DNA molecules." Although they addressed the general possibility that "new DNA elements . . .
might possibly become widely disseminated among human, bacterial, plant, or animal
populations with unpredictable effects," their recommendations to laboratory scientists
were limited to a few specific types of experiments. A moratorium was proposed on the

[5]S.N. Cohen, A.C.Y. Chang, H.W. Boyer, R.B. Helling, "Construction of biologically functional plasmids in vitro," *Proceedings of the National Academy of the Sciences of the USA* 70 (1973): 3240–3244.

introduction of new antibiotic resistance or bacterial toxin genes into bacteria that did not normally carry these genes, and on the introduction of DNA from tumor viruses or other animal viruses into autonomously reproducing DNA elements.[6]

The same committee convened an international meeting at Asilomar, Califor- 8 nia, early the next year, whose goal was to devise safeguards "so evidently tight that no one could accuse scientists of [being] self-serving," as the senior British delegate eventually persuaded the conferees. The Berg committee also proposed that the director of the National Institutes of Health (NIH) appoint a committee to advise him on establishing safety procedures for these studies within the United States. These standards would be enforced through the NIH and other government agencies that disburse government research grants.

The 1975 international meeting at Asilomar established the safety principles 9 for DNA studies that were eventually adopted in the U.S. (as the "NIH guidelines") and in most other countries. The two guiding principles were: *containment* of the experiments within specially constructed laboratories, based on the established practices of scientists working with contagious diseases and tumor viruses; and the use of *enfeebled vectors* (carrier organisms) for the recombinant DNA molecules. The vectors consist of mutated strains of the intestinal bacteria E. coli which, even if they should escape the experiment and enter a human gut, could survive only a very short time.[7]

Having established these principles, the Asilomar conference also voted to end 10 the voluntary moratorium on recombinant DNA experiments. The conferees were well aware that their recommendations were going to be questioned outside the scientific community, in fact, one of the main reasons for drawing them up was the concern, voiced by Stanley Cohen of Stanford, that "if the collected wisdom of this group doesn't result in recommendations, the recommendations may come from other groups less well qualified." Despite this pressure, the scientific community generally felt that these scientists had performed a valuable public service. Writing about Paul Berg, who chaired the Asilomar conference, the science journalist Nicholas Wade wrote, "Probably few other people could have asked for a moratorium, got it to stick worldwide, and then handled the issue with the openness and disinterest that disarmed resentment and led the world's scientific community to a notable and generally harmonious consensus."[8]

Washington Waits And Watches

In November 1975 the NIH advisory committee published its own proposed 11 guidelines, which followed the Asilomar principles of containment and enfeebled vectors, but which were considerably stricter about the levels of safety protection required for particular types of experiments. At this point, NIH invited public comment on the guidelines before they went into effect. What came forth was severe apprehension about

---

[6]P. Berg et al., letter to the editor: "Potential biohazards of recombinant DNA molecules," *Science* 185 (1974): 303.

[7]P. Berg et al., "Asilomar conference on recombinant DNA molecules," *Science* 188 (1975): 991–994.

[8]N. Wade, "Genetics: Conference sets strict rules to replace moratorium," *Science* 187 (1975): 931–935.

the entire technology, fears of worldwide cataclysm, and calls to stop this research entirely, or at least to establish multiple and restrictive levels of regulation. These criticisms were repeatedly voiced in scientific journals and public forums, and before legislative committees. For example, Dr. Erwin Chargaff wrote to *Science* that:

> a bizarre problem is posed by recent attempts to make so-called genetic engineering palatable to the public . . . what seems to have been disregarded completely is that we are dealing here much more with an ethical problem than with one in public health, and that the principal question to be answered is whether we have the right to put an additional fearful load on generations that are not yet born. I use the adjective 'additional' in view of the unresolved and equally fearful problem of the disposal of nuclear waste. Our time is cursed with the necessity for feeble men, masquerading as experts, to make enormously far-reaching decisions. Is there anything more far-reaching than the creation of new forms of life? . . . But beyond all this, there arises a general problem of the greatest significance, namely, the awesome irreversibility of what is being contemplated. You can stop splitting the atom; you can stop visiting the moon; you can stop using aerosols; you may even decide not to kill entire populations by the use of a few bombs. But you cannot recall a new form of life . . . An irreversible attack on the biosphere is something so unheard-of, so unthinkable to previous generations, that I could only wish that mine had not been guilty of it. The hybridization of Prometheus with Herostratus is bound to give evil results.[9]

Dr. Robert Sinsheimer, a participant in the Asilomar conference who later 12 came out in favor of a permanent moratorium on recombinant DNA experiments because of their evolutionary danger, criticized scientists who proclaimed a right to free inquiry, yet were oblivious to the evolutionary and social dangers of this particular inquiry. A governmental authority, he argued, must take responsibility for and restrain this "great and terrible power."[10] Numerous other calls for regulation were voiced by environmentalists, by radical groups such as Science for the People, and by others.

These views found a measure of support in Washington. Senators Edward Kennedy and Jacob Javits wrote to President Ford in July 1976, shortly after the NIH guidelines were officially released, that they were: 13

> gravely concerned that these relatively stringent [NIH] guidelines may not be implemented in all sectors of the domestic and international research communities and that the public will therefore be subjected to undue risk . . . We urge you to implement these [NIH] guidelines immediately whenever possible by executive directive and/or rulemaking, and to explore every possible mechanism to assure compliance . . .[11]

---

[9]E. Chargaff, letter to the editor: "On the dangers of genetic meddling," *Science* 192 (1976): 938–939.

[10]L.R. Sinsheimer, "Two lectures on recombinant DNA research" in *The Recombinant DNA Debate*, eds. Jackson and Stich.

[11]J.P. Swazey, J.R. Sorenson, C.B. Wong, "Risks and benefits, rights and responsibilities: A history of the recombinant DNA research controversy," *Southern California Law Review* 51 (1978): 1019–1078.

Senator Kennedy favored more public participation in science, and had been critical of scientists for making public policy in private. Several bills submitted to Congress in 1977 had provisions for federal licensing and inspection of laboratories, complex reporting systems, and fines of thousands of dollars for scientists who violated the rules.[12]

The bill proposed by Senator Kennedy would have established an independent 14 national regulatory commission specifically for recombinant DNA research. It was to be comprised primarily of nonscientists, and would control all research in this field (except that local communities could set more severe restrictions, or ban the research altogether). Barbara J. Culliton remarked in *Science* that, in the minds of many biologists, Kennedy's bill assumed the character of a monster as fearsome as any biological mutant one could imagine coming from a recombinant DNA laboratory.

During most of 1977 there was a scramble among government agencies to ac- 15 quire this new regulatory territory. Fortunately, however, disagreements among legislators prevented any one of the proposed bills from being passed quickly. For during that year, a consensus developed among many scientists that the risks of recombinant DNA research were, at worst, very much smaller than they themselves had previously estimated, and perhaps nonexistent. This consensus grew after S. Chang and S.N. Cohen demonstrated that recombinant DNA is also produced in nature.[13] Cohen and other scientists succeeded in gaining the attention of several concerned Senators, including Senator Kennedy, and impressed them with these new scientific assessments. In September, Senator Adlai Stevenson called on the Senate to put off legislation in order not to act in haste, and Senator Kennedy withdrew support from his own bill, joining with the view that the hazards were questionable rather than imminent.

The paper by Chang and Cohen was a scientific turning point in the debate be- 16 cause it demonstrated that recombinant DNA production is not an unprecedented tampering with the balance of nature. In retrospect, it is surprising that scientists assumed for so long that recombinant DNA production, a process that depends on natural biological products such as the restriction endonucleases, would have occurred only in the laboratory.[14] Perhaps most importantly, the research and the warnings of hazard had gone on for years, but *nothing had happened.* By the end of 1978, only the most activist

---

[12]The historical account here relies heavily on the cited reports by three reporters for the journal *Science:* Nicholas Wade, Barbara J. Culliton, and Eliot Marshal.

[13]Chang and Cohen, "In vivo site-specific genetic recombination promoted by EcoRI restriction endonuclease."

[14]Even before the restriction enzymes were discovered, there were numerous examples in nature of gene transfer between species. Many viral infections of bacteria, plants, and animals require that the genes of the virus be spliced onto the genes of the host cell on infection, and out of the infected cells on release of the virus. Often host genes are carried out from one host by viruses capable of infecting another. A plant globin gene has since been identified in nitrogen fixing plants whose functioning genetic code as well as nonfunctioning intervening code sequences are identical to animal globin, which demonstrates, in a most ancient example, evolution accommodating gene transfer between two higher organisms. It may be argued that a very large number of gene exchanges are possible, too many to expect that any gene combination a scientist might produce has already occurred in nature. But this is now a quantitative argument of how often it occurs, rather than an argument that, absent our laboratories, recombination would never occur. We live in a planet where life is very ancient, so that an astronomical number of genetic recombinations will have time to occur over the course of a billion and a half years of evolution, and this implies that the random probability of deleterious exchanges (that is, of the accidentally cataclysmic kind feared by Chargaff) must be vanishingly low.

environmentalist groups were opposing recombinant DNA research, and even they were under severe internal criticism from scientists who were prominent trustees of groups such as Friends of the Earth and the Natural Resources Defense Council. The environmentalist movement was accused of scaremongering, willfully disregarding all evidence, singlemindedly pursuing a general interest in slowing down technology, and protecting its political investment in hobbling DNA research. James D. Watson wrote in the *Washington Post* that "such groups thrive on bad news, and the more the public worries about the environment, the more likely we are to keep providing them with the funds that they need to keep their organizations going. So if they do not watch themselves, they will always opt for the worst possible scenario."[15]

No Apocalypse

Enough time has passed to state that no catastrophe was truly imminent at the 17 time of the great controversies (leaving aside speculation that the course of history will eventually provide the predicted disaster). It is therefore appropriate to ask how the Cassandras of genetic disaster came to be so wrong in their expectations, and what else might have alarmed and misled them.

Fear and hostility toward science and technology were rampant in the United 18 States at the time of the recombinant DNA debate, and in the pronouncements (and presumably the minds) of the alarmists there was a fusion of fears: fear of nuclear wastes, fear of chemical pollution of the earth and its atmosphere, and fear of evil, ambitious, and self-serving scientists and doctors. These led to the numerous apocalyptic predictions and distortions of judgment that only fear and hostility can promote. During the same period we were told by responsible committees and observers that there would be worldwide famine by 1975, that the majority of cancers was caused by pollution, that the ozone layer of the atmosphere would disappear, and that we would never again have enough petroleum. Each of these predictions was false. I would not characterize all predictions of holocaust and cataclysm as psychological distortions of judgment, but in hindsight these clearly were.

Many of the strongest opponents of recombinant DNA studies—such as Jon 19 Beckwith, George Wald, and the Science for the People organization—were already firmly established in the intellectual American left. The militant environmentalists who continued to oppose the research after 1978 find their roots and support in the same political outlook. Coming as they do from the political left, their arguments and proposals rest on two premises. The first is that governmental control (by the right government) is progressive and will serve the interests of "the people." The second—a profoundly conservative belief that underlies much of the American left's approach to technology—is summed up in the words of M.B. Williams: "Damage resulting from natural processes which humans might have prevented is morally preferable to damage resulting from human action."[16] This second premise stands in opposition to a pragmatic weighing of costs and benefits; subscribers to it will feel perfectly justified in magnifying potential

---

[15]J.D. Watson, *Washington Post* (May 14, 1978).
[16]M.B. Williams, "Ethical theories underlying the recombinant DNA controversy," in *Recombinant DNA: Science Ethics and Politics,* ed., J. Richards (New York: Academic Press, 1978) pp. 177–190.

dangers and ignoring potential benefits. Daniel Callahan argued the point this way: "There might be a loss to human progress if the research is not pursued, but it is difficult to see how there could be a claim that a failure to pursue the research would be in itself immoral . . . it is *our* lives which may be gambled with . . . *our* decision to make."[17] Of course, there is no logical basis for preferring one kind of damage or loss to another, and there is no justification for the moral superiority Callahan and others arrogate to themselves. (The argument, however, is especially compatible with the temperament of the American left, which views science and technology as aspects of American society that are antithetical to its interests and philosophy, and which despairs of all benefits, and detects all manner of dangers, in science.)

If we take the arguments of those who would have restricted DNA experiments 20 as predictions of what would happen if the research were to proceed, the predictions were uniformly wrong—not only about the dangers involved, but also about the uses of the research results. There was the charge that DNA research would lead to genetic stigmatization for political purposes, and that genetics research would divert funds and attention from true health needs. Yet the first human genetic disorder diagnosed by recombinant DNA methods was sickle cell anemia, which is found mainly among blacks, and which can be diagnosed *in utero* only by DNA technology. These findings are now universally considered a welcome clinical advance. There is no one to my knowledge who has raised the issue of "stigmatization" with regard to this or other genetic diseases (mainly hematologic and immunologic disorders) which are now being diagnosed by these techniques.

And the contribution of science and medical technology to the health of the 21 American people over the past fifty years can hardly be questioned. The problems for which scientific advances have proved crucial could not have been solved by redistribution of care or environmental manipulation; rather, these advances depended on a sympathetic political and economic climate for basic research. The long delay between the discovery of penicillin in the 1920s and its application to human disease in the 1940s is largely attributable to the withering away of medical research during the Great Depression. The eradication of polio depended on live virus research during the 1950s that might have been discouraged in today's political environment; in which case, it has been said, we might now have hundreds of thousands of well-functioning, miniaturized iron lungs instead of an eradicated disease.

The costs to scientific progress of a prolonged moratorium only become evi- 22 dent if a moratorium is unsuccessful, or when it ends. Had the moratorium of 1974–75 been made permanent, either voluntarily or by legislative fiat, the cost would have been the loss of the medical benefits we now enjoy. These are most impressive: They include new diagnostic methods and investigative techniques in medicine and agriculture; new availability in large quantities of biological products such as interferon and certain human hormones; and non-infective viral proteins for use as vaccines. Moreover, the potential application of this technology to virtually every area of biology, medicine, and agriculture seems even more promising now than then.

---

[17]D. Callahan, "Ethical prerequisites for examining biological research: the case of recombinant DNA," in *Recombinant DNA: Science Ethics and Politics,* ed., J. Richards, pp. 135–148.

Should We Regulate the Future?

If it is made into an ethical principle, the belief in popular (or governmental) 23 control over all scientific activity can undermine a realistic assessment of how much control can actually be exercised. The degree to which prohibited activities will escape all controls may be underestimated, and the ability of scientific research to proceed in the face of controls and moratoria will be overestimated.

When Congress considered new laws regulating DNA research, the legislative 24 remedies all consisted of regulations on the conduct of experiments and reporting requirements, at the very minimum extending the recently enacted NIH guidelines to research activity not supported by NIH. It is hard to imagine rules such as these protecting us against the risk that somewhere in the world someone will conduct an experiment that will destroy us all. After all, the materials and equipment needed to set up such experiments on a small scale are very modest (perhaps $150,000 startup costs, $100,000 yearly expenses, and two persons working full-time). The international multibillion-dollar traffic in illicit drugs is testimony to the impossibility of complete regulation of the genetic recombination technology, since such technology also has enormous commercial appeal and ready availability of materials and knowledge.

From a certain point of view, however, legislative and administrative regula- 25 tion seemed a compelling necessity in 1977, and the agonized protests of scientists in the field seemed foolish. During that year a legislative aide to a congressional subcommittee on Health and the Environment, expecting legislative regulation to prevail, described the scientists' response to proposed legislation in this way:

> Nevertheless, the greatest fear response exhibited by any group came from the scientists as soon as legislation was proposed. It was particularly frustrating for me to deal with a barrage of protests so fraught with a nearly total lack of understanding of administrative law, often a lack of knowledge of the content of particular bills and a failure to distinguish between the various House and Senate bills. The extent to which bills are misunderstood, misinterpreted and false conclusions drawn from them was unbelievable.
>
> . . . The most offensive features of this reaction of scientists was not their initial ignorance and naivity—that can be forgiven—but their subsequent refusal to learn. Numerous briefings were held and memoranda written to explain in detail how each section of the House bill should be interpreted, but a significant segment of the scientific establishment resolutely held steadfast to their misconceptions and false conclusions. This was something worse than hubris and basically unforgivable. . . .
>
> . . . one must conclude that this was purely an instinctive, emotional and defensive response to fear . . . But fear of what? How could the mere extension of safety standards by law pose such a threat?
>
> Clearly, if the purpose and content of legislation had been understood in the first place, it wouldn't have been perceived as a threat at all. But since it was somehow regarded as control of the content of scientific research, where scientists were to be sent to jail for forgetting to plug a pipette, no wonder such a frozen state of emotional intransigence resulted.[18]

---

[18]B.K. Zimmerman, "Beyond recombinant DNA—Two views of the future," in *Recombinant DNA: Science Ethics and Politics*, ed., J. Richards, pp. 273–301.

But from another point of view, the fears that were truly unreasonable were the 26 fears of imminent genetic catastrophe. The scientists were engaging in political debate and a lobbying effort that was well within the American tradition, and which was ultimately successful. The worst thing that could have happened in 1977, from their viewpoint (and, I believe, from the viewpoint of the public interest), was for legislation to be enacted. No matter how carefully worded, by its very existence legislation would have been a triumph for the cataclysmic fears and the political ideology of the left.

The scientists did not fear the NIH guidelines, which were more easily subject 27 to modification as new knowledge developed, whereas modifying legislation is a more cumbersome process. Legislation would have reified the existing guidelines just at the point when they seemed less and less scientifically justifiable. In succeeding years the NIH guidelines have gradually eased on the basis of the scientific knowledge developed since the original concerns came up. In 1981, the NIH Director's recombinant DNA advisory committee recommended that virtually all the remaining *requirements* be converted to *recommendations,* since federal controls no longer seemed necessary.

Yet because of the existing regulatory burdens of the NIH guidelines, there still 28 may be hidden costs that we are in fact not paying. No American university or hospital committee has seen fit to approve a human gene-transplantation experiment. The only scientist known to have attempted this was severely censured, and suffered loss of grant support for violating NIH guidelines.[19] The clinical trials have been described as unduly heroic and unjustifiably premature, but not as having endangered the two terminally-ill patients who participated. Since the guidelines existed as official policy, it was wrong to violate them, but his censure may prevent him or other like-minded physicians from in fact making a breakthrough. Absent the NIH regulations, the experiment might still have been criticized, but trials of this kind might not have been so effectively inhibited.

The Art of Scientific Discovery

The nature of scientific creativity is such that the effects of a moratorium or 29 overly-strict regulation can be devastating, and not quickly reversed. Science, like the arts, intensely absorbs the individual. The creative agonies in science—with its manic-depressive extremes of elation and depression, and the very immediate and personal rewards for scientific achievement—are much like those in the arts. For virtually all scientists who have made great discoveries, there are a few good years of great activity during which most of their important work is done; later they create mainly through their younger colleagues. To forbid a scientist those early years is to ruin the work of a lifetime. What Beckwith and his colleagues gave up in their moratorium is something of great personal value to a scientist, and is not easily yielded.

Consider the resistance to censorship of artists in totalitarian countries. Some 30 of them manage to continue, but art does not flourish. Like the arts, genetic research and thought have been under severe political pressure during much of this century. The

---

[19]G.B. Kolata and N. Wade, "Human gene treatment stirs new debate," *Science* 210 (1980): 407; N. Wade, "UCLA gene therapy racked by friendly fire," *Science* 210 (1980): 509–511; N. Wade, "Gene therapy caught in more entanglements," *Science* 212 (1981): 24–25.

triumph of environment over genetics—as embodied in the suppression of Mendelian genetics and the stranglehold of Lysenko—was proclaimed as official Soviet dogma during the time of Stalin. Lysenko's role was not weakened until after the ouster of Khrushchev. As a result, agricultural breeding efforts, which should have been cut and dried scientific experiments, were uniformly unsuccessful, and the Green Revolution began elsewhere. Soviet scientists are still struggling to overcome this lag in genetics. Nazism, whose ideology was a perversion of genetic and evolutionary science, has led to an intellectual inability to confront human genetic diversity today, and so contributed to anti-scientific movements against human genetics.

A Retrospective Judgment

In the light of our current knowledge, the moratorium of 1974–75 and the reg- 31 ulatory mechanism that emerged afterwards can be seen as successful and sober responses to nature and to political realities. The moratorium may have been the product of apocalyptic fears, but it did give rise to a careful judgment of the possible environmental hazards. The scientists involved managed to find a way to avoid paralyzing an important human endeavor, and through their irreproachably responsible actions managed to maintain public confidence in their activities. The bureaucratic structure set up by the U.S. government through the NIH regulations was successful in developing a scientific consensus, involving the public, and capable of being modified with great flexibility in response to new scientific findings. On the other hand, the radical opposition to recombinant DNA research should be judged harshly for the political agenda behind its ostensibly environmental concerns, and for its gross failure to evaluate correctly the actual dangers and benefits of recombinant DNA research.

Questions

1. What aspects of the recombinant DNA controversy does Gershon stress in his account? Does he suggest that the controversy is different from past controversies over scientific research?
2. What is Gershon's own argument in favor of recombinant DNA research?
3. In noting that genetic engineering will continue to produce valuable products like interferon, is Gershon implying that these gains justify possible risks, or does he deny that a risk exists?
4. Does Gershon dispute the statement of Dr. Erwin Chargaff that "Our time is cursed with the necessity for feeble men, masquerading as experts, to make enormously far-reaching decisions"? Does he say or imply that adequate safeguards against incompetence or malice now exist, or that they are unnecessary?
5. What is the "political agenda" of opponents of recombinant DNA, according to Gershon, and why should this opposition "be judged harshly"?
6. What has been the value or usefulness of the controversy, according to Gershon?
7. What assumptions concerning science and research shape Gershon's argument? Are these assumptions stated or implied?
8. How persuasive do you find Gershon's argument?

Suggestions for Writing

1. Discuss whether Gershon's argument in favor of continuing research into recombinant DNA is consequential or deontological or both. See T. H. Murray's discussion of these types of ethical argument.
2. Many argue that scientific experiments and processes that pose a risk to future generations should be strictly controlled or banned by the government. Should limits be imposed by the government or the scientific community in the United States or the world on research into biological and chemical toxins? Should scientists refuse to participate in research into weapons of war or possible pollutants? Focus your argument on a single example pertinent to the issue—for example, recombinant DNA or the production of nuclear power. Present information on potential risks from various sources (books, journal articles, newspaper and magazine articles). Document your sources carefully.

Additional Reading

Huxley, Aldous. *Brave New World.* New York: Harper and Row, 1932.
———. *Brave New World Revisited.* New York: Harper and Row, 1965.
Nossal, G. J. V. *Reshaping Life: Key Issues in Genetic Engineering.* New York: Cambridge University Press, 1985.

The Hazards of Science

Lewis Thomas

Dr. Lewis Thomas writes about scientific research from long experience as a physician and medical researcher. He practiced medicine and taught at various hospitals and medical schools before becoming chairman of pathology and medicine and dean of New York University–Bellevue Medical Center. He also has served as chairman of the pathology department and dean of Yale Medical School, and as chancellor of Memorial Sloan–Kettering Cancer Center in New York City. His numerous essays in the New England Journal of Medicine *have been collected in* Lives of a Cell *(1974),* The Medusa and the Snail *(1979), and* Late Night Thoughts on Listening to Mahler's Ninth Symphony *(1983). In* The Youngest Science *(1983), his account of his scientific career, Dr. Thomas makes the following assessment:*

> Human beings are getting themselves, and the rest of the world, into deeper and deeper trouble, and I would not lay heavy odds on our survival unless we begin maturing soon. Up to now, we have been living through the equivalent of an early childhood for our species. . . .

Thermonuclear war is the worst case to contemplate, enough in itself to cause the crash of the species, but we have other threats to make against our lasting existence: overpopulation and crash, deforestation and crash, pollution and crash, a long list of possible bad dreams come true, the sounds, always outside the window offstage, of the destruction of the orchard. With luck we may come through. The luck will have to be incalculable, and unbelievably on our side over the next few decades. The good thought I have about this is that we are, to begin with, the most improbable of all the earth's creatures, and maybe it is not beyond hope that we are also endowed with improbable luck.

The code word for criticism of science and scientists these days is "hubris." 1 Once you've said that word, you've said it all; it sums up, in a word, all of today's apprehensions and misgivings in the public mind—not just about what is perceived as the insufferable attitude of the scientists themselves but, enclosed in the same word, what science and technology are perceived to be doing to make this century, this near to its ending, turn out so wrong.

"Hubris" is a powerful word, containing layers of powerful meaning, derived 2 from a very old world, but with a new life of its own, growing way beyond the limits of its original meaning. Today, it is strong enough to carry the full weight of disapproval for the cast of mind that thought up atomic fusion and fission as ways of first blowing up and later heating cities as well as the attitudes which led to strip-mining, offshore oil wells, Kepone, food additives, SSTs, and the tiny spherical particles of plastic recently discovered clogging the waters of the Sargasso Sea.

The biomedical sciences are now caught up with physical science and technol- 3 ogy in the same kind of critical judgment, with the same pejorative word. Hubris is responsible, it is said, for the whole biological revolution. It is hubris that has given us the prospects of behavior control, psychosurgery, fetal research, heart transplants, the cloning of prominent politicians from bits of their own eminent tissue, iatrogenic disease, overpopulation, and recombinant DNA. This last, the new technology that permits the stitching of one creature's genes into the DNA of another, to make hybrids, is currently cited as the ultimate example of hubris. It is hubris for man to manufacture a hybrid on his own.

So now we are back to the first word again, from "hybrid" to "hubris," and the 4 hidden meaning of two beings joined unnaturally together by man is somehow retained. Today's joining is straight out of Greek mythology: it is the combining of man's capacity with the special prerogative of the gods, and it is really in this sense of outrage that the word "hubris" is being used today. That is what the word has grown into, a warning, a code word, a shorthand signal from the language itself: if man starts doing things reserved for the gods, deifying himself, the outcome will be something worse for him, symbolically, than the litters of wild boars and domestic sows were for the ancient Romans.

To be charged with hubris is therefore an extremely serious matter, and not to 5 be dealt with by murmuring things about antiscience and antiintellectualism, which is what many of us engaged in science tend to do these days. The doubts about our enterprise have their origin in the most profound kind of human anxiety. If we are right and the critics are wrong, then it has to be that the word "hubris" is being mistakenly employed, that this is not what we are up to, that there is, for the time being anyway, a fundamental misunderstanding of science.

I suppose there is one central question to be dealt with, and I am not at all sure 6 how to deal with it, although I am quite certain about my own answer to it. It is this: are there some kinds of information leading to some sorts of knowledge that human beings are really better off not having? Is there a limit to scientific inquiry not set by what is knowable but by what we *ought* to be knowing? Should we stop short of learning about some things, for fear of what we are, or someone, will do with the knowledge? My own answer is a flat no, but I must confess that this is an intuitive response and I am neither inclined nor trained to reason my way through it.

There has been some effort, in and out of scientific quarters, to make recombi- 7 nant DNA into the issue on which to settle this argument. Proponents of this line of research are accused of pure hubris, of assuming the rights of gods, of arrogance and outrage; what is more, they confess themselves to be in the business of making live hybrids with their own hands. The mayor of Cambridge and the attorney general of New York have both been advised to put a stop to it, forthwith.

It is not quite the same sort of argument, however, as the one about limiting 8 knowledge, although this is surely part of it. The knowledge is already here, and the rage of the argument is about its application in technology. Should DNA for making certain useful or interesting proteins be incorporated into *E. coli* plasmids or not? Is there a risk of inserting the wrong sort of toxins or hazardous viruses, and then having the new hybrid organisms spread beyond the laboratory? Is this a technology for creating new varieties of pathogens, and should it be stopped because of this?

If the argument is held to this level, I can see no reason why it cannot be set- 9 tled, by reasonable people. We have learned a great deal about the handling of dangerous microbes in the last century, although I must say that the opponents of recombinant-DNA research tend to downgrade this huge body of information. At one time or another, agents as hazardous as those of rabies, psittacosis, plague, and typhus have been dealt with by investigators in secure laboratories, with only rare instances of self-infection of the investigators themselves, and no instances at all of epidemics. It takes some high imagining to postulate the creation of brand new pathogens so wild and voracious as to spread from equally secure laboratories to endanger human life at large, as some of the arguers are now maintaining.

But this is precisely the trouble with the recombinant-DNA problem: it has be- 10 come an emotional issue, with too many irretrievably lost tempers on both sides. It has lost the sound of a discussion of technological safety, and begins now to sound like something else, almost like a religious controversy, and here it is moving toward the central issue: are there some things in science we should not be learning about?

There is an inevitably long list of hard questions to follow this one, beginning 11 with the one which asks whether the mayor of Cambridge should be the one to decide, first off.

Maybe we'd be wiser, all of us, to back off before the recombinant-DNA issue 12 becomes too large to cope with. If we're going to have a fight about it, let it be confined to the immediate issue of safety and security, of the recombinants now under consideration, and let us by all means have regulations and guidelines to assure the public safety wherever these are indicated or even suggested. But if it is possible let us stay off that question about limiting human knowledge. It is too loaded, and we'll simply not be able to cope with it.

By this time it will have become clear that I have already taken sides in the 13 matter, and my point of view is entirely prejudiced. This is true, but with a qualification. I am not so much in favor of recombinant-DNA research as I am opposed to the opposition to this line of inquiry. As a longtime student of infectious-disease agents I do not take kindly the declarations that we do not know how to keep from catching things in laboratories, much less how to keep them from spreading beyond the laboratory walls. I believe we learned a lot about this sort of thing, long ago. Moreover, I regard it as a form of hubris-in-reverse to claim that man can make deadly pathogenic microorganisms so easily. In my view, it takes a long time and a great deal of interliving before a microbe can become a successful pathogen. Pathogenicity is, in a sense, a highly skilled trade, and only a tiny minority of all the numberless tons of microbes on the earth has ever been involved itself in it; most bacteria are busy with their own business, browsing and recycling the rest of life. Indeed, pathogenicity often seems to me a sort of biological accident in which signals are misdirected by the microbe or misinterpreted by the host, as in the case of endotoxin, or in which the intimacy between host and microbe is of such long standing that a form of molecular mimicry becomes possible, as in the case of diphtheria toxin. I do not believe that by simply putting together new combinations of genes one can create creatures as highly skilled and adapted for dependence as a pathogen must be, any more than I have ever believed that microbial life from the moon or Mars could possibly make a living on this planet.

But, as I said, I'm not at all sure this is what the argument is really about. Be- 14 hind it is that other discussion, which I wish we would not have to become enmeshed in.

I cannot speak for the physical sciences, which have moved an immense dis- 15 tance in this century by any standard, but it does seem to me that in the biological and medical sciences we are still far too ignorant to begin making judgments about what sorts of things we should be learning or not learning. To the contrary, we ought to be grateful for whatever snatches we can get hold of, and we ought to be out there on a much larger scale than today's, looking for more.

We should be very careful with that word "hubris," and make sure it is not used 16 when not warranted. There is a great danger in applying it to the search for knowledge. The application of knowledge is another matter, and there is hubris in plenty in our technology, but I do not believe that looking for new information about nature, at whatever level, can possibly be called unnatural. Indeed, if there is any single attribute of human beings, apart from language, which distinguishes them from all other creatures on earth, it is their insatiable, uncontrollable drive to learn things and then to exchange the information with others of the species. Learning is what we do, when you think about it. I cannot think of a human impulse more difficult to govern.

But I can imagine lots of reasons for trying to govern it. New information about 17 nature is very likely, at the outset, to be upsetting to someone or other. The recombinant-DNA line of research is already upsetting, not because of the dangers now being argued about but because it is disturbing, in a fundamental way, to face the fact that the genetic machinery in control of the planet's life can be fooled around with so easily. We do not like the idea that anything so fixed and stable as a species line can be changed. The notion that genes can be taken out of one genome and inserted in another is unnerving. Classical mythology is peopled with mixed beings—part man, part animal or plant—and most of them are associated with tragic stories. Recombinant DNA is a reminder of bad dreams.

The easiest decision for society to make in matters of this kind is to appoint an 18 agency, or a commission, or a subcommittee within an agency to look into the problem and provide advice. And the easiest course for a committee to take, when confronted by any process that appears to be disturbing people or making them uncomfortable, is to recommend that it be stopped, at least for the time being.

I can easily imagine such a committee, composed of unimpeachable public fig- 19 ures, arriving at the decision that the time is not quite ripe for further exploration of the transplantation of genes, that we should put this off for a while, maybe until next century, and get on with other affairs that make us less discomfited. Why not do science on something more popular, say, how to get solar energy more cheaply? Or mental health?

The trouble is, it would be very hard to stop once this line was begun. There 20 are, after all, all sorts of scientific inquiry that are not much liked by one constituency or another, and we might soon find ourselves with crowded rosters, panels, standing committees, set up in Washington for the appraisal, and then the regulation, of research. Not on grounds of the possible value and usefulness of the new knowledge, mind you, but for guarding society against scientific hubris, against the kinds of knowledge we're better off without.

It would be absolutely irresistible as a way of spending time, and people would 21 form long queues for membership. Almost anything would be fair game, certainly anything to do with genetics, anything relating to population control, or, on the other side, research on aging. Very few fields would get by, except perhaps for some, like mental health, in which nobody really expects anything much to happen, surely nothing new or disturbing.

The research areas in the greatest trouble would be those already containing a 22 sense of bewilderment and surprise, with discernible prospects of upheaving present dogmas.

It is hard to predict how science is going to turn out, and if it is really good sci- 23 ence it is impossible to predict. This is in the nature of the enterprise. If the things to be found are actually new, they are by definition unknown in advance, and there is no way of telling in advance where a really new line of inquiry will lead. You cannot make choices in this matter, selecting things you think you're going to like and shutting off the lines that make for discomfort. You either have science or you don't, and if you have it you are obliged to accept the surprising and disturbing pieces of information, even the overwhelming and upheaving ones, along with the neat and promptly useful bits. It is like that.

The only solid piece of scientific truth about which I feel totally confident is 24 that we are profoundly ignorant about nature. Indeed, I regard this as the major discovery of the past hundred years of biology. It is, in its way, an illuminating piece of news.

It would have amazed the brightest minds of the eighteenth-century Enlightenment to be told by any of us how little we know, and how bewildering seems the way ahead. It is this sudden confrontation with the depth and scope of ignorance that represents the most significant contribution of twentieth-century science to the human intellect. We are, at last, facing up to it. In earlier times, we either pretended to understand how things worked or ignored the problem, or simply made up stories to fill the gaps. Now that we have begun exploring in earnest, doing serious science, we are getting glimpses of how huge the questions are, and how far from being answered. Because of this, these are hard times for the human intellect, and it is no wonder that we are depressed. It is not so bad being ignorant if you are totally ignorant; the hard thing is knowing in some detail the reality of ignorance, the worst spots and here and there the not-so-bad spots, but no true light at the end of any tunnel nor even any tunnels that can yet be trusted. Hard times, indeed.

But we are making a beginning, and there ought to be some satisfaction, even 25 exhilaration, in that. The method works. There are probably no questions we can think up that can't be answered, sooner or later, including even the matter of consciousness. To be sure, there may well be questions we can't think up, ever, and therefore limits to the reach of human intellect which we will never know about, but that is another matter. Within our limits, we should be able to work our way through to all our answers, if we keep at it long enough, and pay attention.

I am putting it this way, with all the presumption and confidence that I can 26 summon, in order to raise another, last question. Is this hubris? Is there something fundamentally unnatural, or intrinsically wrong, or hazardous for the species in the ambition that drives us all to reach a comprehensive understanding of nature, including ourselves? I cannot believe it. It would seem to me a more unnatural thing, and more of an offense against nature, for us to come on the same scene endowed as we are with curiosity, filled to overbrimming as we are with questions, and naturally talented as we are for the asking of clear questions, and then for us to do nothing about it or, worse, to try to suppress the questions. This is the greater danger for our species, to try to pretend that we are another kind of animal, that we do not need to satisfy our curiosity, that we can get along somehow without inquiry and exploration and experimentation, and that the human mind can rise above its ignorance by simply asserting that there are things it has no need to know. This, to my way of thinking, is the real hubris, and it carries danger for us all.

Questions

1. How does Thomas establish that the point at issue in the debate over recombinant DNA is not the risks involved? Does he say that recombinant DNA presents no risks?
2. Does Thomas say or imply that the scientist should be unconcerned about the consequences of his research? How does Thomas define the chief purpose of science?
3. Is the discussion of the Greek word *hubris* central to the argument, or does Thomas use it only to introduce the central issue?
4. Where does Thomas state his thesis? Does he restate it in the course of the essay?
5. Do Thomas and Gershon agree on the nature of science and on proposed restrictions on scientific investigation?

Suggestions for Writing

1. Abraham Flexner says the following in his essay "The Usefulness of Useless Knowledge":

> It is to dynamite that we owe our progress in mining, in the making of such railroad tunnels as those which now pierce the Alps and other mountain ranges; but of course dynamite has been abused by politicians and soldiers. Scientists are, however, no more to blame than they are to blame for an earthquake or a flood. The same thing can be said of poison gas.

Would Thomas agree with this statement?

2. Thomas asks:

> Is there something fundamentally unnatural, or intrinsically wrong, or hazardous for the species in the ambition that drives us all to reach a comprehensive understanding of nature, including ourselves?

What is your answer to this question? Is the quest for knowledge a sufficient reason for the government to support the construction of high-energy accelerators or space exploration and perhaps a manned flight to Mars? Or should government support depend on the practical uses of these enterprises in peacetime or wartime? State and defend your assumptions and beliefs.

Additional Reading

Thomas, Lewis. *Late Night Thoughts on Listening to Mahler's Ninth Symphony.* New York: Viking, 1983.

———. *The Lives of a Cell: Notes of a Biology Watcher.* New York: Viking, 1974.

———. *The Medusa and the Snail: More Notes of a Biology Watcher.* New York: Viking, 1979.

———. *The Youngest Science: Notes of a Medicine Watcher.* New York: Viking, 1983.

RESPONSIBILITIES OF THE DOCTOR

*T*he issue on which Dr. Mack Lipkin and Sissela Bok focus in their essays is what doctors should tell patients about their illnesses. Written by a physician and a philosopher of law, these essays present contrasting ways of defining the issue and answering the question. In his comedy *Knock,* Jules Romains explores this same issue from a much different perspective and in a highly original way. First performed in 1923, *Knock* is pertinent to other contemporary issues in medicine, including what we mean by "a healthy person."

The two other readings in this section explore questions related to doctors and their responsibilities to patients. In his story "Jean Beicke," William Carlos Williams explores the relationship between a doctor and a patient who may be too ill to benefit from medical attention. A doctor as well as a poet and writer of fiction, Williams draws on both his medical experience and his imagination in describing the doctor's encounter with a difficult patient. In his essay on deciding which patients to treat when medical resources are scarce, James F. Childress discusses an ethical issue that helps to clarify the meaning of medical responsibility.

On Lying to Patients

Mack Lipkin, M.D.

Dr. Mack Lipkin is Emeritus Professor of Family Practice and Psychiatry (Medicine) at the University of Oregon Medical School. His essay on lying to patients defines the issue from the perspective of medicine in the 1970s. Dr. Lipkin does not limit his discussion to situations created by recent advances in medical technology; placebos have long

*been used by doctors, and doctors have long been concerned with how
to counsel cancer patients and their families. Dr. Lipkin is chiefly concerned with the contexts, the concrete situations, of medical decisions.
His attack on "the fallacy of misplaced concreteness" is particularly
interesting to the general reader as well as the medical ethicist.*

Should a doctor always tell his patients the truth? In recent years there has 1
been an extraordinary increase in public discussion of the ethical problems involved in
this question. But little has been heard from physicians themselves. I believe that gaps
in understanding the complex interactions between doctors and patients have led many
laymen astray in this debate.

It is easy to make an attractive case for always telling patients the truth. But 2
as Dr. J. Henderson, the great Harvard physiologist-philosopher of decades ago, commented: "To speak of telling the truth, the whole truth and nothing but the truth to a
patient is absurd. Like absurdity in mathematics, it is absurd simply because it is
impossible . . .The notion that the truth, the whole truth and nothing but the truth can
be conveyed to the patient is a good specimen of that class of fallacies called by White-
head 'the fallacy of misplaced concreteness.' It results from neglecting factors that cannot be excluded from the concrete situation and that are of an order of magnitude and
relevancy that make it imperative to consider them. Of course, another fallacy is also
often involved, the belief that diagnosis and prognosis are more certain than they are.
But that is another question."

Words, especially medical terms, inevitably carry different implications for dif- 3
ferent people. When these words are said in the presence of anxiety-laden illness, there
is a strong tendency to hear selectively and with emphases not intended by the doctor.
Thus, what the doctor means to convey is obscured.

Indeed, thoughtful physicians know that transmittal of accurate information to 4
patients is often impossible. Patients rarely know how the body functions in health and
disease, but instead have inaccurate ideas of what is going on; this hampers the attempts to "tell the truth."

Take cancer, for example. Patients seldom know that while some cancers are 5
rapidly fatal, others never amount to much, some have a cure rate of 99 percent, others
less than 1 per cent, a cancer may grow rapidly for months and then stop growing for
years; may remain localized for years or spread all over the body almost from the beginning; some can be arrested for long periods of time, others not. Thus, one patient thinks
of cancer as curable, the next thinks it means certain death.

How many patients understand that "heart trouble" may refer to literally hun- 6
dreds of different abnormalities ranging in severity from the trivial to the instantly fatal?
How many know that the term "arthritis" may refer to dozens of different types of joint
involvement? "Arthritis" may raise a vision of the appalling disease that made Aunt
Eulalee a helpless invalid until her death years later; the next patient remembers
Grandpa grumbling about the damned arthritis as he got up from his chair. Unfortunately but understandably, most people's ideas about the implications of medical terms
are based on what they have heard about a few cases.

The news of serious illness drives some patients to irrational and destructive 7 behavior; others handle it sensibly. A distinguished philosopher forestalled my telling him about his cancer by saying, "I want to know the truth. The only thing I couldn't take and wouldn't want to know about is cancer." For two years he had watched his mother die slowly of a painful form of cancer. Several of my physician patients have indicated they would not want to know if they had a fatal illness.

Most patients should be told "the truth" to the extent that they can compre- 8 hend it. Indeed, most doctors, like most other people, are uncomfortable with lies. Good physicians, aware that some may be badly damaged by being told more than they want or need to know, can usually ascertain the patient's preferences and needs.

Discussions about lying often center about the use of placebos. In medical 9 usage, a "placebo" is a treatment that has no specific physical or chemical action on the condition being treated, but is given to affect symptoms by a psychologic mechanism, rather than a purely physical one. Ethicists believe that placebos necessarily involve a partial or complete deception by the doctor, since the patient is allowed to believe that the treatment has a specific effect. They seem unaware that placebos, far from being inert (except in the rigid pharmacological sense), are among the most powerful agents known to medicine.

Placebos are a form of suggestion, which is a direct or indirect presentation of 10 an idea, followed by an uncritical, i.e., not thought-out, acceptance. Those who have studied suggestion or looked at medical history know its almost unbelievable potency; it is involved to a greater or lesser extent in the treatment of every conscious patient. It can induce or remove almost any kind of feeling or thought. It can strengthen the weak or paralyze the strong, transform sleeping, feeding, or sexual patterns, remove or induce a vast array of symptoms, mimic or abolish the effect of very powerful drugs. It can alter the functions of most organs. It can cause illness or a great sense of well-being. It can kill. In fact, doctors often add a measure of suggestion when they prescribe even potent medications for those who also need psychologic support. Like all potent agents, its proper use requires judgment based on experience and skill.

Communication between physician and the apprehensive and often confused 11 patient is delicate and uncertain. Honesty should be evaluated not only in terms of a slavish devotion to language often misinterpreted by the patient, but also in terms of intent. *The crucial question is whether the deception was intended to benefit the patient or the doctor.*

Physicians, like most people, hope to see good results and are disappointed 12 when patients do poorly. Their reputations and their livelihood depend on doing effective work; purely selfish reasons would dictate they do their best for their patients. Most important, all good physicians have a deep sense of responsibility toward those who have entrusted their welfare to them.

As I have explained, it is usually a practical impossibility to tell patients "the 13 whole truth." Moreover, often enough, the ethics of the situation, the true moral responsibility, may demand that the naked facts not be revealed. The now popular complaint that doctors are too authoritarian is misguided more often than not. Some patients who insist on exercising their right to know may be doing themselves a disservice.

Judgment is often difficult and uncertain. Simplistic assertions about telling 14 the truth may not be helpful to patients or physicians in times of trouble.

Questions

1. How does Dr. Lipkin define "the fallacy of misplaced concreteness"? Why is the fallacy central to his discussion of the issue of the essay?
2. How is the outright rejection of placebos an example of the fallacy? How would the requirement that cancer patients be given all the facts of their illness be another example of the fallacy?
3. What does Dr. Lipkin suggest as a sound basis for deciding whether to tell a patient the truth?
4. Is the decision for Dr. Lipkin consequential or deontological, as Thomas H. Murray distinguishes ethical considerations (p. 436)? Could it be both?
5. Should a cancer patient be given all the facts, in your view? And do you believe a doctor has the right to give placebos? Why or why not?

Suggestions for Writing

1. Explain why you agree or disagree with Dr. Lipkin on the question of telling patients the whole truth or that of giving them placebos. Identify and defend your assumptions and beliefs.
2. Discuss the problem of telling the whole truth to people in situations other than illness. Focus the major part of your discussion on a specific situation in which telling the truth might harm the person.

Additional Reading

Beauchamp, Tom L., and James F. Childress. *Principles of Biomedical Ethics.* 2nd ed. New York: Oxford University Press, 1983.

Engelhardt, H. Tristram, Jr., and Daniel Callahan, eds. *Knowledge, Value, and Belief.* Hastings-on-Hudson, N.Y.: Hastings Center, 1977.

———. *Morals, Science, and Sociality.* Hastings-on-Hudson, N.Y.: Hastings Center, 1978.

Fletcher, Joseph. *Morals and Medicine; The Moral Problems of: the Patient's Right to Know the Truth, Contraception, Artificial Insemination, Sterilization, Euthanasia.* Princeton: Princeton University Press, 1979.

Pellegrino, Edmund D. *Humanism and the Physician.* Knoxville: University of Tennessee Press, 1979.

Ramsey, Paul. *Ethics at the Edge of Life: Medical and Legal Intersections.* New Haven: Yale University Press, 1970.

Veatch, Robert M. *A Theory of Medical Ethics.* New York: Basic Books, 1981.

Lies to the Sick and Dying

Sissela Bok

Born in Stockholm in 1934, Sissela Bok came to the United States in 1955 and earned graduate degrees from George Washington and Harvard universities. She has lectured on medical ethics at M.I.T. and Harvard, and from 1971 to 1977 was director of the Population Council in New York City. She now teaches at Brandeis University. Her books include Lying: Moral Choice in Public and Private Life *(1978) and* Secrets: On the Ethics of Concealment and Revelation *(1982).*

This essay on lying to sick people represents part of Bok's broader consideration of the ethics of lying. She examines the consequences of lying, but her main concern is with the reasons doctors and nurses give for lying. Her ethical basis for judging these reasons invites comparison with Dr. Mack Lipkin's argument.

The face of a physician, like that of a diplomatist, should be impenetrable. Nature is a benevolent old hypocrite; she cheats the sick and the dying with illusions better than any anodynes.[. . .]

Some shrewd old doctors have a few phrases always on hand for patients that will insist on knowing the pathology of their complaints without the slightest capacity of understanding the scientific explanation. I have known the term "spinal irritation" serve well on such occasions, but I think nothing on the whole has covered so much ground, and meant so little, and given such profound satisfaction to all parties, as the magnificent phrase "congestion of the portal system."

—Oliver Wendell Holmes, *Medical Essays*

This deception tortured him—their not wishing to admit what they all knew and what he knew, but wanting to lie to him concerning his terrible condition, and wishing and forcing him to participate in that lie. Those lies—lies enacted over him on the eve of his death and destined to degrade this awful, solemn act to the level of their visitings, their curtains, their sturgeon for dinner—were a terrible agony for Ivan Ilych.

—Leo Tolstoy, *The Death of Ivan Ilych*

When a man's life has become bound up with the analytic technique, he finds himself at a loss altogether for the lies and the guile which are otherwise so indispensable to a physician, and if for once with the best intentions he attempts to use them he is likely to betray himself. Since we demand strict truthfulness from our patients, we jeopardize our whole authority if we let ourselves be caught by them in a departure from the truth.

—Sigmund Freud, *Collected Papers*, II

Deception as Therapy

A forty-six-year-old man, coming to a clinic for a routine physical check-up 1 needed for insurance purposes, is diagnosed as having a form of cancer likely to cause him to die within six months. No known cure exists for it. Chemotherapy may prolong life by a few extra months, but will have side effects the physician does not think warranted in this case. In addition, he believes that such therapy should be reserved for patients with a chance for recovery or remission. The patient has no symptoms giving him any reason to believe that he is not perfectly healthy. He expects to take a short vacation in a week.

For the physician, there are now several choices involving truthfulness. Ought 2
he to tell the patient what he has learned, or conceal it? If asked, should he deny it? If he decides to reveal the diagnosis, should he delay doing so until after the patient returns from his vacation? Finally, even if he does reveal the serious nature of the diagnosis, should he mention the possibility of chemotherapy and his reasons for not recommending it in this case? Or should he encourage every last effort to postpone death?

In this particular case, the physician chose to inform the patient of his diagno- 3
sis right away. He did not, however, mention the possibility of chemotherapy. A medical student working under him disagreed; several nurses also thought that the patient should have been informed of this possibility. They tried, unsuccessfully, to persuade the physician that this was the patient's right. When persuasion had failed, the student elected to disobey the doctor by informing the patient of the alternative of chemotherapy. After consultation with family members, the patient chose to ask for the treatment.

Doctors confront such choices often and urgently. What they reveal, hold back, 4
or distort will matter profoundly to their patients. Doctors stress with corresponding vehemence their reasons for the distortion or concealment: not to confuse a sick person needlessly, or cause what may well be unnecessary pain or discomfort, as in the case of the cancer patient; not to leave a patient without hope, as in those many cases where the dying are not told the truth about their condition; or to improve the chances of cure, as where unwarranted optimism is expressed about some form of therapy. Doctors use information as part of the therapeutic regimen; it is given out in amounts, in admixtures, and according to timing believed best for patients. Accuracy, by comparison, matters far less.

Lying to patients has, therefore, seemed an especially excusable act. Some 5
would argue that doctors, and *only* doctors, should be granted the right to manipulate the truth in ways so undesirable for politicians, lawyers, and others.[1] Doctors are trained to help patients; their relationship to patients carries special obligations, and they know much more than laymen about what helps and hinders recovery and survival.

Even the most conscientious doctors, then, who hold themselves at a distance 6
from the quacks and the purveyors of false remedies, hesitate to forswear all lying. Lying is usually wrong, they argue, but less so than allowing the truth to harm patients. B.C. Meyer echoes this very common view:

> [O]urs is a profession which traditionally has been guided by a precept that
> transcends the virtue of uttering truth for truth's sake, and that is, "so far as
> possible, do no harm."[2]

Truth, for Meyer, may be important, but not when it endangers the health and 7
well-being of patients. This has seemed self-evident to many physicians in the past—so much so that we find very few mentions of veracity in the codes and oaths and writings by physicians through the centuries. This absence is all the more striking as other principles of ethics have been consistently and movingly expressed in the same documents.

The two fundamental principles of doing good and not doing harm—of benefi- 8
cence and nonmaleficence—are the most immediately relevant to medical practition-
ers, and the most frequently stressed. To preserve life and good health, to ward off illness, pain, and death—these are the perennial tasks of medicine and nursing. These
principles have found powerful expression at all times in the history of medicine. In the
Hippocratic Oath physicians promise to:

> use treatment to help the sick . . . but never with a view to injury and wrong-
> doing.[3]

And a Hindu oath of initiation says:

> Day and night, however thou mayest be engaged, thou shalt endeavor for the
> relief of patients with all thy heart and soul. Thou shalt not desert or injure
> the patient even for the sake of thy living.[4]

But there is no similar stress on veracity. It is absent from virtually all oaths, 9
codes, and prayers. The Hippocratic Oath makes no mention of truthfulness to patients
about their condition, prognosis, or treatment. Other early codes and prayers are
equally silent on the subject. To be sure, they often refer to the confidentiality with
which doctors should treat all that patients tell them; but there is no corresponding reference to honesty toward the patient. One of the few who appealed to such a principle
was Amatus Lusitanus, a Jewish physician widely known for his skill, who, persecuted,
died of the plague in 1568. He published an oath which reads in part:

> If I lie, may I incur the eternal wrath of God and of His angel Raphael, and may
> nothing in the medical art succeed for me according to my desires.[5]

Later codes continue to avoid the subject. Not even the Declaration of Geneva, 10
adopted in 1948 by the World Medical Association, makes any reference to it. And the
Principles of Medical Ethics of the American Medical Association[6] still leave the matter
of informing patients up to the physician.

Given such freedom, a physician can decide to tell as much or as little as he 11
wants the patient to know, so long as he breaks no law. In the case of the man mentioned at the beginning of this chapter, some physicians might feel justified in lying for
the good of the patient, others might be truthful. Some may conceal alternatives to the
treatment they recommend; others not. In each case, they could appeal to the A.M.A.
Principles of Ethics. A great many would choose to be able to lie. They would claim that
not only can a lie avoid harm for the patient, but that it is also hard to know whether
they have been right in the first place in making their pessimistic diagnosis; a "truthful"
statement could therefore turn out to hurt patients unnecessarily. The concern for curing and for supporting those who cannot be cured then runs counter to the desire to be
completely open. This concern is especially strong where the prognosis is bleak; even
more so when patients are so affected by their illness or their medication that they are
more dependent than usual, perhaps more easily depressed or irrational.

Physicians know only too well how uncertain a diagnosis or prognosis can be. 12
They know how hard it is to give meaningful and correct answers regarding health and
illness. They also know that disclosing their own uncertainty or fears can reduce those
benefits that depend upon faith in recovery. They fear, too, that revealing grave risks,
no matter how unlikely it is that these will come about, may exercise the pull of the

"self-fulfilling prophecy." They dislike being the bearers of uncertain or bad news as much as anyone else. And last, but not least, sitting down to discuss an illness truthfully and sensitively may take much-needed time away from other patients.

These reasons help explain why nurses and physicians and relatives of the sick 13 and dying prefer not to be bound by rules that might limit their ability to suppress, delay, or distort information. This is not to say that they necessarily plan to lie much of the time. They merely want to have the freedom to do so when they believe it wise. And the reluctance to see lying prohibited explains, in turn, the failure of the codes and oaths to come to grips with the problems of truth-telling and lying.

But sharp conflicts are now arising. Doctors no longer work alone with pa- 14 tients. They have to consult with others much more than before; if they choose to lie, the choice may not be met with approval by all who take part in the care of the patient. A nurse expresses the difficulty which results as follows:

> From personal experience I would say that the patients who aren't told about their terminal illness have so many verbal and mental questions unanswered that many will begin to realize that their illness is more serious than they're being told.[. . .]
> Nurses care for these patients twenty-four hours a day compared to a doctor's daily brief visit, and it is the nurse many times that the patient will relate to, once his underlying fears become overwhelming.[. . .]This is difficult for us nurses because being in constant contact with patients we can see the events leading up to this. The patient continually asks you, "Why isn't my pain decreasing?" or "Why isn't the radiation treatment easing the pain?"[. . .] We cannot legally give these patients an honest answer as a nurse (and I'm sure I wouldn't want to) yet the problem is still not resolved and the circle grows larger and larger with the patient alone in the middle.[7]

The doctor's choice to lie increasingly involves co-workers in acting a part they 15 find neither humane nor wise. The fact that these problems have not been carefully thought through within the medical profession, nor seriously addressed in medical education, merely serves to intensify the conflicts.[8] Different doctors then respond very differently to patients in exactly similar predicaments. The friction is increased by the fact that relatives often disagree even where those giving medical care to a patient are in accord on how to approach the patient. Here again, because physicians have not worked out to common satisfaction the question of whether relatives have the right to make such requests, the problems are allowed to be haphazardly resolved by each physician as he sees fit.

The Patient's Perspective

The turmoil in the medical profession regarding truth-telling is further aug- 16 mented by the pressures that patients themselves now bring to bear and by empirical data coming to light. Challenges are growing to the three major arguments for lying to patients: that truthfulness is impossible; that patients do not want bad news; and that truthful information harms them.

The first of these arguments was already discussed in Chapter I. It confuses 17 "truth" and "truthfulness" so as to clear the way for occasional lying on grounds supported by the second and third arguments. At this point, we can see more clearly that it is a strategic move intended to discourage the question of truthfulness from carrying much weight in the first place, and thus to leave the choice of what to say and how to say it up to the physician. To claim that "since telling the truth is impossible, there can be no sharp distinction between what is true and what is false"[9] is to try to defeat objections to lying before even discussing them. One need only imagine how such an argument would be received, were it made by a car salesman or a real estate dealer, to see how fallacious it is.

In medicine, however, the argument is supported by a subsidiary point: even if [18] people might ordinarily understand what is spoken to them, patients are often not in a position to do so. This is where paternalism enters in. When we buy cars or houses, the paternalist will argue, we need to have all our wits about us; but when we are ill, we cannot always do so. We need help in making choices, even if help can be given only by keeping us in the dark. And the physician is trained and willing to provide such help.

It is certainly true that some patients cannot make the best choices for them- [19] selves when weakened by illness or drugs. But most still can. And even those who are incompetent have a right to have someone—their guardian or spouse perhaps—receive the correct information.

The paternalistic assumption of superiority to patients also carries great dan- [20] gers for physicians themselves—it risks turning to contempt. The following view was recently expressed in a letter to a medical journal:

> As a radiologist who has been sued, I have reflected earnestly on advice to obtain Informed Consent but have decided to "take the risks without informing the patient" and trust to "God, judge, and jury" rather than evade responsibility through a legal gimmick.[. . .]
>
> [I]n a general radiologic practice many of our patients are uninformable and we would never get through the day if we had to obtain their consent to every potentially harmful study.
>
> [. . .]We still have patients with language problems, the uneducated and the unintelligent, the stolid and the stunned who cannot form an Informed Opinion to give an Informed Consent; we have the belligerent and the panicky who do not listen or comprehend. And then there are the Medicare patients who comprise 35 percent of general hospital admissions. The bright ones wearily plead to be left alone.[. . .]As for the apathetic rest, many of them were kindly described by Richard Bright as not being able to comprehend because "their brains are so poorly oxygenated."[10]

The argument which rejects informing patients because adequate truthful in- [21] formation is impossible in itself or because patients are lacking in understanding, must itself be rejected when looked at from the point of view of patients. They know that liberties granted to the most conscientious and altruistic doctors will be exercised also in the "Medicaid Mills"; that the choices thus kept from patients will be exercised by not only competent but incompetent physicians; and that even the best doctors can make choices patients would want to make differently for themselves.

The second argument for deceiving patients refers specifically to giving them [22] news of a frightening or depressing kind. It holds that patients do not, in fact, generally want such information, that they prefer not to have to face up to serious illness and death. On the basis of such a belief, most doctors in a number of surveys stated that they do not, as a rule, inform patients that they have an illness such as cancer.

When studies are made of what patients desire to know, on the other hand, a 23 large majority say that they *would* like to be told of such a diagnosis.[11] All these studies need updating and should be done with larger numbers of patients and non-patients. But they do show that there is generally a dramatic divergence between physicians and patients on the factual question of whether patients want to know what ails them in cases of serious illness such as cancer. In most of the studies, over 80 percent of the persons asked indicated that they would want to be told.

Sometimes this discrepancy is set aside by doctors who want to retain the view 24 that patients do not want unhappy news. In reality, they claim, the fact that patients say they want it has to be discounted. The more someone asks to know, the more he suffers from fear which will lead to the denial of the information even if it is given. Informing patients is, therefore, useless; they resist and deny having been told what they cannot assimilate. According to this view, empirical studies of what patients say they want are worthless since they do not probe deeply enough to uncover this universal resistance to the contemplation of one's own death.

This view is only partially correct. For some patients, denial is indeed well es- 25 tablished in medical experience. A number of patients (estimated at between 15 percent and 25 percent) will give evidence of denial of having been told about their illness, even when they repeatedly ask and are repeatedly informed. And nearly everyone experiences a period of denial at some point in the course of approaching death.[12] Elisabeth Kübler-Ross sees denial as resulting often from premature and abrupt information by a stranger who goes through the process quickly to "get it over with." She holds that denial functions as a buffer after unexpected shocking news, permitting individuals to collect themselves and to mobilize other defenses. She describes prolonged denial in one patient as follows:

> She was convinced that the X-rays were "mixed up"; she asked for reassurance that her pathology report could not possibly be back so soon and that another patient's report must have been marked with her name. When none of this could be confirmed, she quickly asked to leave the hospital, looking for another physician in the vain hope "to get a better explanation for my troubles." This patient went "shopping around" for many doctors, some of whom gave her reassuring answers, others of whom confirmed the previous suspicion. Whether confirmed or not, she reacted in the same manner; she asked for examination and reexamination. . . .[13]

But to say that denial is universal flies in the face of all evidence. And to take 26 any claim to the contrary as "symptomatic" of deeper denial leaves no room for reasoned discourse. There is no way that such universal denial can be proved true or false. To believe in it is a metaphysical belief about man's condition, not a statement about what patients do and do not want. It is true that we can never completely understand the possibility of our own death, any more than being alive in the first place. But people certainly differ in the degree to which they can approach such knowledge, take it into account in their plans, and make their peace with it.

Montaigne claimed that in order to learn both to live and to die, men have to 27 think about death and be prepared to accept it.[14] To stick one's head in the sand, or to be prevented by lies from trying to discern what is to come, hampers freedom—freedom to consider one's life as a whole, with a beginning, a duration, an end. Some may request to be deceived rather than to see their lives as thus finite; others reject the information which would require them to do so; but most say that they want to know. Their concern for knowing about their condition goes far beyond mere curiosity or the wish to make isolated personal choices in the short time left to them; their stance toward the entire life they have lived, and their ability to give it meaning and completion, are at stake.[15] In lying or withholding the facts which permit such discernment, doctors may reflect their own fears (which, according to one study,[16] are much stronger than those of laymen) of facing questions about the meaning of one's life and the inevitability of death.

Beyond the fundamental deprivation that can result from deception, we are 28 also becoming increasingly aware of all that can befall patients in the course of their illness when information is denied or distorted. Lies place them in a position where they no longer participate in choices concerning their own health, including the choice of whether to be a "patient" in the first place. A terminally ill person who is not informed that his illness is incurable and that he is near death cannot make decisions about the end of his life: about whether or not to enter a hospital, or to have surgery; where and with whom to spend his last days; how to put his affairs in order—these most personal choices cannot be made if he is kept in the dark, or given contradictory hints and clues.

It has always been especially easy to keep knowledge from terminally ill pa- 29 tients. They are most vulnerable, least able to take action to learn what they need to know, or to protect their autonomy. The very fact of being so ill greatly increases the likelihood of control by others. And the fear of being helpless in the face of such control is growing. At the same time, the period of dependency and slow deterioration of health and strength that people undergo has lengthened. There has been a dramatic shift toward institutionalization of the aged and those near death. (Over 80 percent of Americans now die in a hospital or other institution.)

Patients who are severely ill often suffer a further distancing and loss of control 30 over their most basic functions. Electrical wiring, machines, intravenous administration of liquids, all create new dependency and at the same time new distance between the patient and all who come near. Curable patients are often willing to undergo such procedures; but when no cure is possible, these procedures merely intensify the sense of distance and uncertainty and can even become a substitute for comforting human acts. Yet those who suffer in this way often fear to seem troublesome by complaining. Lying to them, perhaps for the most charitable of purposes, can then cause them to slip unwittingly into subjection to new procedures, perhaps new surgery, where death is held at bay through transfusions, respirators, even resuscitation far beyond what most would wish.

Seeing relatives in such predicaments has caused a great upsurge of worrying 31 about death and dying. At the root of this fear is not a growing terror of the *moment* of death, or even the instants before it. Nor is there greater fear of *being* dead. In contrast to the centuries of lives lived in dread of the punishments to be inflicted after death, many would now accept the view expressed by Epicurus, who died in 270 B.C.:*

---

*See Diogenes Laertius, *Lives of Eminent Philosophers,* p. 651. Epicurus willed his garden to his friends and descendants, and wrote on the eve of dying:

"On this blissful day, which is also the last of my life, I write to you. My continual sufferings from strangury and dysentery are so great that nothing could augment them; but over against them all I set gladness of mind at the remembrance of our past conversations." (Letter to Idomeneus, *Ibid,* p. 549.)

Death, therefore, the most awful of evils, is nothing to us, seeing
that, when we are death is not come, and, when death is come, we are not.

The growing fear, if it is not of the moment of dying nor of being dead, is of 32
all that which now precedes dying for so many: the possibility of prolonged pain, the increasing weakness, the uncertainty, the loss of powers and chance of senility, the sense
of being a burden. This fear is further nourished by the loss of trust in health professionals. In part, the loss of trust results from the abuses which have been exposed—the Medicaid scandals, the old-age home profiteering, the commercial exploitation of those who
seek remedies for their ailments;[17] in part also because of the deceptive practices
patients suspect, having seen how friends and relatives were kept in the dark; in part,
finally, because of the sheer numbers of persons, often strangers, participating in the
care of any one patient. Trust which might have gone to a doctor long known to the patient goes less easily to a team of strangers, no matter how expert or well-meaning.

It is with the working out of all that *informed consent*** implies and the infor- 33
mation it presupposes that truth-telling is coming to be discussed in a serious way for
the first time in the health professions. Informed consent is a farce if the information
provided is distorted or withheld. And even complete information regarding surgical
procedures or medication is obviously useless unless the patient also knows what the
condition is that these are supposed to correct.

Bills of rights for patients, similarly stressing the right to be informed, are now 34
gaining acceptance.[18] This right is not new, but the effort to implement it is. Nevertheless, even where patients are handed the most elegantly phrased Bill of Rights, their
right to a truthful diagnosis and prognosis is by no means always respected.

The reason why even doctors who recognize a patient's right to have informa- 35
tion might still not provide it brings us to the third argument against telling all patients
the truth. It holds that the information given might hurt the patient and that the concern for the right to such information is therefore a threat to proper health care. A patient, these doctors argue, may wish to commit suicide after being given discouraging
news, or suffer a cardiac arrest, or simply cease to struggle, and thus not grasp the small
remaining chance for recovery. And even where the outlook for a patient is very good,
the disclosure of a minute risk can shock some patients or cause them to reject needed
protection such as a vaccination or antibiotics.

The factual basis for this argument has been challenged from two points of 36
view. The damages associated with the disclosure of sad news or risks are rarer than
physicians believe; and the *benefits* which result from being informed are more substantial, even measurably so. Pain is tolerated more easily, recovery from surgery is quicker,
and cooperation with therapy is greatly improved. The attitude that "what you don't
know won't hurt you" is proving unrealistic; it is what patients do not know but vaguely
suspect that causes them corrosive worry.

---

*The law requires that inroads made upon a person's body take place only with the informed voluntary con-
sent of that person. The term "informed consent" came into common use only after 1960, when it was used
by the Kansas Supreme Court in *Nathanson vs. Kline*, 186 Kan. 393,350,p. 2d, 1093 (1960). The patient is
now entitled to full disclosure of risks, benefits, and alternative treatments to any proposed procedure, both
in therapy and in medical experimentation, except in emergencies or when the patient is incompetent, in
which case proxy consent is required.

It is certain that no answers to this question of harm from information are the 37 same for all patients. If we look, first, at the fear expressed by physicians that informing patients of even remote or unlikely risks connected with a drug prescription or operation might shock some and make others refuse the treatment that would have been best for them, it appears to be unfounded for the great majority of patients. Studies show that very few patients respond to being told of such risks by withdrawing their consent to the procedure and that those who do withdraw are the very ones who might well have been upset enough to sue the physician had they not been asked to consent beforehand.[19] It is possible that on even rarer occasions especially susceptible persons might manifest physical deterioration from shock; some physicians have even asked whether patients who die after giving informed consent to an operation, but before it actually takes place, somehow expire because of the information given to them.[20] While such questions are unanswerable in any one case, they certainly argue in favor of caution, a real concern for the person to whom one is recounting the risks he or she will face, and sensitivity to all signs of distress.

The situation is quite different when persons who are already ill, perhaps already quite weak and discouraged, are told of a very serious prognosis. Physicians fear 38 that such knowledge may cause the patients to commit suicide, or to be frightened or depressed to the point that their illness takes a downward turn. The fear that great numbers of patients will commit suicide appears to be unfounded.[21] And if some do, is that a response so unreasonable, so much against the patient's best interest that physicians ought to make it a reason for concealment or lies? Many societies have allowed suicide in the past; our own has decriminalized it; and some are coming to make distinctions among the many suicides which ought to be prevented if at all possible, and those which ought to be respected.[22]

Another possible response to very bleak news is the triggering of physiological 39 mechanisms which allow death to come more quickly—a form of giving up or of preparing for the inevitable, depending on one's outlook. Lewis Thomas, studying responses in humans and animals, holds it not unlikely that:

> [. . .]there is a pivotal movement at some stage in the body's reaction to injury or disease, maybe in aging as well, when the organism concedes that it is finished and the time for dying is at hand, and at this moment the events that lead to death are launched, as a coordinated mechanism. Functions are then shut off, in sequence, irreversibly, and while this is going on, a neural mechanism, held ready for this occasion, is switched on. . . .[23]

Such a response may be appropriate, in which case it makes the moments of 40 dying as peaceful as those who have died and been resuscitated so often testify. But it may also be brought on inappropriately, when the organism could have lived on, perhaps even induced malevolently, by external acts intended to kill. Thomas speculates that some of the deaths resulting from "hexing" are due to such responses. Lévi-Strauss describes deaths from exorcism and the casting of spells in ways which suggest that the same process may then be brought on by the community.[24]

It is not inconceivable that unhappy news abruptly conveyed, or a great shock 41 given to someone unable to tolerate it, could also bring on such a "dying response," quite unintended by the speaker. There is every reason to be cautious and to try to know ahead of time how susceptible a patient might be to the accidental triggering—however rare—of such a response. One has to assume, however, that most of those who have survived long enough to be in a situation where their informed consent is asked have a very robust resistance to such accidental triggering of processes leading to death.

When, on the other hand, one considers those who are already near death, the 42 "dying response" may be much less inappropriate, much less accidental, much less unreasonable. In most societies, long before the advent of modern medicine, human beings have made themselves ready for death once they felt its approach. Philippe Ariès describes how many in the Middle Ages prepared themselves for death when they "felt the end approach." They awaited death lying down, surrounded by friends and relatives. They recollected all they had lived through and done, pardoning all who stood near their deathbed, calling on God to bless them, and finally praying. "After the final prayer all that remained was to wait for death, and there was no reason for death to tarry."[25]

Modern medicine, in its valiant efforts to defeat disease and to save lives, may 43 be dislocating the conscious as well as the purely organic responses allowing death to come when it is inevitable, thus denying those who are dying the benefits of the traditional approach to death. In lying to them, and in pressing medical efforts to cure them long past the point of possible recovery, physicians may thus rob individuals of an autonomy few would choose to give up.

Sometimes, then, the "dying response" is a natural organic reaction at the 44 time when the body has no further defense. Sometimes it is inappropriately brought on by news too shocking or given in too abrupt a manner. We need to learn a great deal more about this last category, no matter how small. But there is no evidence that patients in general will be debilitated by truthful information about their condition.

Apart from the possible harm from information, we are coming to learn much 45 more about the benefits it can bring patients. People follow instructions more carefully if they know what their disease is and why they are asked to take medication; any benefits from those procedures are therefore much more likely to come about.* Similarly, people recover faster from surgery and tolerate pain with less medication if they understand what ails them and what can be done for them.*

Respect and Truthfulness

Taken all together, the three arguments defending lies to patients stand on 46 much shakier ground as a counterweight to the right to be informed than is often thought. The common view that many patients cannot understand, do not want, and

---

*Barbara S. Hulka, J. C. Cassel, et al. "Communication, Compliance, and Concordance between Physicians and Patients with Prescribed Medications," *American Journal of Public Health,* Sept. 1976, pp. 847–53. The study shows that of the nearly half of all patients who do not follow the prescriptions of the doctors (thus foregoing the intended effect of these prescriptions), many will follow them if adequately informed about the nature of their illness and what the proposed medication will do.

†See Lawrence D. Egbert, George E. Batitt, et al., "Reduction of Post-operative Pain by Encouragement and Instruction of Patients," *New England Journal of Medicine,* 270, pp. 825–827, 1964.

   See also: Howard Waitzskin and John D. Stoeckle, "The Communication of Information about Illness," *Advances in Psychosomatic Medicine,* Vol. 8, 1972, pp. 185–215.

may be harmed by, knowledge of their condition, and that lying to them is either morally neutral or even to be recommended, must be set aside. Instead, we have to make a more complex comparison. Over against the right of patients to knowledge concerning themselves, the medical and psychological benefits to them from this knowledge, the unnecessary and sometimes harmful treatment to which they can be subjected if ignorant, and the harm to physicians, their profession, and other patients from deceptive practices, we have to set a severely restricted and narrowed paternalistic view—that *some* patients cannot understand, *some* do not want, and *some* may be harmed by, knowledge of their condition, and that they ought not to have to be treated like everyone else if this is not in their best interest.

Such a view is persuasive. A few patients openly request not to be given bad news. Others give clear signals to that effect, or are demonstrably vulnerable to the shock or anguish such news might call forth. Can one not in such cases infer implied consent to being deceived? [47]

Concealment, evasion, withholding of information may at times be necessary. But if someone contemplates lying to a patient or concealing the truth, the burden of proof must shift. It must rest, here, as with all deception, on those who advocate it in any one instance. They must show why they fear a patient may be harmed or how they know that another cannot cope with the truthful knowledge. A decision to deceive must be seen as a very unusual step, to be talked over with colleagues and others who participate in the care of the patient. Reasons must be set forth and debated, alternatives weighed carefully. At all times, the correct information must go to *someone* closely related to the patient. [48]

The law already permits doctors to withhold information from patients where it would clearly hurt their health. But this privilege has been sharply limited by the courts. Certainly it cannot be interpreted so broadly as to permit a general practice of deceiving patients "for their own good." Nor can it be made to include cases where patients might calmly decide, upon hearing their diagnosis, not to go ahead with the therapy their doctor recommends.[26] Least of all can it justify silence or lies to large numbers of patients merely on the grounds that it is not always easy to tell what a patient wants. [49]

For the great majority of patients, on the contrary, the goal must be disclosure, and the atmosphere one of openness. But it would be wrong to assume that patients can therefore be told abruptly about a serious diagnosis—that, so long as openness exists, there are no further requirements of humane concern in such communication. Dr. Cicely Saunders, who runs the well-known St. Christopher's Hospice in England, describes the sensitivity and understanding which are needed: [50]

> Every patient needs an explanation of his illness that will be understandable and convincing to him if he is to cooperate in his treatment or be relieved of the burden of unknown fears. This is true whether it is a question of giving a diagnosis in a hopeful situation or of confirming a poor prognosis.
>
> The fact that a patient does not ask does not mean that he has no questions. One visit or talk is rarely enough. It is only by waiting and listening that we can gain an idea of what we should be saying. Silences and gaps are often more revealing than words as we try to learn what a patient is facing as he travels along the constantly changing journey of his illness and his thoughts about it.

[. . .]So much of the communication will be without words or given indirectly. This is true of all real meeting with people but especially true with those who are facing, knowingly or not, difficult or threatening situations. It is also particularly true of the very ill.

The main argument against a policy of deliberate, invariable denial of unpleasant facts is that is makes such communication extremely difficult, if not impossible. Once the possibility of talking frankly with a patient has been admitted, it does not mean that this will always take place, but the whole atmosphere is changed. We are then free to wait quietly for clues from each patient, seeing them as individuals from whom we can expect intelligence, courage, and individual decisions. They will feel secure enough to give us these clues when they wish.[27]

Above all, truthfulness with those who are suffering does not mean that they should be deprived of all hope: hope that there is a chance of recovery, however small; nor of reassurance that they will not be abandoned when they most need help. 51

Much needs to be done, however, if the deceptive practices are to be eliminated, and if concealment is to be restricted to the few patients who ask for it or those who can be shown to be harmed by openness. The medical profession has to address this problem. Those who are in training to take care of the sick and the dying have to learn how to speak with them, even about dying. They will be helped to do so if they can be asked to consider alternative approaches to patients, put themselves in the situation of a patient, even confront the possibility of being themselves near death. 52

Until the day comes when patients can be assured that they can trust what doctors tell them, is there anything they can do to improve the chances for themselves? How can they try to avoid slipping into a dependent relationship, one in which they have no way of trusting what anyone tells them? Is there any way in which they can maintain a degree of autonomy, even at a time of great weakness? 53

Those who know who will take care of them when they become seriously ill or approach death can talk this matter over well ahead of time. If they do, it is very likely that their desires will be respected. Growing numbers are now signing statements known as *living wills,* in which they can, if they so wish, specify whether or not they want to be informed about their condition. They can also specify conditions under which they do not want to have their lives prolonged.[28] Still others, who may not have thought of these problems ahead of time, can insist on receiving adequate information once they are in need of care. It is the great majority—those who are afraid of asking, of seeming distrustful—who give rise to the view that patients do not really want to know since they never ask. 54

The perspective of needing care is very different from that of providing it. The first seems the most fundamental question for patients to be whether they can trust their care-takers. It requires a stringent adherence to honesty, in all but a few carefully delineated cases. The second sees the need to be free to deceive, sometimes for genuinely humane reasons. It is only by bringing these perspectives into the open and by considering the exceptional cases explicitly that the discrepancy can be reduced and trust restored. 55

Notes

1. Plato, *The Republic,* 389 b. [Bok's notes throughout.]
2. B. C. Meyer, "Truth and the Physician," *Bulletin of the New York Academy of Medicine* 45 (1969): 59–71. See, too, the quotation from Dr. Henderson in Chapter I of this book (p. 12).
3. W. H. S. Jones, trans, *Hippocrates,* Loeb Classical Library (Cambridge, Mass.: Harvard University Press, 1923), p. 164.
4. Reprinted in M. B. Etziony, *The Physician's Creed: An Anthology of Medical Prayers, Oaths and Codes of Ethics* (Springfield, Ill.: Charles C. Thomas, 1973), pp. 15–18.
5. See Harry Friedenwald, "The Ethics of the Practice of Medicine from the Jewish Point of View," *Johns Hopkins Hospital Bulletin,* no. 318 (August 1917), pp. 256–61.
6. "Ten Principles of Medical Ethics," *Journal of the American Medical Association* 164 (1957): 1119–20.
7. Mary Barrett, letter, *Boston Globe,* 16 November 1976, p. 1.
8. Though a minority of physicians have struggled to bring them to our attention. See Thomas Percival, *Medical Ethics,* 3d ed. (Oxford: John Henry Parker, 1849), pp. 132–41; Worthington Hooker, *Physician and Patient* (New York: Baker and Scribner, 1849), pp. 357–82; Richard C. Cabot, "Teamwork of Doctor and Patient through the Annihilation of Lying," in *Social Service and the Art of Healing* (New York: Moffat, Yard & Co., 1909), pp. 116–70; Charles C. Lund, "The Doctor, the Patient, and the Truth," *Annals of Internal Medicine* 24 (1946): 955; Edmund Davies, "The Patient's Right to Know the Truth," *Proceedings of the Royal Society of Medicine* 66 (1973): 533–36.
9. Lawrence Henderson, "Physician and Patient as a Social System," *New England Journal of Medicine* 212 (1955).
10. Nicholas Demy, Letter to the Editor, *Journal of the American Medical Association* 217 (1971): 696–97.
11. For the views of physicians, see Donald Oken, "What to Tell Cancer Patients," *Journal of the American Medical Association* 175 (1961): 1120–28; and tabulations in Robert Veatch, *Death, Dying, and the Biological Revolution* (New Haven and London: Yale University Press, 1976), pp. 229–38. For the view of patients, see Veatch, *ibid.;* Jean Aitken-Swan and E. C. Easson, "Reactions of Cancer Patients on Being Told Their Diagnosis," *British Medical Journal,* 1959), pp. 779–83; Jim McIntosh, "Patients' Awareness and Desire for Information about Diagnosed but Undisclosed Malignant Disease," *The Lancet* 7 (1976): 300–303; William D. Kelly and Stanley R. Friesen, "Do Cancer Patients Want to Be Told?," *Surgery* 27 (1950): 822–26.
12. See Avery Weisman, *On Dying and Denying* (New York: Behavioral Publications, 1972); Elisabeth Kübler-Ross, *On Death and Dying* (New York: The Macmillan Co., 1969); Ernest Becker, *The Denial of Death* (New York: Free Press, 1973); Philippe Ariès, *Western Attitudes toward Death,* trans. Patricia M. Ranum (Baltimore and London: Johns Hopkins University Press, 1974); and Sigmund Freud, "Negation," *Collected Papers,* ed. James Strachey (London: Hogarth Press, 1950), 5:-181–85.
13. Kübler-Ross, *On Death and Dying,* p. 34.
14. Michel de Montaigne, *Essays,* bk. I, chap. 20.
15. It is in literature that these questions are most directly raised. Two recent works where they are taken up with striking beauty and simplicity are May Sarton, *As We Are Now* (New York: W. W. Norton & Co., 1973); and Freya Stark, *A Peak in Darien* (London: John Murray, 1976).
16. Herman Feifel et al., "Physicians Consider Death," *Proceedings of the American Psychoanalytical Association,* 1967, pp. 201–2.

17. See Ivan Illich, *Medical Nemesis* (New York: Pantheon, 1976), for a critique of the iatrogenic tendencies of contemporary medical care in industrialized societies.
18. See, for example, "Statement on a Patient's Bill of Rights," reprinted in Stanley Joel Reiser, Arthur J. Dyck, and William J. Curran *Ethics in Medicine* (Cambridge, Mass., and London: MIT Press, 1977), p. 148.
19. See Ralph Aphidi, "Informed Consent: A Study of Patient Reaction," *Journal of the American Medical Association* 216 (1971): 1325–29.
20. See Steven R. Kaplan, Richard A. Greenwald, and Arvey I. Rogers, Letter to the Editor, *New England Journal of Medicine* 296 (1977): 1127.
21. Oken, "What to Tell Cancer Patients"; Veatch, *Death, Dying, and the Biological Revolution;* Weisman, *On Dying and Denying.*
22. Norman L. Cantor, "A Patient's Decision to Decline Life-Saving Treatment: Bodily Integrity versus the Preservation of Life," *Rutgers Law Review* 26:228–64; Danielle Gourevitch, "Suicide among the Sick in Classical Antiguity," *Bulletin of the History of Medicine* 18 (1969): 501–18; for bibliography, see Bok, "Voluntary Euthanasia."
23. Lewis Thomas, "A Meliorist View of Disease and Dying," *The Journal of Medicine and Philosophy* I (1976): 212–21.
24. Claude Levi-Strauss, *Structural Anthropology* (New York: Basic Books, 1963), p. 167; See also Eric Cassell, "Permission to Die," in John Behnke and Sissela Bok, eds., *The Dilemmas of Euthanasia* (New York: Doubleday, Anchor Press, 1975), pp. 121–31.
25. Aries, *Western Attitudes toward Death,* p. 11.
26. See Charles Fried, *Medical Experimentation: Personal Integrity and Social Policy* (Amsterdam and Oxford: North Holland Publishing Co. 1974), pp. 20–24.
27. Cicely M. S. Saunders, "Telling Patients," in Resier, Dyck, and Curran, *Ethics in Medicine,* pp. 238–40.
28. "Personal Directions for Care at the End of Life," Sissela Bok, *New England Journal of Medicine* 295 (1976): 367–69.

Questions

1. Why does lying to patients seem "an especially excusable act" to some doctors and nurses? What special difficulties do doctors and nurses encounter?
2. Does Bok say or imply that illness and dying present extraordinary moral situations, different in kind from those people encounter in ordinary life?
3. What is the underlying assumption of the argument that "truthfulness is impossible" with the sick and dying? Is this assumption the only basis for Bok's rejection of the argument?
4. What evidence does Bok present in rebutting the argument that "patients do not want bad news"? What are the negative consequences of lying to patients to avoid giving them bad news?
5. How does Bok refute the argument that truthful information harms the patient? What evidence does she cite in support of her argument?
6. Why does Bok present and respond to the three arguments in favor of lying in the order she does? Do the arguments increase in importance or complexity?
7. Do you agree with Bok's reasons for not lying to patients?

Suggestions for Writing

1. Discuss what Bok would say about Dr. Mack Lipkin's argument on the same issue. Cite evidence from both essays.
2. State what your own expectations would be in a situation of serious illness. Would you want doctors and nurses to tell you the whole truth about your illness?

Additional Reading

Bok, Sissela. *Lying: Moral Choice in Public and Private Life.* New York: Pantheon, 1978.
————. *Secrets: On the Ethics of Concealment.* New York: Pantheon, 1982.

Jean Beicke

William Carlos Williams

> *William Carlos Williams (1883–1963) was born in Rutherford, New Jersey, where he lived most of his life—practicing medicine and writing poetry and fiction. Williams attended the medical college at the University of Pennsylvania, interned in New York City, and studied pediatrics for a year in Leipzig, Germany, before returning to Rutherford to begin his practice. During his years at the University of Pennsylvania, he met the poets Ezra Pound and Hilda Doolittle, whose ideas on imagism and the theory of poetry strongly influenced his writing. His first collection of poems was published in 1909, and books of poetry, essays, and fiction appeared in the years following. In 1946 Williams published the first volume of* Paterson, *an epic poem about the United States; additional volumes followed between 1948 and 1958. In his autobiography (1951), Williams discusses the relationship between the writing of poetry and the practice of medicine:*

> The cured man, I want to say, is no different from any other. It is a trivial business unless you add the zest, whatever that is, to the picture. That's how I came to find writing such a necessity, to relieve me from such a dilemma. I found by practice, by trial and error, that to treat a man as something to which surgery, drugs and hoodoo applied was an indifferent matter; to treat him as material for a work of art made him somehow come alive to me.
> —"Of Medicine and Poetry"

> *Later in the same essay Williams defines his purpose in writing poetry:*

> This immediacy, the thing, as I went on writing,
> living as I could, thinking a secret life I wanted to tell
> openly—if only I could—how it lives, secretly about us as
> much now as ever.

The effort to capture the immediacy of the day-to-day life of the doctor is apparent in the story "Jean Beicke."

The ethical situation for the doctor in the 1930s, the time of the episode described in "Jean Beicke," was different from what it is today. Drugs to fight serious infections had not yet come into use. The introduction of sulfa drugs toward the end of the 1930s began a revolution in the treatment of bacterial diseases. Lewis Thomas describes his own feelings at the news:

> I remember the astonishment when the first
> cases of pneumococcal and streptococcal septicemia were
> treated in Boston in 1937. The phenomenon was almost
> beyond belief. Here were moribund patients, who would
> surely have died without treatment, improving in their ap-
> pearance within a matter of hours of being given the medi-
> cine and feeling entirely well within the next day or so.
> —*The Youngest Science: Notes of a Medicine-Watcher*

Before the development of antibiotics and life-support machines, doctors, patients, and their families expected that certain diseases would take their course. With advances in medical technology, ethical problems in medicine grew more and more complex, particularly as the belief grew that doctors could save patients with the proper drugs and medical devices. Today doctors can keep more patients healthy and alive than could doctors in the nineteenth century or during the 1930s. In 1987, approximately ten thousand people in the United States are kept alive mechanically in a "persistent vegetative state," at a minimum cost of $100,000 annually (Newsweek, January 26, 1987).

This change has made the decisions doctors face even more complex. Increasingly, they are forced to make decisions—and take responsibility for the decisions—that patients and their families made in earlier days. In his story, Williams shows how doctors and nurses define their responsibilities to patients and deal with their feelings about illness and death under circumstances different from today's.

During a time like this, they kid a lot among the doctors and nurses on the obstetrical floor because of the rushing business in new babies that's pretty nearly always going on up there. It's the Depression, they say, nobody has any money so they stay home nights. But one bad result of this is that in the children's ward, another floor up, you see a lot of unwanted children.

The parents get them into the place under all sorts of pretexts. For instance, we have two premature brats, Navarro and Cryschka, one a boy and one a girl; the mother died when Cryschka was born, I think. We got them within a few days of each other, one weighing four pounds and one a few ounces more. They dropped down below four pounds before we got them going but there they are; we had a lot of fun betting on their daily gains in weight but we still have them. They're in pretty good shape though now. Most of the kids that are left that way get along swell. The nurses grow attached to them and get a real thrill when they begin to pick up. It's great to see. And the parents sometimes don't even come to visit them, afraid we'll grab them and make them take the kids out, I suppose.

A funny one is a little Hungarian Gypsy girl that's been up there for the past month. She was about eight weeks old maybe when they brought her in with something on her lower lip that looked like a chancre. Everyone was interested but the Wassermann was negative. It turned out finally to be nothing but a peculiarly situated birthmark. But that kid is still there too. Nobody can find the parents. Maybe they'll turn up some day.

Even when we do get rid of them, they often come back in a week or so— sometimes in terrible condition, full of impetigo, down in weight—everything we'd done for them to do over again. I think it's deliberate neglect in most cases. That's what happened to this little Gypsy. The nurse was funny after the mother had left the second time. I couldn't speak to her, she said. I just couldn't say a word I was so mad. I wanted to slap her.

We had a couple of Irish girls a while back named Cowley. One was a red head with beautiful wavy hair and the other a straight haired blonde. They really were good looking and not infants at all. I should say they must have been two and three years old approximately. I can't imagine how the parents could have abandoned them. But they did. I think they were habitual drunkards and may have had to beat it besides on short notice. No fault of theirs maybe.

But all these are, after all, not the kind of kids I have in mind. The ones I mean are those they bring in stinking dirty, and I mean stinking. The poor brats are almost dead sometimes, just living skeletons, almost, wrapped in rags, their heads caked with dirt, their eyes stuck together with pus and their legs all excoriated from the dirty diapers no one has had the interest to take off them regularly. One poor little pot we have now with a thin purplish skin and big veins standing out all over its head had a big sore place in the fold of its neck under the chin. The nurse told me that when she started to undress it it had on a shirt with a neckband that rubbed right into that place. Just dirt. The mother gave a story of having had it in some sort of home in Paterson. We couldn't get it straight. We never try. What the hell? We take 'em and try to make something out of them.

Sometimes, you'd be surprised, some doctor has given the parents a ride before they bring the child to the clinic. You wouldn't believe it. They clean 'em out, maybe for twenty-five dollars—they maybe had to borrow—and then tell 'em to move on. It happens. Men we all know too. Pretty bad. But what can you do?

And sometimes the kids are not only dirty and neglected but sick, ready to die. You ought to see those nurses work. You'd think it was the brat of their best friend. They handle those kids as if they were worth a million dollars. Not that some nurses aren't better than others but in general they break their hearts over those kids, many times, when I, for one, wish they'd never get well.

I often kid the girls. Why not? I look at some miserable specimens they've dolled up for me when I make the rounds in the morning and I tell them: Give it an enema, maybe it will get well and grow up into a cheap prostitute or something. The country needs you, brat. I once proposed that we have a mock wedding between a born garbage hustler we'd saved and a little female with a fresh mug on her that would make anybody smile.

Poor kids! You really wonder sometimes if medicine isn't all wrong to try to do anything for them at all. You actually want to see them pass out, especially when they're deformed or—they're awful sometimes. Every one has rickets in an advanced form, scurvy too, flat chests, spindly arms and legs. They come in with pneumonia, a temperature of a hundred and six, maybe, and before you can do a thing, they're dead.

This little Jean Beicke was like that. She was about the worst you'd expect to find anywhere. Eleven months old. Lying on the examining table with a blanket half way up her body, stripped, lying there, you'd think it a five months baby, just about that long. But when the nurse took the blanket away, her legs kept on going for a good eight inches longer. I couldn't get used to it. I covered her up and asked two of the men to guess how long she was. Both guessed at least half a foot too short. One thing that helped the illusion besides her small face was her arms. They came about to her hips. I don't know what made that. They should come down to her thighs, you know.

She was just skin and bones but her eyes were good and she looked straight at you. Only if you touched her anywhere, she started to whine and then cry with a shrieking, distressing sort of cry that no one wanted to hear. We handled her as gently as we knew how but she had to cry just the same.

She was one of the damnedest looking kids I've ever seen. Her head was all up in front and flat behind, I suppose from lying on the back of her head so long the weight of it and the softness of the bones from the rickets had just flattened it out and pushed it up forward. And her legs and arms seemed loose on her like the arms and legs of some cheap dolls. You could bend her feet up on her shins absolutely flat—but there was no real deformity, just all loosened up. Nobody was with her when I saw her though her mother had brought her in.

It was about ten in the evening, the interne had asked me to see her because she had a stiff neck, and how! and there was some thought of meningitis—perhaps infantile paralysis. Anyhow, they didn't want her to go through the night without at least a lumbar puncture if she needed it. She had a fierce cough and a fairly high fever. I made it out to be a case of broncho-pneumonia with meningismus but no true involvement of the central nervous system. Besides she had inflamed ear drums.

I wanted to incise the drums, especially the left, and would have done it only the night superintendent came along just then and made me call the ear man on service. You know. She also looked to see if we had an operative release from the parents. There was. So I went home, the ear man came in a while later and opened the ears—a little bloody serum from both sides and that was that.

Next day we did a lumbar puncture, tapped the spine that is, and found clear fluid with a few lymphocytes in it, nothing diagnostic. The X-ray of the chest clinched the diagnosis of broncho-pneumonia, there was an extensive involvement. She was pretty sick. We all expected her to die from exhaustion before she'd gone very far.

I had to laugh every time I looked at the brat after that, she was such a funny looking one but one thing that kept her from being a total loss was that she did eat. Boy! how that kid could eat! As sick as she was she took her grub right on time every three hours, a big eight ounce bottle of whole milk and digested it perfectly. In this depression you got to be such a hungry baby, I heard the nurse say to her once. It's a sign of intelligence, I told her. But anyway, we all got to be crazy about Jean. She'd just lie there and eat and sleep. Or she'd lie and look straight in front of her by the hour. Her eyes were blue, a pale sort of blue. But if you went to touch her, she'd begin to scream. We just didn't, that's all, unless we absolutely had to. And she began to gain in weight. Can you imagine that? I suppose she had been so terribly run down that food, real food, was an entirely new experience to her. Anyway she took her food and gained on it though her temperature continued to run steadily around between a hundred and three and a hundred and four for the first eight or ten days. We were surprised.

When we were expecting her to begin to show improvement, however, she didn't. We did another lumbar puncture and found fewer cells. That was fine and the second X-ray of the chest showed it somewhat improved also. That wasn't so good though, because the temperature still kept up and we had no way to account for it. I looked at the ears again and thought they ought to be opened once more. The ear man disagreed but I kept after him and next day he did it to please me. He didn't get anything but a drop of serum on either side.

Well, Jean didn't get well. We did everything we knew how to do except the right thing. She carried on for another two—no I think it was three—weeks longer. A couple of times her temperature shot up to a hundred and eight. Of course we knew then it was the end. We went over her six or eight times, three or four of us, one after the other, and nobody thought to take an X-ray of the mastoid regions. It was dumb, if you want to say it, but there wasn't a sign of anything but the history of the case to point to it. The ears had been opened early, they had been watched carefully, there was no discharge to speak of at any time and from the external examination, the mastoid processes showed no change from the normal. But that's what she died of, acute purulent mastoiditis of the left side, going on to involvement of the left lateral sinus and finally the meninges. We might, however, have taken a culture of the pus when the ear was first opened and I shall always, after this, in suspicious cases. I have been told since that if you get a virulent bug like the streptococcus mucosus capsulatus it's wise at least to go in behind the ear for drainage if the temperature keeps up. Anyhow she died.

I went in when she was just lying there gasping. Somehow or other, I hated to see that kid go. Everybody felt rotten. She was such a scrawny, misshapen, worthless piece of humanity that I had said many times that somebody ought to chuck her in the garbage chute—but after a month watching her suck up her milk and thrive on it—and to see those alert blue eyes in that face—well, it wasn't pleasant. Her mother was sitting by the bed crying quietly when I came in, the morning of the last day. She was a young woman, didn't look more than a girl, she just sat there looking at the child and crying without a sound.

I expected her to begin to ask me questions with that look on her face all doctors hate—but she didn't. I put my hand on her shoulder and told her we had done everything we knew how to do for Jean but that we really didn't know what, finally, was killing her. The woman didn't make any sign of hearing me. Just sat there looking in between the bars of the crib. So after a moment watching the poor kid beside her, I turned to the infant in the next crib to go on with my rounds. There was an older woman there looking in at that baby also—no better off than Jean, surely. I spoke to her, thinking she was the mother of this one, but she wasn't.

Before I could say anything, she told me she was the older sister of Jean's mother and that she knew that Jean was dying and that it was a good thing. That gave me an idea—I hated to talk to Jean's mother herself—so I beckoned the woman to come out into the hall with me.

I'm glad she's going to die, she said. She's got two others home, older, and her husband has run off with another woman. It's better off dead—never was any good anyway. You know her husband came down from Canada about a year and a half ago. She seen him and asked him to come back and live with her and the children. He come back just long enough to get her pregnant with this one then he left her again and went back to the other woman. And I suppose knowing she was pregnant, and suffering, and having no money and nowhere to get it, she was worrying and this one never was formed right. I seen it as soon as it was born. I guess the condition she was in was the cause. She's got enough to worry about now without this one. The husband's gone to Canada again and we can't get a thing out of him. I been keeping them, but we can't do much more. She'd work if she could find anything but what can you do with three kids in times like this? She's got a boy nine years old but her mother-in-law sneaked it away from her and now he's with his father in Canada. She worries about him too, but that don't do no good.

Listen, I said, I want to ask you something. Do you think she'd let us do an autopsy on Jean if she dies? I hate to speak to her of such a thing now but to tell you the truth, we've worked hard on that poor child and we don't exactly know what is the trouble. We know that she's had pneumonia but that's been getting well. Would you take it up with her for me, if—of course—she dies.

Oh, she's gonna die all right, said the woman. Sure, I will. If you can learn anything, it's only right. I'll see that you get the chance. She won't make any kick, I'll tell her.

Thanks, I said.

The infant died about five in the afternoon. The pathologist was dog-tired from a lot of extra work he'd had to do due to the absence of his assistant on her vacation so he put off the autopsy till next morning. They packed the body in ice in one of the service hoppers. It worked perfectly.

Next morning they did the postmortem. I couldn't get the nurse to go down to it. I may be a sap, she said, but I can't do it, that's all. I can't. Not when I've taken care of them. I feel as if they're my own.

I was amazed to see how completely the lungs had cleared up. They were almost normal except for a very small patch of residual pneumonia here and there which really amounted to nothing. Chest and abdomen were in excellent shape, otherwise, throughout—not a thing aside from the negligible pneumonia. Then he opened the head.

It seemed to me the poor kid's convolutions were unusually well developed. I kept thinking it's incredible that that complicated mechanism of the brain has come into being just for this. I never can quite get used to an autopsy.

The first evidence of the real trouble—for there had been no gross evidence of meningitis—was when the pathologist took the brain in his hand and made the long steady cut which opened up the left lateral ventricle. There was just a faint color of pus on the bulb of the choroid plexus there. Then the diagnosis all cleared up quickly. The left lateral sinus was completely thrombosed and on going into the left temporal bone from the inside the mastoid process was all broken down.

I called up the ear man and he came down at once. A clear miss, he said. I think if we'd gone in there earlier, we'd have saved her.

For what? said I. Vote the straight Communist ticket.

Would it make us any dumber? said the ear man.

Questions

1. What attitudes does the doctor express toward the poor children he treats? Does he say or imply that he or other doctors or nurses do more to save the life of one child than another?
2. How much can the doctors and nurses of the hospital do for Jean Beicke? What can they not do? Do they seem aware of their limitations?
3. How different in attitude toward Jean are the mother and the aunt? Does the aunt ask the doctor not to intervene and let Jean die? Or is she merely expressing hope that the child will die?
4. What is the implication of the concluding exchange with the ear specialist? Are these statements of anger or despair over the failure to save the child? Or do they show that the doctor and the specialist are callous?
5. Do you have the sense that the narrator speaks for the author of the story—that they share the same attitudes and feelings? Or do you sense that the author stands at a distance from his narrator and asks the reader not to accept the narrator's values or judgments about people?
6. Does the story have a point or a thesis? Does Williams want to generate a particular attitude in the reader toward doctors or the poor? Or is he presenting an episode of medical practice that the reader will find interesting but not necessarily instructive?

Suggestions for Writing

1. Discuss what is gained by the author through the first-person narration. How different would "Jean Beicke" be if the story were told through an undramatized third-person narrator?
2. Discuss the ethical questions that the doctor faces in treating Jean Beicke and dealing with her mother and aunt. Does Williams raise these questions directly?
3. Characterize the doctor on the basis of his statements about patients and how he performs his job. Then describe the attitude that Williams generates toward the doctor.
4. Compare the attitude of the doctor toward his patients with that of the doctor in one of the stories or poems listed here. Use this comparison to state an idea or a thesis about the two works.
   a. Anton Chekhov, "Ward 6"
   b. Nathaniel Hawthorne, "Dr. Heidigger's Experiment"
   c. Franz Kafka, "The Country Doctor"
   d. Sylvia Plath, "The Surgeon at 2 A.M."
   e. William Carlos Williams, "The Use of Force"

Additional Reading

Rosenthal, A. L., ed. *William Carlos Williams Reader.* New York: New Directions, 1969.
Williams, William Carlos. *Autobiography.* New York: Random House, 1951.
———. *Collected Earlier Poems.* New York: New Directions, 1951.
———. *Collected Later Poems.* Rev. ed. New York: New Directions, 1962.
———. *The Doctor Stories.* New York: New Directions, 1984.
———. *Paterson: A Long Poem.* New York: New Directions, 1968.
———. *Selected Essays.* New York: New Directions, 1969.

Who Shall Live when Not All Can Live?

James F. Childress

James F. Childress is Kyle Professor of Religious Studies and Professor of Medical Education at the University of Virginia, where he has taught since 1968. He has also taught at the Kennedy Institute of Ethics at Georgetown University, Princeton University, Columbia University, and other schools. He is the author of numerous articles and books, including Priorities in Biomedical Ethics *(1981),* Moral Responsibility in Conflicts: Essays on Nonviolence, War, and Conscience *(1982), and* Who Should Decide? Paternalism in Health Care *(1982).*

In this article, first published in 1970, Childress considers an issue generated by the scarcity of dialysis machines, which were then coming into use. As Childress notes in his opening paragraph, the issue was not a new one; it had been confronted more than sixty years earlier in George Bernard Shaw's play The Doctor's Dilemma. *The doctor in the play can accept only a limited number of patients for an experimental treatment of tuberculosis, and he argues that he must choose between two sick men on the basis of their character and usefulness to society:*

> Try to think of those ten patients as ten shipwrecked men on a raft—a raft that is barely large enough to save them—that will not support one more. Another head bobs up through the waves at the side. Another man begs to be taken aboard. He implores the captain of the raft to save him. But the captain can only do that by pushing one of his ten off the raft and drowning him to make room for the new comer. That is what you are asking me to do.

He adds:

> In every single one of those ten cases I have had to consider, not only whether the man could be saved, but whether he was worth saving.

*The issue that Shaw raises in the statement just quoted con-
tinues to occupy medical doctors and ethical philosophers. Childress
centers his discussion on a famous lifeboat incident in 1841, to which
Shaw was possibly referring in the quoted passage. The question of
whether the doctor should consider who is "worth saving" is the subject of Childress's essay. The notes throughout are his.*

Who shall live when not all can live? Although this question has been urgently 1
forced upon us by the dramatic use of artificial internal organs and organ transplanta-
tions, it is hardly new. George Bernard Shaw dealt with it in "The Doctor's Dilemma":

> SIR PATRICK. Well, Mr. Savior of Lives: which is it to be? that honest decent
> man Blenkinsop, or that rotten blackguard of an artist, eh?
> RIDGEON. It's not an easy case to judge, is it? Blenkinsop's an honest decent
> man; but is he any use? Dubedat's a rotten blackguard; but he's a genuine
> source of pretty and pleasant and good things.
> SIR PATRICK. What will he be a source of for that poor innocent wife of his,
> when she finds him out?
> RIDGEON. That's true. Her life will be a hell.
> SIR PATRICK. And tell me this. Suppose you had this choice put before you:
> either to go through life and find all the pictures bad but all the men and
> women good, or go through life and find all the pictures good and all the men
> and women rotten. Which would you choose?[1]

A significant example of the distribution of scarce medical resources is seen in 2
the use of penicillin shortly after its discovery. Military officers had to determine which
soldiers would be treated—those with venereal disease or those wounded in combat.[2] In
many respects such decisions have become routine in medical circles. Day after day physicians and others make judgments and decisions "about allocations of medical care to
various segments of our population, to various types of hospitalized patients, and to specific individuals,"[3] for example, whether mental illness or cancer will receive the higher
proportion of available funds. Nevertheless, the dramatic forms of "Scarce Life-Saving
Medical Resources" (hereafter abbreviated as SLMR) such as hemodialysis and kidney
and heart transplants have compelled us to examine the moral questions that have been
concealed in many routine decisions. I do not attempt in this paper to show how a resolution of SLMR cases can help us in the more routine ones which do not involve a conflict of life with life. Rather I develop an argument for a particular method of determining who shall live when not all can live. No conclusions are implied about criteria and
procedures for determining who shall receive medical resources that are not directly
related to the preservation of life (e.g. corneal transplants) or about standards for allocating money and time for studying and treating certain diseases.

Just as current SLMR decisions are not totally discontinuous with other medi- 3
cal decisions, so we must ask whether some other cases might, at least by analogy, help
us develop the needed criteria and procedures. Some have looked at the principles at
work in our responses to abortion, euthanasia, and artificial insemination.[4] Usually they
have concluded that these cases do not cast light on the selection of patients for artificial and transplanted organs. The reason is evident: in abortion, euthanasia, and artificial insemination, there is no conflict of life with life for limited but indispensable re-

sources (with the possible exception of therapeutic abortion). In current SLMR decisions, such a conflict is inescapable, and it makes them so morally perplexing and fascinating. If analogous cases are to be found, I think that we shall locate them in moral conflict situations.

Analogous Conflict Situations

An especially interesting and pertinent one is *U.S. v. Holmes.*[5] In 1841 an 4
American ship, the *William Brown,* which was near Newfoundland on a trip from Liverpool to Philadelphia, struck an iceberg. The crew and half the passengers were able to escape in the two available vessels. One of these, a longboat, carrying too many passengers and leaking seriously, began to founder in the turbulent sea after about twenty-four hours. In a desperate attempt to keep it from sinking, the crew threw overboard fourteen men. Two sisters of one of the men either jumped overboard to join their brother in death or instructed the crew to throw them over. The criteria for determining who should live were "not to part man and wife, and not to throw over any women." Several hours later the others were rescued. Returning to Philadelphia, most of the crew disappeared, but one, Holmes, who had acted upon orders from the mate, was indicted, tried, and convicted on the charge of "unlawful homicide."

We are interested in this case from a moral rather than a legal standpoint, and 5
there are several possible responses to and judgments about it. Without attempting to be exhaustive I shall sketch a few of these. The judge contended that lots should have been cast, for in such conflict situations, there is no other procedure "so consonant both to humanity and to justice." Counsel for Holmes, on the other hand, maintained that the "sailors adopted the only principle of selection which was possible in an emergency like theirs,—a principle more humane than lots."

Another version of selection might extend and systematize the maxims of the 6
sailors in the direction of "utility"; those are saved who will contribute to the greatest good for the greatest number. Yet another possible option is defended by Edmond Cahn in *The Moral Decision.* He argues that in this case we encounter the "morals of the last days." By this phrase he indicates that an apocalyptic crisis renders totally irrelevant the normal differences between individuals. He continues,

> In a strait of this extremity, all men are reduced—or raised, as one may choose to denominate it—to members of the genus, mere congeners and nothing else. Truly and literally, all were "in the same boat," and thus none could be saved separately from the others. I am driven to conclude that otherwise—that is, if none sacrifice themselves of free will to spare the others—they must all wait and die together. For where all have become congeners, pure and simple, no one can save himself by killing another.[6]

Cahn's answer to the question "who shall live when not all can live" is "none" unless the voluntary sacrifice by some persons permits it.

Few would deny the importance of Cahn's approach although many, including 7
this writer, would suggest that it is relevant mainly as an affirmation of an elevated and, indeed, heroic or saintly morality which one hopes would find expression in the voluntary actions of many persons trapped in "borderline" situations involving a conflict of

life with life. It is a maximal demand which some moral principles impose on the individual in the recognition that self-preservation is not a good which is to be defended at all costs. The absence of this saintly or heroic morality should not mean, however, that everyone perishes. Without making survival an absolute value and without justifying all means to achieve it, we can maintain that simply letting everyone die is irresponsible. This charge can be supported from several different standpoints, including society at large as well as the individuals involved. Among a group of self-interested individuals, none of whom volunteers to relinquish his life, there may be better and worse ways of determining who shall survive. One task of social ethics, whether religious or philosophical, is to propose relatively just institutional arrangements within which self-interested and biased men can live. The question then becomes: which set of arrangements—which criteria and procedures of selection—is most satisfactory in view of the human condition (man's limited altruism and inclination to seek his own good) and the conflicting values that are to be realized?

There are several significant differences between the *Holmes* and SLMR cases, 8 a major one being that the former involves *direct* killing of another person, while the latter involve only *permitting* a person to die when it is not possible to save all. Furthermore, in extreme situations such as *Holmes,* the restraints of civilization have been stripped away, and something approximating a state of nature prevails, in which life is "solitary, poor, nasty, brutish and short." The state of nature does not mean that moral standards are irrelevant and that might should prevail, but it does suggest that much of the matrix which normally supports morality has been removed. Also, the necessary but unfortunate decisions about who shall live and die are made by men who are existentially and personally involved in the outcome. Their survival too is at stake. Even though the institutional role of sailors seems to require greater sacrificial actions, there is obviously no assurance that they will adequately assess the number of sailors required to man the vessel or that they will impartially and objectively weigh the common good at stake. As the judge insisted in his defense of casting lots in the *Holmes* case: "In no other than this [casting lots] or some like way are those having equal rights put upon an equal footing, and in no other way is it possible to guard against partiality and oppression, violence, and conflict." This difference should not be exaggerated since self-interest, professional pride, and the like obviously affect the outcome of many medical decisions. Nor do the remaining differences cancel *Holmes'* instructiveness.

Criteria of Selection for SLMR

Which set of arrangements should be adopted for SLMR? Two questions are in- 9 volved: Which standards and criteria should be used? and, Who should make the decision? The first question is basic, since the debate about implementation, e.g. whether by a lay committee or physician, makes little progress until the criteria are determined.

We need two sets of criteria which will be applied at two different stages in the 10 selection of recipients of SLMR. First, medical criteria should be used to exclude those who are not "medically acceptable." Second, from this group of "medically acceptable" applicants, the final selection can be made. Occasionally in current American medical practice, the first stage is omitted, but such an omission is unwarranted. Ethical and social responsibility would seem to require distributing these SLMR only to those who have some reasonable prospect of responding to the treatment. Furthermore, in transplants such medical tests as tissue and blood typing are necessary, although they are hardly fully developed.

"Medical acceptability" is not as easily determined as many non-physicians assume since there is considerable debate in medical circles about the relevant factors (e.g., age and complicating diseases). Although ethicists can contribute little or nothing to this debate, two proposals may be in order. First, "medical acceptability" should be used only to determine the group from which the final selection will be made, and the attempt to establish fine degrees of prospective response to treatment should be avoided. Medical criteria, then, would exclude some applicants but would not serve as a basis of comparison between those who pass the first stage. For example, if two applicants for dialysis were medically acceptable, the physicians would *not* choose the one with the *better* medical prospects. Final selection would be made on other grounds. Second, psychological and environmental factors should be kept to an absolute minimum and should be considered only when they are without doubt critically related to medical acceptability (e.g., the inability to cope with the requirements of dialysis which might lead to suicide).* 11

The most significant moral questions emerge when we turn to the final selection. Once the pool of medically acceptable applicants has been defined and still the number is larger than the resources, what other criteria should be used? How should the final selection be made? First, I shall examine some of the difficulties that stem from efforts to make the final selection in terms of social value; these difficulties raise serious doubts about the feasibility and justifiability of the utilitarian approach. Then I shall consider the possible justification for random selection or chance. 12

Occasionally criteria of social worth focus on past contributions but most often they are primarily future-oriented. The patient's potential and probable contribution to the society is stressed, although this obviously cannot be abstracted from his present web of relationships (e.g., dependents) and occupational activities (e.g., nuclear physicist). Indeed, the magnitude of his contribution to society (as an abstraction) is measured in terms of these social roles, relations, and functions. Enough has already been said to suggest the tremendous range of factors that affect social value or worth.† Here we encounter the first major difficulty of this approach: How do we determine the relevant criteria of social value? 13

The difficulties of quantifying various social needs are only too obvious. How does one quantify and compare the needs of the spirit (e.g., education, art, religion), political life, economic activity, technological development? Joseph Fletcher suggests that 14

---

*For a discussion of the higher suicide rate among dialysis patients than among the general population and an interpretation of some of the factors at work, see H. S. Abram, G. L. Moore, and F. B. Westervelt, "Suicidal Behavior in Chronic Dialysis Patients," *American Journal of Psychiatry* 127 [March 1971], 1199–1204. This study shows that even "if one does not include death through not following the regimen the incidence of suicide is still more than 100 times the normal population."

†I am excluding from consideration the question of the ability to pay because most of the people involved have to secure funds from other sources, public or private, anyway.

"some day we may learn how to 'quantify' or 'mathematicate' or 'computerize' the value problem in selection, in the same careful and thorough way that diagnosis has been."[7] I am not convinced that we can ever quantify values, or that we should attempt to do so. But even if the various social and human needs, in principle, could be quantified, how do we determine how much weight we will give to each one? Which will have priority in case of conflict? Or even more basically, in the light of which values and principles do we recognize social "needs"?

One possible way of determining the values which should be emphasized in selection has been proposed by Leo Shatin.[8] He insists that our medical decisions about allocating resources are already based on an unconscious scale of values (usually dominated by material worth). Since there is really no way of escaping this, we should be self-conscious and critical about it. How should we proceed? He recommends that we discover the values that most people in our society hold and then use them as criteria for distributing SLMR. These values can be discovered by attitude or opinion surveys. Presumably if fifty-one percent in this testing period put a greater premium on military needs than technological development, military men would have a greater claim on our SLMR than experimental researchers. But valuations of what is significant change, and the student revolutionary who was denied SLMR in 1970 might be celebrated in 1990 as the greatest American hero since George Washington.

Shatin presumably is seeking criteria that could be applied nationally, but at the present, regional and local as well as individual prejudices tincture the criteria of social value that are used in selection. Nowhere is this more evident than in the deliberations and decisions of the anonymous selection committee of the Seattle Artificial Kidney Center where such factors as church membership and Scout leadership have been deemed significant for determining who shall live.[9] As two critics conclude after examining these criteria and procedures, they rule out "creative nonconformists, who rub the bourgeoisie the wrong way but who historically have contributed so much to the making of America. The Pacific Northwest is no place for a Henry David Thoreau with bad kidneys."[10]

Closely connected to this first problem of determining social values is a second one. Not only is it difficult if not impossible to reach agreement on social values, but it is also rarely easy to predict what our needs will be in a few years and what the consequences of present actions will be. Furthermore it is difficult to predict which persons will fulfill their potential function in society. Admissions committees in colleges and universities experience the frustrations of predicting realization of potential. For these reasons, as someone has indicated, God might be a utilitarian, but we cannot be. We simply lack the capacity to predict very accurately the consequences which we then must evaluate. Our incapacity is never more evident than when we think in societal terms.

Other difficulties make us even less confident that such an approach to SLMR is advisable. Many critics raise the spectre of abuse, but this should not be overemphasized. The fundamental difficulty appears on another level: the utilitarian approach would in effect reduce the person to his social role, relations, and functions. Ultimately it dulls and perhaps even eliminates the sense of the person's transcendence, his dignity as a person which cannot be reduced to his past or future contribution to society. It is not at all clear that we are willing to live with these implications of utilitarian selection. Wilhelm Kolff, who invented the artificial kidney, has asked: "Do we really subscribe to the principle that social standing should determine selection? Do we allow patients to be treated with dialysis only when they are married, go to church, have children, have a job, a good income and give to the Community Chest?"*

The German theologian Helmut Thielicke contends that any search for "objec- 19 tive criteria" for selection is already a capitulation to the utilitarian point of view which violates man's dignity.[11] The solution is not to let all die, but to recognize that SLMR cases are "borderline situations" which inevitably involve guilt. The agent, however, can have courage and freedom (which, for Thielicke, come from justification by faith) and can

> go ahead anyway and seek for criteria for deciding the question of life or death
> in the matter of the artificial kidney. Since these criteria are . . . questionable,
> necessarily alien to the meaning of human existence, the decision to which
> they lead can be little more than that arrived at by casting lots.[12]

The resulting criteria, he suggests, will probably be very similar to those already employed in American medical practice.

He is most concerned to preserve a certain *attitude* or *disposition* in SLMR— 20 the sense of guilt which arises when man's dignity is violated. With this sense of guilt, the agent remains "sound and healthy where it really counts."[13] Thielicke uses man's dignity only as a judgmental, critical, and negative standard. It only tells us how all selection criteria and procedures (and even the refusal to act) implicate us in the ambiguity of the human condition and its metaphysical guilt. This approach is consistent with his view of the task of theological ethics: "to teach us how to understand and endure— not 'solve'—the borderline situation."[14] But ethics, I would contend, can help us discern the factors and norms in whose light relative, discriminate judgments can be made. Even if all actions in SLMR should involve guilt, some may preserve human dignity to a greater extent than others. Thielicke recognizes that a decision based on any criteria is "little more than that arrived at by casting lots." But perhaps selection by chance would come the closest to embodying the moral and nonmoral values that we are trying to maintain (including a sense of man's dignity).

The Values of Random Selection

My proposal is that we use some form of randomness or chance (either natural, 21 such as "first come, first served," or artificial, such as a lottery) to determine who shall be saved. Many reject randomness as a surrender to non-rationality when responsible and rational judgments can and must be made. Edmond Cahn criticizes "Holmes'

---

*"Letters and Comments," *Annals of Internal Medicine,* 61 (Aug. 1964), 360. Dr. G. E. Schreiner contends that "if you really believe in the right of society to make decisions on medical availability on these criteria you should be logical and say that when a man stops going to church or is divorced or loses his job, he ought to be removed from the programme and somebody else who fulfills these criteria substituted. Obviously no one faces up to this logical consequence" (G.E.W. Wolstenholme and Maeve O'Connor, eds. *Ethics in Medical Progress: With Special Reference to Transplantation,* A Ciba Foundation Symposium [Boston, 1966], p. 127).

judge" who recommended the casting of lots because, as Cahn puts it, "the crisis involves stakes too high for gambling and responsibilities too deep for destiny."[15] Similarly, other critics see randomness as a surrender to "non-human" forces which necessarily vitiates human values. Sometimes these values are identified with the process of decision-making (e.g., it is important to have persons rather than impersonal forces determining who shall live). Sometimes they are identified with the outcome of the process (e.g., the features such as creativity and fullness of being which make human life what it is are to be considered and respected in the decision). Regarding the former, it must be admitted that the use of chance seems cold and impersonal. But presumably the defenders of utilitarian criteria in SLMR want to make their application as objective and impersonal as possible so that subjective bias does not determine who shall live.

Such criticisms, however, ignore the moral and nonmoral values which might 22 be supported by selection by randomness or chance. A more important criticism is that the procedure that I develop draws the relevant moral context too narrowly. That context, so the argument might run, includes the society and its future and not merely the individual with his illness and claim upon SLMR. But my contention is that the values and principles at work in the narrower context may well take precedence over those operative in the broader context both because of their weight and significance and because of the weaknesses of selection in terms of social worth. As Paul Freund rightly insists, "The more nearly total is the estimate to be made of an individual, and the more nearly the consequence determines life and death, the more unfit the judgment becomes for human reckoning . . . Randomness as a moral principle deserves serious study."[16] Serious study would, I think, point toward its implementation in certain conflict situations, primarily because it preserves a significant degree of *personal dignity* by providing *equality* of opportunity. Thus it cannot be dismissed as a "non-rational" and "non-human" procedure without an inquiry into the reasons, including human values, which might justify it. Paul Ramsey stresses this point about the *Holmes* case:

> Instead of fixing our attention upon "gambling" as the solution—with all the frivolous and often corrupt associations the word raises in our minds—we should think rather of *equality* of opportunity as the ethical substance of the relations of those individuals to one another that might have been guarded and expressed by casting lots.[17]

The individual's personal and transcendent dignity, which on the utilitarian ap- 23 proach would be submerged in his social role and function, can be protected and witnessed to by a recognition of his equal right to be saved. Such a right is best preserved by procedures which establish equality of opportunity. Thus selection by chance more closely approximates the requirements established by human dignity than does utilitarian calculation. It is not infallibly just, but it is preferable to the alternatives of letting all die or saving only those who have the greatest social responsibilities and potential contribution.

This argument can be extended by examining values other than individual dig- 24 nity and equality of opportunity. Another basic value in the medical sphere is the relationship of trust between physician and patient. Which selection criteria are most in accord with this relationship of trust? Which will maintain, extend, and deepen it? My contention is that selection by randomness or chance is preferable from this standpoint too.

Trust, which is inextricably bound to respect for human dignity, is an attitude 25
of expectation about another. It is not simply the expectation that another will perform
a particular act, but more specifically that another will act toward him in certain ways—
which will respect him as a person. As Charles Fried writes:

> Although trust has to do with reliance on a disposition of another person, it
> is reliance on a disposition of a special sort: the disposition to act morally, to
> deal fairly with others, to live up to one's undertakings, and so on. Thus to
> trust another is first of all to expect him to accept the principle of morality in
> his dealings with you, to respect your status as a person, your personality.[18]

This trust cannot be preserved in life-and-death situations when a person expects decisions about him to be made in terms of his social worth, for such decisions violate his
status as a person. An applicant rejected on grounds of inadequacy in social value or virtue would have reason for feeling that his "trust" had been betrayed. Indeed, the sense
that one is being viewed not as an end in himself but as a means in medical progress
or the achievement of a greater social good is incompatible with attitudes and relationships of trust. We recognize this in the billboard which was erected after the first heart
transplants: "Drive Carefully. Christiaan Barnard Is Watching You." The relationship of
trust between the physician and patient is not only an instrumental value in the sense
of being an important factor in the patient's treatment. It is also to be endorsed because
of its intrinsic worth as a relationship.

Thus the related values of individual dignity and trust are best maintained in 26
selection by chance. But other factors also buttress the argument for this approach.
Which criteria and procedures would men agree upon? We have to suppose a hypothetical situation in which several men are going to determine for themselves and their families the criteria and procedures by which they would want to be admitted to and excluded from SLMR if the need arose.* We need to assume two restrictions and then ask
which set of criteria and procedures would be chosen as the most rational and, indeed,
the fairest. The restrictions are these: (1) The men are *self-interested*. They are
interested in their own welfare (and that of members of their families), and this, of
course, includes survival. Basically, they are not motivated by altruism. (2) Furthermore, they are *ignorant* of their own talents, abilities, potential, and probable contribution to the social good. They do not know how they would fare in a competitive situation, e.g., the competition for SLMR in terms of social contribution. Under these
conditions which institution would be chosen—letting all die, utilitarian selection, or
the use of chance? Which would seem the most rational? the fairest? By which set of criteria would they want to be included in or excluded from the list of those who will be
saved? The rational choice in this setting (assuming self-interest and ignorance of one's
competitive success) would be random selection or chance since this alone provides
equality of opportunity. A possible response is that one would prefer to take a "risk" and

---

*My argument is greatly dependent on John Rawls's version of justice as fairness, which is a reinterpretation
of social contract theory. Rawls, however, would probably not apply his ideas to "borderline situations." See
"Distributive Justice: Some Addenda," *Natural Law Forum*, 13 (1968), 53. For Rawls's general theory, see
"Justice as Fairness," *Philosophy, Politics and Society* (Second Series), ed. by Peter Laslett and W. G.
Runciman (Oxford, 1962), pp. 132–157 and his other essays on aspects of this topic.

therefore choose the utilitarian approach. But I think not, especially since I added that the participants in this hypothetical situation are choosing for their children as well as for themselves; random selection or chance could be more easily justified to the children. It would make more sense for men who are self-interested but uncertain about their relative contribution to society to elect a set of criteria which would build in equality of opportunity. They would consider selection by chance as relatively just and fair.*

An important psychological point supplements earlier arguments for using chance or random selection. The psychological stress and strain among those who are rejected would be greater if the rejection is based on insufficient social worth than if it is based on chance. Obviously stress and strain cannot be eliminated in these borderline situations, but they would almost certainly be increased by the opprobrium of being judged relatively "unfit" by society's agents using society's values. Nicholas Rescher makes this point very effectively:

> a recourse to chance would doubtless make matters easier for the rejected patient and those who have a specific interest in him. It would surely be quite hard for them to accept his exclusion by relatively mechanical application of objective criteria in whose implementation subjective judgment is involved. But the circumstances of life have conditioned us to accept the workings of chance and to tolerate the element of luck (good or bad): human life is an inherently contingent process. Nobody, after all, has an absolute right to ELT [Exotic Lifesaving Therapy]—but most of us would feel that we have "every bit as much right" to it as anyone else in significantly similar circumstances.†

Although it is seldom recognized as such, selection by chance is already in operation in practically every dialysis unit. I am not aware of any unit which removes some of its patients from kidney machines in order to make room for later applicants who are better qualified in terms of social worth. Furthermore, very few people would recommend it. Indeed, few would even consider removing a person from a kidney machine on the grounds that a person better qualified *medically* had just applied. In a discussion of the treatment of chronic renal failure by dialysis at the University of Virginia Hospital Renal Unit from November 15, 1965 to November 15, 1966, Dr. Harry Abram writes: "Thirteen patients sought treatment but were not considered because the program had reached its limit of nine patients."[19] Thus, in practice and theory, natural chance is accepted at least within certain limits.

My proposal is that we extend this principle (first come, first served) to determine who among the medically acceptable patients shall live or that we utilize artificial

---

*Occasionally someone contends that random selection may reward vice. Leo Shatin (op. cit., p. 100) insists that random selection "would reward socially disvalued qualities by giving their bearers the same special medical care opportunities as those received by the bearers of socially valued qualities. Personally I do not favor such a method." Obviously society must engender certain qualities in its members, but not all of its institutions must be devoted to that purpose. Furthermore, there are strong reasons, I have contended, for exempting SLMR from that sort of function.

†Nicholas Rescher, "The Allocation of Exotic Medical Lifesaving Therapy," *Ethics,* 79 (April 1969), 184. He defends random selection's use only after utilitarian and other judgments have been made. If there are no "major disparities" in terms of utility, etc., in the second stage of selection, then final selection could be made randomly. He fails to give attention to the moral values that random selection might preserve.

chance such as a lottery or randomness. "First come, first served" would be more feasible than a lottery since the applicants make their claims over a period of time rather than as a group at one time. This procedure would be in accord with at least one principle in our present practices and with our sense of individual dignity, trust, and fairness. Its significance in relation to these values can be underlined by asking how the decision can be justified to the rejected applicant. Of course, one easy way of avoiding this task is to maintain the traditional cloak of secrecy, which works to a great extent because patients are often not aware that they are being considered for SLMR in addition to the usual treatment. But whether public justification is instituted or not is not the significant question: it is rather what reasons for rejection would be most acceptable to the unsuccessful applicant. My contention is that rejection can be accepted more readily if equality of opportunity, fairness, and trust are preserved, and that they are best preserved by selection by randomness or chance.

This proposal has yet another advantage since it would eliminate the need for 30 a committee to examine applicants in terms of their social value. This onerous responsibility can be avoided.

Finally, there is a possible indirect consequence of widespread use of random 31 selection which is interesting to ponder, although I do *not* adduce it as a good reason for adopting random selection. It can be argued, as Professor Mason Willrich of the University of Virginia Law School has suggested, that SLMR cases would practically disappear if these scarce resources were distributed randomly rather than on social worth grounds. Scarcity would no longer be a problem because the holders of economic and political power would make certain that they would not be excluded by a random selection procedure; hence they would help to redirect public priorities or establish private funding so that life-saving medical treatment would be widely and perhaps universally available.

In the framework that I have delineated, are the decrees of chance to be taken 32 without exception? If we recognize exceptions, would we not open Pandora's box again just after we had succeeded in getting it closed? The direction of my argument has been against any exceptions, and I would defend this as the proper way to go. But let me indicate one possible way of admitting exceptions while at the same time circumscribing them so narrowly that they would be very rare indeed.

An obvious advantage of the utilitarian approach is that occasionally circum- 33 stances arise which make it necessary to say that one man is practically indispensable for a society in view of a particular set of problems it faces (e.g., the President when the nation is waging a war for survival). Certainly the argument to this point has stressed that the burden of proof would fall on those who think that the social danger in this instance is so great that they simply cannot abide by the outcome of a lottery or a first come, first served policy. Also, the reason must be negative rather than positive; that is, we depart from chance in this instance not because we want to take advantage of this person's potential contribution to the improvement of our society, but because his immediate loss would possibly (even probably) be disastrous (again, the President in a grave national emergency). Finally, social value (in the negative sense) should be used as a standard of exception in dialysis, for example, only if it would provide a reason strong enough to warrant removing another person from a kidney machine if all machines were taken. Assuming this strong reluctance to remove anyone once the commitment has been made to him, we would be willing to put this patient ahead of another applicant for a vacant machine only if we would be willing (in circumstances in which all machines are being used) to vacate a machine by removing someone from it. These restrictions would make an exception almost impossible.

While I do not recommend this procedure of recognizing exceptions, I think 34 that one can defend it while accepting my general thesis about selection by randomness or chance. If it is used, a lay committee (perhaps advisory, perhaps even stronger) would be called upon to deal with the alleged exceptions since the doctors or others would in effect be appealing the outcome of chance (either natural or artificial). This lay committee would determine whether this patient was so indispensable at this time and place that he had to be saved even by sacrificing the values preserved by random selection. It would make it quite clear that exception is warranted, if at all, only as the "lesser of two evils." Such a defense would be recognized only rarely, if ever, primarily because chance and randomness preserve so many important moral and nonmoral values in SLMR cases.*

Notes

1. George Bernard Shaw, *The Doctor's Dilemma* (New York, 1941), pp. 132–133. [Childress's notes throughout.]
2. Henry K. Beecher, "Scarce Resources and Medical Advancement," *Daedalus* (Spring 1969), pp. 279–280.
3. Leo Shatin, "Medical Care and the Social Worth of a Man," *American Journal of Orthopsychiatry,* 36 (1967), 97.
4. Harry S. Abram and Walter Wadlington, "Selection of Patients for Artificial and Transplanted Organs," *Annals of Internal Medicine,* 69 (September 1968), 615–620.
5. *United States v. Holmes* 26 Fed. Cas. 360 (C.C.E.D. Pa. 1842). All references are to the text of the trial as reprinted in Philip E. Davis, ed., *Moral Duty and Legal Responsibility: A Philosophical-Legal Casebook* (New York, 1966), pp. 102–118.
6. *The Moral Decision* (Bloomington, Ind., 1955), p. 71.
7. Joseph Fletcher, "Donor Nephrectomies and Moral Responsibility," *Journal of the American Medical Women's Association,* 23 (Dec. 1968), p. 1090.
8. Leo Shatin, op. cit., pp. 96–101.
9. For a discussion of the Seattle selection committee, see Shana Alexander, "They Decide Who Lives, Who Dies," *Life,* 53 (Nov. 9, 1962). 102. For an examination of general selection practices in dialysis see "Scarce Medical Resources," *Columbia Law Review* 69:620 (1969) and Harry S. Abram and Walter Wadlington, op. cit.
10. David Sanders and Jesse Dukeminier, Jr., "Medical Advance and Legal Lag: Hemodialysis and Kidney Transplantation," *UCLA Law Review* 15:367 (1968) 378.

---

*I read a draft of this paper in a seminar on "Social Implications of Advances in Biomedical Science and Technology: Artificial and Transplanted Internal Organs," sponsored by the Center for the Study of Science, Technology, and Public Policy of the University of Virginia, Spring 1970. I am indebted to the participants in that seminar, and especially to its leaders, Mason Willrich, Professor of Law, and Dr. Harry Abram, Associate Professor of Psychiatry, for criticisms which helped me to sharpen these ideas. Good discussions of the legal questions raised by selection (e.g., equal protection of the law and due process), which I have not considered can be found in "Scarce Medical Resources," *Columbia Law Review,* 69:620 (1969); "Patient Selection for Artificial and Transplanted Organs," *Harvard Law Review,* 82:1322 (1969); and Sanders and Dukeminier, op. cit.

11. Helmut Thielicke, "The Doctor as Judge of Who Shall Live and Who Shall Die," *Who Shall Live?* ed. by Kenneth Vaux (Philadelphia, 1970), p. 172.
12. Ibid., pp. 173–174.
13. Ibid., p. 173.
14. Thielicke, *Theological Ethics,* Vol. I, *Foundations* (Philadelphia, 1966), p. 602.
15. Cahn, op. cit., p. 71.
16. Paul Freund, "Introduction," *Daedalus* (Spring 1969), xiii.
17. Paul Ramsey, *Nine Modern Moralists* (Englewood Cliffs, N.J., 1962), p. 245.
18. Charles Fried, "Privacy," In *Law, Reason, and Justice,* ed. by Graham Hughes (New York, 1969), p. 52.
19. Harry S. Abram, M.D., "The Psychiatrist, the Treatment of Chronic Renal Failure, and the Prolongation of Life: II" *American Journal of Psychiatry* 126:157–167 (1969), 158.

Questions

1. How do the alternatives discussed in paragraphs 6–8 help Childress define the point at issue in the debate over selection?
2. What difficulties in the idea of "medical acceptibility" does Childress explore? Why should "medical criteria" not be the basis for deciding who receives treatment?
3. Childress introduces the utilitarian standard in paragraph 6 (see p. 87)—the determination of "who will contribute to the greatest good for the greatest number"—and returns to it in paragraphs 14–20. What does he show to be the difficulties in the criterion of "social value"?
4. Does Childress disagree with the German theologian Thielicke that a "sense of guilt" ought to be encouraged in people and maintained?
5. What criterion for selection does Childress propose, and why does he consider it superior to other criteria?
6. How does Childress respond to the criticism that his criterion ignores the problem of "moral and nonmoral values" (paragraph 22)? What chief value would his criterion preserve, and how does Childress defend this value?
7. How does Childress respond to other criticisms in paragraphs 26–34?
8. Why must we assume the two "restrictions" that humans are "self-interested" and that they are "ignorant" of what they can contribute to the public good (paragraph 26)?

Suggestions for Writing

1. If you were in charge of a dialysis clinic and had too few machines for the number of patients, would you give preference to a scientist working on a cure for cancer over a person holding an ordinary job—perhaps an accountant or a waitress? What would be your criterion in making this decision, and how would you defend it against objections?

2. Are there circumstances when the welfare of society should take precedence over the welfare of the individual in allocating life-saving medical resources? If a shortage of insulin should arise, should people serving life sentences for murder be denied the drug? Or should "chance" govern the decision?

Additional Reading

Childress, James F. *Moral Responsibility in Conflicts: Essays on Nonviolence, War, and Conscience.* Baton Rouge: Lousiana State University Press, 1982.

———. *Who Should Decide?: Paternalism in Health Care.* New York: Oxford University Press, 1982.

Katz, Jay, and Alexander Morgan Capron. *Catastrophic Disease—Who Decides What?: A Psychosocial and Legal Analysis of the Problems Posed by Hemodialysis and Organ Transplantation.* New York: Russell Sage Foundation, 1975.

World Health Organization. *Health Aspects of Human Rights: With Special Reference to Developments in Biology and Medicine.* Geneva: World Health Organization, 1976.

*Knock**

The French novelist, poet, and dramatist Jules Romains (1885–1972) was trained as a scientist and philosopher, and he taught philosophy before World War I and for several years after his discharge from the army. He is best known among English readers for a series of twenty-seven novels. Men of Good Will, *published between 1932 and 1946. In these novels set in the social and political world of France between 1908 and 1933, Romains illustrates the personal philosophy that he called "Unanimism"—the belief that when individuals are united by a common emotion they can guide their lives for good rather than evil. However, the same "collective soul," Romains pointed out, can make people vulnerable to charismatic leaders and charlatans of many kinds. Romains wrote a number of comedies after the First World War to warn against this danger. In the 1930s he argued for a strong League of Nations and urged French men and women to unite against Nazi Germany. During the Second World War he lived in the United States and Mexico, returning to France in 1946.*

Perhaps no profession has been more admired and more feared or ridiculed—sometimes in the same periods—as the medical

---

*Translated from the French by James B. Gidney

profession. In ancient Greece, the physician seems to have been a revered figure—associated with the legendary Asclepius, described by Homer in the Iliad *as "the blameless physician." According to some legends, Asclepius was the son of Apollo and a local deity; in other legends, Asclepius is a mortal who became a god. Shrines to Asclepius were temples of healing in which the sick person might be cured through the agency of the healing gods during sleep. The sick person thus had access to supernatural as well as natural cures.*

In recent times, the "touch" of the physician has often been thought sufficient to heal the sick person. At times when no natural means of cure was available, the physician need only be present at the bedside of the patient or be able to predict the outcome of an illness— for example, in standing vigil to watch for the turn of a fever. By definition, the physician cannot always diagnose and cure illnesses. Indeed, the claim of being able to diagnose and cure every illness had been one definition of quackery. Encouraging unquestioning belief in the doctor has been another. The Irish dramatist George Bernard Shaw suggests in his satire on doctors, The Doctor's Dilemma, *that such faith might be a superstition. The basis for this faith, Shaw states in the preface to the play, is belief itself:*

> There is no harder scientific fact in the world than the fact that belief can be produced in practically unlimited quantity and intensity, without observation or reasoning, and even in defiance of both, by the simple desire to believe founded on a strong interest in believing.

This belief might be invested in "science," without knowledge of particular techniques and therapies or of their limitations. For Shaw, the doctor was to be judged by standards that applied to all people:

> As to the honor and conscience of doctors, they have as much as any other class of men, no more and no less. And what other men dare pretend to be impartial where they have a strong pecuniary interest on one side?

Romains raises similar questions in his comedy on medicine, Knock (1923). *His purpose is obviously to say something about belief in doctors, but his title character raises other important questions for modern readers. For many, the early scenes—in particular, the various ways Knock creates a profitable medical practice—establish the character of the man clearly. For others, the claims Knock makes for "medicine" late in the play suggest complex motives and attitudes. The reader will find many ideas and interpretations to consider as the play progresses.*

CHARACTERS

KNOCK, doctor
PARPALAID, doctor
MADAME PARPALAID, his wife
JEAN, Parpalaid's chauffeur

THE TOWN CRIER
MOUSQUET, pharmacist
BERNARD, schoolteacher
THE LADY IN BLACK, middle-aged farm woman
THE LADY IN PURPLE, elderly aristocrat
THE TWO YOUNG FELLOWS, town wags
MADAME REMY, landlady at the Key Hotel
SCIPIO, orderly
THE MAID at the Key Hotel
MARIETTE, nurse (heard offstage)

*The action takes place in and near the
        village of St. Maurice*

ACT I *In Dr. Parpalaid's car*
ACT II *Knock's office. A few days later*
ACT III *The Key Hotel. Three months later*

ACT I

The action takes place in and around a very old automobile, vintage 1900–1902. Enormous tonneau of the double phaeton type but with a tapering rear end. Lots of copperwork. Small hood that looks like a warming-pan.

During a part of the act the car is in motion. It starts from the vicinity of a small railroad station and climbs up a mountain road.

Four persons are about to get into the car—KNOCK, DR. PARPALAID, MME. PARPALAID, *and* JEAN, *the driver.*

DR. PARPALAID: (*to* KNOCK) Have you got all your bags, Doctor?
KNOCK: Yes, everything, Dr. Parpalaid.
DR. PARPALAID: Jean will stow them up front. We can all three fit easily into the back. The tonneau is so roomy and the bucket-seats are so comfortable! It doesn't cramp you like the things they're turning out today.
KNOCK: (*to* JEAN *who is stowing a large box*) Watch out for that box. I put some instruments in it. They're breakable.
(JEAN *puts* KNOCK'S *baggage into the car*)
MME. PARPALAID: I'd certainly miss this roadster if we were ever so foolish as to sell it.
(KNOCK *looks at car in surprise*)
DR. PARPALAID: That's what it is really—a roadster with the advantages of the old double phaeton.
KNOCK: I suppose so.
(*The entire front seat disappears under the luggage*)
DOCTOR: See how easily your bags fit in. They won't be in Jean's way at all. It's even too bad you didn't bring more so you could get a better idea of the comfort my car offers.
KNOCK: Is St. Maurice very far?

DOCTOR: About seven miles. Being so far from the railroad has its points. It keeps your patients faithful. They don't go off to the county seat to consult someone else.

KNOCK: Isn't there a bus?

DOCTOR: Yes, there is, but it's a mechanism so appalling in its dilapidation you'd rather walk.

MME. PARPALAID: You really can't get along without a car here.

DOCTOR: Especially in the profession.

(KNOCK *remains courteous but noncommittal*)

JEAN: (*to* DOCTOR) Shall I get her started?

DOCTOR: By all means, begin your preparations.

(JEAN *begins a series of manoeuvres: opening the hood, unscrewing the spark plugs, pumping in gasoline, etc.*)

MME. PARPALAID: The scenery along the way is wonderful. Zénaïde Fleuriot described it in one of her best novels—I forget its name. (*She gets into car. To her husband*) Why don't you take the bucket seat? Dr. Knock can sit in the back with me and enjoy the view.

(KNOCK *sits at* MME. PARPALAID'S *left*)

DOCTOR: The interior is so roomy that three can be quite comfortable in the back seat. But of course you want to stretch out to enjoy the view. (*approaching* JEAN) Is everything ready? Have you got the gas in all right? In both cylinders? Did you remember to wipe the plugs? It's a good precaution after a seven mile trip. And be sure to wrap up the carburetor. An old scarf would do better than that rag. (*as he moves toward rear*) That's just fine! Fine! (*gets into car—to* KNOCK) Pardon me, I'll sit on this big bucket seat which is actually a folding armchair.

MME. PARPALAID: The road climbs all the way to St. Maurice. It would be a terrible walk with all that baggage. But in the car it's a delight.

DOCTOR: (*to* KNOCK) At one time, Doctor, I courted the muse. I composed a sonnet of fourteen verses on the scenic magnificence you're about to behold. I'm damned if I can remember it. "Oh, valleys deep, oh, pastoral shades . . ."

(JEAN *turns the crank desperately*)

MME. PARPALAID: Albert, for several years you've been saying "valleys." It was "chasms deep" the way you wrote it.

DOCTOR: That's right, it was. "Chasms deep." (*an explosion*) Listen to that smooth motor, Doctor. Just a few turns of the crank to get it going, it hits on one cylinder, then on the other, and that's all there is to it. We're off.

(JEAN *gets in. The car begins to jolt. The landscape changes slowly.*)

DOCTOR: (*after a few moments of silence*) Well, from this moment you're my successor and believe me, you've done well for yourself. From now on my practice is yours. If one of my patients should manage to spot me in spite of the speed we're making and call on me to apply the healing art, I'd bow out. I'd say, "You've made a mistake. *This* is the local doctor." And believe me, I'd stay out of it (*backfiring of motor*) unless you formally invited me to consult. (*more backfiring*) You just had the luck to run into a man who was determined to indulge himself in a caprice.

MME. PARPALAID: My husband has always wanted to end his career in a big city.

DOCTOR: Sing my swan song on a large stage, so to speak. Ridiculous bit of vanity, isn't it? I dreamed of Paris, but Lyon will do.

MME. PARPALAID: Instead of going on making his fortune peacefully here!

(KNOCK *observes them alternately, thoughtfully, glances at the scenery*)

DOCTOR: Don't make fun of me, Doctor. Thanks to this whim you've got my practice for a song.

KNOCK: You think so?

DOCTOR: Obviously.

KNOCK: Well, I didn't haggle.

DOCTOR: No, you didn't. I liked your straightforwardness. I also liked the way you handled the whole thing by correspondence without even coming down here till the papers were signed. That struck me as chivalrous, even American. But I congratulate you just the same on a windfall. Because that's what it is. Steady work, no fluctuations.

MME. PARPALAID: No competition.

DOCTOR: A pharmacist who knows his place.

MME. PARPALAID: Nothing to spend your money on.

DOCTOR: Not a single expensive entertainment.

MME. PARPALAID: In six months you'll have saved twice what you owe my husband.

DOCTOR: And I'm letting you pay it in four quarterly installments. I really think I'd have finally turned you down if it weren't for my wife's rheumatism.

KNOCK: (*to* MME. PARPALAID) You suffer from rheumatism, Madame?

MME. PARPALAID: Unfortunately, yes.

DOCTOR: The climate is very healthful in general but it isn't good for her.

KNOCK: Do many people have rheumatism in these parts?

DOCTOR: Doctor, you'd do better to ask if there are many who don't have it.

KNOCK: That's very interesting.

DOCTOR: Yes, for someone who wants to study rheumatism.

KNOCK: (*softly*) I meant from the point of view of the practice.

DOCTOR: Oh no, people around here would no more go to a doctor for rheumatism than you'd go to a priest for rain.

KNOCK: That's too bad.

MME. PARPALAID: Look at that view, Doctor. You'd think we were in Switzerland.

(*sharper backfiring*)

JEAN: (*in* DOCTOR'S *ear*) Sir, there's something wrong. I'd better check the fuel pipe.

DOCTOR: (*to* JEAN) All right! (*to others*) As a matter of fact I was going to suggest a brief stop here.

MME. PARPALAID: Why?

DOCTOR: (*giving her a look*) Don't you think the scenery is worth it?

MME. PARPALAID: But if you want to stop there's a better view when we get a little higher.

(*Car lurches to halt.* MME. PARPALAID *understands*)

DOCTOR: Well, we can stop up there too. We can stop three or four times if we want to. Thank God, we're not out to set any records. (*to* KNOCK) Notice how gently the car stops, Doctor. You can always control your speed and that's important in mountainous country. (*as they climb out*) You'll be converted to mechanical transportation and sooner than you think. But watch out for the shoddy stuff they're turning out now. They don't put the steel in them that they used to.

KNOCK: If you can't do anything with rheumatism, you ought to make it up with pneumonia and pleurisy.

DOCTOR: (*to* JEAN) You might take advantage of our stop to clean out the fuel pipe. You were speaking of pneumonia and pleurisy, Doctor. They're rare up here. The climate is severe, as you know. All the sick babies die in the first six months, without the doctor's ever being called in, of course. The ones that survive are pretty rugged. On the other hand we have apoplexy and heart cases. But they never suspect it. They collapse and die all of a sudden around fifty.

KNOCK: You haven't made your fortune out of sudden death?

DOCTOR: Obviously not. (*thinks about it*) Well, we still have . . . first, influenza. Not the ordinary flu. That doesn't bother them. In fact, they welcome it. They think it drives out the evil vapors. I mean the world-wide epidemics of influenza.

KNOCK: Good God, do I have to wait for the next world-wide epidemic?

DOCTOR: I've lived through two of them myself: in 89 and 90 and in 1918.

MME. PARPALAID: In 1918 we had a very high mortality rate, higher than in the big cities. (*to her husband*) Didn't we? You compared the figures.

DOCTOR: Yes, percentagewise we were ahead of 83 departments.

KNOCK: Did they call you?

DOCTOR: Oh yes, mostly toward the end.

MME. PARPALAID: And we collected a lot of fees on St. Michael's Day.

(JEAN *crawls under the car*)

KNOCK: I beg your pardon?

MME. PARPALAID: Up here the patients pay on St. Michael's Day.

KNOCK: But what does that mean? Mañana, or something like that?

DOCTOR: (*from time to time glances at* JEAN) Of course not, Doctor. St. Michael's Day is one of the best known dates on the calendar. It comes at the end of September.

KNOCK: (*changing his tone*) And October has just begun. Whew! You picked a good time to sell out. (*paces about, thinking*) Look, if someone comes for an office visit, he pays you then, doesn't he?

DOCTOR: No, on St. Michael's Day. That's the custom.

KNOCK: But if he only comes for a single visit? Suppose you don't see him the rest of the year.

DOCTOR: On St. Michael's Day.

MME. PARPALAID: On St. Michael's Day.

(KNOCK *stares at them—silence*)

MME. PARPALAID: As a matter of fact, people around here almost always come for a single visit.

KNOCK: What!

MME. PARPALAID: That's the way it is.

(DR. PARPALAID *looks disturbed*)

KNOCK: But how about regular patients?

MME. PARPALAID: What do you mean, regular patients?

KNOCK: The patients you visit several times a week or several times a month.

MME. PARPALAID: (*to her husband*) Did you hear what the doctor said? Regular customers like the butcher and the baker. The doctor has his illusions like all beginners.

DOCTOR: (*putting his hand on* KNOCK'S *arm*) Believe me, Doctor, you've got the best kind of patients here—the kind that leave you free.

KNOCK: Free? That's a good one!

DOCTOR: Let me explain myself. I mean you're not at the mercy of a few patients who may get well from one day to the next and throw your budget out of kilter. When you're dependent on everybody, you're not dependent on anybody. See what I mean?

KNOCK: You mean I should have brought some bait and fishing tackle. Maybe I can get them here. (*paces about thinking, goes over to car, stares at it—half turning around*) The situation is becoming clear, Doctor. You've turned over to me—for several thousands, which I still owe you—a practice which is on a par with this car (*pats it affectionately*) of which it may be said that it's not too high at nineteen francs but at twenty-five it's overpriced. (*looking at it like a connoisseur*) Look, I like to do things in a big way. I'll give you thirty for it.

DOCTOR: Thirty francs for my roadster! I wouldn't sell it for six thousand.

KNOCK: As I expected. (*looking again at the car*) So I can't buy it.

DOCTOR: Well, if you'd at least make me a serious offer!

KNOCK: Too bad! I could have used it for storage. (*coming back to them*) I'd give up your patients with as little bitterness if it weren't too late.

DOCTOR: Doctor, I'm afraid you're the victim of a . . . a false impression.

KNOCK: I'm afraid it's you I'm the victim of . . . However, I'm not the kind to complain and when I'm swindled, I don't blame anyone but myself.

MME. PARPALAID: "Swindled!" Don't put up with that, Albert! . . . Aren't you going to protest?

DOCTOR: I'd rather straighten out Dr. Knock's misconceptions.

KNOCK: As for your installments, unfortunately they're on a quarterly basis in a climate in which the patients are on an annual basis. We'll have to straighten *that* out. In any case, don't worry about me. I dislike being in debt but I can stand it. It's a lot less painful than lumbago, for example, or a boil on the rear end.

MME. PARPALAID: You mean you're not going to pay us on the due dates?

KNOCK: I'd like nothing better than to pay you, Madame, but I have no control over the calendar. I can't change St. Whosit's Day.

MME. PARPALAID: St. Michael's.

KNOCK: St. Michael's.

DOCTOR: Don't you have any savings?

KNOCK: None: I live on my earnings. Or rather, I'm looking forward to living on them. I regret the mythical character of your patients all the more because I had been counting on using some entirely new methods on them. (*after a moment's reflection, speaking as if to himself*) Actually the problem merely presents itself in a somewhat different light.

DOCTOR: In that case, Doctor, you'd be very wrong to give way to a discouragement which is merely the outgrowth of your inexperience. Medicine is a rich soil but it doesn't yield its harvest unaided. You've been led astray by your youthful dreams.

KNOCK: Doctor, your remarks teem with errors. In the first place, I'm forty years old. Whatever dreams I may have aren't youthful.

DOCTOR: That may well be, but you've never practiced.

KNOCK: You're wrong there too.

DOCTOR: Didn't you tell me that you had just had your thesis accepted last summer?

KNOCK: Yes, I did. Thirty-two pages in-octavo entitled "On So-called Good Health," with this epigraph which I attributed to Claude Bernard: "Healthy people are sick people who don't know it."

DOCTOR: Then we don't disagree.

KNOCK: On my theory?

DOCTOR: No, on the fact that you're a beginner.

KNOCK: I beg your pardon. My studies are quite recent but I began practicing twenty years ago.

DOCTOR: What were you, a health officer? They went out years ago.

KNOCK: No, I had my bachelor's degree.

MME. PARAPALAID: There aren't any bachelor's degrees in health.

KNOCK: In liberal arts, Madame.

DOCTOR: You mean you practiced on the sly, without a license?

KNOCK: On the contrary, I practiced out in the open—and not in some provincial hole but over a space of 4500 miles.

DOCTOR: I don't understand.

KNOCK: It's simple enough. Twenty years ago I was forced to give up my studies in romance languages. I became a clerk in a Marseilles department store. At the tie counter. I lost my job. One day-I was walking along the docks when I saw an announcement: Steamship 1700 tons destination India wants doctor, license not required. What would you have done in my place?

DOCTOR: Nothing, obviously.

KNOCK: True, you had no real call. I had. I applied. I hate being in a false position, so I told them right away: "Gentlemen, I could tell you that I'm a doctor but I'm not. What's worse, I haven't even chosen a subject for my thesis." They replied that they didn't insist on my being a doctor and they didn't give a good God damn about my thesis. Then I said, "Although I'm not a doctor, I'd like, for the sake of prestige and discipline, to be called 'Doctor' on board." They said, "Naturally." Nonetheless I put in twenty minutes explaining why I had wrestled with my conscience and ended up by asking for a title to which I really had no right. We had only three minutes left to discuss salary.

DOCTOR: But you really had no knowledge of medicine?

KNOCK: I didn't say that. From my earliest childhood I had a passion for medical and pharmaceutical advertisements and for reading the Directions for Using on the bottles and pill boxes my parents bought. At the age of nine I had learned by heart a number of speeches on the faulty elimination of the constipated. And I can still recite a remarkable letter, written in 1897 by the widow P . . . of Bourges to the Shakers' American Tonic. Would you like to hear it?

DOCTOR: No, thanks, I'll take your word for it.

KNOCK: Through the study of these texts I acquired at an early age a medical style. But above all they enabled me to penetrate to the true meaning and goal of medicine, which the medical schools have buried under a pile of scientific rubbish. I think I may say that by the time I was twelve I had the right feel for medicine. My present method has been derived from it.

DOCTOR: Oh, you have a method? I'd be interested to know what it is.

KNOCK: I'm not promoting it. After all, it's the results that count. Today you're turning over to me a practice which, by your own admission, is worthless.

DOCTOR: Worthless! Really! I beg your pardon!

KNOCK: Come back in a year and see what I've done with it. The evidence will be conclusive. In forcing me to start from scratch you have increased the interest of the experiment.

JEAN: Sir . . . (DR. PARPALAID *goes over to him*) I think I'll have to take out the carburetor too.

DOCTOR: All right, go ahead. (*returns to* KNOCK) Since we have a good deal to say to one another, I've told the boy to give the carburetor its monthly cleaning.

MME. PARPALAID: But how did you get away with it when you were on your boat?

KNOCK: The last two nights before going on board I put in a lot of time thinking. My six months' practice proved the soundness of my ideas. That's more or less the hospital procedure.

MME. PARPALAID: How many people were you responsible for?

KNOCK: The crew and seven passengers of a very humble sort. Thirty-five in all.

MME. PARPALAID: That's a good number.

DOCTOR: Any deaths?

KNOCK: Not one. As a matter of fact, that's against my principles. I believe in reducing mortality.

DOCTOR: We all do.

KNOCK: You too? I wouldn't have thought it. In a word, I believe that in spite of all temptations to the contrary, we should try to save the patient.

MME. PARPALAID: There's something in what he says.

DOCTOR: Did you have many patients?

KNOCK: Thirty-five.

DOCTOR: The whole lot?

KNOCK: The whole lot.

MME. PARPALAID: How did the boat keep going?

KNOCK: Oh, we worked out a rotation.

(*silence*)

DOCTOR: Are you really a doctor now? . . . Because here you've got to have your license and you'd cause us a great deal of embarrassment . . . If you aren't a doctor, you ought to make a clean breast of it . . .

KNOCK: I am really and doctorally a doctor. When I saw how well my methods worked in practice, I couldn't wait to try them out on terra firma. I knew I'd have to go through the formality of a degree.

MME. PARPALAID: But you said you'd finished your course just recently?

KNOCK: I wasn't able to start right away. In order to live I was obliged for a time to trade in peanuts. (MME. PARPALAID *is startled*) Oh, I didn't sell them by the bag, I set up an office to supply retailers. If I'd kept at it ten years I'd have been a millionaire. But it was dull. As a matter of fact, almost all professions get to be a bore after a while. I found that out. Actually, medicine is the only true profession, except maybe politics, finance, and the priesthood which I haven't tried yet.

MME. PARPALAID: Do you think you can use your methods here?

KNOCK: If I didn't, I'd get out of here as fast as I could and you'd never catch up with me. Obviously I'd rather be in a city.

MME. PARPALAID: (*to her husband*) Before we leave for Lyon, why don't you find out something about the doctor's methods? You wouldn't commit yourself to anything.

DOCTOR: Doctor Knock doesn't seem to want to divulge them.

KNOCK: (*after reflection*) To accommodate you I'll make you this proposition. Instead of paying you, God knows when, in cash, I'll pay you in kind. You can stay with me for a week and learn how I do things.

DOCTOR: (*annoyed*) You're not serious, Doctor. More likely you'll be writing me in a week for advice.

KNOCK: I won't wait that long. I'd like to get some from you right now.

DOCTOR: I'm at your service.

KNOCK: Is there a town crier in St. Maurice?

PARPALAID: You mean a fellow who rings a big bell and makes announcements in public?

KNOCK: Exactly.

DOCTOR: Yes, there is. He makes announcements for the town council. He doesn't have any private clients except people who have lost their pocketbooks or now and then an out-of-town merchant who's having a sale of pottery.

KNOCK: Good! What's the population?

DOCTOR: Thirty-five hundred in the village, I believe, and almost six thousand in the township.

KNOCK: How about the county?

DOCTOR: Oh, at least twice as many.

KNOCK: Are they poor?

MME. PARPALAID: On the contrary, they're very well fixed, you might even say rich. There are some large farms. A number of people have private incomes or live off their lands.

DOCTOR: Awfully stingy though.

KNOCK: Any industry?

DOCTOR: Very little.

KNOCK: Trade?

MME. PARPALAID: Oh, there are plenty of shops.

KNOCK: Are the traders completely wrapped up in business?

DOCTOR: Anything but. For most of them it's extra income or a way to put in their spare time.

MME. PARPALAID: While the wife keeps the shop the husband steps out.

DOCTOR: Or the reverse.

MME. PARPALAID: You'll admit it's usually the husband. Besides, the women haven't anywhere to go. The men have hunting, fishing, and ninepins—and in winter, the café.

KNOCK: Are the women very devout? (DR. PARPALAID *laughs*) It's an important question for me.

MME. PARPALAID: A lot of them go to mass.

KNOCK: But does God play any considerable part in their everyday thoughts?

MME. PARPALAID: Don't be silly!

KNOCK: Fine. (*thinks*) No great vices?

DOCTOR: Such as?

KNOCK: Opium, cocaine, the black mass, sodomy, political convictions?

DOCTOR: You mix things up so. I've never heard of opium or the black mass but people are interested in politics like anywhere else.

KNOCK: But do you know any who'd torture their parents to get the party ballot or the income tax?

DOCTOR: Thank God, they're not like that.

KNOCK: How about adultery?

DOCTOR: How do you mean?

KNOCK: I mean, has it undergone an exceptional development? Is it particularly active?

DOCTOR: You ask some strange questions. No doubt there are deceived husbands, like anywhere else, but it's not excessive.

MME. PARPALAID: Besides, it's not easy. People know everything you do . . .

KNOCK: Good. Is there anything else I should know? For example, religious sects, superstitions, secret societies?

MME. PARPALAID: At one time some of the women went in for spiritualism.

KNOCK: Ah! (*this interests and disturbs him*)

MME. PARPALAID: They used to get together with the lawyer's wife and do some table tapping.

KNOCK: That's bad. Very bad.

MME. PARPALAID: But I think they've given it up.

KNOCK: I hope so. And there's no magician or faith healer? No smelly old farmer who cures people by the laying on of hands?

DOCTOR: There may have been at one time but now now.

(*From time to time* JEAN *may be seen desperately turning the crank and wiping his forehead*)

KNOCK: (*excitedly rubbing his hands and walking about*) In a word, the town is on the threshold of the medical age. (*going to car*) Doctor, would it be inhuman to ask one more effort from this vehicle? I have a great urge to get to St. Maurice.

MME. PARPALAID: It came on suddenly.

KNOCK: Please, let's get going.

DOCTOR: What exerts such a powerful attraction on you?

KNOCK: (*walks back and forth several times in silence*) Doctor, I have a feeling that you've muffed a marvellous opportunity and, to use your own style, brought forth a harvest of weeds where you might have had a burgeoning garden. You should be leaving here with gold coming out of your pockets, sitting on a pile of gilt-edged securities as thick as a mattress, you, Madame, with three strings of pearls around your neck, and the two of you riding in a shiny limousine instead of this monument to the first creative efforts of modern genius.

MME. PARPALAID: Is this a joke, Doctor?

KNOCK: It would be a cruel joke.

MME. PARPALAID: Then it's horrible! Did you hear him, Albert?

DOCTOR: What I heard is that Dr. Knock is a visionary and perhaps a manic depressive. He plunges from one extreme to the other. A few minutes ago the practice wasn't worth anything; now it's a bonanza. (*shrugs his shoulders*)

MME. PARPALAID: Yes, but how about you? You're too sure of your opinions. How many times have I told you that we could do better than vegetate in St. Maurice if you only knew how to go about it?

DOCTOR: All right, all right. I'll come back in three months for my first installment. We'll see how Dr. Knock is getting along.

KNOCK: That's fine. Come back in three months. We'll have time to talk about it then. But now, please, let's go.

DOCTOR: (*nervously, to* JEAN) Are you ready?

JEAN: (*whispering*) Oh, *I'm* ready. But this time I don't think we'll get it started by ourselves.

DOCTOR: (*whispering*) What's the matter?

JEAN: (*shaking his head*) It would take stronger men than we are to crank it.

DOCTOR: Suppose we give it a push?

JEAN: (*without conviction*) Maybe.

DOCTOR: Why not? We've got sixty feet of level ground. I'll steer; you push.

JEAN: All right.

DOCTOR: And try to jump on the running-board at the right moment. (*goes back to others*). All aboard, Doctor, all aboard. Jean, who's a young Hercules, wants to see if he can start us without the crank. It's a game with him—a kind of self-starter in which electrical energy is replaced by muscular energy . . . which is much the same thing if you come to think of it.

(JEAN *braces himself against the body of the car*)

CURTAIN

ACT II

Former Home of PARPALAID. KNOCK *has moved in temporarily. Tables, chairs, combination cupboard-bookshelf, sofa, blackboard, wash-basin. Anatomical and histological sketches on wall.* KNOCK, *seated, writing; town crier standing.*

KNOCK: (*looking up*) You're the town crier?

CRIER: Yes, sir.

KNOCK: Call me "Doctor." When you answer me, say "Yes, Doctor" and "No, Doctor."

CRIER: Yes, Doctor.

KNOCK: And when you talk about me outside, be sure to say "the doctor said," "the doctor did" . . . It's important. When you talked about Dr. Parpalaid among yourselves, what did you say?

CRIER: We said, "He's a good man but he doesn't amount to much."

KNOCK: That's not what I meant. Did you say "the doctor"?

CRIER: No, we said "M. Parpalaid" or sometimes "Ravachol."

KNOCK: (*puzzled*) "Ravachol"? Why did you call him that?

CRIER: It's just a name he'd picked up. I don't know how.

KNOCK: And you thought he didn't amount to much?

CRIER: He did all right for me but I guess not for everybody.

KNOCK: Hm!

CRIER: When you went to see him, he didn't know.

KNOCK: Didn't know what?

CRIER: What you had. Nine times out of ten he'd say, "It's nothing. You'll be all right tomorrow."

KNOCK: He would?

CRIER: Or he'd hardly listen to you, just say "hm, hm" and start talking about something else for an hour. His car, for example.

KNOCK: As if you'd come to him for that!

CRIER: Then he'd prescribe something real cheap—a tonic or something like that. You know, when people pay eight francs to go to a doctor, they don't want a four-sou prescription. And no matter how dumb you are, you don't need a doctor to tell you to take camomile.

KNOCK: What you've told me is most disturbing. But I sent for you to get some information. How much did you charge Dr. Parpalaid for an announcement?

CRIER: (*bitterly*) He never gave me an announcement.

KNOCK: What! In all the thirty years he was here?

CRIER: Not one announcement in thirty years.

KNOCK: (*getting up, holding piece of paper*) I just can't believe it. You must have forgotten. Well, what are your prices?

CRIER: Three francs for the little round and five francs for the big round. You may think that's too high but I'd advise you, sir . . .

KNOCK: Doctor.

CRIER: I'd advise you, Doctor, if you can spare the extra two francs, to take the big round. You get much better coverage.

KNOCK: What's the difference?

CRIER: On the little round I stop five times: in front of the town hall, at the post office, at the Key Hotel, at Thieves' Corners, and on the market corner. On the big round I stop eleven times: at . . .

KNOCK: All right, I'll take the big round. Are you free this morning?

CRIER: Right away, if you like.

KNOCK: I do. Here's the announcement. (*gives him paper*)

CRIER: (*looking it over*) I'm used to all sorts of writing but I'd rather you read it to me first.

(*The* CRIER *listens professionally*)

KNOCK: (*slowly*) "Dr. Knock, successor to Dr. Parpalaid, presents his compliments to the people of the city and township of St. Maurice and is pleased to announce that, in the interest of the welfare of the community and with the objective of arresting the progress of diseases of all kinds which have been encroaching in recent years on this formerly healthful region . . .

CRIER: That's the God's truth!

KNOCK: ". . . his services will be available to the residents of the city and township without any charge from 9:30 to 11 A.M. every Monday. Non-residents will be charged the regular fee of eight francs."

CRIER: (*taking the announcement with respect*) Well, that's a wonderful idea! It will be well received. You'll see! You're a public benefactor! (*changing tone*) But you know this is Monday. If I announce this today, they'll start coming in here in five minutes.

KNOCK: As quick as that? You really think so?

CRIER: Besides, it may not have occurred to you that Monday is market day. Half the township is in town. They'll all hear this. You'll be swamped.

KNOCK: I'll try to handle them.

CRIER: What's more, you've got your best chance for patients on market day. Dr. Parpalaid hardly ever saw them on any other day. (*familiarly*) If you give it to them free . . .

KNOCK: Please understand that my chief desirė is for people to take care of themselves. If I wanted to make money, I'd set up practice in Paris—or New York.

CRIER: You hit the nail on the head! We don't take enough care of ourselves. We won't listen to anybody. We drive ourselves too hard. When we're sick we just make ourselves keep going. We might as well be so many animals.

KNOCK: I see you reason very clearly.

CRIER: (*swelling up*) Oh, I can reason all right. I haven't as much education as I ought to have. But there are plenty of educated people I don't have to take a back seat to. The mayor can tell you. Why, would you believe it, sir . . .

KNOCK: Doctor.

CRIER: Doctor! . . . One day when the prefect himself was at the town hall, in the big reception room, and all the big shots were there, you can ask any of them, the chief deputy, or M. Michalon, or any of them, and . . .

KNOCK: And the prefect saw right away who was who and he said the town crier reasoned things out better than some who thought they were too good for him. And the mayor didn't have a word to say.

CRIER: (*delighted*) That's exactly it! Every word! I'd swear you were hidden somewhere and heard the whole thing.

KNOCK: I wasn't there.

CRIER: Then somebody must have told you. Somebody high up? (KNOCK *makes gesture of diplomatic reticence*) You can't tell me you haven't been talking to the prefect recently. (KNOCK *smiles*)

KNOCK: (*getting up*) Well, I'm counting on you. And give it a lot of voice, will you?

CRIER: (*hesitantly*) I won't be able to get back this morning or if I do, I'll get here too late. Would you be good enough to . . . give me my consultation now?

KNOCK: Uh . . . all right. But we'll have to hurry. I have appointments with M. Bernard, the schoolteacher, and M. Mousquet, the pharmacist. I'll have to see them before the patients start coming in. What's the matter with you?

CRIER: Let me think! (*laughs*) Well, sometimes after I've eaten I feel a kind of itch here. (*puts hand on upper part of stomach*) It tickles . . . or scratches.

KNOCK: (*deep concentration*) Let's be clear about it. Does it tickle or does it scratch?

CRIER: It scratches. (*thinks it over*) But it tickles too, sort of.

KNOCK: Show me exactly where.

CRIER: Here.

KNOCK: Here? Where's here?

CRIER: Here . . . or maybe here. Or in between.

KNOCK: Halfway between? . . . Wouldn't it be just a little to the left, where my finger is?

CRIER: I think so.

Responsibilities of the Doctor 523

KNOCK: Does it hurt when I press?

CRIER: Yes, I'd say it hurts.

KNOCK: (*grave manner*) Ah! Doesn't it scratch worse when you've eaten calf's head vinaigrette?

CRIER: I never eat it. But I think if I ate it, it would scratch worse.

KNOCK: Hm! That's important. Hm! How old are you?

CRIER: Fifty-one, going on fifty-two.

KNOCK: Nearer fifty-one or fifty-two?

CRIER: (*gradually getting worried*) Fifty-two. I'll be fifty-two in November.

KNOCK: (*putting hands on* CRIER'S *shoulders*) Go about your work today as you always do. But get to bed early tonight and stay in bed tomorrow. I'll stop by to see you. My visits will be free. But don't tell anyone about it. I'm just doing it for you.

CRIER: (*anxiously*) It's very good of you, Doctor. But do you think I've got something serious?

KNOCK: It's not very serious yet. We've caught it in time to treat it. Do you smoke?

CRIER: (*taking out his handkerchief*) No, I chew.

KNOCK: Absolutely no chewing. Do you drink wine?

CRIER: A reasonable amount.

KNOCK: Not a drop of wine. Are you married?

CRIER: (*mops his forehead*) Yes, Doctor.

KNOCK: Total abstinence there.

CRIER: Can I eat?

KNOCK: Today, while you're working, you can have a bowl of soup. Tomorrow we'll have to be stricter. For now, just stick to what I've told you.

CRIER: (*mopping himself again*) Wouldn't it be better to get to bed right away? I really don't feel good.

KNOCK: (*opening door*) By no means! In a case like yours it's unwise to go to bed between sunrise and sunset. Make your announcements just as if nothing was wrong and wait till this evening. (*shows him out*)

(*Enter schoolteacher,* M. BERNARD)

KNOCK: How do you do, M. Bernard? I hope I haven't inconvenienced you too much by asking you to stop by at this hour.

BERNARD: No, no, that's all right, Doctor. I have a moment. My assistant takes over for recess.

KNOCK: I was very anxious to have a talk with you. We have so many things to do together. Urgent things too. I wouldn't want to break up the valuable collaboration that existed between you and my predecessor.

BERNARD: Collaboration?

KNOCK: I'm not the kind of man who insists on imposing his own ideas or on tearing down everything that's been built up beforehand. At the outset I'll follow your lead.

BERNARD: I don't see . . .

KNOCK: Let's leave things as they are for now. We can make improvements as we go along if we need to. (*sits down*)

BERNARD: But . . .

KNOCK: Whether it's printed material, or lectures, or our meetings together, I'd like to do things your way. You set the time and I'll adjust my schedule to it.

BERNARD: I'm afraid I don't understand, Doctor.

KNOCK: I simply mean that I'd like to maintain the connection even while I'm getting started.

BERNARD: There must be something I don't grasp . . .

KNOCK: Oh, come! You were in regular contact with Dr. Parpalaid, weren't you?

BERNARD: I saw him now and then at the bar in the Key Hotel. We sometimes played a game of billiards together.

KNOCK: That's not the kind of contact I mean.

BERNARD: We didn't have any other.

KNOCK: But . . . but . . . how did you divide up responsibility for community instruction in hygiene? Or family education? and I don't know what all—the hundreds of things a doctor and schoolteacher can only do in cooperation?

BERNARD: We didn't divide up anything.

KNOCK: You mean you really preferred acting independently?

BERNARD: It's much simpler than that. Neither of us ever gave it a thought. This is the first time I've heard of such a thing in St. Maurice.

KNOCK: (*with all the signs of being flabbergasted and in deep distress*) If I weren't hearing it from your own lips, I wouldn't believe it.

(*silence*)

BERNARD: I'm sorry to be such a disappointment to you, but you'll agree that it wasn't up to me to take the initiative in such a matter, even if I'd thought of it and my teaching duties had left me much more spare time than they do.

KNOCK: Obviously it wasn't. You waited for a summons that never came.

BERNARD: Whenever I've been asked to lend a hand, I've always tried to do it.

KNOCK: I know, I know, M. Bernard. (*silence*) Then from the point of view of hygiene and preventive medicine, these poor people have been left entirely to their own devices.

BERNARD: I should say so!

KNOCK: I'll bet they drink water without ever thinking of the millions of bacteria they take in at every swallow.

BERNARD: Oh, absolutely.

KNOCK: Do they even know what a microbe is?

BERNARD: I doubt it. Some of them know the word but they probably think it's a kind of insect.

KNOCK: (*getting up*) It makes me shudder to think of it. Listen, M. Bernard! You and I can't make up in a week for years of . . . let's say carelessness. But we must do something.

BERNARD: I'm willing but I'm afraid I won't be of much help to you.

KNOCK: M. Bernard, I've been told by one who knows you well that you have one great fault—modesty. You're the only one who doesn't know that you have an unusual personal influence and moral authority here. Forgive me for embarrassing you by mentioning it. But I can't do anything without you.

BERNARD: Doctor, you're exaggerating.

KNOCK: Yes, of course. I can take care of my patients without you. But who'll help me fight disease itself? Who'll help me bring it out into the open? Who'll teach these poor people the dangers that lie in wait for them every second of the day? Who'll teach them they shouldn't wait until they're dead to call a doctor?

BERNARD: They're very negligent, no doubt about it.

KNOCK: (*becoming more and more animated*) Let's start at the beginning. I have material for several popular lectures: complete notes, some good slides, and a lantern. You know how to set up that sort of thing. To start out, a lecture—it's all written out and very entertaining—on typhoid fever—the unsuspected forms it takes, its many carriers: water, bread, milk, shellfish, green vegetables, salads, dust, breath, etc. . . . the weeks and months of incubation before it suddenly breaks out and kills you, the frightful complications it brings with it . . . all very attractively worked up with pictures: enlarged shots of bacilli, details of the excreta of typhoid victims, and not just black and white, but pink, chestnut, yellow, and greenish white. You can imagine. (*sits down*)

BERNARD: (*highly upset*) I'm too impressionable. If I got into anything like that, I wouldn't be able to sleep.

KNOCK: That's just what we want. I mean—that's just the way we want it to hit our audiences. *You'll* get used to it. But don't let *them* sleep! (*leaning toward him*) That's what's wrong with them. They're asleep. Asleep with a false sense of security from which the sudden, shattering blow of disease awakens them, too late.

BERNARD: (*trembling*) I've never been very strong. My parents had a hard time nursing me through childhood. I know the microbes on your slides are just pictures, but still . . .

KNOCK: (*as if he hadn't heard*) For those who aren't shaken up by our first lecture, I've got another. The title is harmless enough: "Germ-carriers." It proves beyond any doubt, by citing actual cases, that you can have good color, rosy tongue, sound appetite, and all the time you're carrying around with you trillions of virulent bacilli, enough to infect half a dozen counties. (*getting up*) On the basis of both theory and experience, I have to suspect anybody of being a germ-carrier. You, for example. I have no way of knowing you aren't one.

BERNARD: (*springing to his feet*) Me! Doctor . . .

KNOCK: I'd like to meet anybody who could go out of that second lecture in a gay mood.

BERNARD: Do you think I'm a germ-carrier, Doctor?

KNOCK: Not you necessarily. I took you as an example. But I think I hear M. Mousquet outside. I'll see you again soon, M. Bernard, and thanks for your support. I felt sure I could count on it.

(*After* BERNARD *has gone out,* MOUSQUET *comes in. He is dressed simply, almost sloppily*)

KNOCK: Please have a seat, M. Mousquet. I just had time to glance inside your pharmacy yesterday. But I saw enough to convince me of its quality. I was impressed by its perfect order and its modernity, down to the last detail.

MOUSQUET: You're too kind, Doctor.

KNOCK: I consider it vital. So far as I'm concerned, a doctor who hasn't the support of a first-class pharmacist is like a general going into battle with no artillery.

MOUSQUET: I'm glad you appreciate the importance of the profession.

KNOCK: And I'm glad that a service like yours is properly rewarded and that you clear at least 25,000 a year.

MOUSQUET: Twenty-five thousand! You mean profit? I wish I could do half as well.

KNOCK: M. Mousquet, you're not talking to a treasury man but to a friend—a colleague, if I may say so.

MOUSQUET: Doctor, I wouldn't insult you by suspecting you. I have all I can do to exceed 10,000.

KNOCK: But that's atrocious! (MOUSQUET *shrugs sadly*) I was thinking of 25,000 as a minimum. You haven't any competition?

MOUSQUET: No, not within several miles.

KNOCK: Then what's the matter? Have you any enemies?

MOUSQUET: Not that I know of.

KNOCK: You haven't a skeleton in the closet? A moment of inattention . . . fifty grams of laudanum in place of castor oil? It can happen in a moment.

MOUSQUET: Believe me, nothing of the sort. Not the slightest accident in twenty years.

KNOCK: Then . . . then I hate to entertain the idea. . . . Was my predecessor . . . wasn't he equal to his task?

MOUSQUET: That depends on your point of view.

KNOCK: Again, M. Mousquet, this is just between ourselves.

MOUSQUET: Dr. Parpalaid is a fine man. We had the most cordial private relations.

KNOCK: But his prescriptions didn't add up to much?

MOUSQUET: That's it.

KNOCK: When I piece together all the things I've heard about him, I wonder if he believed in medicine at all.

MOUSQUET: At the start I did everything I could. When people told me they didn't feel good, if it seemed at all serious, I sent them to him. But that was the end of it. They never came back.

KNOCK: That upsets me a great deal, I'll have to admit. M. Mousquet, ours are the two noblest of professions. It's criminal to allow them to slip from the level of influence and prosperity to which our predecessors have brought them. "Sabotage" is not too strong a word.

MOUSQUET: You're right. Aside from the question of money, you feel you're sinking below the tinker and the grocer. Doctor, my wife couldn't afford the hats and the silk stockings the tinker's wife parades around in every day of the week.

KNOCK: Stop, please, it's too painful. It's as if you told me that a judge's wife had to do the baker's washing to get bread.

MOUSQUET: If Mme. Mousquet were here, she'd be much affected by what you're saying.

KNOCK: Why, in a town like this, you and I shouldn't be able to handle all the work.

MOUSQUET: That's true.

KNOCK: It's a matter of principle with me to regard the entire population as our patients. Ipso facto.

MOUSQUET: The entire population! That's asking a lot.

KNOCK: I say the entire population.

MOUSQUET: Of course anyone can become our patient from time to time.

KNOCK: Not from time to time. A regular patient! A faithful patient!

MOUSQUET: Well, he's got to get sick first.

KNOCK: "Get sick" is an old idea. It can't stand up to modern science. "Health" is a word which we could just as well erase from our vocabularies. For me there are only people more or less sick of more or less numerous diseases progressing at a more or less rapid rate. Naturally, if you tell them they're well, they're only too glad to believe you. But you're deceiving them. The only possible excuse is that you already have so many patients to take care of that you can't possibly take any more.

MOUSQUET: It's a good theory anyway.

KNOCK: A profoundly modern theory, M. Mousquet. If you think it over, you'll be struck by its relation to the admirable concept of the nation in arms, a concept from which our modern states derive their strength.

MOUSQUET: You're a thinker, Dr. Knock, and no matter what the materialists say, thought rules the world.

KNOCK: (*getting up*) Listen to me! (*Both standing.* KNOCK *takes* MOUSQUET'S *hands*) Perhaps I'm overconfident. There may be some bitter disillusionment in store for me. But if at the end of a year, you haven't cleared the 25,000 francs you ought to be making, if Mme. Mousquet doesn't have the dresses, hats, and stockings which her station requires, you can come in here and tell me off and I'll turn both cheeks to be slapped.

MOUSQUET: Doctor, I thank you from the bottom of my heart. I'd be ungrateful if I didn't help you in any way I can.

KNOCK: Good. You can count on me. I'm counting on you.

(MOUSQUET *goes out*)

KNOCK: (*at the door*) Now for my patients. (*calling out*) A dozen already? Please tell any that come in from now on that I can't see them after 11:30, at least not free. (*to lady in black as she enters*) Are you the first, Madame? (*closes door behind her*) Are you a resident of the county?

LADY IN BLACK: (*She is 45 and exudes an atmosphere of peasant greed and constipation*) Yes, I live in the township, in the big farm on the Luchère road.

KNOCK: Do you own it?

LADY IN BLACK: Yes, with my husband.

KNOCK: If you work it yourselves, you must be kept busy.

LADY IN BLACK: I should think so, sir! Eighteen cows, two bulls, two steers, the mare and the colt, six goats, a dozen hogs, not to mention the chickens.

KNOCK: Good Lord! Don't you have help?

LADY IN BLACK: Of course we have. Three men and a woman and some extras by the day at harvest time.

KNOCK: You really have your hands full. I'm afraid you don't have much time to take care of yourselves.

LADY IN BLACK: Oh, no!

KNOCK: And yet you're sick.

LADY IN BLACK: Not "sick" exactly. I'm really just tired.

KNOCK: That's what you call it. (*going up to her*) Let's see your tongue. You probably don't have much appetite.

LADY IN BLACK: No.

KNOCK: You're constipated.

LADY IN BLACK: Yes, some.

KNOCK: (*puts stethoscope to her chest*) Put your head down. Breathe. Cough. You didn't by any chance fall off a ladder when you were little?

LADY IN BLACK: I don't remember.

KNOCK: (*thumping her upper back, applying pressure to her lower back*) Do you ever have pain here when you go to bed? Any lameness?

LADY IN BLACK: Yes, sometimes.

KNOCK: (*continuing to listen to stethoscope*) Try to remember. It must have been a big ladder.

LADY IN BLACK: It could have been.

KNOCK: (*very positive*) It was about ten feet, leaning against a wall. You fell off backwards. You took most of the impact on your left side, fortunately.

LADY IN BLACK: Oh, yes.

KNOCK: You must have consulted Dr. Parpalaid about it.

LADY IN BLACK: No, I never did.

KNOCK: Why not?

LADY IN BLACK: He never gave free consultations. (*silence*)

KNOCK: (*gestures for her to sit down*) Do you realize the condition you're in?

LADY IN BLACK: No.

KNOCK: (*sits down facing her*) So much the better. Do you want to get well or don't you?

LADY IN BLACK: Yes.

KNOCK: I must warn you before we go any further that it will take a long time and cost a good deal.

LADY IN BLACK: Oh, no! Why should it?

KNOCK: Because it takes more than a few minutes to cure something you've had for forty years.

LADY IN BLACK: Forty years!

KNOCK: Yes, from the time you fell off the ladder.

LADY IN BLACK: How much will it cost?

KNOCK: What are your calves worth currently?

LADY IN BLACK: That depends on their weight and the market. But the good ones should bring at least four to five hundred francs.

KNOCK: How about your hogs?

LADY IN BLACK: Some of them more than a thousand.

KNOCK: It will cost you about two calves and two hogs.

LADY IN BLACK: Oh, oh, oh! Almost three thousand francs. Holy Mother of God, that will ruin us.

KNOCK: If you'd rather make a pilgrimage, I won't stand in your way.

LADY IN BLACK: Oh, a pilgrimage is expensive too and usually doesn't work. (*pause*) What have I got that's so terrible?

KNOCK: (*very courteously*) I think I can make it clear very quickly with the help of the blackboard (*goes to board and starts sketching*). Here's your spinal column in cross-section—very rough, of course. This is your Turck's nexus and this is your Clarke's column. Do you follow me? Now, when you fell off the ladder your Turck and your Clarke slipped in opposite directions by a fraction of an inch (*drawing arrows*). You may think that's not much but in this location, it's enough. You've got a continual strain on your multipolars. (*wipes his fingers*)

LADY IN BLACK: (*groaning*) Oh, oh, Mother of God!

KNOCK: Don't let it upset you. You won't die of it right away. You've got time.

LADY IN BLACK: (*still groaning*) Oh, oh, I never should have fallen off that ladder.

KNOCK: I'm not sure it wouldn't be better to leave things as they are. You have to work so hard to earn anything. Old age, on the other hand, is no bargain. You don't get much fun out of it.

LADY IN BLACK: Isn't there a less expensive way to do it? Something a bit cruder? Provided it cures me, of course.

KNOCK: What I propose is to put you under observation. It will cost you almost nothing. After a few days you can see how your illness is progressing and decide for yourself.

LADY IN BLACK: All right.

KNOCK: Good. You can go home now. Did you come in a car?

LADY IN BLACK: No, I walked.

KNOCK: (*writing prescription, seated at table*) We'll have to try to find you a car. Go to bed when you get home. In a room where you can be alone as much as possible. Close the shutters and draw the curtains so the light won't bother you. Don't let anyone talk to you. No solid food for a week. A glass of Vichy water every two hours and, if you need it, a half a cracker soaked in milk morning and evening. But I'd rather you'd get along without the cracker if you can. You can't say I'm prescribing an expensive cure! We'll see how you feel in a week. If you're strong and full of life it will mean that things aren't as bad as they seem. If, on the other hand, you're weak and drowsy, have a hard time getting up, then there's no doubt about it and we'll have to start the treatment. All right?

LADY IN BLACK: (*sighing*) Whatever you say.

KNOCK: (*indicating paper on which he has been writing*) Here are your instructions. I'll stop by to see you in the next few days. (*gives her paper and leads her to the door; calling out*) Mariette, please help Madame downstairs and get her a car.

(*Through the door several patients may be seen. The appearance of the* LADY IN BLACK *as she goes out impresses them and frightens them a little. Enter the* LADY IN PURPLE. *She is 60. Her entire costume is the same shade of purple. She leans rather majestically on a sort of alpenstock.*)

LADY IN PURPLE: (*grandly*) You must be surprised to see me here, Doctor.

KNOCK: A little, yes.

LADY IN PURPLE: It's not often that a Mme. Pons, by birth a Lempousas, comes to a doctor for a free consultation.

KNOCK: It's very flattering.

LADY IN PURPLE: You may see in it a sign of the degeneracy of the times when a crowd of hog butchers and vulgarians drive their own carriages and swill champagne with actresses, while a Lempousas, whose family goes back unbroken to the thirteenth century and once owned half the province, and who is related to all the nobility and the better people of this part of the country, has to wait in line with the town paupers. We've seen better times, haven't we, Doctor?

KNOCK: Too true, Madame, all too true.

LADY IN PURPLE: I won't pretend that my income is what it used to be nor that I've been able to maintain the household of six servants or the stable of four horses that were traditional in the family until the death of my uncle. Last year I even had to sell an estate of 400,000 acres which came to me from my maternal grandmother. It's called La Michouille, of Greek and Latin origin, according to our priest, who derives it from *mycodium,* hatred of the mushroom, because nobody has ever found a mushroom on the estate. It's as if the soil couldn't stand them. As a matter of fact, what with taxes and upkeep, it brought in very little, particularly after my husband died. The tenants took advantage of me. They were always arguing and begging for reductions or delays in the rent. I got so sick of it! Just sick to death! Don't you think I was right to get rid of it, everything considered?

KNOCK: (*he has been completely attentive throughout this speech*) Undoubtedly, Madame. Especially if you like mushrooms and above all, if you've invested the proceeds wisely.

LADY IN PURPLE: Ah, you've put your finger on the sore spot! I keep asking myself if I invested wisely. I doubt it, I very much doubt it. I took the advice of that nincompoop of a lawyer. A dear man but about as much sense as his wife's coffee-table which, as you may have heard, was used for a time for some spiritualist hocus-pocus. I put a good deal of it into coal mining stocks. What do you think of them, Doctor?

KNOCK: In general they're good buys. A bit speculative perhaps. They go up for no reason at all and then go down the same way.

LADY IN PURPLE: Oh, you make my flesh creep. I must have bought them when they were up. Fifty thousand francs worth. It's madness to put so much into coal mining when you haven't a large fortune.

KNOCK: I agree it should never be more than a tenth of your capital.

LADY IN PURPLE: If it's only a tenth, it's not really mad?

KNOCK: Not at all.

LADY IN PURPLE: Thank you, Doctor. You've set my mind at rest. I needed it. You don't know how much I worry about the management of my pittance. I sometimes think I need other worries to drive that one away. Humankind is a frail vessel, Doctor. We're fated to get rid of one anxiety only by replacing it with another. But we do get some relief from the change. I'd like to stop thinking the whole day about my tenants and my investments. But at my age I can hardly go in for love affairs (*sighing*) or start out on a trip around the world. But you must be impatient to know why I've been waiting in line for a free consultation.

KNOCK: Whatever your reason, I'm sure it was a good one.

LADY IN PURPLE: It's simple. I wanted to set an example. I thought your idea was fine and noble. But I know these people. I thought to myself: "They just aren't accustomed to such a thing and they won't go. The doctor will be left high and dry with his generosity." Then I thought: "But if they see that a Mme. Pons, by birth a Lempousas, is willing to lead the way, they won't be ashamed to follow suit." Everything I do is noticed and discussed, naturally.

KNOCK: Your decision was most praiseworthy, Madame. I thank you for it.

LADY IN PURPLE: (*gets up as if to leave*) I'm delighted to have made your acquaintance, Doctor. I'm at home in the afternoons. A few people drop in to call. We hold a salon around an old Louis Quinze teapot I inherited from my grandmother. There will always be a cup for you. (KNOCK *bows. She continues toward the door*) You know, I'm really terribly worried by my tenants and my investments. I can't sleep nights. I get terribly worn out. You wouldn't have a secret that would help me sleep, I suppose?

KNOCK: Have you suffered from insomnia a long time?

LADY IN PURPLE: A very long time.

KNOCK: Did you tell Dr. Parpalaid about it?

LADY IN PURPLE: Yes, more than once.

KNOCK: What did he say?

LADY IN PURPLE: He told me to read three pages of the Civil Code. It was a joke to him. He never took it seriously.

KNOCK: He may have been wrong. Some cases of insomnia are extremely serious.

LADY IN PURPLE: Are they really?

KNOCK: Insomnia may be the result of a basic malfunction of the intracerebral circulation, particularly a degenerative change in the blood vessels which we call the "pipestem" formation. It's possible your cerebral arteries are pipestems.

LADY IN PURPLE: Good heavens! Pipestems! Would tobacco have anything to do with it? I take a bit of snuff now and then.

KNOCK: That's something we'd have to look into. Insomnia can also come from a deep, sustained assault on the gray matter by nevroglia.

LADY IN PURPLE: That must be horrible. Please explain it to me, Doctor.

KNOCK: (*calmly*) Can you picture a crab or a squid or a giant spider nibbling or sucking or pecking away at your brain?

LADY IN PURPLE: Ohh! (*collapses horrified into an armchair*) That's horrible. It's enough to make one faint. That must be what's wrong with me. It's just the way I feel. Doctor, please kill me right away. Give me a hypodermic. No, no, don't desert me. I've reached the ultimate in horror. (*pause*) I suppose it's fatal and absolutely incurable?

KNOCK: No, it's not.

LADY IN PURPLE: There's hope for recovery?

KNOCK: Yes, in time.

LADY IN PURPLE: Don't deceive me, Doctor. I want to know the truth.

KNOCK: It all depends on taking regular treatments and keeping at it.

LADY IN PURPLE: But what are you cured of? The pipe-stem thing or the spider? I'm pretty sure it's the spider in my case.

KNOCK: You can be cured of either. I might not dare offer any hope to an ordinary patient who wouldn't have either the time or the means for the most up-to-date methods. It's different with you.

LADY IN PURPLE: Oh, I'll be a very good patient, Doctor. I'll be as docile as a pet dog. I'll go anywhere you say. If only it isn't too painful.

KNOCK: It's not painful at all. We'll use radioactivity. The difficulty is having the patience to stick to it for two or three years and finding a doctor who's willing to give constant supervision while the cure is in progress. It involves minute calculations of the dosage of radioactivity—and almost daily visits.

LADY IN PURPLE: Oh, I'll be patient. But you aren't going to want to give me as much time as you'd have to.

KNOCK: So far as desire is concerned, I ask nothing better. But ability is another thing. Do you live far?

LADY IN PURPLE: No, just down the street. Across from the public scales.

KNOCK: I'll try to stop in every day. Except Sunday. And Monday because of my office hours.

LADY IN PURPLE: Won't that be too long? Two days in a row? Won't I be practically without treatment from Saturday to Tuesday?

KNOCK: I'll leave detailed instructions. And perhaps I can find a minute to drop in Sunday morning or Monday afternoon.

LADY IN PURPLE: Oh, that's good. What should I do now?

KNOCK: Go home and stay in bed. I'll call tomorrow morning and give you a more complete examination.

LADY IN PURPLE: Shouldn't I take some medicine today?

KNOCK: Uh . . . yes. (*scribbles prescription*) Stop in at the pharmacy and ask M. Mousquet to make up this prescription right away as a starter.

(*Lady goes out*)

KNOCK: (*at door, calling*) Mariette, who are all these people? (*looking at his watch*) Didn't you tell them there would be no free visits after 11:30?

VOICE OF MARIETTE: (*offstage*) Yes, I did, but they insisted on staying.

KNOCK: Well, who's next? (*Two young fellows come forward. They are holding back their laughter, nudging and winking at each other, suddenly exploding. Behind them the crowd is enjoying their horseplay and becoming noisy. Doctor pretends to notice nothing.*) Which one?

FIRST YOUNG FELLOW: (*glancing away, hiding laughter, slightly nervous*) Hee hee hee! Both of us. Hee hee hee!

KNOCK: You aren't coming in together?

FIRST YOUNG FELLOW: Oh, yes, we are. Hee hee hee. Yes.

KNOCK: I can't see you both at the same time. You'll have to decide between you. Anyway, I don't think I've seen you before. There are others ahead of you.

FIRST YOUNG FELLOW: They're letting us go first. Ask them. (*laughs under his breath*)

SECOND YOUNG FELLOW: We always go together. We're a regular pair. Hee hee hee.

(*laughter all around*)

KNOCK: (*very coldly, biting his lip*) Come in. (*closes door—to first young fellow*) Get undressed. (*to second, pointing to a chair*) Sit down there! (*They continue to make signs to each other and snigger but with a bit of an effort.*)

FIRST YOUNG FELLOW: (*in trousers and shirt*) Do I have to take everything off?

KNOCK: Just your shirt. (*young fellow takes off shirt, appears in flannel undershirt*) That will do. (*Approaches, walks around him, prods him, thumps him, listens to heart and lungs with stethoscope, draws his skin tight, turns back eyelids and lips. Then takes out laryngoscope with reflector, puts it on slowly, suddenly shines light in young fellow's face, down his throat, into his eyes. When the patient has been sufficiently browbeaten, points to sofa*) Stretch out here. All right. Raise your knees. (*prods his stomach, applies stethoscope in various places*) Hold out your arm. (*takes pulse and blood pressure*) All right. Get dressed. (*silence as young fellow gets dressed*)

KNOCK: Is your father living?

FIRST YOUNG FELLOW: No, he's dead.

KNOCK: Died suddenly?

FIRST YOUNG FELLOW: Yes.

KNOCK: Um-hum. He wasn't very old?

FIRST YOUNG FELLOW: No, only forty-nine.

KNOCK: As old as that? (*Long pause. The two young fellows have lost all desire to laugh.* KNOCK *rummages behind a piece of furniture and brings out some large posters showing the main body organs in an advanced stage of alcoholism and in their normal state. To young fellow courteously*) I'd like to show you what state your most important organs are in. Here are an ordinary man's kidneys. Here are yours. (*with pauses*) Here's your liver. Here's your heart. But in your case the heart is farther gone than it looks here. (KNOCK *calmly replaces posters*)

FIRST YOUNG FELLOW: Maybe I should stop drinking?

KNOCK: That's up to you. (*silence*)

FIRST YOUNG FELLOW: Is there anything I can take for it?

KNOCK: It would hardly be worth while. (*to second young fellow*) It's your turn now.

FIRST YOUNG FELLOW: If you want, Doctor, I'll come back for a regular visit—and pay.

KNOCK: It wouldn't do any good.

SECOND YOUNG FELLOW: There's nothing wrong with me, Doctor.

KNOCK: What do you know about it?

SECOND YOUNG FELLOW: (*staggering back fearfully*) I'm in good health, Doctor.

KNOCK: Then why did you come here?

SECOND YOUNG FELLOW: (*continues to tremble*) To keep my friend company.

KNOCK: Isn't he big enough to come by himself? Come on, get undressed!

SECOND YOUNG FELLOW: (*moving toward door*) No, no, not today, Doctor. I'll come back.

(*Silence.* KNOCK *opens the door. Noise of crowd beginning to laugh.* KNOCK *watches the young fellows go out. They look haggard and terrified as they pass through the crowd which becomes as silent as a funeral.*)

CURTAIN

ACT III

Main lobby of Key Hotel. Atmosphere is that of a hotel in a county seat turning into a sanatorium. Commercial calendars are still around, but the nickel plating, enamel ware, and scrubbed linen of modern hygiene are creeping in.

MME. REMY: Has the car come, Scipio?

SCIPIO: Yes.

MME. REMY: I heard the road was blocked by snow.

SCIPIO: Pooh! Fifteen minutes' delay.

MME. REMY: Whose bags are these?

SCIPIO: A lady who's come from Livron to see the doctor.

MME. REMY: But we weren't expecting her until this evening.

SCIPIO: You're wrong. It's the lady from St. Marcellin who's coming this evening.

MME. REMY: How about this suitcase?

SCIPIO: It's Ravachol's.

MME. REMY: What? Is M. Parpalaid here?

SCIPIO: He was right behind me.

MME. REMY: What's he here for? Not trying to get his old job back, is he?

SCIPIO: He probably wants to consult the doctor.

MME. REMY: But we have nothing open except 9 and 14. I'm holding 9 for the lady from St. Marcellin and putting the lady from Livron in 14. Why didn't you tell Ravachol there was nothing left?

SCIPIO: Because 14 was left. I had no authority to decide between Ravachol and the lady from Livron.

MME. REMY: That puts me in a bad spot.

SCIPIO: Try to get out of it! I'll be busy with my patients.

MME. REMY: No, wait a minute, Scipio. You stay here and explain to M. Parpalaid that there aren't any more rooms. I can't tell him myself.

SCIPIO: Very sorry, but I've just got time to get into my coat. Dr. Knock will be here in a few minutes. I've got to get urine samples from 5 and 8, a saliva specimen from 2, temperature from 3, 4, 12, 17, and 18 and I don't know what all. I'm not anxious to catch hell.

MME. REMY: Can't you even take the lady's bags upstairs?

SCIPIO: What's the maid doing? Stringing pearls? (*goes out*)

(MME. REMY, *catching sight of* PARPALAID, *follows* SCIPIO *out*)

PARPALAID: Hm, nobody around? Mme. Rémy! . . . Scipio! . . . That's strange . . . Here's my suitcase. . . . Scipio!

MAID: (*in nurse's uniform*) Did you call, sir?

PARPALAID: I wanted to see the landlady.

MAID: Why, sir?

PARPALAID: So she could give me a room.

MAID: Oh, I wouldn't know about that. Are you one of the patients we've been expecting?

PARPALAID: I'm not a patient; I'm a doctor.

MAID: Oh, then you've come to help the doctor. He certainly needs it.

PARPALAID: Don't you know me, Mademoiselle?

MAID: No, I don't.

PARPALAID: Dr. Parpalaid. I was the doctor of St. Maurice until three months ago. You're a stranger, I suppose?

MAID: No, I'm not, but I didn't know we had a doctor here before Dr. Knock. (*silence*) Please excuse me, sir. The landlady will be along any minute. I've got to get my pillow-cases sterilized. (*goes out*)

PARPALAID: Something funny has happened to this hotel.

MME. REMY: (*peeping in cautiously*) He's still there! (*taking bull by the horns*) Hello, M. Parpalaid. You're not looking for a room, I hope.

PARPALAID: As a matter of fact, I was. How are you, Mme. Rémy?

MME. REMY: I'm sorry, we haven't a room.

PARPALAID: Is there a fair?

MME. REMY: No, it's just an ordinary day.

PARPALAID: Since when have you been full on ordinary days? Where do all your guests come from?

MME. REMY: They're patients.

PARPALAID: Patients?

MME. REMY: Yes, patients. People who are taking treatments.

PARPALAID: Why are they staying here?

MME. REMY: Because it's the only hotel in St. Maurice. Anyway, they've no cause to complain about being put up here while we're waiting for our new quarters. They get all their treatments right here in the hotel and observe all the rules of modern hygiene.

PARPALAID: But where do they come from?

MME. REMY: The patients? Recently they've been coming from all over. At first they were just transients.

PARPALAID: I don't follow you.

MME. REMY: People who were in St. Maurice on business. They heard about Dr. Knock and took the opportunity to consult him. Of course they didn't know the condition they were in but they must have had a presentiment or something. It's lucky they happened to be in St. Maurice or some of them would be dead today.

PARPALAID: Why would they be dead today?

MME. REMY: Because, since they didn't suspect anything, they'd have gone right on eating and drinking and all sorts of crazy things.

PARPALAID: Did they all stay here?

MME. REMY: Yes. When they came back from seeing Dr. Knock they went right to bed and began taking treatments. Now it's all different of course. The people that come make a special trip for it. Unfortunately, we don't have space for all of them. We're expecting to build.

PARPALAID: But this is amazing!

MME. REMY: (*after thinking about it*) It must seem amazing to you. If you had to lead the kind of life Dr. Knock does, you couldn't take it.

PARPALAID: What kind of life does he lead?

MME. REMY: He works like a slave. As soon as he's up, he's off on his visits. He stops in here at ten. You'll see him in about five minutes. Then he goes to his office for consultations. After that more visits all over the township. Of course he has his car, a beautiful new one, and he drives like a fiend. But I dare say there are lots of times he has nothing but a sandwich for lunch.

PARPALAID: That's just the way it is with me in Lyon.

MME. REMY: Is it? When you were here you lived a pretty quiet life. (*joshing tone*) Remember your billiard games in the bar?

PARPALAID: Apparently people enjoyed better health when I was here.

MME. REMY: Oh, no, they didn't. We just didn't take care of ourselves. That's not the same thing. Some people think we country folk are still savages who don't care about our bodies, that we just wait for our time to die like animals, that cures, diets, machines, and other progressive things are only for the big cities. That's a bad mistake, M. Parpalaid. We value ourselves as much as anybody and while we don't like to throw money around, we're willing to pay for what we need. You're still living in the time of the peasants who squeezed a sou until it bled and would rather lose an eye or a leg than spend three francs on medicine. Times have changed, thank God.

PARPALAID: Well, if people are tired of good health and willing to pay for bad, they might as well. It's all profit for the doctor.

MME. REMY: (*much excited*) Well, just don't try to tell anyone that Dr. Knock is in it for money. He started the free visits. We never had such a thing before. He makes people pay if they can, which is only right, but he doesn't take anything from the poor. He'll drive all the way across the township, spend ten francs on gas, and park his big, shiny car in front of a shanty to help some old woman who can't even pay him in goat's cheese. And don't insinuate that he makes people think they're sick when they're not. Take me, for example! He's probably examined me ten times since he started coming in here every day. He's always patient. Every time he listens to me from top to toe with the stethoscope and uses all his other instruments too. It takes him a good quarter of an hour. He's told me every time there's nothing wrong with me, nothing to worry about, I can eat and drink what I like. And he won't take a centime for it. The same with M.

Bernard, the schoolteacher, who got it into his head somehow that he was a germ-carrier. He was going crazy over it. Just to put his mind at rest Dr. Knock analyzed his excreta three times. Besides, here's M. Mousquet who's coming to take blood with the doctor from the patient in 15. You can ask him. (*thinks*) Anyway, give me your suitcase. I'll try to squeeze you in somewhere.

MOUSQUET: (*now fashionably dressed*) Has the doctor come in? Ah, Dr. Parpalaid! A ghost from the tomb. We haven't seen you in a long while.

PARPALAID: What do you mean, a long while? It's only three months.

MOUSQUET: You're right. Three months! It seems an age. (*a bit patronizing*) Are things going well for you in Lyon?

PARPALAID: Very well, thanks.

MOUSQUET: Good, good. I'm glad to hear it. Did you pick up a ready-made clientele?

PARPALAID: Uh . . . I've increased it by a third . . . Is Mme. Mousquet well?

MOUSQUET: Yes, she's much better.

PARPALAID: Has she been sick?

MOUSQUET: Don't you remember those migraine headaches she complained about? You never thought they were important. Dr. Knock diagnosed them right away—a deficiency of ovarian secretions. He prescribed a course of ovotherapy which has done wonders.

PARPALAID: Is she all right now?

MOUSQUET: No more trouble from migraine, none at all. The headaches she has now come from overwork. That's natural enough. We're terribly rushed. I need an assistant. Do you know anyone you could recommend?

PARPALAID: I don't at the moment but I'll keep it in mind.

MOUSQUET: Life isn't tame here the way it used to be. I don't get to bed until 11:30 and still I haven't filled all my prescriptions.

PARPALAID: In short, a gold mine.

MOUSQUET: Oh, I'm taking in five times what I used to and I don't complain about that. But there are other satisfactions than money. You know, Doctor, I like my work and I like to feel useful. I'd rather be on the go than sitting around. It's just the way I am. . . . But here's the doctor.

KNOCK: (*coming in*) (*to* MOUSQUET) Hello. Hello, Dr. Parpalaid. I was wondering about you. Did you have a good trip?

PARPALAID: Fine, thanks.

KNOCK: Did you drive?

PARPALAID: No, I came by train.

KNOCK: Ah, that's good. You want your payment, I suppose.

PARPALAID: I thought that while I'm here . . .

MOUSQUET: I'll have to leave you. (*to* KNOCK) I'll be in 15. (*goes out*)

PARPALAID: I hope you no longer think I swindled you.

KNOCK: You did your best, Doctor.

PARPALAID: You can't deny I gave up my practice to you and the practice was worth something.

KNOCK: Oh, you could have stayed. We would hardly have bothered one another. Has M. Mousquet told you of our early results?

PARPALAID: I've heard about them.

KNOCK: (*fumbling in his pocketbook*) Please keep this confidential, but here are some of my statistics. You'll see how they relate to our conversation of three months ago. First, consultations. This curve reflects the weekly figures. We start from your weekly average. I didn't know it but I put it at approximately five.

PARPALAID: Five consultations a week? Twice that, Doctor.

KNOCK: As you like. Here are my figures. Naturally they don't include the free consultations on Mondays. Mid-October: 37. End of October: 90. End of November: 128. End of December: not yet tallied but it will exceed 150. From now on the consultation curve will have to be sacrificed in the interests of the treatment curve. Consultation in itself doesn't interest me much. It's a rather rudimentary art, like fishing with a net. Treatment is more like fish hatchery.

PARPALAID: Pardon me, Doctor, but are your figures scrupulously accurate?

KNOCK: Scrupulously.

PARPALAID: You mean that in a week there were 150 people in St. Maurice who took the trouble to go to a doctor's office and wait their turns—and paid for it? They weren't forced to do it? No pressure of any kind?

KNOCK: No help from the police or the militia.

PARPALAID: Amazing!

KNOCK: Let's look at the treatment curve. Early October, the situation I inherited from you, regular home patients: none, wasn't it? (*Feeble gesture of protest from* PARPALAID) End of October: 32. End of November: 121. End of December: It will be between 245 and 250.

PARPALAID: I can't help feeling that you're taking advantage of my credulity.

KNOCK: I, on the other hand, don't consider these figures particularly large. After all, the township has 2853 homes among which 1502 have a gross income of more than 12,000 francs.

PARPALAID: What has their income got to do with it?

KNOCK: (*going to wash basin*) You can't expect a family to take care of a permanent invalid on an income of less than 12,000 francs. That would be imposing on them. Even above 12,000 you can't prescribe the same treatment for everybody. I use a sliding scale with four categories. The lowest, for those from twelve to twenty thousand, get one visit a week and about 50 francs of pharmaceuticals per month. At the top, the de luxe treatment, for incomes in excess of 50,000 francs, involves at least four visits a week and three hundred francs of additional expenditure: x-rays, radium, diathermy, analysis, medication, etc.

PARPALAID: But how do you know your patients' incomes?

KNOCK: (*begins meticulous washing of hands*) Not from the treasury department, fortunately. While my calculations indicate that there are 1502 incomes over 12,000 francs, the collector of internal revenue counts 17. The highest income on his list is 20,000; on mine it's 120,000. We never agree. Of course he's working for the government.

PARPALAID: Where do you get your information?

KNOCK: (*smiling*) From a variety of sources. It's a big job. I spent most of October on it. And I'm constantly revising. Take a look at this! Nice-looking, isn't it?

PARPALAID: It looks like a map of the township. But what do those red dots mean?

KNOCK: It's a map of medical conquest. Every red dot represents a regular patient. A month ago you'd have seen a big white patch—the Chabrières patch.

PARPALAID: What's that?

KNOCK: Named for the one-horse town in the middle of it. I've concentrated on it in the last few weeks. The patch hasn't entirely disappeared, but I've made some inroads, haven't I? In fact, you can hardly see it.

(*silence*)

PARPALAID: Doctor, I couldn't hide my astonishment if I wanted to. I can't doubt your results. They've been confirmed from several sources. You're a remarkable man. Others might be unwilling to concede as much, but they'd think it nonetheless. They wouldn't be doctors if they didn't. But forgive me if I ask an embarrassing question.

KNOCK: Please! Go right ahead.

PARPALAID: Well, if I used your method . . . if I was as skilled at it as you are . . . if I had only to put it into practice . . .

KNOCK: Go on.

PARPALAID: Wouldn't I have to rid myself of some scruples? (*pause*) Answer me, please.

KNOCK: It seems to me it's up to you to answer.

PARPALAID: I don't want to be dogmatic about it. It's a very delicate point. (*silence*)

KNOCK: I'm afraid I don't quite understand you.

PARPALAID: You may think me too much of a stickler for ethical standards, but doesn't your method subordinate the interest of the patient just a bit to that of the doctor?

KNOCK: Dr. Parpalaid, you're forgetting that there is an interest which is greater than either.

PARPALAID: What?

KNOCK: The interest of medicine. I serve that interest and that alone.

(*Silence.* PARPALAID *is thoughtful*)

PARPALAID: Yes, yes, I suppose so.

(*From this point to the final curtain the stage becomes lighted more and more by the Light of Medical Science which, as everyone knows, contains more greens and violets than ordinary Earthly Light.*)

KNOCK: You've given me a township inhabited by several thousand neutral individuals, individuals without direction. My function is to direct them, to lead them into a life of medicine. I put them to bed and see what can be made of them: tuberculosis, neurasthenia, arteriosclerosis, whatever you like, but *something,* for God's sake. Nothing gets on my nerves like that indeterminate nonentity called a healthy man.

PARPALAID: But you can't put the whole township to bed!

KNOCK: That remains to be seen. I've known a family of five, all sick in bed at the same time, who got along all right. You remind me of those economists who claimed that a big, modern war couldn't last more than six weeks. The truth is we're all too timid. Nobody, not even I, will go all the way and put the whole population to bed, just to see. So all right, I agree there have to be a few healthy people if only to take care of the sick and constitute a kind of reserve behind the lines of disease. What I can't stand is good health putting on airs. You'll admit that's going too far. We can wink at a certain number of cases, we can allow a certain number of people to maintain a façade of well-being. But when they start flaunting it in our faces, that's when I lose patience. That's what happened to M. Raffalens.

PARPALAID: That behemoth! The fellow who claims to be able to carry his mother-in-law around at arm's length?

KNOCK: The same. He defied me for three months . . . but I've put him in his place.

PARPALAID: How?

KNOCK: He's taken to his bed. His boasts were undermining the medical spirit of the population.

PARPALAID: I still see a serious difficulty.

KNOCK: What is it?

PARPALAID: You think only of medicine . . . but how about other things? If your methods became general, wouldn't there be a considerable diminution in other activities of society, some of which are of some interest, after all?

KNOCK: That's not my business. I serve medicine.

PARPALAID: I suppose when an engineer is laying out a railroad right of way, he doesn't worry what the country doctor thinks of it.

KNOCK: I should think not. (*goes stage rear and looks out window*) Just take a look out there, Dr. Parpalaid. You know the view from this window. You can't have failed to notice it between billiard games. Right in the middle Mt. Aligre marks the limit of the township. To the left you can see the villages of Mesclat and Trébures. On this side you could see all the valley towns strung out in a row if the houses of St. Maurice weren't in the way. All you saw in the scene was its natural beauty of which you're quite a connoisseur. It was a rude landscape, scarcely human. Today it is alive to medicine, you might say drenched in medicine, sustained by the subterranean fires of our art. The first time I stood here, the day after my arrival, I felt quite humble. My presence didn't seem to count for much. This expanse of earth was getting along quite well without me or anyone like me. Today I am as much at ease in this spot as an organist at his mighty keyboard. In two hundred fifty of those houses—you can't quite make them out because of the distance and the foliage—there are two hundred fifty rooms in which someone is confessing his faith in medicine, two hundred fifty beds in which a human body bears witness that life has meaning and, thanks to me, the meaning is medical. It's still more beautiful at night because of the lights. Most of the lights are my doing. Those who aren't sick sleep in darkness. They're blotted out. But the sick have their lamps burning. The night spares me the annoyance of anything outside the sphere of medicine, shields me from its defiance. The township yields to a firmament of which I am the continual creator. Not to mention the church bells! Their primary mission is to remind all these people of my prescriptions. The bells are thus my voice. For example, in a few minutes it will be ten o'clock. For all my patients ten o'clock means the second reading of rectal temperature. In a few minutes, two hundred fifty thermometers will penetrate in unison . . .

PARPALAID: (*seizing his arm excitedly*) Doctor, I have a proposal for you.

KNOCK: What?

PARPALAID: This provincial town is no place for you. A man like you should have a great city to work in.

KNOCK: I'll have it sooner or later.

PARPALAID: But you're at the height of your powers. In a few years they'll begin to decline. Believe me, I speak from experience.

KNOCK: Well?

PARPALAID: So you shouldn't wait.

KNOCK: Do you know a practice to which you could refer me?

PARPALAID: Mine. I'll give it to you. How could I better show my admiration for you?

KNOCK: What would become of you?

PARPALAID: Oh, me? I'd content myself with my old practice in St. Maurice.

KNOCK: Ah, yes!

PARPALAID: I'll go further. We'll forget the few thousand francs you owe me. I'll make you a gift of them.

KNOCK: Of course. You're really not as dumb as people say.

PARPALAID: What do you mean by that?

KNOCK: You don't produce much but you know how to buy and sell. The qualities of a tradesman.

PARPALAID: Believe me . . .

KNOCK: You're even a rather sharp psychologist. You perceive that I don't care much about money as soon as I get to the point where I'm making a lot of it, and that the medical conquest of a district or two in Lyon would drive the graphs of St. Maurice right out of my mind. Well, I have no intention of growing old here! But I'm not ready to snap up the first offer!

(MOUSQUET *starts to cross the room discreetly to get to the door.* KNOCK *stops him.*)

KNOCK: Wait a minute, M. Mousquet. Do you know what Dr. Parpalaid is proposing? An exchange of practices. I would take his place in Lyon and he'd come back here.

MOUSQUET: He's kidding.

KNOCK: Not at all. He's made me a very serious offer.

MOUSQUET: I'll be damned. . . . You're refusing, of course?

PARPALAID: Why should Dr. Knock refuse?

MOUSQUET: Because if people have any sense they don't trade a two thousand franc shotgun for a compressed air pistol. You might as well offer to trade cars.

PARPALAID: I assure you I have a first-rate practice in Lyon. I succeeded Dr. Merlu, who was well known, with a fine reputation.

MOUSQUET: Yes, but that was three months ago. You can cover a lot of ground in three months. And you cover it faster going down than up. (*to* KNOCK) Anyway, Doctor, the people of St. Maurice won't accept it.

PARPALAID: What business is it of theirs? We haven't asked for their opinion.

MOUSQUET: You'll get it just the same. I don't say they'll throw up barricades. That's not the custom here and anyway we haven't any pavements. But they could start you back to Lyon. (*sees* MME. REMY *approaching*) Here's your chance to see for yourself.

(MME. REMY *comes in carrying pile of plates*)

MOUSQUET: Mme. Rémy, you're just in time to hear the good news. Dr. Knock is leaving us and Dr. Parpalaid is coming back.

(MME. REMY *lets go the plates but manages to catch them and clasp them to her bosom like a fan*)

MME. REMY: No, no! Not on your life! (*to* KNOCK) They'll have to take you away in a plane in the middle of the night because I'll tell everybody and they won't let you go. We'll puncture your tires. As for you, Dr. Parpalaid, if that's what you came here for, I'm sorry to say I haven't a single room left and even though it's the fourth of January, you'll have to sleep outside.

(*goes to table to deposit plates*)

PARPALAID: (*highly upset*) Very well, very well! If that's the attitude of these people toward a man who devoted twenty-five years of his life to them! Since there's no longer room for anything but quackery in St. Maurice, I prefer to earn my living honestly in Lyon—not only honestly but rather comfortably, I don't mind saying. The idea of resuming my old practice did cross my mind, I admit, but only because of my wife's health. She can't accustom herself to city air. Dr. Knock, let's settle our accounts as soon as possible. I'll be leaving this evening.

KNOCK: You won't offend us in that way, I'm sure, Doctor. In her surprise at hearing an item of news which wasn't true and in her fear of dropping her plates, Mme. Rémy lost control of her language. She didn't mean what she said. You see, now her plates are safe, she's her old good-natured self again. You may read in her eyes the gratitude she shares with all of St. Maurice for your twenty-five years of silent ministry.

MME. REMY: Of course M. Parpalaid has always been a fine man. And he served as well as anyone as long as we didn't need a doctor. The only bad time was during the epidemic. You can't tell me a real doctor would have let so many people die of Spanish influenza.

PARPALAID: A real doctor! What a thing to say! Do you think that a "real doctor" can fight a worldwide epidemic? It's like expecting the rural constable to stop an earthquake. Just wait for the next one and see if Dr. Knock makes out any better.

MME. REMY: Dr. Knock . . . Listen, M. Parpalaid, I'm not going to talk cars with you because I don't know anything about them. But I'm beginning to know something about sick people. Let me tell you that with all the weak ones already in bed, we're ready for your worldwide epidemic. It's just like M. Bernard said in his lecture the other day— the terrifying thing is a clap of thunder in a blue sky.

MOUSQUET: I wouldn't advise you to start any arguments around here, Doctor. The pharmaco-medical spirit is flourishing all over the place. Everyone has his own ideas about it and they'll all give you a battle.

KNOCK: Let's not become involved in scholarly disputations. Mme. Rémy and Dr. Parpalaid may have differing opinions and still maintain courteous relations with one another. (*to* MME. REMY) You have a room for the doctor, haven't you?

MME. REMY: No, I haven't. You know perfectly well we hardly have room for our patients. If a patient came along I might be able to do the impossible and crowd him in. That would only be doing my duty.

KNOCK: Suppose I told you the doctor won't be in condition to leave this afternoon and that, medically speaking, he needs at least a day of rest.

MME. REMY: That's another thing entirely . . . But . . . M. Parpalaid didn't come for a consultation, did he?

KNOCK: If he had, professional ethics would hardly allow me to say so publicly.

PARPALAID: Now what are you up to? I'm leaving tonight. That's all there is to it.

KNOCK: (*looking him over*) Doctor, I'm serious. You're very much in need of a day's rest. I'd advise you against leaving today. If necessary, I'll go on record as opposing it.

MME. REMY: All right, Doctor, I didn't know. Don't worry, we'll get M. Parpalaid a bed. Shall we take his temperature?

KNOCK: We'll discuss that a little later.

(MME. REMY *goes out*)

MOUSQUET: I'll have to leave you for a moment. (*to* KNOCK) I broke a needle. I'm going to pick up another at the pharmacy. (*goes out*)

PARPALAID: What was that, a joke? (*short pause*) Thanks anyway. It wouldn't be fun starting out on another eight hours' trip tonight. (*pause*) I'm not twenty years old any more and I'm beginning to feel it. (*pause*) It's wonderful the way you keep a straight face. You looked at me just now . . . (*getting up*) Even though I knew it was a joke—

after all, I know the tricks of the trade—still you had a look on your face . . . as if you were looking right into my insides. It's very effective.

KNOCK: I'm sorry. I can't help it. As soon as I meet someone, I feel a diagnosis coming on, no matter how useless or out of place it may be. (*confidentially*) It's gone so far I avoid looking at myself in a mirror.

PARPALAID: What do you mean, a diagnosis? An imaginary diagnosis, or what?

KNOCK: Imaginary! Let me tell you, as soon as I look at a face, without even thinking about it, I begin noting a number of hardly perceptible signs: skin, eyeballs, capillaries, rate of breathing, hair, and I don't know how many others. My diagnostic machinery starts running by itself. I have to watch it. It's becoming ridiculous.

PARPALAID: In that case . . . I'm sorry to be so insistent, but I have a reason for it . . . When you said I needed a day's rest, were you joking or . . . or were you? Again I apologize for insisting, but I've been a bit worried. I've noticed several things about myself lately . . . and even if my curiosity is purely academic, I'd be interested in knowing if your involuntary diagnosis corresponds with my own observations.

KNOCK: Let's leave that for later, if you don't mind, Doctor. (*bells*) It's ten o'clock. I have to make my rounds. We'll have lunch together, if you'll be so kind. As for your health and any decisions it may entail, we can talk about them in a more leisurely way this afternoon in my office.

(KNOCK *goes out. After ten strokes the bells are silent.* PARPALAID, *crumpled up in a chair, remains lost in thought.* SCIPIO, *the* MAID, *and* MME. REMY *enter carrying ritual instruments. They pass silently across the stage, bathed in the light of Medical Science.*)

CURTAIN

Questions

1. Has Dr. Parpalaid engaged in a swindle, as Dr. Knock suggests, or does he have another reason for selling his practice and moving to Lyon? Why is he willing at the end to cancel the contract with Dr. Knock and return to St. Maurice?
2. What does Dr. Knock mean by the phrase, the "interest of medicine," in answering the question of whether his methods subordinate the patient's interest to that of the doctor? Why is the contented or happy man an "indeterminate nonentity" and a challenge to the doctor according to Dr. Knock?
3. Does Dr. Knock buy the practice only because he wants to make money? Or should we accept his statement in the final act that he wants to make the citizens of St. Maurice "alive to medicine"? Does Romains show these to be contradictory goals?
4. How is Dr. Parpalaid's view of health and medicine different from Dr. Knock's? How does Romains reveal this difference in the course of the play?
5. Is Romains satirizing Dr. Parpalaid? Or does Dr. Parpalaid represent the ideal doctor in what he has done for the citizens of St. Maurice—a standard by which we are to judge Dr. Knock? Or does Romains want us to admire Dr. Knock and laugh at Dr. Parpalaid? Is the effort to make all citizens of St. Maurice patients very different from what we today call "preventive medicine"?

6. What qualities in the citizens of St. Maurice does the play satirize? Is Romains suggesting that they are better or worse than most people, or do they typify people in general?
7. What is the chief theme of the play, and how do the plot and the characters develop it? Does the play have subordinate themes?

Suggestions for Writing

1. Discuss what Romains seems to believe is good medicine and bad medicine. How do you know this from the play?
2. If a doctor or a lawyer is highly skilled in the practice of medicine or law but has chosen one of these professions to make money, is the person therefore a bad doctor or lawyer? Is an unskilled or untrained doctor or lawyer a quack by definition, or could a skilled doctor or lawyer also be a quack?
3. The nineteenth-century English social critic John Ruskin writes the following in his essay "The Roots of Honor":

> Not less is the respect we pay to the lawyer and physician, founded ultimately on their self-sacrifice. Whatever the learning or acuteness of a great lawyer, our chief respect for him depends on our belief that, set in a judge's seat, he will strive to judge justly, come of it what may. Could we suppose that he would take bribes, and use his acuteness and legal knowledge to give plausibility to iniquitous decisions, no degree of intellect would win for him our respect. Nothing will win it, short of our tacit conviction, that in all important acts of his life justice is first with him; his own interest, second.
>
> In the case of a physician, the ground of the honor we render him is clearer still. Whatever his science, we should shrink from him in horror if we found him regard his patients merely as subjects to experiment upon; much more, if we found that, receiving bribes from persons interested in their deaths, he was using his best skill to give poison in the mask of medicine.

Do you agree with Ruskin on what defines the honor of the physician? What other attitudes and acts define the honor of the physician for you?

Additional Reading

Boak, Denis. *Jules Romains.* New York: Twayne, 1974.
Norrish, P. J. *Drama of the Group: A Study of Unanimism in the Plays of Jules Romains.* Cambridge, England: Cambridge University Press, 1958.

POPULATION
AND HUMAN LIFE

The issue of population control was widely discussed in the 1960s and is an important topic again in the 1980s. The threat of a rapidly increasing world population is sometimes cited by proponents of abortion—probably the most heated issue of the 1980s—and denied by its opponents. The increasing scarcity of natural resources has intensified concerns about overpopulation. When Jonathan Swift published "A Modest Proposal" in 1729, many fewer people existed in Ireland and the world—the total population at that time has been estimated at well under a billion people. In the 1980s the population of the world is five times as large—just under five billion, with China alone containing more than a billion people. The rate of acceleration has been enormous since 1729: the world population doubled between 1600 and 1900, and a second doubling occurred only eighty years later, in 1980. In 1965, it was estimated that 180,000 babies were being born every day—in contrast to 40,000 a day in 1900. This means that 125 babies were born each minute, 7,500 each hour, a million each week at that time. By one current estimate, the world population will be between six and seven billion by the year 2000. In 1972 Barbara Ward and René Dubos gave this account of the impact on population growth:

> This rate of growth of population in the twentieth century has been accompanied by the settlement of virtually all the naturally inhabitable parts of the globe and an increase of more than a billion people in urban settlements of over 20,000 inhabitants, by a quadrupling of energy consumption, and a virtually uncountable increase in the consumption of depletable resources. Today it has been estimated that, on the average, a citizen in the world's wealthiest country—the United States—carries eleven tons of steel around with him in cars and household equipment and produces each year one ton of waste of all sorts. Even these brief indications are enough to show that the impact of man and his technology on his natural environment and resources is already radically different from anything yet experienced in human history.
> —*Only One Earth*

The topic of population density and human life is obviously a broad one, encompassing such issues as abortion and "triage"—the policy of allocating food and other scarce resources to some people and not to others. The five writers in this section examine related issues from different perspectives. René Dubos first discusses the general implications of population growth in our own time. Jonathan Swift's 1729 essay offers a solution to overpopulation as an alternative to solutions that he believed his English readers were unwilling to consider. Richard Selzer considers the issue of abortion—a medical as well as a social issue—from the perspective of a surgeon. Garrett Hardin discusses the broader issue of scarcity of natural resources. Finally, the nineteenth-century poet Arthur Hugh Clough gives us a rendering of the Ten Commandments fitted to the modern world. The perspectives of the essays and poem in this section are widely varied. These writers' assumptions are different, and so are their approaches to the related issues.

Population Density and Human Life

René Dubos

René Jules Dubos was associated with Rockefeller University from 1927 until his death in 1982. A world-renowned bacteriologist and biochemist, Dubos found new ways to treat bacterial infections through antibiotics and contributed much to the fight against tuberculosis. Dubos was also an environmentalist, concerned with the relationship between the social and physical environment and the control of disease. His numerous books include Only on Earth *(written in 1972 with Barbara Ward),* So Human an Animal *(1968)—awarded the Pulitzer Prize—and* Man Adapting *(1965), from which the essay reprinted here is taken.*

In Man Adapting *Dubos considers adaptations that control populations of other species. He states:*

> The innate biological and social wisdom that keeps animal populations from multiplying to the extent that they destroy their habitat no longer seems to operate in man. Yet the time has come when he too finds himself in the absolute necessity of regulating his numbers.

In the section of the book reprinted here, Dubos considers the consequences of overpopulation.

Overpopulation and Ways of Life

Of the many dangers created by overpopulation, the most frequently discussed   1
are those arising from shortages of food and raw materials; even water may soon come to be in short supply in our communities. Famine is commonly regarded as the first

likely consequence of overpopulation. It is true indeed that approximately one-third of the people now living do not have enough to eat, and even more have a qualitatively inadequate diet. As we have seen, however, food production could be increased quantitatively manyfold, and improved qualitatively, by many different technological procedures. Just like synthetic materials in industrial processes today, proteins, amino acids, and vitamins produced by an industrialized form of agriculture, or even by chemical techniques, might come to play an essential role in the nutrition of the crowded world.

Present-day agricultural methods, even when carried out with modern equip- 2 ment, still remain close in principle to the ancient practices of land utilization developed almost 10,000 years ago during the Neolithic period.[1] The real change in food production will probably depend more on the introduction of truly new technologies unrelated to Neolithic farming than on more powerful tractors to till the land, or more widespread use of fertilizers and pesticides. The extraction of concentrated proteins from crude and otherwise inedible plant materials, a more efficient utilization of solar energy in photosynthesis, and the application of chemical techniques to the production of synthetic foodstuffs may come to occupy with regard to traditional agriculture the same position that automated work occupies today with regard to the skill of the eighteenth-century craftsman. Farming and gardening will of course persist, but less from economic necessity than for the satisfaction of traditional values. To a large extent, the modernized forms of ancient agricultural practices will survive as hobbies, just as do deer-hunting, trout-fishing, and home cabinet work, which are still actively pursued only because man finds it hard to cast away the habits and skills on which his survival depended for so long.

According to recent estimates, the application of present scientific knowledge 3 to agriculture would permit producing enough food to support the existence of 50 billion human beings on earth—almost 20 times the present level! Barring unforeseen technical difficulties and natural disasters, it is therefore unlikely that the food supply will soon constitute a limiting factor in the growth of the world population. Man will need simply to adapt himself, as he certainly can, to consider that roast beef, sweet corn, tender lettuce, and tasty fruit are not essential to good nutrition, but need be used only as adornments to diets made up of foodstuffs designed and produced for their nutritional value, rather than for their taste or traditional meaning.

However, the necessity to modify nutritional habits is only one of the many 4 qualitative changes in human life that can be expected to result in the near future from the population avalanche. In fact, the most disturbing problems that will arise from a larger world population may not be amenable to technological solutions. As he populates more and more of the earth, man will have to eliminate all forms of wildlife that would compete with him for space and food; he will increasingly have to flood deserts and fell forests in order to create more farm land, factories, houses, and roads; in brief, he will tolerate wild animals, wild plants, and wild landscapes only to the extent that they serve his needs. Highways, factories, and dwellings will occupy much of the scenery; all natural resources, including water, will have to be carefully husbanded.

---

[1]Neolithic period: last Stone Age period, during which humans used implements and weapons of polished stone and tended cattle. [Ed.]

Most disturbing perhaps are the behavioral consequences likely to ensue from 5 overpopulation. The ever-increasing complexity of the social structure will make some form of regimentation unavoidable; freedom and privacy may come to constitute antisocial luxuries and their attainment to involve real hardships. In consequence, there may emerge by selection a stock of human beings suited genetically to accept as a matter of course a regimented and sheltered way of life in a teeming and polluted world, from which all wilderness and fantasy of nature will have disappeared. The domesticated farm animal and the laboratory rodent on a controlled regimen in a controlled environment will then become true models for the study of man.

Thus, it is apparent that food, natural resources, supplies of power, and other 6 elements involved in the operation of the body machine and of the industrial establishment are not the only factors to be considered in determining the optimum number of people that can live on earth. Just as important for maintaining the *human* qualities of life is an environment in which it is possible to satisfy the longing for quiet, privacy, independence, initiative, and some open space. These commodities will be in short supply long before there is a critical shortage of the materials and forces that keep the human machine going and industry expanding. In the words of Stuart Mill a century ago: "A population may be too crowded, though all be amply supplied with food and raiment. It is not good for man to be kept perforce at all times in the presence of his species. A world from which solitude is extirpated, is a very poor ideal."

The question then is not so much how many mouths can be fed, or how many 7 bodies can be accommodated, as what can be done to maintain the qualities that give to human life its peculiar characteristics. In other words, the optimum size of the world population cannot be discussed without consideration of predetermined objectives. There are many possible choices of goals open to a wealthy and enlightened community. The most difficult problem is to select what to do among all the things that could be done, many of which cry out for attention.

From the simple materialistic point of view, the creation of wealth is the most 8 obvious goal; but the provision for continued growth, or rather for continued change, is equally important because happiness depends more on variety of outlook than on wealth itself. The development of military and other forms of power is probably justified, because it is required for the protection of national freedom, in the present state of the world at least. The conservation and improvement of resources for future generations is also an essential part of social responsibility, unfortunately much overlooked at the present time. Improvements of human health, in quality and longevity; the development of social institutions, of education, and of culture; a deeper understanding of man's nature and his place in the cosmos; all these criteria must be considered in deciding the optimum population density.

Because the importance of family control appears so self-evident, it is at first 9 sight difficult to understand why certain populations continue to grow after reaching a density that results not only in shortages of food and other resources but also in a hopeless outlook for their children. The fundamental reason is that human beings regard life as the supreme good, even though it involves privations and suffering. The love for life, and the desire to expand it through the creation of children, is not a rational attitude based on thought or learning, but a motivation more powerful because antecedent and spontaneous, indeed primeval, in nature.

The two large obstacles that stand in the way of fertility control are therefore 10 independent of familiarity with contraceptive techniques. One is the primeval urge for the creation of new life, and the other a deep uncertainty as to the future of the human condition. This uncertainty calls to mind the question from *Alice in Wonderland:* "Cheshire Puss, would you tell me please, which way I ought to go from here?" To which question the very proper answer was, "That depends a great deal on where you want to get to." The great weakness of the campaigns for population control is that everyone knows where one should *not* go, but no one has a clear notion of what to substitute for the satisfactions that human nature derives from sharing the experience of children, and for the feeling of safety afforded by the company of numerous human beings. Birth control techniques are only means to an end, and they will be used only if they serve a purpose judged worthwhile. For this reason, campaigns for the limitation of family size will make little headway until people are given a convincing and clear vision of goals as appealing as the creation of more life.

The Human Qualities of Life

Everyone realizes that quality is a better criterion than quantity in formulating 11 population goals, but the qualities judged most desirable for human existence depend on ill-defined and highly subjective value judgments. Human beings readily agree on the need for improvements in health, longevity, comfort, and conformity with social mores. However, other aspects of the qualities of life raise questions that cannot be answered conclusively, in part because they involve a kind of scientific knowledge not yet available, and more importantly because they raise philosophical and ethical considerations that have not yet been made objective.

In a community where most children survive into adulthood, population stabil- 12 ity demands of course that family size be strictly limited. For example, with a life expectancy at birth of 60 years, the population will stop growing only if the birth rate does not exceed 16.7 per 1,000. With the death rates now prevailing in most of the Western world, even as low a figure as three children per family would cause an approximate doubling of the population every 50 years. Clearly then, population control will demand a limitation of family size much more stringent than the average practice in the United States at the present time. It is not unlikely that such strict limitation would interfere somewhat with the play of the selective forces that operated in the past, which helped to minimize the spread of certain genetic defects in the population. Unfortunately, knowledge of human genetics is not sufficiently developed to warrant predictions as to the distant consequences of real population control.

Concern with the possibility of genetic deterioration and a desire to improve 13 the qualities of the human stock have led some geneticists to advocate a program of eugenics aimed at favoring the spread in the general population of traits they consider beneficial. But it would take a soothsayer to design the ideal human being, since the only thing known about the future is that it will certainly differ greatly from the present. Science cannot specify the goal toward which evolution should proceed or the kind of environment best for human life, because this involves value judgments that transcend objective knowledge. The wiser course for the time being is probably to favor the greatest possible diversity among the human population, in the form of genetic polymorphism, so as to make it easier for the human race to take best advantage of unpredictable conditions. In a changing world, it is more important to be adaptable than to be perfectly adapted.

Fortunately, the medical aspects of the population problem are somewhat sim- 14 pler and clearer than those faced by geneticists and sociologists. As emphasized earlier and contrary to what is so often stated, the population avalanche is not the consequence of medical action. It began before modern medicine could exert any significant influence on either death or birth rates, and it is reaching its most disturbing intensity in areas where medical services are the most deficient. Indeed, improvements in public health might well be the most effective way to slow down population growth. The people in primitive and poor societies have learned through long experience that most of their children will die before reaching adulthood, and that the surviving progeny will be sufficiently large only if many more children are born than are desired. However, it is now within the power of preventive medicine to change this passive acceptance of fatality, by showing that the majority of newborn can be made to survive through the use of relatively inexpensive techniques applicable everywhere.

Modern medicine can also help in changing attitudes toward the population 15 problem by improving the general state of health. As everyone knows, planning for the future demands a kind of stamina rarely possessed by the sick and malnourished. For social groups as well as for individual persons, mental apathy is a common consequence of malnutrition and debilitating diseases. Improvements in nutrition and health will go very far toward helping people in low-income countries to change their ways of life and in particular to raise their sights beyond the dismal present. Larger hopes and aspirations will render people who are now lethargic and passive more receptive to birth control teaching, by providing them with the vision of a future different from the dreary past they have known, in which the mere experience of being alive was the only reward of life.

One can take it for granted that man will not rest content until he has estab- 16 lished permanent settlements all over the earth. For this reason, increases in the world population are inevitable. A larger population, however, need not imply true overpopulation since the increases can come about through the occupation of new territories, as DDT made possible in Ceylon, and as canalization of water made possible in the American Southwest.

It is equally certain, on the other hand, that the demographic expansion cannot 17 continue very long. If men allow themselves to continue breeding like rabbits, their fate will inevitably be to live like rabbits, a precarious and limited existence. The greatest dangers posed by overpopulation do not arise from shortages of food and resources for industrial development. Immensely complex as it is, the world population problem can be seen nevertheless as a fairly simple pattern in which the material aspects of living are interwoven with the aspirations of man's nature. Long before the world population has reached the maximum level for which the earth can provide material support, there will be other forms of scarcity, less obvious but more important in the long run. The most critical commodities are not the material ones, but those which condition the qualities human life must preserve if it is to remain above the brutish level and retain its superiority over the rest of animal life.

The undisciplined increase in population is obviously an evil, but as Malthus[2] 18 himself stated in the final paragraph of his first essay, "Evil exists in the world, not to create despair, but activity." At the present time, activity in this regard should be directed not only to the development of birth control techniques but also to creating a motivation, based on social goals, appealing enough to substitute for the emotional satisfactions derived from the mere creation of more life. Health improvement will facilitate population control by giving underprivileged people the confidence that children can be saved from early death. It will give them the vigor necessary to visualize and create the future, instead of passively accepting life as the dreary experience of the day.*

Questions

1. Why does Dubos characterize his own argument as qualitative?
2. How does he explain the fact that populations continue to grow in spite of shortages of food and other resources? How does this fact support his argument?
3. Does Dubos suggest ways of controlling population growth? Does the discussion suggest that he might approve of abortion as a means of controlling the population or that he would approve of medical advances that keep people alive while the world's population is rising?
4. What personal values emerge in the course of the discussion? Does Dubos state these values?

Suggestions for Writing

1. Discuss the sacrifices that Americans should impose on themselves to conserve the rapidly diminishly natural resources worldwide. Should restrictions be imposed on energy use in order to conserve fossil fuels? Should the consumption of meat, paper, and other products that require wooded land to be cleared or trees to be cut be reduced in order to conserve the world's forests?

---

²Thomas Robert Malthus (1766–1834): English clergyman who argued in *An Essay on the Principle of Population* (1978) that population increases faster than the available supply of food and therefore must be checked by governments. [Ed.]

*After I completed this chapter, the Honorable Quintin Hogg, then Minister of Science and Education of Great Britain, published an article in which he discussed the "foreseeable impacts of science on political life." The following quotation is taken from the section of his article dealing with the world population problem:

> even though it [a magic contraceptive pill] were found to exist, its use in the conditions of Indian, African or Amer-Indian village life is problematical. What is certain to my mind is that the high birth-rate in the developing countries is less the product of the absence of such methods (since cruder methods of control have existed since the dawn of history) as of the simple desire for children in a society not yet used to low infant mortality rates and accustomed to regard a quiverful of offspring as a poor man's old age pension, a personal bodyguard or the answer to the servant problem. Social insurance, monogamy, later marriage, improved living and housing conditions, and a higher degree of personal security will, in my judgment, do more in the long term to lower the birth-rate than all the contraceptive pills in the world. These conditions will, I believe, follow on the development of agriculture and industry and an intelligent social policy.

2. Do you agree or disagree with Dubos that "some form of regimentation is unavoidable" in controlling overpopulation? Should the government regulate the size of families, or is such regulation not the proper role of government?

Additional Reading

Appleman, Philip. *The Silent Explosion.* Boston: Beacon Press, 1965.

Dubos, René Jules. *beast or Angel?: Choices That Make Us Human.* New York: Scribner's, 1974.

————. *So Human an Animal.* New York: Scribner's, 1968.

————. *Man Adapting.* New Haven: Yale University Press, 1965.

————. *The Wooing of Earth.* New York: Scribner's, 1980.

Ward, Barbara Jackson, and René Dubos. *The Care and Maintenance of a Small Planet.* New York: Norton, 1972.

Abortion

Richard Selzer

Richard Selzer is a surgeon and member of the faculty of Yale Medical School. Born in 1928, he grew up in Troy, New York, where his father practiced medicine. He graduated from Union College and Albany Medical College and later from the Surgical Training Program at Yale. Selzer's first publication was a collection of stories, Rituals of Surgery *(1974), some of which explore unusual aspects of medical practice. His reputation as a major writer on medicine was established with* Mortal Lessons: Notes on the Art of Surgery *(1976).* Confessions of a Knife *(1979) and* Letters to a Young Doctor *(1982) also contain essays on the art of medicine.*

In an autobiographical essay, "Down from Troy," Selzer describes his father, a physician impoverished by the Depression in the early 1930s. "He did no raving in the dead of night," Selzer writes. "Nor did he violate the oath of Hippocrates with secret abortion, that unspeakable act of the day. Instead he went furtive—through his empty waiting room, to his desk—and took up his pen to write fiction." Selzer then comments on his own vocation as a writer: "Now that I too have been reduced to the anguish of writing fiction, it should be my holy scripture, my beacon, and my emblem. As it is, I am a writer unmoored, in search of a heritage, catching at stray ancestors."

Horror, like bacteria, is everywhere. It blankets the earth, endlessly lapping to find that one unguarded entryway. As though narcotized, we walk beneath, upon, through it. Carelessly we touch the familiar infected linen, eat from the universal dish; we disdain isolation. We are like the newborn that carry immunity from their mothers' wombs. Exteriorized, we are wrapped in impermeable membranes that cannot be seen. Then one day, the defense is gone. And we awaken to horror.

In our city, garbage is collected early in the morning. Sometimes the bang of the cans and the grind of the truck awaken us before our time. We are resentful, mutter into our pillows, then go back to sleep. On the morning of August 6, 1975, the people of 73rd Street near Woodside Avenue do just that. When at last they rise from their beds, dress, eat breakfast and leave their houses for work, they have forgotten, if they had ever known, that the garbage truck had passed earlier that morning. The event has slipped into unmemory, like a dream.

They close their doors and descend to the pavement. It is midsummer. You measure the climate, decide how you feel in relation to the heat and the humidity. You walk toward the bus stop. Others, your neighbors, are waiting there. It is all so familiar. All at once you step on something soft. You feel it with your foot. Even through your shoe you have the sense of something unusual, something marked by a special "give." It is a foreignness upon the pavement. Instinct pulls your foot away in an awkward little movement. You look down, and you see . . . a tiny naked body, its arms and legs flung apart, its head thrown back, its mouth agape, its face serious. A bird, you think, fallen from its nest. But there is no nest here on 73rd Street, no bird so big. It is rubber, then. A model, a . . . joke. Yes, that's it, a joke. And you bend to see. Because you must. And it is no joke. Such a gray softness can be but one thing. It is a baby, and dead. You cover your mouth, your eyes. You are fixed. Horror has found its chink and crawled in, and you will never be the same as you were. Years later you will step from a sidewalk to a lawn, and you will start at its softness, and think of that upon which you have just trod.

Now you look about; another man has seen it too. "My God," he whispers. Others come, people you have seen every day for years, and you hear them speak with strangely altered voices. "Look," they say, "it's a baby." There is a cry. "Here's another!" and "Another!" and "Another!" And you follow with your gaze the index fingers of your friends pointing from the huddle where you cluster. Yes, it is true! There *are* more of these . . . little carcasses upon the street. And for a moment you look up to see if all the unbaptized sinless are falling from Limbo.

Now the street is filling with people. There are police. They know what to do. They rope off the area, then stand guard over the enclosed space. They are controlled, methodical, these young policemen. Servants, they do not reveal themselves to their public master; it would not be seemly. Yet I do see their pallor and the sweat that breaks upon the face of one, the way another bites the lining of his cheek and holds it thus. Ambulance attendants scoop up the bodies. They scan the street; none must be overlooked. What they place upon the litter amounts to little more than a dozen pounds of human flesh. They raise the litter, and slide it home inside the ambulance, and they drive away. You and your neighbors stand about in the street which is become for you a battlefield from which the newly slain have at last been bagged and tagged and dragged away. *But what shrapnel is this? By what explosion flung, these fragments that sink into the brain and fester there?* Whatever smell there is in this place becomes for you the stench of death. The people of 73rd Street do not then speak to each other. It is too soon for outrage, too late for blindness. It is the time of unresisted horror.

Later, at the police station, the investigation is brisk, conclusive. It is the hospital director speaking: ". . . fetuses accidentally got mixed up with the hospital rubbish . . . were picked up at approximately eight fifteen A.M. by a sanitation truck. Somehow, the plastic lab bag, labeled HAZARDOUS MATERIAL, fell off the back of the truck and broke open. No, it is not known how the fetuses got in the orange plastic bag labeled HAZARDOUS MATERIAL. It is a freak accident." The hospital director wants you to know that it is not an everyday occurrence. Once in a lifetime, he says. But you have seen it, and what are his words to you now?

He grows affable, familiar, tells you that, by mistake, the fetuses got mixed up with the other debris. (Yes, he says *other;* he says *debris.*) He has spent the entire day, he says, trying to figure out how it happened. He wants you to know that. Somehow it matters to him. He goes on:

Aborted fetuses that weigh one pound or less are incinerated. Those weighing over one pound are buried at a city cemetery. He says this. Now you see. It *is* orderly. It *is* sensible. The world is *not* mad. This is still a civilized society.

There is no more. You turn to leave. Outside on the street, men are talking things over, reassuring each other that the right thing is being done. But just this once, you know it isn't. You saw, and you know.

And you know, too, that the Street of the Dead Fetuses will be wherever you go. You are part of its history now, its legend. It has laid claim upon you so that you cannot entirely leave it—not ever.

I am a surgeon. I do not shrink from the particularities of sick flesh. Escaping blood, all the outpourings of disease—phlegm, pus, vomitus, even those occult meaty tumors that terrify—I see as blood, disease, phlegm, and so on. I touch them to destroy them. But I do not make symbols of them. I have seen, and I am used to seeing. Yet there are paths within the body that I have not taken, penetralia where I do not go. Nor is it lack of technique, limitation of knowledge that forbids me these ways.

It is the western wing of the fourth floor of a great university hospital. An abortion is about to take place. I am present because I asked to be present. I wanted to see what I had never seen.

The patient is Jamaican. She lies on the table submissively, and now and then she smiles at one of the nurses as though acknowledging a secret.

A nurse draws down the sheet, lays bare the abdomen. The belly mounds gently in the twenty-fourth week of pregnancy. The chief surgeon paints it with a sponge soaked in red antiseptic. He does this three times, each time a fresh sponge. He covers the area with a sterile sheet, an aperture in its center. He is a kindly man who teaches as he works, who pauses to reassure the woman.

He begins.

A little pinprick, he says to the woman.

He inserts the point of a tiny needle at the midline of the lower portion of her abdomen, on the downslope. He infiltrates local anesthetic into the skin, where it forms a small white bubble.

The woman grimaces.

That is all you will feel, the doctor says. Except for a little pressure. But no more pain.

She smiles again. She seems to relax. She settles comfortably on the table. The worst is over.

The doctor selects a three-and-one-half-inch needle bearing a central stylet. He places the point at the site of the previous injection. He aims it straight up and down, perpendicular. Next he takes hold of her abdomen with his left hand, palming the womb, steadying it. He thrusts with his right hand. The needle sinks into the abdominal wall.

Oh, says the woman quietly.

But I guess it is not pain that she feels. It is more a recognition that the deed is being done.

Another thrust and he has speared the uterus.

We are in, he says.

He has felt the muscular wall of the organ gripping the shaft of his needle. A further slight pressure on the needle advances it a bit more. He takes his left hand from the woman's abdomen. He retracts the filament of the stylet from the barrel of the needle. A small geyser of pale yellow fluid erupts.

We are in the right place, says the doctor. Are you feeling any pain? he asks.

She smiles, shakes her head. She gazes at the ceiling.

In the room we are six: two physicians, two nurses, the patient, and me. The participants are busy, very attentive. I am not at all busy—but I am no less attentive. I want to see.

I see something! It is unexpected, utterly unexpected, like a disturbance in the earth, a tumultuous jarring. I see a movement—a small one. But I have seen it.

And then I see it again. And now I see that it is the hub of the needle in the woman's belly that has jerked. First to one side. Then to the other side. Once more it wobbles, is *tugged,* like a fishing line nibbled by a sunfish.

Again! And I *know!*

It is the *fetus* that worries thus. It is the fetus struggling against the needle. Struggling? How can that be? I think: *that cannot be.* I think: the fetus feels no pain, cannot feel fear, has no *motivation.* It is merely reflex.

I point to the needle.

It is a reflex, says the doctor.

By the end of the fifth month, the fetus weighs about one pound, is about twelve inches long. Hair is on the head. There are eyebrows, eyelashes. Pale pink nipples show on the chest. Nails are present, at the fingertips, at the toes.

At the beginning of the sixth month, the fetus can cry, can suck, can make a fist. He kicks, he punches. The mother can feel this, can *see* this. His eyelids, until now closed, can open. He may look up, down, sideways. His grip is very strong. He could support his weight by holding with one hand.

A reflex, the doctor says.

I hear him. But I saw something in that mass of cells *understand* that it must bob and butt. And I see it again! I have an impulse to shove to the table—it is just a step—seize that needle, pull it out.

We are not six, I think. We are *seven*.

Something strangles *there*. An effort, its effort, binds me to it.

I do not shove to the table. I take no little step. It would be . . . well, madness. Everyone here wants the needle where it is. Six do. No, *five* do.

I close my eyes. I see the inside of the uterus. It is bathed in ruby gloom. I see the creature curled upon itself. Its knees are flexed. Its head is bent upon its chest. It is in fluid and gently rocks to the rhythm of the distant heartbeat.

It resembles . . . a sleeping infant.

Its place is entered by something. It is sudden. A point coming. A needle!

A spike of *daylight* pierces the chamber. Now the light is extinguished. The needle comes closer in the pool. The point grazes the thigh, and I stir. Perhaps I wake from dozing. The light is there again. I twist and straighten. My arms and legs *push*. My hand finds the shaft—grabs! I *grab*. I bend the needle this way and that. The point probes, touches on my belly. My mouth opens. Could I cry out? All is a commotion and a churning. There is a presence in the pool. An activity! The pool colors, reddens, darkens.

I open my eyes to see the doctor feeding a small plastic tube through the barrel of the needle into the uterus. Drops of pink fluid overrun the rim and spill onto the sheet. He withdraws the needle from around the plastic tubing. Now only the little tube protrudes from the woman's body. A nurse hands the physician a syringe loaded with a colorless liquid. He attaches it to the end of the tubing and injects it.

Prostaglandin, he says.

Ah well, prostaglandin—a substance found normally in the body. When given in concentrated dosage, it throws the uterus into vigorous contraction. In eight to twelve hours, the woman will expel the fetus.

The doctor detaches the syringe but does not remove the tubing.

In case we must do it over, he says.

He takes away the sheet. He places gauze pads over the tubing. Over all this he applies adhesive tape.

I know. We cannot feed the great numbers. There is no more room. I know, I know. It is a woman's right to refuse the risk, to decline the pain of childbirth. And an unwanted child is a very great burden. An unwanted child is a burden to himself. I know.

And yet . . . there is the flick of that needle. I *saw* it. I saw . . . I *felt*—in that room, a pace away, life prodded, life fending off. I saw life avulsed—swept by flood, blackening—then *out*.

There, says the doctor. It's all over. It wasn't too bad, was it? he says to the woman.

She smiles. It is all over. Oh, yes.

And who would care to imagine that from a moist and dark commencement six months before there would ripen the cluster and globule, the sprout and pouch of man?

And who would care to imagine that trapped within the laked pearl and a dowry of yoke would lie the earliest stuff of dream and memory?

It is a persona carried here as well as a person, I think. I think it is a signed piece, engraved with a hieroglyph of human genes.

I did not think this until I saw. The flick. The fending off.

Later, in the corridor, the doctor explains that the law does not permit abortion beyond the twenty-fourth week. That is when the fetus may be viable, he says. We stand together for a moment, and he tells of an abortion in which the fetus *cried* after it was passed.

What did you do? I ask him.

There was nothing *to* do but let it live, he says. It did very well, he says. A case of mistaken dates.

Questions

1. What experience led Selzer to write his essay on abortion? On what aspects of this experience does he give the most details, and why?
2. Does Selzer argue for or against abortion in the essay? Does he want to change the minds of readers about abortion? Does he want just to give the facts about abortion and the related ethical issues? Or does he want only to express his personal feelings, without arguing a thesis or presenting facts?
3. What impression do you get of Selzer as a writer and a person from the essay?

Suggestions for Writing

1. Many people have objected to recent advertisements that graphically depict the fetus in the course of an abortion. Selzer is equally graphic in his details. How graphic do you believe the producer or writer should be in arguing for or against abortion? How much illustration and detail do you considerable permissible? Defend the standards on which you base your judgment.
2. Discuss your response to Selzer's essay on abortion—the feelings and ideas it evokes, your opinion as to what Selzer wishes to accomplish in writing the essay, and his success or failure in doing so.

Additional Reading

Callahan, Daniel. *Abortion: Law, Choice, and Morality.* New York: Macmillan, 1970.

Selzer, Richard. *Confessions of a Knife.* New York: Simon and Schuster, 1979.

————. *Letters to a Young Doctor.* New York: Simon and Schuster, 1982.

————. *Mortal Lessons: Notes on the Art of Surgery.* New York: Simon and Schuster, 1976.

————. *Rituals of Surgery.* New York: Simon and Schuster, 1974.

Tooley, Michael. *Abortion and Infanticide.* New York: Oxford University Press, 1984.

A Modest Proposal

For Preventing the Children of Poor People in Ireland from Being a Burden to Their Parents or Country, and for Making Them Beneficial to the Public

Jonathan Swift

The Irish satirist Jonathan Swift (1667–1745) was born in Dublin and educated at Trinity College in that city. Ordained in the Church of England in 1694, he lived in Ireland and England—writing satirical books, supervising the publication of the writings of his patron Sir William Temple, increasing his circle of friends (which included his cousin John Dryden and other important writers of the day), seeking help from the Whig government for Irish clergymen, and engaging himself in other causes. Disapproving of Whig policy toward the Anglican Church, Swift allied himself with the Tory Party and through his political writings greatly influenced political events. When the Whigs returned to power after the death of Queen Anne, he returned to Dublin. In 1773 he had been appointed Dean of St. Patrick's Cathedral in Dublin. Swift continued his writing—on occasion attacking policies of the English government toward the Irish. His most famous work, Gulliver's Travels, *was published in 1726. In his final years, Swift suffered illness and senility. His reputation had grown with the Irish people, and at his death in 1745 he was widely mourned.*

The reader of "A Modest Proposal" should keep in mind that Swift was a Protestant writing about the largely Catholic Irish poor. The situation in Ireland in 1729, the year "A Modest Proposal" was published, was unusually desperate for the poor, and things had been bad for them for half a century. The population of Ireland was predominantly Roman Catholic, and the Protestant English rulers had dealt severely with political rebellion. As in England, Catholics suffered severe penalties. After 1691 Catholic schools were outlawed, and some priests were deported. Irish Catholics were not allowed to own land and the lands of those who did were confiscated. They were seldom able to find redress for crimes in the courts. The established Church of Ireland was Protestant, and though the membership represented one-seventh of the population, it depended on tithes from the Catholic majority. Not surprisingly, half the Catholic population had emigrated by the middle of eighteenth century. Many more were to emigrate in the next century when the potato crop failed in the 1840s, and thousands starved or became homeless.

Swift alludes to these facts. However, his chief concern is with the restrictions on commerce that made it impossible for the Irish to feed and clothe themselves. The Irish woolen industry was destroyed

*by English legislation of 1699 that forbade exports; heavy duties made
it impossible for the Irish to export goods except to England. Other restrictions were so severe that Irish agriculture languished. Acts of 1665
and 1680 had forbidden the entry of Irish cattle, sheep, and swine and
the flesh of these animals into England; importing butter and cheese
from Ireland was also forbidden. Furthermore, Irish products that
could be exported had to be carried in English ships. Much of the land
was held by English owners; one-third of the rents collected from tenants was spent in England. The Irish were by these means
impoverished—numerous paupers roamed the country, famine was
frequent. The English by contrast prospered—government revenues
rose with the increase in manufacture and exports.*

*It is these conditions that Swift addresses in "A Modest Pro-
posal" through a "proposer" who offers a surprising, though perhaps
not original, solution to the problems of a starving country. Though
Swift does not address us directly, we hear his voice throughout the
essay. He forces us in various ways to look beyond the proposer to the
author who created him.*

It is a melancholy object to those who walk through this great town, or travel 1
in the country, when they see the streets, the roads, and cabin-doors crowded with beggars of the female sex, followed by three, four, or six children, all in rags, and importun-
ing every passenger for an alms. These mothers, instead of being able to work for their
honest livelihood, are forced to employ all their time in strolling to beg sustenance for
their helpless infants: who, as they grow up, either turn thieves for want of work, or
leave their dear native country to fight for the Pretender in Spain, or sell themselves to
the Barbadoes.

I think it is agreed by all parties, that this prodigious number of children in the 2
arms, or on the backs, or at the heels of their mothers, and frequently of their fathers,
is in the present deplorable state of the kingdom, a very great additional grievance; and,
therefore, whoever could find out a fair, cheap, and easy method of making these children sound and useful members of the commonwealth, would deserve so well of the
public, as to have his statue set up for a preserver of the nation.

But my intention is very far from being confined to provide only for the chil- 3
dren of professed beggars; it is of a much greater extent, and shall take in the whole
number of infants at a certain age, who are born of parents in effect as little able to support them as those who demand our charity in the streets.

As to my own part, having turned my thoughts for many years upon this im- 4
portant subject, and maturely weighed the several schemes of other projectors, I have
always found them grossly mistaken in their computation. It is true, a child, just
dropped from its dam, may be supported by her milk for a solar year with little other
nourishment; at most, not above the value of two shillings, which the mother may certainly get, or the value in scraps, by her lawful occupation of begging; and it is exactly
at one year old that I propose to provide for them in such a manner, as, instead of being
a charge upon their parents or the parish, or wanting food and raiment for the rest of
their lives, they shall, on the contrary, contribute to the feeding, and partly to the clothing, of many thousands.

There is likewise another great advantage in my scheme, that it will prevent 5 those voluntary abortions, and that horrid practice of women murdering their bastard children, alas, too frequent among us, sacrificing the poor innocent babes, I doubt more to avoid the expense than the shame, which would move tears and pity in the most savage and inhuman breast.

The number of souls in this kingdom being usually reckoned one million and 6 a half, of these I calculate there may be about two hundred thousand couples whose wives are breeders; from which number I subtract thirty thousand couples, who are able to maintain their own children (although I apprehend there cannot be so many, under the present distresses of the kingdom); but this being granted, there will remain an hundred and seventy thousand breeders. I again subtract fifty thousand for those women who miscarry, or whose children die by accident or disease within the year. There only remain a hundred and twenty thousand children of poor parents annually born. The question therefore is how this number shall be reared and provided for? which, as I have already said, under the present situation of affairs, is utterly impossible by all the methods hitherto proposed. For we can neither employ them in handicraft or agriculture; we neither build houses (I mean in the country) nor cultivate land: they can very seldom pick up a livelihood by stealing until they arrive at six years old, except where they are of towardly parts; although I confess they learn the rudiments much earlier; during which time they can, however, be properly looked upon only as probationers; as I have been informed by a principal gentleman in the county of Cavan, who protested to me, that he never knew above one or two instances under the age of six, even in a part of the kingdom so renowned for the quickest proficiency in that art.

I am assured by our merchants that a boy or a girl before twelve years old is no 7 salable commodity; and even when they come to this age they will not yield above three pounds or three pounds and half-a-crown at most, on the exchange; which cannot turn to account either to the parents or kingdom, the charge of nutriment and rags having been at least four times that value.

I shall now, therefore, humbly propose my own thoughts, which I hope will not 8 be liable to the least objection.

I have been assured by a very knowing American of my acquaintance in London, that a young healthy child, well nursed, is, at a year old, a most delicious, nourishing, and wholesome food, whether stewed, roasted, baked, or boiled; and I make no doubt that it will equally serve in a fricassee or a ragout.

I do therefore humbly offer it to public consideration, that of the hundred and 10 twenty thousand children already computed, twenty thousand may be reserved for breed, whereof only one-fourth part to be males; which is more than we allow to sheep, black cattle, or swine; and my reason is, that these children are seldom the fruits of marriage, a circumstance not much regarded by our savages, therefore one male will be sufficient to serve four females. That the remaining hundred thousand may, at a year old, be offered in sale to the persons of quality and fortune through the kingdom; always advising the mother to let them suck plentifully in the last month, so as to render them plump and fat for a good table. A child will make two dishes at an entertainment for friends; and when the family dines alone, the fore or hind quarter will make a reasonable dish, and, seasoned with a little pepper or salt, will be very good boiled on the fourth day, especially in winter.

I have reckoned, upon a medium, that a child just born will weigh twelve 11 pounds, and in a solar year, if tolerably nursed, increaseth to twenty-eight pounds.

I grant this food will be somewhat dear, and therefore very proper for land- 12 lords, who, as they have already devoured most of the parents, seem to have the best title to the children.

Infants' flesh will be in season throughout the year, but more plentifully in 13 March, and a little before and after: for we are told by a grave author, an eminent French physician, that fish being a prolific diet, there are more children born in Roman Catholic countries about nine months after Lent than at any other season; therefore, reckoning a year after Lent, the markets will be more glutted than usual, because the number of popish infants is at least three to one in this kingdom; and therefore, it will have one other collateral advantage, by lessening the number of papists among us.

I have already computed the charge of nursing a beggar's child (in which list 14 I reckon all cottagers, labourers, and four-fifths of the farmers) to be about two shillings per annum, rags included; and I believe no gentleman would repine to give ten shillings for the carcass of a good fat child, which, as I have said, will make four dishes of excellent nutritive meat, when he has only some particular friend, or his own family, to dine with him. Thus, the squire will learn to be a good landlord, and grow popular among his tenants; the mother will have eight shillings net profit, and be fit for work till she produces another child.

Those who are more thrifty (as I must confess the times require) may flay the 15 carcass; the skin of which artificially dressed, will make admirable gloves for ladies, and summer-boots for fine gentlemen.

As to our city of Dublin, shambles[1] may be appointed for this purpose in the 16 most convenient parts of it, and butchers we may be assured will not be wanting; although I rather recommend buying the children alive, and dressing them hot from the knife, as we do roasting pigs.

A very worthy person, a true lover of his country, and whose virtues I highly 17 esteem, was lately pleased, in discoursing on this matter, to offer a refinement upon my scheme. He said, that many gentlemen of this kingdom, having of late destroyed their deer, he conceived that the want of venison might be well supplied by the bodies of young lads and maidens, not exceeding fourteen years of age, nor under twelve; so great a number of both sexes in every country being now ready to starve for want of work and service; and these to be disposed of by their parents, if alive, or otherwise by their nearest relations. But, with due deference to so excellent a friend, and so deserving a patriot, I cannot be altogether in his sentiments; for as to the males, my American acquaintance assured me from frequent experience, that their flesh was generally tough and lean, like that of our schoolboys, by continual exercise, and their taste disagreeable; and to fatten them would not answer the charge. Then as to the females, it would, I think, with humble submission, be a loss to the public, because they soon would become breeders themselves: and besides, it is not improbable that some scrupulous people might be apt to censure such a practice (although indeed very unjustly) as a little bordering upon cruelty; which, I confess hath always been with me the strongest objection against any project, how well soever intended.

---

[1]Butcher shops.

But in order to justify my friend, he confessed that this expedient was put into [18] his head by the famous Psalmanazar,[2] a native of the island Formosa, who came from thence to London above twenty years ago; and in conversation told my friend, that in his country, when any young person happened to be put to death, the executioner sold the carcass to persons of quality as a prime dainty; and that in his time the body of a plump girl of fifteen, who was crucified for an attempt to poison the emperor, was sold to his Imperial Majesty's prime minister of state, and other great mandarins of the court, in joints from the gibbet, at four hundred crowns. Neither indeed can I deny, that if the same use were made of several plump young girls in this town, who, without one single groat to their fortunes, cannot stir abroad without a chair, and appear at playhouse and assemblies in foreign fineries which they never will pay for, the kingdom would not be the worse.

Some persons of a desponding spirit are in great concern about that vast num- [19] ber of poor people who are aged, diseased, or maimed; and I have been desired to employ my thoughts what course may be taken to ease the nation of so grievous an encumbrance. But I am not in the least pain upon that matter, because it is very well known, that they are every day dying, and rotting, by cold and famine, and filth and vermin, as fast as can be reasonably expected. And so to the younger labourers, they are now in almost as hopeful a condition: they cannot get work, and consequently pine away for want of nourishment, to a degree, that if at any time they are accidentally hired to common labour, they have not strength to perform it; and thus the country and themselves are happily delivered from the evils to come.

I have too long digressed, and therefore shall return to my subject. I think the [20] advantages by the proposal which I have made are obvious and many, as well as of the highest importance.

For first, as I have already observed, it would greatly lessen the number of pa- [21] pists, with whom we are yearly overrun, being the principal breeders of the nation as well as our most dangerous enemies; and who stay at home on purpose with a design to deliver the kingdom to the Pretender, hoping to take their advantage by the absence of so many good Protestants, who have chosen rather to leave their country than stay at home and pay tithes against their conscience to an idolatrous Episcopal curate.[3]

Secondly, the poorer tenants will have something valuable of their own, which [22] by law may be made liable to distress, and help to pay their landlord's rent; their corn and cattle being already seized, and money a thing unknown.

Thirdly, whereas the maintenance of an hundred thousand children, from two [23] years old and upwards, cannot be computed at less than ten shillings a piece per annum, the nation's stock will be thereby increased fifty thousand pounds per annum; besides the profit of a new dish introduced to the tables of all gentlemen of fortune in the kingdom who have any refinement in taste. And the money will circulate among ourselves, the goods being entirely of our own growth and manufacture.

---

[2]A French writer, George Psalmanazar, who posed as a native of Formosa in a fake book he published about that country in 1704, in England.
[3]Swift is attacking prejudice against Irish Catholics and the motives of a number of Protestant dissenters from the Church of England. "The Pretender" was James Stuart (1688–1766), son of the Catholic James II, deposed in 1688.

Fourthly, the constant breeders, besides the gain of eight shillings sterling per 24 annum by the sale of their children, will be rid of the charge of maintaining them after the first year.

Fifthly, this food would otherwise bring great custom to taverns; where the 25 vintners will certainly be so prudent as to procure the best receipts for dressing it to perfection, and, consequently, have their houses frequented by all the fine gentlemen, who justly value themselves upon their knowledge in good eating: and a skillful cook, who understands how to oblige his guests, will contrive to make it as expensive as they please.

Sixthly, this would be a great inducement to marriage, which all wise nations 26 have either encouraged by rewards, or enforced by laws and penalties. It would increase the care and tenderness of mothers towards their children, when they were sure of a settlement for life to the poor babes, provided in some sort by the public, to their annual profit instead of expense. We should soon see an honest emulation among the married women, which of them could bring the fattest child to the market. Men would become as fond of their wives during the time of their pregnancy, as they are now of their mares in foal, their cows in calf, or sows when they are ready to farrow; nor offer to beat or kick them (as is too frequent a practice) for fear of a miscarriage.

Many other advantages might be enumerated. For instance, the addition of 27 some thousand carcasses in our exportation of barrelled beef; the propagation of swine's flesh, and improvement in the art of making good bacon, so much wanted among us by the great destruction of pigs, too frequent at our tables, which are no way comparable in taste or magnificence to a well-grown, fat yearling child, which, roasted whole, will make a considerable figure at a Lord Mayor's feast, or any other public entertainment. But this, and many others, I omit, being studious of brevity.

Supposing that one thousand families in this city would be constant customers 28 for infants' flesh, besides others who might have it at merry meetings, particularly weddings and christenings, I compute that Dublin would take off annually about twenty thousand carcasses; and the rest of the kingdom (where probably they will be sold somewhat cheaper) the remaining eighty thousand.

I can think of no one objection that will possibly be raised against this proposal, 29 unless it should be urged, that the number of people will be thereby much lessened in the kingdom. This I freely own, and it was indeed one principal design in offering it to the world. I desire the reader will observe that I calculate my remedy for this one individual kingdom of Ireland, and for no other that ever was, is, or I think ever can be, upon earth. Therefore let no man talk to me of other expedients: of taxing our absentees at five shillings a pound: of using neither clothes nor household-furniture except what is of our own growth and manufacture: of utterly rejecting the materials and instruments that promote foreign luxury: of curing the expensiveness of pride, vanity, idleness, and gaming in our women; of introducing a vein of parsimony, prudence, and temperance: of learning to love our country, wherein we differ even from Laplanders, and the inhabitants of Topinamboo:[4] of quitting our animosities and factions, nor act any longer like the Jews, who were murdering one another at the very moment their

---

[4] A district of Brazil notorious for its barbarism and ignorance.

city was taken:[5] of being a little cautious not to sell our country and consciences for nothing: of teaching landlords to have at least one degree of mercy towards their tenants: lastly, of putting a spirit of honesty, industry, and skill into our shopkeepers; who, if a resolution could now be taken to buy only our native goods, would immediately unite to cheat and exact upon us in the price, the measure, and the goodness, nor could ever yet be brought to make one fair proposal of just dealing, though often and earnestly invited to it.

Therefore I repeat, let no man talk to me of these and the like expedients, till 30 he hath at least some glimpse of hope that there will ever be some hearty and sincere attempt to put them in practice.

But, as to myself, having been wearied out for many years with offering vain, 31 idle, visionary thoughts, and at length utterly despairing of success, I fortunately fell upon this proposal; which, as it is wholly new, so it hath something solid and real, of no expense and little trouble, full in our own power, and whereby we can incur no danger in disobliging England. For this kind of commodity will not bear exportation, the flesh being of too tender a consistence to admit a long continuance in salt, although perhaps I could name a country which would be glad to eat up our whole nation without it.

After all, I am not so violently bent upon my own opinion as to reject any offer 32 proposed by wise men which shall be found equally innocent, cheap, easy, and effectual. But before something of that kind shall be advanced in contradiction to my scheme, and offering a better, I desire the author, or authors, will be pleased maturely to consider two points. First, as things now stand, how they will be able to find food and raiment for a hundred thousand useless mouths and backs? And, secondly, there being a round million of creatures in human figure throughout this kingdom, whose whole subsistence put into a common stock would leave them in debt two millions of pounds sterling, adding those who are beggars by profession, to the bulk of farmers, cottagers, and labourers, with the wives and children who are beggars in effect; I desire those politicians who dislike my overture, and may perhaps be so bold as to attempt an answer, that they will first ask the parents of these mortals, whether they would not at this day think it a great happiness to have been sold for food at a year old, in the manner I prescribe, and thereby have avoided such a perpetual scene of misfortunes as they have since gone through, by the oppression of landlords, the impossibility of paying rent without money or trade, the want of common sustenance, with neither house nor clothes to cover them from the inclemencies of weather, and the most inevitable prospect of entailing the like, or greater miseries, upon their breed for ever.

I profess, in the sincerity of my heart, that I have not the least personal interest 33 in endeavouring to promote this necessary work, having no other motive than the public good of my country, by advancing our trade, providing for infants, relieving the poor, and giving some pleasure to the rich. I have no children by which I can propose to get a single penny; the youngest being nine years old, and my wife past child-bearing.

---

[5]Swift is referring to the fall of Jerusalem in 70 A.D.

Questions

1. Were you surprised by the "modest proposal"? If not, why not? If you were surprised, why were you? Because the proposer does not seem likely to make a shocking proposal? Because the tone of the essay led you to expect another proposal?
2. How would you characterize the proposer? Does he seem a cruel and insensitive person, hostile to the Irish poor? Or is he sympathetic to the Irish, persuaded that his proposal will cause less pain than that being suffered by Irish parents and children? Or is the proposer being ironic—pretending that his proposal is worthy of consideration?
3. In what tone of voice does he address the English? What does this tone suggest about his attitude toward them? Does he state his attitude directly? Does he believe the English are capable of considering the alternatives suggested by the proposer?
4. What does Swift gain in speaking about Ireland through his proposer rather than in his own person?
5. How successful is Swift in realizing his purpose in writing the essay? Should the essay be judged a success if the English adopted the proposal? Should it be judged a failure if they did nothing to alleviate the poverty and suffering of the Irish?

Suggestions for Writing

1. Discuss how the character and motives of the proposer emerge in the course of the essay. Toward the end of your essay, discuss the attitude Swift wishes the reader to take toward the proposer, and tell how you know.
2. Write your own "modest proposal" to remedy a current situation that you consider intolerable. Give details about this situation in the course of making the proposal, as Swift does. Present the proposal in your person or through an invented character like Swift's proposer.
3. Swift attacked the English in the *Drapier Letters* (1724), occasioned by the decision of the English to allow debased coins to circulate in Ireland. *Gulliver's Travels* and Swift's earlier writings under the pseudonym Isaac Bickerstaff show other satirical techniques. These and other satirical writings are contained in *The Prose Works*, edited by Herbert Davis (1939). Compare the methods Swift uses in "A Modest Proposal" with those in one of these other writings—for example, his satire of the European powers in Book 2 of *Gulliver's Travels*.

Additional Reading

Beckett, James G. *The Making of Modern Ireland: 1603–1923*. New York: Knopf, 1966.

Ehrenpreis, Irvin. *Swift: The Man, His Works, and the Age*. 2 vols. Cambridge: Harvard University Press, 1962–1967.

Oliver, Watkins Ferguson. *Jonathan Swift and Ireland*. Urbana: University of Illinois Press, 1962.

Swift, Jonathan. *Gulliver's Travels*. Ed. Robert A. Greenberg. New York: Norton Critical Editions, 1967.

————. *The Prose Works.* Ed. Herbert Davis. 16 vols. Oxford, England: Shakespeare Head Press, 1939–1974.
Woodham-Smith, Cecil. *The Great Hunger: 1845–1849.* London: Hamish Hamilton, 1962.

*Triage**

Garrett Hardin

As a professor of biology at the University of California at Santa Barbara, Garrett Hardin studied protozoa, algae, photosynthesis, and antibiotics. Much of his writing concerns the problem of scarcity and the demands of populations on natural resources. The word triage *(French, "sorting"), Hardin states, originated in the First World War to describe the assignment of scarce medical resources on the basis of need.*

The idea of triage, James F. Childress shows, has been a controversial one: the criteria for selection have been widely debated, and so has the need of triage in the allocation of food. One argument against triage is that of the British economist Barbara Ward, who rejects the Malthusian theory that overpopulation leads to disaster. Ward argues that "if parents are given work, responsibility, enough food, and safe water, they have the sense to see that they do not need endless children as insurance against calamity." She states:

> It may be that this positive strategy of stabilizing population by sustained, skilled and well-directed investment in food production, and in clean water suggests less drama than the hair-raising images of inexorably rising tides of children eating like locusts the core out of the whole world's food supplies.

Ward particularly objects to the implication that selection is inevitable in resources of all kinds because the world is a battlefield:

> But perhaps we should be wise to prefer relevance to drama. In "triage," there is, after all, a suggestion of the battlefield. If this is how we see the world, are we absolutely certain who deserves to win—the minority of guzzlers who eat 2,000 pounds of grain, or the majority of despairing men of hunger who eat 400 pounds?
>
> —"Triage"

Ward points out that history gives "uncomfortable answers." The barbarians eventually conquered the comfortable Romans.

---

*Pronounced trē äzh'.

"Is this the battlefield we want? And who will
'triage' whom?" —"Triage"

These are the issues that engage Hardin in his essay on triage.

"Hard cases make bad law," said Justice Holmes.[1] Perhaps so; but they make 1
good science and, I submit, good ethics. What is considered a hard case in ethics is usually one that pits a Promethean approach (which we resist) against an Epimethean
(which we slip into all too gratefully). Nowhere is this more apparent than in the problem of allocating scarce resources. One way to do this is by the system called "triage."
If there are not enough medical officers to save all the wounded soldiers, whom shall we
save *first?* If we don't have enough food to save all the starving people of the world, to
whom shall we give the food *first?* Triage gives answers to problems like these.

No full treatment of triage has yet been written. The recently published four- 2
volume *Encyclopedia of Bioethics*[2] treats the subject in a superficial and desultory fashion. For reasons that should become clear as we go along, there is great reluctance to
discuss this topic. It may be that the popular media will steal a march on the scholars.
For a number of years the Korean War television show M*A*S*H, has introduced the
term "triage" into the dialogue about once every two months (by my estimate). The
word is usually just thrown out in passing; it no doubt escapes the notice of most view-
ers because they are not familiar with it. But in January of 1979 the producers used
about five minutes of the program to explain the procedure of medical triage in a dramatically justified context. Their treatment might be criticized for not sufficiently emphasizing the controversial aspects of the system, but it was a good introduction to the
subject.

The formerly rare word "triage" was introduced to the general public by the 3
Paddock brothers in 1967, thus starting an argument that is still with us. In their book
Famine—1975! William Paddock, an agricultural expert specializing in tropical problems, and Paul Paddock, a retired officer of the U.S. Department of State, defended a
simple thesis: America cannot possibly save everyone in the world from starving, so we
will have to make choices, following the method of selection known to the military as
triage.[3] What is triage?

"Triage," said Lord Ritchie-Calder some time later, "is a relentless two-syllable 4
word. It is a French term dredged up from the mud of the First World War, of the
Marne, the Somme, Verdun, Passchendaele and Chateau-Thierry."[4] If we hope to make
progress in dealing with so vital an issue we had better refrain from using such emotional language. Let us be advised by Spinoza.

Non ridere, non lugere, neque detestari, sed intelligiere.[5]

"Not to laugh, not to lament, neither to curse, but to understand"—this should be our
policy and our goal. It should be noted that Lord Ritchie-Calder gained his reputation
and his peerage from his work as a journalist: the significance of this vocation will be
touched on later.

Before evaluating the Paddocks' proposal to apply triage in the distribution of 5
food let us see how the practice is carried out in a strictly military situation, relying on

the excellent discussion by Stuart W. Hinds in a symposium on *Lifeboat Ethics.*[6] Military triage is a system of assigning priority for the treatment of the wounded after a battle *WHENEVER the need for medical attention exceeds the supply of medical personnel and facilities.* (The italicized phrase is important but often overlooked.) In such cases the wounded can be categorized into three groups:

Group One: Those so seriously wounded that they either cannot survive, or can be saved only if served by an unreasonably large allotment of medical resources.

Group Two: Those who can be saved by a reasonable amount of care, but would die without it.

Group Three: Those who will survive without treatment (though possibly with some pain)—the so-called "walking wounded." In any event, their treatment can be postponed to a later time when the activity is less hectic.

A system of military triage was described and first consciously used by Baron Dominique Jean Larrey (1766–1842), Napoleon's surgeon-in-chief. I say "consciously used" because I suspect that such a judgmental scheme has often been employed in times of scarcity: triage is common sense. It is worth noting that Baron Larrey also introduced the field ambulance to military medicine, for which hundreds of thousands of soldiers have been thankful.

As with so many human innovations, the *naming* of triage in medicine did not come until long after its rationale was explained. The literature on military triage is not large; the very paucity of it throws light on human motives and the origin of taboos. The word "triage" does not occur in the indexes of either *Military Medicine* (twenty-five volumes) or *Military Surgeon* (ninety-three volumes), the two journals devoted exclusively to military medicine. The word does not appear in any articles dealing with war casualties, the evacuation of casualties, first aid, or the treatment of battle casualties. Instead, we find the words "sorting," "selection," "selective tagging," and the like.

"Triage" is not found in the index of any of the fourteen volumes of the British *History of the Second World War,* but it does occur a score of times in the American equivalent. (Why the national difference?) On one occasion a British military surgeon remarked:

> The word "triage" has been quite rightfully condemned. I think it is outlived,
> and some more sensible word such as grouping, or selection is the word of
> choice. I don't think it matters very much that we have three groups a, b and
> c; or one, two and three. That, after all, is intended only as a guide for one who
> hasn't faced it before. It is . . . sense that matters.

Plainly the commentator is disturbed only by the word, not the fact. "Words," said Thomas Hobbes, "are wise men's counters,—they do but reckon by them; but they are the money of fools." How, then, is a wise man to counsel with fools? If the counterfeit is accepted as genuine, ideas will be lost through confusion; but if the counterfeit is publicly identified for what it is, passions may be so aroused that ideas are rejected without examination.

Part of the emotional reaction to triage stems, I think, from a mistaken assumption as to the etymology of the word. "Triage" looks like it comes from "tri-" or three, and this suggests a necessary division into three groups, with the subsequent absolute rejection of one group, the "hopelessly wounded." Absolute rejection frightens 9 us: to reword an old saw, we fear that the life that is rejected may be our own.

But "triage" has quite a different origin: it comes from the French *trier* which 10 means to sort, sort out, screen, pick, choose, cull, select. When someone speaks against triage but in favor of sorting or selection he is guilty of etymological nonsense. Sorting is sorting, whatever the word used, and the word "triage" was used for the sorting of wools and coffee beans long before it was applied to the sorting of human casualties.

The three-way sorting scheme is a good pedagogical tool for explaining the 11 logic of triage, but trifurcation is not necessary. Alternatively we can arrange the candidates for help into a single hierarchical list based on efficiency, where efficiency is measured by the "amount of life" (L) saved per unit effort (E), as expressed in the L/E ratio. The individuals we earlier spoke of as Group Two will be at the head of the list, because their L/E values are high. Below them will be the other two groups: Group One—the desperately wounded—have a low L/E value because E is so great; Group Three—the "walking wounded"—have a low L/E value because L is so small. (It is understood, of course, that L stands not for life itself, but for "life saved"—the life that would, without intervention, be lost.) Using an efficiency analysis the pedagogical trifurcation disappears.

Triage is, then, the most efficient procedure, the procedure that saves the max- 12 imum number of lives. Some sensitive people may react adversely to the *word* "efficient" applied to the saving of human lives, but I think it unlikely that such people will reject the *ideal* of saving the maximum number of lives possible. Though the military strategist may want to do this for strictly military reasons, the most compassionate pacifist reaches the same conclusion by another route. Triage is also the philosophy of choice in civilian medicine whenever need overwhelms medical resources, as it may following a massive catastrophe. *No close student of the problems of either military medicine or civilian medicine has ever proposed an alternative to triage.*

We are now ready to turn to the application of triage in allocating the "surplus" 13 food of a rich country to poor countries in need. The book *Famine—1975!* was a shocker to reviewers. The book reviewer of the *Christian Science Monitor*[7] was repelled by its "self-righteousness," pointing to its subtitle, "America's Decision: Who Will Survive?" The facts behind this title are simple: America exports about half of the cereal grains it produces, and more than half of the grain in international trade is produced by the United States. If we sell grain, its distribution is determined by market mechanisms; but when we give it away, if there are more requests than we can fulfill, how can we avoid deciding who gets how much? In years when demand exceeds supply we must triage the distribution—yes, triage is now an English verb—and the most hopeless countries would have to do without. The internationalist Richard Falk has objected to *our* making such decisions:

> Such an approach involves a radical repudiation of human solidarity, requires standing aside while millions perish, and naturally induces the society called "hopeless" to adopt the most desperate strategies of self-preservation. As such, *triage* is dangerously naive about political consequences.[8]

Without undue simplification I think the issues raised by Falk can be fairly 14 dealt with in a few words. First let us take up the matter of political naivety. If we are thinking of war we must remember that modern warfare is so expensive that even the richest nations cannot afford it: the "Yom Kippur War" in 1973, waged in proxy for the Soviet Union and the United States, though it lasted only eighteen days, nearly bank-rupted us. For poor countries, *invasive* foreign wars are out of the question. As for ter-rorism, the threat of it will be with us as long as envy exists—that is, forever—so we have to find ways to deal with it anyway. The threat of terrorism, like other forms of blackmail, cannot be bought off; police action, imperfect though it be, is the principal recourse of a society that is determined to survive.

Falk says that resorting to triage "requires standing aside while millions per- 15 ish." But if a 100 million ton supply of surplus grain encounters a 200 million ton de-mand, what more can we do than "stand aside"? Further activity would, at best, be a waste of resources; and at worst, counter-productive. The implication of "standing aside" is that we do so callously. Critics of triage sometimes sound as though their prin-cipal concern is that the rich should suffer. (The critics assume the role of deputies of envy.) But what is the good of emotional suffering? *Com-passion* literally means "sym-pathy with." Does compassion that leads to no useful action do the unfortunate any good? Triage may be enriched with compassion, or it may not be. If you had to choose between people practicing the two kinds of triage, which would you choose? If you had to be operated on, what would you look for first in your surgeon—competence or com-passion?

There are those who reject triage on the grounds that it is not necessary. Of 16 course if it isn't, if there is no real scarcity, then there is no need to triage the appli-cants. But the denial of scarcity is generally made *sotto voce.* When Falk discusses the group to be left out of the distribution of goods in international triage he uses quotation marks to surround the word "hopeless" thus impugning the idea of scarcity.

The reviewer in the *Monitor* denied the grounds for triage in a different way: 17 "Since we cannot condemn India—or Haiti or Egypt—to death, since countries and people cannot simply vanish from the face of the earth, what heroic answer must be found?" What a multi-edged sword language is! "Condemn" suggests sentencing under criminal law, but the reason for the discrimination of triage is not to condemn but to maximize the number of lives saved. "Condemn" is an Epimethean judgment that takes no account of the successful Promethean strategy of triage. As for any countries and people vanishing from the face of the earth, nations—a non-living abstraction—have vanished before, and they will continue to vanish. *Individual* people may die "before their time," but the abstraction called *the people* is almost ineradicable. Twenty-five percent of the European populace was extinguished by plague in the middle of the four-teenth century, but "the people" continued and are now more numerous than ever.

Those who cannot bring themselves to admit the Promethean rationality of tri- 18 age are inclined to befuddle the issue by professing a pretty faith in counterfactual con-ditionals. The *Monitor* reviewer's "what heroic answer must be found?" implies that there *is* a "heroic" and painlessly acceptable answer. Aurelio Peccei, a rich industrialist turned internationalist,[9] speaking of the making of triage decisions, asserts that "the right to make such decisions cannot be left to just a few nations, because it would lend them ominous power over the life of the world's hungry. However, the world has yet to see any international mechanism to cope with these human, moral and political dilem-mas."[10] In other words, triage decisions must be turned over to a supranational authority—which does not exist! And if no one is empowered to carry out triage, more lives will be lost.

There is an old folk saying that should be worked into a sampler to hang in 19 the study of every idealist: *"If it's and and's were pots and pans, there'd be no need for tinkers."*

People who refuse to face squarely the challenge of scarcity are apt to find 20 themselves in embarrassing positions. I cite two instances, the first from a newspaper account:

> An Irish nun is visiting Bangladesh, staying at a Christian hostel in Dacca. On her second evening in the city, she steps outside for a breath of air and finds an emaciated baby deserted on the doorstep. She takes the baby in, feeds it, doctors it, bathes it, and then goes out searching for the mother, who is nowhere to be found.
>
> The next morning the nun finds a second starving baby lying in the street in front of the hostel. So she takes the second baby in. Then she goes off to the local police station to report the missing babies and to seek advice.
>
> The advice is to put the babies back in the street or, the police officer says, you will find four more babies tomorrow.
>
> "What on earth am I to do?" the nun says later in the day. "Am I to put them out to starve?"[11]

Note that the moral is left dangling. Whether or not the nun finally saw the 21 light, it is contrary to the traditions of journalism to reach a conclusion in such an emotionally threatening situation. We are lucky when a newspaper even clearly points out the problem.

The second account is of Mother Teresa, the European nun who has devoted a 22 lifetime to bringing comfort to the poor of Calcutta. It is commonly estimated that a quarter of a million of India's poorest people sleep on the streets of Calcutta. Many of them die every night, and are removed by municipal drays. Many others, near death, have trouble moving the next morning. Some of these are picked up by Mother Teresa's workers and carried away to her rest home where they are bathed, put in clean apparel, and fed. The idea is to give them a dignified death. One cannot but admire the selfless service of these nuns, carrying out duties that would appall most of us. Yet there is irony in the consequences.

Normally the Indian who is so treated dies within a few days; he was selected 23 for this treatment because he appeared to be a terminal case. But judgment is difficult, and some of the rescued survive. What then? The bed of a survivor is needed for a new candidate for death (for Calcutta's nocturnal sidewalks and alcoves furnish a more than bountiful supply). So the recovered Indian is put out on the sidewalks—"to try again," as it were. Sooner or later he will fulfill the implied contract. In the meantime Mother Teresa, rejecting conventional triage, is forced to practice a sort of triage of her own. Proponents of traditional triage see an ironical justice in this punishment. We cannot refrain from asking, Does Mother Teresa increase or decrease the amount of suffering in the world?

Unwillingness to make hard decisions extends to other species. When the 24 *Torrey Canyon* oil-tanker wrecked off British shores, the spilled oil covered the feathers of thousands of birds. British volunteers, great bird-lovers, flocked to save the birds by cleaning the oil off their feathers. Experts, assessing the results later, found that most of the birds perished before they were cleaned, and that most of the few that survived the cleaning process died when they were released. One of the directors of the project

told the London *Sunday Times:* "These bird-rescue centres have been established because we haven't the guts to say there is nothing we can do. It is only a public-relations
exercise."[12]

Public relations is a great breeder of hypocrisy. The *appearance* of compassion 25
pays—as every actor, preacher, politician, and public relations specialist knows very
well, though it is to his hypocritical interest not to dwell on the fact. The profession of
journalism also selects for the appearance of compassion (accompanied, we can grant,
by some genuine feeling).

Of every well-intentioned proposal we must ask the Promethean question *And* 26
then what? for time is of the essence. An act is generally identified as compassionate if
it diminishes suffering *right now:* we seldom demand of a compassionate act that it diminish suffering a decade from now. Those who pride themselves on compassionately
rejecting triage do so because they hold it unthinkable to ask people to suffer in the
present for the sake of a brighter future for others or for themselves.

Journalism, by its nature, is oriented almost wholly toward the present, a very 27
narrow present indeed for daily newspapers. It is perfectly natural that journalists
should be strong on present-oriented compassion and weak on Promethean concern for
the future consequences of present action. Journalist Lord Ritchie-Calder's abhorrence
of the word "triage" is easily understandable in terms of his occupation, as is also his
opinion that M*A*S*H is a heartless and inhumane television program.[13] He is much
disturbed by the joking that goes on among the doctors during the hectic operating
scenes. Mankind's never-ending struggle against hypocrisy would be helped if Lord
Ritchie-Calder would listen to Lord Byron:

> And if I laugh at any mortal thing,
> 'Tis that I may not weep.[14]

There is much unpreventable tragedy in the world, and bitter laughter comes 28
naturally to those whose vocation requires prolonged attendance at scenes of tragedy.
Taking a cue from Sir Toby Belch who asked, "Dost thou think, because thou art virtuous, there shall be no more cakes and ale?"[15] we might well ask, *"Because thou art com-*
passionate, shall there be no more gales of laughter?" There are times when laughter
is desperately needed to enable us to retain our sanity in this tragic world. But it must
be admitted that the cause of our laughter can be easily misunderstood by compassionate men and women who have not squarely faced the implications of scarcity.

As the Promethean approach to ethics gains in acceptance we will become ever 29
more aware of tragedy and the necessity of weighing the good of present actions against
their contingent future consequences. The vocational ethics of the physician—as presently conceived—require that he focus only on the present person. Who, then, speaks
for posterity? This Promethean problem has been poignantly stated by the English phys-
iologist A. V. Hill:

> The dilemma is this. All the impulses of decent humanity, all the dictates of
> religion and all the traditions of medicine insist that suffering should be re-
> lieved, curable diseases cured, preventable disease prevented. The obligation is
> regarded as unconditional: it is not permitted to argue that the suffering is
> due to folly, that the children are not wanted, that the patient's family would
> be happier if he died. All that may be so; but to accept it as a guide to action

would lead to a degradation of standards of humanity by which civilization would be permanently and indefinitely poorer. . . .

Some might [take] the purely biological view that if men will breed like rabbits they must be allowed to die like rabbits. . . . Most people would still say no. But suppose it were certain now that the pressure of increasing population, uncontrolled by disease, would lead not only to widespread exhaustion of the soil and of other capital resources but also to continuing and increasing international tension and disorder, making it hard for civilization itself to survive: Would the majority of humane and reasonable people then change their minds? If ethical principles deny our right to do evil in order that good may come, are we justified in doing good when the foreseeable consequence is evil?[16]

The compassionate Promethean is not satisfied by the mere saving of a present 30 life: he wants us to find some way of taking account of the future and of posterity's needs.[17] The Promethean cannot forget that the life we save today breeds more lives in need of saving tomorrow.

This insight is not new. Tertullian, in the third century, spoke of "the vast pop- 31 ulation of the earth to which we are a burden," saying that "she scarcely can provide for our needs." In modern terms, all population theory must begin with the concept of the carrying capacity of the territory (the earth, for example).[18] "Our demands grow greater," said Tertullian*. Does it occur to us to moderate our demands by bringing supply and demand into balance? No, not even in Tertullian's day: "Our complaints against nature's inadequacy are heard by all." In other words, don't blame ourselves, blame someone else (Nature). If that is the best we can do, we recognize a bitter justification for Tertullian's conclusion:

> The scourges of pestilence, famine, wars, and earthquakes have come to be regarded as a blessing to overcrowded nations, since they serve to prune away the luxuriant growth of the human race.[19]

The concept of carrying capacity is one which any agriculturist understands— 32 notice the verb "to prune" in Tertullian's statement. This understanding was pretty well lost during the hundred and fifty years after Malthus, a time that saw the rise of the idea of progress, an increase in urbanization, and the flowering of urbanized economics, which is the economics of the man who buys his food at the store. Urbanized economics says that the supply of anything can always be increased by raising the price. Urban economists have lost sight of the substantive source of food—the land. Of course technology has tremendously increased the carrying capacity of the land, but it cannot do so indefinitely. And technology is powerless to increase the supply of some goods, for instance wild beauty and natural solitude.

Economists are only now coming to recognize that today's economic interpre- 33 tation of "scarcity" and "supply" is unecological. Kicking and screaming every inch of the way economists are being dragged into the twenty-first century.[20] They must recapture the vision (blotted out after John Stuart Mill) that economics is above all else the science of the allocation of scarce resources.

---

*Tertullian (160? B.C.–A.D. 230): early father of the Christian church. [Ed.]

To prune, to thin, to cull, to sort out, to screen, to pick, to choose, to select— 34 every one of these actions takes time into account. We renounce some present good for the sake of the future. To the critic who is deficient in a feeling for the future, selection processes bespeak a lack of compassion. But those who have the courage to select, and to live with the consequences of selection, believe that only Promethean, time-oriented decisions deserve the name of compassion.

Every system of ethics (like all logical systems) rests on unexamined assump- 35 tions. Throughout this discussion I have assumed that it is desirable to minimize suffering. When it comes to the saving of lives most people, given the choice of saving many lives or few, would choose many. The theory of triage seeks to maximize the number of lives saved. The philosopher John Taurek[21] has argued that triage is not the best policy. Taurek's hints of the mathematical form of his argument are here developed explicitly.

Nowhere in his discussion does Taurek use the word "triage." Whether this is 36 through ignorance or semantic distaste does not matter: he is clearly talking about triage, which he contrasts with another system. In comparing these two systems I use the terms "Triage Policy" and "Parity Policy." The reason for the second name will presently be explained.

Suppose that we have 5 units of a life-saving medicine; that there are 5 persons 37 in Group I, each of whom requires 1 unit to save his life; and that Group II has only 1 person in it, and that he requires 5 units of the medicine to save his life. Using this model, let us compare the two policies.

Triage Policy: Seeking to maximize the saving of lives we allocate all 5 units of 38 medicine to Group I, thus saving 5 lives. The single person in Group II gets no medicine. Triage Policy saves 5 of the 6 lives at risk. Triage specifically recognizes the inequality of individuals, the significant inequality in this connection being the inequality of demands on environmental resources. (The resources are environmental because they are not internal to the individual making the demands.) If the relevant sector of the environment is controlled by the community, the right of allocation may be reserved to the community, acting through its legitimate authorities.

Parity Policy: Taurek maintains that policy should be built on equal concern 39 for each person, regardless of the inequality of the demands (needs). (Here we hear an echo of Marx's "to each according to his needs.") I think it is fair to call Taurek's proposal a Parity Policy. Such a policy seeks to give each petitioner an equal chance at life, no matter how large his demands on the resources of the environment. To do this Taurek proposes that we begin by flipping a coin to see whether the 5 units of medicine are to be assigned wholly to Group I or wholly to Group II. In that way, everyone is given a 50-50 chance of being saved. No one is penalized because his need is greater.

How many lives are saved under this policy? We must bring probability theory 40 into play, employing the concept of "mathematical expectation" (M.E.).

Fifty percent of the time 5 lives are saved. This gives a partial M.E. of $(\frac{1}{2})$ 41 $(5) = 2\frac{1}{2}$.

Fifty percent of the time 1 life is saved. Partial M.E. $= (\frac{1}{2}) (1) = \frac{1}{2}$.   42

The sum of the above two answers is the total M.E. Total M. E. $= (2\frac{1}{2}) +$ 43 $(\frac{1}{2}) = 3$.

So the Parity Policy saves—on the average, over the long run—just 3 lives 44 instead of 5.

The efficiency of the Triage Policy, relative to the Parity Policy, is: 5 ÷ 3 = 45 1.67, or 67 percent more efficient in saving lives.

One might suppose that the superiority of the Triage Policy in the saving of 46 human lives would make the philosopher doubt the propriety of his Parity Policy, but he goes out of his way to let us know that he has no doubts. He would pursue it, he says, even if the number 5 were replaced by the number 50 (with the necessary changes). Let us follow him up this path.

We have 50 units of life-saving medicine.   47

Each of the 50 persons in Group I requires 1 unit to have his life saved.   48

The single person in Group II requires 50 units.   49

Triage Policy: All 50 units are supplied to Group I, thus saving 50 lives.   50

Parity Policy: Each group gets all the medicine 50 percent of the time. On the 51 average, the number of lives saved is (½) (50) + (½) (1) = 25 + ½ = 25½.

The relative efficiency of the Triage Policy is now: 50 ÷ 25½ = 1.96, or 96 52 percent more efficient.

Now let us carry this argument to the limit. Let: n = the number of persons 53 in Group I; and n = the number of units of medicine available, where: (a) each person in Group I requires 1 unit; and (b) the single person in Group II requires n units.

Following the same line of reasoning as before we find that the relative superi- 54 ority (in saving lives) of the Triage Policy is given by the expression:

$$n \div \frac{n}{2} + \tfrac{1}{2}.$$

As the variable n becomes indefinitely large, the constant (½) becomes rela- 55 tively less and less important. In the limit, as $n \rightarrow \infty$, the relative efficiency of Triage Policy becomes:

$$n \div \frac{n}{2} = \frac{2n}{n} = 2,$$

i.e., the Triage Policy, in the limit, is 100 percent better than the Parity Policy.

One of the clearest trends of the past two centuries has been the steady increase 56 in the value placed on the individual human life, independent of its social status or social worth. Laws governing the liability of employers and public officials, medical malpractice judgments, attitudes toward national military service—in these and many other areas there has been a steady growth in the presumption that the individual human life is infinitely precious. Considering that the number of human lives has now swelled to nearly five billion; considering that world population is increasing faster than it ever has before (by about 90 million per year); considering that the earth still has only the 5.983×10^{21} metric tons of matter that it started with when life began about three billion years ago—considering all these facts, as we approach closer and closer the limit of the earth's ability to support the all too abundant human lives, it is rather ironical that we should become more and more concerned about the preservation and well-being of each and every individual human life. Our concern does the heart credit; but

I doubt if the mythical Man-from-Mars would have predicted this paradoxical coincidence of historical trends. If the Man-from-Mars is anything of an economic determinist he might well question whether the coincidence will long continue.

How are we to view Taurek's Parity Policy in the light of historical trends? On the one hand it seems to represent a reversal, inasmuch as it assigns more value to the *feelings* of the people being judged than it does to their lives. Parity Policy seeks to maximize concern for feelings, whereas Triage Policy maximizes the number of human lives saved. (Should those who strive for population control lobby for Parity Policy? An interesting suggestion!)

On the other hand, if we ask, "What is the relation of policy to the *individual* human life?" emphasizing "individual" rather than "life," we realize that Taurek's proposal is in the mainstream of increasing individualism in the Western world. As an individual I may want to live forever, to be freed of competitive pressures, and to have my needs taken care of no matter how great the drain on community resources, no matter how many other lives must be sacrificed that I may live. Accused of egotism by others I could conceivably back down on my personal demands. Instead (if I am a thoroughgoing Western-style individualist), I am more likely to take the other tack and recommend that we all support each other in unmitigated individualistic demands, even when the universalizing of these demands proves counter-productive. The replacement of a Triage Policy by a Parity Policy reduces the number of lives saved, or (in less extreme situations) the average quality of people's lives. The true Promethean, concerned with a distant future in which he may no longer be an actor, inevitably is less concerned with individuals *as such* (including himself), and more concerned with the good that accrues to individuals through their membership in a community. In an increasingly more crowded community, in a world pressing ever harder against physical and psychological limits, a true Promethean cannot but support the rationalism of triage policies which, by their very nature, acknowledge the limitedness of the available resources and the limitlessness of time.

At the beginning of this chapter I said that hard cases make good ethics. The scarcity case is a good example. Exploring the implications of the Parity Policy we have discovered that the wisdom of triage can be fully appreciated only if we recognize the inevitability of competition; and competition between members of the same species is inescapable so long as death is not a sufficiently effective thinning agent—which we prevent it from being with our fantastic medical advances. Life, cooperation, and compassion are all good things, but we can have too much of any one good thing, considered in isolation and elevated to the status of an absolute good. The central problem—both philosophically and practically—is to find acceptable ways of weighing opposing goods (under a variety of circumstances and with due regard for the interests of our posterity) so that we—and our descendants—can lead healthy and balanced lives. In this search, Prometheus should be our guide.

Notes

1. Oliver Wendell Holmes, Jr., 1904. *Northern Securities Co. v. United States, 193 U.S. 197,400.* "Great cases like hard cases make bad law," is what Holmes actually said, which implies that the second part of the quotation is older than Holmes. A case is great when it threatens the culture. The ability of even the wisest jurists to make a balanced cultural change with a single

court judgment is severely limited—this is F. A. Hayek's point in "The Three Sources of Human Ethics," in *Law, Legislation, and Liberty,* vol. 2 (Chicago: University of Chicago Press, 1979)—and so the judgment made in a great case makes bad law in the sense that it has to be followed by a swarm of other judgments and legislation before any new sort of cultural stability is achieved. Consider, for instance, the still unfinished cascade of consequences of the Supreme Court decision in *Brown v. Board of Education,* 1954. [Hardin's notes except where noted.]

2. Warren T. Reich, ed., 1978. *Encyclopedia of Bioethics* (New York: Free Press).
3. William and Paul Paddock, 1967. *Famine—1975! America's Decision: Who Will Survive?* (Boston: Little, Brown).
4. From "Triage," a dialogue discussion paper for the Center for the Study of Democratic Institutions, Santa Barbara, California, 4 April 1975.
5. I do not know the original source. This passage serves as the epigraph of Ernest Becker, 1973. *The Denial of Death* (New York: Free Press).
6. George R. Lucas, Jr., and Thomas W. Ogletree, eds., 1976. *Lifeboat Ethics: The Moral Dilemmas of World Hunger* (New York: Harper & Row).
7. Henrietta Buckmaster, *Christian Science Monitor,* 9 November 1967.
8. Richard A. Falk, 1971. *This Endangered Planet* (New York: Random House).
9. Peccei is the founder and *primum inter pares* of the informal "Club of Rome," which catalyzed the production of the *Limits to Growth* study by a group at the Massachusetts Institute of Technology.
10. Aurelio Peccei, 1977. *The Human Quality* (New York: Pergamon Press).
11. *The Wall Street Journal,* 27 November 1974, p. 1.
12. Noël Mostert, 1974. "Supertankers," *The New Yorker,* 20 May, p. 84.
13. I have heard him express this opinion twice at small conferences. Whether this is in print or not I do not know.
14. George Noel Gordon, Lord Byron, 1821. *Don Juan,* canto 4, stanza 4.
15. William Shakespeare, 1600. *Twelfth-Night,* act 2, scene 3, line 124.
16. A. V. Hill, 1952. "The Ethical Dilemma of Science," *Nature* 170:388-93. As a further footnote let me report that at a symposium in which I took part Lord Ritchie-Calder cited this passage of Lord Hill's as a particularly obnoxious one.
17. This is a fantastically subtle and recalcitrant problem. I have scratched the surface of it in chapter 4 of *The Limits of Altruism* (Bloomington: Indiana University Press, 1977).
18. See chapter 3 of *The Limits of Altruism.*
19. Tertullian. *De Anima.*
20. Herman E. Daly, 1978. *Steady-State Economics* (San Francisco: W. H. Freeman). This is an excellent introduction to the new economics.
21. John M. Taurek, 1977. "Should the Numbers Count?" *Philosophy and Public Affairs* 6 (4):293-316. After completing his analysis Taurek discovered that similar conclusions had been reached by G.E.M. Anscombe, 1967. "Who is Wronged?" *Oxford Review,* no. 5.

Questions

1. Does Hardin discuss the military meaning of *triage* because he assumes the world is a battlefield? Or is he concerned only with tracing the meaning of the word?
2. Why does Hardin discuss the connotation of the word in paragraphs 9 and 10?
3. What point is Hardin making through the discussion of triage in civilian medicine in paragraph 12?

4. How does Hardin respond to the objection that, in the distribution of American grain to other countries, triage "requires standing aside while millions perish" (paragraph 15)? What point is he making about the word *condemn* in paragraph 17?
5. How does the discussion of compassion in paragraphs 20–26 develop the argument that Hardin is making for triage?
6. What is the Promethean solution that Hardin urges we make? What support does he find for it in the past? (An Epimethean solution is one based on afterthought.)
7. What is the difference between "Triage Policy" and "Parity Policy"? Does Hardin reject "Parity Policy" on statistical grounds alone?
8. Does Hardin say or imply in paragraph 58 that good is achieved by individuals *only* "through their membership in a community"? Is he arguing that the general good of the community has priority over the good of the individual?

Suggestions for Writing

1. Discuss whether Hardin would agree with any one of the following statements:
   a. Rich nations have an obligation to feed as many of the needy in the world as possible.
   b. The basis for allocating scarce grain should be the political stability of the government in need.
   c. The basis for allocation of food should be the quality of roads and transportation of the country in need.
   d. Dialysis machines should not be assigned to those who have had cancer or who have a history of heart trouble.
2. Does Hardin persuade you that making a selection for triage is better policy than flipping a coin?

Additional Reading

Benjamin, Walter W. "A Challenge to the Eco-Doomsters." *Christian Century,* March 24, 1979.

Cousins, Norman. "Of Life and Lifeboats." *Saturday Review,* March 8, 1975.

Ehrlich, Paul, et al. *Ecoscience: Population, Resources, Environment.* San Francisco: W. H. Freeman, 1977.

Hardin, Garrett. *Exploring New Ethics for Survival: The Voyage of the Spaceship Beagle.* New York: Viking, 1972.

———. *Filters against Folly: How to Survive Despite Economists, Ecologists, and the Merely Eloquent.* New York: Viking, 1985.

———. *The Limits of Altruism: An Ecologist's View of Survival.* Bloomington: Indiana University Press, 1977.

———. *Promethean Ethics: Living with Death, Competition, and Triage.* Seattle: University of Washington Press, 1980.

The Latest Decalogue

Arthur Hugh Clough

The English poet Arthur Hugh Clough (1819–1861) was not as well known in his time as his contemporaries Alfred Tennyson, Robert Browning, and his friend Matthew Arnold. Born in Liverpool, England, he lived for a time in Charleston, South Carolina. Returning to England, he attended Rugby where he was a favorite student of the headmaster, educational reformer Dr. Thomas Arnold (the father of Matthew Arnold), whose emphasis on conduct as the mark of the Christian strongly influenced him. Clough later attended Oxford University, resigning a fellowship because of religious doubts. Outspoken about the religious and moral issues of the Victorian age, Clough has found a large audience in this century through poems such as "The Latest Decalogue" that seem unusually contemporary in subject and outlook.

Thou shalt have one God only; who
Would be at the expense of two?
No graven images may be
Worshiped, except the currency.
Swear not at all; for, for thy curse
Thine enemy is none the worse.
At church on Sunday to attend
Will serve to keep the world thy friend.
Honor thy parents; that is, all
From whom advancement may befall.
Thou shalt not kill; but need'st not strive
Officiously to keep alive.
Do not adultery commit;
Advantage rarely comes of it.
Thou shalt not steal; an empty feat,
When it's so lucrative to cheat.
Bear not false witness; let the lie
Have time on its own wings to fly.
Thou shalt not covet, but tradition
Approves all forms of competition.

The sum of all is, thou shalt love,
If anybody, God above:
At any rate shall never labor
More than thyself to love thy neighbor.

Questions

1. Why does the speaker begin the penultimate line with the words "At any rate" and emphasize the word *more* in the final line?
2. Why does the speaker add the words "if anybody" to line 21? Is the phrase needless or redundant?
3. How are the concluding four lines the "sum" of the advice given in lines 1–20?
4. What does the speaker mean by "all forms of competition?"
5. What is the general tone of the poem? Is the tone the same throughout, or does it change in the course of the poem?
6. What attitudes and beliefs explain the condition of the world for the speaker? Does the speaker identify these attitudes and beliefs or allude to them?

Suggestions for Writing

1. Discuss the purpose of the poem and the means by which Clough realizes this purpose. Give particular attention to the voice that you hear in the poem—the tone of the speaker.
2. Compare Clough's commentary on modern religious belief with that in one of the following poems or another of your choosing. Note similarities and differences in attitude and treatment of the theme. Use your comparison to develop an idea or thesis.
   a. Matthew Arnold, "Dover Beach"
   b. William Butler Yeats, "The Second Coming"
   c. T. S. Eliot, "The Hollow Men"
   d. Edith Sitwell, "A Canticle of the Rose"
   e. Philip Larkin, "Church Going"

Additional Reading

Houghton, Walter E. *The Poetry of Clough.* New Haven: Yale University Press, 1963.
Greenberger, Evelyn Barish. *Arthur Hugh Clough: The Growth of a Poet's Mind.* Cambridge: Harvard University Press, 1970.
Lowry, H. F., A. P. P. Norrington, and F. L. Mulhauser, eds. *The Poems of Arthur Hugh Clough.* London: Oxford University Press, 1951.

WAR

"*A*ll wars are made for the sake of getting money," Plato states in his dialogue *Phaedo.* Wars are bred, he suggests in the *Republic,* because societies "are not content with necessities, but give themselves up to getting unlimited wealth" and thus aggress against their neighbors. War can be justified against the enemies of Greece, Plato further suggests, but not "civil strife" between Greeks. Indeed, reason might govern in the internal affairs of a country, for human beings are not incorrigible:

> As Greeks they will not devastate the soil of Greece or burn the homesteads;
> nor will they allow that all the inhabitants of any state, men, women, and chil-
> dren, are their enemies, but only the few who are responsible for the quarrel.
> The greater number are friends, whose land and houses, on all these accounts,
> they will not consent to lay waste and destroy.

War for Plato, then, need not be a constant of human life. In an ideal world, human beings would live by reason.

In the seventeenth century, the English philosopher Thomas Hobbes expressed what many who had survived the ferocious religious wars of the previous hundred years knew to be true: The state of nature, Hobbes wrote in *Leviathan,* finds "the life of man solitary, poor, nasty, brutish, and short." The natural condition of life is war. A monarchist, Hobbes believed in the necessity of a strong central government that would put a curb on intractable human nature.

> If a covenant be made, wherein neither of the parties perform presently, but
> trust one another; in the condition of mere Nature (which is a condition of
> war of every man against every man), upon any reasonable suspicion it is void.
> But if there be a common power set over them both, with right and force suffi-
> cient to compel performance, it is not void.

In the twentieth century, Fascism and Nazism glorified war as an expression of what was thought best in human nature—the will to power, ruthless qualities that expressed, in the phrase of Adolf Hitler, "the iron logic of Nature." For Hitler, war was necessary because the higher, racially pure "Aryan" race could survive only by master over and finally the extermination of lower, impure races: "Those who want to live, let them fight, and those who do not want to fight in this world of eternal struggle do not deserve to live."

The contrary view is that the world need not be an arena of perpetual struggle and that war might be controlled through a nonauthoritarian government or world organization. This possibility was indeed suggested in 1795 by the German philosopher Immanuel Kant in his essay "Perpetual Peace." Kant states a premise much like that of Hobbes: "The state of peace among men living side by side is not the natural state; the natural state is one of war." But Kant reaches a different conclusion in arguing that where the civil constitution of the state is republican, war may be curbed:

> If the consent of the citizens is required in order to decide that war should be declared (and in this constitution it cannot but be the case), nothing is more natural than that they would be very cautious in commencing such a poor game, decreeing for themselves all the calamities of war.

The idea of a parliament of nations is not a recent one, and in our time it has been attempted and has also been thought a fantasy. The failure of the League of Nations and the alleged failures of its successor, the United Nations, have led many to despair that war can be prevented through reason, as Plato supposed, rather than through vigilant national defense. For many years the argument over nuclear disarmament in the United States has been whether regional or world pacts can lessen the need of an arsenal of nuclear weapons. Some people today argue for total disarmament, and a few argue, as Nigel Calder indicates, that totalitarian government is preferable to the extinction of human life through nuclear war.

The essays, story, and poem in this section present different views of war. In the opening essay, Nigel Calder discusses present realities—the preparations nations have undertaken to fight a war with nuclear weapons. The chapters from Niccolo Machiavelli's *The Prince* show how war was viewed by a diplomat and political writer of the sixteenth century. Writing at the beginning of the twentieth century, the psychologist and philosopher William James discusses the possibility of abolishing war. Two selections represent contemporary views. Lewis Mumford discusses the origins of war from the perspective of modern history and social anthropology; in his encyclical, Pope John XXIII discusses the possibilities for peace from the perspective of church doctrine and religious philosophy. Finally, Herbert Read's poem about the First World War explores the impact of war on individuals.

Looking for the Exit

Nigel Calder

A graduate of Cambridge University, the science writer Nigel Calder worked as a physicist before becoming a journalist. In 1956 he joined the editorial staff of the journal New Scientist, *serving as editor*

from 1962 to 1966. From 1959 to 1962, he was also the science corre-
spondent for the British periodical The New Statesman. *Calder has pro-*
duced a number of distinguished television series and books on scien-
tific subjects, including The Violent Universe *(1969),* The Mind of Man
(1970), The Key to the Universe *(1977), and* Spaceships of the Mind
(1978). He is also the author of other books on modern science, includ-
ing Einstein's Universe *(1979) and* Nuclear Nightmares *(1979), from*
which this essay is taken.

In this postscript to Nuclear Nightmares, *Calder discusses the*
state of mind that nuclear war has produced in the world. He discusses
the psychological as well as political realities that guide the nuclear
powers as they consider ways to survive nuclear war.

The Swiss, like the Chinese, think that a nuclear world war is entirely possible. 1
They consider that the risks now warrant a great effort to protect themselves; so, while
China digs tunnels, Switzerland has embarked on a costly program of domestic shelters.
Every man who is not in the army must serve in the civil defense organization and the
cantonal governments have their wartime bunkers. Large public shelters have been
prepared—for example, under the skating rink at Bern and in the motorway tunnel that
runs through Luzern. In a suburb of Bern I saw a shelter hospital magnificently
equipped and quite unused; Switzerland already has more than seventy thousand hospital beds and a thousand operating theaters, underground.

Every new house in Switzerland must have a shelter in its foundation—and not 2
merely an improvised fallout shelter. The law requires a strong structure with massive
sealed doors and an air-filtration system, built to government specifications that make
it resistant to the blast from a one-megaton H-bomb at a distance of 1.6 miles. In peacetime the government encourages use of the shelter as a wine cellar or storage room, but
if war threatens, it will have to be cleared out and, within twenty-four hours, supplied
with bunks, food, water, a radio, and digging tools. The occupants have to be prepared
to stay in the shelter for days or weeks, venturing outside only briefly, with the permission of the civil defense authorities. By 1978, 4 million Swiss had places in modern shelters and another 1.8 million could be accommodated in older shelters; altogether 90
percent of the Swiss population had protection of one sort or the other. The aim is to
have bed space in a modern shelter for every citizen.

Neutral Switzerland is one of the least likely places in Europe to suffer direct 3
hits from nuclear weapons, but the inhabitants are taking no chances. When the fallout
blows in from Stuttgart, Lyon, or Turin, the Swiss will be sitting out the war and its af-
termath in shelters built precisely for that purpose and which far surpass any available
to the populations of the countries more likely to be belligerent. That is one Western nation's response, carefully considered and executed, to the threat of nuclear war. It is not
encouraging for the rest of us, least of all when you remember that Switzerland plays
host to many disarmament conferences and evidently has scant confidence in their
fruitfulness.

I have tried to understand, and to explain in this book, a cluster of dangers fac- 4
ing the world, but understanding is clouded as soon as diagnosis gives way to advocacy.
By picking and choosing among the facts and theories I could write speeches for the

fiercest militarist ("If there's going to be a first strike let's do it right!") or the most thoroughgoing pacifist ("Get rid of the bomb before it gets rid of us!"). But any glibness about this appalling and complex subject is unpardonable, so my feelings are those of a busybody who has shouted "Fire!" in the theater and now cannot point to the safe way out.

The abolition of war itself remains a long-term objective, but it seems an unat- 5 tainable way of escaping from immediate perils, because it presupposes the transformation of the world into a utopian planet of universal contentment. As long as any real or apparent injustice persists, people will fight against it. Between the main power blocs the perception of injustice is permanent: the West sees in the Soviet Union the built-in political injustice and repression associated with the privileges of membership in the Communist party; the Soviets see in the West the built-in economic injustice and repression associated with the privileges of private wealth.

The leading "peacemakers" are the well-to-do in the rich northern industrial 6 lands, who imagine that there is nothing to fight about. They could change their attitude overnight if, for example, the Middle Eastern producers refused to supply them with the oil on which their prosperity so precariously depends. People can be much more militaristic than they imagine possible in peacetime. The British, for example, are the most combative nation on earth, having been, by historical record, involved in more wars than anyone else in the past one hundred fifty years. Twice in this century, the United Kingdom has adapted enthusiastically and victoriously to total war and is now curiously valiant about being one of the countries most intensively targeted for nuclear war.

The prospect of universal death may nevertheless concentrate human minds 7 sufficiently to produce a shift in attitudes toward nuclear weapons. A fundamental question for Westerners is whether nuclear weapons are compatible with their moral codes and their political systems. "Nukes" are totalitarian weapons that look far more convincing in the hands of dictators than of democrats. A ruthless Stalin with SS-18s might all too easily prevail by nuclear threat over nations that value the personal lives of their citizens more highly than he does. "Give me liberty or give me death" is a fine sentiment for an individual or an army but not for a nation, and every sane Westerner knows in his heart that his children, at least, would be "better red than dead."

For internal reasons, too, the preservation of Western-style democracy may be 8 a forlorn hope in a nation armed with nuclear weapons. The all-important decisions about nuclear warfighting cannot be subject to parliamentary debate. Civilian citizens are like front-line troops in nuclear warfare, but they are really worse off than privates because they have not the slightest control over the course of events and are denied even the limited satisfaction of fighting back. The peacetime rituals of deterrence and governmental negotiations with potential adversaries require "rational" and consistent policies quite incompatible with the democratic rights of voters or legislators to change their minds or to challenge the government's judgment. Erratic influences of "hawks" and "doves" in the U.S. Congress are horrifying for anyone preoccupied with avoiding nuclear war, yet suppressing them would negate democracy.

The future of cities is also in question because they are such inviting targets for 9 nuclear weapons. Theodore Taylor, a former weapon maker, thinks that we should take advantage of modern technology to disperse into self-sufficient villages, "so that there

aren't targets like Tokyo and London and Leningrad any more." The snag is that to target villages is just a matter of subdividing the payloads of missiles into more and more
independently targetable warheads, or else relying upon radioactive fallout to kill people
over huge areas. A village and even a city would be safer from attack or threat of attack
if it were not part of a nation-state, and the nation-state itself may disappear in the nuclear age. It could conceivably give way to a world empire run by one power with a monopoly on nuclear weapons, or a global police state engineered by frightened consensus,
or a benign and nonbureaucratic world government ministering to Taylor's "globe of
villages."

Such possibilities, though, are scarcely on the agenda for the virulent 1980s. 10
As remedies for present dangers they are as ineffectual as other suggestions with long
"lead times," such as discouraging small boys from playing with toy bombers, or transferring all warmaking to a scaled-down replica of the earth on the moon. In the short
run the only courses open to nations for altering the present tendencies are to rearm,
to change their commitments, or to disarm. And well-intended actions may, unfortunately, produce disastrous reactions elsewhere.

Rearmament is the most widespread response discernible today. In the Third 11
World the nuclear proliferators are busy and the arms salesmen are prospering more
than ever in deals for the supply of conventional weapons. The Russians have new missiles in the developmental pipeline and their arms program has been extremely vigorous
for a long time. Although some congressmen would like to see a much larger program,
the United States is busy pursuing the cruise missiles and the Trident submarine-
launched missile system. For the strategic contest between the United States and the
Soviet Union new systems like the MX missile (which, their advocates say, will ease the
counterforce problem) take years to engineer and deploy. An intensified competition in
existing types of strategic weapons could not take away the capacity of both sides to use
their multiple warheads and gain a big advantage by striking first.

Conventional weapons can be built more rapidly and young men can be con- 12
scripted instantaneously. One region where massive conventional rearmament might
arguably reduce the risk of nuclear war is in Europe, where NATO stands on its ram-
shackle edifice of nuclear deterrence, waiting now for the neutron bomb and the newer
Pershings. But West Europeans will hesitate about consigning their sons to huge and
expensive armies unless the payoff is substantial—a Europe purged of nuclear weapons,
for example.

If avoiding death traps were the overriding purpose, the safest course for the 13
Americans and the Russians would be to change their postures, give up acting as big
brothers to the world, abandon their allies, withdraw into the shells of their own territories, and glare at each other across the North Pole. Pessimists in Washington fear that
Soviet superiority in strategic missile forces could drive the United States into that position, so that the Communists might then win the struggle for world domination without firing a shot. The United States took over the role of Western policeman from the
British after 1945 and finds itself supporting corrupt, dictatorial, feudal, and belligerent
regimes in the name of protecting democracy. The Soviet Union now challenges the
Americans in every continent, largely by supporting the national liberation movements
to which those "rotten apple" regimes naturally give rise. There is no hint that fear of

the American nuclear arsenal will stop the Soviet Union from pursuing this policy. As the Chinese put it, rudely but equitably, the Americans and Russians cannot forbear to interfere in world events and are therefore doomed to fight. Yet any abrupt switch by either or both of the superpowers to a more isolationist policy could encourage the proliferation of nuclear weapons and regional turmoil.

Consider an admission by the Americans that they really do not want to start 14 a nuclear war. It could take the form of an uplifting declaration of "no first use" by the U.S. president, saying that in no circumstances will he be the first to employ the bomb. Many thoughtful people, including scientists in the Pugwash movement, have for a long time urged both superpowers to declare "no first use." The promise could not be entirely reliable, of course, but it would force the abandonment of policies that openly contradict it, soothe rather than aggravate the mounting fears of a "disabling first strike," and strengthen the idea of deterrence by admitting that one is deterred oneself. In principle it would be an excellent, logically necessary step.

An American "no first use" declaration would, though, pull out the rug from 15 under NATO's "first use" policy, which threatens to employ nuclear weapons, mainly American, against Soviet tanks attacking Western Europe. Would the Europeans then rely upon the British nuclear weapons to sustain the "first use" strategy in Germany? That is doubtful, even though the safety of the United Kingdom is directly at stake in a European war. If the United States confesses to being deterred from "first use," the British David confronting the Soviet Goliath looks unimpressive. More likely consequences of an American declaration of "no first use" would be the dissolution of NATO and a rush by the nations of Western Europe to adopt the French policy of looking after oneself. West Germany might make its own nuclear weapons within a matter of days and that, as we have seen, could precipitate the big war in Europe.

The same result might ensue if the United Kingdom gave up its nuclear 16 weapons—not an unreasonable decision for an extremely vulnerable island unable to afford advanced weapons technology. Regardless of the merits of that idea, the Germans look to the British weapons as their second line of nuclear defense in the not implausible event of the Americans holding back. I hate to say so, but even a failure to modernize the British nuclear forces—a process due to begin in the early 1980s—might drive the Germans toward the bomb. We all live in a house of cards and any rearrangement of the pieces, however sensible in the long run, could bring everything crashing down.

Negotiated disarmament remains the chief hope of carefully dismantling the 17 house of cards, but it will not help us in the next few crucial years. Nuclear disarmament recedes almost out of reach as the superpowers multiply their warheads and more and more countries acquire the bomb. As recently as 1978, at the special U.N. session on disarmament, the governments vowed unanimously to work for complete disarmament, and after that moving experience, the presidents and prime ministers all went home to order new battle tanks and submarines. Nations that will gladly get rid of useless weapons will not, except to a token degree, interfere with the weapons that matter to them. Nobody listened when an old warrior like President Eisenhower said: "The alternative is so terrible that any risks there might be in advancing to disarmament are as nothing." Instead, the American people voted for John Kennedy, who accused the Eisenhower administration of letting the Russians gain an advantage in missiles.

There is a simple and formidable reason why disarmament negotiations keep 18
stalling. Progress is continuously sabotaged because each nation taking part in a negotiation is really an ensemble of conflicting interests. It is enough to distinguish between
the diplomats who may genuinely want to go down in history as peacemakers and their
military advisers who are professional pessimists, wary about tricks and cheats. In the
seesaw of proposal and counterproposal there is almost never a moment when all parties
on all sides can concur, and the peacemakers are often regarded as near-traitors by their
military colleagues, who greatly outnumber them at home. The budget of the U.S. Arms
Control and Disarmament Agency, for example, is less than half of what the U.S. Defense Department spends on military bands.

The story of Soviet-American disarmament talks since 1945 is so tedious and 19
tragic that one must doubt whether either side was ever very serious. Agreements and
declarations by the superpowers have banned a succession of weapons that were technically difficult to contrive, or of doubtful military value: orbiting H-bombs, antiballistic
missiles, biological weapons, environmental weapons, and the like. Useful though such
self-denial may be in fringe areas, it does not slow down the main arms race. The Strategic Arms Limitation Talks only regulated the rate of growth in strategic warheads, and
laid out some rules within which the game of "counterforce" could continue without
the players' fellow countrymen growing excessively uneasy about the danger and the
cost. The SALT I negotiators carefully agreed *not* to prevent "mirving," and the number
of multiple warheads allowed under SALT II is far too generous. None of this is to deny
the importance of SALT in keeping the conversation going between the superpowers.
Winston Churchill's dictum still holds good: "Jaw, jaw is better than war, war."

If the Americans and Russians remain on speaking terms, they can continue to 20
work toward a ban on the deployment of antisatellite systems. An agreement on that
would help to slow down an arms race that has no logical termination this side of Mars,
and it would also make the two sides less nervous about an attack on their early-warning
and communications satellites as a concomitant to a possible first strike. There also exists a pair of proposals that might be agreed upon fairly quickly and which could lessen
the risk of nuclear war by causing both sides to lose confidence in their weapons. The
first is the Comprehensive Test-Ban Treaty already under negotiation between the
Americans, the Russians, and the British, which would ban all nuclear test explosions
by the three countries, even underground. To prevent cheating, the intention is to distribute seismic monitoring stations that will detect the shock of an explosion and distinguish it from an earthquake. Such a treaty may be the minimal requirement, as a small
step toward nuclear disarmament, for encouraging non-nuclear-weapon nations to stick
to the nonproliferation treaty. But the protests from the weapon makers are also a sign
that it will be an effective measure of arms control in its own right.

The most obvious consequence of a comprehensive test-ban treaty is that novel 21
types of bombs could not be tested. If the weapon makers have bright ideas for "fission-
free H-bombs" and the like, *tant pis*. The development of new missiles might also be im-
peded, at least a little, by the inability to fully test newly designed or refigured weapons
intended to ride in them. But the key point is that the fighting services like to take an
occasional warhead out of the missiles and bombers on alert, and explode it to satisfy
themselves that their weapons have not been quietly corroding away over the years.

Given a ban on testing, the Soviet Union and the United States would, as the years passed, begin to doubt their warheads. The deterrent second-strike value of the weapons would scarcely be impaired, because in a retaliatory attack a few unexploded bombs make little difference to the overall violence. But both sides would soon stop even thinking about perpetrating a disabling first strike because of the risk of botching it, and fears of a strike from the other side would recede as well.

Missiles, too, tend to deteriorate in their silos and the same reasoning inspires 22 the missile-test quota, strongly advocated by Sidney Drell. The idea is that each side should be allowed only a specified number of tests of strategic missiles in the course of a year—a dozen, say. As early-warning satellites can instantly detect a missile launch anywhere in the world, and both superpowers spy systematically on each other's missile tests, it would be an arms-control measure very easy to verify.

The first effect of the quota would be to make the introduction of new missiles 23 and the modification of old ones a slower and more difficult process. It would quickly affect existing weapons too. Missile accuracy of the kind needed for a counterforce strike is a delicate matter of statistics, and to have good statistics you need plenty of tests. Restricted by the quota, the generals and admirals would not care to bet the fate of nations on the reliability and accuracy of their aging missiles. George Kistiakowsky, who was President Eisenhower's science adviser at the start of the missile contest, endorses these measures, which undermine confidence in strategic weapons on both sides. As Kistiakowsky says succinctly: "Let them rot!"

The avoidance of nuclear war in the 1980s, when proliferation in the Middle 24 East coincides with a peak in counterforce opportunities for the superpowers, will depend on the rate at which the planet generates deadly quarrels. If a grave crisis comes in the next few years, we shall just have to hope that the Soviet Union is indeed deterred from attempting a nuclear "counterbattery" strike by unassailable American missile-carrying submarines, and that the United States will show moral restraint. Do not undervalue moral attitudes: few national leaders want to commit the worst atrocity of all time, and that thought, rather than deterrence, may be what has saved us so far. And the simple touchstone of morality about nuclear warfare is that it remains unthinkable.

Yet it only takes one madman, one politician or soldier growing weary or impa- 25 tient with peace, or one fool who misunderstands a crisis, to bring Northern civilization to an abrupt end. The post-1945 generation is now taking over the reins of power—individuals who did not experience the shock of Hiroshima and regard nuclear weapons as normal gadgets. Some scientists say that whatever test-ban treaties and disarmament measures may be devised, a multimegaton weapon should be exploded in the atmosphere every few years in front of the assembled leaders of the world's nations, so that they will stand in awe of its incomprehensible heat and force. Even at a safe distance of thirty miles or more they will feel it like the opening of an oven door, or the gates of hell.

Questions

1. What attitude does Calder believe most of his readers hold toward the risks of nuclear war? Does Calder describe *your* attitude toward nuclear war in paragraph 7?

2. Why do totalitarian societies have an advantage in nuclear warfare? Why are nuclear weapons a threat to Western-style democracy?
3. Why is it not possible to abolish war under present circumstances?
4. What other political circumstances make the control of nuclear weapons difficult?
5. What current proposals for preventing nuclear war does Calder criticize? What is his criticism of them?
6. What obstacles stand in the way of negotiated disarmament, according to Calder? Does Calder suggest other ways to reduce the risk of nuclear war?
7. What additional risks will the 1980s present?

Suggestions for Writing

1. Discuss the circumstances and realities in the world that make nuclear war a possibility for Calder. Does Calder say or imply that the abolition of war is impossible?
2. How much has the threat of nuclear war affected your own life—has it limited your goals or influenced your choice of a career, for example? If the threat has had no effect, how do you explain that?
3. Use the *New York Times, U.S. News and World Report, Foreign Affairs,* and other sources to find current arguments for and against nuclear disarmament or a related issue. How different is discussion of the issue today from Calder's in 1980?

Additional Reading

Blainey, Geoffrey. *The Causes of War.* New York: The Free Press, 1973.
Bundy, William P., ed. *The Nuclear Controversy: A Foreign Affairs Reader.* New York: New American Library, 1985.
Calder, Nigel. *Nuclear Nightmares: An Investigation into Possible Wars.* New York: Viking, 1980.
Dyson, Freeman J. *Weapons and Hope.* New York: Harper and Row, 1984.
Herken, Gregg. *Counsels of War.* New York: Knopf, 1985.
Smoke, Richard. *War: Controlling Escalation.* Cambridge: Harvard University Press, 1977.

The Art of War, from Book 1*

Niccolo Machiavelli

*The diplomat and politician Nicolo Machiavelli was born in
1469, the son of a lawyer who was a minor functionary in the government of Florence, a powerful state of fifteenth-century Italy. In 1498,
Machiavelli was appointed secretary to the Council of Ten for War.
During the fourteen years he served in this position, he traveled on diplomatic missions to Milan and later to France, from where he sent back
reports on the court of Louis XII. In 1502, Machiavelli was sent on a
mission to Cesare Borgia, the ruler of Urbino, and observed Cesare's
brutal quelling of a conspiracy against him. This cruel, inventive military leader instantly won Machiavelli's admiration; Cesare became the
model for the successful prince Machiavelli described in his most famous book,* The Prince.*

Back in Florence, having overcome suspicion that he had
been scheming with Cesare Borgia, Machiavelli persuaded the Council
to form a citizen militia, and in 1508 he led the militia to victory over
neighboring Pisa. On a mission to France in 1510, he formed the idea
of uniting the many independent states of Italy into a confederation
modeled upon Switzerland. In 1495 Florence had become a republic
and had deposed its Medici rulers; in 1512 Pope Julius II attacked the
Republic, hoping to restore the Medici rule. Machiavelli's militia fled
from their defense of Florence. With the return of the Medicis to power,
Machiavelli lost his post. Implicated in a plot against the Medicis, he
was imprisoned, tortured, and finally released because of insufficient
evidence. For the remainder of his life, he lived with his wife and children in his ancestral home outside of Florence. It was there that Machiavelli wrote* The Prince, *his discourse on war, the history of Florence,
and other books and essays.*

At the end of* The Prince *Machiavelli asks how Italy might defend herself without the use of mercenary soldiers and what strategies
and arms would best defend the country.* The Art of War, *written in
1521, answers these questions. The short preface defines the responsibilities of a citizen in a republic and defends the necessity of warfare.
The discourse that follows is in the form of a dialogue between Cosimo
Ruccellai and his friends and a mercenary general, Fabrizio Colonna,
who had just returned from a campaign in northern Italy. The scene of
the dialogue is the garden of Cosimo's house in Florence. Book 1 of the
dialogue begins with a discussion of which actions and policies of the
ancient Greeks and Romans the Italians should imitate. Fabrizio gives
this answer:*

---

*Translated by Allen H. Gilbert

To honor and reward excellence, not to despise poverty, to
esteem the methods and regulations of military discipline,
to oblige the citizens to love one another, to live without
factions, to esteem private less than public good, and other
like things that could easily fit in without times.

*In the excerpts from Book 1 reprinted here, Fabrizio discusses profes-
sional and citizen soldiers. Machiavelli's idea of civic virtue and his
conception of warfare—suggested in the preface to the book—emerge
in this discussion. In the preface, Machiavelli addresses Lorenzo di
Filippo Strozzi, a Florentine nobleman, to whom he dedicated the
work.*

Preface

In the past, Lorenzo, many have held and now still hold this opinion: that no 1
two things are more out of harmony with one another or differ more from one another
than civilian life and military life. Because of this we often see one who plans to excel
in the soldier's calling at once not merely changing his dress, but also in habits, manners, voice and presence departing widely from every civilian custom, because he does
not believe that civilian dress can be worn by one who strives to be active and ready for
any and every violent deed. Nor can civilian habits and manners be used by one who
thinks those habits effeminate and those manners not helpful in his activities; nor does
it seem suitable for him to retain normal bearing and speech when with his beard and
his curses he intends to make other men afraid. This makes the opinion I have mentioned seem in these times very true. But if we consider ancient ways, we shall not find
things that are more closely united, more in conformity, and of which one, necessarily,
so much loves the other as do these, because all the arts that are provided for in a state
for the sake of the common good of men, all the statutes made in it so that men will
live in fear of the laws and of God, would be vain if for them there were not provided
defenses, which when well ordered, preserve them, even though they themselves are not
well ordered. And so, on the contrary, good customs, without military support, suffer
the same sort of injury as do the rooms of a splendid and kingly palace, even though ornamented with gems and gold, when, not being roofed over, they have nothing to protect them from the rain. And if for every other order of men in cities and kingdoms
every diligence should be used to keep them faithful, peaceful, and full of the fear of
God, in the army it should be redoubled. Because from what man ought his native land
to expect greater fidelity than from that one who has to promise to die for her? In whom
ought there to be more love of peace than in him who can get nothing but injury from
war? In whom ought there to be more fear of God than in a man who every day, being
exposed to countless perils, has great need for his aid? This necessity, well considered
both by those who give laws to empires and by those who are put in charge of military
training, would bring it about that the life of soldiers would be praised by other men and
with great zeal followed and imitated. But since military customs are wholly corrupted
and have greatly diverged from ancient methods, about them have sprung up injurious
opinions, which make everybody hate soldiering and avoid association with those who
engage in it.

But judging from what I have seen and read that it is not impossible to bring 2
military practice back to ancient methods and to restore some of the forms of earlier excellence, and wishing not to pass these my times of leisure without doing something,
I have determined, for the pleasure of those who love ancient deeds, to write out what
I have learned about the art of war. And though it is a rash thing to treat material with
which one has not dealt professionally, nonetheless, I do not believe I err in holding
with words alone an office that many, with greater presumption, have held with actions,
because the errors I make as I write can without damage to anybody be corrected; but
those which the others make as they act cannot be recognized except through the ruin
of their governments. You, then, Lorenzo, will consider the qualities of these labors of
mine and give them, according to your judgment, such censure or such praise as you
think they merit. These I send to you both to show that I am grateful—though my capa-
bility does not measure up to the benefits I have received from you—and also because,
since it is the custom to honor with such works those who through nobility, riches, intelligence, and liberality shine brightly, I know that in riches and nobility you do not
have many equals, in intelligence few, and in liberality none.

FABRIZIO. I wish to begin with your words, in which you said to me that in war, 3
which is my profession, I have not used any ancient methods. On this I say that because
this is a profession by means of which men cannot live virtuously at all times, it cannot
be practiced as a profession except by a republic or a kingdom; and neither of these,
when they have been well regulated, has ever allowed one of its citizens or subjects to
practice it as a profession, nor has any good man ever engaged in it as his special profession. Because he will never be reckoned a good man who carries on an occupation in
which, if he is to endeavor at all times to get income from it, he must be rapacious,
fraudulent, violent, and must have many qualities which of necessity make him not
good; nor can men who practice it as a profession, the big as well as the little, be of any
other sort, because this profession does not support them in time of peace. Hence they
are obliged either to hope that there will be no peace, or to become so rich in time of
war that in peace they can support themselves. And neither one of these two expectations is to be found in a good man, because from the desire to support themselves at all
times come the robberies, the deeds of violence, the murderous acts that such soldiers
commit as much against their friends as against their enemies; and from not wishing
peach come the deceits that the generals practice against those by whom they are employed, in order that a war may last; and if peace does come, it often happens that the
generals, being deprived of their stipends and of their living, lawlessly set up their en-
signs as soldiers of fortune and without any mercy plunder a region.

It is not in your historical records that when there were many soldiers in Italy 4
without pay because the wars were finished, several groups joined together, which were
called Companies, and kept exacting money from the cities and plundering the country,
and there was no remedy? Have you not read how the Carthaginian soldiers, at the end
of the first war they had with the Romans, under Matho and Spendius, two leaders re-
belliously chosen by them, waged a more dangerous war against the Carthaginians than
the one they had finished with the Romans? In the time of our fathers, Francesco

---

[1]Francesco Sforza (1401–1466): soldier who became Duke of Milan by force of arms and ruled parts of northern Italy from 1450 to his death.

Sforza[1], in order to be able to live sumptuously in times of peace, not merely deceived the Milanese by whom he was employed, but took away their liberty and became their prince. Like him have been all the other soldiers of Italy who have practiced warfare as their personal profession, and if they have not, by means of their evil deeds, become dukes of Milan, they merit so much the more to be blamed, because without so much gain, they all, if you examine their lives, have the same faults. Sforza, the father of Francesco, forced Queen Giovanna to throw herself into the arms of the King of Aragon, having suddenly abandoned her and left her unarmed in the midst of her enemies, merely to satisfy his ambition or to exact money from her or to take away her kingdom. Braccio[2], with the same efforts, tried to occupy the Kingdom of Naples, and if he had not been defeated and killed at Aquila, would have succeeded. Such outrages do not come from anything else than that there have been men who practiced the trade of the soldier as their special profession. Do you not have a proverb reinforcing my reasons that runs: "War makes thieves and peace hangs them?" Because those who do not know how to live by any other occupation and do not find anybody who will support them in soldiering and do not have so much ability that they can join together to carry out an honorable villainy, are forced by necessity to rob on the highway, and justice is forced to wipe them out.

COSIMO. For me, you have made this profession of the soldier become almost nothing, and I had thought it the most excellent and the most honorable there could be. Hence, if you do not explain it better, I shall not be satisfied, because, if it is as you say, I do not know whence comes the glory of Caesar, of Pompey, of Scipio, of Marcellus, and of so many Roman generals whom fame praises as though they were gods. 5

FABRIZIO. I have not yet finished discussing all that I have laid out, for there were two things: one, that a good man is not able to carry on this activity as his profession; the second, that a well-ordered republic or kingdom would never permit her subjects and her citizens to make it their profession. About the first I have said all that has occurred to me. It remains for me to speak of the second, in which I shall arrive at an answer to this last question of yours. So I say that Pompey and Caesar and almost all the Roman generals after the last Carthaginian war gained fame as brave men but not as good ones, while those who lived before them gained fame as brave and good. This came about because the latter did not take the waging of war for their profession, and those I first named did practice it as their profession. And while the republic continued without reproach, no great citizen ever presumed, by means of such an activity, to retain power in time of peace, so as to break the laws, plunder the provinces, usurp and tyrannize over his native land and in every way gain wealth for himself. Nor did anybody of low estate dream of violating his oath, forming parties with private citizens, ceasing to fear the Senate, or carrying out any tyrannical injury in order to live at all times by means of warfare as a profession. But the generals, satisfied with their triumph, eagerly returned to private life; and those who were privates laid down their arms with greater eagerness than they took them up, and each one turned to the occupation by means of which he had supported his life. Nor was there ever anybody who hoped by plunder and by means of this profession to make his living. About this one can make, as to the great citizens, an obvious inference by means of Regulus Attilius, who, when he was general 6

---

[2]Braccio da Montone (c. 1370–1424): a powerful Italian *condottiere* or professional soldier of the early fifteenth century.

of the Roman armies in Africa and had almost conquered the Carthaginians, asked from the Senate leave to return home to take care of his fields, which were ruined by his laborers. From this it is clearer than sunlight that if he had practiced war as his profession and by means of that had expected to gain profit, he would not, when he had as booty so many provinces, have asked leave to return to take care of his fields, because every day he would have gained more than the value of all of them.

But because these good men, who did not practice war as their profession, did 7 not expect to get from it anything except labor, peril, and fame, when they were famous enough, they wished to come home and live by their profession. As to the men of low rank and the mass of soldiers, it is evidently true that each one was in the same condition, for everyone gladly left such a pursuit and, when he was not soldiering, was willing to be a soldier, and when he was soldiering, wanted to be dismissed. This is verified in many ways, and especially because among the chief privileges the Roman people gave to a citizen was that he would not be forced against his will to serve as a soldier. Rome, then, while she was well governed (which was up to the time of the Gracchi[3] did not have any soldier who took up this pursuit as his profession, and for that reason she had few bad ones, and all of those were severely punished. A well-ordered city will then decree that this practice of warfare shall be used in times of peace for exercise and in times of war for necessity and for glory, and will allow the public alone to practice it as a profession, as did Rome. Any citizen who in such an activity has another purpose is not a good citizen, and any city that conducts itself otherwise is not well governed.

COSIMO. I am well pleased and satisfied with what you have said up to now and 8 am much gratified with this conclusion you have drawn, and so far as it deals with a republic, I believe it is true, but as to a king, I do not at all know, because I should suppose a king would wish to have around him those who would especially take as their profession this pursuit.

FABRIZIO. So much the more will a well-governed kingdom avoid such profes- 9 sionals, because they alone are the ruin of its king and are altogether servants of tyranny. Do not bring up to me in reply any kingdom of the present. I shall deny that they are well-governed kingdoms, because the kingdoms that have good laws do not give absolute command to their king except in their armies; in this place alone sudden decision is necessary, so in it there must be one and only one authority. In other things he cannot do anything without consultation, and they are obliged to fear—those who give him advice—that he will have somebody near him who in time of peace will desire war, being unable to get his living without it.

But I wish to carry this matter a little further and not to seek out a kingdom 10 wholly good but one like those that exist today, where likewise the king needs to be afraid of those who for their profession take warfare, because the might of armies, without any doubt, is their infantry. Hence if a king does not manage in such a way that his infantrymen in time of peace are glad to return home and live by their occupations, he will necessarily be ruined, because there is no more dangerous infantry than that composed of men who carry on war as their profession, because you are obliged either to make war always, or to pay them always, or to be subject to the danger that they will deprive you of your kingdom. To make war always is not possible; to pay them always is not possible; so necessarily you run into danger of losing your power.

---

[3]Gracchi: first-century noble Roman family that championed the small farmer, urging agrarian reforms.

My Romans, as I have said, while they were wise and good, never allowed their 11 citizens to take this pursuit as their profession, notwithstanding that they would have been able to support them at all times, because at all times they made war. But to avoid the injury that could be done them by this continual employment, since the times did not vary, they varied the men, and they observed the time in such a way for their legions that always in fifteen years they had renewed them; and thus they made use of men in the flower of their lives, that is, from eighteen to thirty-five years, a time in which the legs, the hands and the eye are in harmony with one another, nor did they wait until their vigor decreased and their malice increased, as later they did in corrupt times. Because Octavian first and then Tiberius[4], thinking more about their own power than about the public advantage, began to disarm the Roman people in order to command them more easily and to keep those same armies continually on the frontiers of the Empire. And because they still did not judge that they would be enough to hold in check the Roman people and Senate, they set up an army called Praetorian, which remained near the walls of Rome and was like a castle over that city. Because they then freely began to allow men chosen for those armies to practice soldiering as their profession, these men soon became arrogant, so that they were dangerous to the Senate and harmful to the Emperor. The result was that many emperors were killed through the arrogance of the soldiers, who gave the Empire to whom they chose, and took it away; sometimes it happened that at the same time there were many emperors established by various armies. From these things resulted, first, division of the Empire, and finally its ruin.

Hence kings, if they wish to live securely, make up their infantry of men who, 12 when it is time to make war, gladly for love of them go into it, and when peace comes, more gladly return home—which will always happen when a king selects men who know how to live by some other profession than this. So he must see to it that when peace comes his chief men return to rule their peoples, his gentlemen to the management of their property, and the infantry to their individual occupations. Each one of these will gladly make war in order to have peace, and will not seek to disturb the peace in order to have war.

COSIMO. Truly this reasoning of yours seems to me well considered. Neverthe- 13 less, since it is almost opposite to what I have up to now supposed, my mind is still not purged of every doubt, because I see many lords and gentlemen support themselves in time of peace by means of the pursuits of war, such as those like yourself who receive pay from princes and from republics. I see also almost all the men-at-arms steadily getting their pay. I see that there are many infantrymen in the garrisons of cities and fortresses. Hence it seems to me that there is a place, in time of peace, for everybody.

FABRIZIO. I do not believe you believe that in time of peace everyone has his 14 place, because, supposing that no other reason could be brought forward, the small number of all those who remain in the places mentioned by you would answer you. What fraction of the infantry needed in war are those used in time of peace? Because the fortresses and the cities that are guarded in time of peace, in war are guarded much more; and to them are to be added the soldiers kept in the field, of which there are a large number, all of whom in peace are dismissed. And as to governmental garrisons,

---

[4]Octavian: Augustus Caesar (63 B.C.–A.D. 14), adopted son of Julius Caesar and first Roman emperor. Tiberius (42 B.C.–A.D. 37): adopted son of Augustus Caesar and second emperor of Rome.

a small number, Pope Julius[5] and you have shown to everybody how much to be feared are those not willing to carry on any other occupation than war; such men because of their arrogance you have rejected from your garrisons, and you have put there Switzers, since they were born and brought up under laws and chosen by their free states, with genuine selection. So hereafter you will not say that in peace there is a place for every man. As to the men-at-arms, since all of them in peace continue to get their pay, any solution of their case seems more difficult. Nevertheless, he who carefully considers the whole finds the answer easy, because this way of keeping the men-at-arms is a method that is corrupt and not good. The reason is that they are men who make war their profession, and every day they would cause a thousand disorders in the states where they are, if supported by a body of sufficient size; but since they are few and unable by themselves to make up an army, they are not so often able to cause grave damage. Nevertheless they have done it many times, as I explained to you about Francesco, and Sforza his father, and Braccio da Perugia. So as to this custom of retaining men-at-arms, I do not approve of it, for it is corrupt and can cause serious troubles.

COSIMO. Would you plan to do without them, or, if you retained them, how 15 would you plan to retain them?

FABRIZIO. By the method of the citizen army; not like that of the King of France, 16 because that is dangerous and unjust like ours, but like that of the ancients, who raised cavalry from their subjects and in time of peace sent them to their homes to live by their occupations, as I shall set forth more at length before this discussion is over. So if now this part of the army is able to live by military activity, even though there is peace, it comes from corrupt method. As to the pay that is reserved for me and the other leaders, I say that this in the same way is a very corrupt method, because a wise republic would not be giving it to anybody; on the contrary it ought to use its citizens as leaders in war, and in time of peace have them return to their professions. So, too, a wise king either ought not to give such pay, or if he does give it, the causes should be either that it is reward for noble deeds or that he wishes to make use of a man as much in peace as in war.

Because you bring up my case, I wish to use myself as an example. I say that 17 I have never practiced war as my profession, because my profession is to govern my subjects and to defend them, and, in order to be able to defend them, to love peace and to know how to make war. And my king rewards me and esteems me not so much because I understand war as because I also can advise him in peace. No king, then, ought to allow around himself anyone who is not of my sort, if he is wise and intends to conduct himself prudently, because if he has around him either too great lovers of peace or too great lovers of war, they will make him err. I cannot, in this my first discourse and according to my proposals, speak further on this; and if what I have said is not enough for you, you must find somebody who will satisfy you better. You can at least see how difficult it is to bring ancient methods back into present wars, and what sort of preparations a wise man ought to make and what opportunities he can hope for that will let him carry them out. But you will gradually understand these things better, if the discourse does not weary you, as we compare some parts of the ancient ways with modern methods.

---

[5]Pope Julius II (1443–1513): Energetic pope who sought to limit the power of Florence and Venice; he started the rebuilding of St. Peter's, employing Michelangelo, Bramante, and other great architects and painters.

COSIMO. If at the beginning we wished to hear you discuss these things, truly 18 what up to now you have said of them has redoubled our desire; so we thank you for what we have had, and for the remainder we ask.

FABRIZIO. Since you are pleased to have it so, I intend to start my treatment of 19 this material at the beginning, so that it may be better understood, for it is possible by that method to explain more at length. The purpose of him who wishes to make war is to be able to fight with any enemy in the field and to be able to win a battle. If he expects to do this, it is necessary to draw up an army. In order to draw up the army, it is necessary to find men, to arm them, to organize them, to train them both in small and in large bodies, to furnish them with quarters, and at last, either by remaining quiet or by marching, to bring them into the enemy's presence. These affairs comprise all the labor of field warfare, which is the most necessary and the most honored. In a man who well understands how to offer battle to the enemy, the other errors he may make in affairs of war will be bearable; but he who lacks this knowledge, though in other particulars he may be very able, will never carry on a war with honor, because a single battle that you win cancels all your other bad actions. So in the same way if you lose one, all the good things you have earlier done have no value.

Since then the men must first be found, it is necessary to come to their selec- 20 tion, for so the ancients called it. We call it drafting, but in order to call it by a name more honored, I wish us to keep for it the name of selection. It is the opinion of those who have given rules for warfare that men should be chosen from temperate countries, in order that they may have spirit and prudence, because a hot country produces the prudent but not the spirited, a cold one the spirited but not the prudent. This rule is well given to one who is prince of all the world and therefore has the opportunity to take men from such places as seem good to him. But if we wish to give a rule that anybody will be able to use, we must say that every republic and every kingdom must draw its soldiers from its own countries, hot or cold or temperate as they happen to be. Because ancient examples show that in every country training can produce good soldiers, because where nature fails, the lack can be supplied by ingenuity, which in this case is more important than nature. And choosing them in other places is not to be called selection, because selection means taking the best from a region and having power to choose those who are not willing as well as those who are willing to serve. It is not, however, possible to make this selection except in places subject to you, because you cannot get those you wish in lands that are not yours, but you must take those who are willing.

COSIMO. Yet it is possible, even among those willing to come, to choose some 21 and to omit some; and therefore it can be called selection.

FABRIZIO. You speak the truth to a certain extent. But consider the defects that 22 such selection has in itself, because many times we even discern that it is not selection. The first thing: those who are not your subjects and who serve willingly are not the best but rather the worst of a region; because if any there are of bad reputation, lazy, uncontrolled, without religion, fugitives from the authority of their fathers, swearers, gamblers, in every way badly brought up, they are the ones who are willing to serve as soldiers. Such habits are as contrary as possible to true and good soldiership. When so many such men offer themselves to you that they exceed the number you have designated, you can choose them, but when the material is bad, the selection cannot be good. Yet many times there are not enough to make up the number of which you have need, so that, since you are forced to take them all, it can no longer be called making a selection, but hiring infantry. With this bad method are formed today the armies in Italy and elsewhere, except in Germany, because nobody is hired by command of the prince but according to the desire of him who wishes to serve. Consider, then, what methods of these ancient armies can now be introduced into an army of men brought together in such a way.

COSIMO. What way can be used, then?   23

FABRIZIO. The one I mentioned: to select them from the prince's subjects and 24
by his authority.

COSIMO. Among those thus selected can some ancient methods be intro- 25
duced?

FABRIZIO. You well know there could, if he who commanded them were their 26
prince or accustomed lord, in a principate, or if he were a citizen and for the time a general, in a republic. Otherwise it is difficult to do anything good.

COSIMO. Why?   27

FABRIZIO. I shall tell you in time. For the present I wish this to be enough for 28
you: namely, that it is not possible to work well in any other way.

COSIMO. Since, then, he must make this selection in his own lands, whence do 29
you judge it would be better to draw them, from the city or from the country?

FABRIZIO. Those who have written on this all agree that it is better to draw them 30
from the country, since they will be men used to hardships; brought up to labor; accustomed to being in the sun, to avoiding the shade; able to use tools, to dig a ditch, to carry a burden, and to be without guile and without malice. But in this matter my opinion would be that since those employed are of two sorts, foot and horse, those on foot should be chosen from the country, and those on horseback from the cities.

COSIMO. At what age would you take them?   31

FABRIZIO. I should take them, when I had to raise a new army, from seventeen 32
to forty years; when it was established and I had to renew it, at seventeen always.

COSIMO. I do not well understand this distinction.   33

FABRIZIO. I shall tell you. If I had to set up an army where there was none, it 34
would be necessary to choose all those men who were most apt, if only they were of military age, so that they could be trained, as I shall explain. But when I should have to make a selection in places where this army had been set up, as additional soldiers I should take those seventeen years old, because the older men would already be selected and enrolled.

COSIMO. Then you would wish to set up a citizen army like that in our lands. 35

FABRIZIO. You are right. It is true that I should arm them, officer them, train 36
them, and organize them in a way that I think may not be that in which you have organized them.

COSIMO. Then you praise the citizen army?   37

FABRIZIO. Why do you suppose I would condemn it?   38

COSIMO. Because many wise men have always found fault with it.   39

FABRIZIO. It is a contradiction to say that a wise man finds fault with the citizen 40
army. He can indeed be thought wise and be misjudged.

COSIMO. The bad showing it has always made will make us hold to such an opin- 41
ion.

FABRIZIO. Beware that the defect is not yours rather than its, as you will recog- 42 nize before we finish this discussion.

COSIMO. You will do something most acceptable. Still I wish to tell you in what 43 respect these men find fault with it, in order that you may be better able to provide its defense. This is what they say: either it will be useless, and to trust ourselves to it will make us lose our power; or it will be effective, and by means of it he who controls it can easily take away our power. They bring up the Romans, who, by means of these forces of their own, lost their liberty. They bring up the Venetians and the King of France, of whom the first, in order not to have to obey one of their citizens, made use of the forces of others; and the King has disarmed his people in order to be able more easily to command them. But they fear uselessness much more than this. For this uselessness they bring up two principal reasons. One is that the men are inexperienced; the other is that they are made to serve by force; because they say that things are not thoroughly learned, and that by force nothing is ever done well.

FABRIZIO. All these reasons you speak of are from men who understand only 44 things that are not far off, as I shall plainly show you. And first, as to the uselessness, I tell you that no military force can be employed that is more useful than one's own, and that one cannot provide one's own army except in this way. And since this gives no possibility for debate, I do not intend to waste time on it, because all the examples of ancient history are with us. And because they bring up inexperience and force, I say it is true that inexperience produces lack of courage, and force produces discontent. But they can be made to gain courage and experience by means of the method of arming them, exercising them, and organizing them, as in the progress of this discourse you will see. But as to force, you must understand that when men are brought into military service on the command of the prince, they will come to it not altogether through force nor altogether voluntarily, because free will alone would cause all the difficulties I spoke of above: namely, that there would not be a selection and there would be few who would go; and likewise pure force would produce evil results. Therefore one ought to take a middle course, in which there would not be force alone nor free will alone, but the men will be so influenced by respect for their prince that they will fear his anger more than immediate inconvenience. And it will always happen that this will be a force mixed with free will in such a way that from it will not arise such discontent as to produce bad effects. I do not at all mean by this that such an army cannot be beaten, because the Roman armies were beaten many times, and the army of Hannibal was beaten, so one can see that an army cannot be organized of which anybody can promise that it never will be defeated. Hence these wise men of yours ought not to measure the uselessness of this army by its having lost once but should believe that just as it loses, so it can conquer and remove the cause of the loss. And if they investigate this situation, they will find that it has not resulted from a defect in method, but from the organization's not having been made perfect. And as I have said, they ought to provide for it not by finding fault with the citizen army but by improving it. How this is to be done you will learn as we proceed.

As to fearing that such an organization may take your state from you by means 45 of one who will be made head of it, I answer that weapons borne by citizens or subjects, given by the laws and well regulated, never do damage; on the contrary they are always an advantage, and cities keep themselves uncorrupted longer by means of those weapons than without them. So Rome was free four hundred years and was armed; Sparta, eight hundred; many other cities have been unarmed and have been free less than forty years. Because cities have need of armies; when they do not have their own forces, they hire foreigners; and foreign forces sooner do injury to the public welfare than native ones, because they are easier to bribe, and a citizen who is trying to become powerful can sooner avail himself of them; and to some extent he has material easier to deal with, since he is to oppress men who are unarmed. Besides this, a city ought to fear two enemies more than one. A city that makes use of foreign armies fears at once the foreigner she hires and the citizen, and as to this fear being necessary, remember what I said a little earlier about Francesco Sforza. A city that uses its own forces, fears only its own citizen. But among all the reasons that can be given, I wish this to serve me: namely, that never did anybody establish a republic or a kingdom who did not suppose that the same persons who inhabited it would need with their weapons to defend it.

Questions

1. Does Machiavelli state the reasons why nations or states engage in war? Or does he merely assume that war is a fact of life?
2. Why does Machiavelli consider professional soldiers undesirable? Does he argue that the citizen soldier is equal to the professional soldier in skill? What advantages does the citizen soldier possess?
3. What conception of the ideal state emerges in Machiavelli's discussion of professional and citizen soldiers? What virtues does the citizen possess in the ideal state?
4. Does Machiavelli suggest that soldiers should never be drafted? Does conscription have disadvantages?

Suggestions for Writing

1. Discuss your agreement or disagreement with the argument made in the dialogue for citizen soldiers or the arguments against professional soldiers. State and defend your own assumptions about the responsibilities of citizenship.
2. Machiavelli asks in the preface: "Because from what man ought his native land to expect greater fidelity than from that one who has to promise to die for her?" State whether you agree or disagree with this statement, and explain why.
3. Discuss the qualities that in your opinion make a good friend and a good leader. Are these qualities incompatible?

Additional Reading

Machiavelli, Niccolo. *The Chief Works of Machiavelli and Others.* 3 vols. Trans. and ed. Allan H. Gilbert. Durham: Duke University Press. 1964. Contains *The Art of War* (1519–20), *The Discourses* (1513), *The Prince* (1513), and Machiavelli's other writings relating to war.

Pocock, J. G. *The Machiavellian Moment: Florentine Political Thought and the Atlantic Republican.* Princeton: Princeton University Press, 1975.
Strauss, Leo. *Thoughts on Machiavelli.* Seattle: University of Washington Press, 1969.

The Moral Equivalent of War

William James

The American psychologist and philosopher William James (1842–1910) graduated from Harvard Medical School in 1869. He began teaching anatomy and physiology at Harvard University in 1872 and in 1881 became a professor of philosophy there. James helped create the school of American philosophy known as pragmatism—in general, the testing of ideas by their consequences or results. His many influential books include The Principles of Psychology *(1890),* The Varieties of Religious Experience *(1902), and* A Pluralistic Universe *(1909).*

In writing "The Moral Equivalent of War" in 1907, James perhaps had the American Civil War of his youth in memory; the United States had more recently been engaged in the war with Spain, begun in 1898. It was during the Spanish-American War that Theodore Roosevelt organized the "Rough Riders" and gained wide popularity as a political leader. The Boer War of 1898–1902 between England and the Afrikaners of the Orange Free State and the Transvaal Republic, in South Africa, had been costly in life to both sides. The Russo-Japanese War had come to an end in 1905 through the efforts of President Theodore Roosevelt, and in the following year Roosevelt persuaded France and Germany to settle their dispute over Morocco at a conference in Algeciras, Spain. Some people felt a world war was imminent, but others believed universal peace was at last a possibility.

James begins his essay with a description of modern war, which he hopes can be avoided by acceptance of a proposal probably inspired by energetic people like Theodore Roosevelt.

The war against war is going to be no holiday excursion or camping party. The military feelings are too deeply grounded to abdicate their place among our ideals until better substitutes are offered than the glory and shame that come to nations as well as to individuals from the ups and downs of politics and the vicissitudes of trade. There is something highly paradoxical in the modern man's relation to war. Ask all our millions, north and south, whether they would vote now (were such a thing possible) to have our war for the Union expunged from history, and the record of a peaceful transition to the present time substituted for that of its marches and battles, and probably hardly a handful of eccentrics would say yes. Those ancestors, those efforts, those memories and legends, are the most ideal part of what we now own together, a sacred spiritual possession worth more than all the blood poured out. Yet ask those same people whether they would be willing in cold blood to start another civil war now to gain another similar possession, and not one man or woman would vote for the proposition. In modern eyes, precious though wars may be, they must not be waged solely for the sake of the ideal harvest. Only when forced upon one, only when an enemy's injustice leaves us no alternative, is a war now thought permissible.

It was not thus in ancient times. The earlier men were hunting men, and to   2 hunt a neighboring tribe, kill the males, loot the village and possess the females, was the most profitable, as well as the most exciting, way of living. Thus were the more martial tribes selected, and in chiefs and people a pure pugnacity and love of glory came to mingle with the more fundamental appetite for plunder.

Modern war is so expensive that we feel trade to be a better avenue to plunder;   3 but modern man inherits all the innate pugnacity and all the love of glory of his ancestors. Showing war's irrationality and horror is of no effect upon him. The horrors make the fascination. War is the *strong* life; it is *in extremis*; war-taxes are the only ones men never hesitate to pay, as the budgets of all nations show us.

History is a bath of blood. The Iliad is one long recital of how Diomedes and   4 Ajax, Sarpedon and Hector *killed.* No detail of the wounds they made is spared us, and the Greek mind fed upon the story. Greek history is a panorama of jingoism and imperialism—war for war's sake, all the citizens being warriors. It is horrible reading, because of the irrationality of it all—save for the purpose of making "history"—and the history is that of the utter ruin of a civilization in intellectual respects perhaps the highest the earth has ever seen.

Those wars were purely piratical. Pride, gold, women, slaves, excitement, were   5 their only motives. In the Peloponnesian war for example, the Athenians ask the inhabitants of Melos (the island where the "Venus of Milo" was found), hitherto neutral, to own their lordship. The envoys meet, and hold a debate which Thucydides gives in full, and which, for sweet reasonableness of form, would have satisfied Matthew Arnold.[1] "The powerful exact what they can," said the Athenians, "and the weak grant what they must." When the Meleans say that sooner than be slaves they will appeal to the gods, the Athenians reply: "Of the gods we believe and of men we know that, by a law of their nature, wherever they can rule they will. This law was not made by us, and we are not the first to have acted upon it; we did but inherit it, and we know that you and all mankind, if you were as strong as we are, would do as we do. So much for the gods; we have told you why we expect to stand as high in their good opinion as you." Well, the Meleans still refused, and their town was taken. "The Athenians," Thucydides quietly says, "thereupon put to death all who were of military age and made slaves of the women and children. They then colonized the island, sending thither five hundred settlers of their own."

---

[1]The Greek historian Thucydides (471?–400 B.C.) described the Peloponnesian War between Athens and Sparta. By "sweet reasonableness" the Victorian poet and critic Matthew Arnold (1822–1888) meant the willingness of a classic writer to examine an issue or conflict from several points of view and to change opinion and admit error.

Alexander's career was piracy pure and simple, nothing but an orgy of power 6
and plunder, made romantic by the character of the hero. There was no rational principle in it, and the moment he died his generals and governors attacked one another. The
cruelty of those times is incredible. When Rome finally conquered Greece, Paulus
Æmilius² was told by the Roman Senate to reward his soldiers for their toil by
"giving" them the old kingdom of Epirus. They sacked seventy cities and carried off a
hundred and fifty thousand inhabitants as slaves. How many they killed I know not; but
in Etolia they killed all the senators, five hundred and fifty in number. Brutus was "the
noblest Roman of them all," but to reanimate his soldiers on the eve of Philippi he similarly promises to give them the cities of Sparta and Thessalonica to ravage, if they win
the fight.

Such was the gory nurse that trained societies to cohesiveness. We inherit the 7
warlike type; and for most of the capacities of heroism that the human race is full of we
have to thank this cruel history. Dead men tell no tales, and if there were any tribes of
other type than this they have left no survivors. Our ancestors have bred pugnacity into
our bone and marrow, and thousands of years of peace won't breed it out of us. The popular imagination fairly fattens on the thought of wars. Let public opinion once reach a
certain fighting pitch, and no ruler can withstand it. In the Boer war both governments
began with bluff but couldn't stay there, the military tension was too much for them.
In 1898 our people had read the word "war" in letters three inches high for three
months in every newspaper. The pliant politician McKinley was swept away by their eagerness, and our squalid war with Spain became a necessity.³

At the present day, civilized opinion is a curious mental mixture. The military 8
instincts and ideals are as strong as ever, but are confronted by reflective criticisms
which sorely curb their ancient freedom. Innumerable writers are showing up the bestial side of military service. Pure loot and mastery seem no longer morally avowable motives, and pretexts must be found for attributing them solely to the enemy. England and
we, our army and navy authorities repeat without ceasing, arm solely for "peace," Germany and Japan it is who are bent on loot and glory. "Peace" in military mouths today
is a synonym for "war expected." The word has become a pure provocative, and no
government wishing peace sincerely should allow it ever to be printed in a newspaper.
Every up-to-date dictionary should say that "peace" and "war" mean the same thing,
now *in posse,* now *in actu.* It may even reasonably be said that the intensely sharp competitive *preparation* for war by the nations *is the real war,* permanent, unceasing; and
that the battles are only a sort of public verification of the mastery gained during the
"peace"-interval.

It is plain that on this subject civilized man has developed a sort of double per- 9
sonality. If we take European nations, no legitimate interest of any one of them would
seem to justify the tremendous destructions which a war to compass it would necessarily entail. It would seem as though common sense and reason ought to find a way to

²The Roman consul Paulus Aemilius died at the battle of Cannae in 216 B.C.
³President William McKinley (1843–1901) conducted the war with Spain in 1898. In Cuba, Theodore Roosevelt led the Rough Riders in the capture of San Juan Hill, and Commodore Dewey took Manila in the Spanish-
occupied Philippine Islands. At the Treaty of Paris in December, Spain gave Puerto Rico and Guam and sold
the Philippines to the U.S. She also freed Cuba.

reach agreement in every conflict of honest interests. I myself think it our bounden duty to believe in such international rationality as possible. But, as things stand, I see how desperately hard it is to bring the peace-party and the war-party together, and I believe that the difficulty is due to certain deficiencies in the program of pacificism which set the militarist imagination strongly, and to a certain extent justifiably, against it. In the whole discussion both sides are on imaginative and sentimental ground. It is but one utopia against another, and everything one says must be abstract and hypothetical. Subject to this criticism and caution, I will try to characterize in abstract strokes the opposite imaginative forces, and point out what to my own very fallible mind seems the best utopian hypothesis, the most promising line of conciliation.

In my remarks, pacificist though I am, I will refuse to speak of the bestial side 10 of the war-*régime* (already done justice to by many writers) and consider only the higher aspects of militaristic sentiment. Patriotism no one thinks discreditable; nor does any one deny that war is the romance of history. But inordinate ambitions are the soul of every patriotism, and the possibility of violent death the soul of all romance. The militarily patriotic and romantic-minded everywhere, and especially the professional military class, refuse to admit for a moment that war may be a transitory phenomenon in social evolution. The notion of a sheep's paradise like that revolts, they say, our higher imagination. Where then would be the steeps of life? If war had ever stopped, we should have to re-invent it, on this view, to redeem life from flat degeneration.

Reflective apologists for war at the present day all take it religiously. It is a sort 11 of sacrament. Its profits are to the vanquished as well as to the victor; and quite apart from any question of profit, it is an absolute good, we are told, for it is human nature at its highest dynamic. Its "horrors" are a cheap price to pay for rescue from the only alternative supposed, of a world of clerks and teachers, of co-education and zoophily, of "consumer's leagues" and "associated charities," of industrialism unlimited and feminism unabashed. No scorn, no hardness, no valor any more! Fie upon such a cattleyard of a planet!

So far as the central essence of this feeling goes, no healthy minded person, it 12 seems to me, can help to some degree partaking of it. Militarism is the great preserver of our ideals of hardihood, and human life with no use for hardihood would be contemptible. Without risks or prizes for the darer, history would be insipid indeed; and there is a type of military character which every one feels that the race should never cease to breed, for every one is sensitive to its superiority. The duty is incumbent on mankind, of keeping military characters in stock—of keeping them, if not for use, then as ends in themselves and as pure pieces of perfection,—so that Roosevelt's weaklings and mollycoddles may not end by making everything else disappear from the face of nature.

This natural sort of feeling forms, I think, the innermost soul of army-writings. 13 Without any exception known to me, militarist authors take a highly mystical view of their subject, and regard war as a biological or sociological necessity, uncontrolled by ordinary psychological checks and motives. When the time of development is ripe the war must come, reason or no reason, for the justifications pleaded are invariably fictitious. War is, in short, a permanent human *obligation*. General Homer Lea, in his recent book "The Valor of Ignorance," plants himself squarely on this ground. Readiness for war is for him the essence of nationality, and ability in it the supreme measure of the health of nations.

Nations, General Lea says, are never stationary—they must necessarily expand 14 or shrink, according to their vitality or decrepitude. Japan now is culminating; and by the fatal law in question it is impossible that her statesmen should not long since have entered, with extraordinary foresight, upon a vast policy of conquest—the game in which the first moves were her wars with China and Russia and her treaty with England, and of which the final objective is the capture of the Philippines, the Hawaiian Islands, Alaska, and the whole of our Coast west of the Sierra Passes. This will give Japan what her ineluctable vocation as a state absolute forces her to claim, the possession of the entire Pacific Ocean; and to oppose these deep designs we Americans have, according to our author, nothing but our conceit, our ignorance, our commercialism, our corruption, and our feminism. General Lea makes a minute technical comparison of the military strength which we at present could oppose to the strength of Japan, and concludes that the islands, Alaska, Oregon, and Southern California, would fall almost without resistance, that San Francisco must surrender in a fortnight to a Japanese investment, that in three or four months the war would be over, and our republic, unable to regain what it had heedlessly neglected to protect sufficiently, would then "disintegrate," until perhaps some Cæsar should arise to weld us again into a nation.

A dismal forecast indeed! Yet not unplausible, if the mentality of Japan's states- 15 men be of the Cæsarian type of which history shows so many examples, and which is all that General Lea seems able to imagine. But there is no reason to think that women can no longer be the mothers of Napoleonic or Alexandrian characters; and if these come in Japan and find their opportunity, just such surprises as "The Valor of Ignorance" paints may lurk in ambush for us. Ignorant as we still are of the innermost recesses of Japanese mentality, we may be foolhardy to disregard such possibilities.

Other militarists are more complex and more moral in their considerations. 16 The "Philosophie des Krieges," by S. R. Steinmetz is a good example. War, according to this author, is an ordeal instituted by God, who weighs the nations in its balance. It is the essential form of the State, and the only function in which peoples can employ all their powers at once and convergently. No victory is possible save as the resultant of a totality of virtues, no defeat for which some vice or weakness is not responsible. Fidelity, cohesiveness, tenacity, heroism, conscience, education, inventiveness, economy, wealth, physical health and vigor—there isn't a moral or intellectual point of superiority that doesn't tell, when God holds his assizes and hurls the peoples upon one another. *Die Weltgeschichte ist das Weltgericht;* and Dr. Steinmetz does not believe that in the long run chance and luck play any part in apportioning the issues.

The virtues that prevail, it must be noted, are virtues anyhow, superiorities 17 that count in peaceful as well as in military competition; but the strain on them, being infinitely intenser in the latter case, makes war infinitely more searching as a trial. No ordeal is comparable to its winnowings. Its dread hammer is the welder of men into cohesive states, and nowhere but in such states can human nature adequately develop its capacity. The only alternative is "degeneration."

Dr. Steinmetz is a conscientious thinker, and his book, short as it is, takes 18 much into account. Its upshot can, it seems to me, be summed up in Simon Patten's word, that mankind was nursed in pain and fear, and that the transition to a "pleasure-economy" may be fatal to a being wielding no powers of defence against its disintegrative influences. If we speak of the *fear of emancipation from the fear-régime,* we put the whole situation into a single phrase; fear regarding ourselves now taking the place of the ancient fear of the enemy.

Turn the fear over as I will in my mind, it all seems to lead back to two 19 unwillingnesses of the imagination, one æsthetic, and the other moral; unwillingness, first to envisage a future in which army-life, with its many elements of charm, shall be forever impossible, and in which the destinies of peoples shall nevermore be decided quickly, thrillingly, and tragically, by force, but only gradually and insipidly by "evolution"; and, secondly, unwillingness to see the supreme theatre of human strenuousness closed, and the splendid military aptitudes of men doomed to keep always in a state of latency and never show themselves in action. These insistent unwillingnesses, no less than other æsthetic and ethical insistencies, have, it seems to me, to be listened to and respected. One cannot meet them effectively by mere counter-insistency on war's expensiveness and horror. The horror makes the thrill; and when the question is of getting the extremest and supremest out of human nature, talk of expense sounds ignominious. The weakness of so much merely negative criticism is evident—pacificism makes no converts from the military party. The military party denies neither the bestiality nor the horror, nor the expense; it only says that these things tell but half the story. It only says that war is *worth* them; that, taking human nature as a whole, its wars are its best protection against its weaker and more cowardly self, and that mankind cannot *afford* to adopt a peace-economy.

Pacificists ought to enter more deeply into the æsthetical and ethical point of 20 view of their opponents. Do that first in any controversy, says J. J. Chapman, *then move the point,* and your opponent will follow. So long as anti-militarists propose no substitute for war's disciplinary function, no *moral equivalent* of war, analogous, as one might say, to the mechanical equivalent of heat, so long they fail to realize the full inwardness of the situation. And as a rule they do fail. The duties, penalties, and sanctions pictured in the utopias they paint are all too weak and tame to touch the military-minded. Tolstoy's pacificism is the only exception to this rule, for it is profoundly pessimistic as regards all this world's values, and makes the fear of the Lord furnish the moral spur provided elsewhere by the fear of the enemy. But our socialistic peace-advocates all believe absolutely in this world's values; and instead of the fear of the Lord and the fear of the enemy, the only fear they reckon with is the fear of poverty if one be lazy. This weakness pervades all the socialistic literature with which I am acquainted. Even in Lowes Dickinson's exquisite dialogue,[4] high wages and short hours are the only forces invoked for overcoming man's distaste for repulsive kinds of labor. Meanwhile men at large still live as they always have lived, under a pain-and-fear economy—for those of us who live in an ease-economy are but an island in the stormy ocean—and the whole atmosphere of present-day utopian literature tastes mawkish and dishwatery to people who still keep a sense for life's more bitter flavors. It suggests, in truth, ubiquitous inferiority.

---

[4]G. Lowes Dickinson, *Justice and Liberty: A Political Dialogue* (New York: McClure, 1908).

Inferiority is always with us, and merciless scorn of it is the keynote of the mili- 21 tary temper. "Dogs, would you live forever?" shouted Frederick the Great. "Yes," say our utopians, "let us live forever, and raise our level gradually." The best thing about our "inferiors" today is that they are as tough as nails, and physically and morally almost as insensitive. Utopianism would see them soft and squeamish, while militarism would keep their callousness, but transfigure it into a meritorious characteristic, needed by "the service," and redeemed by that from the suspicion of inferiority. All the qualities of a man acquire dignity when he knows that the service of the collectivity that owns him needs them. If proud of the collectivity, his own pride rises in proportion. No collectivity is like an army for nourishing such pride; but it has to be confessed that the only sentiment which the image of pacific cosmopolitan industrialism is capable of arousing in countless worthy breasts is shame at the idea of belonging to *such* a collectivity. It is obvious that the United States of America as they exist today impress a mind like General Lea's as so much human blubber. Where is the sharpness and precipitousness, the contempt for life, whether one's own, or another's? Where is the savage "yes" and "no," the unconditional duty? Where is the conscription? Where is the blood-tax? Where is anything that one feels honored by belonging to?

Having said thus much in preparation, I will now confess my own utopia. I de- 22 voutly believe in the reign of peace and in the gradual advent of some sort of a socialistic equilibrium. The fatalistic view of the war-function is to me nonsense, for I know that war-making is due to definite motives and subject to prudential checks and reasonable criticisms, just like any other form of enterprise. And when whole nations are the armies, and the science of destruction vies in intellectual refinement with the sciences of production, I see that war becomes absurd and impossible from its own monstrosity. Extravagant ambitions will have to be replaced by reasonable claims, and nations must make common cause against them. I see no reason why all this should not apply to yellow as well as to white countries, and I look forward to a future when acts of war shall be formally outlawed as between civilized peoples.

All these beliefs of mine put me squarely into the anti-militarist party. But I do 23 not believe that peace either ought to be or will be permanent on this globe, unless the states pacifically organized preserve some of the old elements of army-discipline. A permanently successful peace-economy cannot be a simple pleasure-economy. In the more or less socialistic future towards which mankind seems drifting we must still subject ourselves collectively to those severities which answer to our real position upon this only partly hospitable globe. We must make new energies and hardihoods continue the manliness to which the military mind so faithfully clings. Martial virtues must be the enduring cement; intrepidity, contempt of softness, surrender of private interest, obedience to command, must still remain the rock upon which states are built—unless, indeed, we wish for dangerous reactions against commonwealths fit only for contempt, and liable to invite attack whenever a centre of crystallization for military-minded enterprise gets formed anywhere in their neighborhood.

The war-party is assuredly right in affirming and reaffirming that the martial 24 virtues, although originally gained by the race through war, are absolute and permanent human goods. Patriotic pride and ambition in their military form are, after all, only specifications of a more general competitive passion. They are its first form, but that is no reason for supposing them to be its last form. Men now are proud of belonging to a conquering nation, and without a murmur they lay down their persons and their wealth, if by so doing they may fend off subjection. But who can be sure that *other aspects of one's country* may not, with time and education and suggestion enough, come to be regarded with similarly effective feelings of pride and shame? Why should men not some day feel that it is worth a blood-tax to belong to a collectivity superior in *any* ideal respect? Why should they not blush with indignant shame if the community that owns them is vile in any way whatsoever? Individuals, daily more numerous, now feel this civic passion. It is only a question of blowing on the spark till the whole population gets incandescent, and on the ruins of the old morals of military honor, a stable system of morals of civic honor builds itself up. What the whole community comes to believe in grasps the individual as in a vise. The war-function has grasped us so far; but constructive interests may some day seem no less imperative, and impose on the individual a hardly lighter burden.

Let me illustrate my idea more concretely. There is nothing to make one indig- 25 nant in the mere fact that life is hard, that men should toil and suffer pain. The planetary conditions once for all are such, and we can stand it. But that so many men, by mere accidents of birth and opportunity, should have a life of *nothing else* but toil and pain and hardness and inferiority imposed upon them, should have *no* vacation, while others natively no more deserving never get any taste of this campaigning life at all,— *this* is capable of arousing indignation in reflective minds. It may end by seeming shameful to all of us that some of us have nothing but campaigning, and others nothing but unmanly ease. If now—and this is my idea—there were, instead of military conscription a conscription of the whole youthful population to form for a certain number of years a part of the army enlisted against *Nature,* the injustice would tend to be evened out, and numerous other goods to the commonwealth would follow. The military ideals of hardihood and discipline would be wrought into the growing fibre of the people; no one would remain blind as the luxurious classes now are blind, to man's relations to the globe he lives on, and to the permanently sour and hard foundations of his higher life. To coal and iron mines, to freight trains, to fishing fleets in December, to dishwashing, clothes-washing, and window-washing, to road-building and tunnel-making, to foundries and stoke-holes, and to the frames of skyscrapers, would our gilded youths be drafted off, according to their choice, to get the childishness knocked out of them, and to come back into society with healthier sympathies and soberer ideas. They would have paid their blood-tax, done their own part in the immemorial human warfare against nature; they would treat the earth more proudly, the women would value them more highly, they would be better fathers and teachers of the following generation.

Such a conscription, with the state of public opinion that would have required 26 it, and the many moral fruits it would bear, would preserve in the midst of a pacific civilization the manly virtues which the military party is so afraid of seeing disappear in peace. We should get toughness without callousness, authority with as little criminal cruelty as possible, and painful work done cheerily because the duty is temporary, and threatens not, as now, to degrade the whole remainder of one's life. I spoke of the "moral equivalent" of war. So far, war has been the only force that can discipline a whole community, and until an equivalent discipline is organized, I believe that war must have its way. But I have no serious doubt that the ordinary prides and shames of social man, once developed to a certain intensity, are capable of organizing such a moral equivalent as I have sketched, or some other just as effective for preserving manliness of type. It is but a question of time, of skilful propagandism, and of opinion-making men seizing historic opportunities.

The martial type of character can be bred without war. Strenuous honor and 27 disinterestedness abound elsewhere. Priests and medical men are in a fashion educated to it, and we should all feel some degree of it imperative if we were conscious of our work as an obligatory service to the state. We should be *owned,* as soldiers are by the army, and our pride would rise accordingly. We could be poor, then, without humiliation, as army officers now are. The only thing needed henceforward is to inflame the civic temper as past history has inflamed the military temper. H. G. Wells, as usual, sees the centre of the situation. "In many ways," he says, "military organization is the most peaceful of activities. When the contemporary man steps from the street, of clamorous insincere advertisement, push, adulteration, underselling and intermittent employment into the barrack-yard, he steps on to a higher social plane, into an atmosphere of service and coöperation and of infinitely more honorable emulations. Here at least men are not flung out of employment to degenerate because there is no immediate work for them to do. They are fed and drilled and trained for better services. Here at least a man is supposed to win promotion by self-forgetfulness and not by self-seeking. And beside the feeble and irregular endowment of research by commercialism, its little short-sighted snatches at profit by innovation and scientific economy, see how remarkable is the steady and rapid development of method and appliances in naval and military affairs! Nothing is more striking than to compare the progress of civil conveniences which has been left almost entirely to the trader, to the progress in military apparatus during the last few decades. The house-appliances of today, for example, are little better than they were fifty years ago. A house of today is still almost as ill-ventilated, badly heated by wasteful fires, clumsily arranged and furnished as the house of 1858. Houses a couple of hundred years old are still satisfactory places of residence, so little have our standards risen. But the rifle or battleship of fifty years ago was beyond all comparison inferior to those we possess; in power, in speed, in convenience alike. No one has a use now for such super-annuated things."[5]

Wells adds[6] that he thinks that the conceptions of order and discipline, the tra- 28 dition of service and devotion, of physical fitness, unstinted exertion, and universal responsibility, which universal military duty is now teaching European nations, will remain a permanent acquisition, when the last ammunition has been used in the fireworks that celebrate the final peace. I believe as he does. It would be simply preposterous if the only force that could work ideals of honor and standards of efficiency into English or American natures should be the fear of being killed by the Germans or Japanese. Great indeed is Fear, but it is not, as our military enthusiasts believe and try to make us believe, the only stimulus known for awakening the higher ranges of men's

---

[5]H. G. Wells, *First and Last Things* (New York: Putnam's, 1908), p. 215.
[6]Wells, p. 226.

spiritual energy. The amount of alteration in public opinion which my utopia postulates is vastly less than the difference between the mentality of those black warriors who pursued Stanley's party on the Congo with their cannibal war-cry of "Meat! Meat!" and that of the "general staff" of any civilized nation.[7] History has seen the latter interval bridged over: the former one can be bridged over much more easily.

Questions

1. How is modern war different from ancient war, according to James? How does he illustrate the nature of ancient war?
2. In what sense do we "inherit the warlike type" embodied in Alexander the Great? Is James referring to genetic or cultural inheritance?
3. If the "popular imagination fairly fattens on the thought of wars," what explains the rising objection to war discussed in paragraph 8? What explains the "double personality" James refers to in paragraph 9?
4. What virtues does war develop and what attractions does it have? Why does James stress these virtues and attractions in his review of the writings of apologists for war in paragraphs 11–19? How does James explain in paragraphs 22–24 why he does not wish to lose the "martial virtues" in the course of ending war?
5. What strategy or approach should pacifists adopt in trying to end war? How does the proposal made by James illustrate this strategy?
6. What examples does James give of "the moral equivalent of war"? Why does he believe the modern world might consider these alternatives?

Suggestions for Writing

1. Do you agree with James that the "martial virtues" are necessary in the modern world? Would you defend military service for men and women on this ground?
2. In the 1980s proposals have been made for national youth service. If the argument were made that they provide a "moral equivalent for war" and develop the characteristics James extolls in the essay, would you agree or disagree?

Additional Reading

Allen, Gay Wilson, ed. *A William James Reader.* Boston: Houghton Mifflin, 1972.
———. *William James: A Biography.* New York: Viking, 1967.
James, William. *Memories and Studies.* New York: Longmans, Green, 1912.
———. *The Will to Believe and Other Essays in Popular Philosophy.* New York: Longmans, Green, 1909.
Perry, Ralph Barton. *The Thought and Character of William James.* Cambridge: Harvard University Press, 1935.

---

[7]The journalist Henry Morton Stanley (1841–1904) led an expedition into the Congo in search of David Livingstone. He made later expeditions into central Africa. His books include *Through the Dark Continent* (1878) and *In Darkest Africa* (1890).

The Origins of War

Lewis Mumford

Lewis Mumford has written numerous books on architecture, city planning, and the effects of technology on modern living. During his long career, he has taught at Stanford University, the University of Pennsylvania, Wesleyan University, and M.I.T., and has written numerous books on a wide range of subjects. His books on contemporary American society, ethics, and technology include Technics and Civilization *(1934),* The Culture of Cities *(1938),* The Conduct of Life *(1951),* The City in History *(1961), and* The Myth of the Machine *(1967). Mumford has received numerous awards including the Presidential Medal of Freedom in 1964 and the National Medal for Literature in 1972.*

In The Pentagon of Power *(1970), Mumford describes modern warfare as a "modernized megamachine" that becomes increasingly lethal as those who control it become dehumanized:*

> Until now, human violence had been limited by the meager physical resources at the disposal of governments. In so far as earlier megamachines were forced to rely upon manpower to exercise control, they were kept to the human scale, and were, what is more, open both to attack from without and to corruption from within. But the new megamachine knows no such limitations; it can command obedience and exert control through a vast battery of efficient machines, with fewer human intermediaries than ever before. To a degree hitherto impossible, the megamachine wears the magic cloak of invisibility; even its human servitors are emotionally protected by their remoteness from the human target they incinerate or obliterate.

In this essay written in 1959, Mumford explores the origins of war from the perspectives of history and psychology.

1   At the time that the first great civilizations of the ancient world were coming into existence, the human race suffered an injury from which it has not yet recovered. If I interpret the evidence correctly, that injury still plays an active part in our lives, and caps our most hopeful dreams about human improvement with nightmares of destruction and extermination.

2   This injury happened at a moment when primitive man's powers, like ours today, had suddenly expanded; and it was due essentially to an aberration, or a series of aberrations, which put his most beneficent inventions at the command of his neurotic anxieties. So far from disappearing with time and being healed by the growth of law and reason, this original injury has only tightened its hold upon the collective actions of tribes and nations.

The aberration I refer to is the institution of war; and my purpose in discussing   3
its origins is to bring into consciousness a group of events and beliefs that have long remained buried, partly through sheer neglect, partly through a repression of painful irrationalities that contradicted civilized man's belief in his own orderly and rational behavior. It is only today, after a century of prodigious research into human origins, that
some of these events have come to light and been thrown open to interpretation.

That early injury had an effect upon civilized life, somewhat comparable to the   4
kind of childhood injury that psychiatrists characterize as a trauma: an injury whose
worst results may not show themselves till far on in adult life. Instead of being buried
in the psyche of an individual, it became embedded in the institutional life of every succeeding city, state, and empire.

In making this analysis, I shall have to start from an assumption that is un-   5
provable; namely, that there is a parallel between the general human situation today
and that faced by the individual, unable to cope with the problems of his life, unable to
make rational decisions, baffled, depressed, paralyzed, because he is still the prey of infantile fantasies he is unable to escape or control. In the case of individuals, we know
that such fantasies, deeply embedded in childhood, may keep on poisoning the whole
system, though the wound has seemingly healed and the scar is hardly visible. Childhood misapprehensions, animosities, and resentments, childhood misinterpretations of
natural events, such as birth, death, separation—all account for the persistence of infantile patterns of conduct. Often, later in life, these patterns overcome the adult and
leave him helpless. He still views present realities through the distorting glasses of his
childhood fantasy.

That something unfortunate once happened to man at the very moment when   6
an immense creativity was released was perhaps recognized in part in the Jewish and
Christian myth of the Fall, which was anticipated by even earlier Egyptian lamentations
over the perverse wickedness of man in going contrary to the gods. Many other peoples,
from China to Greece, looked back to a golden age when war and strife were unknown,
and when, as Lao-tse put it, one village might look at the smoke rising from the chimneys of another nearby, without envy or rivalry.

There is now enough anthropological and archaeological evidence to show that   7
there is at least a partial basis for these wistful memories of a more peaceful past, when
scarcity of food, violence, danger, and death were mainly the results of natural disasters,
not the deliberate products of man. If civilization's first great achievements awakened
new fears and anxieties, we must understand how and why this happened; for these fears
and anxieties still press on us. As long as the source of our irrational acts remains hidden, the forces that are still driving us to destruction will seem uncontrollable. The
worst part about civilized man's original errors and the most threatening aspect of our
present situation are that we regard some of our most self-destructive acts as normal
and unavoidable.

There is a close parallel between our own age, exalted yet stunned by the seem-   8
ingly limitless expansion of all its powers, and the epoch that marked the emergence of
the earliest civilizations in Egypt and Mesopotamia. In his pride over his present accomplishments, it is perhaps natural for modern man to think that such a vast release of
physical energy and human potentiality had never taken place before. But on examination this proves a too flattering illusion: the two ages of power, modern and ancient, are

bound together by many similar characteristics, both good and evil, which set them apart from other phases of human history.

Just as the prelude to the nuclear age came with the large-scale introduction 9 of water, wind, and steam power, so the first steps toward civilization were taken in the neolithic domestication of plants and animals. This agricultural revolution gave man food, energy, security, and surplus manpower on a scale no earlier culture had known. Among the achievements that mark this transformation from barbarism to civilization were the beginnings of astronomy and mathematics, the first astronomical calendar, the sailboat, the plow, the potter's wheel, the loom, the irrigation canal, the man-powered machine. Civilized man's emotional and intellectual potentialities were raised further through the invention of writing, the elaboration of the permanent record in painting, sculpture, and monuments, and the building of walled cities.

This great leap forward came to a climax about 5000 years ago. A like mobiliza- 10 tion and magnification of power did not again take place until our own era. For most of recorded history, mankind has lived on the usufruct of that early advance, making many piecemeal additions and widening the province held by civilization, but never essentially changing the original pattern.

There was probably an important religious side to this whole transformation. 11 With the priestly observations that produced the measured months and years, people became conscious, as never before, of human dependence upon the cosmic forces, the sun, the moon, the planets, on whose operations all life depended. Planetary movement of "clockwork" regularity gave man his first glimpse of an orderly, repetitive, impersonal world, utterly reliable, but benignly productive only within the frame of its inflexible laws.

With this new cosmic theology there came a sudden fusion of sacred and secu- 12 lar power, in the person of the all-powerful king, standing at the apex of the social pyramid. The king was both a secular ruler and the chief priest or even, in the case of the Egyptians, a living god. He no longer needed to follow village tradition and customs, like the village council of elders. His will was law. Kingship by divine right claimed absolute powers and evoked piously obedient collective responses.

What kingly power could not do solely by intimidation, and what magical rites 13 and orderly astronomical observation could not do alone by successful prediction, the two in combination actually did accomplish. Large assemblages of men moved and acted as if they were one, obedient to the royal command, fulfilling the will of the gods and rulers. People were driven to heroic physical efforts and sacrifices beyond all precedent. Throughout history, the major public works—canals, embankments, roads, walls, "pyramids" in every form—have been built with forced labor, either conscripted for part of the year or permanently enslaved. The enduring symbol of this vast expansion and regimentation of power is of course the Great Pyramid of Cheops, built without wheeled vehicles or iron tools, by relays of 100,000 men working over a limited span of years.

Should we be surprised that the achievements of our own age of nuclear power 14 appeared first at this period as myths and fantasies associated with the gods? Absolute power, power to create and annihilate, became the attribute of a succession of deities. Out of his own substance the Egyptian sun god, Atum, created the universe. Instantaneous communication, remote control, the collective incineration of whole cities (Sodom and Gomorrah), and germ warfare (one of the plagues of Egypt) were freely practiced by a succession of inhumane deities in order to insure that their commands would be obeyed. Human rulers, who still lacked the facilities to carry out these dreams on a great scale, nevertheless sought to counterfeit them. With the growth of an efficient bureaucracy, a trained army, systematic taxation, and forced labor, this early totalitarian system showed all the depressing features that similar governments show in our own day.

An overconcentration on power as an end in itself is always suspect to the psy- 15 chologist. He reads in it attempts to conceal inferiority, anxiety, and impotence. Perhaps early civilized man was justifiably frightened by the forces he himself had brought into existence, in the way that many people are frightened now by nuclear power. In neither case was the extension of physical power and political command accompanied by a complementary development of moral direction and humane control.

There were further grounds for doubt and fear among men of that early civili- 16 zation. Though they had achieved a hitherto unattainable security and wealth, the very growth of population and the extension of trade made their whole economy more subject to conditions and forces they could not control.

Our age knows how difficult it is to achieve equilibrium and security in an 17 economy of abundance. But the early fabric of civilization was far more precariously balanced, since the welfare of the whole was based on the magical identification of the king and the community in the beliefs and rites of their religion. The king personified the community; he was the indispensable connecting link between ordinary men and the cosmic powers they must propitiate and obey. While the king assumed full responsibility for the life and welfare of his subjects, the community, in turn, waxed and waned with the life of its ruler.

That magic identification produced a further occasion for anxiety, far deeper 18 than any threat of actual floods or bad crops; for despite their claims to divine favor and immortality, kings too were subject to mortal accidents and misfortunes. So constant was this anxiety that the Egyptian Pharaoh's name could not be uttered without interjecting the prayer, "Life! Prosperity! Health!" This identification of the king's life with the community's fate produced an even more sinister perversion. To avert the wrath of the gods, indicated by any natural mischance, the king himself must be slain as a sacrifice. At this early stage, dream and fact, myth and hallucination, religion and science formed a confused welter. One lucky change in weather after a ritual sacrifice might give sanction to a long-repeated chain of ritualistic slaughters.

To save the king from this discouraging fate, which might lessen the attrac- 19 tions of the office, a further trick of religious magic came into play. A stand-in would be chosen and temporarily treated with all the honors and privileges of a king, in order to perform the final role of sacrificial victim on the altar. As the demand for such victims increased in times of trouble, these substitutes were sought outside the community, by violent capture. And what began as a one-sided raid for captives in time brought about the collective reprisals and counterraids that became institutionalized as war. Back of war lay this barbarous religious sanction: only by human sacrifice can the community be saved.

War, then, was a specific product of civilization—often if not always, mainly if 20 not solely, the outcome of an organized effort to obtain captives for a magical blood sacrifice. In time, armed might itself took on a seemingly independent existence, and the extension of power became an end in itself, a manifestation of the "health" of the state. But underneath the heavy overlays of rationalization, war remained colored by the original infantile misconception that communal life and prosperity could be preserved only by sacrificial expiation. Civilized man's later efforts to impute the origin of war to some primal animal instinct toward murderous aggression against his own kind are empty rationalizing. Here the words of the anthropologist, Bronislaw Malinowski, are decisive, "If we insist that war is a fight between two independent and politically organized groups, war does not occur at a primitive level."

What is most remarkable about the spread of war as a permanent institution is 21 that the collective anxiety that originally brought about the ritual of human sacrifice seems to have deepened with material progress. And as anxiety increased, it could no longer be appeased by a mere symbolic sacrifice at the altar, for the ritual itself produced hatred, fear, and a natural desire for revenge among the peoples victimized. In time even greater numbers, with more effective weapons, were drawn into the brutal ceremony, so that what was at first a preliminary, one-sided raid before the sacrifice became the essential sacrifice itself. The alternative to permitting the mass slaughter of one's own people was the destruction of the enemy's city and temple and the enslavement of the population. These acts periodically eased anxiety and enhanced power. War provided a kind of self-justification in displacing neurotic anticipations by actual dangers—that return to reality seems to restore human equipoise. Psychiatrists observed during the Blitz in London that the need for facing real dangers often removed a patient's load of neurotic anxiety. But war performs this service at a ghastly price. Psychologically healthy people have no need to court dismemberment and death.

The growth of law and orderly behavior and morals, which improved the rela- 22 tion of men in cities, was not transferred to the collective relations of communities; for the ability to produce disorder, violence, and destruction itself remained a symbol of royal power. From the relatively peaceful Egyptians to the bloodthirsty Assyrians and Mongolians, one monument after another boasts of kings humiliated, prisoners killed, cities ruined. The solemn association of kingship, sacred power, human sacrifice, and military effectiveness formed a dominant complex that governed human behavior everywhere. But in time the search for sacrificial captives took on a utilitarian disguise—if spared as slaves, they added to the labor force. So the secondary products of military effort—slaves, booty, land, tribute—supplanted and concealed the original anxiety motive. Since a general expansion of productive power and culture had accompanied kingship and human sacrifice, people were conditioned to accept the evil as the only way of securing the good. The repeated death of civilizations from internal disintegration and outward assault underscores the fact that the evil elements in this amalgam largely canceled the goods and blessings.

This perception is not a discovery of modern historians. After the eighth cen- 23 tury B.C. the working principles of a power-centered civilization were boldly challenged by a long series of religious prophets, from Amos and Isaiah to Lao-tse and Mo Ti. Whatever their differences the exponents of these new ideas scorned the notion of a mere increase of power and material wealth as the central purpose of life. In the name of peace and love they rejected irrational human sacrifice in every form—on the altar or on the battlefield. Christianity went even further. Alone among the religions, instead of sacrificing human beings to appease the divine wrath, it sacrificed its God, renouncing

His power in behalf of love, in order to save mankind by cleansing the sinner of anxiety and guilt.

But the power complex, embedded in the routines of civilization, was not dis- 24 lodged by even this challenge. Ironically, Christianity itself supplanted its pagan rivals by seizing the power of the state under Constantine (A.D. 313) and utilizing all its engines of compulsion. As in the times of Moloch and Bel, the bloodiest collective sacrifices in history were those made in wars to establish the supremacy of a state religion.

How are we to explain the persistence of war, with its victories that turn out 25 as disastrous as its defeats, its just causes that produce unjust or contradictory consequences, and its heroic martyrdoms sullied and betrayed by the base, selfish conduct of the survivors? There seem to me two general answers. One is that the original pattern of civilization, as it took form in the walled city and in turn produced the "walled" state, has remained unaltered until modern times. War was an integral part of the constellation of civilized institutions, held in tension within the city, on the basis of a division of classes, slavery and forced labor, and religious uniformity. To remove any part of this fabric seemed, to the rulers of men, a threat to every other part. They exalted the sacrifices of war because they wanted to maintain their own power.

There was an additional mitigating factor: until recent times, only a small part 26 of the world's population accepted the terms of civilized life and its constant involvement with war; moreover, the amount of damage any army could inflict was limited. In Christian nations the human cost of war had been further reduced by the acceptance of a military code that limited violence to armed soldiers and generally exempted civilians and even their property from capture or deliberate destruction. Finally, the greater part of the world's population, living in rural communities, immune by their feebleness and poverty from the rapacious temptations of urbanized power, constituted a reservoir of vitality and sanity.

These mitigations and compensations progressively reduced the evils of total 27 war as practiced by the early empires; but neither the needs of commerce, nor the admonitions of religion, nor the bitter experience of bereavement and enslavement altered the basic pattern. By any reasonable standard, war should early have been classed with individual murder, as an unqualified collective crime or an insane act, but those who held power never permitted any subversive judgment on the irrationality of the method even if applied to rational ends. The fact that war has persisted and now threatens, at the very peak of our advances in science and technology, to become all-enveloping and all-destructive, points to the deep irrationality that first brought it into existence. This irrationality springs not only from the original aberration but from the unconscious depths of man, plagued with repressed guilt and anxiety over the godlike powers he presumptuously has learned to wield.

Western culture during the last four centuries has produced an explosive re- 28 lease of human potentialities and powers. Unfortunately the irrationalities of the past have been subjected to a similar projection and magnification.

The most formidable threat we confront, perhaps, is the fact that the fantasies 29 that governed the ancient founders of civilization have now become fully realizable. Our most decisive recent inventions, the atom bomb and the planetary rocket, came about through a fusion of secular and "sacred" power, similar to their ancient union. Without the physical resources of an all-powerful state and the intellectual resources of an all-knowing corps of scientists, that sudden command of cosmic energy and interplanetary space would not have been possible. Powers of total destruction that ancient man dared impute only to his gods, any mere Russian or American air-force general can now command. So wide and varied are the means of extermination by blast and radiation burns, by slow contamination from radioactive food and water, to say nothing of lethal bacteria and genetic deformities, that the remotest hamlet is in as great peril as a metropolis. The old factor of safety has vanished.

As our agents of destruction have reached cosmic dimensions, both our tangi- 30 ble fears and our neurotic apprehensions have increased until they are so terrifying to live with that they are involuntarily repressed. This repression is particularly notable in America, where it is marked by the virtual absence of any discussion or critical challenge of either our nuclear weapons or our ultimate aims. This is perhaps an indication of the unconscious guilt we feel for developing and actually using the atom bomb. Along with an unwillingness to face our own conduct or search for alternative courses, our behavior presents an even more dangerous symptom—an almost pathological sense of compulsion to pyramid our errors. This drives us to invest ever-increasing quantities of intelligence and energy in the building of ever more dangerous absolute weapons, while devoting but an insignificant fraction of this same energy and intelligence to the development of indispensable political and moral controls. We are in fact using our new knowledge and our new powers to re-enforce ancient errors and prolong the life of obsolete institutions that should long ago have been liquidated.

During the last dozen years every responsible head of government has con- 31 fessed openly that with our present readiness to use methods of atomic, bacterial, and chemical extermination, we might bring an end to civilization and permanently deform, if not destroy, the whole human race. Our failure to act on this warning, as an animal would act in the face of a comparable danger, gives the measure of our neurotic compulsions. So even the prudent thought of our own retributory, collective death offers no guarantee against the misuse of our powers so long as the engines of total annihilation remain available and the neurosis itself persists.

The two principal nuclear powers have been acting as if each was all-powerful 32 and could dictate the terms of existence to the rest of the planet. In the name of absolute sovereignty they have actually achieved impotence. What has been called the "stalemate of terror" is in fact a deliberate checkmate of those humane gifts and adroit moves that might save us. This precarious stalemate may be ended at any moment by a careless gesture, which could upset the board itself and sweep away all the pieces. It can be effectively ended only by both sides acknowledging their paralyzing inability to move and agreeing to start a new game.

To conceive this new game, which can no longer be played under the old rules 33 with the old pieces, both powers must take their eyes off each other and address themselves to the common task of saving the world from the threatened catastrophe they have impetuously brought within range. Instead, these governments with the connivance of their allies have been seeking to normalize their neurosis and have made participation in their infantile plans and infantile fantasies a test of political sanity. By now, a respected official in charge of Civil Defense finds it easier to envisage a whole nation of 180,000,000 people living permanently underground than to conceive of any means of delivering the world of its diabolical hatreds and collective paranoias. Strangely, such a national burial is put forward as an ingenious method for combating possible Russian blackmail. This failure to recognize when the remedy is worse than the disease is one of the score of current symptoms of mental disorder in apparently orderly minds.

If no great changes were yet visible in the general pattern of civilization, this 34 picture would be extremely dismal; for as long as the old institutions remain operative, war will continue an integral expression of the anxieties and tensions they produce. Fortunately, this original structure has undergone a profound change during the past four centuries; and a large part of it is no longer acceptable. The old urban container has in fact exploded, leaving behind only a few citadels of absolute power on the ancient pattern, like the Kremlin and the Pentagon. What is even more important, the invisible walls between classes and castes have been breaking down steadily during the last several decades—more rapidly in the United States perhaps than in Communist countries.

What applies to the division of classes also applies to the disparity between na- 35 tions. Neither knowledge nor power nor material goods can be monopolized by any privileged class or privileged country. Those Americans who fancied we had a permanent monopoly of atomic energy and technical skill recently found this out to their dismay; but the moral is not that we must "catch up with the Russians," but that we must accept the duties and demands of living in an open world among our equals. The real world of modern man has become porous and penetrable: every part of it is more closely interrelated than ever before and therefore more dependent upon the good will and sympathy and self-restraint of the rest of mankind. St. Paul's injunction to the little Christian congregations that everyone should be "members one of another," has now become a practical necessity of survival among the nations.

If so many other institutions of civilization, which held together solidly for 36 6000 years, have been crumbling away and are being replaced, is it likely that war will escape the same fate? The logic of history suggests it will not—if history has a logic. Our own military leaders have wryly admitted that in any large-scale war neither side can hope for a victory; indeed they have not the faintest notion of how such a war, once begun, might be ended, short of total extermination for both sides. Thus we are back at the very point at which civilization started, but at an even lower depth of savagery and irrationality. Instead of a token sacrifice to appease the gods, there would now be a total sacrifice, merely to bring an end to our neurotic anxieties.

In short, only the irrational, superstitious, magical function of war remains as 37 a live possibility—the propitiation of gods in whom we do not believe by a sacrifice that would nullify the meaning of human history. In that surviving pocket of festering irrationality lies our chief, if not our only, enemy.

What are the possibilities of mankind's acquiring a fresh grip on reality and 38 shedding the compulsive fantasies that are pushing us to destruction? There is little question of what measures must be taken to avoid a general nuclear catastrophe. Every intelligent observer understands the minimum precautions necessary for securing physical safety and for enabling a reconstituted United Nations to operate, not as a feeble hand brake on power politics, but as an active agent of international justice and comity. The only vital problem now is whether we can liberate ourselves from our irrational attitudes and habits, so that we may firmly take the necessary steps. It is not enough to appeal to human reason alone, as intelligent people often so earnestly do, to avert a general holocaust. We must first bring our long-buried sacrificial fantasies into the open before they erupt once more through internal pressure. Only exposure will counteract their power over us.

As with a neurotic patient, one of the conditions for resuming control and 39 making rational decisions, free from pathological deformation, is the continued existence of large areas of conduct that are still orderly, cooperative, harmonious, life-directed. Once the patient has the courage to unburden himself of his disruptive experiences and recognize them for what they are, the sound parts of his personality can be brought into play. Fortunately, much of our life is still conducted on wholly rational and humane terms; furthermore, modern man is closer to confronting his hidden irrationalities than ever before. Scientific curiosity, which led to the discovery of the hidden structure of matter, also led to the exploration of the hidden structure of the human psyche. We now begin to understand the actual meaning of the morbid dreams, fantasies, and myths that have repeatedly undermined the highest human achievements.

With the knowledge that the biologist and the psychologist have furnished us, 40 we must now perceive that both the original premises of civilization and those of our own so-called Nuclear, or Space, Age are humanly obsolete—and were always false. In purely physical terms, we now have possession of absolute power of cosmic dimensions, as in a thermonuclear reaction. But "absolute power" belongs to the same magic-religious scheme as the ritual of human sacrifice itself: living organisms can use only limited amounts of power. "Too much" or "too little" is equally fatal to life. Every organism, indeed, possesses a built-in system of automatic controls which governs its intake of energy, limits its excessive growth, and maintains its equilibrium. When those controls do not operate, life itself comes to an end. When we wield power extravagantly without respect to other human goals we actually upset the balance of the organism and threaten the pattern of the whole organic environment. Unqualified power diminishes the possibilities for life, growth, development. More than a century ago Emerson wrote, "Do not trust man, great God! with more power until he has learned to use his little power better."

The test of maturity, for nations as for individuals, is not the increase of power, 41 but the increase of self-understanding, self-control, self-direction, and self-transcendence. For in a mature society, man himself, not his machines or his organizations, is the chief work of art.

The real problem of our age is to search into the depths of the human soul, 42 both in the present generation and in the race's history, in order to bring to light the devious impulses that have deflected man for so long from his fullest development. For the human race has always lived and flourished, not by any one-sided exhibition of power, but by the constant sustenance and co-operation of the entire world of living beings. Not to seize power, but to protect and cherish life is the chief end of man; and the godlike powers that the human race now commands only add to its responsibilities for self-discipline and make more imperative a post-magical, post-mechanical, post-nuclear ideology which shall be centered, not on power, but on life.

Can such a new approach become operative in time to liberate man from war 43 itself, as he was once liberated by his own efforts from incest, cannibalism, the blood feud and slavery? It is too early to answer this question, and it is perhaps almost too late to ask it. Admittedly it may take an all-out fatal shock treatment, close to catastrophe, to break the hold of civilized man's chronic psychosis. Even such a belated awakening would be a miracle. But with the diagnosis so grave and the prognosis so unfavorable, one must fall back on miracles—above all, the miracle of life itself, that past master of the unexpected, the unpredictable, the all-but-impossible.

Questions

1. What analogy does Mumford propose between society and the individual in paragraphs 1–5?
2. What evidence does Mumford present for the injury discussed in paragraph 6? Does he suggest that the disposition to war is an inherited one—originating in the "injury" suffered by the human race in the ancient world?
3. What similarities between our age and that of ancient Egypt and Mesopotamia does Mumford discuss in paragraphs 8–17?
4. What does Mumford mean by the statement in paragraph 14 that "the achievements of our own age of nuclear power appeared first at this period as myths and fantasies associated with the gods"? What are these myths and fantasies?
5. What produced the anxiety and fear in ancient people that Mumford discusses in paragraphs 15–18? How did war originate in this anxiety and fear? How did war change in its end or goal?
6. According to paragraph 22, how was war later rationalized?
7. How does Mumford explain the fact that the development of law and morals of people in cities "was not transferred to the collective relations of communities" (paragraph 22)?
8. How does Mumford explain the persistence of war in paragraphs 21 and 25–28?
9. What view of the origin of war does Mumford reject in paragraph 20? Why does he stress the error of this view? What can the modern world gain from knowledge of ancient history?
10. What solution to the problem of war does Mumford find in his parallel with the individual? What general lessons do the parallels developed in the essay teach?

Suggestions for Writing

1. Does the analogy between the individual and society seem to you a strong one? Do the differences weaken or qualify the analogy, or are they insignificant to the argument?
2. Compare the kind of evidence Mumford presents in his explanation for war with the evidence presented by one of the following writers. Discuss whether the two writers reach similar or different conclusions based on similar or much different evidence.
   a. Hannah Arendt, *On Violence*
   b. Sigmund Freud, "Why War?"
   c. John U. Nef, *War and Human Progress*
   d. Arnold Toynbee, *War and Civilization*
   e. Quincy Wright, *A Study of War*

Additional Reading

Mumford, Lewis. *The Condition of Man.* New ed. New York: Harcourt Brace Jovanovich, 1973.

———. *Interpretations and Forecasts, 1922–1972: Studies in Literature, History, Biography, Technics, and Contemporary Society.* New York: Harcourt Brace Jovanovich, 1973.

———. *The Myth of the Machine. Volume 1: Technics of Human Development. Volume 2: Pentagon of Power.* New York: Harcourt Brace Jovanovich, 1967–1974.

———. *Technics and Civilization.* New York: Harcourt Brace Jovanovich, 1964.

Pacem in Terris, Parts III and IV

Pope John XXIII

Pope John XXIII was born Angelo Giuseppe Roncalli in 1881 near Bergamo, in northern Italy. He served as army chaplain in the First World War and afterwards in various church posts—including service as Apostolic Delegate in Athens and Turkey from 1934 to 1944. Appointed cardinal in 1953, he served as Patriarch of Venice until his election as Pope John XXIII in 1958. During his papacy, Pope John convened the Second Vatican Council that produced momentous changes in the Catholic Church. In 1963 he was awarded the United States Presidential Medal of Freedom. When he died of cancer in 1963, he was mourned throughout the world as a great peacemaker and humanitarian.

Pope John's encyclical letter Pacem in Terris *("Peace on Earth"), published on April 11, 1963, opens with a statement on order in the universe:*

> The progress of learning and the inventions of technology clearly show that, both in living things and in the forces of nature, an astonishing order reigns, and they also bear witness to the greatness of man, who can understand that order and create suitable instruments to harness those forces of nature and use them to his benefit.

The first two parts of the encyclical discuss the proper order between persons and between the person and the state. The encyclical warns against the use of physical force in governing society:

> Wherefore, a civil authority which uses as its only or its chief means either threats and fear of punishment or promises of rewards cannot effectively move men to promote the common good of all. Even if it did so move them, this would be altogether opposed to their dignity as men, endowed with reason and free will.

Pope John states that authorities must instead appeal to conscience and the sense of duty to the common good. Laws that oppose the moral law and will of God are not binding on the conscience of the individual citizen. Government, the encyclical states further, must take responsibility for the social and economic welfare of citizens, create employment, and make it possible for all citizens to "share as far as they are able in their country's cultural advantages." It states this general principle:

> For experience has taught us that, unless these authorities take suitable action with regard to economic, political and cultural matters, inequalities between the citizens tend to become more and more widespread, especially in the modern world, and as a result human rights are rendered totally ineffective and the fulfillment of duties is compromised.

These statements are the basis for the consideration of relations between states and the world community in Parts III and IV—the sections of the encyclical reprinted here.

Part III

Relations between States

Subjects of rights and duties

Our Predecessors have constantly maintained, and We join them in reasserting, that nations are reciprocally subjects of rights and duties. This means that their relationships also must be harmonized in truth, in justice, in a working solidarity, in liberty. The same natural law, which governs relations between individual human beings, serves also to regulate the relations of nations with one another.

81. This is readily clear to anyone if he would consider that the heads of states can in no way put aside their natural dignity while they represent their country and provide for its welfare, and that they are never allowed to depart from the natural law by which they are bound and which is the norm of their conduct.

82. Moreover, it is inconceivable that men because they are heads of government are forced to put aside their human endowments. On the contrary, they occupy this place of eminence for the very reason that they have earned a reputation as outstanding members of the body politic in view of their excellent intellectual endowments and accomplishments.

83. Indeed it follows from the moral order itself that authority is necessary for civil society, for civil society is ruled by authority; and that authority cannot be used to thwart the moral order without instantly collapsing because its foundation has been destroyed. This is the warning of God Himself: *A word, then, for the kings' ears to hear, kings' hearts to heed: a message for you, rulers, wherever you be! Listen well, all you that have multitudes at your command, foreign hordes to do your bidding. Power is none but comes to you from the Lord, nor any royalty but from One who is above all. He it is that will call you to account for your doings with a scrutiny that reads your inmost thoughts.*[1]

84. Lastly it is to be borne in mind that also in the regulating of relations between states, authority is to be exercised for the achievement of the common good, which constitutes the reason for its existence.

85. But a fundamental factor of the common good is acknowledgment of the moral order and exact observance of its commands. *A well established order among nations must be built upon the unshakable and unchangeable rock of the moral law, made manifest in the order of nature by the Creator Himself and by Him engraved on the hearts of men with letters that can never be effaced. . . . Like the rays of a gleaming beacon, its principles must guide the plans and policies of men and nations. From its signals, which give warning and point out the safe and sure course, they must get their norms and guidance if they would not see all their laborious efforts to establish a new order condemned to tempest and shipwreck.*[2]

In truth

86. First among the rules governing the relations between states is that of truth. This calls, above all, for the elimination of every trace of racism, and the consequent recognition of the principle that all states are by nature equal in dignity. Each of them accordingly is vested with the right to existence, to self-development, to the means fitting to its attainment, and to be the one primarily responsible for this self-development. Add to that the right of each to its good name, and to the respect which is its due.

87. Very often, experience has taught us, individuals will be found to differ enormously, in knowledge, power, talent and wealth. From this, however, no justification is ever found for those who surpass the rest to subject others to their control in any way. Rather they have a more serious obligation which binds each and everyone to lend mutual assistance to others in their efforts for improvement.

88. Likewise it can happen that one country surpasses another in scientific progress, culture and economic development. But this superiority, far from permitting it to rule others unjustly, imposes the obligation to make a greater contribution to the general development of the people.

89. In fact, men cannot by nature be superior to others since all enjoy an equal natural dignity. From this it follows that countries too do not differ at all from one another in the dignity which they derive from nature. Individual states are like a body whose members are human beings. Furthermore, we know from experience that nations are wont to be very sensitive in all matters which in any way concern their dignity and honor, and rightly so.

90. Truth further demands that the various media of social communications made available by modern progress, which enable the nations to know each other better, be used with serene objectivity. That need not, of course, rule out any legitimate emphasis on the positive aspects of their way of life. But methods of information which fall short of the truth, and by the same token impair the reputation of this people or that, must be discarded.[3]

In justice

91. Relations between nations are to be further regulated by justice. This implies, over and above recognition of their mutual rights, the fulfillment of their respective duties.

92. Since nations have a right to exist, to develop themselves, to acquire a supply of the resources necessary for their development, to defend their good name and the honor due to them, it follows that they are likewise bound by the obligation of effectively guarding each of these rights and of avoiding those actions by which these rights can be jeopardized. As men in their private enterprises cannot pursue their own interests to the detriment of others, so too states cannot lawfully seek that development of their own resources which brings harm to other states and unjustly oppresses them. This statement of St. Augustine seems to be very apt in this regard: *What are kingdoms without justice but large bands of robbers.*[4]

93. Not only can it happen, but it actually does happen that the advantages and conveniences which nations strive to acquire for themselves become objects of contention; nevertheless, the resulting disagreements must be settled, not by force, nor by deceit or trickery, but rather in the only manner which is worthy of the dignity of man, i. e., by a mutual assessment of the reasons on both sides of the dispute, by a mature and objective investigation of the situation, and by an equitable reconciliation of differences of opinion.

The treatment of minorities

94. Closely related to this point is the political trend which since the nineteenth century has gathered momentum and gained ground everywhere, namely, the striving of people of the same ethnic group to become independent and to form one nation. Since this cannot always be accomplished for various reasons, the result is that minorities often dwell within the territory of a people of another ethnic group, and this is the source of serious problems.

95. In the first place, it must be made clear that justice is seriously violated by whatever is done to limit the strength and numerical increase of these lesser peoples; the injustice is even more serious if vicious attempts of this kind are aimed at the very extinction of these groups.

96. It is especially in keeping with the principles of justice that effective measures be taken by the civil authorities to improve the lot of the citizens of an ethnic minority, particularly when that betterment concerns their language, the development of their natural gifts, their ancestral customs, and their accomplishments and endeavors in the economic order.[5]

97. It should be noted, however, that these minority groups, either because of their present situation which they are forced to endure, or because of past experiences, are often inclined to exalt beyond due measure anything proper to their own people, and to such a degree as to look down on things common to all mankind as if the welfare of the human family must yield to the good of their own ethnic group. Reason rather demands that these very people recognize also the advantages that accrue to them from their peculiar circumstances; for instance, no small contribution is made toward the development of their particular talents and spirit by their daily dealings with people who have grown up in a different culture since from this association they can gradually make their own the excellence which belongs to the other ethnic group. But this will happen only if the minorities through association with the people who live around them make an effort to share in their customs and institutions. Such, however, will not be the case if they sow discord which causes great damage and hinders progress.

Active solidarity

98. Since the mutual relations among nations must be regulated by the norm of truth and justice, they must also derive great advantage from an energetic union of mind, heart and resources. This can be effected at various levels by mutual cooperation in many ways, as is happening in our own time with beneficial results in the economic, social, political, educational, public health and sports spheres. We must remember that, of its very nature, civil authority exists, not to confine its people within the boundaries of their nation, but rather to protect, above all else, the common good of that particular civil society, which certainly cannot be divorced from the common good of the entire human family.

99. So it happens that civil societies in pursuing their interests not only must not harm others, but must join their plans and forces whenever the efforts of an individual government cannot achieve its desired goals; but in the execution of such common efforts, great care must be taken lest what helps some nations should injure others.

100. Furthermore, the universal common good requires that in every nation friendly relations be fostered in all fields between the citizens and their intermediate societies. Since in many parts of the world there are groups of people of varying ethnic backgrounds, we must be on our guard against isolating one ethnic group from its fellow men. This is clearly inconsistent with modern conditions since distances which separate people from each other have been almost wiped out. Neither are we to overlook the fact that men of every ethnic group, in addition to their own characteristic endowments by which they are distinguished from the rest of men, have other important gifts of nature in common with their fellow men by which they can make more and more progress and perfect themselves, particularly in matters that pertain to the spirit. They have the right and duty therefore to live in communion with one another.

The proper balance between population, land and capital

101. Everyone certainly knows that in some parts of the world there is an imbalance between the amount of arable land and the size of the population, and in other parts between the fertility of the soil and available farm implements. Consequently, necessity demands a cooperative effort on the part of the people to bring about a quicker exchange of goods, or of capital, or the migration of people themselves.

102. In this case We think it is most opportune that as far as possible employment should seek the worker, not vice versa. For then most citizens have an opportunity to increase their holdings without being forced to leave their native environment and seek a new home with many a heartache, and adopt a new state of affairs and make new social contacts with other citizens.

The problem of political refugees

103. The sentiment of universal fatherhood which the Lord has placed in Our heart makes Us feel profound sadness in considering the phenomenon of political refugees: a phenomenon which has assumed large proportions and which always hides numberless and acute sufferings.

104. Such expatriations show that there are some political regimes which do not guarantee for individual citizens a sufficient sphere of freedom within which their

souls are allowed to breathe humanly; in fact, under those regimes even the lawful existence of such a sphere of freedom is either called into question or denied. This undoubtedly is a radical inversion of the order of human society, because the reason for the existence of public authority is to promote the common good, a fundamental element of which is the recognition of that sphere of freedom and the safeguarding of it.

105. At this point it will not be superfluous to recall that such exiles are persons, and that all their rights as persons must be recognized, since they do not lose those rights on losing the citizenship of the states of which they are former members.

106. Now among the rights of a human person there must be included that by which a man may enter a political community where he hopes he can more fittingly provide a future for himself and his dependents. Wherefore, as far as the common good rightly understood permits, it is the duty of that state to accept such immigrants and to help to integrate them into itself as new members.

107. Wherefore, on this occasion, We publicly approve and commend every undertaking, founded on the principles of human solidarity and Christian charity, which aims at making migration of persons from one country to another less painful.

108. And We will be permitted to signal for the attention and gratitude of all right-minded persons the manifold work which specialized international agencies are carrying out in this very delicate field.

Disarmament

109. On the other hand, it is with deep sorrow that We note the enormous stocks of armaments that have been and still are being made in more economically developed countries, with a vast outlay of intellectual and economic resources. And so it happens that, while the people of these countries are loaded with heavy burdens, other countries as a result are deprived of the collaboration they need in order to make economic and social progress.

110. The production of arms is allegedly justified on the grounds that in present-day conditions peace cannot be preserved without an equal balance of armaments. And so, if one country increases its armaments, others feel the need to do the same; and if one country is equipped with nuclear weapons, other countries must produce their own, equally destructive.

111. Consequently, people live in constant fear lest the storm that every moment threatens should break upon them with dreadful violence. And with good reason, for the arms of war are ready at hand. Even though it is difficult to believe that anyone would dare bring upon himself the appalling destruction and sorrow that war would bring in its train, it cannot be denied that the conflagration can be set off by some unexpected and unpremeditated act. And one must bear in mind that, even though the monstrous power of modern weapons acts as a deterrent, there is nevertheless reason to fear that the mere continuance of nuclear tests, undertaken with war in mind, can seriously jeopardize various kinds of life on earth.

112. Justice, then, right reason and consideration for human dignity and life urgently demand that the arms race should cease; that the stockpiles which exist in various countries should be reduced equally and simultaneously by the parties concerned; that nuclear weapons should be banned; and finally that all come to an agreement on a fitting program of disarmament, employing mutual and effective controls. In the

words of Pius XII, Our Predecessor of happy memory: *The calamity of a world war, with the economic and social ruin and the moral excesses and dissolution that accompany it, must not be permitted to envelop the human race for a third time.*[6]

113. All must realize that there is no hope of putting an end to the building up of armaments, nor of reducing the present stocks, nor, still less—and this is the main point—of abolishing them altogether, unless the process is complete and thorough and unless it proceeds from inner conviction: unless, that is, everyone sincerely cooperates to banish the fear and anxious expectation of war with which men are oppressed. If this is to come about, the fundamental principle on which our present peace depends must be replaced by another, which declares that the true and solid peace of nations consists not in equality of arms but in mutual trust alone. We believe that this can be brought to pass, and we consider that, since it concerns a matter not only demanded by right reason but also eminently desirable in itself, it will prove to be the source of many benefits.

114. In the first place, it is an objective demanded by reason. There can be, or at least there should be, no doubt that relations between states, as between individuals, should be regulated not by the force of arms but by the light of reason, by the rule, that is, of truth, of justice and of active and sincere cooperation.

115. Secondly, We say that it is an objective earnestly to be desired in itself. Is there anyone who does not ardently yearn to see dangers of war banished, to see peace preserved and daily more firmly established?

116. And finally, it is an objective which will be a fruitful source of many benefits, for its advantages will be felt everywhere, by individuals, by families, by nations, by the whole human family. The warning of Pius XII still rings in our ears: *Nothing is lost by peace; everything may be lost by war.*[7]

117. Since this is so, We, the Vicar on earth of Jesus Christ, Savior of the World and Author of Peace, and as interpreter of the very profound longing of the entire human family, following the impulse of Our heart, seized by anxiety for the good of all, We feel it Our duty to beseech men, especially those who have the responsibility of public affairs, to spare no pain or effort until world events follow a course in keeping with man's destiny and dignity.

118. In the highest and most authoritative assemblies, let men give serious thought to the problem of a peaceful adjustment of relations between political communities on a world level: an adjustment founded on mutual trust, on sincerity in negotiations, on faithful fulfillment of obligations assumed. Let them study the problem until they find that point of agreement from which it will be possible to commence to go forward towards accords that will be sincere, lasting and fruitful.

119. We, for Our part, will not cease to pray God to bless these labors so that they may lead to fruitful results.

In liberty

120. It has also to be borne in mind that relations between states should be based on freedom, that is to say, that no country may unjustly oppress others or unduly meddle in their affairs. On the contrary, all should help to develop in others a sense of responsibility, a spirit of enterprise, and an earnest desire to be the first to promote their own advancement in every field.

The evolution of economically underdeveloped countries

121. Because all men are joined together by reason of their common origin, their redemption by Christ, and their supernatural destiny, and are called to form one Christian family, We appealed in the Encyclical *Mater et Magistra* to economically developed nations to come to the aid of those which were in the process of development.[8]

122. We are greatly consoled to see how widely that appeal has been favorably received; and We are confident that even more so in the future it will contribute to the end that the poorer countries, in as short a time as possible, will arrive at that degree of economic development which will enable every citizen to live in conditions more in keeping with his human dignity.

123. But it is never sufficiently repeated that the cooperation, to which reference has been made, should be effected with the greatest respect for the liberty of the countries being developed, for these must realize that they are primarily responsible, and that they are the principal artisans in the promotion of their own economic development and social progress.

124. Our Predecessor Pius XII already proclaimed that *in the field of a new order founded on moral principles, there is no room for violation of freedom, integrity and security of other nations, no matter what may be their territorial extension or their capacity for defense. It is inevitable that the powerful states, by reason of their greater potential and their power, should pave the way in the establishment of economic groups comprising not only themselves but also smaller and weaker states as well. It is nevertheless indispensable that in the interests of the common good they, as all others, should respect the rights of those smaller states to political freedom, to economic development and to the adequate protection, in the case of conflicts between nations, of that neutrality which is theirs according to the natural, as well as international, law. In this way, and in this way only, will they be able to obtain a fitting share of the common good, and assure the material and spiritual welfare of their people.*[9]

125. It is vitally important, therefore, that the wealthier states, in providing varied forms of assistance to the poorer, should respect the moral values and ethnic characteristics peculiar to each, and also that they should avoid any intention of political domination. If this is done, *a precious contribution will be made towards the formation of a world community, a community in which each member, whilst conscious of its own individual rights and duties, will work in a relationship of equality towards the attainment of the universal common good.*[10]

Signs of the times

126. Men are becoming more and more convinced that disputes which arise between states should not be resolved by recourse to arms, but rather by negotiation.

127. We grant indeed that this conviction is chiefly based on the terrible destructive force of modern weapons and a fear of the calamities and frightful destruction which such weapons would cause. Therefore, in an age such as ours which prides itself on its atomic energy it is contrary to reason to hold that war is now a suitable way to restore rights which have been violated.

128. Nevertheless, unfortunately, the law of fear still reigns among peoples, and it forces them to spend fabulous sums for armaments, not for aggression they

affirm—and there is no reason for not believing them—but to dissuade others from aggression.

129. There is reason to hope, however, that by meeting and negotiating, men may come to discover better the bonds that unite them together, deriving from the human nature which they have in common; and that they may also come to discover that one of the most profound requirements of their common nature is this: that between them and their respective peoples it is not fear which should reign but love, a love which tends to express itself in a collaboration that is loyal, manifold in form and productive of many benefits.

Part IV

Relationship of Men and of Political Communities with the World Community

Interdependence between political communities

The recent progress of science and technology, since it has profoundly influenced human conduct, is rousing men everywhere in the world to more and more cooperation and association with one another. Today the exchange of goods and ideas, travel from one country to another have greatly increased. Consequently, the close relations of individuals, families, intermediate associations belonging to different countries have become vastly more frequent and conferences between heads of states are held at shorter intervals. At the same time the interdependence of national economies has grown deeper, one becoming progressively more closely related to the other, so that they become, as it were, integral parts of the one world economy. Finally, the social progress, order, security and peace of each country are necessarily connected with the social progress, order, security and peace of all other countries.

131. Given these conditions, it is obvious that individual countries cannot rightly seek their own interests and develop themselves in isolation from the rest, for the prosperity and development of one country follows partly in the train of the prosperity and progress of all the rest and partly produces that prosperity and progress.

Insufficiency of modern states to ensure the universal common good

132. No era will destroy the unity of the human family since it is made up of human beings sharing with equal right their natural dignity. For this reason, necessity, rooted in man's very nature, will always demand that the common good be sought in sufficient measure because it concerns the entire human family.

133. In times past, it seemed that the leaders of nations might be in a position to provide for the universal common good, either through normal diplomatic channels, or through top-level meetings, or through conventions or treaties, by making use of methods and instruments suggested by natural law, the law of nations, or international law.

134. In our time, however, relationships between states have changed greatly. On the one hand, the universal common good poses very serious questions which are difficult and which demand immediate solution especially because they are concerned

with safeguarding the security and peace of the whole world. On the other hand the heads of individual states, inasmuch as they are juridically equal, are not entirely successful no matter how often they meet or how hard they try to find more fitting juridical instruments. This is due not to lack of goodwill and initiative but to lack of adequate power to back up their authority.

135. Therefore, under the present circumstances of human society both the structure and form of governments as well as the power which public authority wields in all the nations of the world, must be considered inadequate to promote the universal common good.

Connection between the common good and political authority

136. Moreover, if we carefully consider the essential nature of the common good on the one hand, and the nature and function of public authority on the other, everyone sees that there is an intrinsic connection between the two. And, indeed, just as the moral order needs public authority to promote the common good in civil society, it likewise demands that public authority actually be able to attain it. From this it follows that the governmental institutions, on which public authority depends and through which it functions and pursues its end, should be provided with such structure and efficacy that they can lead to the common good by ways and methods which are suitably adapted to various contingencies.

137. Today the universal common good poses problems of world-wide dimensions, which cannot be adequately tackled or solved except by the efforts of public authority endowed with a wideness of powers, structure and means of the same proportions: that is, of public authority which is in a position to operate in an effective manner on a world-wide basis. The moral order itself, therefore, demands that such a form of public authority be established.

Public authority instituted by common consent and not imposed by force

138. This public authority, having world-wide power and endowed with the proper means for the efficacious pursuit of its objective, which is the universal common good in concrete form, must be set up by common accord and not imposed by force. The reason is that such an authority must be in a position to operate effectively; yet, at the same time, its action must be inspired by sincere and real impartiality: it must be an action aimed at satisfying the universal common good. The difficulty is that there would be reason to fear that a supra-national or world-wide public authority, imposed by force by the more powerful nations might be an instrument of one-sided interests; and even should this not happen, it would be difficult for it to avoid all suspicion of partiality in its actions, and this would take from the force and effectiveness of its activity. Even though there may be pronounced differences between nations as regards the degree of their economic development and their military power, they are all very sensitive as regards their juridical equality and the excellence of their way of life. For that reason, they are right in not easily yielding obedience to an authority imposed by force, or to an authority in whose creation they had no part, or to which they themselves did not decide to submit by their own free choice.

The universal common good and personal rights

139. Like the common good of individual states, so too the universal common good cannot be determined except by having regard for the human person. Therefore,

the public and universal authority, too, must have as its fundamental objective the recognition, respect, safeguarding and promotion of the rights of the human person; this can be done by direct action when required, or by creating on a world scale an environment in which leaders of the individual countries can suitably maintain their own functions.

The principle of subsidiarity

140. Moreover, just as it is necessary in each state that relations which the public authority has with its citizens, families and intermediate associations be controlled and regulated by the principle of subsidiarity, it is equally necessary that the relationships which exist between the world-wide public authority and the public authorities of individual nations be governed by the same principle. This means that the world-wide public authority must tackle and solve problems of an economic, social, political or cultural character which are posed by the universal common good. For, because of the vastness, complexity and urgency of those problems, the public authorities of the individual states are not in a position to tackle them with any hope of a positive solution.

141. The world-wide public authority is not intended to limit the sphere of action of the public authority of the individual state, much less to take its place. On the contrary, its purpose is to create, on a world basis, an environment in which the public authorities of each state, its citizens and intermediate associations, can carry out their tasks, fulfill their duties and exercise their rights with greater security.[11]

Modern developments

142. As is known, the United Nations Organization (U.N.O.) was established on June 26, 1945, and to it there were subsequently added specialized agencies consisting of members designated by the public authority of the various countries with important international tasks in the economic, social, cultural, educational and health fields. The United Nations Organization had as its essential purpose the maintenance and consolidation of peace between peoples, fostering between them friendly relations, based on the principles of equality, mutual respect, and varied forms of cooperation in every sector of human endeavor.

143. An act of the highest importance performed by the United Nations Organization was the Universal Declaration of Human Rights, approved in the General Assembly of December 10, 1948. In the preamble of that Declaration, the recognition and respect of those rights and respective liberties is proclaimed as a goal to be achieved by all peoples and all countries.

144. We are fully aware that some objections and reservations were raised regarding certain points in the Declaration, and rightly so. There is no doubt, however, that the document represents an important step on the path towards the juridical-political organization of all the peoples of the world. For in it, in most solemn form, the dignity of a human person is acknowledged to all human beings; and as a consequence there is proclaimed, as a fundamental right, the right of every man freely to investigate the truth and to follow the norms of moral good and justice, and also the right to a life worthy of man's dignity, while other rights connected with those mentioned are likewise proclaimed.

145. It is therefore our ardent desire that the United Nations Organization—in its structure and in its means—may become ever more equal to the magnitude and

nobility of its tasks, and may the time come as quickly as possible when every human being will find therein an effective safeguard for the rights which derive directly from his dignity as a person, and which are therefore universal, inviolable and inalienable rights. This is all the more to be hoped for since all human beings, as they take an ever more active part in the public life of their own country, are showing an increasing interest in the affairs of all peoples, and are becoming more consciously aware that they are living members of the whole human family.

Notes

1. *Wisdom,* 6, 1–4.
2. Cf. Radio Message of Pius XII, Christmas Eve, 1941, *Acta Apostolical Sedis* XXXIV, 1942, p.16.
3. Cf. Radio Message of Pius XII, Christmas Eve, 1940, A.A.S. XXXIII, 1941, pp. 5–14.
4. *De civitate Dei,* Book IV, ch. 4; Patrologia Latina, 41, 115; cf. Radio Message of Pius XII, 1939, A.A.S. XXXII, 1940, pp. 5–13.
5. Cf. Radio Message of Pius XII, Christmas Eve, 1941, A.A.S. XXXIV, 1942, pp. 10–21.
6. Cf. Radio Message, Christmas Eve, 1941, A.A.S. XXXIV, 1942, p. 17; and Exhortation of Benedict XV to the rulers of peoples at war, August 1, 1917, A.A.S. IX, 1917, p. 418.
7. Cf. Radio Message, August 24, 1939, A.A.S. XXXI, 1939, p. 334.
8. A.A.S. LIII, 1961, pp. 440–441.
9. Cf. Radio Message, Christmas Eve, 1941, A.A.S. XXXIV, 1942, pp. 16–17.
10. Encyclical *Mater and Magistra* of John XXIII, A.A.S. LIII, 1961, p. 443.
11. Cf. Address of Pius XII to youths of Catholic Action from the dioceses of Italy gathered in Rome, September 12, 1948, A.A.S., XL, p. 412.

Questions

1. How does the encyclical define the moral law in the discussion of the obligations of authorities to their citizens and of educated and prosperous people to those less fortunate?
2. What does the encyclical identify as the causes of dispute between states? Which of these causes originated in the twentieth century?
3. What attitudes can reduce if not eliminate these tensions and causes?
4. Does the encyclical state or imply that democratic government is superior to other kinds?
5. What is the meaning of the statement in paragraph 102 that "employment should seek the worker"?
6. Under what conditions can permanent disarmanent occur? Does the encyclical suggest how nations can guarantee their "freedom, integrity, and security" in a state of disarmament?
7. What political conditions in the modern world work against the common good? Does the encyclical suggest that unity is more possible in the twentieth century than in previous centuries?
8. What is "the principle of subsidiarity," and what responsibilities does it entail?

Suggestions for Writing

1. The encyclical suggests that the problems facing the modern world are interrelated ones. Identify these problems and explain how the encyclical shows their interrelations.
2. Discuss the changes that would have to occur in relations between the nuclear powers to bring about the world order enjoined by the encyclical.

Additional Reading

John XXIII. *Journal of a Soul.* New York: McGraw-Hill, 1965.
Johnson, Paul. *Pope John XXIII.* Boston: Little, Brown, 1974.

The Execution of Cornelius Vane

Herbert Read

The English poet and critic Herbert Read (1893–1968) was born in Yorkshire, England, the son of a farmer. Read served in the infantry in the First World War, earning the Military Cross and the Distinguished Service Order. His first books of poems, many of them based on his war experiences, appeared in 1915 and 1919. After the war Read continued to write poetry and literary criticism. Through his work as a curator at the Victoria and Albert Museum, he gained knowledge of modern art and wrote several influential books on the subject. Read taught fine art at Edinburgh University and was Norton Professor of Poetry at Harvard University. His poems are collected in several volumes, including Collected Poems *(1946) and* Moon's Farm *(1955). His books on literature include* Form in Modern Poetry *(1932),* The True Voice of Feeling: Studies in English Romantic Poetry *(1953), and* Poetry and Experience *(1967).* The Innocent Eye *(1933) and* The Contrary Experience *(1963) are biographical. "The Execution of Cornelius Vane" first appeared in 1919.*

Le combat spirituel est aussi brutal que la bataille d'hommes; mais la vision de la justice est le plaisir de Dieu seul.[1]

Arthur Rimbaud

---

[1]The strife of the spirit is as brutal as the strife among men; but only God has the pleasure of seeing justice.

Arraign'd before his worldly gods
He would have said:
'I, Cornelius Vane,
A fly in the sticky web of life,
Shot away my right index finger.
I was alone, on sentry, in the chill twilight after dawn,
And the act cost me a bloody sweat.
Otherwise the cost was trivial—they had no evidence.
And I lied to the wooden fools who tried me.
When I returned from hospital
They made me acompany cook:
I peel potatoes and other men fight.'

For nearly a year Cornelius peeled potatoes
And his life was full of serenity.
Then the enemy broke our line
And their hosts spread over the plains
Like unleash'd beads.
Every man was taken—
Shoemakers, storemen, grooms—
And arms were given them
That they might stem the oncoming host.

Cornelius held out his fingerless hand
And remarked that he couldn't shoot.
'But you can stab,' the sergeant said,
So he fell in with the rest, and, a little group,
They marched away towards the enemy.

After an hour they halted for a rest.
They were already in the fringe of the fight:
Desultory shells fell about them,
And past them retreating gunteams
Galloped in haste.
But they must go on.

Wounded stragglers came down the road,
Haggard and limping
Their arms and equipment tossed away.
Cornelius Vane saw them, and his heart was beating wildly,
For he must go on.

At the next halt
He went aside to piss,
And whilst away a black shell
Burst near him:

Hot metal shrieked past his face;
Bricks and earth descended like hail,
And the acrid stench of explosive filled his nostrils.

Cornelius pitched his body to the ground
And crouched in trembling fear.
Another shell came singing overhead,
Nowhere near.

But Cornelius sprang to his feet, his pale face set.
He willed nothing, saw nothing, only before him
Were the free open fields:
To the fields he ran.

He was still running when he began to perceive
The tranquillity of the fields
And the battle distant.
Away in the north-east were men marching on a road;
Behind were the smoke-puffs of shrapnel,
And in the west the sun declining
In a sky of limpid gold.

When night came finally
He had reached a wood.
In the thickness of the trees
The cold wind was excluded,
And here he slept a few hours.

In the early dawn
The chill mist and heavy dew
Pierced his bones and wakened him.
There was no sound of battle to be heard.
In the open fields again
The sun shone sickly through the mist
And the dew was icy to the feet.
So Cornelius ran about in that white night,
The sun's wan glare his only guide.

Coming to a canal
He ran up and down like a dog
Deliberating where to cross.
One way he saw a bridge
Loom vaguely, but approaching
He heard voices and turned about.
He went far the other way,
But growing tired before he found a crossing,

Plunged into the icy water and swam.
The water gripped with agony;
His clothes sucked the heavy water,
And as he ran again
Water oozed and squelched from his boots
His coat dripped and his teeth chattered.

He came to a farm.
Approaching cautiously, he found it deserted.
Within he discarded his sopping uniform, dried himself and donned
Mufti[2] he found in a cupboard.
Dark mouldy bread and bottled cider he also found
And was refreshed.
Whilst he was eating,
Suddenly,
Machine-guns opened fire not far away,
And their harsh throbbing
Darkened his soul with fear.

The sun was more golden now,
And as he went—
Always going west—
The mist grew thin.

About noon,
As he skirted the length of a wood
The warmth had triumphed and the spring day was beautiful.
Cornelius perceived with a new joy
Pale anemones and violets of the wood,
And wished that he might ever
Exist in the perception of these woodland flowers
And the shafts of yellow light that pierced
The green dust.

Two days later
He entered a village and was arrested.
He was hungry, and the peace of the fields
Dissipated the terror that had been the strength of his will.
He was charged with desertion
And eventually tried by court-martial.

The evidence was heavy against him,
And he was mute in his own defence.
A dumb anger and a despair
Filled his soul.

---

[2]Civilian clothes.

He was found guilty.
Sentence: To suffer death by being shot.

The sentence duly confirmed,
One morning at dawn they led him forth.
He saw a party of his own regiment,
With rifles, looking very sad.
The morning was bright, and as they tied
The cloth over his eyes, he said to the assembly:
'What wrong have I done that I should leave these:
The bright sun rising
And the birds that sing?'

Questions

1. Who are the "worldly gods" that might have arraigned Cornelius Vane? What would he have justified in his arraignment?
2. Why does Cornelius run from the battlefield?
3. Does he feel shame or guilt over deserting his regiment? Is he defending or justifying his desertion in his final words?
4. What is the significance to the poem of the epigraph from Rimbaud on the strife of the spirit?
5. Is this poem about war, or human justice, or merely about one person's life and death?

Suggestions for Writing

1. Discuss what "The Execution of Cornelius Vane" suggests to you about the author's values and view of people and life.
2. Compare the ways Herbert Read and one of the following poets convey their attitude toward war:
   a. Alfred Lord Tennyson, "The Charge of the Light Brigade"
   b. A. E. Housman, "Epitaph on an Army of Mercenaries"
   c. Thomas Hardy, "Channel Firing"
   d. Wilfred Owen, "Dulce et Decorum Est"
   e. Randall Jarrell, "The Death of the Ball Turret Gunner"

Additional Reading

Read, Herbert. *Annals of Innocence and Experience*. London: Faber and Faber, 1946.
————. *Collected Poems*. London: Faber and Faber, 1946.
————. *The Contrary Experience*. New York: Horizon Press, 1973.

Copyrights and Acknowledgments

The author wishes to thank the copyright holders of the selections in this book, which are listed below in order of their appearance:

Author Index

Angelou, Maya, 32
Arendt, Hannah, 378
Auden, W. H., 177
Bok, Sissela, 475
Calder, Nigel, 582
Camus, Albert, 249
Childress, James F., 496
Clough, Arthur Hugh, 579
Coles, Robert, 321
Douglass, Frederick, 24
Dubos, René, 546
Emerson, Ralph Waldo, 182
Feldman, Irving, 427
Forster, E. M., 207
Freud, Sigmund, 155
Gershon, Elliot S., 453
Gordimer, Nadine, 411
Gould, Stephen Jay, 312
Greene, Graham, 241
Hardin, Garrett, 566
Hawthorne, Nathaniel, 42
Herberg, Will, 223
James, William, 601
John XXIII, Pope, 621
King, Martin Luther, Jr., 329
Lipkin, Mack, 471
Machiavelli, Niccolo, 590
Mead, Margaret, 102

Milgram, Stanley, 390
Mill, John Stuart, 87
Montaigne, Michel de, 8
Morris, Wright, 348
Mumford, Lewis, 611
Murray, Thomas H., 433
Orwell, George, 370
Plato, 142
Read, Herbert, 633
Rifkin, Jeremy, 446
Romains, Jules, 509
Rousseau, Jean-Jacques, 67
Schweitzer, Albert, 16, 201
Selzer, Richard, 552
Solzhenitsyn, Alexander, 163
Steffens, Lincoln, 129
Swift, Jonathan, 558
Thomas, Dylan, 56
Thomas, Lewis, 464
Thoreau, Henry David, 354
Tillich, Paul, 215
Tolstoy, Leo, 259
Toth, Susan Allen, 111
Welty, Eudora, 343
Williams, William Carlos, 489
Wollstonecraft, Mary, 300
Wordsworth, William, 134